POPULATION MATTERS

Population Matters

Demographic Change, Economic Growth, and
Poverty in the Developing World

Edited by
NANCY BIRDSALL
ALLEN C. KELLEY
STEVEN W. SINDING

OXFORD
UNIVERSITY PRESS

OXFORD
UNIVERSITY PRESS

Great Clarendon Street, Oxford OX2 6DP

Oxford University Press is a department of the University of Oxford.
It furthers the University's objective of excellence in research, scholarship,
and education by publishing worldwide in

Oxford New York

Athens Auckland Bangkok Bogotá Buenos Aires Cape Town
Chennai Dar es Salaam Delhi Florence Hong Kong Istanbul Karachi
Kolkata Kuala Lumpur Madrid Melbourne Mexico City Mumbai Nairobi
Paris São Paulo Shanghai Singapore Taipei Tokyo Toronto Warsaw
with associated companies in Berlin Ibadan

Oxford is a registered trade mark of Oxford University Press
in the UK and in certain other countries

Published in the United States
by Oxford University Press Inc., New York

British Library Cataloguing in Publication Data
Data available

Library of Congress Cataloging in Publication Data
Population matters : demographic change, economic growth, and poverty in the
developing world / edited by Nancy Birdsall, Allen C. Kelley, Steve Sinding.
p. cm.
Includes bibliographical references and index.
1. Developing countries—Population—Economic aspects.   2. Poverty—Developing
countries.   3. Demographic transition—Developing countries.   I. Birdsall, Nancy.
II. Kelley, Allen C.   III. Sinding, Steven W.
HB884 .P575 2001   304.6′09172′4–dc21   2001024734

ISBN 0-19-924407-3

1 3 5 7 9 10 8 6 4 2

Typeset by Newgen Imaging Systems (P) Ltd, Chennai, India
Printed in Great Britain
on acid-free paper by
Biddles Ltd., www.biddles.co.uk

Foreword

Two central questions have dominated debates about the place of population in efforts to spur social and economic development: is rapid population growth an important contributor to poverty, inequality, and lagging development (the Debate about Whether)? And, if so, what is the best way to bring down rapid population growth (the Debate about How)? The Debate about How produced much rancor and uncertainty. Was 'development the best contraceptive', as was colorfully asserted in the early 1970s, or should direct interventions, such as family planning services, receive the higher priority?

The debate was largely resolved at the 1994 International Conference on Population and Development in Cairo. The nations of the world committed themselves at Cairo to a comprehensive approach that includes both high quality reproductive health services, including family planning, *and* broad development efforts—to improve educational levels, reduce infant and maternal mortality, and bring about greater gender equality.

Meanwhile, on the Debate about Whether, economists through the 1970s and early 1980s were questioning whether the data supported the neo-Malthusian concern that rapid population growth would undermine development. By the late 1980s there was considerable doubt among economists that population growth deserved the high priority it had been receiving. An influential report of the US National Research Council, *Population Growth and Economic Development: Policy Questions*, presented the view, characterized by a co-author of this volume, Allen C. Kelley, as 'revisionist': '*On balance*, we reach the *qualitative* conclusion that slower population growth *could* be beneficial to economic development for *most* of the developing countries'. Perhaps as a result, the Cairo conference gave little attention to any macroeconomic rationale for public concern with continuing high population growth in many developing countries.

It was against this background that Dr Nafis Sadik, Executive Director of the United Nations Population Fund (UNFPA) asked the Rockefeller Foundation and the David and Lucile Packard Foundation to sponsor a workshop on recently accumulated new evidence on demography and economic development. The workshop was to be part of the preparatory process for a special session of the UN General Assembly in June 1999 to assess progress in implementing the Cairo Programme of Action. For its part, the Rockefeller Foundation was pleased to be able to offer as the venue for the workshop its Bellagio Study and Conference Center, the site of many significant meetings on population over the years. The workshop was organized by Steven W. Sinding, Director of Population Sciences at the Foundation, along with, at his initiative, Nancy Birdsall, Senior Associate at the Carnegie Endowment for International Peace. As this book reveals, the workshop was highly successful, and I am grateful to Dr Sinding and his colleagues for their commitment and hard work.

Particular recognition is due Dr Sarah Clark, Director of the Population Program at the Packard Foundation, for Packard's strong support for the workshop and her keen interest in the proceedings. Thanks are also due to UNFPA staff, in particular Dr Sadik and Catherine Pierce. Both played key roles in identifying non-academic participants from the world of policy whose insights and commentary contributed to the policy relevance of this volume. Finally, the Rockefeller Foundation, which for nearly 90 years has been committed to the application of scientific knowledge to development policies and programs, takes pride and pleasure in having helped make possible this important new contribution to our understanding of how demographic change affects both population growth and poverty.

I believe that this volume represents a state of the art report that can serve as the basis for a more confident set of policy recommendations, not only with respect to economic growth but, even more importantly, in my view, in the struggle to overcome poverty and economic inequality. Collectively, the chapters in this volume tell us, as the title implies, that policies aimed at reducing high fertility in poor countries through humane and ethical programs can significantly contribute to economic growth, poverty alleviation, and greater equity—a considerably more clear and hopeful statement than was possible a decade ago.

New York   Gordon Conway
7 June 2000   *President, The Rockefeller Foundation*

Preface

This book has its origins in a conversation between Nafis Sadik, Executive-Director of the UN Population Fund (UNFPA) and Steven W. Sinding, then Director for Population Sciences at the Rockefeller Foundation, in the spring of 1998. Despite the enormous success of the 1994 International Conference on Population and Development (ICPD), over which she had presided in Cairo in 1994, Dr Sadik was concerned that the promised resources to implement the Cairo Programme of Action were not forthcoming.

The Cairo conference was a remarkable success in so far as it produced a broad and deep consensus on needed actions in the field of population and reproductive health. But Sadik worried that an important underpinning of the strong political and budgetary support for international cooperation in the field of population that had existed since the original World Population Conference in Bucharest in 1974 was missing from Cairo: the *macroeconomic rationale.* Cairo was mostly about the *how* of population programs, and less about the *why.* The Programme of Action lacked the sense of urgency of earlier conferences about dealing effectively with rapid population growth because of its potential negative consequences—for the well-being of individual families, the environment, and economic development. Now, Dr Sadik felt, as the UN was preparing for its five-year review and assessment of implementation of the Cairo Programme of Action, it would make sense also to review what had been learned in recent years about the impact of population growth on economic development.

The last thoroughgoing review of the demographic-economic equation was a 1986 study by the prestigious US National Research Council of the National Academy of Sciences (NAS)—*Population Growth and Economic Development: Policy Questions.*[1] A very carefully conducted and cautious statement, the NAS report represented the closest one could come to scientific consensus amount economist-demographers in the mid-1980s on the demographic-economic relationship. While generally supportive of efforts to bring down very high rates of population growth in developing countries, the NAS volume placed considerably less importance on population as a cause of economic stagnation than had such earlier writings as a 1971 report by the same Academy[2] and an influential volume by Coale and Hoover in the late 1950s.[3] The 1986 report had had a significant influence on the thinking of development

---

[1] National Research Council, National Academy of Sciences (1986). Washington: National Academy Press.

[2] National Academy of Sciences (1971). *Rapid Population Growth: Consequences and Policy Implications* 2 vols. Baltimore: Johns Hopkins Press for the National Academy of Sciences.

[3] Coale, A. J., and E. M. Hoover (1958). *Population Growth and Economic Development in Low-Income Countries.* Princeton University Press, Princeton, NJ.

economists around the world—in finance and development ministries in the developing world, in donor agencies, and in such influential lending institutions as the World Bank and the regional development banks. In general, these institutions now seemed to give population less priority than they had in the earlier period.

Sinding readily agreed that an objective reappraisal was timely. Enough time had passed since the 1986 NAS review to warrant a look at new data. Furthermore, several groups of economists, working quite independently of one another, had recently examined in detail the role of fertility reduction in the Asian 'economic miracle'. He suggested that the Rockefeller Foundation, in collaboration with one or two other funders, could make its conference center in Bellagio, Italy available for a meeting at which leading researchers and scholars could review the demographic-economic state of the art. He approached the David and Lucile Packard Foundation whose population program director, Dr Sarah Clark, agreed the review was important and that Packard would help support the meeting. They and Sadik agreed that Dr Nancy Birdsall would be the ideal organizer of such a meeting. Birdsall, then Executive Vice President of the Inter-American Development Bank, was a leading expert among economists on population questions. She had spent many years at the World Bank and had directed the Bank's seminal 1984 *World Development Report*, regarded by many as the most comprehensive volume on population and development up to that time. Dr Birdsall agreed to organize the meeting and quickly identified most of the key participants whose contributions appear in this volume. She also brought to the agenda a critical additional dimension: the relationship between demographic change and poverty. Dr Sadik arranged for the conference to be an official 'expert meeting' as part of the preparatory process for the June 1999 UN General Assembly Special Session to review progress in implementing the ICPD Programme of Action.

Thus, on 2–6 November 1998 the Symposium on Population Change and Economic Development took place at the Rockefeller Foundation's Villa Serbelloni on the shores of Lake Como. Most of the participants agreed it was the most stimulating set of papers and discussions on the subject they had participated in for many years—in some cases, ever. All agreed the results warranted a new publication, reflecting the evolution in thinking that had taken place since the 1986 NAS review. We hope readers of this volume will agree with that assessment.

NB
ACK
SWS

Acknowledgements

The editors of this volume are grateful to the participants in the conference at Bellagio, Italy which provided the original forum for discussion of the issues on which the chapters in this book are based. Special thanks go to those who raised the central policy questions which the technical work herein is meant to address. These include Martha Campbell, Geeta Rao Gupta, Cecilia Lopez, Nora Lustig, Ernst Lutz, Mohammed Nizamuddin, Christiana Okoije, and in particular Nafis Sadik, head of the United Nations Population Fund (UNFPA). We also want to thank early supporters of the idea of the conference, including the Packard Foundation's Sarah Clark and Catherine Pierce of UNFPA, and all of our contributors, who in addition to the work on their own papers, shared generously their comments on each others' papers and on the editors' contributions. Nancy Birdsall and Steven Sinding are especially grateful to their co-editor Allen Kelley for his thoughtful and thorough reviews of the original Chairmen's Report of the Bellagio conference, which provided the basis for Chapter 1 of this book. We could not have begun the work without the organizational help of Janet O'Connell of the Rockefeller Foundation in setting up the Bellagio conference, and we could not have completed the book without the expert logistical support of Marygold Severn-Walsh, Brain Deese, and Delores Bigby of the Carnegie Endowment for International Peace, and the encouragement of colleagues in Carnegie's Global Policy Program, including Thomas Carothers, and the assistance of Gail McKinnis of Duke University. We want also to acknowledge the financial support of the Rockefeller Foundation, the David and Lucile Packard Foundation, the United Nations Population Fund, Columbia University's Mailman School of Public Health, and the Carnegie Endowment for International Peace.

Contents

Contents

List of Contributors

Editors

Nancy Birdsall is Senior Associate and Director of the Economic Reform Project at the Carnegie Endowment for International Peace. She was the Executive Vice President of the Inter-American Development Bank from 1993 until 1998. She holds a doctorate in economics from Yale University and was previously the Director of the Policy Research Department of the World Bank. Dr Birdsall has been a senior adviser to the Rockefeller Foundation and a member of various study committees of the National Academy of Sciences. She has written extensively about development issues, most recently on the causes and effects of inequality in a globalizing world.

Allen C. Kelley is James B. Duke Professor of Economics at Duke University. A Ph.D. graduate of Stanford University in 1964, Kelley assumed an appointment at the University of Wisconsin at Madison in 1965, and at Duke University in 1973. His visiting appointments have included Harvard, Yale, International Institute for Applied Systems Analysis (Vienna), University of Melbourne, Australian National University, and Esmee Fairbairn Research University (Edinburgh). Kelley's research program focused on economic demography, development, and history.

Steven W. Sinding is Professor of Clinical Public Health at the Mailman School of Public Health of Columbia University, a position he assumed in September 1999. He is directing a three-year study on the future of development cooperation and assistance, with a special emphasis on reproductive health and population program assistance. From 1991 to 1999, he served as Director of the Population Sciences program at the Rockefeller Foundation. He has written extensively on international population issues and is called upon frequently to lecture to both academic and general audiences on international population issues. Sinding received his bachelor's degree from Oberlin College in Ohio in 1965 and his Ph.D. in political science from the University of North Carolina at Chapel Hill in 1970.

Contributors

Jere R. Behrman is the W. R. Kenan, Jr. Professor of Economics and Director of the Population Studies Center at the University of Pennsylvania, where has been on the faculty since 1965. He has undertaken research on a broad range of human resource and demographic issues, particularly in developing countries and has published over 230 professional articles and 25 books primarily on such topics.

David Bloom is the Clarence James Gamble Professor of Economics and Demography at Harvard University's School of Public Health. Bloom received a BS in Industrial and Labor Relations from Cornell University in 1976, an MA in Economics from Princeton University in 1978, and a Ph.D. in Economics and Demography from Princeton in 1981. He has published over 80 articles and books in the fields of economics and demography, and his current research interests include labor economics, health, demography, and the environment.

John Bongaarts is Vice President, Policy Research Division of the Population Council. His research has focused on the determinants of fertility, population-environmental relationships, and population policy options. He is a member of the Royal Dutch Academy of Sciences and a fellow of the AAAS. He received the Robert J. Lapham Award and the Mindel Sheps Award from the Eindhoven Institute of Technology, the Netherlands, and a Ph.D. in Biomedical Engineering from the University of Illinois.

David Canning is a Professor of Economics at Queen's University Belfast. He has a Ph.D. in economics from Cambridge University and has held faculty positions at the London School of Economics, Cambridge University, and Columbia University. He has also worked on development issues as a Development Associate at the Harvard Institute for International Development. His current research focuses on economic growth in developing countries, in particular its interaction with demographic and health factors.

Robert Eastwood is Lecturer in Economics at Sussex University. He has worked on small firm behavior poverty, and income distribution in developing countries. Recent papers include 'The Impact of Changes in Human Fertility on Poverty', *Journal of Development Studies*, 1999 (with Michael Lipton) and Directed Credit and Investment in Small Scale Industry in India: Evidence from Firm-Level Data 1965–78', *Journal of Development Studies* 1999 (with Renu Kohli). He has worked as an adviser for UNDP and IFAD.

Ricardo Hausmann is Professor of the Practice of Economic Development at Harvard's Kennedy School of Government. Previously, he served as the first Chief Economist of the Inter-American Development Bank (1994–2000), where he created the Research Department. He has served as Minister of Planning of Venezuela (1992–93) and member of the Board of the Central Bank of Venezuela. He also served as Chairman of the IMF–World Bank Development Committee. His research interests include issues of growth, macroeconomic stability, international finance, and the social dimensions of development. He holds an MA, and Ph.D. in Economics from Cornell University.

Ronald D. Lee is Professor of Demography and Economics at the University of California at Berkeley. His recent work studies flows of resources across ages, and the interactions of these flows with changing population age structures. He also works on probabilistic forecasts of mortality, population, Social Security finances, and general government budgets. He is a member of the US National Academy of Sciences and Corresponding Member of the British Academy.

Michael Lipton is Research Professor of Economics, Poverty Research Unit at Sussex University. He has worked on agricultural research, nutrition economics, poverty, and economic demography in developing countries, including Bangladesh, Botswana,

India, Sierra Leone, Sri Lanka, and South Africa. He has advised the World Bank, UNDP, and other organizations, and is currently Lead Scholar for IFAD's forthcoming Rural Poverty report.

Andrew Mason is Chair and Professor of Economics at the University of Hawaii at Manoa and Senior Fellow and former Director of the Program on Population at the East-West Center. The focus of his research is the economic impact of demographic change. He has just completed a study on the role of demography in East Asian economic success. He recently co-edited *Sharing the Wealth: Demographic Change and Economic Transfers between Generations*, published by Oxford University Press.

Thomas Merrick is Senior Population Adviser—Population, Human Development Network (HDN), the World Bank. He works with the Bank's Health, Nutrition and Population Sector Board to strengthen the Bank's capacity and effectiveness in addressing population, family planning, and related reproductive health concerns. Prior to joining the Bank in 1992, he served as President of the Washington-based Population Reference Bureau for eight years. From 1976 to 1984, he directed the Center for Population Research and chaired the Department of Demography at Georgetown University, where he was also Associate Professor of Demography.

Tim Miller is a demographer at the Center for the Economics and Demography of Aging (CEDA). The Center, established by the National Institute of Aging, is located at the University of California at Berkeley. His research at CEDA has focused on analysis, forecasting, and simulation of population aging. Three major areas of interest have been health demography, inter-age transfers, and immigration.

Ricardo Paes de Barros is the Director of Social Policy and Research at the National Institute for Applied Economic Research (IPEA) in Brazil. He has been a researcher at IPEA for over 20 years, and is the author of numerous books and scientific publications on labor and human development economics in Brazil. He holds a Ph.D. in Economics from the University of Chicago, USA, and a Masters in Statistics from the Institute of Pure and Applied Mathematics (IMPA), Rio de Janeiro, Brazil. He has also conducted postdoctoral research at both the Chicago University and Yale University.

John Pender, a research fellow, joined IFPRI in 1995 after working as an Assistant Professor of Economics at Brigham Young University. His research at IFPRI focuses on the causes and effects of agricultural change in fragile lands, particularly the hillsides of Central America and the highlands of East Africa. Pender received a bachelor's degree from the California Institute of Technology, a Master of Public Policy degree from the University of California, Berkeley, and a Ph.D. in Agricultural Economics from Stanford University.

Robert M. Schmidt is an Associate Professor of Economics at the University of Richmond where he also holds the CSX Chair of Accounting and Finance. His Masters and Ph.D. are from Duke University; his BA in Economics is from the University of Wisconsin. He has held a visiting appointment at the International Institute for Applied Systems Analysis near Vienna; and has received research assistance from the

National Science Foundation, the World Bank, and the US Department of Education, among others.

Miguel Székely obtained a D.Phil. and a Masters in Economics from Oxford University (1992–96) as well as a Masters in Public Policy at ITAM, Mexico (1989–91). He was lecturer and researcher at the Center for Economic Studies at el Colegio de Mexico, and he is currently a research economist at the Research Department of the Inter-American Development Bank. His areas of expertise include income distribution, poverty, education economics, and household saving. He has published several journal articles and book chapters on these issues.

Jeffrey G. Williamson is the Laird Bell Professor of Economics at Harvard University. He is also Faculty Fellow at the Harvard Center for International Development and Research Associate at the National Bureau of Economic Research. A Ph.D. from Stanford University, Professor Williamson taught at the University of Wisconsin for 20 years before joining the faculty at Harvard in 1983. The author of more than 20 scholarly books and nearly 150 articles on economic history and development, Professor Williamson recently served as President of the Economic History Association (1994–95) and as Chairman of the Harvard Economics Department (1997–2000).

PART I

SETTING THE STAGE

For more than 200 years, ever since the Revd Thomas Malthus produced his famous *First Essay on Population*, scholars and intellectuals have been debating the question of whether population growth inhibits improvements in the social and economic conditions of societies. The debate acquired special urgency in the second half of the twentieth century as population growth reached rates higher than had ever been previously recorded in country after country, and policy-makers demanded to know whether or not they should intervene directly. Unfortunately, scientific research has not provided particularly useful guidance to policy over the last half century. Practitioners of the various disciplines differed strongly among themselves and produced widely divergent, often contradictory advice to policy-makers.

The part that follows traces some of the history of recent debates between economists and members of other disciplines, and among economists themselves. Birdsall and Sinding summarize the principal conclusions that emerged from the symposium from which this book derives. Foremost among the findings is a shift in the view of most economists who have studied the demographic/economic development relationship in recent years—from a view that the relationship is neutral to mildly negative to one that finds considerable evidence that high fertility often inhibits growth and that successful efforts to reduce fertility can accelerate economic development.

Allen Kelley traces the evolution of academic inquiry on the significance of population growth for development, from alarmism to what he calls 'revisionism', to a more nuanced form of revisionist thought—from the 1950s and 1960s population crisis mentality, to the 1980s view that population growth is a 'neutral' phenomenon, to the contemporary view (which is encapsulated in the title of this book) that *population does matter*. He points out that the key factor distinguishing the various assessments is the time period over which population impacts are assessed. The impacts highlighted during the 'alarmist period' were distinctly direct, and short run, in which demographic impacts are relatively strong. The impacts during the 'neutralist' period were long run in focus, allowing time for adjustments and feedbacks to occur. Demography had smaller roles in this time frame. In the 1990s, an intermediate time perspective is adopted—a few decades of the demographic transition—so the impacts found, not surprisingly, are somewhere in between: population does matter, but it is not all determining, nor can or should it be ignored.

John Bongaarts helps to lay the groundwork for understanding *why* population matters by explaining the rapid shifts in dependency burdens that occur during the transition from high to low mortality and fertility. Early in the transition, populations are very young and the size of the young age cohort (under age 15), compared to the economically active one (15–65), is very large. At the middle stages of the transition, as fertility falls, the proportions begin to shift in favor of a relatively large workforce in comparison with both the under-15 and over-65 age groups. Finally, at the end of the transition, the proportion of the population in the older dependent age group rises relative to both young and working age. These shifts can have profound implications for the economy and for families, as the chapters in Parts II and III demonstrate.

1

How and Why Population Matters: New Findings, New Issues

NANCY BIRDSALL AND STEVEN W. SINDING

INTRODUCTION: THE BELLAGIO SYMPOSIUM

No social phenomenon has attracted more attention in the last half-century than the 'population explosion'—that surge of population numbers rising almost threefold from 2.5 billion in 1950 to over 6 billion at the turn of the millennium, and continuing at a diminishing pace to level out at as much as 11 billion in the middle of the twenty-second century. Given the exceptional complexity and diversity of the various impacts of rapid demographic change and rising population numbers, assessments of the consequences of the population explosion have varied widely, ranging all the way from the view that more population growth leads to more prosperity to forecasts that rapid population growth would precipitate wide-ranging catastrophes (famines, ecological collapses, wars, natural resource depletion, and the like).[1]

The range of views has spurred an outpouring of research, much of it by economists and economic demographers. Focusing on the effects of the developing countries' extraordinarily rapid population growth on their economic growth and on the economic and social welfare of their peoples, economists have addressed two big questions: has the rapid population growth of the last half-century been good or bad for these countries' economic prospects? If bad, what government policies and programs to encourage lower fertility and thus slower population growth, if any, make sense—for the economy and for individual and family welfare?

The debate about these questions has been fruitful and contentious, both among economists and between economists and other social scientists. It has been fruitful in the traditional academic sense, in contributing to increasingly sophisticated work based on a stream of new theoretical and modeling insights and on exploitation of ever-improving data. It has been contentious because of its policy relevance. Officialdom has looked to researchers, and particularly to economists, for guidance on policies in poor countries that affect the most personal and critical decisions of families—regarding marriage, women's status, and of course childbearing itself, and for guidance on programs of foreign assistance by rich countries to poor countries.

---

[1] For example, for the positive view Simon (1977) for the negative view, Ehrlich (1975).

While knowledge on the big questions has proceeded slowly, distinct and measured progress has been made. At various times—once or twice a decade since 1950—groups of scholars have taken stock of the research—usually at the behest of the United Nations, the World Bank, USAID, and other official organizations concerned with economic development prospects in the Third World.[2] The present volume, resulting from a Symposium on Population Change and Economic Development held in Bellagio, Italy on 2–6 November 1998, represents the first installment in the new millennium of the continuing compendia of research on population issues by economists and economic demographers.[3] It brings to the fore some notable new findings and highlights a new set of questions.

This chapter is an introduction to the volume as a whole. It draws both upon the papers prepared for the Bellagio Symposium, and equally important, on the Symposium deliberations. The deliberations were of particular value because the Symposium brought together two groups of participants. The first represented economists actively involved in various aspects of economic-demographic research. The papers they presented were assessed not only by their peers at the Symposium, but also by the second group of participants, policy analysts representing various constituencies working on development and population issues. The purpose of an exchange between these groups was to push the research community to contemplate the policy implications of new findings and to help frame the critical policy questions that new research was shaping. At the same time, it encouraged the policy community to incorporate more quickly and more effectively into new programs the implications of new research findings. The papers themselves and the deliberations allow us in this first chapter to vary from the usual format of an edited volume which typically summarizes the results of each chapter. Instead, we have chosen to organize this chapter around several key arguments and empirical results bearing on the two big questions set out above. This permits us, while assessing and updating the literature on the basis of the reported research, to also lay the groundwork for a discussion of the implications of this most recent and sophisticated research for policy. There were, however, no papers at the Symposium that focused primarily on policy and no session that systematically linked the latest research findings to policy. To rectify this gap, one of us has compiled a short concluding chapter, drawing from her previous work and integrating the insights and findings of the Bellagio participants.

Finally, while we have attempted to be faithful to the research essays and to the discussion they catalyzed, judgments on what to include and emphasize have obviously

[2] Kelley, in Chapter 2 of this book, provides an extensive review of these official reviews as well as of the research on which the reviews were based.

[3] The Bellagio Symposium was organized by Nancy Birdsall of the Carnegie Endowment for International Peace, with the support of the Rockefeller and Packard Foundations and the United Nations Population Fund (UNFPA). The sessions were chaired by Nancy Birdsall and Steven Sinding (then of Rockefeller).

been necessary.[4] Moreover, this format for an introductory chapter has the drawback that it greatly understates and downplays the richness of the individual chapters presented in the volume. We therefore hope our readers, particularly those who are scholars and researchers in this field, will give those chapters the detailed scrutiny they merit.

THEMES AND NEW FINDINGS

The chapters in this volume address four questions: what have been the effects of fertility and mortality decline and other demographic changes in the developing countries in the postwar period

- on economic growth?
- on poverty and inequality? and
- on sustainable use of natural resources in agriculture?

What are the implications for economic, social, and population policies and programs?

These are, of course, only a subset of themes that merit consideration, but they arguably represent some of the more important areas of inquiry. First, assessments focusing on aggregate economic growth have attracted attention in past debates about population growth in developing countries (some would say inordinate attention), and the results of this type of assessment are bound to affect future policy and future new research efforts. Secondly, poverty reduction and the distribution of the fruits of economic progress represent critical dimensions of welfare advancement in the Third World; yet research on the impact of population growth and demographic change on poverty and income distribution by economists has been surprisingly limited. Thirdly, the agricultural sector has dominated the activity of most Third World residents; the environment is increasingly under stress; and interactions among the environment, poverty, and population are of special importance in the rural sector. These three themes—aggregate growth, distribution and poverty, and agriculture and the environment—thus represent especially important areas in which to take stock. Finally, debate among economists about the effects of population growth has often clouded rather than clarified policy; an objective of this volume is to reflect upon the implications of new evidence for future development programs and policies.

Like those collective research assessments that have gone before, the findings in this volume strike some new themes (in this case in the assessment of the impacts

---

[4] This chapter is a revision and expansion of our original report on the Symposium. Drafts of the original report were shared with each participant. Their inputs were then incorporated where we felt appropriate, and a revised document was circulated to each participant for information. The final Symposium Report, like this chapter itself, rests solely with the authors. (Allen Kelley joined as a co-editor to the present volume; he focused mainly on providing feedback to the authors.) The authors of this Introduction are especially grateful to our co-editor, Allen Kelley, for his extensive and extremely useful comments on the Symposium Report and on the original draft of this chapter.

of rapid demographic change on aggregate output growth, and on poverty), and reinforce others (in this case the impacts of population on the rural economy and the environment).

First, in contrast to assessments over the last several decades, rapid population growth is found to have exercised a quantitatively important negative impact on the pace of aggregate economic growth in developing countries. The finding, as discussed below, bodes well for the future, as population growth rates decline, even as it helps account for low economic growth in the past.

Secondly, rapid fertility decline is found to make a quantitatively relevant contribution to reducing the incidence and severity of poverty. Though an association between poverty and high fertility has long been noted, research in this area has rarely gone beyond association to causality, and has advanced slowly given the challenges of empirical assessment. The new findings suggest more strongly than before that past high fertility in poor countries has been a partial cause of the persistence of poverty— both for poor families that are large, and via the kinds of economy-wide effects that Malthus theorized about, for poor families even if they are small. As with the finding that rapid population growth affects economic growth, this bodes well for the future, since fertility is declining almost everywhere in the developing world.

Finally, the impact of rapid demographic change on the rural environment and development is found to be mixed—above all, a minor player in a much larger story about initial conditions and broad policy effects. This finding calls attention to the relevance of development policy writ large—of policies having to do with agricultural prices, rural infrastructure, the urban labor market, and the financial sector—to whether demographic change and more narrowly defined 'population policies' affect for good or ill rural residents, still the majority in the developing world.

We turn now to some specifics about these effects of demographic change, and then to the implications for policy as seen by economists through the lens of their economic analyses.

SETTING THE STAGE: DEMOGRAPHIC CHANGE AND ECONOMIC REVISIONISM

Recounting the at times fitful progress of economic research on population over many decades, Allen Kelley (Ch. 2) emphasizes the triumph of what he calls 'revisionism'. He refers not to a particular quantitative assessment of the effect of rapid population growth—positive, negative, or neutral—but to a particular approach to research. That approach emphasizes the long run, and the possibility over the long run that the initial impact of demographic change will be modified by feedback within social and economic systems. With this approach, the net impact of a demographic change depends on the period allowed for such feedbacks, the importance of the feedbacks themselves, and the extent to which feedbacks moderate or reinforce initial impacts.

Economists have tended to emphasize the relevance of *compensating* technology and institutions in *moderating* initial negative impacts of, for example, the effect of a growing population; this is a point that Pender makes in Chapter 12, and that

Ester Boserup made in her classic study of how population growth in African agricultural societies catalyzed the change from shifting fallow to higher yielding settled agriculture.[5] The attention to compensating and thus moderating factors comes naturally for economists concerned with general equilibrium effects in large markets, where for example a new scarcity due to a perturbation in one part of the system should lead to a price increase in the scarce good, leading in turn to reduced demand for that good. However, in models of the effects of demographic change, economists have more recently also noted the potential for *reinforcing effects*, where an initial perturbation such as a decline in mortality has a long-run positive impact—potentially more than offsetting any short-run negative 'crowding' effect of the initial rise in population growth. Bloom and Canning in Chapter 7 note that an exogenous increase in life expectancy can spur economic growth because longer expected life encourages private investment in education which raises country economic growth, and that additional economic growth may then induce an additional increase in life expectancy.

Moreover, economists generally expect initial negative effects of a demographic change to be moderated and initial positive effects to be reinforced, the more effective are markets, governments, and institutions. So the initial negative impact on the economy of an exogenous demographic change such as a decline in infant mortality (due to new health technology) will be greater, unfortunately, in low-income countries, where these three institutions are relatively weak. And in turn the initial positive effect of a decline in fertility (say due to increased education of mothers) in reducing local pressure on school spending is likely to be reinforced where labor markets and school systems are working well and parents are prepared to invest in their children's education. Similarly, economic models will take into account the possibility that the initial impact of a demographic change, whether positive or negative, can pale in comparison to the effect of its interaction with markets and policies, so that the strength or weakness of the latter turns out to be the critical determinant of the ultimate outcome in terms of people's well-being.

The analysis of revisionism presented by Kelley clarifies and puts in perspective the contributions of the Bellagio papers. Specifically, the key findings of the Bellagio papers are all amassed using revisionist methodologies by economists who examine demographic impacts over long time periods, who account for some feedbacks of demography within societies, and who find, contrary to some previous revisionist studies, a negative net impact on measures of economic growth and poverty reduction.

Finally, it is worth noting one additional element of the revisionist approach, namely that over the long run the different components of demographic change can have offsetting, and thus moderating effects. Change in the rate of population growth is the result of change in one or both of fertility and mortality decline, and in some settings of migration, and the aggregate change in population growth brings over time changes in the size of population, in density, and in age composition. Moreover, because demographic change occurs slowly (at least compared to economic and political change), the separate effects of these different components of

[5] Boserup (1965).

demographic change matter immensely for understanding the overall effects of population on the economy. One of the long-run changes that follows from change in fertility and mortality in a population is the gradual, gradually shifting, and computationally complicated (while essentially straightforward) working through to changes in the age composition of that population. The latter half of the twentieth century has witnessed changes in age composition of populations on a dramatic scale, in both developing and developed countries. Though the changes have come slowly in terms of the short scholarly life of individual researchers, they have been stunningly rapid in historical terms, and highly differentiated across countries—making it possible to assess the impact of those changes over time and across countries. The studies in this book reflect the new prominence of age composition as a factor in economists' latest models of long-run economic growth, after many years of relative neglect.[6]

John Bongaarts's analysis of dependency burdens in the developing world (Ch. 3) is thus a critical starting-point for much of what follows in this volume. Bongaarts emphasizes that declining fertility, now under way to one degree or another in all regions of the world, will result in substantially changed age structures and distribution, with gradually reduced proportions of the population under age 15 and enlarged proportions over age 65. As countries move through the demographic transition of falling mortality followed eventually by falling fertility, they face first a period of increasing child-dependency ratios, then of decreasing child-dependency ratios as a larger proportion of the population moves through the working ages, and eventually of increasing old-age-dependency ratios.

The effect of fertility decline in the second intermediate stage (through which virtually all developing countries have passed and will be passing in the latter twentieth and early twenty-first centuries) is a one-time 'demographic bonus' or 'window of opportunity'—a period of as many as 50 years during which an initially high ratio of the working age to the dependent population gradually declines. After a country has passed through this period, it returns to a more or less stable child-dependency ratio (and a higher aged-dependency ratio), at new lower levels of both fertility and mortality.

Changes in the dependency ratio are driven mostly by fertility decline and less by changes in mortality. This is simply because mortality affects all parts of the age distribution while the fertility effect has a strong immediate impact on the child-dependency ratio, and then gradually works its way through the entire age distribution. In some developing countries, however, where the initial phase of mortality decline has concentrated on infants and youth, the mortality decline has reinforced the impact on age distribution of fertility decline.

So the duration and pace of fertility decline, and the extent to which mortality decline is disproportionately concentrated on infants and children, affect both the

---

[6] Of course there have been exceptions. Because age composition affects savings rates, economists have tried to assess the impact of age composition change on changes in savings. Early efforts to use cross-country data as a proxy for change in countries (e.g. Leff 1969) were unconvincing.

duration and impact of the so-called window of opportunity. The faster the decline, the larger the potential benefits of a relatively high ratio of working-age to dependent ages, but the shorter the period the window will remain open. The period of the window of opportunity is characterized by (1) more workers producing more total output, *if* they are productively employed; (2) greater accumulation of wealth, *if* savings occur and are productively invested; and (3) a larger supply of human capital, *if* appropriate investments are made in its formation.

Bongaarts traces the shift in dependency ratios that accompanies the demographic transition across the major regions of the developing world, showing that the shift occurred earliest in East Asia, followed shortly thereafter by Latin America, and considerably later by Africa. The Middle East and South Asia are at intermediate points between Latin America and Africa.

POPULATION CHANGE AND THE ECONOMY

Allen Kelley's chapter with Robert Schmidt (Ch. 4) brings together and systematically assesses the results of the major recent studies of the effects of rapid population growth on per capita income growth over the last 35 years. Referring to recent studies using aggregate country data to assess the influence of population growth in the developing world on increases in country-level GDP per capita, Kelley and Schmidt conclude: 'We arrive at the *qualified* judgment: rapid population growth, and its associated demographic components, appears to have exerted a fairly strong, adverse effect on the pace of economic growth over the period 1960–1995' (emphasis added).

Economists for a decade or more have hesitated to make strong statements about the magnitude of effects of population growth on economic development. To quote from the 1986 National Academy of Sciences report: '*On balance*, we reach the *qualitative* conclusion that slower population growth would be beneficial to economic development for *most* developing countries' (emphasis added). In his review of the history of the population debate (Ch. 2), Kelley explains why economists now have more confidence in the clearer results of more recent analyses. These more recent analyses—of the last five years or so—are based on better-specified models (in which demographic variables are now incorporated into the growth models developed by economists in the last decade). Compared to the 1980s, they exploit the longer period of time over which it has been possible to observe the effect of reduced fertility, changing labor force size, and lower youth dependency on economic growth.

These recent analyses, including those in this volume by Jeffrey Williamson (Ch. 5) as well as by Kelley and Schmidt, represent an advance over earlier analyses because they distinguish carefully among the effects of changes in the various components of demographic change and population growth—including fertility, mortality, and the dependency ratio—rather than looking only at population growth in the aggregate, and because they also take into account changes in population size and density. These analyses indicate that among demographic changes of the last three decades, increases in population density and size and increases in the relative size of the working-age population are positively associated with economic growth, while increases in the size of the age group 0 to 15 are negatively associated with growth.

Kelley and Schmidt use their statistical results to examine not only the positive or negative effects of the different components of demographic change, but the quantitative magnitude of these effects, taking into account the size of the actual demographic changes over the 35-year period 1960–95. Over that period, demographic trends have been strongly favorable to economic growth for the average country. Declining fertility and mortality, and to a much smaller extent, larger populations and higher densities, have all spurred economic growth. The only trend that has apparently slowed growth for the average country is a decline in the growth rate of the working age population. Of course many of the poorest developing countries that are still in a relatively early stage of fertility decline can look forward to increases in the size of the working-age population for many years to come.

Why should a relatively larger working-age population contribute to positive economic growth? Economists have long theorized that savings contribute to higher levels of per capita income (by financing higher investment and thus higher output per person), and more recently that higher savings and investment may contribute to sustained rates of income growth as well. In their chapter (Ch. 6) Ronald Lee, Andrew Mason, and Tim Miller, using household survey data from Taiwan on earnings, estimated savings, and fertility and mortality, simulate increases in savings rates and in accumulated wealth on the basis of a life-cycle model of savings behavior. The life-cycle model is driven by the kinds of changes in the youth-dependency ratio and the rapid increases in working-age population that Taiwan and other East Asian countries have experienced in the postwar period due to their rapid fertility declines. (It also assumes that individuals cannot rely on the kind of 'transfer wealth' that pay-as-you-go systems of retirement represent, but must save themselves to finance their own retirement.)

The simulation model generates substantial increases in savings rates and in wealth during the period of demographic transition as the working-age population increases (under the assumptions of a constant rate of interest or return to capital, and a constant productivity rate). The simulation also generates much higher savings rates and wealth–income ratios at the end compared to the beginning of the long demographic transition, implying higher sustained rates of economic growth at lower levels of fertility and mortality. The results of the simulation track reasonably well actual data on increasing savings rates in Taiwan. This result is consistent with the conclusion of Williamson in this volume and of others who, though differing on the magnitude of the demographic effect, see changes in age structure in East Asia in the least three decades as an important contributor to that region's large upward swings in savings and investment over the same period. The resulting high savings and investment levels were one of many factors that set the stage for that region's long and sustained period of historically unprecedented economic growth. Williamson concludes from cross-country statistical analysis that demographic changes, especially the increase in the working-age population and the increase in savings induced by changes in dependency, can be associated with as much as one-third of the total average annual per capita growth rate of about 6 percent in East Asia in that period.

Four issues need to be considered when assessing the relationship between demographic change and economic performance.

First, the effect is conditioned by the level of development. Kelley and Schmidt's analysis of evidence based on data for the 1980s suggests that the lower the initial level of per capita income, the greater the net positive impact of demographic changes, especially of fertility decline.

Secondly, the positive effect of the demographic changes associated with the demographic transition probably depends strongly on the economic policy which accompanies the transition. The East Asian countries were able to exploit the opportunity presented by the 'demographic bonus' because of a combination of policies including fiscal discipline, relatively open and competitive markets, and substantial public investments in basic education that ensured healthy returns to physical and human capital and to participation in the labor force. In contrast, rapid demographic change in Latin America, including rapid fertility decline in the last two decades, has not been so clearly associated with improved economic performance. Participants agreed that fertility decline and other demographic changes may encourage economic growth but are far from sufficient to guarantee growth. A sound policy regime is essential.

Thirdly, though fertility decline is the primary impetus to the change in age composition that generates the demographic bonus, the statistical results point to mortality decline as an important factor in raising economic growth rates, despite the obvious initial and partial result of higher population growth.[7] Mortality decline has long been assumed by demographers to catalyze, with a lag, a subsequent fertility decline—this is at the heart of the theory of the demographic transition. In addition, the economic models suggest that mortality decline more directly improves growth prospects—possibly by increasing the private incentives to invest in human capital, or because it is associated with morbidity declines that raise productivity.

Fourthly, it is clear from many other studies that the key components of the change in age composition highlighted above, mortality and fertility decline, are not only a possible cause of more rapid economic growth (through their effects during the transition of reducing dependency ratios) but are *outcomes* of factors associated with economic growth, including increased education, better functioning markets, and so forth. If this reverse causality is not taken into account, statistical estimates of the effect of lower or declining mortality and fertility on growth may be overstated. Recent analyses do a much better job of correcting for this possible reverse causality, but cannot fully eliminate it. (It is in part for this reason that Kelley and Schmidt refer to their judgment quoted above, regarding the effects of rapid population growth, as 'qualified'.)

---

[7] Debate continues about whether mortality decline in developing countries has been in part exogenous to economic growth, that is, triggered by factors such as better health technologies that were independent of growth itself, or not. This is a separate issue from the question of the effect of mortality decline on growth.

At the same time, the likelihood of reverse causality out there in the world raises another issue. Reverse causality (to repeat, meaning that fertility and mortality decline may be outcomes as well as or instead of causes of economic growth) creates a methodological problem. On the one hand, its likely presence has led careful scholars to avoid making strong statements about the size of any effect of fertility or mortality change or any other demographic change on economic growth. At the same time, reverse causality if present implies that even an initially small impact of fertility decline in raising growth prospects (by reducing youth dependency for example) could, over time, induce a mutually reinforcing process with larger cumulative effects, as the resulting economic growth contributes to further fertility decline, leading to more economic growth and so on. So while reverse causality, unaccounted for, implies that the long-run effect of an initial fertility decline and the resulting initial boost to growth is *overstated*, two-way causality with feedback implies that the effect is *understated*. (Similarly reverse causality implies that an initially small impact of mortality decline in raising youth dependency could generate a downward spiral of reduced growth, unless followed by reduced fertility, with offsetting effects in lowering youth dependency. In many developing countries, in fact, the sequence of declining mortality which once the larger cohorts reach about age 15 years actually improves dependency ratios, followed by declining fertility, has in fact meant both demographic effects have combined to produce the demographic bonus described above.

Of course these dynamics also make any specific prediction of future high or low economic growth due to demographic triggers foolhardy—because magnitudes are so sensitive to initial estimates and to the effects of elusive and multiple interactions with many non-demographic factors. Having said that, modeling of dynamic, two-way relationships has been largely absent in the economic demography literature. In Chapter 7 of this volume, David Bloom and David Canning set out the theoretical basis for these dynamics. They argue that not only do higher income (and education and other positive correlates of income) lead to lower mortality and fertility, a reasonably well-documented finding, but that lower mortality and fertility can contribute to rising income. Lower mortality and longer life expectancy for example create an environment for higher household investment, including in education, and obviously allow longer periods of productive work per person.[8] Using long time series of demographic and economic data for a large sample of countries, they explore empirically the possibility of two-way causality between economic growth on the one hand, and mortality as well as fertility decline on the other, given a consistently positive link at the country level between declines in mortality and fertility and changes in average country per capita income. Bloom and Canning illustrate the possibility of a reinforcing or 'accelerator' effect of two-way causality. However, they are not able to establish definitively the underlying causal mechanisms nor the quantitative magnitude of two-way causality; it is for the next round of research to hone in better on its quantitative relevance.

---

[8] Of course, there are also offsetting forces such as age-distribution changes, highlighted in their work, where averted infant/child deaths can attenuate or even offset, at least for 15 years, the positive impacts of extending life expectancy.

Another point: even the latest and most technically careful aggregate macro models do not take explicitly into account the potential powerful impact of female labor force participation on economic growth, and the link between declining fertility and increased female labor force participation. Declining fertility and rising female labor force participation may both be the outcome of increases in the opportunity cost of women's time in child-rearing, in turn due to rising levels of education and/or to increasing demand for labor in the formal sector. Rising female labor force participation means that the growth in total work participation increases even faster than the growth in the size of working-age population. The 'demographic bonus' thus may be realized not only through shifts in the age structure but through increases in the participation of women in the formal labor force that fertility decline encourages or at least permits.

Of course the effect of such increases on income growth is overstated to the extent that national accounts include monetary income earned by women but not the real income represented by women's work at home. This raises still another issue that needs to be considered in assessing the effects of population change on economic growth. As with the effects of increased participation in the labor force of women, measured increases in economic growth per capita exaggerate real income gains to the extent that they reflect unsustainable degradation of natural resource wealth, or fail to reflect such 'costs' associated with income growth as pollution which are not subtracted from measured gains in current systems of national accounts.[9]

With all these points in mind, and notwithstanding very important conditioning or mediating factors, there is today stronger evidence than ever before that first, reductions in the dependency ratio due to declining fertility during the demographic transition can, if policy circumstances are favorable, have a strong positive effect on economic growth; and, secondly, that lower fertility (as well as lower mortality), along with the small positive effects of greater density and a larger population resulting from earlier higher population growth, can also lead to higher economic growth rates.[10]

This conclusion, measured as it is, represents a significant departure from the typically more agnostic position of economists on this relationship over the last two decades.

FERTILITY, POVERTY, AND THE FAMILY

Malthus noted at the level of entire societies that high fertility would likely worsen income distribution and increase poverty by increasing the price of food and reducing the price of labor—economic effects in large interacting markets that need to be examined at the macroeconomic level. Along with these effects at the macro level,

[9] National accounts may also fail to measure adequately changes in knowledge, improvements in the quality of life due to new products, and so forth that work in the opposite direction.

[10] Higher-aged dependency, once the transition is complete, could eventually reduce and even offset the positive effect on economic growth during the transition. It is too soon to judge whether higher-aged dependency in Japan, Europe, and eventually in China, will reduce their rates of growth.

there may also be effects at the micro level—of lower fertility within families on the family's own economic and social welfare.

Macro Effects   The literature on income growth and demographic change discussed above indicates that across countries and over many decades declines in fertility and mortality have contributed to income growth. Have these declines also helped reduce poverty and improve the distribution of income? Surprisingly little empirical work has been done on the effects of country-level fertility decline, now a fact for so many developing countries, on changes in country measures of poverty. What has been done is, less surprisingly, generally inconclusive,[11] given the lack of comparable data on country poverty until recently and the inability to test directly such key connections between aggregate demographic change and poverty as the effects of lower fertility on labor demand and wages.

These deficiencies are in part addressed in the chapter by Robert Eastwood and Michael Lipton (Ch. 9). Based on analysis of economic and demographic data for 45 developing countries, they estimate that high fertility increases absolute levels of poverty both by retarding economic growth (thus slowing growth-induced poverty reduction) and by skewing the distribution of consumption against the poor. They estimate that had the average country in this group of 45 countries reduced its birth rate by 5 per 1,000 throughout the 1980s (as in fact many countries did) the average country poverty incidence of 18.9 percent in the mid-1980s would have been reduced to 12.6 percent between 1990 and 1995.[12] The statistical work suggests that about half the estimated decline in poverty over the period in the countries studied can be attributed to increases in economic growth and half to changes in the distribution of consumption that helped the poor.

Eastwood and Lipton also show that the poorer the country and the higher its initial level of fertility, the greater the effect of declining fertility on a decline in absolute poverty. Moreover, the beneficial effects increase as the demographic transition proceeds. The effects of the transition on reductions in poverty are, as with the effects on economic growth, different at different stages of the transition—harmful to poverty reduction in the early stages as population growth accelerates due primarily to mortality decline that occurs disproportionately among infants and children, and helpful in the later stages as fertility declines and aggregate population growth slows.

It follows that during the early stages of the demographic transition, income differentials between poor and non-poor households may in fact become greater. But as the transition extends to all groups in the society, so that fertility as well as mortality begins to decline, and the fertility decline spreads to poor households, the poverty-reducing

---

[11] For a useful survey of work or population and poverty, see Ahlburg (1996). He concludes that there is little direct evidence using economy-wide data to tie population growth to poverty incidence; he goes on to review evidence of indirect links, e.g. through effects on education, and evidence at the family level.

[12] The authors' definition of the poor for this estimate is persons in households where consumption per adult is below that estimated as the minimum needed for adequate food-energy. This definition is a stricter one than the now-conventional definition used for example by the World Bank, of those households where income per person per day is $1 or less.

and inequality-reducing effects increase. As the dependency ratio within families declines and the cost of childbearing declines, more income is available for consumption and savings, particularly where women enter the labor force and contribute to increased family incomes.[13] The analysis (Ch. 11) of Ricardo Paes de Barros and colleagues for Brazil, a country already in the later stages of the transition to lower fertility, illustrates this point. Paes de Barros *et al.* use a series of household surveys in Brazil to study long-term changes in household size and age structure (resulting from various demographic changes, especially fertility decline) and their effects on the incidence of poverty. They estimate that with the age structure of households 70 years ago but today's average income by age of household members, 37 percent of people would be classified as poor, compared to today's actual 25 percent. Put another way, they estimate that the poverty level of the cohort born in 1970 is 12 percentage points lower than it would have been had it experienced the fertility level of the cohort born in 1900. The decline in poverty associated with what has been a dramatic reduction in fertility and thus in household size in Brazil is equivalent to what would have been produced by a 0.7 percent greater annual increase in per capita GDP.

In summary, recent evidence, which exploits improved data on poverty changes at the country level, as well as the fact that a larger number of countries are experiencing some fertility decline, indicates that reductions in fertility may well be contributing to a decline in poverty rates and intensity. Whether this result is robust and whether the impacts are large depend critically on other factors, for example how changes in wage rates affect labor force and fertility decisions of the poor, that need to be studied at the country and at the family level. This brings us to the next topic.

Effects of Large Family Size on Family Welfare   There is little debate that poverty and large family size go hand in hand. Eastwood and Lipton's study and Thomas Merrick's (Ch. 8) refer to dozens of empirical analyses confirming that in today's developing countries larger households have higher poverty incidence. Moreover, among poor households, those that have more children invest less in children's education and health, and systematically see worse health outcomes associated with pregnancy for mothers.[14]

But scientists have long cautioned that the associations observed do not in themselves indicate causality. High fertility in poor families may reflect parents' sensible

---

[13] Lipton points out that this distribution effect of declining fertility can itself be due to two factors. First, there may be a dependency effect—if a reduction in country-level fertility is associated with a greater reduction in the dependency ratio of poor households than of rich households (usually in the later stages of a country's fertility decline—as in the Brazil case above). Secondly, there may be an 'acquisition' effect whereby a decline in fertility improves the ability or willingness of poor households to raise their consumption levels (per non-dependent) for example by raising their labor supply or by raising their savings rate (if their own household size declines with lower fertility) or at the level of markets by reducing the demand for land and increasing the scarcity of labor—both Malthusian-style benefits for the relatively poor whether their own fertility declines or not.

[14] The size of the impact on education enrollment and attainment is typically small, but does not take into account the likely reality that poor families, particularly in rural areas, probably have access to lower quality schooling.

decisions to trade off current consumption for greater future family income when children begin work, or for greater old age security, or it may simply reflect parents' decisions to enjoy children rather than other forms of consumption. The fact that large families tend to have lower incomes should not be construed as meaning that they either are, or that they regard themselves as being, objectively 'worse off'. Indeed, Ricardo Hausmann and Miguel Székely (Ch. 10) emphasize that the fertility decision is embedded in a set of decisions at the family level which are influenced by many aspects of the economic environment, and which make sense given that environment.

On the other hand, studies over the last decade raise several countervailing arguments, increasingly shifting the burden of proof from those who argue that high fertility is chosen (implicitly if not explicitly) by poor couples and should be assumed to reflect optimal levels of welfare for the family, to those who argue that at least some fertility among the poor may not be optimal to family welfare. Many of the arguments are summarized in the chapter by Merrick. They include:[15]

- Severely (indeed often tragically) limited choices of very poor parents. The very poor (the approximately 1 billion households—20 percent of the population of developing countries—that subsist on $1 per day per person or less) have severely constrained choices. For the very poor, the alternative of fewer but 'higher quality' children who might have better prospects does not really exist. The risks—that a child will fail in school, suffer poor health, or even die—are too great, and the rewards too few in an uncertain future. The resources to finance good health and schooling, even to finance a healthy diet, do not exist. In the face of poor capital and other markets, poor households cannot borrow against the future earnings of better-educated children, and ironically therefore cannot afford to choose few children, even recognizing that their fewer children might face a better future.

- A lack of critical information available to the poor. Given the poor state of markets for information, poor households are likely to lack information on the changing probability of infant mortality, on increasing returns to schooling, on improving financial markets as a mechanism for old-age security—that is, on a variety of changing conditions that would lead them to choose fewer children. Such information is in a real sense more costly to acquire for the less educated, and very poor parents are usually without much education. (And of course, whatever information is available, from government officials, for example, on improvement in mortality rates or in the trustworthiness of banks, might reflect an average state of affairs which the poor might reasonably discount as applying to them.)

- The fact that men may dominate in the choice of number of children, while not fully sharing the costs—a kind of intra-familial externality that is assumed away in traditional unitary household utility functions.[16] Cultural and institutional factors

---

[15] The following discussion also reflects the authors' own analyses, including Birdsall and Griffin (1993), Chomitz and Birdsall (1991), and Birdsall (1994). The possibility that men and women have different interests in fertility decisions was raised frequently in the deliberations at the Bellagio Symposium.

[16] Models with individual utility functions and bargaining among household members would better reflect the underlying mechanisms leading to the intra-household allocation of resources.

may lead to differing interests among household members and unequal capacity to participate in household decisions, particularly for women. The reality in many low-income settings may be one of gender imbalances in decision-making regarding whom and when to marry, who in the household gets access to health care and education, when and what kind of contraception to use, and the power to negotiate safe sex when the risk of sexually transmitted diseases and HIV/AIDS infection is high.[17]

• The evidence of higher prevalence of unwanted pregnancies among the poor,[18] combined with evidence that when births are not planned, investments in children, for example in their education, are systematically lower.[19]

• The evidence that in the last decade, fertility has fallen (and contraceptive use risen) even among very poor, uneducated women in Bangladesh and Kenya, who had good access to health and family planning information and services.[20]

In short, on the one hand it is altogether likely that household poverty is a cause as much or more than a consequence of high fertility (or that poverty and high fertility do not cause each other but are both caused by other factors such as poor education). On the other hand, as was the case with aggregate demographic change and aggregate economic growth, it is also likely that there is two-way causation, with poverty and high fertility unfortunately reinforcing each other in a vicious circle. In fact, both theory and improved and expanded empirical efforts support the likelihood that high fertility of poor parents is contributing to their and their children's poverty. In Chapter 14 below Birdsall sets out the implications for policy of this new evidence linking demographic change to poverty decline.

POPULATION, AGRICULTURE, AND NATURAL RESOURCE USE

Of all the possible effects of population size and demographic change on natural resource use, effects on land use in agriculture are probably the most relevant for the developing world. It is in use of land for agriculture that a syndrome of high population growth interacting with poverty to generate pressures for natural resource degradation is most likely.[21]

[17] There is evidence that in some cultures women have little autonomy in sexual and reproductive decision making. See e.g. Mane *et al.* (1994).

[18] See e.g. Bongaarts (1990). The evidence of unwanted pregnancies is ample—based not only on more than two decades of surveys but even more convincingly on the continuing high incidence of abortion, including among the poor, even where abortion is illegal and dangerous. For a skeptical view on measuring unmet needs, see Behrman and Knowles (1998).

[19] The latter evidence is from studies of outcomes for twins (where the extra birth is presumably unanticipated) and of outcomes for children of parents with high biological propensity to conceive. See e.g. Rosenzweig and Wolpin (1980); Rosenzweig and Schultz (1987).

[20] Cleland *et al.* (1994) for Bangladesh; Cross *et al.* (1991) and National Research Council (1993), for Kenya.

[21] An emphasis on land use, particularly farming systems and forest use, was implicitly supported by the 1986 National Academy of Sciences report, which concluded that any problem of population is

In his chapter on this issue John Pender (Ch. 12) reviews the growing empirical literature and provides an example from Honduras of the kind of new study needed. He concludes that though rapid population increase may encourage technological innovation that leads to increased output, such population increase can also have a negative impact, especially in the absence of an adequate policy and institutional environment—that is, an environment that creates incentives for individuals and societies to manage natural resources in a sustainable manner. On the one hand, the potential negative effect of population growth has been and can be mediated by policy and practices. This is particularly the case with respect to output and land productivity.[22] On the other hand, as Pender puts it, *without* collective action, population density can make things worse in terms of agricultural output, land productivity, and most important in terms of human welfare. (Pender also notes that even where population increases catalyze increases in production and land productivity,[23] the outcome in terms of labor productivity and thus consumption and income per person may not be in net terms positive.)

Collective action includes in this instance the capacity of societies to develop the necessary policies, for example protection of property rights and appropriate pricing of water, and the necessary institutions, including rules for sustainable use of common property resources. There remains the question of whether collective action is itself catalyzed or undermined by rapid increases in population in local settings—a question which also seems to depend on many other factors. And as Pender notes, if population increase does raise the likelihood of collective action, it does so necessarily at some cost, administrative and organizational as well as financial, if extant welfare levels are to be sustained. The costs will be particularly high in settings where land is sparsely populated in area terms, so that a society cannot take advantage of the positive effect of a denser population on say the cost of infrastructure, and at the same time densely populated in terms of effective productive land, so that there are negative effects on output per worker as population increases. This combination of a sparse population over space with a dense population per effective agricultural unit prevails in many parts of Africa.[24]

In the end, though the theory and the concepts are clear, in the absence of a richer body of empirical work, in many different settings and over substantial time periods, a simple and general conclusion about the effect of population on natural resource use and sustainability remains elusive. This is unfortunate. Estimates of the costs of environmental damage in developing countries often reach several percentage points

more likely to be associated with unsustainable use of renewable resources such as land, rather than with non-renewable mineral resources.

[22] Pender emphasizes the lack of any convincing evidence that even with favorable (Boserupian) technological change, labor productivity and thus income per worker has also been sustained or increased.

[23] This is the effect that Boserup (1965) outlined.

[24] A possible net negative effect of density in some settings is not inconsistent with the Kelley and Schmidt (Ch. 4) finding that, over many countries and several decades, size and density of population have positive but rather small effects on economic growth.

of GDP, thus qualifying the record of economic growth in developing countries.[25] To the extent that population does play a role in environmental damage, it represents another kind of demographic bonus from reductions in its growth rate, and a further externality far from the calculus (implicit or explicit) affecting individual couples' fertility behavior.

Moreover, there is evidence of a close link between *poverty* and environmental damage; to the extent population growth adds to the difficulty of reducing poverty, it is implicated, if only indirectly, as a factor in environmental degradation.[26] Quite aside from population change, the poor are often driven by lack of options to unsustainable exploitation of natural resources, and in turn, households and entire communities are less able to escape poverty where environmental damage has reduced their access to natural resources. Worse, the vicious cycle may start and is often sustained not because the poor damage the environment, but because their poverty impedes their political ability to resist unsustainable exploitation by others of resources on which they depend.

Still, a simple conclusion about the effects of population change on natural resource use, and the role of poverty interacting with population change, is not warranted. The problem is that the necessary empirical work is unusually challenging. To tease out any effect in a particular setting requires observations over a long time period, if only because changes in population size proceed slowly (at least compared to changes due to natural disasters, price changes, and so on). Over a long time period, of course, the possibility of confounding compensatory or reinforcing adjustments increases, disguising any population effect or confusing its apparent magnitude. For example outmigration may serve as a safety valve out of agriculture if natural resource problems constrain production, or in-migration may occur where resources are managed well. Similarly government investments and interventions may be reinforcing or compensating—an apparent result in Pender's Honduran setting. In this area, there seems to remain no alternative to more detailed and probably more country-specific studies over longer periods of the type the Pender chapter represents. Meanwhile, the one point that is clear is the following: the effects of markets and institutions— sometimes good, sometimes bad—can easily swamp the effect of population change on resource use, degradation, and depletion. The implications for policy thus go far beyond the traditional 'population' arena.

CONSEQUENCES OF RAPID POPULATION GROWTH: A NEW BOTTOM LINE

While over the last several decades major scholarly assessments have generally concluded that rapid population growth has an adverse impact on economic growth in the

---

[25] In addition, high population growth in developing countries for given greenhouse gas emissions per person implies a negative global externality, if emissions contribute to global warming. Of course, any increases will be small relative to accumulated emissions of the rich countries. Birdsall (1993) notes that there are multiple routes for reducing the potential contribution of population growth to global warming.

[26] World Bank (1992).

Third World, especially in the poorest countries where markets are relatively under-developed and government policies too often ill advised, previous studies have for the most part been cautious about providing a *quantitative* assessment. The Bellagio Symposium breaks from this tradition. The Symposium studies expose more clearly than before some of the linkages between components of demographic change and economic growth, and indicate that the size of the impact of rapid population growth may be larger than that attributed to it in the past. The Bellagio results also bring more closely into focus the impact of demographic change on poverty reduction, and underscore the potential (but as yet by no means fully revealed) impacts, both positive and negative, of rapid demographic change in the rural environment.

ECONOMICS AND DEMOGRAPHY: POLICY IMPLICATIONS

We noted at the beginning of this chapter that debate about the effects of population growth on economic growth in poor countries has been particularly contentious. The reason is straightforward: if the effects of the extraordinarily rapid population growth of the last half-century in developing countries have been to constrain their growth and hamper their development, then it is easy (indeed, as we discuss below, too easy) to conclude that government policies to induce people to have fewer children, in the interests of society, make perfect sense. A conclusion that population growth has been harmful seems to invite government to intervene to affect fertility, a sensitive and highly personal arena of family behavior. (The alternative mechanism of slowing population growth via higher mortality is not on the table because it is so obviously not in the interests of individuals or society. Moreover, as the studies in this volume indicate, lowering infant and child mortality is not only an objective in itself and a means to lower fertility as parents seek a desired family size, but also with some lag, a factor in increasing the proportion of the working-age population, with the potential benefits to the economy and on poverty reduction discussed above.)

Along these lines, economists have long emphasized that a finding at the macro level that high fertility impedes economic growth does not necessarily justify public intervention to alter individual micro-level behavior, unless it can be shown that individual childbearing preferences are consistent with lower fertility in the aggregate. In the same spirit, Bellagio participants noted that economic growth is not an end in itself but a means to the larger objective of improved well-being.[27] Thus, it is likely to be counterproductive to push for lower fertility against the wishes of families even if there is a benefit in terms of growth. Economists thus find absolutely no justification for policies that *coerce* people toward specific fertility outcomes.

More formally, as emphasized by Behrman in Chapter 13 of this volume, the central justification for a policy intervention is the *difference* between the private and the social costs (net of benefits; or benefits net of costs) of high (or low) fertility. Any

---

[27] Sen (1999) is most eloquent on the point that an objective of development as well as a means to development, is individual freedom.

difference between private and social costs in whatever realm is usually the outcome of some market failure—for example in the case of pollution, where the polluter passes on costs to others. High fertility may or may not represent a gap between the private and social costs of having children: parents may not only be choosing children over other consumption and investment options; they may also be fully absorbing the costs of those children. If parents absorb fully the cost of children, the resulting reduction in their household per capita income (and thus in aggregate per capita income) does not necessarily justify public intervention. Where parents either cannot or will not absorb the full cost of their children, or where they are bearing children in excess of their desired fertility goals, there may be justification for non-coercive policies that encourage—or make it easier for parents to attain the goal of—smaller families. In any case, the new and more convincing evidence that high fertility constrains growth does not *in itself* provide a rationale for public interventions to reduce fertility.

Behrman's chapter thus provides a link between the conclusions from the earlier chapters regarding the consequences of population change, and the issue of whether and how to intervene in order to improve people's lives. Indeed, all of the 'macro' as well as 'micro' chapters are rooted in 'micro' models of human behavior: in Lee *et al.* about savings decisions at different ages; in Eastwood and Lipton about effects on consumption and work of changes in family size; in Pender about farmers' behavior, and so on. Policy interventions need to be justified and shaped by an understanding of those 'micro' choices people make, and of how public policies and programs affect those choices. As Birdsall suggests in the concluding Chapter 14, the essays in this volume do point to a conclusion which links concern about population growth and change more directly to concern about the welfare of millions of people in the developing world. In their entirety they put together a newly compelling set of arguments and evidence indicating that high fertility exacerbates poverty or, better put, that high fertility makes poverty reduction more difficult and less likely. Given new evidence about the potential benefits of declining fertility for reducing poverty and about the effects of declining mortality and fertility on growth, itself a critical factor in reducing poverty, she argues that a set of policies—ranging broadly from sensible macroeconomic regimes to public financing for certain education, health, and family planning services—are likely to make sense. They make sense because while reducing fertility (and mortality), they also have broad social and economic benefits for relatively low costs, and pose no trade-off in terms of improving individual well-being.

In summary, the chapters in this volume, almost all of which focus on the consequences of demographic change without direct allusion to specific policy implications, strengthen the proposition that the demographic transition and the reductions in rates of population growth throughout most of the developing world in the last few decades have contributed and are contributing to improvement in the lives of that world's poor. Along with some simple application of welfare economics and common sense about the goals of development, they also strengthen the argument for policies that will further improve the lives of the poor in developing countries. Those policies can contribute to development in many ways; we show in this volume that they do so in part by reinforcing the social and economic changes that are speeding the demographic transition.[28]

References

Ahlburg, Dennis A. 1996. 'Population Growth and Poverty'. In Dennis A. Ahlburg, Allen Kelley and Karen Oppenheim Mason eds., *The Impact of Population Growth on Well-Being in Developing Countries*. New York: Springer, 219–58.

Behrman, Jere R. 1996. *Demographic Changes, Poverty and Income Distribution*. Washington: Overseas Development Council.

——— and James Knowles. 1998. 'Population and Reproductive Health: An Economic Framework for Policy Evaluation'. *Population and Development Review*. 24 (4) (Dec.), 697–738.

Birdsall, Nancy. 1993. 'Another look at Population and Global Warming'. World Bank Policy Research Working Paper No. 1020.

——— 1994. 'Government, Population and Poverty: A Win-Win Tale'. In Robert Cassen, ed., *Population and Development: Old Debate, New Conclusions*. Washington: Overseas Development Council, 253–74.

——— and Charles Griffin. 1993. 'Population Growth, Externalities and Poverty'. In Michael Lipton and Jacques van der Gaag, eds., *Including the Poor*. New York: Oxford University Press for the World Bank.

Bongaarts, John. 1990. 'The Measurement of Wanted Fertility'. *Population and Development Review*. 16 (3) (Sept.), 487–506.

Boserup, Ester. 1965. *The Conditions of Agricultural Growth*. Chicago: Aldine.

Cain, Mead T. 1991. 'Widows, Sons, and Old-Age Security in Rural Maharashtra: A Comment'. *Population Studies*. 45 (3) (Nov.), 519–28.

Chomitz, Kenneth M., and Nancy Birdsall. 1991. 'Incentives for Small Families: Concepts and Issues'. In Stanley Fischer, Dennis de Tray, and Shekhar Shah, eds., *Proceedings of the World Bank Annual Conference on Development Economics 1990*. Washington: World Bank, 309–39.

Cleland, John, James F. Phillips, Sajeda Amin, and Golam M. Kamal. 1994. *The Determinants of Reproductive Change in Bangladesh*. Washington: The World Bank.

Coale, Ansley J., and Edgar M. Hoover. 1958. *Population Growth and Economic Development in Low-Income Countries*. Princeton: Princeton University Press.

Cross, Anne R., Walter Obungu, and Paul Kizito. 1991. 'Evidence of a Transition to Lower Fertility in Kenya'. *International Family Planning Perspectives*. 17 (1), 4–7.

Ehrlich, Paul R. 1975. *The Population Bomb*. Rivercity, Mass.: Rivercity Press.

Leff, Nathaniel H. 1969. 'Dependency Rates and Savings Rates'. *American Economic Review*. 59 (5) (Dec.). 885–96.

Mane, Purnima, Geeta Rao Gupta, and Ellen Weiss. 1994. 'Effective Communication between Partners: AIDS and the Risk Reduction for Women'. *AIDS*. 8 (1), 325–32.

National Academy of Sciences. 1986. *Population Growth and Economic Development*. Washington: National Academy of Sciences.

---

[28] This statement remains true even for those developing countries, including China, which will face new challenges associated with the increasing aged-dependency burden, the result in part of past fertility decline. A 'birth dearth' will not in itself justify public interventions any more than a seeming birth glut did in the past.

National Research Council. 1993. *The Population Dynamics of Kenya.* Washington: National Academy Press.

Rosenzweig, Mark R., and Paul T. Schultz. 1987. 'Fertility and Investment in Human Capital: Estimates of the Consequences of Imperfect Fertility Control in Malaysia'. *Journal of Econometrics.* 36 (1/2) (Sep./Oct.). 163–84.

—— and Kenneth I. Wolpin. 1980. 'Testing the Quantity-Quality Fertility Model: The Use of Twins as a Natural Experiment'. *Econometrica.* 48 (1) (Jan.). 227–40.

Sen, Amartya. 1999. *Development as Freedom.* New York: Alfred A. Knopf.

Simon, Julian. 1977. *The Economics of Population Growth.* Princeton: Princeton University Press.

World Bank. 1990. *World Development Report: Poverty.* New York: Oxford University Press.

—— 1992. *World Development Report: Development and the Environment.* New York: Oxford University Press.

2

The Population Debate in Historical Perspective: Revisionism Revised

1. REVISIONISM AND THE POPULATION DEBATE

1.1. *Setting*

Debates surrounding the consequences of population growth on the pace of economic development have, since Malthus, been both vigorous and contentious. While pessimism—indeed alarmism—over the adverse consequences of rapid population growth has dominated the lexicon of popular and, to a lesser extent, scientific discourse, swings in thinking have from time to time occurred. During the Great Depression, Alvin Hansen and the stagnationists cited slow population growth as a cause of aborted or anemic economic recovery. During recent decades the 'birth dearth' in developed countries has motivated writers like Ben Wattenberg to forecast long-term economic decline, waning political clout, and the demise of Western values and influence. And during the 1980s the so-called 'population revisionists' downgraded the prominence of rapid population growth as a source of, or a constraint on, economic prosperity in the Third World.[1]

This population revisionism appeared to represent a notable retreat from the widely held 'traditionalist', or sometimes 'population-alarmist', view of the 1960s and 1970s, that rapid population growth constitutes a strong deterrent to per capita economic growth and development. In contrast, the revisionists have: (1) downgraded the relative importance of population growth as a source of economic growth, placing it along with several other factors of equal or greater importance; (2) assessed the consequences over a longer period of time; and (3) taken indirect feedbacks within economic and political systems into account.[2]

It is to be emphasized that the distinguishing feature of population revisionism is *not* the direction of the net assessment of population consequences—indeed, most

---

[1] Hansen (1939), Wattenberg (1987), National Research Council (1986).

[2] Hodgson (1988) refers to the pre-revisionist period as one of population 'orthodoxy', which refers both to hypotheses about family planning, and to the assumption that 'rapid population growth in nonindustrial societies is a significant problem' (p. 542). Demeny (1986) characterizes revisionism succinctly: 'The more typical revisionist views, however, merely put the problem in its presumed deserved place: several drawers below its former niche' (p. 474).

revisionists conclude that many, if not most, Third World countries would benefit from slower population growth. Rather, revisionism is distinguished by more moderate conclusions about the impacts of population growth, considered smaller than in assessments by traditionalists. This result derives directly from the *methodological perspective* of revisionists that highlights the intermediate to longer run, taking into account both direct and indirect impacts, and feedbacks within economic, political, and social systems.[3]

A striking example of the apparent change in thinking during the 1950–90 period is illustrated by a comparison of the summary statements on the impacts of rapid population growth found in two major studies undertaken by the prestigious National Academy of Sciences (NAS) in the United States. On the one hand, the executive summary of the 1971 Report, *Rapid Population Growth: Consequences and Policy Implications*, cites a large number of adverse impacts of population growth, provides almost no qualifications as to the negative effects, and fails to enumerate possible positive or countervailing impacts.[4] On the other hand, the summary assessment of the 1986 Report, *Population Growth and Economic Development: Policy Questions*, is moderate in tone and substantially qualified: 'On balance, we reach the qualitative conclusion that slower population growth would be beneficial to economic development of most developing countries' (p. 90). Examining this carefully worded statement in detail is instructive because it exemplifies several attributes of revisionism: (1) there are both important positive and negative impacts of population growth (thus, 'on balance'); (2) the actual size of the net impact—and even whether it is strong or weak—cannot be determined given existing evidence (thus, 'qualitative'); (3) only

---

[3] Based on the broader view of the development process held by the revisionists, the strong reliance on family planning to confront so-called 'population problems' such as rapid urbanization and food deficiencies has also been challenged. Elevated emphasis is instead placed on policies that appear to address the more important causes of these problems, and the justification for family planning has shifted to other factors as a result. These justifications include the desirability of reducing the large number of 'unwanted' births, the adverse impact of large families (and close child spacing) on child and maternal health, the flexibility and greater administrative ease in managing a slower pace of development, the adverse consequences of population pressures on selected environmental resources, the impact of population growth on the distribution of income, and the burden of child-rearing on women.

[4] The 1971 NAS report classifies population impacts into five major categories. (1) *Economically*, rapid population growth slows the growth of per capita incomes in the less developed countries (LDCs), perpetuates inequalities of income distribution, holds down saving and capital investment, increases unemployment and underemployment, shifts workers into unproductive pursuits, slows industrialization, holds back technological change, reduces demand for manufactured goods, inhibits development and utilization of natural resources, deteriorates the resource base, and distorts international trade. (2) *Socially*, rapid population growth results in rapid urbanization, strains intergenerational relationships, impedes social mobility, and widens gaps between traditional and other sectors. (3) *Politically*, rapid population growth worsens ethnic/religious/linguistic conflicts, administrative stresses, and political disruption. (4) In terms of *family welfare*, rapid population growth inhibits the quality and quantity of child education, lowers maternal and child health, retards child development, and produces crowded housing and urban slums with associated illnesses. (5) And in terms of the *environment*, rapid population growth stimulates agricultural expansion which in turn results in soil erosion, water deterioration, destruction of wildlife and natural areas, and pollution; and pesticides poison people, and domestic and wild animals (NAS 1971: 1–4).

the direction of the impact from high current growth rates can be discerned (thus, 'slower', and not 'slow'); and (4) the net impact varies from country to country—in most cases it will be negative, in some it will be positive, and in others it will have little impact one way or the other (thus, 'most developing countries').

It is intriguing to speculate as to what explains this significant change in thinking. Below we will argue that a *major* change in thinking did not in fact occur among most American *economists* engaged in scholarly research on the consequences of population growth. Rather, what we may be observing is an increase in the relative influence of the economists *vis-à-vis* the non-economists in the *summary assessments* of the major reports, and in public debate. As a result, highlighting a significant shift toward 'revisionism' *among economists* in the 1980s may be inappropriate. Most prominent American economic-demographers, especially those with an historical bent, have for decades embraced the perspectives of population revisionism—arguably the dominant posture in economics in the post-World War II period.

There are several hypotheses accounting for an elevation of the influence of economists, and revisionists, in the population debate in the 1980s. First, a gradual accumulation of empirical research weakened the foundations of the traditionalist case. Secondly, the theory of economic growth itself changed: it elevated the importance of human capital accumulation and technical change *vis-à-vis* land and natural resources; and it downgraded the relative role of physical capital accumulation.[5]

Thirdly, the importance of institutions—in particular, the roles of governments and economic policies, markets, and property rights—as sources of growth has diverted attention from some specific factors in development, including population. Fourthly, the analysis of demographic factors has been broadened to include indirect, as well as direct, effects, and to encompass the intermediate to longer run.

And finally, the elevated influence of the ideas of Julian L. Simon (1981) on the Reagan Administration's population policies, which were unsupportive of family planning, in part triggered the commissioning of the 1986 National Academy assessment of population consequences.[6] This assessment was undertaken almost entirely by economists, the revisionists. Interestingly, among non-economists, revisionist orthodoxy has never gained a notable foothold. This group is sizeable and includes demographers, biologists/ecologists, and sociologists. By numbers, then, the economist/revisionists have exercised exceptional influence in the debates over the last decade, a phenomenon this chapter assists to understand and place in perspective.

1.2. *Goals*

The primary goal of the present chapter is to identify and assess those key aspects of the population debate that have since 1950 influenced the prominence of population revisionism among scholars in the United States. This focus delimits the chapter.

---

[5] The traditionalist argument relied heavily on the concern that high fertility and thus high dependency rates would reduce investment in physical capital, thus reducing growth.

[6] For details on the NAS Report, see Sect. 2.4 and fn. 17.

First, rather than surveying the large literature on the consequences of population growth, we will highlight only those areas where research and events appear to have most influenced the prominence of revisionism.[7] Secondly, we will focus somewhat narrowly on the American debate. Finally, we will examine only the roles of academics, and mainly the roles of economists. The swings in thinking about population matters may have been influenced much more by the United States Agency for International Development, the United Nations Fund for Population Activities, the Population Council, the Ford and Rockefeller Foundations, and key leaders associated with these and other institutions. The roles of these institutions, and their interactions with academics, are both important and complex, and constitute a central place in a full assessment of the history of the population debate.[8]

Another goal of the present chapter is to provide the background needed to place the choice of topics and the various findings of the Bellagio Symposium in perspective. We attempt to accomplish this by reading the literature on the population debate through the filter of 'revisionism', a history-of-thought, stage-setting exercise that is hopefully both interesting and enlightening.

1.3. *Argument*

Section 2 documents the proposition that the perspective of revisionism has in fact been the dominant posture of economic-demographers since 1950. This is in spite of an apparent ebb and flow of 'traditionalism' versus 'revisionism' over this period— a swing in ideas we consider to be more illusory than substantive. Our approach is to review four benchmark studies that provide a reasonably comprehensive overview of the literature: the 1953 and 1973 United Nations Reports on *The Determinants and Consequences of Population Trends*, and the 1971 and 1986 National Academy of Sciences Reports cited above.

Insight into the reasons for the apparent ebb and flow of ideas centers on three hypotheses: (1) swings in the relative number of economists *vis-à-vis* other scholars participating in the population assessments (Sect. 2); (2) the stimulus (and some of the results) of Julian L. Simon's *The Ultimate Resource* in 1981, as well as a waning

---

[7] Surveys are provided by Birdsall (1988), Kelley (1988), McNicoll (1984), National Research Council (1986), Srinivasan (1988), and World Bank (1984).

[8] On the formulation of US population policy toward the Third World, and the role of the United States Agency for International Development, see Donaldson (1990) and Piotrow (1973). On the role of the Ford Foundation, see Caldwell and Caldwell (1986) and Harkavy (1995). On the potent and pervasive impacts of funding agencies on the scope of social science research, see Demeny (1988), who issues a vivid assessment: 'Social science research directed to the developing countries in the field of population has now become almost exclusively harnessed to serve the narrowly conceived short-term interests of programs that embody the existing orthodoxy . . . the population industry professes no interest in social science research that may bear fruit, if at all, in the relatively remote future. . . . It seeks, and with the power of the purse enforces, predictably, control, and subservience. . . . Research so characterized is an oxymoron' (p. 471). And on the forces that caused the metamorphosis of the scholar-scientist-demographer of the early 1950s into the policy oriented-programmatic/nuts-and-bolts family-planning activist in the ensuing decades, see Hodgson (1983).

influence of the seminal 1958 study by Ansley J. Coale and Edgar M. Hoover (Sect. 3); and (3) the impact of accumulated empirical evidence from the 1970s and early 1980s, summarized in several survey papers in the 1980s that qualified the traditionalist case (Sect. 4). Research in the early 1990s leading up to the Cairo Population Conference did not notably modify this assessment, although a somewhat greater emphasis on microeconomic outcomes emerged, as well as some new macroeconomic results (Sect. 5).

2. BENCHMARK REPORTS

This section provides evidence to support the interpretation that the wide swing away from, and then back toward, population revisionism, as reflected in four of the major reports on the consequences of population growth since 1950, is more apparent than real.[9] In fact, this 'swing' is largely an artefact explained by the anomalous executive summary to the 1971 NAS Report. In contrast, the swing in thinking by economists who contributed to this, and the other reports, is much narrower.

2.1. *United Nations (1953)*

The 1953 UN Report represents the most systematic and comprehensive assessment of the consequences of population growth since Malthus. Balanced in scope, it took both positive and negative effects of population into account, distinguished between short- and long-run impacts, and reckoned both direct and indirect effects. The Report offers a guarded net-impact assessment, stressing diversity according to country-specific conditions.

The chapters on the economic consequences of population are authored mainly by Professor Joseph J. Spengler, who can be considered the founder of modern economic demography in the United States.[10] The Report embraces the three distinguishing attributes of population revisionism.

1. On differentiating between short- and long-run impacts of population due to 'fixed' supplies of natural resources in the face of diminishing returns, the Malthusian dilemma, the Report observes:

Natural conditions are of two sorts: 'constants', which are to a certain extent beyond man's control, and 'variables', which are 'revealed' by human ingenuity and imagination. There is no fundamental dichotomy between the two. In different times and places, variable factors may be considered a constant, and vice versa. Modern industrial societies are continuously transforming what were long considered negative binding conditions into positive variables which can be manipulated. (p. 181)

---

[9] While the *World Development Report 1984* (taken up below) also represents a watershed publication in the development of revisionist thinking, we elect to focus on the UN and NAS reports here since the timing of their assessments (15 to 20 years apart) more clearly shows the evolution of thinking over time.

[10] Spengler wrote the chapters on the consequences of demographic change on (1) natural resources, (2) migration and distribution, and most importantly, (3) per capita output. He in addition wrote the chapter on the history of population theory.

Similarly, and referring to capital–labor ratios as expressed in production-function equations, the Report observes:

An increase in the population and labor force, with all other circumstances unchanged, would tend to reduce per capita output by reducing the amount of physical resources and equipment employed per worker. . . . the value of such equations as expressions of the relationships between population and output is rather limited, because the assumption that other factors remain constant is unrealistic. In real life, all factors affecting output change simultaneously; hence it is necessary to ask: what change in the non-human factors of production may accompany given changes in population and in the labor force? The answer depends on many circumstances . . . . (p. 237)

This longer-run perspective permeated the Report, and played an important role in accounting for its somewhat eclectic and moderate assessment of the net impact of population.

2. On employing a balanced assessment of the connections between population and development, the Report lists some 21 economic-demographic linkages.[11] The impact of population on some factors is judged to be positive (scale, organization); on some, negative (diminishing returns); and on some, neutral (technology and social progress).

3. On taking indirect impacts of population into account, the Report is clear:

For the purpose of analyzing the relative importance of demographic and other factors bearing on output, a nearly complete list of them is required. Otherwise the partial and current influence of some factors may not adequately be taken into account. Such a list guards against the neglect of significant variables, especially when the factors are many and somewhat interdependent. (p. 221)

Based on these three elements of the revisionist perspective—attention to the longer run, numerous positive and negative impacts, and considering indirect effects—the Report's bottom-line assessment follows. It mirrors current revisionist assessments (including the 1986 National Academy of Sciences Report) that emphasize the diversity of impacts, although a negative net impact of undetermined size is considered by the UN Report to be likely in much of the Third World:

An increase of population may tend to raise per capita output in industrialized countries having a tendency towards unemployment, or in countries with ample undeveloped resources that can readily be put to use. On the other hand, in countries where for any reason it is difficult to match population increase with a corresponding development of non-human resources, the effect of population growth may be to hinder the rise of per capita output, in particular where it hinders the formation of capital. (p. 237)

Two factors play a significant role in explaining the guarded nature of the Report's eclectic assessment: uncertainty regarding the importance of mismatches of non-human resources to labor and of the impacts of population on saving and investment.

---

[11] This taxonomy, which effectively established the research agenda of economic demographers over the coming decades, was originally expounded in Spengler (1949).

On mismatches, the Report stresses the role of international trade and migration in conditioning and mitigating population impacts.[12] On saving and investment, the Report observes the theoretical ambiguities resulting when indirect linkages are taken into account and emphasizes the need for empirical analyses into the postulated relationships. This second qualification in fact turned out to represent a primary research emphasis in population assessments for the next two decades. The results of this research played an important role in tilting the population debate toward revisionism in the 1980s.

2.2. *United Nations (1973)*

Updating the earlier UN Report, the 1973 volume veers somewhat from the revisionist thinking. The bottom-line assessment of the consequences of population growth is more pessimistic as a result. However, this assessment is notably qualified by the empirical studies of Simon Kuznets.

. . . rapid population growth in developing countries may impose a heavy burden on society. . . . growth of income would be faster, the slower the growth of population. These findings, however, are not completely corroborated by the available empirical findings. Country data show no consistent association between the rate of growth of population and the rate of growth of total product during the 1950s and 1960s. . . . rapid population growth does not preclude economic improvement. While the rate of population growth may not be one of the predominant factors determining the rate of economic growth, there appears to be a consensus that high population growth rates have held back advances in levels of living . . . . (p. 6)

   The basis of the Report's greater pessimism is uncertain since, in terms of empirical analysis, the summary statements are quite guarded.

. . . the effect of demographic trends on economic development . . . is a complex one involving so many interdependent factors that it has not proved possible to isolate the demographic influences. . . . systematic study of the relationship of demographic trends to the many factors influencing productivity—methods of production, specialization, economies of scale, skills of the labor force, advances in technology, etc.—is not yet far advanced. . . . relatively few hypotheses and models have been established to explain the interrelationships among population, education, and economic development. (p. 8)

Possibly it is the alleged adverse impacts of population growth on the food balance and on capital formation, as represented in two of the background papers, that accounts for the Report's somewhat pessimistic assessment.[13]

---

[12] ' . . . the world's ability to support a growing population on a rising level of living would be improved by the easing of restrictions on international trade and migration . . . ' (p. 193).

[13] In a conversation with Dr Leon Tabah (3 Sept. 1991), who arrived at the UN in time to head the compilation of the final report, he reported that the overview chapter was authored by several persons in the Population Division, was vetted widely within the UN, and benefitted in particular from feedback solicited from Professors Ansley J. Coale and Nathan Keyfitz. These distinguished scholars, known for their significant concerns about the adverse consequences of rapid population growth, may have played a role in tilting the 1973 Report away from the more eclectic posture of the 1953 UN volume.

With respect to the food balance, where the Report forecasts a trend of diminishing per capita food production in the Third World, the traditionalist methodology is clear: 'Whereas population growth increases requirements for food and . . . is also by far the main factor in the growth of the demand for food, there is no such *direct* relationship between population and the growth of production' (emphasis added) (p. 433).

The analysis is sensitive to the focus on the direct impacts of population growth, and to a shorter-run technological orientation that downplays indirect impacts in the longer run due to price responses, and induced innovation and institutional change.

With respect to capital formation, the Report concludes that: '*other factors being equal,* a decrease in saving capacity occurs as the size of the family . . . increases' (emphasis added) (p. 503). Again, this represents a short-run perspective. Induced indirect impacts on family labor supply and substitutions in consumption are downplayed. While the background paper by Paul Demeny qualifies the quantitative importance of the possible savings impacts of large families and of capital shallowing when other factors are taken into account, these two impacts represent the only unequivocal (negative) population-economic connections in the paper's summary. Moreover, they were central to the traditionalist analytical perspective of the then-popular and influential Coale–Hoover model, discussed below. As a result, they plausibly carried considerable weight in the deliberations.

The most significant new contribution to the population debate in the 1973 Report was the finding by Simon Kuznets that, based on simple correlations, a net negative impact of population on per capita output growth was not obvious in the data. This result qualified the *quantitative* importance of population's hypothesized net (and negative) impact and played a major role in the deliberations. (Around half of the Report's summary assessment is devoted to presenting and interpreting Kuznets's qualifications.) Given the strong priors of demographers and policy-makers that the negative impacts of population growth on development were large, the inability to easily 'confirm' this hypothesis through simple, albeit inconclusive, correlations more than any other factor kept the population debate alive and encouraged the elevation of population revisionism during the next two decades.[14]

In sum, the 1973 Report tilted away from population revisionism, as we characterize it. Two of the three background papers highlight direct, shorter-run impacts, although the one by Demeny is qualified. The remaining paper by Kuznets is distinctly revisionist—long run in orientation and based on a broad theoretical and historical perspective. It effectively provides a counterbalance to the Report's net assessment, which is broadly faithful to the background papers.

---

[14] Kuznets's findings have been replicated in over a dozen studies. For a summary and assessment of this literature, see Kelley (1988: 1700–1). While such correlations are sufficiently difficult to interpret so as to be almost meaningless, ironically had they 'confirmed' the negative priors, it is likely that the debate would have been largely put to rest. For an early application of these correlations to the debate, see Richard A. Easterlin (1967). For an update on the correlations literature, see Kelley and Schmidt (1994).

2.3. *National Academy of Sciences (1971)*

The same cannot be said for the Report by the National Academy of Sciences in 1971 which, in the history of the major studies of population growth, seemingly represents the most traditionalist (and in this case population-alarmist) in perspective. Caution in arriving at a firm judgment on this matter results from the striking gap between the assessment found in the 'Overview' summary in volume I (ch. 1), and the results found in the research papers in volume II. The reason for the dichotomy between the executive summary (the 'Overview') and the scientific papers constitutes a major puzzle which we pursued by an exhaustive inquiry into the process of compiling the report. The results of this investigation are documented in an appendix to this chapter—a set of findings important to assessing not only the evolution of thinking about population research, but also the impacts of the political environment on the interpretation and use of the results.

The assessment in volume I (ch. 1) is highly pessimistic, citing a large number of ways in which 'high fertility and rapid population growth have serious adverse social and economic effects' (p. 1).[15] This seriousness is underscored by a quantitative speculation that a one-quarter reduction in birth rates from 40 to 30 could raise per capita income growth rates by one-third (p. 25). Most of the impacts that are listed are unqualified, and no significant positive contributions of additional population numbers are noted. The Report explicitly employs traditionalist methodology that highlights direct impacts in the short run. Indeed, the preface notes that 'We have limited ourselves to relatively short-term and clear-cut issues' (p. vi).

In contrast, the research papers that take up the economic consequences of population in volume II are in general much less pessimistic, and they employ the perspective of revisionism. Three examples suffice.

Theodore Schultz's paper on 'The Food Supply-Population Growth Quandary' is reasonably optimistic, forecasting increases in per capita food production (assuming governments do not return to their former cheap food policies). The paper discounts the scientific validity of many of the pessimistic food-balance projection models for failing to incorporate appropriate price and induced supply responses. Schultz notes that, while rapid population growth leaves little room for complacency, the major food-balance problems relate to non-demographic factors.

Harvey Leibenstein's paper on the 'Impact of Population Growth on Economic Welfare—Nontraditional Elements' highlights the role of human capital in economic growth and the advantages of a youthful population that incorporates relatively large amounts of up-to-date human capital (denoted as the 'replacement effect'). Given the then postulated importance of non-traditional (or 'residual') factors as sources of economic growth, Leibenstein concludes that the positive impact of the replacement effect may be quantitatively large. While he felt that, on average, rapid population

---

[15] See above, fn. 4.

growth likely deters economic development, he held that the size of this impact was uncertain.[16]

Paul Demeny's paper on 'The Economics of Population Control', while dealing mainly with externalities, is highly skeptical about summary assessments of population's net impact, since

An adequate treatment . . . would have to embrace virtually all important problems having to do with the economics of development and could be handled satisfactorily only in a general equilibrium framework involving fertility itself as a dependent variable. No such treatment yet exists or is in sight . . . . (p. 202)

Moreover, Demeny is critical of current assessments since 'the emphasis that has been given to short-term considerations appears to have been disproportionately strong' (p. 205), a proposition supported by revisionism.

In summary, while the background research papers by the economists participating in the 1971 study are revisionist in orientation, a traditionalist and strongly alarmist assessment is presented in the summary Overview. This represents a watershed in population pessimism in the period since 1950.

2.4. *National Academy of Sciences (1986)*

In striking contrast, the next NAS Report returned to revisionist thinking and, as noted above, provided a guarded and qualified assessment on the net impact of population growth on development. Three factors account for this about-face.

First, the Report emphasizes both individual and institutional responses to initial impacts of population change—conservation in response to scarcity, substitution of abundant for scarce factors of production, innovation and adoption of technologies to exploit profitable opportunities, and the like. These responses are considered to be pervasive and they are judged to be important. According to the report-writers: 'the key [is the] mediating role that human behavior and human institutions play in the relation between population growth and economic processes' (p. 4).

Secondly, empirical studies that had appeared in the literature since the 1971 Report qualified many of the hypotheses central to the population debate. This is true, for example, of the impacts of children on household saving, as well as the impacts of population growth and size on government spending and on educational enrollments.

Thirdly, unlike previous summary reports, the 1986 study was compiled almost entirely by economists whose summary assessments in the overview volume are

---

[16] Leibenstein's posture can be characterized as 'leaning against the wind' of population pessimism. '. . . even in developing countries, there may be situations and periods for which relatively high rates of population growth *may* involve some demographic effects that are helpful to economic growth. Whether the beneficial effects are ever the predominant ones is hard to say . . .' (p. 194). '. . . even the positive replacement effect must be considered as only one element among many—most of which probably inhibit economic growth. The positive replacement effect is delineated primarily in the interest of achieving a balanced approach . . .' (p. 195).

faithful to the background papers, also compiled mainly by economists.[17] Economists' understanding of, and faith in, the potential for market-induced responses to modify initial direct impacts of population change is far greater than that of other social and biological scientists, who were prominent contributors to previous NAS reports.[18] In this regard, it is not surprising that the negative impact of population growth highlighted in the 1986 Report takes the form of renewable resource degradation. It is here that markets can fail since property rights are difficult to assign or maintain, especially for rain forests, fishing areas, and the like.

2.5. *Bottom Line: Reports and the Economists*

Since 1950, several of the major reports on the consequences of population growth in the Third World have appeared to move between the guarded revisionist assessments of 1951 and 1986, and the stronger- to strong-traditionalist assessments in the 1973 UN and 1971 NAS reports, respectively. In contrast, most of the background papers commissioned for these reports and written by economic-demographers can be classified as revisionist, *including* the papers for the 1971 NAS study. As a result, deviations from the revisionist tradition tend to be attributable more to the changing influence of non-economists than to changes in the thinking of economists. Revisionism appears to be the dominant methodological perspective among economic-demographers in assessments of the consequences of population growth.

3. FOUNDATIONS AND CHALLENGE

In assessing the changing prominence of revisionism since 1950, the contributions of three scholars merit particular attention: Ansley J. Coale and Edgar M. Hoover, who

[17] The Working Group on Population Growth and Economic Development included D. Gale Johnson (co-chair), Ronald D. Lee (co-chair), Nancy Birdsall, Rodolfo A. Bulatao, Eva Mueller, Samuel H. Preston, T. Paul Schultz, T. N. Srinivasan, and Anne D. Williams. The study was originally proposed by Steven Sinding, then Director of the Office of Population at USAID, to Robert Lapham and David Goslin. Eugene Hammel chaired the Committee on Population (1983–85). The Working Group was primarily economists since the study's focus was ostensibly 'economic development'. The Working Group set the scope and outline of the project. The background papers were presented at a workshop at Woods Hole, attended mainly by the authors and the NAS working group. The first draft of the summary Report was primarily written by Samuel Preston, although Ronald Lee wrote the first draft of chapter 4, and Geoffrey Green parts of chapter 8. This draft was reviewed, page-by-page, at meetings of the Working Group. In the end, one member would not 'sign off' until three issues had been resolved. Because the report was considered to be potentially controversial, it received exceptionally diligent assessment through the standard reviewing process of the National Academy of Sciences. It is notable that this process and the writing of the executive summary, unlike the setting at the NAS in 1971, was largely absent the external pressures of USAID. This was due to the active participation by the academics in the process (including the writing of the executive summary), and to the role of Steven Sinding at USAID. I am grateful to Sam Preston and Gene Hammel for providing detailed background relating to the 1986 NAS study.

[18] The 1971 committee of 12 members contained 3 economists. Of the 18 persons acknowledged as contributing to the study, 3 were economists. And 4 of the 19 background papers were written by economists.

helped establish the foundations of traditionalism in the 1950s; and Julian L. Simon, who helped mount the revisionist challenge.

3.1. *Ansley J. Coale and Edgar M. Hoover*

No single publication has had a greater impact on the population debate since 1950 then *Population Growth and Economic Development in Low-Income Countries*, the Coale and Hoover (1958) study on Mexico and India. Pioneering in several dimensions, this book: (1) articulated several theoretical linkages between population and economic growth that were consistent with the economic-growth paradigms of the time (e.g. an emphasis on physical capital formation); (2) formalized these linkages in a mathematical model that was parameterized and simulated to generate forecasts of alternative fertility scenarios over the intermediate run; and (3) provided a case study of an important country whose prospects were considered by many analysts to be grim. The Coale–Hoover framework was transparent and easy to understand, the assumptions were made explicit and qualified, and the findings were clearly expounded and accessible to a wide readership.

The model identified, and the simulations quantified, three adverse impacts of population growth: (1) capital-shallowing—a reduction in the ratio of capital to labor because there is nothing about population growth *per se* that increases the rate of saving; (2) age-dependency—an increase in youth-dependency, which raises the requirements for household consumption at the expense of saving, while diminishing the rate of saving; and (3) investment diversion—a shift of (mainly government) spending into areas such as health and education at the expense of (assumed-to-be) more productive, growth-oriented investments.

These hypotheses had a substantial impact on thinking. They formed the basis of most modeling of population up through the 1970s. They figured prominently in the 1973 UN Report. And, according to political scientist and policy analyst Phyllis T. Piotrow (1973), the Coale–Hoover thesis 'eventually provided the justification for birth control as a part of United States foreign policy' (p. 15).

The Coale–Hoover framework both established and sustained the traditionalist perspective over the 1960s and 1970s. The model: (1) focused on the short to intermediate run when adverse consequences of population are greatest; (2) abstracted from induced feedbacks through economizing or substitution in the face of population pressures; and (3) omitted any direct positive impacts of population on per capita output growth (e.g. scale economies). Even though advances in economic theory in the 1960s and 1970s greatly diminished the model's relevance (e.g. theory elevated the roles of human capital, non-traditional factor inputs, technical change, and policies and institutions as sources of growth), and even though accumulating evidence discounted the quantitative importance of the hypotheses relating to capital-shallowing and the adverse impacts on saving, the model's influence did not wane until the 1980s.

3.2. *Julian L. Simon*

The decline in the model's influence was in part the result of the writings of Julian L. Simon. First, his book *The Ultimate Resource* in 1981 attracted enormous attention to the population debate. This was due both to his conclusion that in the intermediate run, rapid population growth was likely to exert a *positive* impact on economic development in many Third World countries; and to the effectiveness of the book's highly accessible exposition and 'debating style'. (The format included goading and prodding, setting up and knocking down of strawmen, and examining albeit popular but some rather extreme anti-natalist positions. Arguably not since the Malthus–Godwin confrontations has this debating style been more effectively used to garner attention to the central elements in the population debate.) While the theoretical linkages and empirical assessments (particularly those relating to technical change) that formed the basis of Simon's optimistic conclusion drew vigorous challenge, it is important to recognize that his results were fundamentally based on the application of the revisionist methodology that had been embraced by most economic-demographers for several decades. In particular, Simon focused on the longer run, and he stressed the importance of feedbacks, especially those resulting from price-induced substitutions in production and consumption in the face of population pressures.

The best example relates to his demonstration that most natural-resource prices (in real or relative terms) trace out a long-run decline in the face of rising demands, stimulated, in part, by expanding populations. Price-induced substitutions in production and consumption, and an expansion of supply, are offered to explain this result. While such a finding is not surprising to economists (see Spengler 1966 and Kuznets 1967), the effectiveness of Simon's writing style and argumentation is nowhere more evident than in his analysis of population-resource interactions.[19]

A second impact of Simon's book derives from its catalytic role in stimulating several systematic re-assessments of the consequences of population growth. These took the form of several literature surveys that brought to light research that had quietly accumulated since the early 1970s. While most of this research (including much of Simon's own work) had exerted a negligible impact on the broader population debates, when collected together, assessed in the context of current theories of economic development, and organized around population themes, the several surveys

---

[19] For example, Simon's population-resource arguments appeared to have been settled in the mind of Spengler and other specialists many years earlier. 'Perhaps the greatest reversal of opinion in the period 1930–65 is that relating to the role played by land and other natural resources in economic development and the disenthralling of populations from Malthusian traps. ... discovery and technological change, together with substitution at producer and consumer levels, have greatly augmented both the visible and the immediately potential stock of fuel, mineral, and related sources of natural-resource services. Man, it is supposed, is confronted by chains of natural-resource substitutes which modern molecular engineering and alchemy can subvert to his purposes, replacing links that weaken and elevating inferior sources (e.g. taconite rock) as well as substituting less expensive for more expensive sources of particular natural resource service needs' (Spengler 1966: 9).

served to elevate the revisionist perspective. All of the surveys turned out to be less pessimistic than those prevailing in the 1970s.

4. 1980s

A review of the methodological emphases and bottom lines of these surveys provides additional confirmation that revisionism was the dominant perspective of the 1980s. While each survey concluded that slower population growth would likely be beneficial to the development of many countries (recall that a net negative assessment is *not* a distinguishing feature of revisionism), none of the surveys was alarmist; none was short run in perspective; all emphasized the multi-dimensional (positive and negative) aspects of population's consequences; several explicitly downplayed the 'traditional' emphasis on diminishing returns, natural resource exhaustion, and negative savings linkages; and all were responsive to updated theoretical perspectives that highlighted human capital, technical change, public policy, and institutional settings.

4.1. *Surveys*

The World Bank's *World Development Report* (1984) may appear at first glance to fall into the 'pessimist' camp of population-consequences assessment. After all, the Report noted upfront that exceptionally rapid 'population growth—at rates above 2 percent . . . —acts as a brake on development' (p. 79). But the Report immediately qualifies that statement: 'Up to a point, population growth can be accommodated', although in terms of advancing economic well-being, there has been 'less progress than might have been' (p. 79). The Report admits a wide diversity of experience. In arriving at its conclusions, it (1) strongly downplays the impact of population growth as a significant deterrent to saving; (2) elevates in importance the likely adverse impacts of population growth on human capital accumulation, and poverty; and (3) recognizes that in some countries larger populations can favorably enhance prosperity through scale economies and market demand. Thus, the 1984 World Bank assessment, like the 1986 National Research Council assessment two years later (discussed above), falls solidly into the revisionist camp. Overall, these two reports, according to Nancy Birdsall (who headed the World Bank Team, and who was also a member of the National Research Council Working Group), conclude that 'rapid population growth can slow development, but only under specific circumstances and generally with limited or weak effects'.[20]

One difference between the reports merits emphasis. The World Bank placed somewhat greater weight on the negative consequences of market and institutional failures, which are in turn exacerbated by population pressures. However, both reports stressed that demography played mainly a contributory, in contrast to a causal, role in accounting for several of the development problems commonly attributed to population growth.

[20] Birdsall (1988: 529).

McNicoll's (1984) survey concludes that 'rapid population growth is a serious burden on efforts to generate sustained increases in per capita product' (p. 212). But he too downplays the traditional saving linkages, recognizes a modest role for scale, and is impressed by positive impacts of population pressures in stimulating innovation. His strongest negative assessments relate to non-economic factors: demographic impacts on kinship structures and international relations. Again, his perspectives are revisionist: longer run in orientation, multi-dimensional, and especially sensitive to a wide array of economic, and especially social and political, feedbacks.

Kelley's (1988) survey concludes that 'economic growth . . . would have been more rapid in an environment of slower population growth, although in a number of countries the impact was probably negligible and in some it may have been positive' (p. 1715). Emphasis is placed on the diversity of settings whereby adverse impacts are likely: specifically, where (1) water and arable land are scarce, (2) property rights poorly defined, and (3) government policies ineffective and biased against labor. Caution is highlighted in treating many popular 'problems' as largely demographic (e.g. unemployment, malnutrition, famine, environmental degradation) since they are mainly caused by more fundamental factors, and are exceptionally sensitive to the appropriateness and efficacy of public policy.

Srinivasan's (1988) survey parallels the conclusions of the 1986 NAS Report discussed above, to which he was an important contributor. He further argues that highlighting pervasive and significant externalities with respect to household fertility decisions is mistaken, and that 'many of the alleged deleterious consequences result more from inappropriate policies and institutions than from rapid population growth. Thus policy reform and institutional change are called for, rather than policy interventions in private fertility decisions to counter these effects' (p. 7).

Birdsall's (1988) survey illustrates well an additional dimension of revisionism. She argues for a broad perspective whereby population consequences are viewed as 'the outcome of many individual decisions at the micro or family level, and thus one aspect of a larger complex system' (p. 493). Accordingly, she not only recognizes and accounts for feedbacks that mitigate problems of resource scarcity due to population pressures, she also extends the analysis to the microeconomic level and emphasizes the endogeneity of parental decisions with respect to family size and investments in children. In this context, she places somewhat greater weight than some others on the possible size of the negative consequences of market and institutional failures that distort parental decision-making with respect to childbearing and rearing.

4.2. *Revisionist Consensus*

One might venture that at the end of the 1980s there was an uneasy consensus among the *economist* participants in the population debate that broadly embraced revisionism.[21] On the one hand, the consensus was held together by considerable agreement

[21] Recall that, for the most part, revisionism has never gained a foothold among non-economists to the population debates.

on several empirical propositions, as well as the identification of areas where population assessments were quite inconclusive. These have been evaluated in the literature surveys of the 1980s (see Sect. 4.2.1 below). In particular, there was a shift away from the concern about the impacts of population growth on resource exhaustion and on physical/human capital accumulation, and a shift toward a concern about renewable resource degradation. On the other hand, the consensus was threatened both by the inconclusive nature of research on some areas of potential impacts (e.g. poverty) of rapid population growth, and by disagreement over the importance of various feedbacks in the analysis of demographic change. Of particular relevance are the ways in which government policies should be viewed, and the importance of population-induced technical change in agriculture. (A summary of the debates on connections between demographic and institutional change is taken up in Sect. 4.2.2.)

4.2.1. *Empirical Propositions*
While there are numerous areas where research has provided a firmer grounding of population impacts, four emerged in the 1980s and notably influenced the elevation of revisionism.[22]

Non-renewable Resource Exhaustion   The concern that population growth results in the exhaustion of non-renewable natural resources is misplaced.[23] The relationship between population growth and global resource use is not as strong as has been assumed.

This conclusion is based on studies of (1) the determinants of resource supply and demand (related most strongly to per capita income); (2) the relative importance of price-induced versus serendipitous technological change on resource discovery and efficiency of use, and lowered costs of extraction; (3) the responsiveness of conservation in the face of resource scarcity; and (4) an assessment of the efficacy of markets and political processes of allocating exhaustible resources over time.[24] Population revisionism, based as it is on a broad theoretical perspective, the longer run, and feedbacks, is no better illustrated than in an analysis of the resource-exhaustion issue.

Saving and Investment   The concern about a substantial reduction of saving due to rapid population growth is not sustained by the data. While some capital-shallowing occurs, the impact of this on economic growth is not particularly strong.

The first conclusion was based on the inability to obtain reasonably conclusive and robust empirical results relating to the impact of population growth and age structure

---

[22] Other areas include assessments of the impact of population growth on unemployment, urbanization, pollution, scale economies, technical change, and the health of children and mothers. In all but the last area the evidence tends to qualify the relatively pessimistic assessments.

[23] Non-renewable resources are mainly minerals, including oil, as opposed to renewable resources like fisheries and forests.

[24] See NAS (1986), Barnett *et al.* (1984), Goeller and Zucker (1984), Leontief *et al.* (1983), MacKellar and Vining, Jr. (1987), and Slade (1987).

on saving.[25] While the data and the modeling leave much to be desired, the failure to 'confirm' the strongly held priors relating to postulated adverse impacts of population growth on saving has diminished the emphasis on this particular linkage. The second conclusion is based on demonstrations with simple growth-theoretic empirical assessments using computable general equilibrium models; it is also illustrated by Kuznets's (1967) analysis of historical trends.[26]

The above two conclusions, which represent qualifications of the Coale–Hoover model (a primarily analytical framework of traditionalism), helped to elevate revisionism in the 1980s. This shift in thinking was further reinforced by a qualification of the Coale–Hoover hypothesis relating to human capital accumulation.

Human Capital Accumulation   The concern that population growth will significantly shift resources from productive physical capital formation into alleged 'less-productive' areas such as education was not sustained by the data. The financing of educational enrollments, which expanded significantly even in the face of population pressures, came from some combination of increases in public (sometimes deficit) spending, reductions in per pupil expenditures, and efficiency gains rather than reduction in investments in other areas. While this allocation plausibly reduced the quality of education, the quantitative importance of this impact was uncertain.

The limited number of studies exploring these issues, based on cross-country comparisons, tended to arrive at the same conclusions.[27]

One example is instructive. T. Paul Schultz's (1987) detailed empirical analysis of schooling in 89 countries over the period 1968–80 revealed that while the overall pace of human capital accumulation in the Third World was exceptional by historic and regional standards (there is, however, a reduction in per pupil expenditures), there did not appear to be a notable (or even measurable) diversion of resources toward education due to demographic factors. In particular, the relative size of the school-age cohort did not appear to exert an independent effect on the share of GNP allocated to education, other things equal, causing Schultz to observe: 'This finding challenges the working assumption of Coale and Hoover (1958) that linked population growth to the share of income allocated by poor countries to "less productive" expenditures on education and social welfare programs' (pp. 458–9).

Resource Degradation   The concern about the effects of population growth on renewable resource degradation where property rights are difficult to assign or maintain (e.g. rain forests, fishing areas) was warranted.

---

[25] With respect to the age-dependency effect, the *World Development Report* concludes: 'Recent empirical studies find only minor support for this view' (World Bank 1984: 82). Timothy King (1985) concurs: 'In the litany of antinatalist argument, however, this one bears little weight. . . . most modern theories suggest that the proportion of children in the population is not very important' (p. 4). Hammer's review of the empirical literature (1985) concludes: 'While there is much evidence to indicate that these two aspects of development [population and saving] are intertwined in many ways, no simple generalizations are justified' (p. 3).

[26] Kelley and Williamson (1974), Keeley (1976), Srinivasan (1988).

[27] Bilsborrow (1978), Schultz (1987), Tait and Heller (1982), Simon and Pilarski (1979).

It is important to recognize that this result, which tends to elevate population pessimism, is also revisionist in orientation, since it explicitly highlighted the role of feedbacks. In this case, however, the market and political feedbacks needed to attenuate excessive resource use were assessed to be weak. These feedbacks would likely remain weak in the intermediate future when substantial, and in some cases irreversible, resource degradation would take place.[28]

4.2.2. *Variables versus Constraints*

Uneasiness in the consensus regarding the merits of revisionism rested less on qualms about the above propositions than on two areas at the heart of revisionism: an assessment of (1) the empirical strength and speed of response of 'feedbacks' (including institutions that are held to attenuate the initial impacts of population growth); and, related to this, (2) the extent to which institutions (e.g. public policy, land tenure systems, social norms) should be considered as 'variables' (revisionism) as opposed to 'constraints' (traditionalism) in the analysis of population.

Government Policies   In no area are the doubts about revisionism better illustrated than in a consideration of the role of the policy-making environment in the Third World. In particular, should public policies be taken as a 'given' in the analysis of population; or should they be considered a variable, possibly even responding to population pressures?

Government policies condition both the form and the size of population impacts on the economy, and these policies respond, in turn, to demographic change.[29] Unfortunately, very little can be said about how government policies relate to rapid population growth because a theory of government behavior that commands substantial empirical support is not available. Models have therefore tended to take the policy-making process to be exogenous (a constraint) in the analyses of demographic change. This approach is defensible so long as it does not downplay the important role of government policies as conditioning variables.

In many Third World countries, government policies have been incompatible with the promotion of economic growth in an environment of rapid population change. Consider three examples. First, policies toward the labor-intensive agricultural sector (especially in Africa) have taken the form of low investment in rural social overhead capital, high taxation of farm outputs (export taxes, and marketing boards that buy output at suppressed prices), high taxation of farm inputs, and exchange rates that encourage primary product imports and discourage exports. Such policies deter productivity-enhancing investments that counter the effects of diminishing returns in agriculture.

Secondly, inward-oriented international trade policies, including exchange rates that favor low-cost imports, have stimulated capital-intensive production in some industries with a corresponding under-utilization of abundant supplies of labor.

---

[28]   National Research Council (1986: ch. 2), World Bank (1984), Keyfitz (1991*a*, 1991*b*).
[29]   This section draws on Kelly (1988: 1717–18).

Finally, policies that favor the location of populations in urban areas have encouraged in-migration and city building that is both capital intensive and expensive.[30]

In general, those countries where government policies have encouraged production patterns at variance with comparative advantage by under-utilizing labor have experienced greater costs and fewer benefits of population growth. Revisionists have drawn attention to these policy-making issues by observing that many of the adverse consequences attributed to rapid population growth (e.g. food shortages, urban squalor, unemployment) are largely the result of unsuitable government policies. A major impact of population growth has been to reveal the adverse consequences of such policies sooner and more dramatically. As such, while population growth 'exacerbates' some problems, it may not be their most important cause. It therefore represents misplaced emphasis to confront such problems with population policies because without a change in economic policies, slower population growth simply postpones the day of reckoning, when the adverse consequences of ill-advised economic policies are tallied.

This is a reasonable set of propositions *if* the argument is one of redressing misplaced emphasis on population policies in those cases where population growth is relatively unimportant. However, one difficulty with the debates has been their tendency to polarize issues toward either-or choices. It is more appropriate to recognize that both population and economic policies exert independent as well as interacting effects on the economy, and that a combination of policy changes may be in order. Two recent statements on the need to develop a balanced perspective that considers population and economic policy interactions are instructive. On redressing possible misplaced emphasis on population policy for solving the short- to intermediate-run problem of starvation, Srinivasan (1987) observes:

The cause of eliminating starvation . . . will be ill-served if, instead of analyzing avoidable policy failure, policy makers turn their attention to attempts at changing an admittedly slow-acting process such as the interaction between population growth and the food economy. This is not to deny the modest improvements . . . resulting from an exogenous reduction in the rate of population growth; rather it is to point out that the pay-off to the correction of policy failures is likely to be more rapid and perhaps greater. (p. 25)

The World Bank (1984) generalizes this point with a stronger emphasis on population policy. It also highlights the need to distinguish between short- and long-run policy impacts.

. . . policies to reduce population growth can make an important contribution to development (especially in the long run), but their beneficial effects will be greatly diminished if they are not supported by the right macroeconomic and sectoral policies. At the same time, failure to address the population problem will itself reduce the set of macroeconomic and sectoral policies that are possible, and permanently foreclose some long-run development options. (p. 105)

At any rate, while it can be demonstrated that 'population problems' are largely due to inappropriate government policies, it is also the case that, *given* these policies,

---

[30] Kelley (1991).

population growth can exert a stronger adverse impact. Since much of the debate has focused on alleged 'population problems', a consensus on population's impact will depend critically on whether such government policies are taken as a constraint, or a variable in the analysis, and whether, even if a constraint, such policies are quantitatively important.

Agricultural Technology The linkages between population growth and size, and labor productivity in agriculture, are particularly important because the substantial majority of the labor force in the Third World, especially in Africa, India, and China, still derives its living from the land. The theoretical relationships are straightforward but ambiguous. Diminishing returns to labor due to a limited supply of land can be offset all or in part by technical change and/or scale economies. As a result, the net impact of population can only be determined empirically. Since in most of the Third World a substantial expansion of land is not presently a viable or economical option, the key linkage pertains to the relationships between population growth and size, and land intensification.[31]

In terms of the empirical record, the picture is varied. For most of Asia, population pressures have encouraged the adoption of new agricultural technologies that are exceptionally productive by historical standards, although there are conspicuous examples where the new technologies have not taken hold.[32] Important lessons have been learned from an analysis of this varied experience. In particular, a major factor explaining variations in country-specific experience has been differences in institutions such as markets, land-tenure arrangements, and government policies. Hayami and Ruttan (1987) place particular emphasis on institutional factors:

The gains from the new technology can be fully realized only if land tenure, water management and credit institutions perform effectively. Markets for inputs that embody new technology— seeds, fertilizer, pesticides—must perform efficiently. Product markets in which prices are

---

[31] In Asia, where most of the Third World resides, land supplies are quite constrained. In Africa, where arable land is relatively and seemingly abundant, costs of reclamation are often high, and the soils are frequently low in nutrients and thus easily degraded. The implications of these soil assessments are uncertain. On the abundance of African land, Nikos Alexandratos's (1986) study of 38 countries concludes that 'a country's capacity of feed its growing population . . . depends only weakly on its land endowments per se' (p. 19). Johnson (1984) is unequivocal on this point: 'there is not the slightest shred of evidence that continued poor performance of food and agriculture in most of Africa is in any way related to resource restraint' (p. 76). On the other hand, with respect to the cost of reclaiming African land, the World Bank (1982) concludes that much of the land is located in areas infested with insects carrying river blindness, sleeping sickness, and malaria. As a result, land intensification can still represent the most economical method of increasing agricultural output. A detailed analysis of the costs of reclaiming land in Africa and India is provided by Binswanger and Pingali (1984), Pingali and Binswanger (1984, 1986, 1987), and Ghatak and Ingersent (1984).

[32] For Asia, see Hayami and Ruttan (1985, 1987). For Africa, see Binswanger and Pingali (1984), Pingali and Binswanger (1984, 1986, 1987), and Boserup (1965, 1981). Agroclimatic conditions in Africa are not as advantageous to known technologies: soils are deficient in key minerals; the hotter climate reduces the efficiency of fertilizer use; a higher clay content reduces water absorption capacity; and closer proximity to the sun results in reduced areas over which a given technology package is appropriate. These factors increase the cost of research and development, and the cost of inputs, (Gourou 1980, and World Resources Institute for Environment and Development 1986).

distorted against either producers or consumers fail to generate the potential gains from the new technology. (p. 94)

Clearly, a key to untangling the relationships between technology and demographic change is the impact of population pressures *on* institutions (e.g. land tenure arrangements, markets, government policies). Regrettably, no generalization is possible here. For example, Rosenzweig, Binswanger, and McIntire (1984) find that output, land, labor, and especially rural credit markets develop in response to higher population densities; and Robert Bates (1983), a political scientist, observes that 'population density promotes the formation of political systems by generating a demand for the vesting of property rights over scarce resources' (p. 35). In contrast, in some areas population pressures result not in land reform, but in land fragmentation.[33] And, with respect to government policies, often biased against technical change and investments in agriculture, a central question is whether governments are more or less likely to undertake appropriate agricultural policies in an environment of slow versus rapid population growth. Srinivasan's (1987) judgment encapsulates our present state of knowledge here:

... it is difficult to assess even qualitatively whether such change [in agricultural systems] will be orderly or whether the burdens of adjustment will be distributed in proportion to the capacity to bear them. ... it is difficult to say whether an easing of demographic pressures will merely postpone the day of political reckoning, or will provide an extended period during which institutions can respond positively. (p. 24)

Again, as was concluded above, the analysis of the impact of population growth depends on whether institutions are considered as 'variables' or 'constraints', and, if variables, the ways and speed with which institutions respond to population pressures. An assessment of these questions is critical since institutions strongly condition the response of technologies in agriculture—the dominant sector of production in the Third World, and technological change represents a (the?) key to Third World development in the coming decades. Badly needed to untangle these issues are stronger theories of institutional change, the considerable input of economic-historical studies in both formulating and testing such theories, and an incorporation of these results into formal modeling efforts (mainly computable general equilibrium models) to assess the role of population size and growth on development. No strong consensus on the population debate can be forthcoming until this occurs.

Bottom Line More than any factor, the strength and nature of 'feedbacks' attenuating or overturning initial impacts of population growth represents a major remaining area of contention in the population debate.[34] Traditionalists tend to assume away

---

[33] For Bangladesh, see Arthur and McNicoll (1978). For a case study of two rural Indonesian villages with contrasting patterns of institutional change in response to rising population densities, see Hayami and Kikuchi (1981).

[34] This assumes that the population debate will continue to focus on economic development and growth, as distinct from distributional issues or welfare.

these feedbacks by considering only the short run, by treating them as 'constraints' in the analysis, or by hypothesizing that their impact is quantitatively unimportant. An example of this posture is the position of Nathan Keyfitz (1991*c*), a distinguished demographer, who, in commenting on 'feedbacks' (denoted as intermediate variables), observes:

The range of these [intermediate variables] is limited only by the imagination of the writer, and the scope for cleverness is wide. Every one of the arguments can be supported by some anecdote, [and] for none is there convincing evidence. I submit that the direct effect is primary, and that the burden of proof is on the one who has introduced some intermediate effect that would upset it. (p. 3)

This statement reflects a strength of skepticism about the importance of feedbacks that causes Keyfitz to propose an empirical test that is unnecessarily constraining (i.e. a one-sided rejection test that implies exceptionally strong theoretical priors). The revisionist methodology does not, and sound science should not, require upsetting direct effects, but only an even-handed analysis that takes feedbacks into account. Keyfitz's statement also reflects the intensity of the debate, the continuing difficulty of achieving a consensus, and the exceptional importance that research in the future be focused on this central dimension of revisionism—the quantitative importance of feedbacks in a general equilibrium framework.

5. 1990s

The above review has been selective, focusing primarily on factors that account for the prominence of revisionism through the 1980s. The present section extends this analysis to the 1990s.

5.1. *The Research Agenda*

Four research themes have been emphasized. The first has been a reassessment of the macro 'correlations' literature that attempts to identify, using cross-country data, statistical relationships between demographic change and the pace of economic growth. This research was motivated by several new studies showing a negative impact of population growth on per capita output growth for the 1980s—a result at variance with the influential findings for the 1960s and 1970s showing no, or at most, a weak relationship.[35] The second research theme has been a review and extension of the microeconomic/social studies exposing impacts of family size on household nutrition, health, and education. This research was motivated by an attempt to reconcile strongly held priors that large families deter personal development with the economy-wide results showing rather weak relationships between educational participation, food availability, and population growth.

---

[35] Barlow (1992), Blanchet (1991), Bloom and Freeman (1988), Brander and Dowrick (1994), and United Nations (1988).

The third research theme has emphasized the impacts of population growth on the environment. This research was motivated both by an elevation of the goal of environmental preservation worldwide, and a realization that providing sufficient food for expanding populations will exact some environmental costs that need to be reckoned. A final research theme has refocused attention on the connections between population pressures and poverty.

5.2. *Leading up to Cairo*

Three studies, commissioned to provide background for the 1994 Cairo Population Conference, represent a convenient basis for summarizing the population research in the early 1990s.

World Bank The first, sponsored by the World Bank and undertaken by Kelley and Schmidt (KS), replicated and confirmed the results of five earlier studies that showed a negative impact of population growth on per capita output growth in the 1980s.[36] In addition, KS extended the modeling in two directions, by (1) appending several demographic embellishments to the popular convergence, or technology-gap, paradigms (e.g. the Barro model); and (2) developing a dynamic model designed to expose the differential impacts of population over the life cycle (e.g. the negative impacts of children versus the positive impacts of working adults on per capita output growth).

This research confirmed the overall negative impact of population growth on per capita output growth in the 1980s across a large number of countries (DCs (developed countries) and LDCs) using a technology-gap model. It moreover revealed that the impact of population growth varied with the *level* of economic development: it was negative in the LDCs and positive in many DCs. An assessment of a net negative impact across all countries appeared in spite of the positive effects found both for population size and density. While no explanation was provided for the new results for the 1980s, the authors explored the hypothesis that the *timing* of demographic effects may have played a role. Since the economic-growth impacts of a new birth vary over a lifetime, modeling of demography should ideally account for the *patterns* of demographic changes, in particular births and deaths, over time. KS (1995) confirmed that some of the earlier 'no-correlation' findings in the literature were related to these dynamics. This interpretation gained additional support from two technology-gap studies by Bloom and Williamson (BW) (1998) and Radelet, Sachs, and Lee (RSL) (1997), whose models emphasize age-distributional patterns.[37] All of these attempts at dynamic modeling are revisionist: all show that demographic change at a given point in time can have positive, negative, or neutral impacts on economic growth

---

[36] Kelley and Schmidt (1994, 1995).

[37] BW emphasize demography and its implications, building upon the RSL core. RSL include a similar demographic specification (which is technically different from BW), and emphasize elements in the core model, as well.

depending, in part, on the timing of the components of (positive) labor force versus (negative) dependent population growth. Only by accounting for this experience over several decades in a way that exposes a wide range of impacts can changes in fertility and mortality (and resulting changes in the age distribution) be adequately assessed.

Overseas Development Council; Government of Australia   Two other studies leading up to Cairo can be considered together since their coverage and authorship have significant overlap. The findings of the first, sponsored by the Overseas Development Council and led by Robert Cassen (with 15 participants), appeared in *Population and Development: Old Debates, New Conclusions*; the findings of the second, commissioned by the Australian government and led by Dennis Ahlburg (with 10 participants), appeared in *The Impact of Population Growth on Well-being in Developing Countries.*

Generally the results of these studies conform broadly with the collective findings of the several surveys examined above for the 1980s. This is hardly surprising since major new empirical findings were not forthcoming given the relatively short intervening period; and notable new interpretations are unlikely given the overlap of the participants with the earlier surveys. Neither of the two new studies is alarmist in tone; both are balanced in their consideration of both short- and long-run impacts of demography, a wide variety of impacts (both positive and negative), and various feedbacks.

The two studies did offer a modified reorientation of past analyses by shifting attention from the macroeconomic impacts of population growth to an elevated emphasis of the microeconomic impacts of large families. Specifically, it was found that large families were disadvantaged in health and nutrition. In addition, several studies revealed adverse impacts of large families on educational attainment and participation, although here the evidence is mixed, precluding strong conclusions. This is because there are a sizeable number of studies showing no, or even positive, impacts of family size and educational outcomes, and seldom are any of the (positive or negative) impacts quantitatively large.[38]

The resulting bottom lines of the two studies, together, are qualified and quite comprehensive. Cassen (1994) concludes: 'At the microeconomic level, . . . there are clear negative effects [of large families] . . . on the health and education of children and mother's health and life opportunities' (p. 20). 'At the macroeconomic level, matters are less definitive; much depends on circumstances' (p. 20). Ahlburg *et al.* (1996) conclude:

. . . slowing of rapid population growth is likely to be advantageous for economic development, health, food availability, housing, poverty, the environment, and possibly education, especially

---

[38] While upwards of 40 separate econometric studies using household data are assessed, the modeling and empirical analysis of most of these studies is problematic. The family-size decision is usually modeled as exogenous and, in all but three studies, the impacts are posited as being linear over the entire range of family size. As a result, this literature is presently quite unsettled, based both on its mixed results and its underlying modeling.

in poor agrarian societies facing pressure on land and resources. For several of these areas, for example poverty, the size of any beneficial effects of slowing population growth is unknown. For other areas, the impacts are relatively small. Such small effects, however, are likely to be synergistic and cumulative (p. 10).

6. RECONCILIATION

It is intriguing that the assessments on the economic consequences of population growth, as found in the seminal 1951 United Nations Report, have not much changed over the intervening five decades. While debates on these consequences have been vigorous and contentious, what we denote in this essay as 'revisionism' has, for the most part, prevailed as the dominant analytical perspective among most economists who have written on population matters. The hallmark of this revisionism is not whether the net impact of population growth is assessed to be negative or positive. It is rather the *way* the analysis is undertaken: focusing on the longer run; accounting for feedbacks, direct and indirect effects; and admitting a wide range of impacts, both positive and negative. In a sense, this broader perspective has attenuated the rancor in the debates; it has provided a reconciliation among a number of participants to the debates that admits a middle ground that is plausibly closer to the truth, and arguably based on sounder scholarship.

The research agenda of revisionists is particularly demanding given the extended time period of analysis and the variety of forces that must be reckoned. Over the last half century this research has expanded at a reasonable pace, resulting in strong qualifications and a downgrading of several empirical propositions of the 'traditionalist/ alarmist' school. It has moreover exposed several areas where most research is needed (e.g. the impacts of rapid population growth on poverty, and the environment; the interactions of policy environments and demographic change).

While the bad news is that in many areas of population assessments, the empirical findings lack precision and strength, the good news is that debates have become less contentious and increasingly productive in outcome. While possibly the only certainty in the 'population debate' may be its continuance, fortunately the elevation of the revisionist perspective has put that debate on a solid footing.

Appendix: Puzzles, Politics, and Population Research: The 1971 NAS Report

In spite of exhaustive inquiries of the NAS, USAID, and seven of the participants in the NAS Report, it has not been possible to identify with certainty the author of 'Overview', chapter 1, volume I ('Summary and Recommendations'). Somewhat surprisingly, NAS archives contain no information on the Report. And according to representatives at the USAID, the relevant files appear to have been retired. Direct participants were later vague about authorship. (I talked with Professor Revelle twice in the summer of 1991 to obtain his impressions on the drafting and vetting of 'Summary and Recommendations' in general, and 'Overview' in particular. While he recalled drafting a version of the summary, his memory was not sufficiently precise to form firm judgments. He died two weeks after our last conversation.) According to one observer, key leadership within USAID was 'unhappy with earlier versions of the summary. . . . There was enormous pressure on the NAS staff to 'deliver' a supportive document'. Ansley Coale, unable to accompany Revelle to an AID briefing on the Report, recalls remarking to Revelle a week later that he (Revelle) must have been disappointed in him. Revelle's response was unambiguous: 'You're damned right I am'. Apparently, AID's reception of the NAS–Revelle draft was not particularly satisfying.

Most participants contacted concluded that the NAS staff drafted the 'Overview'. None remembers reviewing that draft. Several participants were surprised by the strong negative orientation of the 'Overview'. One wrote with respect to a major section in the 'Summary and Recommendations': 'As I go back to the book and look at the two parts which pertain to the puzzle, I am as baffled as you are as to who might be responsible for having run them'. Another participant, who examined the 'Overview' in detail, noted: 'I am deeply offended that a product put together with a lot of effort to avoid simplistic traps was perverted by ad hoc interference with the highly visible first few pages. I didn't see the "Overview" until I got a copy of the book, and I didn't examine it with care until your phone call'. His review revealed several inconsistences between the 'Overview' and the research chapters.

The above analysis, pieced together from notes on numerous conversations with, and letters from, participants in the NAS report, has been subsequently corroborated by documents received from Professor George Stolnitz, a central figure in the drafting of volume I. The Stolnitz documents included Revelle's (1969) draft of the executive summary (entitled 'The Consequences of Population Change, and Their Implications for National and International Policies'), which was dramatically different in tone and conclusions from the published 'Overview'.

According to Stolnitz, the Revelle draft 'didn't pass muster' with Murray Todd (and with persons Todd consulted), the NAS staff professional attached to the project. Stolnitz was asked by Todd to so inform Revelle, and to work with Revelle (and other committee members) on a revision. The Revelle draft was non-alarmist in tone and represented a guarded treatment. For example, after considering population's commonly-cited negative impacts on natural resource use, investment, savings, and dependency, Revelle concluded: 'All of the above effects taken together are relatively small' (Revelle 1969: 13). In terms of overall assessment, Revelle concluded: 'There is, as yet, little public or expert agreement about the nature and extent of the effects of rapid population growth, their importance relative to other factors of development, their interrelations with these factors . . . . Hence, it is difficult to determine the direction and relative level of effort that should be given to programs aimed toward the reduction of population growth . . . ' (Revelle 1969: 5). Revelle emphasized the need for objective assessment of population impacts, and warned against one-sided alarmism. 'Discussions of the population problem are too often highly charged with emotion, fear and passion. Drastic predictions of widespread famine . . . are commonly made and widely believed. . . . the problem of sufficient food for the world's growing population probably can be solved, and its solution involves many factors besides slowing down rates of population growth' (Revelle 1969: 8). Given these various statements, it is difficult to believe that Revelle would have embraced the resulting 'Overview' which is decidedly one-sided, and alarmist in orientation. (There is evidence he had read 'Overview'. Revelle 1971: 1.)

Based on a careful review and analysis of a sizeable number of documents relating to the NAS study, Stolnitz concludes that it is almost certain that chapter 1 was written by Murray Todd. Apparently early on (Oct. 1969), the planning committee sought, as is characterized by Oscar (Bud) Harkavy's paraphrased rendering in a memorandum written by Todd (1969), 'a number of crisply stated propositions on the consequences of population growth' (p. 1). (The final 'Overview' in fact took this format.) Additionally, the planning committee sought 'the opportunity to set to rest some of the popular myths that currently surround the population question, for example that world famine can confidently... [blurred in manuscript] in the 1970's' (Todd 1969: 1). (The final 'Overview' did not in fact include this material.)

Stolnitz concludes that 'The indicated pile-up of unfavorable aspects of Third World population change in chapter 1, presented in staccato fashion, [is] an editor's expository ploy to catch the attention of the hurried, abbreviated perusals to be expected by D.C. and other targeted doers and shakers' (Stolnitz 1991: 1). Why such a rendering passed Revelle's scrutiny, why it was not vetted by the remaining committee members, and why it was so one-sided—given the desire to qualify 'myths' (equally eye-catching)—remain as puzzles.

A final observation on Todd's role should be recorded. If, as is highly likely, Todd drafted (and/or negotiated) the executive summary, it is clear that he was under extensive pressure from powerful population activists in the Department of State, USAID, and some NGOs. It may be unreasonable to expect a person in such a role to fully withstand such pressure.

I am grateful for feedback on aspects of this Report from Ansley J. Coale, Moye Freyman, Oscar Harkavy, Hans Landsberg, Thomas Merrick, Carol Pichard, Roger Revelle, Norman Ryder, Steve Sinding, T. W. Schultz, and Myron Weiner. Both the NAS and USAID were completely cooperative in attempting to locate documentation relating to the NAS Report. I especially thank George Stolnitz, who sorted through and commented on hundreds of pages of manuscript materials relating to the NAS study, available in his personal files. His detailed analysis of these documents provided pivotal insights into assessing the relationship of the 'Overview' chapter (summarizing the NAS study) to the positions of the analysts associated with the report, and the background papers.

References

Ahlburg, D. A., A. C. Kelley, and K. Oppenheim Mason. 1996. *The Impact of Population Growth on Well-being in Developing Countries*. Berlin: Springer-Verlag.

Alexandratos, Nikos. 1986. 'Population Carrying Capacity of African Lands: A Re-Assessment'. Paper presented at the Seminar on Economic Consequences of Population Trends in Africa, International Union for the Scientific Study of Population. Nairobi, Kenya, Dec., mimeo.

Arthur, W. Brian, and Geoffrey McNicoll. 1978. 'An Analytical Survey of Population and Development in Bangladesh'. *Population and Development Review*. 4 (1), 23–80.

Barlow, Robin. 1992. 'Demographic Influences on Economic Growth'. Ann Arbor: University of Michigan, mimeo.

Barnett, H. J., G. M. van Muiswinkel, M. Scheichter, and J. J. Myers. 1984. 'The Global Trend in Nonfuel Minerals'. In J. L. Simon and H. Kahn, eds., *The Resourceful Earth: A Response to Global 2000*. New York: Basil Blackwell, 316–38.

Bates, Robert H. 1983. *Essays on the Political Economy of Rural Africa*. Cambridge: Cambridge University Press.

Bilsborrow, Richard E. 1978. 'The Relationship between Population Growth and the Expansion of Education Systems in Developing Countries, 1950–1970'. *Pakistan Development Review*. 17 (2), 212–32.

Binswanger, Hans P., and Prabhu L. Pingali. 1984. 'The Evolution of Farming Systems and Agricultural Technology in Sub-Saharan Africa'. World Bank Discussion Paper ARU-23. Washington: World Bank.

Birdsall, Nancy. 1988. 'Economic Approaches to Population Growth and Development'. In Hollis B. Chenery and T. N. Srinivasan, eds., *Handbook of Development Economics*. Amsterdam: Elsevier Science Publications.

Blanchet, Didier. 1991. 'Estimating the Relationship between Population Growth and Aggregate Economic Growth in LDC's: Methodological Problems'. In *Consequences of Rapid Population Growth in Developing Countries*. Proceedings of the United Nations Institut national d'études demographiques Expert Group Meeting, New York, 23–6 Aug. 1988. New York: Taylor and Francis, 67–99.

Bloom, David E., and Richard B. Freeman. 1988. 'Economic Development and the Timing and Components of Population Growth'. *Journal of Policy Modeling* 10 (1) (Special Issue: Modeling Demographic and Economic Dynamics, Dominick Salvatore, guest ed.): 57–81.

—— and Jeffrey G. Williamson. 1998. 'Demographic Transitions and Economic Miracles in Emerging Asia'. *World Bank Economic Review*. 12 (3), 419–55.

Boserup, Ester. 1965. *The Conditions of Agricultural Growth*. Chicago: Aldine.

—— 1981. *Population and Technological Change*. Chicago: University of Chicago Press.

Brander, James A., and Steve Dowrick. 1994. 'The Role of Fertility and Population in Economic Growth: Empirical Results from Aggregate Cross-national Data'. *Journal of Population Economics*. 7: 1–25.

Caldwell, John C., and Pat Caldwell. 1986. *Limiting Population Growth and the Ford Foundation Contribution*. Dover, NH: Francis Pinter.

Cassen, Robert, ed. 1994. *Population and Development: Old Debates, New Conclusions*. Overseas Development Council, US–Third World Policy Perspectives No. 19. New Brunswick, NJ: Transaction Publishers.

Coale, Ansley J., and Edgar M. Hoover. 1958. *Population Growth and Economic Development in Low-Income Countries*. Princeton: Princeton University Press.

Demeny, Paul. 1986. 'Population and the Invisible Hand'. *Demography*. 23 (4), 473–88.

—— 1988. 'Social Science and Population Policy'. *Population and Development Review*. 14 (3), 451–79.

Donaldson, Peter J. 1990. *Nature Against Us: The United States and the World Population Crisis 1965–1980*. Chapel Hill, NC: University of North Carolina Press.

Easterlin, Richard A. 1967. 'Effects of Population Growth on the Economic Development of Developing Countries'. *Annals of the American Academy of Political and Social Science*. 369: 98–108.

Ghatak, Subrata, and Ken Ingersent. 1984. *Agriculture and Economic Development*. Baltimore: Johns Hopkins University Press.

Goeller, H. E., and A. Zucker. 1984. 'Infinite Resources: The Ultimate Strategy'. *Science*. 223:456–62.

Gourou, Pierre. 1980. *The Topical World: Its Social and Economic Conditions and its Future Status*. 5th edn. New York: Longman.

Hansen, Alvin H. 1939. 'Economic Progress and Declining Population Growth'. *American Economic Review*. 29 (1, pt. 1), 1–15.

Hammer, Jeffrey S. 1985. 'Population Growth and Savings in Developing Countries: A Survey'. World Bank Staff Working Paper, No. 687. Washington.

Harkavy, Oscar. 1995. *Curbing Population Growth: An Insider's Perspective on the Population Movement*. New York: Plenum Press.

Hayami, Yujiro, and Masao Kikuchi. 1981. *Asian Village Economy at the Crossroads: An Economic Approach to Institutional Change*. Baltimore: Johns Hopkins University Press, and Tokyo: University of Tokyo Press.

Hayami, and Ruttan, Vernon. 1985. *Agricultural Development: An International Perspective*. Baltimore: Johns Hopkins Press.

—— 1987. 'Population Growth and Agricultural Productivity'. In D. Gale Johnson and Ronald D. Lee, eds., *Population Growth and Economic Development: Issues and Evidence*. Madison: University of Wisconsin Press.

Hodgson, Dennis. 1983. 'Demography as Social Science and Policy Science'. *Population and Development Review*. 9 (1), 1–34.

—— 1988. 'Orthodoxy and Revisionism in American Demography'. *Population and Development Review*. 14 (4), 541–69.

Johnson, D. Gale. 1984. 'World Food and Agriculture'. In Julian Simon and Herman Kahn, eds., *The Resourceful Earth: A Response to Global 2000*. New York: Basil Blackwell, 67–112.

Keeley, Michael C. 1976. 'A Neoclassical Analysis of Economic-Demographic Simulation Models'. In Michael C. Keeley, ed., *Population, Public Policy and Economic Development*, New York: Praeger, 25–45.

Kelley, Allen C. 1988. 'Economic Consequences of Population Change in the Third World'. *Journal of Economic Literature*. 26 (Dec.), 1685–1728.

—— 1991. 'African Urbanization and City Growth: Perspectives, Problems and Policies'. Paper presented at INED/UNPD Conference, Development and Rapid Demographic Growth: A New Look at the Future of Africa. Paris, France, 2–6 Sept. 1991.

—— and Robert M. Schmidt. 1994. 'Population and Income Change: Recent Evidence'. World Bank Discussion Papers 249. Washington: World Bank.

—— —— 1995. 'Aggregate Population and Economic Growth Correlations: The Role of the Components of Demographic Change'. *Demography*. 32 (4), 543–55.

—— and Jeffrey G. Williamson. 1974. *Lessons from Japanese Development: An Analytical Economic History*. Chicago: University of Chicago Press.

Keyfitz, Nathan. 1991*a*. 'Population and Development Within the Ecosphere: One View of the Literature'. *Population Index*. 57 (1), 5–22.

—— 1991*b*. 'Population Growth can Prevent the Development that would Slow Population Growth'. In Jessica Tuchman Mathews, ed., *Preserving the Global Environment*. New York: W. W. Norton and Company, 39–77.

—— 1991*c*. 'Why Population is Said to be Unimportant for Environment and Development: Or How to Make the Population Problem Disappear'. Paper presented at the Population Association of America, Washington.

King, Timothy. 1985. 'Population and Development: Back to First Principles'. In *Population Trends and Public Policy* (Population Reference Bureau). 7: 2–11.

Kuznets, Simon. 1967. 'Population and Economic Growth'. *Proceedings of the American Philosophical Society*. 111 (3), 170–93.

Leontief, W., J. Koo, S. Nasar, and I. Sohn. 1983. *The Future of Nonfuel Minerals in the U.S. and World Economy*. Lexington, Mass.: D. C. Heath.

MacKellar, F. Landis, and David R. Vining, Jr. 1987. 'Natural Resource Scarcity: A Global Summary'. In D. Gale Johnson and Ronald D. Lee, eds., *Population Growth and Economic Development: Issues and Evidence*. Madison: University of Wisconsin Press, 259–329.

McNicoll, Geoffrey. 1984. 'Consequences of Rapid Population Growth: An Overview and Assessment'. *Population and Development Review*. 10 (2), 177–240.

National Academy of Sciences. 1971. *Rapid Population Growth: Consequences and Policy Implications*. 2 vols. Baltimore: Johns Hopkins Press for the National Academy of Sciences.

National Research Council. 1986. *Population Growth and Economic Development: Policy Questions.* Washington: National Academy Press.

Pingali, Prabhu L., and Hans P. Binswanger. 1984. 'Population Density and Farming Systems: The Changing Focus of Innovations and Technical Change'. Paper prepared for the IUSSP Seminar on Population, Food and Rural Development. New Delhi, India.

—— —— 1986. 'Population Density, Market Access and Farmer-Generated Technical Change in Sub-Saharan Africa'. Paper presented at the Seminar on the Consequences of Population Trends in Africa. IUSSP, Nairobi, Kenya.

—— —— 1987. 'Population Density and Agricultural Intensification: A Study of the Evolution of Technologies in Tropical Agriculture'. In D. Gale Johnson and Ronald Lee, eds., *Population Growth and Economic Development: Issues and Evidence.* Madison: University of Wisconsin Press, 27–56.

Piotrow, Phyllis T. 1973. *World Population Crisis: The United States Response.* New York: Praeger.

Radelet, Steven, Jeffrey Sachs, and Jong-Wha Lee. 1997. 'Economic Growth in Asia'. Harvard Institute for International Development, Development Discussion Paper No. 609.

Revelle, Roger. 1969. 'The Consequences of Population Change, and their implications for National and International Policies'. Mimeo.

—— 1971. Memo to Members of the NAS Study Committee on the Consequences of Rapid Population Growth. 1 Mar.

Rosenzweig, Mark R., Hans P. Binswanger, and John McIntyre. 1984. 'From Land-Abundance to Land-Scarcity: The Effects of Population Growth on Production Relations in Agrarian Economies'. Paper prepared for the IUSSP Conference on Population, Food, and Rural Development. New Delhi, India.

Schultz, T. Paul. 1987. 'School Expenditures and Enrollments, 1960–1980: The Effects of Income, Prices and Population Growth'. In D. Gale Johnson and Ronald D. Lee, eds., *Population Growth and Economic Development: Issues and Evidence.* Madison: University of Wisconsin Press, 413–76.

Simon, Julian L. 1981. *The Ultimate Resource.* Princeton: Princeton University Press.

—— and Pilarski, Adam M. 1979. 'The Effect of Population Growth upon the Quantity of Education Children Receive'. *Review of Economics and Statistics.* 61 (4), 572–84.

Slade, M. E. 1987. 'Natural Resources, Population Growth and Economic Well-Being'. In D. Gale Johnson and Ronald D. Lee, eds., *Population Growth and Economic Development: Issues and Evidence.* Madison: University of Wisconsin Press.

Spengler, Joseph J. 1949. 'Theories of Socio-Economic Growth'. In National Bureau of Economic Research, *Problems in the Study of Economic Growth.* New York: National Bureau of Economic Research, 46–115.

—— 1966. 'The Economist and the Population Question'. *American Economic Review.* 56 (1), 1–24.

Srinivasan, T. N. 1987. 'Population and Food'. In D. Gale Johnson and Ronald D. Lee, eds., *Population Growth and Economic Development: Issues and Evidence.* Madison: University of Wisconsin Press, 3–26.

—— 1988. 'Population Growth and Economic Development'. *Journal of Policy Modeling.* 10 (1) (Spring), 7–28.

Stolnitz, George J. 1991. Letter to Allen C. Kelley. 16 Nov.

Tait, Alan A., and Heller, Peter S. 1982. 'International Comparisons of Government Expenditure'. International Monetary Fund Occasional Paper No. 10. Washington: IMF.

Todd, W. Murray. 1969. Memo to Members of the Executive Committee of the NAS Study on the Consequences of Population Growth and their Policy Implications. 31 Oct.

United Nations. 1953. *The Determinants and Consequences of Population Trends.* Department of Social Affairs, Population Division, Population Studies No. 17. New York: United Nations.

—— 1973. *The Determinants and Consequences of Population Trends.* Department of Economic and Social Affairs, Population Studies No. 50. 2 vols. New York: United Nations.

—— 1988. *World Population Trends and Policies: 1987 Monitoring Report.* Department of International Economic and Social Affairs, Population Studies No. 103. ST/ESA/SER.A/103. New York: United Nations.

Wattenberg, Ben J. 1987. *The Birth Dearth.* New York: Pharos Books.

World Bank. Selected Years. *World Development Report.* New York: Oxford University Press.

World Resources Institute and International Institute for Environment and Development. 1986. *World Resources 1986.* New York: Basic Books.

3

Dependency Burdens in the Developing World

JOHN BONGAARTS

The developing world is currently going through a period of very rapid demographic change. The best-known trend is the unprecedented increase in population size, but other demographic variables are also changing at a rapid pace. Birth rates have dropped steeply in recent decades as women are having smaller families, and death rates are now a fraction of the levels that prevailed a century ago. One important consequence of these trends in fertility and mortality is a substantial and not well-appreciated change in the distribution of the population by age. Broadly speaking, a population 'ages' as a country moves through the demographic transition.

This introductory chapter focuses on the dependency burden which is defined as the ratio of dependent young and old to the population of working age. The dependency burden varies over time and among populations in ways that have important economic and social consequences, as described in later chapters in this volume. Before turning to a discussion of demographic dimensions of dependency, I will first briefly review broad demographic trends, because they are the causes of variation in the dependency burden.

COMPLETING THE DEMOGRAPHIC TRANSITION

The term 'demographic transition' refers to a fairly well-defined pattern of change in birth, death, and population growth rates that accompanies the process of development. Before the transition's onset, population growth is near zero as high death rates more or less offset the high birth rates typically found in traditional agricultural societies. Population growth is again near zero after the completion of the transition as birth and death rates both reach low levels in modern industrialized societies. During the transition period between these demographic equilibria, large increases in population occur because the death rate drops before the birth rate (see Fig. 3.1).

The demographic transition of the developing world is now about half complete. The recent period of rapid expansion of human numbers began in the late nineteenth century and led to an increase of 4 billion from nearly 1 billion in 1850 to 4.8 billion today. Population size is expected to grow by an additional 5 billion, approaching 10 billion in the twenty-second century, according to recent projections by the United Nations (1998) and the World Bank (1998). Over the past three decades population

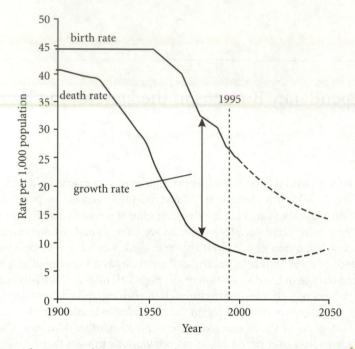

Figure 3.1. *The Demographic Transition in the Developing World, Estimates and Projections*
Source: UN (1996); author's estimates.

size has increased by a record 2 billion, and the same increase is projected over the next 30 years, thus making the period from 1970 to 2030 the peak of the transition.

The acceleration of population growth during the twentieth century was caused primarily by a sustained reduction in mortality. Improved living standards, better nutrition, greater investments in sanitation and clean water supplies, expanded access to health services, and wider application of low-cost public health measures such as immunization have yielded very rapid mortality reductions, especially since World War II. By the late 1960s, the average annual death rate had dropped to 15 per 1,000 population which is less than half the pre-transitional level. Together with a still largely unchanged birth rate of 40 per 1,000, this yielded a growth rate of 25 per 1,000 or 2.5 percent per year (see Fig. 3.1). Since then, birth rates have declined sharply, particularly in Asia and Latin America, and the average number of births per woman has been cut in half—from six in the 1960s to three today. As a consequence, the annual population growth rate in 1990–95 declined to 1.8 percent. Because this slowly declining growth rate is applied to a rapidly growing population base, the absolute annual increment in population size has actually continued to rise—from 64 million in the late 1960s to 76 million in the early 1990s. It is expected to remain near this level until 2025.

The timing of the onset and the duration of demographic transitions differs widely from region to region and from country to country. Some African countries are still

Table 3.1. *Total Population Estimates (1950–1995) and Projections (2000–2050), by Region*

Country	Population (billions)				
	1950	1995	2000	2025	2050
Africa	0.22	0.72	0.82	1.45	2.05
Asia[a]	1.32	3.32	3.57	4.68	5.34
Latin America	0.17	0.48	0.51	0.69	0.81
Developing world	1.71	4.52	4.90	6.82	8.20

Note: [a]Excluding Japan, Australia, and New Zealand, but including Oceania.

Source: UN (1996).

in the early transitional stages because they have experienced only modest declines in death rates and virtually no change in birth rates, but there are also a few countries, primarily in East Asia, where the transition is virtually complete. In general, the more developed a country is, the further it has progressed through the transition.

Because transitions in most countries are far from complete, further growth is expected for the foreseeable future in all regions of the developing world. Table 3.1 summarizes key results from regional projections made by the United Nations (UN). In 1995, Asia's population size of 3.3 billion represented more than two-thirds of the LDC total (and more than half of the world total), and this number is expected to reach 5.3 billion by 2050—a 58 percent increase. Africa, with 0.58 billion inhabitants in 1995, is likely to experience by far the most rapid expansion, nearly tripling in size by 2050. Latin America, with 0.48 billion in 1995, is the smallest of the major regions; this is expected to remain the case with a growth pattern similar to Asia's. The developing world as a whole is projected to reach 8.2 billion in 2050.

The future growth expected in these projections is primarily attributable to three factors (the minor role of migration is ignored):

1. *Fertility above Replacement*   Fertility is at replacement when each generation of women exactly replaces the previous one (i.e. every newborn girl on average gives birth to one daughter over her lifetime). Replacement represents a critical threshold because it equals the fertility level that, if maintained over time, produces zero population growth. Positive or negative deviations from replacement lead in the long run to persistent population growth or decline, respectively. Currently, replacement fertility equals 2.36 births per woman (bpw) in the developing world. This level exceeds 2 because children who die before reaching the reproductive ages have to be replaced with additional births, and because the sex ratio at birth slightly exceeds one (typically 1.05 male for every female birth). Despite rapid recent declines in many countries, fertility remains well above the replacement level in all regions in the South with fertility ranging from a high of 5.3 bpw in Africa to 2.7 bpw in Asia and Latin America. This implies that fertility remains one of the key forces contributing to further population growth.

The UN projections assume fertility to decline in the future, eventually stabilizing at the replacement level before 2040. Once a country has reached replacement it is assumed to remain there; this assures that population growth reaches zero at the end of the transition (assuming constant mortality and zero migration).

2. *Declining Mortality*   Life expectancy in the developing world has risen from an average of 40 years in 1950 to 64 years today. Latin America, which now has a life expectancy of 70 years, has reached mortality levels similar to those in the developed world in the 1960s, and Asia is not far behind. Sub-Saharan Africa's mortality has been highest, and its current life expectancy is just 54 years.

Over the next half century the UN projections assume life expectancy to continue to rise in all regions. By 2050 Asia and Latin America are both expected to have mortality conditions similar to those in the developed world today, but Africa will continue to lag, in part because the continent is most heavily affected by the AIDS epidemic.

3. *Young Age Structure*   Even if fertility could immediately be brought to the replacement level with constant mortality and zero migration, population growth would continue in developing countries. The reason for this is a young age structure, which is the result of high fertility and rapid population growth in recent decades. With a large proportion of the population under age 30, further growth over the coming decades is assured because these young people will produce more births than deaths as they build families and grow old, even if their fertility is at replacement. This age-structure effect is called population momentum (Keyfitz 1971).

The contribution of each of these three demographic factors to future population growth in the developing world was estimated in a recent study (Bongaarts and Bulatao, 1999). It found that the momentum inherent in the current young age structure of the developing world accounts for a larger proportion of future population growth than either above-replacement fertility or declining mortality. Momentum is clearly the largest component of future growth in Asia and Latin America, but not in Africa where high fertility is slightly more important. These findings provide one demonstration of the crucial role played by the changing age structure in population dynamics.

THE DEPENDENCY BURDEN

The declines in fertility and mortality that occur over the course of the demographic transition are accompanied by important changes in the distribution of the population by age. Countries in the early stages of the transition have a younger age structure than countries that have reached the end of the transition. This trend over time is illustrated in Figure 3.2 which presents the estimated distribution by age in 1950 and 1975 and the projected distribution for 2000, 2025, and 2050 for the developing world. The proportion of the population under age 15 is expected to decline from 37.8 percent in 1950 to 21.0 percent in 2050, while the population over age 65 is projected to rise from 3.9 percent to 13.8 percent over the same period. The age distribution changed relatively little between 1950 and 1975 despite a rapid decline in mortality

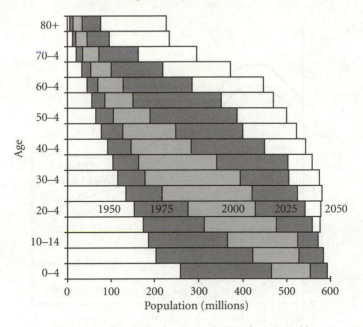

Figure 3.2. *Population by Age in the Developing World*
Source: UN (1996).

during this period. Changes in mortality generally affect the age distribution much less than changes in fertility because mortality declines typically affect all ages, while fertility declines affect the number of new entrants into the population pyramid at age 0.

The most widely used indicator of the dependency burden is the age dependency ratio (ADR) (Shryock and Siegel 1973). The ADR of a population at a given point in time is defined as the ratio of the population in the ages below 15 (P_{15}) and over 65 (P_{65}) to the population between ages 15 and 65 (P_{15-65}):

$$ADR = (P_{15} + P_{65})/P_{15-65}$$

This ratio aims to measure how many 'dependents' there are for each person in the 'working' age groups. Obviously, not every person below 15 and over 65 is a dependent and not every person between ages 15 and 65 is at work, but despite the crudeness of this indicator it is the most common measure used to document broad trends in the age composition and dependency burden.

Over the course of a demographic transition the ADR shows a characteristic pattern of change. Figure 3.3 presents this pattern as estimated from 1950 to 1995 and projected from 1995 to 2050 for the developing world. Early in the transition the ADR typically first rises slightly as more births survive infancy. Next, the ADR falls sharply as the decline in fertility reduces the proportion of the population under age 15. Finally, at the end of the transition the ADR increases again as the proportion of the

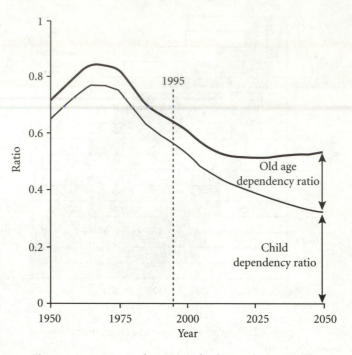

Figure 3.3. *Age Dependency Ratio for the Developing World*
Source: UN (1996).

Table 3.2. *Age Dependency Ratio for the Developing World in 2050 by Age at Onset of Old Age Dependence and Age at End of Child Dependence*

Age at end of child dependence	Age at onset of old-age dependence		
	65	60	55
15	0.53	0.72	0.96
20	0.67	0.90	1.19
25	0.85	1.13	1.50

population over age 65 rises. These changes are clearly reflected in the corresponding trends in the child dependency ratio (P_{15}/P_{15-65}) and the old-age dependency ratio (P_{65}/P_{15-65}) which are also plotted in Figure 3.3.

It should be noted that the age dependency ratio is highly sensitive to the ages that mark the end of dependency for the young and the return to dependency among the old. Table 3.2 presents estimates of the ADR for different assumptions about these ages. The conventional ADR is projected to reach 0.53 in 2050 in the developing world, but if the working age groups are assumed to be 20–60 then the ADR reaches 0.9 and if it is 25–55 then the ADR reaches 1.5. The latter estimate implies a dependency

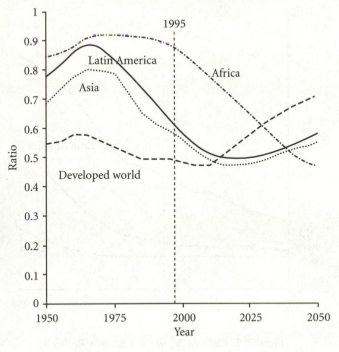

Figure 3.4. *Age Dependency Ratio by Region*
Source: UN (1996).

burden that is nearly three times as large as the conventional one. The reason for this high sensitivity of the ADR to variations in the ages at the beginning and end of the working ages is that any change in these ages affects both the numerator and the denominator of the ADR and these effects reinforce each other.

Figure 3.4 gives past and projected future trends in ADR by region. The broad patterns over time are similar to those for the developing world as a whole: an initial small increase, followed by a period of several decades during which the dependency burden declines substantially, and finally an upturn as the transition ends. However, the different regions are at very different stages of their transitions and these patterns are therefore not synchronous. Africa is still relatively early in its transition and its dependency burden remains high, although it is expected to decline steadily and substantially over the next several decades. Asia and Latin America entered their transitions earlier than Africa and these regions already have experienced about a quarter century of declines in their dependency burdens. This trend will continue into the early part of the next century before leveling off and eventually turning up again. There are important differences in these patterns among subregions and countries; for example, East Asia entered the fertility transition earlier than South Asia. The ADR for the developed world is included in Figure 3.4 for comparison. It has been lower than in any region of the developing world for the past several decades,

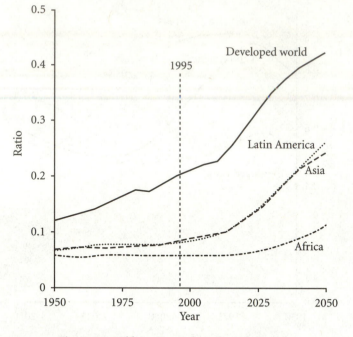

Figure 3.5. *Old-Age Dependency Ratio by Region*
Source: UN (1996).

but is expected to turn sharply upward early in the next century due to an increase in the proportion of the population over age 65.

The upturn in the dependency at the end of the transition is primarily the consequence of a rise in the old-age dependency ratio (OADR). As shown in Figure 3.3, the OADR of the developing world has been a small part of the overall dependency burden in the past and it has been relatively stable over time. Figure 3.5 plots the OADRs for regions and confirms this pattern at the regional level. It also demonstrates that the OADR of all LDC regions is small relative to that of the developed world. In Asia and Latin America old-age dependency is expected to turn upward after 2010, but even then it will remain well below the level in the developed world. The OADR of Africa is not projected to turn up until about 2030.

As already noted, the downturn in the dependency burden in the middle of the transition is related to the decline in the level of fertility. This is to be expected because the population under age 15 at a particular point in time consists of the survivors of births that have occurred over the preceding 15 years. The relationship between the ADR and the total fertility rate for the preceding 15 years in South Korea is plotted in Figure 3.6. As was the case for a number of other East-Asian countries South Korea experienced an extremely rapid fertility decline between 1965 and 1990 and the decline in the ADR has been equally rapid. The tight link between fertility and the

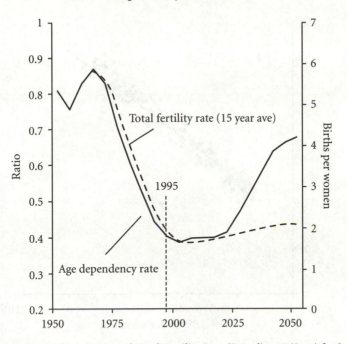

Figure 3.6. *Age Dependency Ratio and Total Fertility Rate (Preceding 15 Years) for South Korea*
Source: UN (1996).

ADR in this country is evident in Figure 3.6 and similar relationships exist in other countries. This conclusion is confirmed by the very high correlation (0.97) between the ADR of countries in 1995 and the average total fertility rate for the period 1980–95 (Fig. 3.7).

CONCLUSION

The demographic transition is accompanied by fairly predictable declines, first in mortality and, after a delay, also in fertility. These well-established trends have less well-known consequences for the distribution of the population by age and for the dependency burden. The age dependency ratio varies widely over the course of the transition but this pattern is quite predictable. Following a modest initial rise the dependency ratio typically experiences a prolonged period of decline during the central part of the transition. The preceding analysis has documented that this decline in dependency is very closely tied to the decline in fertility. Variations in the dependency burden among contemporary developing countries are almost entirely explained by variations in recent fertility. Similarly, the timing, duration, and magnitude of the decline in the dependency rate in mid-transitional societies are largely determined by the timing, duration, and magnitude of the fertility declines.

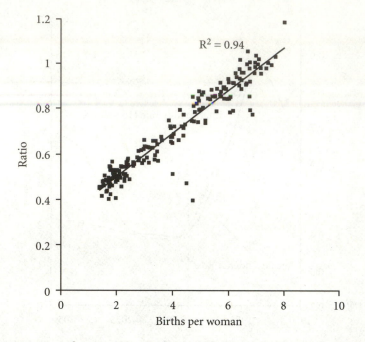

Figure 3.7. *Age Dependency Ratio in 1995 by Total Fertility Rate 1980–1995 for 184 Countries*
Source: UN (1996).

References

Bongaarts, John and Rodolfo Bulatao. 1999. 'Completing the Demographic Transition'. *Population and Development Review*. 25(3): 515–29.

Keyfitz, Nathan. 1971. 'On the Momentum of Population Growth', *Demography*. 8 (1), 71–80.

Shryock, Henry S., and Jacob S. Siegel. 1973. *The Methods and Materials of Demography*. Washington: US Dept. of Commerce, Bureau of the Census, 1973.

United Nations. 1996. *World Population Prospects: The 1996 Revision. Annex I: Demographic Indicators*. New York: United Nations Department for Economic and Social Information and Policy Analysis, Population Division.

—— 1998. *World Population Projections to 2150*. New York: United Nations Department for Economic and Social Information and Policy Analysis Population Division, United Nations.

World Bank. 1998. *World Development Indicators 1998*. Washington: World Bank.

PART II

POPULATION CHANGE AND
THE ECONOMY

This part reports on the results of four studies of the relationship between population change and macroeconomic performance. Together, they represent an important shift from the findings of earlier studies: demographic variables loom larger in explaining economic performance than they did in earlier research. This is true for at least three reasons. First, constant improvements in data make it easier to detect trends which may have been obscured by earlier data deficiencies. Secondly, significant differences among countries may have emerged in the 1980s that in fact were less pronounced earlier. And finally, new explanatory models have resulted in analytic approaches that may be revealing heretofore unseen relationships.

Kelley and Schmidt present further analysis of work they undertook in the early 1990s. Their findings are stated clearly, if highly conditionally: the effect of population growth, which showed little or no effect on economic growth in the 1960s and 1970s, is 'negative, statistically significant, and large in the 1980s'. The coefficient varies with level of economic development—negative in developing countries; positive for many developed countries. Kelley and Schmidt also found that population density is consistently positively associated with economic growth across time and across all countries; that population size is positively associated with economic growth during some time periods; and that the 'net' impact of demography over the 1980s was negative. The authors urge readers not to make too much of these results; they are based on data and models which are still far from perfect. None the less, they are consistent with other research findings that have emerged in recent years and they appear to show real change in the 1980s.

Possibly the most striking result from the Kelley–Schmidt chapter is the finding that the size of the impact of demographic change is not only fairly large, but that it does not vary between different demographic renderings—whether those of Barro (who focused on total fertility), earlier Kelley–Schmidt (who focused on crude birth and death rates), or Bloom and Williamson (who focused on the relative size of the population of working ages). The consistency of population impacts between these different perspectives is likely due to the fact that most measures of demography are highly correlated. Still, the bottom-line results of Kelley and Schmidt showing similar assessments across different models add additional confidence to findings that population matters.

Jeffrey Williamson looks at the impact of the demographic transition on economic growth, capital flows, and income distribution in some selected cases. His model depends heavily on the issue raised in Bongaarts's chapter: changes in the age distribution. Essentially, Williamson argues, as the size of the working-age population *relative to* the dependent population rises during the demographic transition, economic growth accelerates. Williamson calls this temporary bulge in the *relative* size of the workforce a 'demographic gift'—more workers supporting a relatively smaller young- and old-age dependent population, therefore higher savings rates, higher investment rates, and a spurt in economic growth. The performance of several East Asian countries from the 1970s to the 1990s generally conforms to this model. Williamson argues that the 'revisionists' failed to detect this relationship because they paid little if any attention to the *sources* of population growth and the *stage* of the demographic transition. Generally, he found in his East Asian analysis, economic growth is slower when the working-age population grows more slowly than the general population does and it is higher when the working-age population grows faster. Thus, both at the early stages of the transition, when the young-age groups are growing fastest, and at the end, when the older-age groups are growing rapidly, economic growth is inhibited. It is during the middle period—the period of the 'demographic gift'—that economic growth is most rapid. Moving on to capital accumulation and distribution, Williamson finds that demographically stimulated savings and investment account for an even larger share of East Asia's economic growth than labor force size and that 'evolution from foreign capital dependence to independence . . . can be explained by the evolution from high youth dependence to low'. Finally, on the issue of demography and income inequality, Williamson finds that income inequality tends to diminish as the relative size of what he calls the 'mature' (as opposed to the young and the old) working-age population increases. In other words, when young adults first enter the workforce, income inequality tends to rise. As this workforce matures, inequalities diminish, but they rise again as the large cohort of workers approaches old age.

David Bloom and David Canning take up where Williamson leaves off. In a speculative essay, they posit that the 'demographic gift' can become what they call a 'virtuous spiral' of falling dependency ratios, greater investment in education, further economic growth, and still lower fertility through *feedbacks*. The notion of feedbacks is important, introducing a more dynamic factor than previous demographic-economic models contained. What is 'cause' at one point in time (e.g. the effect of demographic change on labor supply and capital accumulation) becomes effect at another (the effect of high employment and productivity on fertility), and so on, recursively over time. Bloom and Canning argue that models that fail to take these feedbacks into account are likely to significantly underestimate the importance of demographic change.

Finally, Lee, Mason, and Miller, employing simulation techniques to model East Asian economic performance, show how life-cycle saving motives, interacting with the demographic transition, may account for a substantial portion of the rise in East Asian savings rates to unprecedented levels.

Taken together, the four chapters in this part all produced by scholars who have held the 'revisionist' view, suggest that the revisionist consensus in mainstream neoclassical economics deserves re-examination, on both empirical and theoretical grounds. The common theme is: '*population does matter*'.

4

Economic and Demographic Change: A Synthesis of Models, Findings, and Perspectives

ALLEN C. KELLEY AND ROBERT M. SCHMIDT

1. PUZZLES, CONTROVERSY, AND THE PROBLEM

1.1. *Puzzles and Controversy*[1]

No empirical finding has been more important to conditioning the 'population debate' than the widely obtained statistical result showing a general *lack* of correlation between the growth rates of population and per capita output. Documented in more than two dozen studies, such a (lack of) statistical regularity flies in the face of strongly held beliefs by those who expect rapid population growth to deter the pace of economic progress. The correlations have therefore become a point of contention. On the one hand, most analysts[2] agree that simple correlations between population and economic growth are difficult to interpret, plagued as they are by failure to adequately account for reverse causation between demographic and economic change, complicated timing relationships associated with the Demographic Transition, excessive reliance on cross-national data, sensitivity to the selection of countries, complexity of economic-demographic linkages that are poorly modeled, spurious correlation, econometric pitfalls, and data of dubious quality. On the other hand, the virtual absence of a systematic relationship in the face of such strongly held priors has quite literally kept the population debate alive. Ronald Lee's early summary evaluation of dozens of studies in this literature is instructive: 'these cross-national studies have not provided what we might hope for: a rough and stylized depiction of the consequences of rapid population growth: unless, indeed, the absence of significant results is itself the result' (1983: 54).

The importance of this finding is exemplified by the evolution of the two major United Nations reports (1953, 1973) on population. The first, in 1953, was eclectic in assessing the relative importance of the various positive and negative impacts

---

[1] This section draws upon Kelley and Schmidt (1994).

[2] E.g. 'these statistical correlations provide little *prima facie* information about the size or nature of the net impact of population growth on economic development' (Kelley 1988: 1701). In a similar vein, see National Research Council (1986: 7) and Blanchet (1991: 4).

of population growth. In contrast, the second, in 1973, came down (in the text) as somewhat anti-natalist; yet this tone was strongly qualified (in the executive summary) by a single study: Simon Kuznets's empirical results that failed to uncover a negative relationship between the pace of population growth and economic development. Kuznets's impeccable research could not be ignored; the UN report's major conclusions had to be qualified.

Confirmation of Kuznets's findings in many studies by numerous researchers of differing perspectives has provided force to the 'revisionist' position that emphasizes a methodology that provides for a balanced and relatively complete assessment of the economic impacts of demographic change—one that accounts for long- as well as short-run impacts of, as well as economic/social/political feedbacks in response to, demographic change. This perspective obtained analytical interpretation and empirical buttressing through an extensive review of the economic-demographic literature in the 1986 National Academy of Sciences report, *Population Growth and Economic Development: Policy Questions*. With this report, and several appearing around the same time, the population debate appeared to turn the corner.[3] The strong anti-natalist arguments of the 1970s were reassessed as alarmist overstatements of the negative consequences of rapid population growth. Depending on one's persuasion, the NAS report represented either a backlash or a balanced rendering that put the debate back on solid footing.[4]

Ironically, while on the one hand the simple empirical correlations between population growth and economic development constituted a major force in causing a reassessment of the impacts of population growth, on the other hand the appearance of 'new' correlations in several recent studies could well cause the pendulum to swing back toward a more cautious (alarmist?) interpretation.[5] These studies appear to reveal a negative association between population and economic growth based on international cross-country data for the early 1980s. Even though the authors of these studies are generally guarded with respect to the strength or importance of this finding, the intriguing question arises: has the impact of population growth changed?

1.2. *The Problem: A First Pass*

Could it be that the negative consequences of rapid population growth associated with diminishing returns to capital and the environment are emerging as relatively

---

[3] McNicoll (1984), Srinivasan (1988), World Bank (1984).

[4] An alternative interpretation is that the alarmist renderings in the 1970s were mainly by non-economists. This is supported, for example, by a careful reading of the 1971 National Academy of Sciences report, *Rapid Population Growth: Consequences and Policy Implications*, often cited as the major scholarly justification for the alarmist view. In fact, this impression results mainly from the short, crisply written executive summary, which is unfaithful to the evidence and argumentation of important scholarly contributions to the study, mainly, but not exclusively, written by the economists. Unfortunately, the executive summary is unauthored, and it was not vetted with most of the participants in the NAS study. An evolution of swings in thinking on population matters, as depicted in several major reports, is provided in Kelley (1991).

[5] These studies include Barlow (1992), Blanchet (1991), Bloom and Freeman (1988), Brander and Dowrick (1994), and United Nations (1988).

more important forces than, say, the positive impacts of scale, induced innova-
tion/technical change, and/or attenuating feedbacks? Or, is it possible that the 1980s—
a period encompassing significant structural adjustments, world recession, wars,
and droughts—constitute an 'exceptional' decade for untangling these economic-
demographic interactions? Are these recent statistical correlations robust, or are they
the result of necessarily arbitrary research decisions that are not yet fully assessed—
decisions relating to choice of statistical procedures, data sets, time periods, countries
included, modeling structures, functional forms, and the like? In short, is a negative
population- and economic-growth correlation emerging? If so, why; and so what?

The Argument A central message of the present study is that neither the results
of the recent studies pertaining to the experience of the 1980s, nor those similar to
them over the last two decades, should carry excessive weight in assessing the net
consequences of demographic change on economic growth. While we believe this
message is compelling, we predict it will be selectively heard, crowded out in the
minds of those who would like to accept or reject the recent (as well as the past)
empirical findings.

Accordingly, it is important that the recent studies be carefully evaluated—at a
minimum, in terms of their econometric and empirical muster; and, to the extent
that they appear to be yielding new findings, that the robustness and meaning of such
findings be uncovered. Timing is important. After all, it was Kuznets's single empirical
finding showing a lack of association of population and economic growth in the early
1970s that profoundly conditioned the population debate for more than a decade.

Veracity and Meaning of Recent Studies What can we make of the recent empirical studies of population- and economic-growth connections? We addressed this
question in considerable detail in a World Bank Study (Kelley and Schmidt 1994),
where the five key studies were replicated and assessed, and some new modeling variants were explored.[6] Generally, the recent evidence is consistent with an impact of
population growth on per capita output growth that:

1. is not statistically significant in the 1960s and 1970s (a finding consistent with a
   wide literature);
2. is negative, statistically significant, and large in the 1980s; and
3. varies with the level of economic development in the 1980s (it is negative in the
   LDCs and positive for many DCs).

In extending these studies, and considering some new variants, we also found that:

4. population density exerts a consistently significant (positive) impact across all
   decades;
5. population size exerts a positive impact in some periods; and
6. the 'net' impact of demography over the decade of the 1980s was negative.

---

[6] The assessments included three data sets (Summers and Heston 1988; United Nations; World Bank),
five country selections, five country groupings, eight periods, and five estimation procedures.

Whether this new finding represents an aberration or a confirmation of an emerging trend is a key question. Providing an explanation will require detailed econometric and demographic modeling. The present study will offer some clues relevant to such modeling.

1.3. *The Problem: A Second Pass*

A beginning is provided in two recent studies that highlight the *dynamics* of demographic change. In particular, since the economic-growth impacts of a new birth vary over a lifetime (the impact is initially negative during the child-rearing years, then positive during the labor force years, and finally (possibly) negative during retirement), modeling of demography must account for the *patterns* of birth and death rate changes over time. In one such study, Kelley and Schmidt (1995; hereafter KS) confirm that some of the early 'no-correlation' findings can plausibly be related to these offsetting effects. This interpretation gains additional support from Bloom and Williamson (1998; hereafter BW), and also from Radelet, Sachs, and Lee (1997; hereafter RSL), who emphasize the same timing issues and show that demographic change at a given point in time can have positive, negative, or neutral impacts on economic growth depending, in part, on the timing of the components of (positive) labor force versus (negative) dependent population growth.

All of these studies draw upon an analytic framework that is commonly denoted as 'convergence' or 'technology-gap' models. These are handy paradigms since they permit an examination of both long- and shorter-run (or transition) impacts of demography. Unfortunately, there is wide variance in the choice of variables (and estimation techniques) in the empirical implementation of these models; moreover, the incorporation of demography has been spotty, so that generalizations, at this point, must be cautious. While the KS and the BW studies have pointed the way in dynamic modeling, much work remains.

This justifies the primary objectives of the present paper, which takes stock of the various ways demography has been incorporated into convergence-type models, and which extends these analyses in several ways by: (1) incorporating and comparing alternative demographic specifications; (2) extending the time period of analysis to the mid-1990s; and (3) assessing the impacts of demography in early and later periods. This will permit us to assess, in a preliminary way, the role of demography on economic growth, at least in the popular convergence-type models.

1.4. *Modus Operandi*

Our methodology will be to append various demographic specifications to a 'core' convergence-type model (Barro 1997), using a common data set, data aggregation, statistical procedure, and country selection. Each of the results will then be subjected to robustness tests. The selection of the demographic specifications draws upon studies by Barro, KS, BW, and others. In addition, we extend two of the modeling formulations to expose economic-demographic linkages in more detail. We end up with eight models that command considerable support. To these we apply the historical experience of the period 1960–95 in order to assess the quantitative importance of the various components of demography, and the *net* impacts of demography in alternative modeling variants.

Since at this stage the present chapter represents an exploratory study, we can provide at most a *qualified* judgment that declines in both mortality and in fertility have notably increased the rate of economic growth. Declines in each component contributed around 0.32 points to changes in per capita output growth over the period 1960–95. This figure corresponds to 21 percent of 1.50 percent, the average annual growth of per capita output, or, alternatively, 22 percent of the combined impacts of changes in non-demographic influences on Y/Ngr. A combination of all components of demographic change roughly doubles this sizeable impact.[7] Apparently the positive impacts of population density, size, and labor force growth are more than offset by the costs of rearing children and maintaining an enlarged youth-dependency age structure. The emphasized 'qualified' caveat relates to robustness tests we have performed, the results of which are discussed below.

2. THEORY AND MODELING

Three approaches dominate the extensive literature on economic-demographic modeling: simple correlations, production functions, and convergence patterns.

2.1. *Simple Correlations*

Simple-correlations studies hypothesize that per capita output growth is influenced by various dimensions of demography:

$$Y/Ngr = f(D), \tag{1}$$

where D is usually taken to be contemporaneous population growth (Y/Ngr), sometimes age structure (youth and aged dependency, working ages), births and/or deaths (e.g. crude birth or death rates, life expectancy, and/or total fertility), migration, and occasionally size (N) and/or density (e.g. N/Land).

Several early studies focused on unconditioned correlations between per capita output and population growth for various country samples and periods of time. Most authors recognized the limitations of such simplistic modeling. Nevertheless, given the exceptional *strength* of the posited negative impacts of population growth on development voiced in many circles, the frequent failure to uncover any notable empirical relationship added a qualifying empirical dimension to the population debates. In the 1980s, however, the debates changed toward a more balanced and complete reckoning of population's many impacts; diminished alarmism

---

[7] For expositional simplicity, we use 'mortality' to refer to life expectancy or CDR and 'fertility' to refer to all other demographic variables in the models (TFR, CBR and its lags, population and working-age, growth rates, age structure, size, and density).

based on somewhat narrow and usually short-run renderings was attenuated, and with it the popularity of the simple correlations studies. Such models were, after all, of limited use since they failed to expose the many channels, as well as the dynamics, through which demography affects the economy. Specifically, the correlations that found little or no impact of population growth did *not* demonstrate the absence of a role for demography; indeed, demographic impacts may well have been important, but simply offsetting. Fortunately, about this time, data were increasingly available for broadening empirical inquiries to account for a wider array of linkages.

2.2. *Production Functions*

Production-function studies are based on estimating variants of a model:

$$Y = g(K, L, H, R, T), \tag{2}$$

where output (Y) is produced by the *stocks* of various factors: physical capital (K), labor (L), human capital (H: education and health), resources (R: land, minerals, and environment), and technology (T). Because data on these stocks are difficult to compile, and in an effort to attenuate possible problems of reverse causality, this equation is usually transformed into growth-rate terms in which attention is focused on more easily observable factor *flows* such as the growth of physical capital (e.g. net investment = gross investment less depreciation). Demographic processes are then linked to the growth of the factor inputs.

These models, however, face formidable difficulties in empirical implementation: estimates of capital depreciation, resource depletion, and human capital growth are difficult to compile; and technology and scale, considered central to economic growth, are exceptionally elusive to assess. It has therefore become necessary to impose constraining assumptions that result in simpler renderings than desired. For example, potentially important demographic linkages through scale, diminishing returns, and technical change are sometimes combined into a single 'residual' which obscures many of the most important linkages between demography and the economy.[8] Thus, although aggregate production functions represent promising analytical frameworks, their empirical renderings have been limited in scope.

2.3. *Convergence Patterns*

Convergence-patterns studies, rooted in neoclassical growth theory,[9] explore the relationships between economic growth and the *level* of economic development. They focus on the pace at which countries move from their current level of labor

---

[8] See Brander and Dowrick (1994) and others they cite in this tradition.
[9] Ramsey (1928), Solow (1956), Cass (1965), and Koopmans (1965). This section benefits from the presentation of RSL (1997: 4–6); see also Barro (1997), and Barro and Lee (1993).

productivity (Y/L) to their long-run, or steady-state equilibrium level of labor productivity ((Y/L)*).[10]

Formally, the usual variant of this model can be written:

$$Y/Lgr = c[\ln(Y/L)^* - \ln(Y/L)].^{[11]} \tag{3}$$

Here the rate of labor productivity growth (Y/Lgr) is proportional to the gap between the logs of the long-run, steady-state $(Y/L)^*$ and the current (Y/L) level of labor productivity. The greater this gap, the greater are the gaps of physical capital, human capital, and technical efficiency from their long-run levels. Large gaps allow for 'catching up' through (physical and human) capital accumulation, and technology creation and diffusion across, and within countries.

Under restrictive assumptions,[12] this model predicts 'unconditional convergence' by all countries to the same long-run level of labor productivity. Were $(Y/L)^*$ the same for all countries, low-income countries would have larger gaps and eqn (3) predicts them to grow faster as a result. In fact, however, *positive* rather than negative correlations are observed between the level and growth rate of labor productivity. The model has, as a result, been modified.

Specifically, models now hypothesize 'conditional convergence' where long-run labor productivity differs across countries depending on country-specific characteristics:

$$\ln(Y/L)^* = a + bZ \tag{4}$$

The actual specification of the determinants of long-run labor productivity (the Z's) varies notably, but the basic model, which combines equations (3) and (4), is the same across scores of empirical studies.

$$Y/Lgr = a' + b'Z - c \ln(Y/L);^{[13]} \tag{5}$$

where $a' = ac$ and $b' = bc$.

---

[10] Most empirical studies highlight per capita rather than per-laborer output. In neoclassical modeling this distinction is sidestepped by the assumption that $L = aN$, where a is usually unity. Theoretically, short of invoking this assumption, the labor-productivity formulation is preferred; and it can be easily transformed into per capita terms, as shown below.

[11] By way of comparison, consider the formulation for continuous growth of Y/L at a constant rate, r, between time periods 0 and T: $Y/L_T = Y/L_0 e^{rT}$. Taking logs, and solving for r, $r = [\ln(Y/L_T) - \ln(Y/L_0)]/T$. This formulation is analogous to that in the convergence model where r corresponds to Y/Lgr; Y/L to Y/L*; Y/L to Y/L; and (1/T) to c.

[12] These assumptions include, for example, perfect factor mobility; identical attitudes toward work, saving and property; identical resource endowments; and identical economic and governmental structures.

[13] Most empirical implementations differ from the theoretical formulation in two important ways. First, the theory models instantaneous growth rates while studies employ five-, ten-, 25-year, or even longer periods. In theory, all variables in eqn (5) are measured at exact instant t. In implementation, measurement of Y/Lgr is over the period while Y/L is at the beginning of the period. The theory dictates (1) that the estimated intercept and convergence parameters are functions of the true convergence parameter, c, and the length of the estimation period; and (2) that the Z vector be calculated as period averages (see RSL 1997: 4–6 for the mathematical details). In practice, studies use beginning-of-period values, lagged values,

What types of Z variables are, and should be, included as determinants of long-run labor productivities? Illustrative are two recent studies. The first, by Radelet *et al.* (1997, RSL), highlights two categories of determinants: economic structure variables (e.g. natural resource and human capital stocks, access to ports, location in tropics, whether landlocked, extent of coastline, etc.), and economic/political policies (e.g. openness to trade, quality of institutions, etc.). The second, by Barro (1997), highlights inflation, size of government, form of political system, terms of trade, human capital, and demography (fertility). (Papers by other authors would expand this list several fold.)[14]

A revealing feature of the convergence-patterns models can be gleaned by considering variables *omitted* by Barro and RSL. In both papers the authors emphasize variables that determine *long-run*, or 'potential' $(Y/L)^*$ labor productivity, and downplay variables that bring about the 'adjustment' or 'transition' to long-run equilibrium. An example of one such omitted variable is investment shares.[15] Putting aside the problem of endogeneity, investment can be viewed as an adjustment variable. The gap between current and long-run labor force productivity largely dictates the return to investment. Investment will flow to those countries with highest returns. Rather than investment accounting for growth *per se*, it can be argued that the 'structural' features of countries that impede or facilitate investment should be highlighted in the modeling of Z (e.g. measures of the risk of expropriation, restrictive licensing, political conditions, etc.). Such features modify long-run potential labor productivity because they impede or encourage investment.

We hasten to observe that there are many defendable perspectives on variable choice, and that much is yet to be learned about the appropriate configuration of 'core variables' to be included in such modeling.[16]

3. DEMOGRAPHY

Incorporating demography into convergence-patterns models has been spotty and ad hoc.[17] Demographic variables that qualify are those that affect $(Y/L)^*$, and those that condition the transition to $(Y/L)^*$. The nature of these two types of demographic variables can be illustrated by examining the studies of: (1) Barro (1997) and Kelley

period averages, and/or period changes for the Z variables, often without convincing rationale. We prefer to use period average or change. In an instance where endogeneity might be an issue, we employ the beginning-of-period value as an instrument.

Secondly, most studies couch eqn (5) in per capita (Y/N) rather than in per worker (Y/L) terms. The nature of the translation from labor productivity to per capita is examined below.

[14] For a survey, see Pritchett (1998), Easterly *et al.* (1998), and Fagerberg (1994).

[15] Barrow and Lee (1993) included investment shares in an earlier model.

[16] Levine and Renelt (1992) find that investment rates constitute the most robust variable in such studies. Pritchett (1998) leans toward production-function type variables, with an emphasis on econometric properties (e.g. their variation across time and space). Sala-i-Martin (1997) is somewhat eclectic, based on his research with around 2 million growth regressions.

[17] In a review of more than two dozen studies, Fagerberg (1994) finds that demography is omitted one-third of the time. Where Ngr is included, its estimated effect is equally split between being significantly negative, and insignificant. More detailed (and appropriate) specifications of demography are sparse.

and Schmidt (1994), which highlight long-run impacts of demography but include a role for transitions; (2) Kelley and Schmidt (1995) which examine both long-run and transition impacts; and (3) Bloom and Williamson (1998), which capture transition-impacts solely, or primarily.

3.1. *Barro's Demography*

Barro (1997) focuses on a single demographic variable, the total fertility rate (TFR).[18] This variable captures both the adverse capital-shallowing impact of more rapid population growth, and the resource costs of raising children versus producing other goods and services. By its very nature the TFR exerts its impacts mainly on long-run labor productivity $(Y/L)^*$ versus the short-run transitions en route to equilibrium. After all, the TFR is a hypothetical construct that represents what the fertility rate 'would be if' the current age-specific fertility rates were maintained over a long period of time.[19]

3.2. *Kelley–Schmidt's Early Demography*

In their early modeling, KS (1994) highlight three dimensions of demography: population growth, size, and density.

Population Growth   To conform with an extensive empirical literature, KS initially examine the impact of population growth, whose 'net' effects on per capita output growth are postulated to be ambiguous. Only in the simplest of growth-theoretic frameworks is there an unequivocal quantitative prediction: that is, population growth affects the level but not the growth of per capita output in the long run.[20] More complex variants that allow for embodied technical change, embellishments for human capital and factor augmentation, population-induced feedbacks, and scale always produce ambiguous assessments.[21]

To this simple demographic specification in Ngr, KS provide an 'augmented' model that includes size and density.

---

[18] He also includes life expectancy at birth (e_0), but mainly as a measure of health, although he recognizes that this variable has demographic interpretations as well.

[19] In some earlier renderings, Barro and Lee (1993) experiment with alternative demographic specifications, including total population growth and the youth-dependency ratio.

[20] Solow (1956), Phelps (1968). In these models technical change is exogenous, and savings rates are exogenous to population growth. The capital-shallowing effect of an increase in population growth eventually drives down the long-run level of capital per worker enough so that it can be sustained by the (fixed) ratio of savings to output.

[21] Formally, if the production function exhibits constant returns to scale, and if one assumes that labor is a constant proportion of population, then O/L depends on the availability of complementary factors and technology. An increase in population growth will reduce the growth of average productivity through diminishing returns—a 'resource-shallowing' effect—if such a population increase does not also affect the growth of complementary factors and/or technology. If population growth diminishes the growth of the other factors and/or technology, labor productivity growth is reduced by even more; if it stimulates the growth of other factors and/or technology (a 'resource-augmenting' effect), labor productivity growth is increased or decreased, depending on the relative importance of the negative resource-diluting versus the positive resource-augmenting effects.

Size and Density   Curiously, even though studies in the economic-demographic tradition have long stressed the importance of population size and density, these influences have been strikingly missing in empirical analyses of growth in recent decades. This is due in part to the finding that resource scarcity (land, natural resources) appears to have played a relatively small role in accounting for growth; to the popularity of neoclassical economics that focuses on physical and human capital; and to the discovery that technological change has largely dominated economic progress. In effect, technology has in many countries relaxed the constraints of fixed resources against which increasing population sizes press, thereby attenuating the adverse impacts of diminishing returns. Still, many studies in agricultural economics, as well as dozens in economic theory, have emphasized the advantages of size, scale, and density.

Building on KS (1994), the present chapter resurrects the size and density variables as a part of the empirical story accounting for economic progress. While our findings are exploratory, they serve to add breadth to the analysis. In the following subsections we therefore review some of the arguments and empirical studies that relate population size and density to output growth. We will conclude that both recent theory and empirical work justify the inclusion of scale and density in empirical studies of growth, but with specifications that are sufficiently flexible to allow for a variety of outcomes.

Economies of Scale[22]   Scale effects are exceptionally elusive to specify and evaluate. At the narrowest level, they refer to *within*-firm variations in productivity when all factors change proportionately. With few exceptions, such economies are usually exhausted by firms of moderate size. At a broader level, scale economies emanate from indivisibilities in lumpy investments, including roads, communications, research and development, and markets. These can be important, especially in agriculture (Boserup 1981). In a still broader framework, scale economies derive from increased specialization and diversification *between* firms (Stigler 1961). While some of these size benefits can be obtained in other ways (e.g. through international trade and/or the linking of regional centers with transport and communications), still, these investments are themselves likely to be more viable with larger populations (Glover and Simon 1975).

A review of the limited empirical literature relating to scale and density leaves one with the assessment that both factors are relevant to growth, but that the *magnitude* of the impacts varies notably from place to place, and over time. For some developed countries (e.g. the United States) where resources have been abundant, institutions strong, and densities relatively sparse, expanding population size has generally been viewed as a positive influence on long-run growth (Abramovitz 1956; Denison 1962).

However, these underlying conditions do not generally prevail in the Third World. First, population sizes are already sufficiently large in many areas to garner most scale economies in manufacturing. Indeed, the distribution and density of population may be relatively more important here (Henderson 1987; James 1987; National Research Council 1986). Secondly, scale effects are usually associated with high capital–labor

---

[22] This section draws upon Kelley (1988).

ratios, a production format at variance with prevailing factor proportions. Thirdly, city sizes are approaching (or in some cases, exceeding) those where additional scale efficiencies from size are available.

It is in agriculture where the positive benefits of population size are most discussed. Higher population densities can decrease per unit costs and increase the efficiency of transportation, irrigation, extension services, markets, and communications. These favorable impacts may be substantial, but they vary from place to place.[23] On the one hand, Asian land densities were likely sufficiently dense decades ago to garner most positive size effects. On the other hand, much of Africa is sparsely settled, and in places some infrastructure investments may not be economical for years to come. Additionally, even in areas where densities are not limiting, institutions often are. Constraining land ownership patterns, poorly developed markets, and imprudent government policies diminish the economic viability of investments and technology. It is not unlikely that differing institutional conditions most differentiate the putative favorable historical experience with scale effects in some developed countries from the apparently less favorable experiences in many Third World nations in the present.

Endogenous Growth   Most theoretical models of technological change in the endogenous-growth literature arrive at a striking conclusion: the pace of technological change is directly related to population size. This is because the fruits of R&D are assumed to be available to all without cost, and there are no constraints on adoption. In effect, there is an R&D industry producing a non-rival stock of knowledge. Holding constant the share of resources used for research, an increase in population size advances technological change without limit.[24] Partly in response to this prediction, a few analysts have recently been developing models that highlight firm-specific innovation and invention processes to include limitations and costs on even the use of non-rival technology. This can give rise to an outcome where population size has little or no impact on the pace of innovation in the long run, although it can have a favorable impact during the 'transition' to the long run.[25]

Evidence   Apart from the historical literature for developed countries, where scale is sometimes held to be positive and important, there are surprisingly few empirical studies that apply to the Third World. The pioneering work is by Chenery and Syrquin (1975). Based on the experience of 101 countries across the income spectrum and over

---

[23] Simon (1975), Glover and Simon (1975), Boserup (1981), Pingali and Binswanger (1987), Hayami and Ruttan (1987).

[24] There are numerous studies in this tradition, including those of Arrow (1962), Grossman and Helpman (1991), Lucas (1988), and Romer (1986, 1990). Citations are greatly expanded in Backus *et al.* (1992), and Dinopoulos and Thompson (1999). These arguments apply mainly to world and not to national populations, although if there are nation-specific impediments to diffusion, country-specific population sizes may matter as well.

[25] Peretto and Smulders (1998) review this emerging literature, and present a paradigm for the development and use of R&D that incorporates dilution effects, spillover networks, and technological distances relating to firm size and numbers. As populations expand, more firms enter the market and become increasingly specialized, using a decreasing portion of the non-rival technology stock.

the period 1950–70, they find that the structure of the development process reveals strong and pervasive scale effects (measured by population size), although these effects vary by stage of development. Basically, small countries develop a modern productive industrial structure more slowly, and later; and large countries have higher levels of accumulation and (presumably) higher rates of technical change.[26]

Taken together, several recent studies also support the relevance of positive scale effects, although the results are not uniform. Backus *et al.* (1992) show that the growth of manufacturing output per worker is strongly related to both scale and measures of intra-industry trade. They fail to unearth scale effects at the economy-wide level (measured by the growth of GDP per capita), a result confirmed by Dinopoulos and Thompson (1999). However, these latter results can be discounted since they represent simple, unconditioned correlations.[27] Also at the aggregate level, and based on a range of historical data and simulations, Kremer (1993) concludes that larger initial populations have tended to have faster technical change and population growth. Finally, at the firm level, it is clear that R&D is positively related to firm size (Cohen and Klepper 1996).

Specifications   Neither theory nor available evidence is sufficiently strong to support a tight empirical specification of the impacts of size and density. Thus, following Chenery and Syrquin (1975), below we evaluate both non-linearities in the variables and in functional forms to allow for diminishing (or even negative) marginal impacts.

3.3. *Kelley–Schmidt Dynamics: Components Demography*

The population growth variable masks important dynamics of demography associated with the *components* of demographic change.[28] While, in a country without international migration, population growth is by definition the difference between the crude birth and death rates (Ngr = CBR − CDR), in practice the impacts of demography can vary depending on: (1) the *levels* of these crude rates (levels imply different age distributions and/or age-specific rates); (2) the *sensitivity* of the economy to the separate

---

[26] Chenery and Syrquin (1975) allow substantial flexibility in isolating population impacts, as measured by two terms: $\ln N$ and $(\ln N)^2$. Scale effects (positive or negative) are posited to decline with size (the logs), although the pace and even the direction of this pattern can vary (the squared term). Thus, while scale effects (usually positive) are found to be pervasive, the quantitative size of the impacts varies widely. For example, positive scale effects in investment and saving rates rise up to populations of sizes of around 30 million (85% of the countries in their sample), but for influences like government expenditures and taxation rates, they rise only to populations of around 15 million. The inflow of foreign capital shows an inverse pattern, and school enrollments reveal no scale effects.

[27] Chenery and Syrquin (1975) demonstrated the importance of conditioning scale effects for relevant interactions.

[28] This section draws on Kelley and Schmidt (1995). These ideas have been explored by others: Simon and Gobin (1980), Coale (1986), Bloom and Freeman (1988), Blanchet (1991), Barlow (1994), and Brander and Dowrick (1994). This microeconomic framework underlies the recent BW models as well.

components (deaths and births can have different impacts); and, importantly, (3) the *timing* of these component changes.

With respect to levels and sensitivity, a similarly low Ngr is observed both before and after the demographic transition. Importantly, however, that low rate is attained in different ways with distinctly different demographic and economic implications. The high birth and death rates during pre-transition imply a younger population than do the low rates during the post-transition. To the extent that age distribution exerts impacts on economic growth, the similar Ngr's will mask the true role of demographic change.

With respect to timing, consider the impacts of *current* births (the CBR) over time. In the short run, the effect of a birth on economic growth is likely to be negative (i.e. children are net 'resource users'). At later stages of the life cycle, the effect of prior births is likely to be positive (working adults are net 'resource creators'). Even later, retired adults may again be net resource users. Moreover, within the 'youth-dependency' cohort (say ages 0–15), the economic impacts can vary notably since caring for babies is exceptionally time-intensive (a negative impact), and older children perform many useful economic functions (a positive impact). Specifying and measuring these various demographic impacts explicitly is potentially important since, given the strong correlation of births across time, exploring only the impacts of current births results in a difficult-to-interpret 'net' rendering across time. Put differently, countries with rapid *current* population growth rates are likely to be those with high *past* population growth rates. Cross-sectional evidence using contemporaneous data on births alone therefore measures *de facto* both the negative impacts of current births and the positive impacts of past births. As a result, the commonly found empirical result showing little or no measured impact of population growth (which is the contemporaneous CBR − CDR) does not necessarily mean that demographic processes are unimportant: it may simply imply that strong intertemporal demographic effects are offsetting.

There are various ways of capturing these dynamics. KS (1994, 1995) focus on the underlying demographic components of births and deaths since this rendering exposes potentially important effects within the youth-dependency cohort.[29] Moreover, from a policy perspective, analysts are typically interested in assessing the impacts of changes in births or deaths, as opposed, say, to policies that target an 'age distribution' *per se*.

Operationally, there are several ways of modeling these dynamics. In KS (1994, 1995), the empirical models measure the differential impacts of CBRs, contemporaneous and lagged 15 years (to capture labor force entry). While this approach was fairly successful, the estimates are plagued by multicollinearity and as a result are less precise

---

[29] An infant death occurring in the same year of birth shows up in both the CBR and CDR but is netted out of Ngr. Furthermore, a surviving birth has different resource implications. For both of these reasons, we believe the appropriate modeling is to net infant deaths out of both CBR and CDR and to include a crude infant death rate (CIDR) as a separate variable. We experimented with that formulation in KS (1995) but found the impact of the CIDR to be trivial and insignificant. The result implies that the pregnancy, delivery, and recovery for these infants has negligible macroeconomic growth effects.

than desired. In the present chapter we advance an alternative specification, posed by Barlow (1992), that postulates an explicit functional form of birth-rate impacts over time. This provides highly interesting estimates of the *differential* impacts of the components of the youth cohort.

3.4. *Bloom/Williamson Dynamics: Transitions Demography*

An alternative methodology for exposing these dynamic relationships has been advanced by Bloom and Williamson (1998; BW hereafter), a demographic framework which is taken up by Radelet, Sachs, and Lee (1997; RSL hereafter), and which builds upon RSL's empirical model of economic growth. Demography in these models follows neatly from a definition that translates the convergence model from one that explains productivity growth into one that explains per capita output growth, the focus of most convergence-patterns studies.

Starting with the definition of output per labor hour,

$$Y/L = (Y/N)(N/L) \tag{6}$$

it can be shown that the basic model of equation (5) can be transformed into per capita terms:

$$(Y/N)gr = a'' + bZ - c'' \ln(Y/N) + d\ln(L/N) + Lgr - Ngr.^{30} \tag{7}$$

The impacts of working-hour growth (Lgr) and population growth (Ngr) cancel each other out when they change at the same rate. This certainly occurs in steady-state growth and is imposed by assumption in most empirical studies. BW note that the 1960s, 1970s, and 1980s were periods of demographic transition for most developing countries. As a result, neither condition holds and differential growth rates will impact observed economic growth. (In an accounting sense, $d = c''$ in this formulation.) BW assume that $d = 0$, an apparent oversight in the translation of the $\ln(Y/L)$ term of eqn (5) into the $\ln(Y/N)$ and $\ln(L/N)$ terms of eqn (7). Thus, in the BW set-up, the workforce share has no impact on output growth.[31]

BW replace Lgr with a pure demographic proxy, the growth rate of the working-age population (WAgr).[32] That is, *if* the only determinant of hours worked were the age distribution of the population, then the relative growth of the working-age

---

[30] As noted in eqn (5) and its fn., the estimated coefficients from this eqn are not the same coefficients as in eqns (3) and (4). Each of these coefficients is a function of the corresponding parameter and the convergence parameter. Furthermore, the coefficients a and c estimated here will decline as the estimation period is extended. See RSL, p. 5, eqn (4).

[31] This was pointed out to us by David Canning; the derivation is based on Bloom *et al.* (BCM), (1998: 8). Interestingly, RSL employ the original $\ln(Y/L)$ term; BW employ the $\ln(Y/N)$ term but not the $\ln(L/N)$ term; while BCM employ both the $\ln(Y/N)$ and $\ln(L/N)$ terms.

[32] Alternatively, one might argue that Lgr is endogenous within this equation. Contemporaneous WAgr could then be viewed as an exogenous instrument for Lgr.

versus full population constitutes the sole impact of demography in their model.[33] Sometimes the impact of demography will be positive, sometimes negative, and sometimes zero. This model highlights the reality that demographic impacts vary during the *transition* to a steady state. The BW theoretical model is silent about any possible impacts of demography on long-run labor productivity; that is, demography does not affect the Z's in eqn (5), and, as noted above, their model omits $\ln(L/N)$.[34] As a result, the BW model has a narrower interpretation than most renderings in the literature, which admit both short- and long-run impacts of demographic change as a part of the theoretical structure. On the other hand, it has the desirable attribute of clarity in interpretation. It stands, moreover, in the post-1985 'revisionist tradition', described above, which highlights the possibility of both positive and negative impacts of demographic change.

To understand the model's implications, it is useful to elaborate on the impacts of demography, and to assess, in particular, the model's predictions of $(1, -1)$ on Lgr and Ngr, respectively. Note first that the model's theoretical predictions are not in terms of the growth of the working-age population (WA), but rather in terms of the growth of total hours worked (L). This measure is affected by age-specific labor force participation rates (LFPR), the working-age population (WA), and employment rates (ER, hours worked per labor force participant). Thus, by definition,

$$L = (WA)(LF/WA)(L/LF) = (WA)(LFPR)(ER). \tag{8}$$

With manipulation it can be shown that the revised model is

$$Y/Ngr = a'' + b'Z - c'' \ln(Y/N) + d \ln(L/N) + ERgr + LFPRgr$$
$$+ WAgr - Ngr. \tag{9}$$

This formulation reveals that the direct impact of demography is $\ln(L/N)$ plus the last two terms, and that two additional variables, the growth in employment (hours worked per laborer per period) and the growth of labor force participation rates, influence per capita output growth as well. Note finally that the predicted parameters on *each* of these last two terms is unity, and that $c'' = d$. (This follows from the definitional feature of the modeling.) Indeed, if the basic 'core model' (i.e. the convergence-pattern framework and the choice of Z's) is correct, it is not even necessary to estimate the sensitivity of output growth to the components of demography: the 'parameters' are predetermined by definition. In practice, however, these parameters in estimation can differ from unity and d can differ from c'' if (1) the variables are mismeasured; (2) omitted terms, say ERgr and/or LFPRgr, are correlated (causally or

---

[33] This implies that two countries with quite different constant age-specific fertility and mortality rates—say one country with a rapid Ngr of 3%, and another with a slow Ngr of 0.5%—will arrive at the *same* level of $(Y/L)^*$ in the long run.

[34] The omission of long-run impacts is recognized by BW (1998) and is taken as a possible explanation of empirical estimates on Ngr and WAgr that may deviate from theoretical expectations. Moreover, while not a formal part of their growth-theoretic modeling structure, their empirical explorations do attempt to isolate demography (age-distributional changes) from other sources of labor force growth.

not) with WAgr and/or Ngr; (3) the Core model and framework is incorrect; and/or (4) the demographic variables affect $(Y/L)^*$ directly (as distinct from their posited sole role in the transition).[35]

These qualifications identify several directions in which the model might be refined to reveal demography's role more fully. Consider two. First, consider interrelationships among the growth of the working-age population, the labor force participation rates, and employment rates. In the short to intermediate run, an increase in the growth of the working-aged population will exert downward pressures on wages and employment rates, other things equal.[36] These negative impacts will be attenuated in the longer run by demand-side feedbacks, but will not likely be overturned. Moreover, fertility may be influenced by labor market conditions (e.g. employment rates), causing a change in the age structure (WAgr).

Secondly, consider the focus of the BW model on the transitional impacts of demographic change. The postulated coefficients of 1 and -1 for WAgr and Ngr, respectively, provide a clear interpretation of the role of demography: relatively rapid growth of the working-age population will speed the transition to long-run economic prosperity, $(Y/L)^*$. However, two countries with the same Z's will ultimately arrive at the same $(Y/L)^*$, irrespective of their demography.[37] BW (1998) acknowledge the possibility that WAgr and/or Ngr might impact $(Y/L)^*$, but they do not model this explicitly. Nor do they include other demographic variables among the Z's.[38] Rather, they note that long-run influences could result in coefficient estimates which deviate from unity.

Such an inquiry into the BW model is instructive. It reveals that both theoretically (e.g. Ngr and LAgr should be included in the Z vector, and $\ln(L/N)$ should be included as a separate variable), and empirically (the determinants of Lgr are correlated with WAgr and Ngr), the resulting estimates of the impacts of demography are hard to interpret. However, highlighting the difference between transition and possible long-run impacts of demographic change is useful.

3.5. *Bloom–Canning–Malaney Dynamics*

David Bloom, David Canning, and Pia Malaney (1998; hereafter BCM) have recently augmented the BW model to include additional demographic impacts ($\ln(L/N)$ and

[35] Bloom *et al.* (1998) have modified the RSL and BW models to include $\ln(WA/N)$, a variable that may represent both transition and longer-run impacts on output growth.

[36] The opposite appears to be occurring in countries like the United States where the relative size of 'traditional' labor force participants (working-age males) is projected to decline. Businesses are preparing for much more diversity in the workplace through, among other things, training programs for females and minorities. Female labor force participation rates and minority employment rates have risen as a consequence.

[37] This implies, for example, that two countries with similar Z's, but each with stable but quite different long-run rates of population growth (e.g. 1% vs. 3%), will arrive at the *same* level of economic prosperity (Y/L) in the long run.

[38] E.g. we have discussed at length the possible impact of population size and density on $(Y/L)^*$. Additionally, dependency rates (D1, D2), determined by earlier WAgr's vs. Ngr's, have been widely studied for their impacts on saving and investment GDP shares. Saving and investment shares, in turn, impact $(Y/L)^*$.

density). The ln(L/N) term is included because of eqn (7)'s specification in per capita rather than per worker terms. The effects of density on output growth are divided between coastal and inland densities as proxies of transportation costs. The impacts of inland (coastal) transport costs on growth are found to be negative (positive). Overall, the BCM model augments the demography of the BW framework. Given our goal of focusing on demographics, the BCM framework will be included below in our empirical assessments.

4. EMPIRICAL SPECIFICATIONS

Our empirical formulations below utilize either of two convergence renderings, ten-year growth periods, and a single set of 'core variables' (the Barro model) to which eight demographic variants have been appended. The first six represent an evolution of the recent literature; the last two are denoted as 'Expanded Dynamics' Models.

4.1. *Convergence Renderings*

Two quite different empirical renderings of the convergence model coexist in the literature. The first, following Barro and Sala-i-Martin (1995), phrases the basic convergence assumption (eqn (3) above) in per capita terms. The second, which we have highlighted in this chapter, follows Radelet, Sachs, and Lee (RSL 1997) and phrases that growth equation in per worker terms. In a mechanical translation into per capita terms, the RSL framework appends three additional terms (ln(L/N), Ngr, and Lgr per BW and BCM) to the single convergence term (ln(Y/N)) of the Barro framework.

Which convergence rendering is appropriate for our estimation? On the one hand, the Barro rendering might be criticized for its implicit assumption of a constant labor force share in the population. On the other hand, the RSL rendering implies very specific, tautological predictions for the additional terms. As noted previously, the predictions of 1 and -1 for Lgr and Ngr suggest that the impact of the demographic transition on economic growth could be calculated without estimating the model.[39] Acknowledging this, the theoretically interesting question of how demography impacts long-run, steady-state levels of per capita income can be addressed in either paradigm.

We remain agnostic in choosing the 'appropriate' convergence rendering. Our first six demographic variants are based on published studies. The last variants extend the two most promising and representative of the dynamic demographic renderings. In each of these, we employ the convergence rendering of the original study.

---

[39] This is an oversimplification. For example, working-age population is used in place of the actual labor force. BW (1998: 22) illustrate an approach for translating working-age growth into labor growth and, with its unitary coefficient, economic growth.

4.2. *Growth-Period Length*

RSL cast their theoretical model at a point in time. Consequently, growth rates are instantaneous and depend upon the values of Y/L and the Z variables at that instant. Correspondingly, the long-run, steady-state productivity level changes as the Z vector values change. This has two important implications for empirical renderings of the model.

First, what is the appropriate length for empirical growth periods? Some studies employ a single cross-section covering the entire period under study (commonly, 1965–90) while others utilize five- or ten-year panels. We have chosen to use ten-year growth periods in a panel setting. Although most of the information is in the cross-sectional dimension, there is information within the time-series dimension as well. While there is a great deal of persistence in many of the variables, some, including several of the demographic variables, do change notably over time. Additionally, several of our demographic renderings focus on transitional impacts which we believe to be modeled better in a panel setting. We have chosen ten-year periods (1960–70, 1970–80, 1980–90), and one five-year period (1990–95) to mute complications of business cycles and other short-run phenomena as well as to maximize the use of 'real' demographic information. (Many annual and five-year values are interpolations, albeit sophisticated ones, of information collected once a decade.) We include period binaries in the model to capture the global economic environment and/or shocks specific to the decade.[40]

Secondly, what changes are wrought when moving from a theoretical model of instantaneous growth to one with growth over ten or 25 years? RSL (1997: 4–5) integrate the model over years 0 through T and note the following.

1. The estimated convergence coefficient, c'', is a function of T and the instantaneous convergence coefficient, c. Specifically, $c'' = (1 - e^{-cT})/T$.
2. Z-vector variables should be calculated as period averages.
3. The estimated intercept, a'', is a function of a, c, and T. Specifically, $a'' = ac''$.

One can retrieve c from c'' and must do so before determining the estimated coefficients for the Z vector. Recall from eqn (6) that the estimated Z-vector coefficient is $b' = bc$. Strangely, these calculations are seldom undertaken in the literature. As a result, and given our interest in providing findings that are comparable with that literature, we will not evaluate the recovered coefficients at this stage. However, we will explore these issues in our ongoing analysis that assesses the robustness of our results.

[40] For additional discussion of the choice of period length, see Barro (1997: 12–13) and Pritchett (1998). Canning (1999) delves into this issue theoretically and empirically. Although his particular emphasis is on human and physical capital, his conclusions are general to any endogenous variable. He concludes that estimated coefficients in cross-country growth regressions are hybrids of parameters from the reduced-form and structural models. Estimates from annual observations will approximate the structural coefficients while those from, say 25- or 35-year periods, replicate the reduced form. Coefficients from our ten-year periods must consequently be interpreted with some care.

4.3. *The Core*

Variables in the Barro (1997) Core model have been defended in several publications (Barro 1991, 1997). While one can easily imagine additional variables for inclusion, suffice it to say that Barro's empirical inquiries have been lengthy and expansive. His latest model represents a reasonable framework on which to graft demographic augmentations.[41] Moreover, from our perspective, it is methodologically appropriate to use Barro's model without modification since our goal is to assess the impacts and merits of alternative demographic specifications. These are plausibly influenced by the Core. As a first pass, we therefore maintain an arm's length in specifying that Core so as not to inadvertently bias our demographic assessments. We will then evaluate the sensitivity of our conclusions to reasonable embellishments of the Barro framework.

In Barro's model the growth rate of output per capita is positively related to:

1. a lower level of per capita income, that is, the convergence hypothesis (with more rapid convergence in countries with higher schooling levels as measured by an interaction term between Y/N and schooling attainment);
2. more schooling (as measured by male secondary attainment), especially at higher secondary levels which facilitate the absorption of new technologies;
3. higher life expectancy, a proxy for better health and human capital in general;
4. terms of trade improvement, posited to generate added employment and income;
5. a lower rate of inflation, leading to better decisions with predictable price expectations;
6. a lower government consumption share, which is posited to release resources for more productive private investment;
7. stronger democratic institutions which promote public, and especially private investments, although at high levels of democracy, growth can be dampened by governments exerting an increasingly active role in redistributing income;
8. a stronger rule of law, which stimulates investment by promoting sanctity of contracts, security of property rights, etc.; and
9. a lower total fertility rate, which attenuates capital-shallowing and adverse saving-rate impacts of high youth dependency (Barro's demography measure).

Variable definitions and sources are compiled in Table A.4.1 (see Appendix).

4.4. *The Demography*

Table 4.1 presents eight demographic specifications which we append to the Core. The models are grouped by increasing detail and complexity. Models 1 and 2 are

---

[41] Most of the Barro variables are continuous. By contrast, many of RSL's Z variables are binaries. These binaries have two disadvantages. They do not capture the full range of experience across countries. More importantly, many of the binaries are time-invariant (e.g. location in the tropics, access to the sea) which substantially weakens inferences from the time-series dimension of the panel; time-varying aspects of the Core are not being held constant.

Table 4.1. *Demographic Specifications*

Model	Variables
1 Barro	ln(TFR)
2 Early KS	Ngr
3 Augmented KS	Ngr, Dns, ln(N)
4 KS Components	CBR, CBR_{-15}, CDR, Dns, ln(N)
5 BW Trns	Ngr, WAgr
6 BCM Trns	Ngr, WAgr, ln(WA/N), Dns
Expanded Dynamics	
7 BCM TrnsExp	Ngr, WAgr, ln(WA/N), Dns, ln N
8 KS CompExp	CBR, CBR_{-5}, CBR_{-10}, CBR_{-15}, CDR, Dns, ln N

Notes: Definitions and expected signs: TFR^- = total fertility rate; $Ngr^{-?}$ = population growth; $Dns^?$ = density; N^+ = population size; CBR^- = crude birth rate less CIDR; CBR^-_{-5}, (lagged 5 years), $CBR^?_{-10}$, CBR^+_{-15}; WA/N^+ = working age/population; CDR^- = crude death rate less CIDR; $WAgr^+$ = working-age growth.

base-line renderings that incorporate the two most popular summary measures of demography: fertility (ln(TFR)), and the population growth rate (Ngr). Model 3 adds density (Dns) and population size (ln(N)).

Models 4 to 6 present three dynamic formulations that highlight the *timing* of demographic impacts. In Model 4, KS isolate the separate impacts of contemporaneous and lagged crude birth rates. This permits separating the negative dependency impacts of births (CBR_t) from the positive impacts on labor force entry of those births that occurred fifteen years earlier (CBR_{t-15}). In Model 5 BW explore a variant of this framework which isolates (or 'factors out') the positive impacts of working-age growth (WAgr) from the (mainly negative) impacts of population growth, leaving Ngr to measure primarily the negative costs of dependency. In Model 6 BCM append the working-age share ln(WA/N) and density to the basic BW framework.[42]

The remaining two models, denoted Expanded Dynamics, extend the dynamic specifications. Model 7 reformulates the BCM formulation to include population size (ln(N)). Model 8 allows for greater flexibility in exposing birth-rate impacts over time. It is hypothesized that children exert differential impacts by age (CBR_t, CBR_{t-5}, CBR_{t-10}, and CBR_{t-15}) with relatively high negative impacts at early ages, and smaller negative or even positive impacts at later ages as they increasingly contribute to productive household and labor force activities.

---

[42] In their 25-year period cross-section estimation, BCM account separately for the impacts of inland and coastal density; in their five-year panel estimation, BCM use total land area. In both measures density is expressed in terms of working-aged population. Separate calculations using the Barro Core indicate that the impacts of density are largely invariant to using WA vs. N.

To accommodate problems due to temporally correlated CBRs, the estimated parameters on each CBR term are constrained by a logarithmic functional form, found to have the best statistical fit compared to linear or quadratic. Operationally, the coefficient for the ith lag is defined as: $\beta_i = \alpha_0 + \alpha_1 \ln(i)$ where $i > 0$. α_0 and α_1 can be estimated directly from variables created as transformations on the CBRs:

Alpha $0 = CBR_t + CBR_{t-5} + CBR_{t-10} + CBR_{t-15};$ and

Alpha $1 = \ln(5)CBR_{t-5} + \ln(10)CBR_{t-10} + \ln(15)CBR_{t-15}.$

4.5. *Endogeneity*

An issue arises with respect to possible reverse causation both in terms of several of the variables in the Barro Core (e.g. inflation, Gcons/Y, democracy) and the demographic variables appended to this framework. Barro elects to attenuate possible endogeneity through instrumentation. While the resulting parameter estimates may be sensitive to his choice of instruments and procedures, we have chosen to adopt his methodology without modification[43] given our strategy of maintaining an arm's length in specifying the Core. Our goal is to minimize possible unintended biases in our demographic assessments.

Problems of reverse causation may plague demographic variables as well, although here the case is less clear. On the one hand, fertility rates are likely to be more sensitive to the *level* than to the *growth* of income. On the other hand, the length of the observations used in the analysis ranges from five to 25 years, resulting in periods sufficiently long that the levels can change notably through growth. Interestingly, both BW and BCM fail to uncover any problems of endogeneity in their long, 25-year periods, yet BCM do encounter reverse causation with their five-year panels. Our analysis below uses an intermediate period (ten years). Consequently, we assessed the need to instrument the demographic change variables through the Wu–Hausman test. In no demographic variant was that test significant at the 5 percent level.[44] As a

---

[43] Barro employs three-stage least-squares estimation, with the third-stage correcting for possible serial correlation. Since he found little evidence of serial correlation, we opted for two-stage estimation instead. Within the Core, we followed Barro in treating the following variables as endogenous: government consumption's share in GDP, democracy and its squared term, and inflation. Because of perceived measurement error, Barro also instruments ln (Y/N) and its interaction with education. The first-stage equations use the following five-year lags as instruments; ln(Y/N), ln(Y/N)'s interaction with contemporaneous education, government consumption's GDP share, and democracy and its squared term. The following exogenous variables from the Core are also used as instruments: education, ln(e$_0$), rule of law, and terms-of-trade change. Finally, binaries for former colonies of Spain and Portugal and former colonies of Great Britain and France are included as instruments for inflation. The first-stage equations are run separately for each period. The second-stage equation is pooled but includes period-specific binaries. The Wu–Hausman test was significant at the 0.1 percent level in all eight demographic variants, indicating that ordinary least-squares will not provide consistent estimates for the indicated Core variables.

[44] Again, to maintain an arm's length from the modeling specification, we assessed reverse causation in the demographic variables by utilizing the instruments proposed by BCM. BCM treat both Ngr and WAgr as endogenous, using as instruments five-year lags for Ngr and Wgr as well as beginning-of-period

result, we do not instrument any of the demographic variables in the results presented below.

5. RESULTS

Appendix Table A.4.2(*a*) presents the two-stage least-squares results for the eight models.

5.1. *The Core*

The Core performs well: all of the estimated parameters are of the expected sign; almost all (71 of 80) are significant at the 5 percent level, and most at the 1 percent level. The parameter estimates are reasonably robust with respect to alternative demographic specifications. The coefficient that changes the most is $\ln(e_0)$, not surprising given its linkages to the demographic variables. Finally, the period effects are plausible and significant: events like OPEC shocks, financial crises, and debt overhang have adversely affected economic growth *vis-à-vis* the 1960s.

5.2. *Demography: A First-Pass Assessment*

The demographic augmentations yield strong and consistent results. All 24 parameter estimates have the anticipated sign, and most are statistically significant at the 5 percent level or better. Overall, demography contributes notably to accounting for economic growth: R^2 increases from 48 percent in the Core model without the TFR and e_0 (not shown in the table) to 54–60 percent in the various models where demography is included.

Population density and size typically reveal significant positive impacts on economic growth. Apparently the stimulus of density on technical change and on reducing the costs of transport/communications, as well as the various positive effects of scale, offset the negative forces of diminishing returns and crowding.[45]

TFR (total fertility rate) and IMR (infant mortality rate). Within that spirit, we included as instruments a lag for the demographic change variable(s) specific to the model as well as TFR and IMR. For the eight demographic variants, the Wu–Hausman test was performed on the following: (1) $\ln$(TFR), (2 and 3) Ngr, (4 and 8) CBR_t, and (5–7) Ngr and WAgr. p-values from these tests are provided in the last line to Table A.4.2(*a*).

[45] These conclusions are invariant to the removal of observations that are statistically identified as strongly 'influential' on these two coefficient estimates. SAS's DFBETAS (scaled measures of changes in each parameter estimate from deleting an observation) were used for making assessments of influential observations within the KS Components Extended model. DFBETAS identified 5 of 344 observations as being influential in estimating the Dns coefficient (one observation each for Chile, Hong Kong, India, Malaysia, and Singapore). By comparison, 24 observations were influential in determining the coefficient on $\ln$(N). India is represented in each of the four decades with the effect of lowering the parameter estimate in three decades but raising it in the 1980s. Paraguay (one negative, two positive) is noted three times; Nicaragua (both positive), Panama and Togo (one positive, one negative) are identified twice; and the remaining are scattered across mainly developing countries.

Several of the remaining measures of population change exert negative impacts on economic growth. This is true, for example, of the TFR and Ngr alone. Of course, the combined effects of Ngr, WAgr, and ln(WA/N) in the Transition Models, and the combined effects of the CBR and CDR in the Components Models, can only be assessed by taking into account realistic changes in the demographic variables, a calculation that is undertaken below.

Transition Dynamics: Models 5 to 7   The estimates give mixed support to the interpretation that the impacts of demography are solely transitional. Recall the predictions of 1 and -1 for WAgr and Ngr, respectively, indicate that the effects of demographic change are offset in long-run steady state. There will be transitional effects on the path to steady state, however. Indeed, BW found substantial transitional effects in East Asia since the mid-1960s. Deviations from 1 and -1 could indicate impacts beyond transitional, and our own estimates are as high as 1.41 and as low as -1.47. However, these coefficients are not statistically different from unity. Statistically, the effects of Ngr and WAgr cannot be said to extend beyond the demographic transition.

On the other hand, additional demographic variables do appear to have long-run impacts. Population size has a significant positive impact in Model 7; density has a positive, but insignificant, impact in Models 6 and 7. More substantively, ln(WA/N) appears to have a strong, positive impact on growth in both Models 6 and 7. Recall that BCM include this variable as part of an algebraic translation from per worker to per capita terms. As such, its coefficient should be the same as that on ln(Y/N). It is not. In fact at 9.52, it is 7.5 times that of ln(Y/N), a difference significant at the 0.1 percent level. This disparity indicates that ln(WA/N) may have a long-run impact on steady-state productivity as well as the immediate impact on growth modeled by BCM. As the complement of dependency, the working-age share in the population can play a quite different role from Ngr and WAgr in the convergence model. The empirical savings literature reveals that dependency can influence both saving and investment. WA/N might be argued to affect labor force quality as well. Both, in turn, plausibly influence Y/N^*.

KS Components Dynamics: Model 8   The complexity of reckoning dependency impacts in a dynamic setting is further illustrated by the Expanded KS Components framework (KS CompEx, Model 8). Here the estimated birth-rate impacts differ notably depending upon the lag. Computing these impacts from the estimated alphas, the parameters on CBR_t, CBR_{t-5}, CBR_{t-10}, CBR_{t-15} turn out to be -1.26, -0.35, 0.04, and 0.27, respectively. The overall impact of reducing the birth rate over the youth-dependency period is therefore positive, and most of this benefit to growth occurs right away. (Very young children are relatively costly, presumably on the mother's time.) After around 10 years, the net impact of a child is estimated to be positive, although up to age 15 (and even abstracting from discounting), this positive impact is not enough to offset the earlier negative costs of dependency. A bottom-line assessment would be that youth dependents have notable costs only for the first few years; thereafter, their net impacts, positive or negative, are substantially offsetting.[46]

It is interesting that the benefits to economic growth of death-rate reductions are substantial, indeed considerably larger than those of birth-rate reductions in the early years. Clearly the *source* of population change matters, as well as its *timing*, and accounting for these dynamics is critical to understanding the impacts of Ngr on Y/Ngr.

5.3. *Demography: A Second-Pass; A Fuller Reckoning*

What are the overall *quantitative* impacts of the various components of demographic change on the pace of economic growth? To answer this question one must account both for the coefficient *size* and the *magnitude* of 'relevant' *changes* in the demographic variables. For the latter, and as one experiment, we examine the impacts of *actual average* changes in demography in our country sample over the 1960s, 1970s, and 1980s. Appendix Table A.4.2(*b*) provides these calculations, obtained by multiplying each estimated parameter by the corresponding average change in the demographic variable over each decade.[47] Since most of the parameters carry signs identical to the trends in the variables, the impacts on per capita output growth are positive (the product of these two factors). Thus, for example, both the decline in the TFR, and an increase in density and size, contribute positively to economic growth.

A question arises on whether or not to include mortality changes (ln (e_0) or CDR) in these calculations. On the one hand, Barro primarily treats life expectancy as a proxy for health, although he recognizes its demographic component. This argues for excluding mortality from our list of 'demographic' variables. On the other hand, ignoring mortality downplays an element of demographic change that merits consideration and reckoning. As a compromise, Table A.4.2(*b*) presents renderings with, and without, mortality change. Our analysis focuses on the total column (Demog w/Mort) that includes the impacts of mortality declines.

Several interesting results emerge.

1. Demographic trends (declining population growth, fertility, mortality; changing age distributions; and rising density and population sizes) have had a sizeable impact on economic growth. Across all eight models the average combined impact (*including* mortality changes) over 30 years on Y/Ngr is 0.64. Declines in fertility and mortality have each contributed around half of this combined impact. Such a figure for each component corresponds to 21 percent of 1.50 percent, the average

---

[46] This assessment, which finds a rather modest resource cost of children during the educational years (ages 5–15), is also consistent with several recent empirical studies (Schultz 1987, 1996; Tan and Mingat 1992; Kelley 1996; and Ahlburg and Jensen 1997) that downplay the quantitative importance of demography on education costs.

[47] For variables measured as period averages, decade changes are calculated as differences between averages of the first five years' experience. Thus, for example, the 1960s are calculated from 1960–64 to 1970–74.

annual Y/Ngr—or, alternatively, 22 percent of combined impacts of changes in non-demographic influences on Y/Ngr.[48]

The consistency of the results across models provides some confidence in this overall assessment.

2. While the overall impact of population growth (Ngr) is negative (per Models 2 and 3), this derives from the *offsetting* forces of fertility and mortality change. The observed declines in fertility/mortality reinforce each other in encouraging economic growth, but offset each other in their impact on decreasing/increasing Ngr. These results underscore the reality that changes in Ngr, *per se*, conceal the size and even the direction of the impacts of Ngr. Increases in Ngr based on mortality declines can stimulate growth while increases in Ngr based on fertility change can attenuate growth. Exposing these differences is important to assessing the impacts of demographic trends.

3. Increasing densities and population sizes contribute a positive but relatively small boost to economic growth, with scale effects dominating density. The lack of importance of density merits qualification given our inability at this stage to compile more appropriate measures of arable land.[49]

4. In most of the models the impact of demography has declined over time. The exceptions are the KS Early and Augmented Models where the average impact in the 1960s, 1970s, and 1980s was 0.60, 0.64, and 0.66, respectively. By contrast, the respective averages for the other six models were 0.77, 0.63, and 0.52. (The contrast is even more stark for the column which excludes mortality.) These disparities highlight the importance of more sophisticated demographic modeling. (For example, many empirical studies have found negligible and insignificant demographic impacts for the 1960s and 1970s, and several have found significant impacts for the 1980s.)

5. Demographic impacts are virtually identical in the 'KS Comp' and 'KS CompEx' models. The extended variant is useful in that it details the lag structure for fertility's impact on economic growth. Nevertheless, the impact for the contemporaneous birth rate in KS Comp turns out to be the sum of the impacts from the contemporaneous, and the specified lags. This is consistent with our earlier argument that the current birth rate, entered alone in a model, will capture the net effects of past fertility because of high levels of persistence in the crude birth rate.

6. Perhaps the most striking aspect of our results is how similar are the combined demographic impacts across the eight models. The simpler Barro and early KS models reveal a combined demographic impact comparable in magnitude to the more sophisticated later models. Of course, the Transition and Components models

[48] Y/Ngr declined at an average rate of -0.80 per decade. Without the positive influence of demographic change, this decline would have been faster ($-1.44 = -0.80 - 0.64$). Demography's impact on economic growth is, then, 44 percent ($0.64/1.44$) of the impact of changes in non-demographic influences. Note also that for expositional simplicity, we use 'mortality' to refer to life expectancy or CDR and 'fertility' to refer to all other demographic variables in the models (TFR, CBR and its lags, population and working-age growth rates, age structure, size, and density).

[49] The FAO estimates of 'potential arable land' are unfortunately available for only a subset of our sample. BCM (1998) find a substantive impact of density when they separate inland from coastal density. Unfortunately, such regional measures are not available in time series.

provide a richer understanding of the underlying processes, even if the bottom-line assessment is little changed.

5.4. *Demography: Bottom-Line Assessments*

Empirical assessments using cross-country data of the impacts of demographic change on the pace of economic growth are presently in a state of flux. This represents a notable change in the literature on this topic which, until the last few years, found only weak or inconclusive empirical relationships. Several factors have changed this situation. (1) Five studies using data for the 1980s appear to reveal reasonably strong negative impacts of rapid population growth and related demographic components on per capita economic growth. (2) Convergence-type frameworks are enlarging the analytical perspectives beyond the simple-correlations and production-functions frameworks. (3) Data have continued to improve and expand in scope. (4) Dynamic specifications that probe the patterns of demographic change are emerging. (5) Applications of appropriate econometric techniques standard in other literatures are increasingly being transferred to demographic studies. (6) Population debates, in the past heated and contentious, are giving way to 'revisionist'[50] renderings that assess these dimensions in a more even-handed and balanced manner. These renderings recognize both positive and negative, and short- and long-run, impacts of demography.

The present chapter is an installment in this research program. Building upon a state-of-the-art Core economic and political model of economic growth, we evaluate the merits of alternative specifications to expose the impacts of demographic change. We arrive at the *qualified* judgment that, given the demographic trends (mainly declining mortality and fertility) over the period 1960–95, economic growth has been favorably impacted by demography. For example, fertility and mortality changes have each contributed around 22 percent to changes in output growth, a figure that corresponds to around 21 percent of 1.50 percent, the average growth of per capita output over the period. More broadly, declining population growth, fertility, and mortality as well as larger populations and higher densities have all spurred growth. The sole growth-inhibiting trend is a decline in the growth of the working-age population. However this trend is not universal. The many emerging economies that are now passing through the beginning stages of the demographic transition can look forward to increases in working-age growth for some time to come. Whether they possess the political and economic conditions to effectively capture the benefits of these favorable demographic trends remains an open issue.

We consider these results to be 'qualified' at this stage since our robustness tests reveal that the *Core Model* findings are sensitive to the periods of aggregation (five versus ten versus 25 or 35 years), although demography is much less sensitive to aggregation, for reasons not fully understood. On the other hand, our conclusions *are* robust with respect to many modeling variants including alternative instrumenting procedures, estimating by OLS, compiling White-corrected standard errors, utilizing

---

[50] For an elaboration of the revisionist methodology and results, see above, Ch. 2.

an LDC sample alone, and assessing results absent observations with exceptional statistical impact. (See Appendix Section B for details.)

In addition to the above assessments of the aggregate macroeconomic paradigms, there is also a significant need to draw upon results of (largely absent) microeconomic analyses. Do poor (mainly rural) households in fact behave according to the life-cycle hypothesis embedded in many of the macro paradigms? Do governments and economies in fact significantly divert resources from productive investments toward relatively unproductive 'demographic spending' in response to population pressures? What are the impacts of demographic changes at the firm and farm levels on the form and pace of technical change? And, what is the quantitative importance of the various determinants of fertility and mortality, and are these determinants exogenous or endogenous with respect to the main arguments in the economic-growth Core?

Happily, the macroeconometrics literature is making steady progress in exposing relationships of long-standing interest. Complementary to maintaining this progress will be an increasing availability of relevant microeconometric studies. The healthy symbiotic relationship between these research programs will predictably bear significant dividends.

Appendix

A. Data and Procedures

Data Sample
The data set consists of 86 countries with populations exceeding 1 million in 1960, which Summers and Heston (1994) classify as market-oriented and for which they provide data on gross domestic product in constant purchasing power. We exclude countries with missing data, extensive resource dependency, and problems with data definitions. For details and a country listing, see Kelley and Schmidt (1994). From that list we exclude Chad, Mauritania, and Somalia due to missing data on educational attainment; and add Taiwan due to its importance in recent studies attempting to explain the 'Asian Tigers'.

Regressions use three decadal (1960–70, 1970–80, 1980–90) and one quinquennial (1990–95) growth period for each country. A panel of 344 observations result.

Variable Definitions and Sources
Table A.4.1 describes the variables used in this study. Within that table, the 'Source' column uses the following key:

BL93   Barro and Lee's data set used in Barro and Lee (1993).
BL96   Barro and Lee (1996) update of their education attainment series.
G   Gastil (1991).
ICRG   International Country Risk Guide.
SH   Summers and Heston Penn World Tables, version 5.6.
Trans   Transformation of Variable described elsewhere in table.
UN   United Nations (1996).
WB   World Bank's 1997 *World Development Indicators* CD-ROM in conjunction with earlier versions for backfilling.

Table A.4.1. *Variables used in the Study*

Variable	Source*	When?	Description
Y/N	SH	BOP	Per capita GDP: purchase-power parity, 1985 international currency units (approximately scaled to US$), chained index.
Y/N_{gr}	Trans	Chg	Per capita GDP percentage growth rate.
TT %chg	WB	Chg	Percentage change in the terms of trade (P_X/P_M).
Gcons/Y	WB, BL93	Avg	Government consumption's (defined as G−education−defense) percentage share in GDP.
Inflatn	WB	Chg	Inflation rate based on the CPI if available, otherwise on the GDP deflator.
e_0	WB	BOP	Life expectancy at birth.
MaleEduc	BL96	Avg	Number of years of secondary plus higher education per adult male, aged 25 and above.
Rule Law	ICRG	Avg	Index of overall maintenance of the rule of law; seven possible rankings rescaled from 0 (low) to 1 (high).
Democrcy	G	Avg	Index of level of democratization; seven possible rankings rescaled from 0 (low) to 1 (high).
TFR	WB	Avg	Total fertility rate.
Ngr	Trans	Chg	Percentage change in population size.
WAgr	UN	Chg	Percentage change in population ages 15–64.
CBR (net)	WB	Avg	Crude birth rate (per 100 population) netted of infant deaths.
Alpha 0	Trans	Avg	See pages 86–7.
Alpha 1	Trans	Avg	See pages 86–7.
CDR (net)	WB	Avg	Crude death rate (per 100 population) netted of infant deaths.
D1	UN	Avg	Youth dependency ratio: ratio of population ages 0–14 to population ages 15–64.
D2	UN	Avg	Elderly dependency ratio: ratio of population ages 65+ to population ages 15–64.
Dns	WB	BOP	Thousands of population per square kilometer.
N	WB	BOP	Thousands of population.

Notes: *Data fills and extrapolations were made by imposing rates of changes from an alternative data set with more complete series. For SH, WB was the primary filling source with UN and IMF as alternatives. WB was generally filled from earlier versions, UN sources, or SH. Fills for ICRG and G are too complicated to describe here; a description is available upon request.

The column headed 'When?' uses the following codes:

Avg	Period average of the annual observations.
BOP	Beginning-of-period value calculated as three-year average centered on the first year of the period.
Chg	Rate of change expressed as a percentage and calculated using the continuous growth formula.

Table A.4.2. *Tables of results*

Table A.4.2(*a*). *Impacts of Demography in Core Convergence Model: Full Sample, 1960–1995*

	Early Models			Exploratory Dynamics			Expanded Dynamics		Mean & StdDev
	Barro (1997) (1)	KS Early (1994) (2)	Augmntd (1994) (3)	KS Comp (1995) (4)	BW Trns (1997) (5)	BCM Trns (1998) (6)	BCM TrnsEx (1999) (7)	KS CompEx (1999) (8)	
The Model Core									
ln(Y/N)	−1.50**	−1.27**	−1.35**	−1.20**	−1.06**	−1.27**	−1.28**	−1.21**	0.85
	(6.01)	(5.00)	(5.50)	(5.02)	(4.13)	(5.08)	(5.18)	(5.07)	(1.03)
TT %chg	0.16**	0.16**	0.16**	0.15**	0.15**	0.15**	0.15**	0.15**	−0.45
	(5.34)	(5.21)	(5.55)	(5.31)	(4.95)	(5.35)	(5.45)	(5.33)	(3.35)
Gcons/Y	−0.10*	−0.12**	−0.05	−0.04	−0.12**	−0.08*	−0.05	−0.04	7.26
	(2.19)	(2.64)	(1.01)	(0.86)	(2.64)	(1.77)	(0.98)	(0.82)	(3.61)
Inflatn	−0.03**	−0.04**	−0.03**	−0.03**	−0.04**	−0.03**	−0.03**	−0.03**	14.95
	(4.12)	(4.43)	(4.09)	(4.18)	(4.58)	(4.05)	(3.94)	(4.13)	(27.82)
ln(e_0)	4.61**	6.44**	6.39**		5.52**	5.01**	5.17**		4.07
	(4.04)	(5.63)	(5.81)		(4.79)	(4.58)	(4.77)		(0.21)
MaleEduc	0.59**	0.65**	0.64**	0.46*	0.52**	0.34	0.36*	0.47*	1.29
	(2.82)	(2.96)	(3.06)	(2.19)	(2.37)	(1.60)	(1.76)	(2.23)	(1.19)
ln(y)*Ed	−0.28*	−0.22*	−0.27*	−0.20	−0.13	−0.11	−0.14	−0.21*	0.95
	(2.30)	(1.71)	(2.14)	(1.62)	(1.01)	(0.88)	(1.16)	(1.69)	(1.48)
Rule Law	1.92*	2.58**	2.42**	1.92*	2.42**	1.80*	2.04**	1.94*	0.56
	(2.27)	(2.96)	(2.83)	(2.31)	(2.86)	(2.16)	(2.49)	(2.33)	(0.24)
Democry	6.82**	7.88**	6.64**	4.95**	6.60**	5.79**	5.51**	4.91**	0.58
	(3.30)	(3.58)	(3.08)	(2.34)	(3.04)	(2.75)	(2.68)	(2.35)	(0.33)
Democ^2	−7.57**	−8.46**	−7.00**	−5.48**	−7.39**	−6.35**	−6.19**	−5.43**	0.44
	(4.04)	(4.21)	(3.41)	(2.75)	(3.73)	(3.19)	(3.16)	(2.75)	(0.38)
The Demography									
ln(TFR)	−2.52**								1.39
	(6.02)								(0.52)

Table A.4.2 (Continued.)

	Early Models			Exploratory Dynamics			Expanded Dynamics		Mean & StdDev
	Barro (1997) (1)	KS Early (1994) (2)	Augmntd (1994) (3)	KS Comp (1995) (4)	BW Trns (1997) (5)	BCM Trns (1998) (6)	BCM TrnsEx (1999) (7)	KS CompEx (1999) (8)	
Ngr		−0.53**	−0.41**		−1.47**	−1.37**	−1.27**		1.92
		(3.64)	(2.85)		(4.61)	(4.49)	(4.14)		(0.99)
WAgr					0.95**	1.41**	1.31**		2.10
					(3.31)	(4.79)	(4.46)		(1.02)
ln(WA/N)						9.52**	8.54**		−0.57
						(4.42)	(3.94)		(0.10)
BR (net)				−1.54**					2.97
				(4.53)					(1.09)
BR lag15				0.23					3.26
				(0.69)					(1.03)
Alpha 0								−1.26**	12.51
								(3.54)	(4.21)
Alpha 1								0.57**	21.14
								(2.68)	(6.92)
Implied BR coefficients									
Current								−1.26	
Lag 5								−0.35	
Lag 10								0.04	
Lag 15								0.27	
DR (net)				−1.71**				−1.75**	0.93
				(3.62)				(3.70)	(0.33)
Dns			0.57**	0.36		0.21	0.31	0.37*	0.17
			(3.04)	(1.93)		(1.15)	(1.70)	(1.97)	(0.61)
ln(N)			0.27**	0.18*			0.18*	0.18*	9.37
			(3.20)	(2.13)			(2.22)	(2.19)	(1.26)

Pd:70–80	−0.83**	−0.60	−0.70*	−0.87**	−1.02**	−0.96**	−1.03**	−0.87**	0.25
	(2.67)	(1.87)	(2.28)	(2.79)	(3.02)	(3.01)	(3.28)	(2.81)	(0.43)
Pd:80–90	−2.46**	−2.07**	−2.26**	−2.40**	−2.47**	−2.54**	−2.64**	−2.41**	0.25
	(7.27)	(5.92)	(6.79)	(7.17)	(6.85)	(7.50)	(7.91)	(7.24)	(0.43)
Pd:90–95	−3.28**	−3.10**	−3.24**	−3.10**	−3.36**	−3.24**	−3.35**	−3.11**	0.25
	(9.55)	(8.65)	(9.46)	(9.34)	(9.40)	(9.56)	(9.99)	(9.37)	(0.43)
Constant	−11.65*	−22.47**	−25.29**	6.76**	−18.42**	−11.72*	−14.89**	6.73**	
	(2.38)	(4.85)	(5.50)	(4.45)	(3.92)	(2.53)	(3.09)	(4.45)	
R Squared	0.57	0.54	0.57	0.60	0.56	0.60	0.61	0.60	
Adj R-Sq.	0.55	0.52	0.55	0.58	0.54	0.58	0.59	0.58	
Std Error	1.67	1.74	1.67	1.63	1.71	1.61	1.60	1.63	
No. of Obs	344	344	344	344	344	344	344	344	
t-values	OLS	OLS	OLS	OLS	OLS	OLS	OLS	OLS	
p-values from tests of joint significance									
DEMOG_GR				0.000**	0.000**	0.000**	0.000**	0.000**	
DNS_LNN			0.001**	0.042*			0.052	0.036*	
EDUC	0.021*	0.008**	0.010*	0.095	0.024*	0.248	0.220	0.088	
DEMOCRCY	0.000**	0.000**	0.003**	0.016*	0.000**	0.005**	0.005**	0.016*	
PERIOD	0.000**	0.000**	0.000**	0.000**	0.000**	0.000**	0.000**	0.000**	
p-values from tests that Ngr = −1 and WAgr = 1: Significance indicates different from −1 or 1.									
NGR_NEG1					0.137	0.232	0.388		
WAGR_ONE					0.850	0.172	0.302		
p-values from tests that ln(Y/N) = − ln(WA/N): Significance indicates they differ in absolute value.									
YCAP_WAN						0.000**	0.001**		
p-values from Durbin–Wu–Hausman Test on Demographic Variables: ln(TFR), Ngr, WAgr, and/or BR. Significance indicates OLS estimates are inconsistent & variable(s) should be instrumented.									
DWT Test	0.091	0.081	0.122	0.891	0.087	0.981	0.967	0.356	

Notes: The dependent variable is Y/Ngr. The full sample includes 86 countries and three decennial periods (1960–70, 1970–80, 1980–90) and one quinquennial period (1990–95). Pooled regressions have been estimated using two-stage least-squares. Variable definitions are presented in Table A.4.1. Pd:70–80, Pd:80–90, and Pd:90–95 are binaries; their coefficients are relative to the 1960s.

Table A.4.2(b). *Demographic Impacts on Changes in Y/Ngr from Decadal Changes*

Model	Year	Demog w/Mort	Demog w/o Mrt	ln(TFR)	ln(e_0)	Ngr	WAgr	ln(WA/N)	CBR	CBR05	CBR10	CBR15	CDR	Dns	ln(N)
Part 1: Period Means															
	1960s			1.65	3.97	2.28	2.04	−0.59	3.39	3.42	3.41	3.41	1.12	0.13	9.06
	1970s			1.52	4.04	2.13	2.37	−0.60	3.14	3.27	3.39	3.42	0.99	0.16	9.27
	1980s			1.34	4.10	2.00	2.34	−0.57	2.92	3.02	3.14	3.27	0.88	0.19	9.48
	1990s			1.18	4.16	1.40	1.64	−0.54	2.62	2.77	2.92	3.02	0.81	0.22	9.68
Part 2: Inter-Period Changes in Means															
	1960s			−0.13	0.07	−0.14	0.33	−0.01	−0.25	−0.15	−0.02	0.02	−0.13	0.03	0.21
	1970s			−0.18	0.07	−0.13	−0.03	0.03	−0.22	−0.25	−0.25	−0.15	−0.11	0.04	0.21
	1980s			−0.16	0.05	−0.60	−0.70	0.03	−0.30	−0.25	−0.22	−0.25	−0.07	0.03	0.20
Part 3: Impact of Inter-Period Changes in Demography															
Barro	1960s	0.66	0.33	0.33	0.32	—	—	—	—	—	—	—	—	—	—
	1970s	0.76	0.45	0.45	0.31	—	—	—	—	—	—	—	—	—	—
	1980s	0.64	0.40	0.40	0.25	—	—	—	—	—	—	—	—	—	—
	Average	0.68	0.39												
KS Early	1960s	0.53	0.08		0.45	0.08	—	—	—	—	—	—	—	—	—
	1970s	0.51	0.07		0.44	0.07	—	—	—	—	—	—	—	—	—
	1980s	0.67	0.32		0.34	0.32	—	—	—	—	—	—	—	—	—
	Average	0.57	0.16												
Augmentd	1960s	0.58	0.13		0.44	0.06	—	—	—	—	—	—	—	0.02	0.06
	1970s	0.56	0.13		0.43	0.05	—	—	—	—	—	—	—	0.02	0.06
	1980s	0.66	0.32		0.34	0.25	—	—	—	—	—	—	—	0.02	0.05
	Average	0.60	0.19												
KS Comp	1960s	0.66	0.43			—	—	—	0.38	—	—	0.00	0.23	0.01	0.04
	1970s	0.55	0.36			—	—	—	0.34	—	—	−0.03	0.19	0.01	0.04
	1980s	0.57	0.45			—	—	—	0.46	—	—	−0.06	0.12	0.01	0.04
	Average	0.59	0.41												

Model	Period														
BW Trns	1960s	0.91	0.52	—	0.38	0.21	0.31	—	—	—	—	—	—	—	—
	1970s	0.54	0.17	—	0.37	0.19	-0.02	—	—	—	—	—	—	—	—
	1980s	0.52	0.22	—	0.30	0.88	-0.66	—	—	—	—	—	—	—	—
	Average	0.66	0.31												
BCM Trns	1960s	0.91	0.56	—	0.35	0.20	0.46	-0.11	—	—	—	—	—	0.01	—
	1970s	0.76	0.42	—	0.34	0.18	-0.04	0.27	—	—	—	—	—	0.01	—
	1980s	0.40	0.13	—	0.27	0.82	-0.98	0.29	—	—	—	—	—	0.01	—
	Average	0.69	0.37												
BCM TrnsEx	1960s	0.92	0.56	—	0.36	0.18	0.43	-0.10	—	—	—	—	—	0.01	0.04
	1970s	0.77	0.42	—	0.35	0.17	-0.03	0.24	—	—	—	—	—	0.01	0.04
	1980s	0.43	0.15	—	0.28	0.76	-0.92	0.26	—	—	—	—	—	0.01	0.04
	Average	0.71	0.38												
KS CompEx	1960s	0.65	0.42	—	—	—	—	—	0.31	0.05	-0.00	0.00	0.23	0.01	0.04
	1970s	0.57	0.37	—	—	—	—	—	0.28	0.09	-0.01	-0.04	0.20	0.01	0.04
	1980s	0.56	0.44	—	—	—	—	—	0.38	0.09	-0.01	-0.07	0.12	0.01	0.04
	Average	0.59	0.41												
AVG EIGHT MODELS		0.64	0.33												

Notes: Demog w/Mort: Total of the line's demographic impacts, including $\ln(e_0)$ and CDR.
Demog w/o Mrt: Total, excluding $\ln(e_0)$ and CDR.
Coefficient estimates used to calculate these impacts are shown in Table A.4.2(a).
Period means in part 1 represent the average value over the indicated decade: e.g. 1960s represents the average over the ten years 1960–69. In part 2 1960s refers to changes between the 1960s and 1970s; 1970s between the 1970s and 1980s; and 1980s between the 1980s and 1990–95. Average is the unweighted average of the indicated column.
(1) $\ln$(TFR), CBR (net of infant deaths), CBR15 (net of infant deaths), CDR (net of infant deaths), Alpha 0, Alpha 1 represent the impact of changes in decadal averages.
(2) Ngr and WAgr represent the impacts of changes in annual growth rates for the decade.
(3) Dns and $\ln$(N) represent the impacts of changes in beginning of decade levels.
(4) Average annual Y/Ngr for the 1960–65, 1970–75, 1980–85 & 1900–95 are 2.96, 2.51, −0.04, and 0.55, respectively. Consequently, the inter-decade changes in Y/Ngr are −0.45, −2.55, and 0.59, respectively; or an average of −0.80.

B. Robustness of the Results

To assess the robustness of our results, Tables A.4.2(*a*) and A.4.2(*b*) have been re-estimated with alternative data sets, time periods, aggregation periods, and statistical procedures. Our goal is not to ascertain whether a few parameters (or their precision) change, but rather to determine whether any changes observed are sufficiently large to modify our conclusions. Such an assessment represents a judgment call that can be evaluated by consulting the 21 re-estimated tables available at our web site URL www.econ.duke.edu/~kelley/Research/Synthesis/synthesis.html.

Our primary conclusions, to be evaluated with respect to alternative specifications, are:

1. The Core economic/social/political model reveals conditional convergence and performs well, with most explanatory variables statistically significant at usual standards.
2. The Core model results are broadly insensitive to the demographic specifications.
3. Declines in fertility and mortality each have a positive impact on Y/Ngr.
4. This total demographic impact is about equally divided between separate impacts deriving from changes in fertility (including associated age, size, and density changes) and changes in mortality.
5. Each separate demographic impact is approximately 22 percent of the combined impacts on Y/Ngr of changes in Core model influences over the period 1960–95, or, alternatively, around 21 percent of the average decadal Y/Ngr.
6. Population size and density commonly exert a positive but small impact on Y/Ngr.

Five sets of tables are initially generated to examine the impacts of:

1. including instrumented demographic variables,
2. estimating by ordinary least squares,
3. compiling White-correlated standard errors,
4. utilizing the LDC sample alone, and
5. assessing the impacts of observations having exceptional statistical impact.

Examining the results reveals that the six conclusions above are generally invariant to these modeling alternatives. Three qualifications merit noting. First, the rate of adjustment in the model Core is somewhat slower in the LDCs. Secondly, while the absolute size of the assessed impacts of demography in the LDCs are similar to those in the full sample, the relative importance of demography is greater in the LDCs given the slower overall growth rate there.[51] Thirdly, among the Core model variables, government consumption appears to be least stable across the tables.

We next re-estimated the basic model to assess the impacts of:

1. three data aggregations (5, 10, and 25/35 years), and
2. two periods (1960–95, 1965–90).

Examining these tables reveals some results that are sensitive to modeling variations.

---

[51] This result merits exploration, including an assessment of the LDC model with respect to the several variants examined in this section. This project is outside our present objectives which focus on comparisons with comparable empirical models in the literature. These focus almost exclusively on a wider country coverage.

Specifically,

1. the impact of demography, as measured by the size of the estimated parameter, increases with the length of data aggregations. However, calculations that show the quantitative size of the impacts, accounting for changes in the variables over time, is not much affected on a *per-year* basis (i.e. when one controls for the difference in period length);
2. the Core model deteriorates substantially with data aggregations of 25 and 35 years.

The latter result is in contrast to findings in the literature that use the Radelet–Sachs–Lee Core, which is fairly insensitive to data aggregation. This is plausibly explained by the limited temporal variation of many of the RSL variables. Still, even with the weak Core performance of the Barro framework for the 25- and 35-year aggregations, the main conclusions with respect to demography (when transformed to account for period-length scaling) are broadly preserved.

Table A.4.3 illustrates the above conclusions. The first two columns present results comparable to those in Table A.4.2(*b*) for two of the eight models, while column three presents a simple average of all eight models (see Table 4.1). The last three columns present the percentage of the total demographic impacts accounted for by 'fertility' which, technically, represents non-mortality impacts. These include, for example, age-structure impacts and the small impacts of population size and density.

Table A.4.3. *Summary of Demographic Impacts*

Model	Dynamic Models		8-Model Average	% Due to 'Fertility'		
	BCMTex	KSCex		BCMTex	KSCex	Avg
1960–1995						
Basic	71/38	59/41	64/33	54	69	52
InstDem	71/39	42/23	62/32	55	55	52
OLS	66/38	55/40	59/32	58	73	54
LDC	79/45	66/44	70/37	57	67	53
DfFits	66/33	55/36	61/28	50	65	46
Basic 5yr	68/32	59/43	64/32	47	73	50
Basic 10yr	71/38	59/41	64/33	54	69	52
Basic 35yr	89/65	62/50	69/43	73	81	62
1965–1990						
Basic 5yr	77/35	64/46	72/35	45	72	49
Basic 10yr	72/39	57/45	66/38	54	79	58
Basic 25yr	80/49	58/45	66/35	61	78	53

Notes: (1) Columns present demographic impacts for the two most detailed demographic models (BCM TransEx and KS CompEx) as well as for the average of the eight demographic variants. (2) Entries in the first three columns represent impacts on Ngr change of demographic change: Total/'Fertility' (i.e. without e_0 and/or CDR). For example, the first entry, 71/38, is listed in Table A.4.2(*b*) under BCM TrnsEx as 0.71 and 0.38. The last three columns present 'Fertility' as a percentage of Total. (3) The 'Basic' model is estimated by two-stage least squares; uses 10-year data aggregations; and instruments selected core, but not demographic, variables (see pp. 85–6 above). 'InstDem' instruments demography as well (see pp. 87–8 above); 'OLS' has been estimated by ordinary least squares using standard as well as White-corrected t-values; 'LDC' uses the LDC sample; 'DfFits' eliminates observations of unusual influence; and the 'Basic' model has been estimated over 5-year, 10-year, and full-period growth periods for the 1960–95 as well as 1965–90 time frames. (4) Full tabular outputs are posted on the World-Wide Web as referenced in the text.

References

Abramovitz, Moses. 1956. 'Resource and Output Trends in the United States Since 1870'. *American Economic Review.* 46 (2): 5–23.

Ahlburg, Dennis A., and Eric R. Jensen. 1997. 'Education and the East Asian Miracle'. Population Series, No. 88-3. East-West Center Working Papers, Aug.

Arrow, Kenneth J. 1962. 'Economic Welfare and the Allocation of Resources for Inventions'. In R. R. Nelson, ed., *The Rate and Direction of Inventive Activity.* Princeton: Princeton University Press for the NBER, 609–25.

Backus D., P. Kehoe, and T. Kehoe. 1992. 'In Search of Scale Effects in Trade and Growth'. *Journal of Economic Theory.* 57: 377–409.

Barlow, Robin. 1992. 'Demographic Influences on Economic Growth'. Ann Arbor: University of Michigan, mimeo.

—— 1994. 'Population Growth and Economic Growth: Some More Correlations'. *Population and Development Review.* 20 (1): 153–65.

Barro, Robert J. 1991. 'Economic Growth in a Cross Section of Countries'. *Quarterly Journal of Economics.* 106 (2), 407–44.

—— 1997. 'Determinants of Economic Growth: A Cross-Country Empirical Study'. Development Discussion Paper No. 579. Harvard Institute for International Development, Apr.

—— and Jong-Wha Lee. 1993. 'Losers and Winners in Economic Growth'. NBER Working Paper No. 4341. Cambridge, Mass.

—— —— 1996. 'International Measures of Schooling Years and Schooling Quality'. *American Economic Review.* 86 (2): 218–23.

—— and Xavier Sala-i-Martin. 1995. *Economic Growth.* New York: McGraw-Hill.

Blanchet, Didier. 1991. 'Estimating the Relationship between Population Growth and Aggregate Economic Growth in LDC's: Methodological Problems'. In *Consequences of Rapid Population Growth in Developing Countries.* Proceedings of the United Nations Institut national d'études demographiques Expert Group Meeting, New York, 23–6 Aug. 1988. New York: Taylor and Francis, 67–99.

Bloom, David E., David Canning, and Pia Malaney. 1988. 'Demographic Change and Economic Growth in Asia'. Mimeo.

—— and Richard B. Freeman. 1988. 'Economic Development and the Timing and Components of Population Growth'. *Journal of Policy Modeling.* 10 (1) (Special Issue: Modeling Demographic and Economic Dynamics, Dominick Salvatore, guest ed.): 57–81.

—— and Jeffrey G. Williamson. 1997. 'Demographic Change and Human Resource Development'. In *Emerging Asia: Changes and Challenges,* ch. 3. Manila: Asian Development Bank.

—— —— 1998. 'Demographic Transitions and Economic Miracles in Emerging Asia'. *World Bank Economic Review.* 12 (3): 419–55.

Boserup, Ester. 1981. *Population and Technological Change.* Chicago: University of Chicago Press.

Brander, James A., and Steve Dowrick. 1994. 'The Role of Fertility and Population in Economic Growth: Empirical Results from Aggregate Cross-national Data'. *Journal of Population Economics.* 7: 1–25.

Canning, David. 1999. 'The Role of Education and Infrastructure in Economics Growth'. Mimeo.

Cass, David. 1965. 'Optimum Growth in an Aggregative Model of Capital Accumulation'. *Review of Economic Studies.* 12: 1–10.

Chenery, Hollis, and Moises Syrquin. 1975. *Patterns of Development: 1950–1970*. Oxford: Oxford University Press.

Coale, Ansley J. 1986. 'Population Trends and Economic Development'. In Jane Mencken, ed., *World Population and U.S. Policy: The Choices Ahead*. New York: W. W. Norton, for the American Assembly, 96–104.

Cohen, W., and S. Klepper. 1996. 'A Reprise of Size and R&D'. *Economic Journal*. 106: 925–51.

Denison, Edward F. 1962. *The Sources of Growth in the United States*. New York: Committee for Economic Development.

Dinopoulos, Elias, and Peter Thompson. 1999. 'Scale Effects in Schumpeterian Models of Economic Growth'. *Journal of Evolutionary Economics*, 9 (2): 157–85.

Easterly, William, Michael Kremer, Lant Pritchett, and Lawrence H. Summers. 1998. 'Good Policy or Good Luck? Country Growth Performance and Temporary Shocks'. World Bank, mimeo.

Fagerberg, Jan. 1994. 'Technology and International Differences in Growth Rates'. *Journal of Economic Literature*. 32 (3): 1147–75.

Gastil, Raymond Duncan. 1991. 'The Comparative Survey of Freedom: Experiences and Suggestions'. In Alex Inkeles, ed., *On Measuring Democracy: Its Consequences and Concomitants*. New Brunswick, NJ: Transaction Publishers, 21–46.

Glover, Donald R., and Julian L. Simon. 1975. 'The Effect of Population Density on Infrastructure: The Case of Road Building'. *Economic Development and Cultural Change*. 23 (3): 453–68.

Grossman, Gene, and Elhanan Helpman. 1991. *Innovation and Growth in the Global Economy*. Cambridge, Mass.: MIT Press.

Hayami, Yujiro, and Vernon W. Ruttan. 1987. 'Population Growth and Agricultural Productivity'. In D. Gale Johnson and Ronald D. Lee, eds., *Population Growth and Economic Development: Issues and Evidence*. Madison: University of Wisconsin Press, 57–101.

Henderson, J. Vernon. 1987. 'Industrialization and Urbanization: International Experience'. In D. Gale Johnson and Ronald D. Lee, eds., *Population Growth and Economic Development: Issues and Evidence*. Madison: University of Wisconsin Press, 189–224.

ICRG. 1982–95. 'International Country Risk Guide'. Political Risk Services; obtained from IRIS Center, University of Maryland.

James, Jeffrey. 1987. 'Population and Technical Change in the Manufacturing Sector of Developing Countries'. In D. Gale Johnson and Ronald D. Lee, eds., *Population Growth and Economic Development: Issues and Evidence*. Madison: University of Wisconsin Press, 225–56.

Kelley, Allen C. 1988. 'Economic Consequences of Population Change in the Third World'. *Journal of Economic Literature*. 26: 1685–728.

—— 1991. 'Revisionism Revisited: An Essay on the Population Debate in Historical Perspective'. Paper presented at the Nobel Symposium in Economics, 5–7 December. Lund, Sweden, mimeo.

—— 1996. 'The Consequences of Population Growth on Human Resource Development: The Case of Education'. In D. A. Ahlburg, A. C. Kelley, and K. Oppenheim Mason, eds., *The Impact of Population Growth on Well-being in Developing Countries*. Berlin: Springer-Verlag, 67–137.

—— and Robert M. Schmidt. 1994. 'Population and Income Change: Recent Evidence'. World Bank Discussion Papers 249. Washington: The World Bank.

———— 1995. 'Aggregate Population and Economic Growth Correlations: The Role of the Components of Demographic Change'. *Demography*. 32 (4): 543–55.

Koopmans, Tjallig C. 1965. 'On the Concept of Optimal Economic Growth'. In *The Economic Approach to Development Planning*. Amsterdam: North-Holland (for Pontificia Acad. Sci.).

Kremer M. 1993. 'Population and Growth: One Million BC to 1990'. *Quarterly Journal of Economics*. 108: 681–716.

Lee, Ronald D. 1983. 'Economic Consequences of Population Size, Structure and Growth'. *IUSSP* (International Union for the Scientific Study of Population) *Newsletter*. 17: 43–59.

Levine, R., and D. Renelt. 1992. 'A Sensitivity Analysis of Cross-Country Growth Regressions'. *American Economic Review*. 82: 942–63.

Lucas, R. E. 1988. 'On the Mechanics of Economic Development'. *Journal of Monetary Economics*. 22: 3–42.

McNicoll, Geoffrey. 1984. 'Consequences of Rapid Population Growth: An Overview and Assessment'. *Population and Development Review*. 10 (2): 177–240.

National Academy of Sciences. 1971. *Rapid Population Growth: Consequences and Policy Implications*. 2 vols. Baltimore: Johns Hopkins University Press for the National Academy of Sciences.

National Research Council. 1986. *Population Growth and Economic Development: Policy Questions*. National Research Council, Working Group on Population Growth and Economic Development, Committee on Population, Commission on Behavioral and Social Sciences and Education. Washington: National Academy Press.

Peretto, Pietro, and Sjak Smulders. 1998. 'Specialization, Knowledge Dilution and Scale Effects in an IO-based Growth Model'. Tilberg University, Center Discussion Paper No. 9802.

Phelps, Edmund S. 1968. 'Population Increase'. *Canadian Journal of Economics*. 1 (3): 497–518.

Pingali, Prabhu L., and Hans P. Binswanger. 1987. 'Population Density and Agricultural Intensification: A Study of the Evolution of Technologies in Tropical Agriculture'. In D. Gale Johnson and Ronald D. Lee, eds., *Population Growth and Economic Development: Issues and Evidence*. Madison: University of Wisconsin Press, 27–56.

Pritchett, Lant. 1998. 'Patterns of Economic Growth: Hills, Plateaus, Mountains, and Plains'. World Bank, mimeo.

Radelet, Steven, Jeffrey Sachs, and Jong-Wha Lee. 1997. 'Economic Growth in Asia'. Harvard Institute for International Development, Development Discussion Papers No. 609.

Ramsey, Frank. 1928. 'A Mathematical Theory of Saving'. *Economic Journal*. 38: 543–59.

Romer, Paul. 1986. 'Increasing Returns and Long-Run Growth'. *Journal of Political Economy*. 94: 1002–37.

—— 1990. 'Endogenous Technological Change'. *Journal of Political Economy*. 98: S71–S103.

Sali-i-Martin, Xavier. 1997. 'I Just Ran Two Million Regressions'. *American Economic Review*. Papers and Proceedings. 87: 178–83.

Schultz, T. Paul. 1987. 'School Expenditures and Enrollments, 1960–1980: The Effects of Income, Prices and Population Growth'. In D. Gale Johnson and Ronald D. Lee, eds., *Population Growth and Economic Development: Issues and Evidence*. Madison: University of Wisconsin Press, 413–76.

—— 1996. 'Accounting for Public Expenditures on Education: An International Panel Study'. In T. Paul Schultz, ed., *Research in Population Economics*, vol. 8. Greenwich, Conn.: JAI Press, 233–64.

Simon, Julian. 1975. 'The Effect of Population Density on Infrastructure: The Case of Road Building'. *Economic Development and Cultural Change*. 23 (3): 453–568.

—— and Roy Gobin. 1980. 'The Relationship between Population and Economic Growth in LDCs'. In J. L. Simon and J. DaVanzo, eds., *Research in Population Economics*, vol. 2. Greenwich, Conn.: JAI Press, 215–34.

Solow, Robert M. 1956. 'A Contribution to the Theory of Economic Growth'. *Quarterly Journal of Economics.* 70 (1): 65–94.

Srinivasan, T. N. 1988. 'Population Growth and Economic Development'. *Journal of Policy Modeling.* 10 (1): 7–28.

Stigler, George J. 1961. 'Economic Problems in Measuring Changes in Productivity'. *Studies in Income and Wealth.* 25: 47–77. Conference on Poverty and Wealth. Princeton: Princeton University Press.

Summers, Robert, and Alan Heston. 1988. 'A New Set of International Comparisons of Real Product and Price Levels: Estimates for 130 Countries, 1950–1985'. *Review of Income and Wealth.* Series 30, No. 2: 207–62.

———— 1994. 'Data Update 5.5'. Computer diskette based on 'The Penn World Table (Mark 5): An Expanded Set of International Comparisons, 1950–1988'.

Tan, Jee-Peng, and Alain Mingat. 1992. *Education in Asia: A Comparative Study of Cost and Financing.* Washington: The World Bank.

United Nations. 1953. *The Determinants and Consequences of Population Trends.* Department of Social Affairs, Population Division, Population Studies No. 17. New York: United Nations.

—— 1973. *The Determinants and Consequences of Population Trends.* Department of Economic and Social Affairs, Population Studies No. 50. 2 vols. New York: United Nations.

—— 1988. *World Population Trends and Policies: 1987 Monitoring Report.* Department of International Economic and Social Affairs, Population Studies No. 103. ST/ESA/SER.A/103. New York: United Nations.

—— 1996. 'Sex and Age Annual 1950–2050 (The 1996 Revision)'. United Nations Population Division (data diskettes).

World Bank. 1984. *World Development Report.* New York: Oxford University Press.

—— 1994. *World Data 1994: World Bank Indicators on CD-ROM.* Washington: The World Bank.

—— 1995. *World Data 1995: World Bank Indicators on CD-ROM.* Washington: The World Bank.

—— 1997. *World Development Indicators 1997 on CD-ROM.* Washington: The World Bank.

5

Demographic Change, Economic Growth, and Inequality

JEFFREY G. WILLIAMSON

THE DEMOGRAPHIC TRANSITION AND WORLD HEALTH CONVERGENCE

The demographic transition describes the change from pre-industrial high fertility and mortality to post-industrial low fertility and mortality. Figure 5.1 offers a stylized view of the transition. Declines in mortality—especially infant and child mortality—mark the beginning of almost all demographic transitions, and the age structure can be strongly influenced since most of these early declines in mortality are enjoyed by infants and children. True, the improved survivor rates for children induces parents to reduce their fertility. If parents adjusted completely and immediately, there would be no youth glut, no acceleration in population growth, and no transition worth talking about. But they do not: their adjustment is slow, so that the youth glut is large and persistent. After a lag, however, fertility begins to decline marking the next stage of the transition. The population growth rate is implicit in the first panel of Figure 5.1 as the difference between fertility and mortality. The second panel makes the population dynamics explicit: the demographic transition must be accompanied by a cycle in population growth *and* the age structure. Figure 5.1 and the rest of this chapter treats the demographic system as if it were closed, and thus

This chapter was originally presented to a Symposium on Population Change and Economic Development co-sponsored by the Rockefeller Foundation, the United Nations Population Fund, and the Packard Foundation, held at the Bellagio Center, Lake Como, Italy, 2–6 November 1998. It draws heavily on completed research published elsewhere by myself: 'Growth, Distribution, and Demography: Some Lessons from History', *Explorations in Economic History* (1998), 241–71. It draws even more heavily on past collaborations: with David Bloom, 'Demographic Transitions and Economic Miracles in Emerging Asia', *World Bank Economic Review* (1998), 419–55; with Matthew Higgins, 'Age Structure Dynamics in Asia and Dependence on Foreign Capital', *Population and Development Review* (1997), 261–93; and with Tarik Yousef, 'Demographic Transitions and Economic Performance: Background Hypotheses and Empirical Findings in MENA', paper presented to the *Conference on Population Challenges in the Middle East and North Africa: Towards the 21st Century*, 2–4 November 1998, Cairo. The chapter also draws on preliminary research with Matthew Higgins on the late twentieth century inequality and demography connection, as well as my own published research dealing with the late nineteenth century ('Globalization and Inequality, Past and Present', *World Bank Research Observer* (1997), 117–35). I want to recognize both Bloom and Higgins for their massive contributions to the ideas and evidence presented in this chapter.

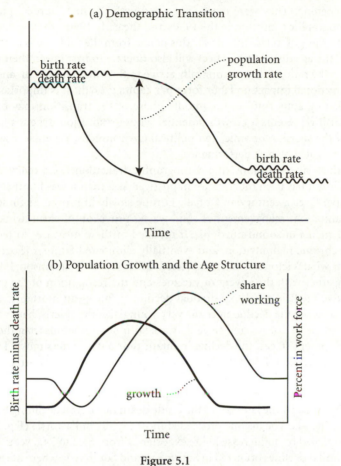

(a) Demographic Transition

birth rate
death rate

population
growth rate

birth rate
death rate

Time

(b) Population Growth and the Age Structure

Birth rate minus death rate

share
working

Percent in work force

growth

Time

Figure 5.1
Source: Bloom and Williamson (1998: Figure 1).

it ignores external migration. Were it quantitatively important and if it responded to cohort gluts and scarcities, external migration might very well mute the impact of demographic transitions, as it did in late nineteenth century Europe (Hatton and Williamson 1998). In the late twentieth century, international migrations are simply not great enough to matter except, perhaps, for the United States and some oil-producing countries in the Middle East. They mattered a great deal, however, when mass migration was relatively unchecked prior to World War I (Williamson 1998).

These components of the demographic transition might have separate influences on economic growth. The population growth rate could influence economic growth, for the reasons asserted by both the population pessimists and optimists. The demographic transition could also affect economic growth through the age distribution. Ansley Coale and Edgar Hoover (1958) coined the term dependency rate to predict the impact of big youth cohorts on low savings, low investment, and slow educational capital-deepening. They were more concerned with the first 'burden' phase of the Asian demographic transition in the 1950s and the early 1960s, so they devoted little attention to the 'gift' phase that drives this paper, from the mid-1960s to the present. Of course, the age distribution effect will also operate to first lower, then raise, then lower again the ratio of the economically active to the total population, and thus will have a transitional impact on labor force per capita growth. It is important to stress that the demographic 'gift' in the middle phase of the transition may or may not be realized; it represents a growth potential whose realization depends upon other features of the social, economic, and political environment. Whether it *was* realized should be revealed by past performance.

Like industrial revolutions, the demographic transition takes many decades to complete, but it has been much faster in postwar Asia than it was in nineteenth century Europe. Over a century and a half, Europe slowly improved its understanding of basic sanitation, management of solid waste, provision of clean drinking water, and the elements of sound nutrition. It invested in these measures to reduce mortality and chronic malnutrition, and eventually eliminated famines (Fogel 1994). It cleaned up what Victorian reformers called 'killer cities' (Williamson 1990). These factors, together with the advent of vaccines and the recognition of the importance of preventive medicine, led to a gradual decline in European mortality. Infant and child mortality led the decline since the very young, like the elderly, have always been most vulnerable to disease, and since they are far more numerous than the elderly at early development stages, the decline in infant mortality matters most. The fertility rate also declined slowly, and the European demographic transition stretched out for more than a hundred years (Coale and Watkins 1986).

Asia's demographic transition followed the stylized model by starting with a decline in mortality rates. By the late-1940s, the crude death rate began declining very rapidly everywhere in Asia. The decline proceeded most rapidly in East Asia (Fig. 5.2) and it was accompanied by an increase in life expectancy from 61.2 to 74.6 years from 1960 to 1992. Similar declines occurred in South East and South Asia where life expectancy improved from 51.6 to 67.2 and from 46.9 to 60.6, respectively. In the 1950s and 1960s, most of the aggregate mortality decline was being driven by the decline in the youngest cohorts (Bloom and Williamson 1997). They also occurred in Latin America (Taylor 1995) and MENA (the Middle East and North Africa: Yousef 1997).

What initiated the Asian demographic transition? What induced that initial fall in child mortality in the 1940s? The health investments and medical technologies that had been developed and put into practice in Europe did not exist in Asia until relatively recently: there was a big gap between best health practice prevailing in industrialized Europe and local health practice prevailing in Asia. The scope for the transmission of health technologies was enormous in the 1940s, since it had been pent up by de-globalization, two world wars, a great depression, and wars of colonial liberation. When the postwar transfer of this pent-up health technology finally took place, it happened in a rush. The process was speeded up even further by investment in health-improving social overhead which was heavily financed by world funding agencies that were non-existent prior to the 1940s. In short, the possibilities for an

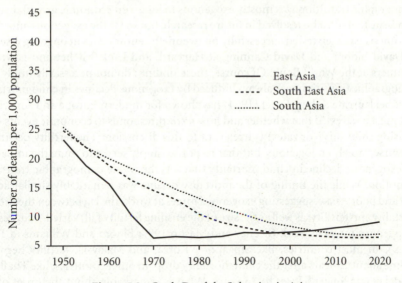

Figure 5.2. *Crude Death by Subregion in Asia*
Source: Bloom and Williamson (1998: figure 2).

Asian catch-up with the West in terms of health and demography were enormous in the late 1940s, and they were driven by factors external to Asia itself. In the half century since then, Asia has exploited the catch-up potential with such enthusiasm that it has produced one of the fastest and most dramatic demographic transitions ever.[1] This has played a big part in a general world health convergence, and it was started in the 1940s by *exogenous* forces.

There are, of course, other competing explanations for the rapid decline in Third World and especially Asian child mortality in the middle of this century, which, after all, was the real force driving the age distribution over the first two phases of the demographic transition. The most important competing explanation suggests that the event was *endogenous*: increased agricultural productivity and trade in food both raised nutrition sufficiently to lower infant mortality dramatically over less than a decade, and did so everywhere in Asia and the rest of the Third World. Perhaps, but it seems unlikely given that the magnitude and timing of the mortality decline was so similar everywhere in Asia, Latin America, and MENA regardless of level of development and productivity performance in agriculture.

Resolving the debate between the view which favors an *exogenous* supply-side-driven fall in infant mortality in the 1940s and 1950s and one which favors an *endogenous* demand-side-driven fall matters since it will influence the extent to which the

---

[1] The language being used in this section is purposely similar to that used in the debate over economic catch-up and convergence (Abramovitz 1986; Baumol 1986; Barro 1991; Sachs and Warner 1995) because I think exactly the same reasoning applies to the demographic transition in Asia and the rest of the Third World.

demographic transition was mostly exogenous to long-run economic growth itself. It is an issue that must be resolved in future research, but so far the exogenous-mortality hypothesis has been tested successfully on twentieth century data in ongoing research by David Bloom and David Canning at Harvard, and Lant Pritchet and Lawrence Summers at the World Bank. Of course, these findings do not necessarily imply that demographic transitions are always induced by exogenous declines in child mortality, as Nobel laureate Robert Fogel (1994) has shown for modern Europe and America.

It must be stressed that whether and how *fertility* responds to economic events (and to rising child survivor rates) is irrelevant to this discussion. The fertility decline is, of course, largely endogenous, but that response simply serves to mute the impact of the exogenous decline in child mortality that sets the whole demographic transition in motion. While the timing of the mortality decline was remarkably similar across rich and poor Asia—suggesting exogenous forces at work, the lag between the drop in mortality and fertility, as well as the size of the ensuing fertility fall, varied—suggesting endogenous forces at work (Feeney and Mason 1997; Bloom and Williamson 1997: fig. 5). In most countries, like Singapore, Korea, and Malaysia, fertility began to decline about 15 years after the child mortality drop. In other countries, like Thailand, the delay was longer, closer to 25 years. What is remarkable about the onset of the Asian fertility decline is the very short period over which it occurred and that it was so dramatic everywhere, even where the pace of economic development was slow (Caldwell and Caldwell 1996).[2]

The pace and timing of the demographic transition has led to enormously divergent trends in population growth and age structure across Asia and the rest of the Third World. Figure 5.3 plots the ratio of the working-age population to the non-working-age population for the three subregions in Asia and MENA (again, the Middle East and North Africa). With only two precocious exceptions, Japan and Sri Lanka, Asia's surge to peak youth dependency rates occurred in the 1960s and 1970s, reflected in Figure 5.3 by the low ratio of working-age population to non-working-age population. The ratio of working-age to non-working-age population has been rising in Asia and MENA since 1975, but this increase has been especially dramatic in East Asia. According to UN projections, the ratio will peak for East Asia in 2010. With the exception of Japan, the elderly dependency rate has been mostly irrelevant to Asia in this century, even to the more economically mature East Asia. It will, of course, become very relevant to these older tigers as they advance further into this new

---

[2] There are, of course, a number of possible explanations for the decline in fertility, and it matters in deciding how much of the decline was endogenously related to the economic miracle itself, and how much was exogenous and driven by policy. Contraceptive use rates vary across Asia (Bloom and Williamson 1997, table 5); government intervention accounts for some of this variance, while family demand, responding in part to economic events, accounts for the remainder. The big debate is over which mattered most. Two well-known demographers argue that government intervention mattered a great deal and that the intervention was distinctly Asian (Caldwell and Caldwell 1996). Another even offered an estimate. Examining the decline in the total fertility rate 1965–75 for 68 developing countries, Boulier (1986) concluded that only 27% was due to economic change while 40% was due to government-supported family planning and 33% to previous fertility decline. The general view seems to be that family planning programs have been central to the decline in Asian fertility, beginning with India in 1951.

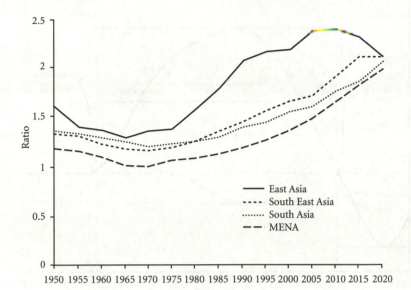

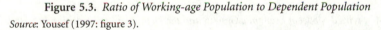

Figure 5.3. *Ratio of Working-age Population to Dependent Population*
Source: Yousef (1997: figure 3).

century. Indeed, Figure 5.3 projects a decline in the ratio of the working-age to the non-working-age population after 2010. This reflects the increase in the elderly dependency rate as the bulge in the age distribution works its way through the East Asian population. However, the elderly dependency rate will not become a dominant demographic force anywhere else in Asia, Africa, and MENA even as late as 2030.

THE ECONOMIC HYPOTHESIS

What matters most in identifying the impact of demographic change on economic performance is the changing age distribution. This chapter argues that in the early stages of the demographic transition, per capita income growth is diminished by large youth dependency burdens and small working-age adult shares: there are relatively few workers and savers. As the transition proceeds, per capita income growth is promoted by smaller youth dependency burdens and larger working-age adult shares: there are relatively many workers and savers. The early burden of having few workers and savers becomes a potential gift: a high share of working-age adults. Later, the economic gift evaporates, as the elderly share rises.

This story argues that some of the slower growth performance prior to 1970 can be attributed to the fact that East Asia was carrying a very heavy youth dependency burden. Without the youth dependency burden, East Asia would have had higher growth rates prior to 1970. As East Asia graduated from demographic burden to gift,

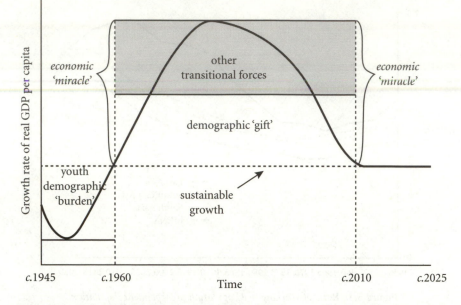

Figure 5.4. *Stylized Model of Economic Growth and the Demographic Transition in East Asia*
Source: Bloom and Williamson (1998: figure 7).

the youth dependency burden decreased and the proportion of working-age adults increased. The result was an acceleration of the growth rate abetted by demographic forces. These transitional demographic forces helped to push the growth rate far above its pre-1970 level to the 'miraculous' rates of the past quarter century. Sometime in the near future, however, the demographic gift in East Asia will evaporate as the share of elderly in the population increases, and, consequently, economic growth will tend to slow down. Once the demographic transition is complete, population growth will no longer affect economic growth.

Figure 5.4 offers a stylized version of the economic hypothesis where the sustainable growth rate is taken to be about 2 percent per annum. Note, however, that the contribution of the demographic transition to the East Asian miracle will also depend on how the miracle is defined. If it is defined as a share of per capita GDP growth between 1960 and 2010 in Figure 5.4, then it accounts for about a third of the miracle; if it is defined as the surplus over the sustainable rate, then it accounts for almost half; and if it is defined as the increase in growth rates from 1945–60 to 1960–2010, then it accounts for almost three-quarters. Now, can Figure 5.4 be defended with evidence?

SIMPLE GROWTH THEORY

The cross-country growth equations reported in the next section were estimated by David Bloom and myself (1998) and they are derived from a conventional Ramsey model. If production per worker (y) takes the form $y = f(k) = Ak^{\alpha}$, then we can derive eqn (1) which will be familiar to any reader of a current advanced macroeconomic textbook (e.g. Barro and Sala-i-Martin 1995). It is also consistent with the empirical growth literature, especially that which focuses on conditional convergence (Barro 1991; Mankiw *et al.* 1992; Sachs and Warner 1995). In the Ramsey model, the average growth rate (g_y) of output per worker between any time T_1 and T_2 is proportional to the logged ratio of income per worker in the steady state (y^*) and income per worker at time T_1 as follows:

$$g_y = \frac{1}{T_2 - T_1} \log\left(\frac{y(T_2)}{y(T_1)}\right) = \alpha \log\left(\frac{y^*}{y(T_1)}\right). \tag{1}$$

Two additional modifications can be made to this generic model. The first involves the formulation of steady-state output. Following Sachs, Radelet, and Lee (1997) in the Asian Development Bank's *Emerging Asia*, assume that y^* is formed as

$$y^* = X\beta \tag{2}$$

where X is a matrix with k determinants of the steady state. Also following Sachs, Radelet, and Lee, let the variables included in X include log level of schooling in the initial period, life expectancy in the initial period, a measure of natural resource abundance, a measure of openness, an index of institution quality, average government savings, and geographical variables indicating the ratio of coastline to land area, whether there is access to major ports, and whether the country is located in the tropics. The second modification involves changing the metric from output per worker (y) to output per capita $(\tilde{y})$. Note that

$$\tilde{y} = \frac{Y}{P} = \frac{Y}{L}\frac{L}{P} = y\frac{L}{P} \tag{3}$$

where P is the total population, L is the number of workers, y is output per worker, and $\tilde{y}$ is output per capita. This expression can easily be converted to growth rates,

$$g_{\tilde{y}} = g_y + g_{workers} - g_{population}. \tag{4}$$

When eqns (1) and (2) are substituted into (4) and a stochastic term is added, the estimation eqn (5) emerges:

$$g_{\tilde{y}} = X\Pi_1 + y(T_1)\Pi_2 + g_{workers}\Pi_3 + g_{population}\Pi_4 + \varepsilon \tag{5}$$

where theoretically, $\Pi_3 = -\Pi_4 = 1$. For a stable population, the growth rate of the workforce equals the growth rate of the population, and net demographic effects vanish. If the population is unstable as during a transition, then demography matters.

ECONOMETRIC RESULTS FOR THE WORLD

The econometric analysis is based on a world sample of 78 countries covering the quarter century from 1965 to 1990 (Bloom and Williamson 1998): Africa 17; Asia 13; Latin America 21; MENA 5; and OECD 22.

Table 5.1. *OLS Regression of Economic Growth on Population Growth, 1965–90 (Dependent variable: growth rate of real GDP per capita, 1965–90, in PPP terms. Sample includes 78 countries.)*

Independent variables	Ordinary least squares estimates	
	(1) Specification 1 Revised	(2) Specification 2 Emerging Asia
GPOP6590	0.16	0.56
	(0.20)	(0.16)
GDP per capita as ratio of US	−1.50	−2.30
GDP per capita, 1965 (logged)	(0.25)	(0.22)
Log life expectancy, 1960		5.81
		(0.98)
Log years of secondary	0.82	0.37
schooling, 1965	(0.18)	(0.15)
Natural resource abundance	−4.68	−2.40
	(1.35)	(1.17)
Openness	2.23	1.88
	(0.47)	(0.36)
Quality of institutions	0.21	0.22
	(0.10)	(0.07)
Access to ports (landlocked)	−0.68	−0.87
	(0.39)	(0.29)
Average gov't savings, 1970–90	0.18	0.15
	(0.04)	(0.03)
Located in the tropics		−1.09
		(0.33)
Ratio of coastline distance to		0.29
land area		(0.12)
Constant	−2.11	−27.38
	(0.92)	(4.3)
Adjusted R²	0.69	0.83

Note: Standard errors are reported in parentheses below coefficient estimates.

Source: Bloom and Williamson (1998: table 2).

We start by asking whether the level of population growth affects economic growth, since that's the (wrong) way the population debate has always been couched. The results appear in Table 5.1. Most of the recent research on economic convergence has focused on the sign of the coefficient on log initial income. If the coefficient is negative, the model predicts conditional convergence: that is, after controlling for the steady-state level of income, poor countries tend to grow faster and approach their steady-state level quicker than rich countries. Consistent with recent research on economic convergence, there is conditional convergence in our sample too. But what about population growth? In the revised specification in Table 5.1 (col. 1), there is no significant relationship between population growth (GPOP6590) and GDP per capita growth, confirming the neutralist position. Note, however, how sensitive this result is to the specification. As soon as log life expectancy in 1960 and two variables controlling for economic geography are added, population is shown to have a positive and significant impact on GDP per capita growth (Table 5.1, col. 2), supporting the optimist position.

Table 5.1 illustrates the kind of mistakes the profession has made when concluding that demography doesn't matter. The conclusion typically fails to pay any attention to the sources of population growth and to the stage of the demographic transition. It matters: a child mortality decline or a baby boom both raise the youth dependent age population; a mortality decline among the elderly increases the retired dependent age cohort; immigration raises the working-age population (because it self-selects young adults); and improved mortality among the population at large has no impact on age structure at all. Since the productive capacity of an economy is directly (and indirectly) linked to the size of its working-age population relative to its total population, it is essential to distinguish between the two components when exploring the impact of demographic change on economic performance.

Table 5.2 conforms to these notions: the growth rate in the economically active population (GEAP6590) joins GPOP6590 in the regression. The growth rate of the working-age population measures the change in the size of the population aged 15 to 64 between 1965 and 1990.[3] Table 5.2 confirms that the growth of the working-age population has had a powerful positive impact on GDP per capita growth, while growth of the total population has had a powerful negative impact. Consider the results reported in the second column of Table 5.2. The coefficient on the growth rate of the working-age population is positive, statistically significant, and big: a 1 per-cent increase in the growth rate of the working age population is associated with a 1.46 percent increase in the growth rate of GDP per capita. The coefficient on the growth rate of the total population is negative, statistically significant, and almost as big: a 1 percent decrease in the growth rate of the dependent population is asso-ciated with about a 1 percent increase in the growth rate of GDP per capita.[4] The third and fourth columns of Table 5.2 show what happens when the impact of the growth rates of the working-age and the entire population are constrained to be equal but of opposite sign. In steady state, when the age distribution is stable, population growth wouldn't matter in either of these two specifications. In transition, when the age distribution changes, demography matters. The coefficient here is big, positive, and significant. Thus, where the growth rate of the economically active exceeds that of the population in our sample, higher GDP per capita growth rates have appeared

---

[3] There are, of course, other variables that help determine the labor participation rate. If they dominated the demographic influences, then we wouldn't have a story to tell. They didn't.

[4] The coefficients of the other variables are similar to those found in Sachs *et al.* (1997), and the interested reader may wish to explore them there. Throughout this chapter, specification 2 refers to their model, while specification 1 refers to a revised version which removes initial life expectancy and two economic geography variables.

Table 5.2. *Effects of Population Growth on Economic Growth, 1965–90 (Dependent variable: growth rate of real GDP per capita, 1965–90, in PPP terms. Sample includes 78 countries.)*

Independent variables	Ordinary least squares estimates			
	(1)	(2)	(3)	(4)
	Specification 1	Specification 2	Specification 1 (constrained)	Specification 2 (constrained)
GEAP6590	1.95	1.46		
	(0.38)	(0.34)		
GPOP6590	−1.87	−1.03		
	(0.43)	(0.40)		
GEAP6590- GPOP6590			1.97	1.68
			(0.38)	(0.35)
GDP per capita as	−1.36	−2.00	−1.39	−1.97
ratio of US GDP	(0.21)	(0.21)	(0.21)	(0.22)
per capita, 1965				
Log life expectancy,		3.96		2.94
1960		(0.97)		(0.97)
Log years of secondary	0.50	0.22	0.50	0.28
schooling, 1965	(0.16)	(0.14)	(0.16)	(0.14)
Natural resource	−4.86	−2.35	−4.86	−2.57
abundance	(1.2)	(1.0)	(1.1)	(1.1)
Openness	2.06	1.92	2.00	1.72
	(0.40)	(0.32)	(0.38)	(0.33)
Quality of institutions	0.23	0.20	0.22	0.15
	(0.08)	(0.07)	(0.08)	(0.07)
Access to ports	−0.35	−0.64	−0.31	−0.40
(landlocked)	(0.34)	(0.07)	(0.32)	(0.27)
Average gov't savings,	0.14	0.12	0.14	0.13
1970–90	(0.03)	(0.03)	(0.03)	(0.03)
Located in the tropics		−1.31		−1.20
		(0.30)		(0.31)
Ratio of coastline		0.24		0.23
distance to land area		(0.11)		(0.12)
Constant	−2.46	−19.5	−2.28	−14.3
	(0.79)	(4.3)	(0.69)	(4.1)
Adjusted R²	0.76	0.86	0.78	0.85

Note: Standard errors are reported in parenthesis below coefficient estimates.

Source: Bloom and Williamson (1998: table 3).

(*ceteris paribus*). Equivalently, where the middle of the age distribution (ages 15–64) grows faster than the tails (ages 15 and below and 65 and above), GDP per capita growth is faster. The opposite is true if the growth rate of the total population exceeds that of the economically active. If the dependent population is growing faster than the workforce, the model predicts slower growth.

Previous contributions to the population debate have, typically, failed to explore the possibility of reverse causality between population growth and economic growth, this despite a literature which suggests that economic events clearly induce demographic responses. Table 5.2 used ordinary least squares (OLS), but the results are the same when instrumental variables (IV) are used to account for possible reverse causality (Bloom and Williamson 1998: table 3).

Table 5.3 reports the results when interaction terms and regional controls are included. The table deals with two issues: first, to see whether the demographic environment has an impact on the role of 'institutional quality' and 'openness' on growth; and secondly, to see whether Asian growth responds differently to the same demographic and economic events compared with other regions. In the first four columns, the unconstrained versions of the model are re-estimated by including interactions between GEAP and a standard proxy for the quality of institutions (Knack and Keefer 1995), on the one hand, and GEAP and a standard proxy for openness (Sachs and Warner 1995), on the other. The last two columns explore whether there is any regional effect remaining. There is no evidence supporting the view that the demographic environment influenced the impact of institutional quality or openness. There is some weak evidence that Asia grew faster than the omitted region, Africa, even after controlling for all of these forces, but there is no strong evidence that suggests that Asia—after controlling for all these forces—grew any faster than North America or Europe. The latter is an even stronger finding than that offered by Paul Krugman a few years ago (Krugman 1994).

The growth of the dependent population slows down economic growth, but does a growing *young*, dependent population have the same impact as a growing *elderly*, dependent population? When the estimation equation is modified by inserting the growth rates of the population under 15 and over 65 in place of the growth rate of the population as a whole, the results serve to clarify which 'dependent' populations contribute to the slow-down: it's the young (Bloom and Williamson 1998: table 5). The coefficient on the population under the age of 15 is negative and significant, such that a 1 percentage point increase in the growth of the population under age 15 is associated with a decrease in the GDP per capita growth of about 0.4 percentage points. In contrast, a small, statistically insignificant, but positive, coefficient emerges for the elderly. It appears that the elderly continue to make important economic contributions by tending the young, by working part-time, and perhaps by still saving. In any case, the elderly are a smaller net drag than are the very young who do not work or save at all.[5] Since the elderly are currently a small minority of the total dependent population in much of the Third World (11% in Asia in 1990), the relationship between the dependent young and GDP per capita growth dominates, accounting for the negative effects that the dependent population as a whole exerts on the growth rate of GDP per capita.

---

[5] It must be said, however, that the data describing their behavior are thin. Long life expectancy is too new to inspire confidence about our ability to predict the behavior of the elderly, especially outside the OECD. This is true for researchers, and it may be true of the new elderly themselves!

Table 5.3. *Effects of Population Growth on Economic Growth under Alternative Specifications, 1965–1990 (Dependent variable: growth rate of real GDP per capita, 1965–90. Sample includes 78 countries.)*

Independent variables	Ordinary least squares estimates					
	(1) Specification 1	(2) Specification 2	(3) Specification 1	(4) Specification 2	(5) Specification 1	(6) Specification 2
GEAP6590	1.94	1.36	2.03	1.43	1.91	1.24
	(0.66)	(0.55)	(0.43)	(0.39)	(0.45)	(0.40)
GPOP6590	−1.87	−1.01	−1.88	−1.02	−1.72	−0.78
	(0.45)	(0.41)	(0.43)	(0.40)	(0.49)	(0.45)
Interaction between GEAP & instit'l quality	0.002	0.01				
	(0.07)	(0.06)				
Interaction between GEAP & openness			−0.12	−0.05		
			(0.31)	(0.25)		
Asia dummy					0.81	0.60
					(0.44)	(0.35)
North American dummy					0.36	0.67
					(0.67)	(0.55)
South American dummy					0.08	0.35
					(0.49)	(0.42)
Europe dummy					1.00	0.53
					(0.60)	(0.50)
Constant	−2.43	−19.3	−2.62	−19.6	−2.89	−20.19
	(1.35)	(4.3)	(0.89)	(4.3)	(1.20)	(4.4)
Adjusted R^2	0.77	0.86	0.77	0.86	0.79	0.86

Notes: Standard errors are reported in parentheses below coefficient estimates. Because of data limitations, our sample does not include any countries in Eastern Europe. Furthermore, countries from the Middle East are included in the Asian dummy. When controlling for the Middle East separately, the coefficients on GEAP6590 and GPOP6590 do not change significantly.

Source: Bloom and Williamson (1998: table 5).

The economic impact of the demographic transition can be summarized this way: economic growth will be less rapid when the growth rate of the working-age population falls short of that of the population as a whole (an event that characterized the first phase of East Asia's postwar demographic transition prior to 1970); economic growth will be more rapid when the growth rate of the working-age population exceeds that of the population as a whole (an event which characterized the second phase of East Asia's postwar demographic transition overlapping the economic miracle over the past quarter century); and economic growth will be less rapid when the growth rate of the working-age population once again falls short of that of the entire population (an event which will dominate East Asia over the next quarter century).

USING WORLD RESULTS TO EXPLAIN ASIAN ECONOMIC MIRACLES

The theory seems to survive test. But what about economic significance? Can these population dynamics explain a significant part of any economic miracle, like the one East (and South East) Asia underwent before the recent financial collapse?

Between 1965 and 1990, the working age population in East Asia grew 2.4 percent per annum, dramatically faster than the 1.6 percent rate for the entire population, yielding a 0.8 percent differential (Table 5.4). The working-age population also grew faster than the entire population in South East Asia, but the differences were almost half of those in East Asia, while in South Asia they were only a quarter of the East Asian figure. These demographic differences help explain at least some of the disparity in growth performance across Asia between 1965 and 1990. Combining the coefficients from the estimated growth equations in Table 5.3 and the growth rates of the working age and total population, Table 5.4 reports that population dynamics can explain between 1.4 and 1.9 percentage points of GDP per capita growth in East Asia, or as much as a third of the miracle (1.9/6.11). If instead the miracle is defined as the difference between current GDP per capita growth—a transitional rate where population dynamics matter—and the estimated steady state of 2 percent—when population is also in steady state, then population dynamics can explain almost half of the miracle (1.9/(6.11−2)). In South East Asia, where the fertility decline took place a little later and the infant mortality decline was a little less dramatic, population dynamics still accounts for 0.9 to 1.8 points of economic growth, or, again, as much as half of their (less impressive) miracle (1.8/3.8). In South Asia, the incipient demographic transition accounts for only 0.4 to 1.3 percentage points of economic growth, but still as much as three-quarters of a poor growth performance (1.3/1.7). These results are fully consistent with Paul Krugman's assertion that the East Asian miracle was driven mainly by high rates of labor force growth and accumulation (Krugman 1994).[6]

---

[6] Krugman relied on the relatively low rates of total factor productivity growth estimated by Alwyn Young (1994a, 1994b) and Jong-Il Kim and Lawrence Lau (1994), but a recent study has found much higher total factor productivity growth rates (Hsieh 1998).

Table 5.4. *Contribution of Demographic Change to Past Economic Growth, 1965–1990*

Regions	Average growth rate of real GDP per capita, 1965–1990	Average growth rate of population, 1965–90	Average growth rate of economically active population, 1965–90	Average growth rate of dependent population, 1965–90	Estimated contribution, 1965–90 (columns correspond to specifications in Table 5.3)			
					(1)	(2)	(3)	(4)
Asia	3.33	2.32	2.76	1.56	1.04	1.64	0.86	0.73
East Asia	6.11	1.58	2.39	0.25	1.71	1.87	1.60	1.37
Southeast Asia	3.80	2.36	2.90	1.66	1.25	1.81	1.07	0.91
South Asia	1.71	2.27	2.51	1.95	0.66	1.34	0.48	0.41
Africa	0.97	2.64	2.62	2.92	0.14	1.10	−0.07	−0.06
Europe	2.83	0.53	0.73	0.15	0.43	0.52	0.39	0.33
South America	0.85	2.06	2.50	1.71	1.03	1.54	0.87	0.74
North America	1.61	1.72	2.13	1.11	0.94	1.34	0.81	0.69
Oceania	1.97	1.57	1.89	1.00	0.74	1.14	0.62	0.53

Note: These averages are unweighted country averages. Estimated contribution is created by multiplying the coefficients on GEAP6590 and GPOP6590 by the regional averages for each of the reported specifications.

Source: Bloom and Williamson (1998: table 7).

Compared with the rest of the world, East Asia was the largest beneficiary of the population dynamics coming from the demographic transition. The magnitudes for South East Asia and MENA were next in size. Europe received only a small post-baby boom boost of 0.3 to 0.5 percentage points. Even Latin America's demographic impact, 0.7 to 1.5 percentage points, was smaller than East Asia's, although the demographic contribution there was almost identical to that of Asia as a whole.

The future will look quite different. Table 5.5 offers a forecast based on the coefficients of the estimated growth model and the UN demographic projections up to the year 2025. In East Asia, the GDP per capital growth attributable to demographic influences is projected to be *negative* between 1990 and 2025, declining from a positive gain of 1.4 to 1.9 percentage points between 1965 and 1990 to a *loss* of 0.1 to 0.4 percentage points up to 2025, a projected retardation of 1.5 to 2.3 percentage points due solely to demographic forces. The demographically induced growth loss is projected to be even bigger in some parts of East Asia. If nothing happens to offset them, demographic events will induce a 2.0 to 2.4 percentage point decline in Hong Kong's GDP per capita growth rate, a 2.5 to 3.0 percentage point decline in Singapore, a 1.9 to 2.2 percentage point decline in Korea, and a 0.9 to 1.1 percentage point decline in Japan. In contrast, South Asia should see a 0.8 to 1.4 percentage point growth rate *gain* as it leaves the 'burden' stage of the demographic transition entirely and enters the 'gift' stage, the biggest gains being for Pakistan and Bangladesh. South East Asia should register a little smaller demographic gift (0.6 to 1.1 percentage points) with a lot of variance across countries in the region: the biggest gainer will be the Philippines while the biggest losers will be Malaysia and Thailand.

Demographic divergence contributed to Asian economic divergence over the past quarter century, South Asia falling behind East Asia. However, demographic convergence should contribute to economic convergence over the next 30 years in the region. Figure 5.5 offers a stylized characterization of those events.

CHANNELS OF IMPACT: DEMOGRAPHY AND LABOR FORCE GROWTH

How much of the fast-growth transition in Asia can be explained by the impact of demography on labor inputs? Some answers have already been reported elsewhere which are only summarized here (Bloom and Williamson 1997: table 6). Our interest, of course, is in labor inputs *per person* (working hours per capita, or H/P), and its growth can be separated into three parts: changing hours worked per worker (H/L); changing labor participation rates among those of working age (L/EAP); and changing shares of the population of working age (EAP/P), the pure demographic effect. Thus, per capita hours worked can be decomposed into $H/P = (H/L)(L/EAP)(EAP/P)$.

How much of fast Asian economic growth can be explained by a rise in labor inputs per capita due to purely demographic forces? Between 1965 and 1975, very little. Between 1975 and 1990, quite a lot. The rising working-age share served to augment labor-input-per-capita growth by about 0.75 percentage points per annum. This implies about 0.4 percentage points of Asia's transitional growth since 1975 explained

Table 5.5. *Contribution of Demographic Change to Future Economic Growth, 1990–2025*

Regions	Projected growth rate of population, 1990–2025	Projected growth rate of economically active population, 1990–2025	Projected growth rate of dependent population, 1990–2025	Estimated contribution, 1990–2025 (columns correspond to specifications in Table 5.3)			
				(1)	(2)	(3)	(4)
Asia	1.36	1.61	0.99	0.61	0.99	0.50	0.43
East Asia	0.43	0.20	0.87	−0.40	−0.14	−0.44	−0.38
Southeast Asia	1.29	1.66	0.63	0.83	1.10	0.73	0.62
South Asia	1.65	2.11	0.90	1.02	1.38	0.90	0.77
Africa	2.40	2.78	1.88	0.98	1.63	0.73	0.68
Europe	0.17	−0.004	0.48	−0.32	−0.16	−0.34	−0.29
South America	1.50	1.87	0.94	0.82	1.15	0.71	0.60
North America	1.28	1.33	1.21	0.21	0.645	0.11	0.10
Oceania	1.08	0.93	1.37	−0.22	0.24	−0.31	−0.26

Note: These averages are unweighted country averages. Estimated contribution is created by multiplying the coefficients on GEAP6590 and GPOP6590 by the regional averages for each of the reported specifications.

Source: Bloom and Williamson (1998: table 8).

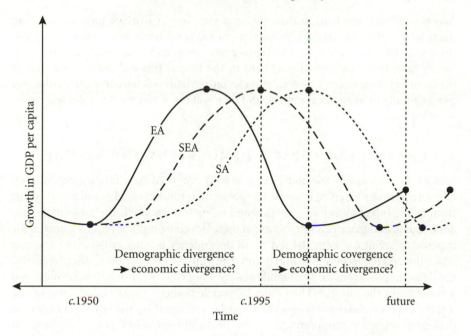

Figure 5.5. *Stylized Model of Economic Growth and the Demographic Transition in Asia*
Source: Bloom and Williamson (1998: figure 7).

(or about a tenth of GDP per capita growth). The figures are much bigger for East Asia: labor-input-per-capita growth due to pure demography was more than 1.1 percentage points per annum, equivalent to 0.6 percentage points of economic growth explained. Since the previous section estimated that demographic forces could account for 1.4 to 1.9 percentage points of the East Asian miracle, their impact on labor inputs per capita must account for about 30 to 40 percent of the total demographic effect. How much of faster growth in East Asia, compared with the OECD, has been due simply to these demographic labor-input-per-capita forces? The answer is almost 0.5 percentage points, or about four-tenths of the gap between East Asia and the OECD.

These demographic labor-input-per-capita forces do not, of course, exhaust all influences on labor supply, nor do they exhaust all demographic transitional influences on the growth rate, but are they likely to persist in the future? It depends on where in Asia we look. The fall in the pure demographic effect will be a huge 1.13 percentage points per annum in East Asia, causing a growth retardation there of about 0.6 percentage points. In sharp contrast, it will raise South Asia's GDP per capita growth rate, although not by much. The demographic influence on labor inputs will by itself foster GDP per capita convergence between the poor South and the rich East, favoring growth in the South by 0.7 percentage points. Whether this potential will be realized by South Asia is, of course, another matter entirely.

Will these purely demographic contributions to growth retardation be offset by Asians working harder, and by their more active participation in the labor force? No.

Asians will work less hard as their incomes rise, just as workers have done before them in the more industrially mature countries. And fewer prime-age Asians will work since they will be able to afford earlier retirement and longer spells of schooling. In any case, if Asians work just as hard in the future, this will reduce that part of the labor-input-per-capita-growth effect to zero. Asians will have to work harder and harder simply to maintain the effect, and they will not if history is any guide.

CHANNELS OF IMPACT: DEMOGRAPHY AND SAVINGS

Almost 40 years ago, Coale and Hoover (1958) proposed their famous dependency hypothesis. It was based on a simple but powerful intuition: rapid population growth from falling infant and child mortality and rising fertility swells the ranks of dependent young, and that demographic event increases consumption requirements at the expense of savings: eventually, the youth dependency burden evolves into a young adult glut and the resulting savings boom contributes to an economic miracle; finally, the demographic transition is manifested by a big elderly burden, low savings, and a deflation of the miracle. The Coale–Hoover hypothesis suggests that some of the impressive rise in Asian savings rates can be explained by the equally impressive decline in dependency burdens, that some of the difference in savings rates between sluggish South Asia and (what used to be) booming East Asia can be explained by their different dependency burdens, and that as the youth dependency rate falls in South Asia and as the elderly dependency rate rises in East Asia over the next three decades, some of the savings rate gaps between the two regions should tend to vanish.

When faced with time series evidence, the Coale and Hoover (1958) hypothesis has had its ups and downs. Nathaniel Leff's (1969) study appeared to place the youth-dependency hypothesis on a solid empirical footing. But later research by Arthur Goldberger (1973), Rati Ram (1982), and others failed to confirm the dependency hypothesis, and thus cast doubt on the validity of the empirical methods employed in the earlier studies. Theoretical developments also seemed to shake the foundations of the dependency hypothesis. James Tobin's (1967) life-cycle model held that the national savings rate should *increase* with faster population growth. The reason is simple at least in that model: faster population growth tilts the age distribution toward young, saving households and away from older, dissaving ones. The representative-agent elaboration of Robert Solow's neoclassical growth model pointed in the same direction as Tobin's, with faster population growth raising savings rates in response to augmented investment demand (Solow 1956). However, the models just described failed to deal adequately with the dynamics implied by the demographic transition. The 'age tilt' in Tobin's steady-state model is owing to the fact that it describes a world restricted to active adults and retired dependents; it would imply a very different tilt if youth dependency were also acknowledged. Similarly, the neoclassical growth models assume fixed labor participation rates, and by implication assume no change in the dependency rate, exactly what one would assume in a model of steady state behavior, but inconsistent with the facts of demographic transition. In effect, both models sacrifice the rich population dynamics implicit in Coale and Hoover's predictions about the demographic *transition*.

The tension between the dependency rate and life-cycle models was addressed in the 1980s by Maxwell Fry and Andrew Mason (1982) and Mason alone (1987, 1988). These authors developed what they called a 'variable rate-of-growth effect' model to link youth dependency and national savings rates. Their new model rests on the premise that a decline in the youth dependency rate may induce changes in the *timing* of life-cycle consumption. If consumption is shifted from child-rearing to later, non-child-rearing stages of the life cycle, aggregate savings rise with a strength that depends directly on the growth rate of national income. As a result, the model argues that the savings rate depends on the *product* of the youth-dependency ratio and the growth rate of national income (the 'growth-tilt effect'), as well as on the dependency ratio itself (the 'level effect').

Under the aegis of this new model, the dependency hypothesis has enjoyed something of a renaissance. The Coale–Hoover intuition has evolved into explicit economic models that, now revised, do very well in accounting for savings in macro time series. Almost all of recent analysis of late twentieth century macro data confirm the Coale–Hoover effects (Masson 1990; Webb and Zia 1990; Collins 1991; Williamson 1993; Higgins 1994, 1998; Kang 1994; Kelley and Schmidt 1995, 1996; Harrington 1996; Lee *et al.* 1997; Taylor 1995), and so does analysis of late nineteenth century macro data (Taylor and Williamson 1994).

The augmented versions of the life-cycle model lie at the heart of these measured Coale and Hoover effects on savings and accumulation. The fact that the life-cycle model receives weak or no support in household cross-sections (e.g. Deaton and Paxson 1997) needs to be reconciled in future research, but some will be offered in a conference volume edited by Andrew Mason (forthcoming). I also will offer some comments on the reconciliation at the end of this chapter.

The biggest macro impacts have been estimated by Matthew Higgins and the present author (1996, 1997) and those results are used in what follows. Higgins and Williamson estimate the effect of changes in population age distribution on changes, not levels, in the savings rate as it deviated around the 1950–92 mean. Thus, East Asia's savings rate was 8.4 percentage points above its 1950–92 average in 1990–92 due to its transition to a much lighter dependency burden. Similarly, East Asia's savings rate in 1970–74 was 5.2 percentage points below its 1950–92 average due to the heavy dependency rate burden at that time. The total demographic swing was an enormous 13.6 percentage points, accounting for *all* of the total rise in the savings rate in East Asia over these 20 years. The figures for South East Asia are similar, but not quite so dramatic. South East Asia's savings rate was 7.9 percentage points higher in 1990–92 than its 1950–92 average due to its lighter dependency burden late in the twentieth century. And South East Asia's savings rate was 3.6 percentage points lower in 1970–74 due to the heavier burden at that time. The total demographic swing was 11.5 percentage points, a smaller figure than for East Asia but still accounting for *all* of the total rise in the savings rate in South East Asia after 1970. The region with the slowest demographic transition has been South Asia, so the far more modest changes in the savings rate there are predictable.

To the extent that domestic savings constrain accumulation, falling dependency rates have played an important role in East Asia's economic miracle since 1970. Indeed, assuming the increase in investment to have been equal to the increase in savings—an assumption rejected in the next section, and assuming a capital–output ratio of 4, it follows that the demographic impact raised accumulation rates in East Asia by 3.4 percentage points, thus augmenting GDP per capita growth by something like 1.5 percentage points. Given that demographic forces have already been estimated to have raised East Asian growth rates by as much as 1.9 percentage points, it looks as if about three-quarters of this is due to accumulation responses. The figure is too high, of course, due to the assumption that domestic savings fully constrained investment.

CHANNELS OF IMPACT: DEMOGRAPHY, INVESTMENT, AND FOREIGN CAPITAL DEPENDENCE

To the extent that East Asia was able to exploit global capital markets over the past quarter century, domestic saving supply is far less relevant than investment demand in determining accumulation performance. As the surviving children of a baby boom or a child mortality decline become young adults, the increase in new workers raises the demand for investment in infrastructure to get them to work, to equip them at work, and to house them as they move away from their parents.

When Matthew Higgins and I (1996, 1997) tested this augmented Coale–Hoover hypothesis on Asia's past, it appeared that changing age distributions had the predicted impact. For East Asia, demographic effects have served to raise investment shares by 8.8 percentage points since the late 1960s. Using the same assumptions made in the previous section on savings, this implies a 1 percentage point rise in the rate of GDP per capita growth. In short, demographic forces contributed 0.6 percentage points to the East Asian miracle via labor inputs per capita and 1 percentage point via capital accumulation per capita, roughly consistent with the total demographic impact estimated using macro growth equations, 1.6 versus 1.4 to 1.9 percentage points. Thus, labor force growth responses might account for about a third of the positive demographic contribution to the miracle (0.6/1.9), accumulation responses for about a half (1/1.9), and other forces for the small remainder.

The interesting question, however, is whether the demographically induced savings responses are less or greater than demographically induced investment responses, and when. Using the parameter estimates for the demographic variables in both the savings and investment equations for Asia, Figure 5.6 reveals the relationship between age distributions and the three national income shares that matter to us here: savings, investment, and the current account balance. The coefficients plotted there are the change in each of the three shares associated with a unit increase in the log age shares, that is, they assess the impact of changes in the age share *ceteris paribus*. Figure 5.6

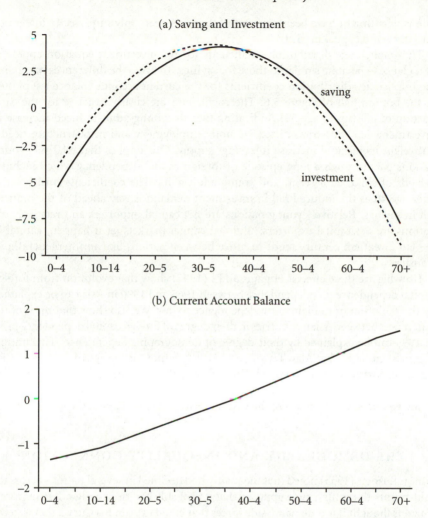

Figure 5.6. *Age Distribution Coefficients on Savings, Investment, and Current Account Balance*

Note: The age distribution coefficients show the change in the national savings rate, etc., associated with a unit increase in the corresponding log age shares. A unit increase means that the age share rises by the factor e.

Source: Higgins and Williamson (1997: figure 1).

shows clearly that youth and old-age dependency have a depressing effect on savings, with the largest impact for ages 0 to 10 and ages above 64. Moreover, the coefficients appear to be consistent with the 'hump' savings pattern predicted by the life-cycle hypothesis, attaining their highest values during mid-life. But they reach a peak rather early in Asia, at age 35 to 39, declining sharply thereafter so as to become negative by age 55 to 59. Yet, the rather young 'center of gravity' found for the savings rate is what might have been expected if Asia has been only imperfectly integrated into the world capital market.[7]

The implicit age distribution coefficients for the investment equation appear at first glance to be quite similar to those for savings. To bring the differences into relief, the implicit age distribution coefficients for the current account balance are plotted in the bottom half of Figure 5.6. The coefficients are clearly negative for the early portion of life (up to age 39), indicating that the young-adult-induced increase in investment demand (transmitted via both employment and infrastructure needs) outweighs its induced increase in savings supply. This implies that relatively young nations pass through a long episode of foreign capital dependency which includes periods of child, adolescent, and young adult gluts. The coefficients turn positive after age 40 as the induced fall in investment demand is way ahead of the induced fall in savings. Relatively young nations are net capital importers and relatively old nations are net capital exporters: if global capital markets let it happen, capital in the late twentieth century tends to move between nations like an intergenerational transfer.

How big are these effects? Higgins and I (1997) show that evolution from foreign capital dependence to independence between 1965 and 1990 in Asia can be explained by the evolution from high youth dependence to low. We also show that most of the differences between Asian countries in their degree of foreign capital dependence prior to 1990 can be explained by their degree of demographic dependence. This finding is consistent with what Alan Taylor and I (1994) found for the age of massive British capital exports just prior to World War I: almost all of that transfer was explained by low demographic dependence in mature Britain and high demographic dependence in the young New World where the vast majority of British capital flowed.

THE DEMOGRAPHY AND INEQUALITY CONNECTION

Simon Kuznets (1955) noted that inequality had declined in several nations across the mid-twentieth century, and supposed that it probably had risen earlier. Furthermore, Kuznets thought it was demand-side forces that could explain his Curve: that is, technological and structural change tended to favor the demand for capital and skills, while saving on unskilled labor. These labor-saving conditions eventually moderated as the rate of technological change (catching up) and the rate of structural change (urbanization and industrialization) both slowed down. Eventually, the labor-saving stopped,

---

[7] Savings supply and investment demand are separately identified in the empirical models developed here only to the extent that countries can borrow and lend on the international capital market without constraint and at a given world interest rate. In the absence of perfect capital mobility, the estimates for savings will reflect a mix of the separate demographic influences on both savings and investment—a lesson made clear by the Higgins–Williamson (1996) simulation model. In this setting, an increase in the share of young adults, who presumably save little, might lead to an increase in the equilibrium quantity of savings by causing an outward shift in the investment demand schedule. Similarly, an increase in the share of the middle-aged might actually reduce savings if any outward shift in savings supply is more than offset by an inward shift in investment demand.

and other, more egalitarian forces were allowed to have their impact. This is what might be called the *strong version* of the Kuznets Curve hypothesis, that income inequality first rises and then declines with development. The *strong version* of the hypothesis is strong because it is unconditioned by any other effects. Demand does it all.

The *weak version* of the Kuznets Curve hypothesis is more sophisticated and should have greater appeal. It argues that these demand forces can be offset or reinforced by any of the remaining Big Three conditional forces.

1. Big Conditional Force One   The forces of some demographic transition at home may glut the labor market with the young and impecunious early in development (as has been true of East Asia, Latin America, the Middle East, and North Africa since the 1970s), reinforcing the rise in inequality. Or emigration to some rich OECD or oil-rich country may have the opposite effect, making the young and impecunious more scarce. It depends on the size of the demographic transition, and it depends on whether labor-scarce parts of the world economy are willing to accommodate mass emigration from the labor-abundant parts (as they did in the late nineteenth century) or whether they are unwilling to do so (as they do today, with the possible exception of the United States).

2. Big Conditional Force Two   A public policy committed to high enrollment rates and to the eradication of illiteracy may greatly augment the supply of skilled and literate labor, eroding the premium on skills and wage inequality, or at least keeping them from rising in the face of the upswing on some derived-demand-induced Kuznets Curve (as was apparently true during the Asian miracle). Or a country might not take this liberal policy stance, allowing instead the skill premium to soar, and wage inequality with it (as has been true of many Latin America and African countries).

3. Big Conditional Force Three   Finally, a commitment to liberal trade policies may allow an invasion of labor-intensive products in rich OECD countries, thus eroding the incomes of those at the bottom of the income hierarchy. Or, governments may protect those interests (as they did between World War I and the 1960s). And a commitment to liberal trade policies in poor countries may allow the export of labor-intensive goods, thus boosting the incomes of common labor at the bottom. Or, they may protect the interests of skilled labor and capital instead (as they did under the ubiquitous import-substitution policies from the 1940s to the 1970s).

The *strong version* of the Kuznets Curve has gotten all the attention, while the *weak version* has gotten little. A phalanx of economists, led by Hollis Chenery and Montek Ahluwalia at the World Bank (Chenery *et al.* 1974; Ahluwalia 1976), looked for unconditional Kuznets Curves in a large sample of countries, as in Figure 5.7. The inequality statistic used by Ahluwalia was simply the income share of the top 20 percent. Based on this 60-country cross-section from the 1960s and 1970s, it looked very much as if there was a Kuznets Curve. True, the more robust portion of the Curve lay to the right; income inequality clearly falls with the development of economically mature economies. The left tail of the Curve appeared to be far less robust; there was enormous variance in inequality experience during earlier stages of

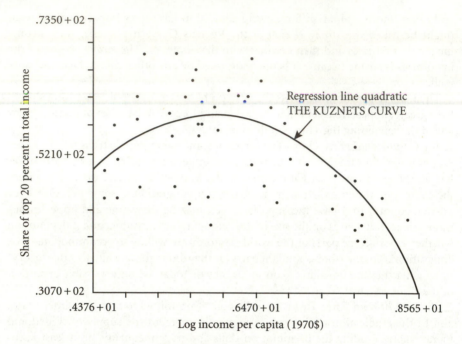

Figure 5.7. *The Kuznets Curve*

Note: Based on international cross-section from the 1960s and 1970s (Ahluwalia 1976: table 8, pp. 340–1).

development. This *strong version* of the Kuznets Curve also seemed to be supported by what historical data was available at that time, some of it reported in Figure 5.8 and some it reported in other sources for the United States (Williamson and Lindert 1980; Lindert 1997) and Britain (Williamson 1985; Lindert 1997).

The attack on the *strong version* of the Kuznets Curve was based right from the start on the quality of the income distribution evidence. The earlier World Bank database was poor: there was simply very little consistency as to how income was measured, how the recipient unit was defined, and how comprehensive the coverage of the units was. Furthermore, it turns out that the Kuznets Curve disappears from Figure 5.7 when one adds regional dummy variables for Asia and Latin America. The latter tends to have higher inequality, and in the 1960s, before the Asian miracle, the Latins were located closer to the middle of the income per capita ranking. The former tends to have lower inequality, the Asians were located closer to the bottom of the income per capita ranking in the 1960s.

Thanks to the recent efforts of Klaus Deininger and Lyn Squire (1996), we now have an excellent inequality data base for 108 countries across various stretches of time between the 1950s and the 1990s, yielding 682 'high quality' observations. Even with this new data base, however, Deininger and Squire were unable to offer any evidence supporting the Kuznets Curve that Ahluwalia saw 25 years ago in Figure 5.6. Once

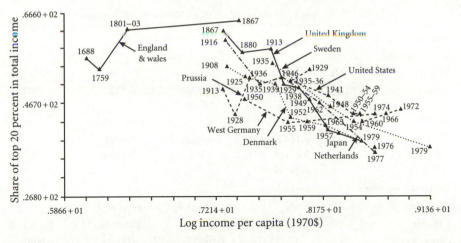

Figure 5.8. *The Kuznets Curve*

Note: Based on historical time series from six OECD countries (Lindert and Williamson 1985: figure 2).

again, the *strong version* of the Kuznets Curve hypothesis fails. While some countries may conform to the Kuznets Curve in the late twentieth century, just as many do not.

But for which countries does the *strong version* of the hypothesis fail, and why? When it does fail is it because demand is being overwhelmed by some combination of the other three forces, or is it that the hypothesized demand forces are absent as often as not? Table 5.6 offers some early and tentative results from an ongoing research project with Matthew Higgins (1999) which uses the Deininger and Squire data. The dependent variable is the Gini coefficient of incomes. The independent variables include a measure of resource abundance, arable land per capita (AGAREA). Resource-abundant economies tend to have unequal incomes. The independent variables also include SWARNER. This is taken from Jeffrey Sachs and Andrew Warner (1995), who argue that the variable measures 'openness'. Since their article appeared, critics have pointed out that SWARNER is dominated instead by whether the country is or was socialist, being 0 if it was. The positive coefficient simply tells us that capitalist countries have more unequal incomes, a result even Ahluwalia was able to document 30 years ago. The other independent variables represent the Big Three listed above. First, education supply is proxied by secondary school enrollment rates (SECENRR). Large educational supplies tend to lower inequality, as predicted. Secondly, demand is proxied by GDP per worker (RGDPW), following convention. The (*weak version* of the) Kuznets Curve hypothesis appears to be alive and well, hidden behind the other Big Conditional Forces contributing to inequality.

Thirdly, and most relevant to this chapter, demographic effects are measured by the share of the adult population between ages 29 and 60 (MATURE). There are two ideas here. First, poor people tend to be either young or old. Secondly, people in fat cohorts tend to get low rewards, and when those fat working-adult cohorts tend

Table 5.6. *Demography and Four Other Determinants of Inequality*

Analysis of variance

Source	DF	Sum of Squares	Mean Square	F Value	Prob > F
Model	6	4.27663	0.71277	26.342	0.0001
Error	147	3.97757	0.02706		
C total	153	8.25420			

Root MSE		0.16449	R-Square	0.5181	
Dep Mean		3.64159	Adj R-SQ	0.4984	
C.V.		4.51710			

Parameter Estimates

Variable	DF	Parameter Estimate	Standard Error	Test for Hypothesis Parameter = 0	Prob > T
INTERCEP	1	4.341497	0.092271	47.052	0.0001
RGDPW	1	0.000035608	0.000006505	5.474	0.0001
RGDPW2	1	$-8.73002E-10$	$1.818821E-10$	-4.800	0.0001
AGAREA	1	0.023945	0.008835	2.710	0.0075
SECENRR	1	-0.003494	0.000868	-4.027	0.0001
SWARNER	1	0.067657	0.035895	1.885	0.0614
MATURE	1	-2.946745	0.378924	-7.777	0.0001

Notes: Inequality data: Deininger and Squire (1996). Dependent variable: Gini. Independent variables: RGDPW = log real GDP per worker; MATURE = [age 30–59]/[age 15–69]; AGAREA = arable land per capita; SECENRR = secondary school enrollment rate; SWARNER = Sachs and Warner (1995) 'open' economy proxy.

Source: Higgins and Williamson 1999.

to lie in the middle of the age-earnings curve where incomes are highest, the age-earnings curve tends to be flattened, and inequality is moderated. When instead the fat cohorts are young or old working adults, the age-earnings curve will rise to and fall from its peak more steeply, and inequality is augmented. This demographic hypothesis has a long tradition in the United States starting with the entry of the baby boomers into the labor market when they faced such poor prospects (Freeman 1979; Welch 1979; Murphy and Welch 1992; Macunovich 1998). Table 5.6 confirms that what has been true of the United States has also been true worldwide: fat mature working-adult cohorts tend to lower inequality while fat young working-adult and/or old working-adult cohorts tend to raise inequality. These inequality effects are not permanent, of course, since they disappear in demographic steady state. But during the industrial revolutions and demographic transitions in the late twentieth century, demography was the strongest force at work accounting for differences in inequality across countries and over time.

A BRIEF CODA

This chapter argues that the primary effect of a demographic transition is to change the age distribution of the population during the transition, that is, to change the center of gravity. If the transition is big enough, the effect on economic variables can also be big. These effects are, of course, transitional rather than permanent, but if the transition spreads over a half century or more, who cares? The economic effects reported in this chapter deal with growth, accumulation, foreign capital dependence, and inequality. Over the past half century, these have been big.

Each of these findings can, and have been, attacked. The unit of observation in the data explored here is in all cases a country during some year. The analysis is macro. Furthermore, the findings are motivated by a strong commitment to versions of the life-cycle model. Since micro data have not been very kind to the life-cycle model, future work will have to reconcile these two conflicting streams of empirical research. Yet, the conflict may be more apparent than real. After all, the micro literature has nothing to say about growth, nor does it allow demographic events to influence commodity and factor markets. Until the micro literature can make these links, I doubt that it can speak with great confidence to the macro issues which drive policy.

References

Abramovitz, Moses. 1986. 'Catching Up, Forging Ahead and Falling Behind'. *Journal of Economic History*. 46: 38–406.

Ahluwalia, Montek. 1976. 'Inequality, Poverty and Development'. *Journal of Development Economics*. 3 (4): 307–42.

Asian Development Bank. 1997. *Emerging Asia*. Manila: Asian Development Bank.

Barro, Robert J. 1991. 'Economic Growth in a Cross Section of Countries'. *Quarterly Journal of Economics*. 106: 407–43.

Barro, Robert J., and Xavier Sala-i-Martin. 1995. *Economic Growth*. New York: McGraw Hill.

Baumol, William J. 1986. 'Productivity Growth, Convergence and Welfare: What the Long-Run Data Show'. *American Economic Review*. 76: 1072–85.

Bloom, David, and Jeffrey G. Williamson. 1997. 'Demographic Transitions, Human Resource Development, and Economic Miracles in Emerging Asia'. In J. Sachs and D. Bloom, eds., *Emerging Asia*. Manila: Asian Development Bank.

———— 1998. 'Demographic Transitions and Economic Miracles in Emerging Asia'. *World Bank Economic Review*. 12(3): 419–55.

Boulier, Brian. 1986. 'Family Planning Programs and Contraceptive Availability: Their Effects on Contraceptive Use and Fertility'. In N. Birdsall *et al.*, eds., *The Effects of Family Planning Programs on Fertility in the Developing World*. World Bank Staff Working Paper No. 677.

Caldwell, John C., and Bruce K. Caldwell. 1996. 'Asia's Demographic Transition'. Background paper for the Emerging Asia project.

Chenery, Hollis B. *et al.* 1974. *Redistribution with Growth*. London: Oxford University Press.

Coale, Ansley J., and Edgar Hoover. 1958. *Population Growth and Economic Development in Low-Income Countries*. Princeton, NJ: Princeton University Press.

——— and Susan C. Watkins. 1986. *The Decline of Fertility in Europe*. Princeton, NJ: Princeton University Press.

Collins, Susan. 1991. 'Saving Behavior in Ten Developing Countries'. In D. Bernheim and J. Shoven, eds., *National Saving and Economic Performance*. Chicago: University of Chicago Press.

Deaton, Angus, and Christina Paxson. 1997. 'The Effects of Economic and Population Growth on National Saving and Inequality'. *Demography*. 34: 97–114.

Deininger, Klaus, and Lyn Squire. 1996. 'A New Data Set Measuring Income Inequality'. *World Bank Economic Review*. 10 (3): 565–91.

Feeney, Griffith, and Andrew Mason. 1997. 'Population in East Asia'. Paper presented to the Conference on Population and the East Asian Miracle, Honolulu, Hawaii (January 7–10).

Fogel, Robert W. 1994. 'Economic Growth, Population Theory, and Physiology: The Bearing of Long-Term Processes on the Making of Economic Policy'. *American Economic Review*. 84: 369–95.

Freeman, Richard. 1979. 'The Effects of Demographic Factors on Age-Earnings Profiles'. *Journal of Human Resources*. 14 (Summer): 289–318.

Fry, Maxwell, and Andrew Mason. 1982. 'The Variable Rate-of-Growth Effect in the Life Cycle Saving Model: Children, Capital Inflows, Interest and Growth in a New Specification of the Life-Cycle Model Applied to Seven Asian Developing Countries'. *Economic Inquiry*. 20: 426–42.

Goldberger, Arthur. 1973. 'Dependency Rates and Savings Rates: Further Comment'. *American Economic Review*. 63: 232–33.

Harrington, Frank. 1996. 'Saving Transitions in Southeast Asia'. Unpublished paper. Manila: Asian Development Bank.

Hatton, Timothy, and Jeffrey G. Williamson. 1998. *The Age of Mass Migration: An Economic Analysis*. New York: Oxford University Press.

Higgins, Matthew. 1994. 'The Demographic Determinants of Savings, Investment, and International Capital Flows'. Ph.D. Dissertation. Cambridge, MA: Harvard University.

—— 1998. 'The Demographic Determinants of Savings, Investment and International Capital Flows'. *International Economic Review*. 39: 343–70.

—— and Jeffrey G. Williamson. 1996. 'Asian Demography and Foreign Capital Dependence'. NBER Working Paper No. 5560. Cambridge, MA: National Bureau of Economic Research.

—— —— 1997. 'Age Structure Dynamics in Asia and Dependence on Foreign Capital'. *Population and Development Review*. 23: 261–93.

—— —— 1999. 'Explaining Inequality the World Around: Cohort Size, Kuznets Curves and Openness, NBER Working Paper no. 7224. Cambridge, MA: National Bureau of Economic Research.

Hsieh, Chang-Tai. 1998. 'What Explains the Industrial Revolution in East Asia? Evidence from Factor Markets'. Unpublished paper, Department of Economics, University of California, Berkeley.

Kang, Kenneth. 1994. 'Why Did Koreans Save So Little and Why Do They Now Save So Much?' *International Economic Journal*. 8: 99–111.

Kelley, Allen C., and Robert M. Schmidt. 1995. 'Aggregate Population and Economic Growth Correlations: The Role of the Components of Demographic Change'. *Demography*. 32: 543–55.

—— —— 1996. 'Savings, Dependency and Development'. *Journal of Population Economics*. 9: 365–86.

Kim, Jong-II and Lawrence Lau. 1994. 'The Sources of Economic Growth of the East Asian Newly Industrialized Countries'. *Journal of the Japanese and International Economies*. 8: 235–71.

Knack, Stephen, and Philip Keefer. 1995. 'Institutions and Economic Performance: Cross-Country Tests Using Alternative Institutional Measures'. *Economics and Politics*. 7: 207–27.

Krugman, Paul. 1994. 'The Myth of Asia's Miracle'. *Foreign Affairs*. 73: 62–78.

Kuznets, Simon. 1954. 'Economic Growth and Income Inequality'. *American Economic Review*. 45 (1): 1–28.

Lee, Ronald, Andrew Mason, and Timothy Miller. 1997. 'Saving, Wealth, and the Demographic Transition in East Asia'. Paper presented at the Conference on Population and the Asian Economic Miracle, East-West Center, Honolulu (January 7–10).

Leff, Nathaniel. 1969. 'Dependency Rates and Savings Rates'. *American Economic Review*. 59: 886–96.

Lindert, Peter H. 1997. 'Three Centuries of Inequality in Britain and America'. In A. B. Atkinson and F. Bourguignon, eds., *Handbook of Income Distribution*. Amsterdam: North Holland.

Lindert, Peter H., and Jeffrey G. Williamson. 1985. 'Growth, Equality and History'. *Explorations in Economic History*. 22 (4): 341–77.

Macunovich, Diane J. 1998. 'Relative Cohort Size and Inequality in the United States'. *American Economic Review*. 88 (2): 259–64.

Mankiw, Greg N., David Romer, and David N. Weil. 1992. 'A Contribution to the Empirics of Economic Growth'. *Quarterly Journal of Economics*. 107: 407–37.

Mason, Andrew. 1987. 'National Saving Rates and Population Growth: A New Model and New Evidence'. In D. G. Johnson and R. Lee, eds., *Population Growth and Economic Development: Issues and Evidence*. Madison, WI: University of Wisconsin Press.

—— 1988. 'Saving, Economic Growth and Demographic Change'. *Population and Development Review*. 14: 113–44.

—— ed. forthcoming. *Population and the East Asian Economic Miracle*. Honolulu: East-West Center.

Masson, Paul. 1990. 'Long-term Macroeconomic Effects of Aging Populations'. *Finance and Development*. 27: 6–9.

Murphy, Kevin, and Finis Welch. 1992. 'The Structure of Wages'. *Quarterly Journal of Economics*. 107 (1): 285–326.

Ram, Rati. 1982. 'Dependency Rates and Aggregate Savings: A New International Cross-Section Study'. *American Economic Review*. 72: 537–44.

Sachs, Jeffrey, Steven Radelet, and Jong-Wha Lee. 1997. 'Economic Growth in Asia'. In J. Sachs and D. Bloom, eds., *Emerging Asia*. Manila: Asian Development Bank.

—— and Andrew Warner. 1995. 'Economic Reform and the Process of Global Integration'. *Brookings Papers on Economic Activity*. 1: 1–118.

Solow, Robert. 1956. 'A Contribution to the Theory of Economic Growth'. *Quarterly Journal of Economics*. 70: 65–94.

Taylor, Alan. 1995. 'Debt, Dependence and the Demographic Transition: Latin America into the Next Century'. *World Development*. 23: 869–79.

—— and Jeffrey G. Williamson. 1994. 'Capital Flows to the New World as an Intergenerational Transfer'. *Journal of Political Economy*. 102: 348–69.

Tobin, James. 1967. 'Life-Cycle Savings and Balanced Economic Growth'. In William Fellner, ed., *Ten Essays in the Tradition of Irving Fischer*. New York: Wiley Press.

United Nations. 1991. *Global Estimates and Projections of Populations by Age and Sex*. New York: United Nations.

Webb, Steven, and Heidi Zia. 1990. 'Lower Birth Rates = Higher Saving in LDCS'. *Finance and Development*. 27: 12–14.

Welch, Finis. 1979. 'Effects of Cohort Size on Earnings: The Baby Boom Babies' Financial Bust'. *Journal of Political Economy*. 87 (5): 565–97.

Williamson, Jeffrey G. 1985. *Did British Capitalism Breed Inequality?* London: George Allen and Unwin.

—— 1990. *Coping with City Growth During the British Industrial Revolution*. Cambridge: Cambridge University Press.

—— 1993. 'Human Capital Deepening, Inequality, and Demographic Events Along the Asia Pacific Rim'. In G. Jones, N. Ogawa, and J. G. Williamson, eds., *Human Resources and Development Along the Asia-Pacific Rim*. Oxford: Oxford University Press.

—— 1997. 'Globalization and Inequality: Past and Present'. *World Bank Research Observer*. 12: 117–35.

—— 1998. 'Growth, Distribution and Demography: Some Lessons from History'. *Explorations in Economic History*. 35: 241–71.

—— and Peter H. Lindert. 1980. *American Inequality: A Macroeconomic History*. New York: Academic Press.

—— and Tarik Yousef. 1998. 'Demographic Transitions and Economic Performance: Background Hypotheses and Empirical Findings in MENA'. Paper presented to the Conference on Population Challenges in the Middle East and North Africa: Towards the 21st Century, Cairo (November 2–4).

Young, Alwyn. 1994*a*. 'Lessons from the East Asian NICS: A Contrarian View'. *European Economic Review*. 38: 964–73.

—— 1994*b*. 'The Tyranny of Numbers: Confronting the Statistical Realities of Asian Growth Experience'. NBER Working Paper No. 4680. Cambridge, MA. National Bureau of Economic Research.

Yousef, Tarik. 1997. 'Demography, Capital Dependency and Growth in MENA'. Paper presented to the conference on Globalization: Challenges and Opportunities for Development in the ERF Region, Kuwait (October 18–20).

6

Saving, Wealth, and Population

RONALD D. LEE, ANDREW MASON, AND TIM MILLER

The connection between saving, population, and economic growth is most easily explained using the neoclassical growth model. Solow (1956) describes an economy in which output per worker is determined by only two variables, capital per worker and the level of technology. Assuming that technology is constant for the moment, economic growth occurs because of an increase in capital per worker or *capital-deepening*. Solow (1956) shows that the rate of capital-deepening is determined by the rate of saving *s* and the rate of population growth *n*. Formally,

$$\dot{k}_t = s y_t - n k_t, \tag{1}$$

where y_t and k_t are output and capital per effective worker, respectively, and $\dot{k}_t$ is the change in k_t per unit of time. The first term on the right-hand side of the equation is the amount of new capital being provided each period by the average worker. The second term is the amount each worker must provide in order to equip new workers at the prevailing capital–labor ratio. If saving exceeds that necessary to equip new workers, the capital–labor ratio increases, that is, capital-deepening occurs.

Given a constant saving rate and a constant population growth rate, the neoclassical model tends toward an equilibrium in which saving is just sufficient to maintain the ratio of capital per worker. The equilibrium occurs when $s y_t = n k_t$ or, in a form that is useful below, when:

$$K^e / Y^e = s/n. \tag{2}$$

If output is a constant returns to scale function of capital and labor and the elasticity of output with respect to capital is β, then equilibrium output per worker is given by:

$$y^e = (s/n)^{\beta/(1-\beta)}. \tag{3}$$

Several important implications follow from the model. First, an increase in the saving rate or a decrease in the population growth rate yields a higher equilibrium capital–output ratio and a higher equilibrium output per worker. Secondly, an increase in the saving rate or a decline in the population growth rate produces a *transitory* increase in the growth rate of output per worker. Thirdly, neither the saving rate nor the population growth rate influences the *rate of growth* of output per worker once equilibrium is established.[1]

Introducing technological change into the model leaves these conclusions intact. In equilibrium, capital per worker and output per worker grow at the rate of technological change, λ. Total capital and total output grow at $\lambda + n$. The equilibrium ratio of capital to output is given by $s/(\lambda + n)$.[2]

The neoclassical model obviously abstracts from important features of the growth process. It neglects, to name a few obvious examples, development policy, the financial sector, and human resources. However, the importance of capital-deepening and the importance of understanding the underlying factors that lead to capital-deepening are borne out by many recent studies of economic growth (e.g. Harberger 1998; Young 1992; Kim and Lau 1994, 1995; World Bank 1993).

The analysis summarized below draws heavily on the experience of Taiwan and other East Asian economies. The rapid increase in capital per worker is one of the distinguishing features of the most successful economies of the post-World War II era. For four East Asian economies for which data are available the annual growth rate in capital per worker from 1965 to *circa* 1990 ranged from 6.6 percent in Thailand to 8.7 percent in Taiwan as compared with only 2.7 percent in the United States (Fig. 6.1).

Estimates of the rates of productivity growth or technological progress vary, but the observed rates of capital-deepening are at least two to three times the rate of technological progress. For example, Harberger (1998) reports total factor productivity growth rates for Taiwan, South Korea, and Thailand in the 2.4 to 3.7 percent range (p. 25). If Young's (1992) more modest estimates of productivity growth in East Asia are accurate, then capital-deepening exceeds technological progress by an even greater factor.

In the Solow framework, two sources can account for capital-deepening that is more rapid than the rate of technological progress: a rise in the saving rate or a decline in the population growth rate. Both have operated to some extent in East Asia. Trends in saving rates are shown for six East Asian economies in Figure 6.2. In 1960, South Korea, Singapore, and Indonesia had gross domestic saving less than 10 percent of gross domestic product. Saving rates in Taiwan and Thailand were below 20 percent. By the early 1990s, saving rates in the 60 to 40 percent range were typical (Fig. 6.2). Capital-deepening in Japan can also be traced to rising saving rates, but they were already quite high by 1960.[3]

Declining population growth rates have also influenced the rate of capital-deepening in East Asia, but the experience is varied. Taiwan and South Korea have both experienced sharp drops in their population growth rates in recent decades. Japan's population growth rate has dropped to near zero, although Japan did not

---

[1] Equations 1 to 3 are not defined when the population growth rate is zero; or, incorporating the rate of technological progress, λ, when $n + \lambda = 0$. In this case, income will grow without limit.

[2] Solow assumes that technological growth is labor-augmenting.

[3] Following Solow, we have to this point ignored international capital flows. The rate of capital-deepening within an economy depends on the investment rate rather than the saving rate. Investment rates have also increased in East Asia although by less than saving rates, particularly in Japan, Taiwan, and Singapore which have had large current account surpluses in recent years.

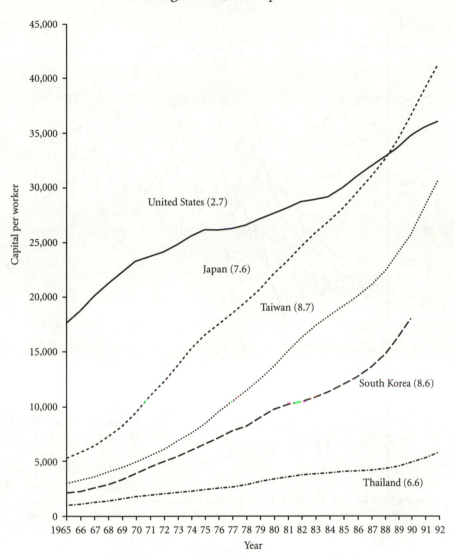

Figure 6.1. *Capital per worker, United States and East Asia*

Note: Annual growth rates of capital per worker in parentheses.

Source: Penn World Tables.

experience population growth as rapid as other Asian countries (Fig. 6.3). Thailand's population growth rate has declined substantially only recently.

Labor force growth rates have not dropped as rapidly as population growth rates in East Asia. In part, this reflects the underlying dynamics of the demographic transition. Populations growth slows from the bottom of the age distribution up, that is, growth

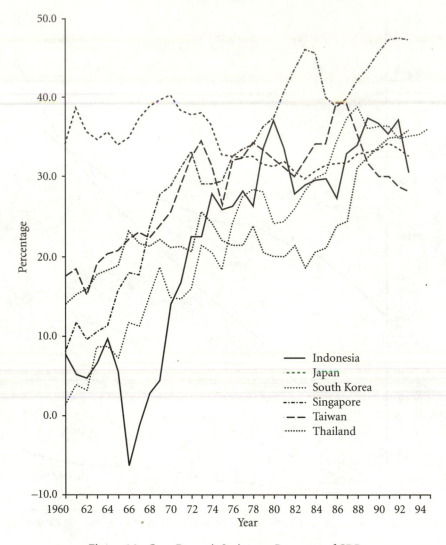

Figure 6.2. *Gross Domestic Saving as a Percentage of GDP*
Source: All countries except Taiwan: World Bank (1999); Taiwan: ROC CEPD (various years).

in the number of children begins to slow earliest, growth in the working ages later. Hence, the population in the working ages has grown more rapidly in East Asia than the general population. In addition, female participation rates have increased substantially in some East Asian populations, including Taiwan and South Korea, helping to sustain a relatively rapid rate of growth in the labor force.

The changes in population growth rates and saving rates in East Asia, and no doubt elsewhere, raise important questions about the neoclassical model. First, can

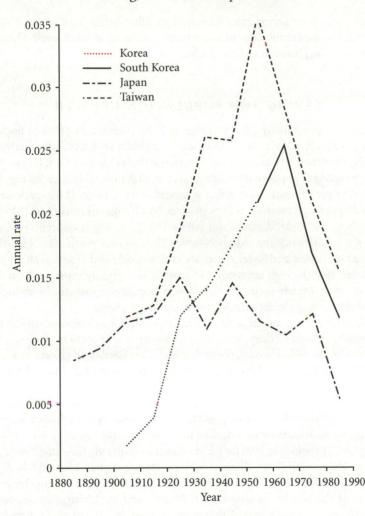

Figure 6.3. *Population Growth Rates*

the decline from a high rate of population growth to a low rate of population growth be characterized as the movement between two equilibria? Probably not. High rates of population growth are a transitory phenomenon in East Asia and elsewhere. Populations before the demographic transition, when population growth rates were low, might be adequately described as in equilibrium. If demographic transition 'theory' proves accurate, populations of the future will reach equilibrium again at a slow population growth rate. If low fertility rates persist in the future, negative population growth may become common. But in the midst of the demographic transition, population growth rates (and population age structures) often change quickly.

Secondly, why have saving rates increased so substantially in East Asia? Are they likely to reach some equilibrium in the future? And, if so, at what level? These issues are taken up in the remainder of this paper.

SAVING AND POPULATION GROWTH

Fisher (1930), among many others, recognized the connection between population and saving. Life-cycle variation in individual productivity leads individuals to vary their saving over their lifetime in order to smooth their consumption. If saving varies by age, then changes in population age structure, that inevitably accompany changes in population growth rates, will affect aggregate saving rates. If life-cycle saving is dominated by pension motives, as hypothesized by Modigliani and others (Modigliani and Brumberg 1954; Modigliani and Ando 1957), saving is concentrated among working-age adults while the elderly dissave. Thus, slower population growth leads to an older population and lower aggregate saving. Coale and Hoover (1958) pointed out, however, that the high costs of child-rearing in a rapidly growing, high fertility population, may impede saving so that slower population growth, by reducing the burden of supporting children, may lead to increased saving.

The life-cycle saving model is readily incorporated into the neoclassical growth model because, in equilibrium, the life-cycle saving rate is constant (see e.g. Mason 1987).[4] As with the Solow model, the saving rate, the population growth rate, and the rate of growth of income and income per worker are all constant. Income per worker grows at the rate of technological progress. However, the impact of population growth on the equilibrium level of income is greater than or less than under the simple neoclassical model with a constant saving rate depending on whether population growth results in an increase or a decline in the saving rate.

Tobin (1967) provides an alternative approach to analyzing life-cycle saving within the neoclassical model. Tobin shows that the aggregate demand for wealth, K/Y, by households governed by life-cycle behavior is constant in equilibrium. He explores the impact of changes in the number of children and the changes in age structure that accompany changes in population growth rates. His calculations, based on US data, show that slower population growth leads to an increase in the K/Y ratio. This implies, in turn, an increase in equilibrium output per worker. Tobin does not consider, however, whether the increase in K/Y is greater than or less than that implied by the simple neoclassical model nor whether the equilibrium saving rate is higher or lower given slower population growth.

The analysis presented here builds on previous studies that have explored the impact of population change on saving and wealth using a life-cycle framework. The

---

[4] A population, closed to migration, will reach an equilibrium or stability when the age-specific probabilities of childbearing and dying are constant for a sufficiently long period of time. Once in equilibrium, the population grows at a constant rate and the age structure of the population is constant. The economy is in equilibrium when the rate of interest is constant, technological progress is constant, i.e., wages shift up by the same percentage in each year, and the age-earnings profile does not change from year to year.

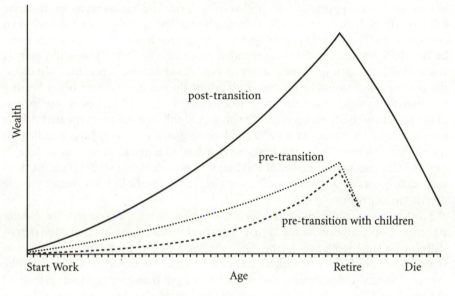

Figure 6.4. *Wealth Profiles*

Source: Lee *et al.* (2000).

accumulation of wealth by households is illustrated in a stylized manner in Figure 6.4 taken from Lee, Mason, and Miller (2000). Adults enter the workforce and begin to accumulate wealth. They continue do so until they retire. Under some circumstances they may continue to accumulate wealth during the early years of their retirement living off interest income. Then, they draw down their wealth supporting themselves in the absence of labor income. Tobin and Modigliani use 'pure' life-cycle models in which households leave no bequests, but Figure 6.4 is drawn to accommodate the possibility that households leave bequests. Uncertainty about time of death may lead people to over-accumulate wealth on average. People may hold additional wealth as a buffer against uncertain income streams or consumption needs, and people may save to provide bequests for their children. The need to provide for old-age consumption is only one of a number of factors that motivates accumulation. Irrespective of the motivation, wealth profiles typically increase with age. The extent to which wealth declines among the elderly is an empirical issue about which there is considerable debate (Hurd 1997).

Over the demographic transition, the number of children rises and then falls. The influence on the age–wealth profile is illustrated, again in highly stylized fashion, in Figure 6.4. If children are, on net, a cost to their parents, an increase in the number of children reduces the average consumption per household member in all years. Because the household smoothes over the life cycle, consumption in years in which there are no child-rearing costs, including retirement years, declines. Hence, less wealth is accumulated to support retirement. A rise in the number of children leads to increased consumption during child-rearing years. The increase is by less than the full cost of children, because parents bear some of the costs by reducing their own consumption. This leads to a wealth profile that is more bowed than would otherwise be the case. Accumulation is concentrated more heavily in the post-child-rearing years. If children are net contributors to household income when they are older, the bowing effect would be reinforced. If adults do not immediately begin bearing children, they would accumulate more wealth early in their adult lives in anticipation of higher future child-rearing costs. The impact of children will be attenuated if there are substantial economies of scale to child-rearing or if parents reduce spending on their other children. (This latter response may lead to lower accumulation of human capital.) Changes in the number of children may also influence other saving motives, such as bequests or uncertainty, affecting the wealth profile in ways that cannot be determined a priori.

Most previous studies of wealth, saving, and population focus on fertility and age structure. But changes in mortality that occur over the demographic transition potentially have a large impact on saving. The retirement motive for wealth accumulation is a relatively weak force in a high mortality, pre-transition population because the expected duration of retirement is so short. For the pre-transition mortality rates used to characterize Taiwan below, a typical individual could expect to live only 0.078 years after age 65 for every year lived between the ages of 20 to 64. A modest level of wealth is sufficient to finance retirement needs in such a population. In a post-transition population, the number of years lived after age 65 are greater by a factor of four or five. To provide the same measure of economic support in old age, wealth also must be substantially greater (Fig. 6.4) by a factor of three to four, as will be shown below.

LIFE-CYCLE WEALTH: TRANSFER WEALTH OR CAPITAL?

The forms of wealth that can resolve life-cycle problems are more varied than frequently envisioned in life-cycle saving models. Working-age people must develop claims on future output beyond their own expected future production. These claims or wealth can be held in three forms: physical wealth (or capital), credit, or transfers. An individual can hold positive wealth in the form of credit, but aggregate credit wealth is always zero because credits and debits are in balance.[5] Transfer wealth is the present value of the difference between the transfers you expect to receive in the future, and the transfers you expect to make. Aggregate transfer wealth can be positive because of transfers from future generations. In traditional societies and in some industrial ones, most people expect to be supported in their old age by their own adult children. Under these circumstances, the wealth represented in Figure 6.4 may consist largely of transfer wealth not capital. Many countries have developed pay-as-you-go social security systems that provide support to the elderly by transferring resources

---

[5] Through foreign lending and borrowing individual countries can create aggregate credit wealth, but global credit wealth must be zero.

from those who are currently workers. These systems also create transfer wealth, rather than capital.

Any form of wealth can be used by the elderly to sustain their consumption, but transfer wealth has no use in economic production. Increasing transfer wealth does not lead to a higher equilibrium output per worker.

Economic development typically, perhaps always, erodes the system of family transfers. If the family system is replaced by a pay-as-you-go public pension system which transfers income from those who are currently working to those who are currently retired, one form of transfer wealth (public) is simply substituted for another form (private). Under these circumstances, the demographic transition increases transfer wealth (or the size of the public pension system), has a fiscal impact (raising taxes on earnings), but has no direct impact on capital formation.

However, if the family transfer system is replaced by a system based on individual responsibility in which workers accumulate real wealth in order to fund their retirement, then demographic transition leads to increased holdings of capital. The institutional form of the individual responsibility system varies from country to country. Farmers and small businessmen may save by investing directly in productive enterprises. Workers may save directly through a variety of financial instruments or by participating in funded company-sponsored pension programs. Some countries, Singapore and Malaysia, for example, have now institutionalized such individual 'life-cycle saving' through large mandatory saving/retirement programs.

The shift away from the traditional family support system is evident in East Asia although family transfers are still considerably more important than is true of the West. The percentage of Japanese elderly living with their children declined by 30 percentage points between 1950 and 1990. About half continued to live with their children in 1990 (Feeney and Mason forthcoming). In 1973, more than 80 percent of Taiwan's elderly lived with their children (Weinstein *et al.* 1994). In 1993, 60 percent of elderly men and 70 percent of elderly women were living with their children (calculated by authors employing the Family Income and Expenditure Survey).

The accumulation of wealth depends more on expectations about support by those who are currently working than by the current arrangements of those who have already retired. Surveys of young Japanese adults indicate that they are increasingly likely to discount the family as a future source of old age support. In 1950, 65 percent of women of childbearing age expected to rely on their children in old age. By 1990, only 18 percent expected to turn to their children for support in the future (Ogawa and Retherford 1993).

Table 6.1 illustrates how the demographic transition and institutional arrangements for old-age support interact to determine saving behavior and capital. The biggest effect on saving rates and on capital formation occurs when the demographic transition is combined with a transition to individual responsibility for old-age support.

In this chapter, we analyze the effect of the demographic transition on savings and capital accumulation under the assumption that the system of individual responsibility has existed throughout. This will exaggerate the effect of a movement down the

Table 6.1. *The Implications of Demographic Transition and Old-Age Support Systems for Saving and Wealth*

	Transfers	Individual responsibility
Pre-Transition	Initial Situation	Small increase in s and K
Post-Transition	Small increase in s and K	Big increase in s and K

left-hand column, passing through the transition while maintaining the system which relies heavily on transfers. It will understate the effect of a movement diagonally from the upper left to the lower right. We believe that this diagonal movement is the most appropriate representation of the changes taking place in East Asia and eventually in other Third World countries. In a number of countries of Latin America, currently switching to mandatory private savings for retirement, the movement to the lower-right cell has already taken place or is in process.

THE SAVING MODEL

The simulation model used in this chapter determines how aggregate saving rates and wealth change during demographic transition if saving by members of the population is governed by life-cycle considerations. The model is described in detail in Lee, Mason, and Miller (forthcoming) and only its main features will be explained here. The demographic component of the model is detailed. The population by single years of age is determined each year based on assumptions about fertility and mortality. Some results presented below are based on mortality and fertility data drawn from Taiwan's experience over the twentieth century. We assume that the population is closed to immigration in all simulations presented here. In earlier work, we treated immigration in a more realistic manner without important implications for the results (see Lee *et al.* forthcoming).

Simulations are intended to track a population from the beginning to the end of its demographic transition. We begin with a low life expectancy at birth (e0) and high total fertility rate (TFR) which remain constant for a period of time sufficient to produce a stable population. Beginning in 1900, life expectancy begins to rise with a speed that varies from one simulation to the next. The total fertility rate begins to decline around 1950 reaching replacement fertility, 2.05 births per woman, with a speed that again varies from simulation to simulation. Age-specific fertility and mortality rates are determined from TFR and e0 assumptions using techniques described in Lee and Carter (1992) and Lee (1993). In none of the simulations do we explore the implications of baby booms or catastrophic increases in mortality.

We assume that children remain in the parental home, pooling their income with that of their parents, until age 25, although some marry and begin childbearing at an earlier age. Until this age, their income is treated as income of their parents, and its disposition is governed by the parents' life-cycle budget constraint and consumption plan. The age of economic independence is based on our work on Taiwan, where, in 1980, only about a quarter of males aged 25 to 29 were household heads. Thus, the actual age of leaving home is typically later than 25. However, we expect (with no direct evidence) that co-resident children would increasingly have control over their earnings as they grow older, whether or not they remain co-resident. Once children establish their economic independence, we assume that they remain independent from their parents for the remainder of their lives.

The household saving model is an extension of Tobin's (1967) formulation and is somewhat similar to Attanasio *et al.* (1997) although their model incorporates uncertainty and precautionary savings in addition to demographic factors. Household behavior is governed by a utility-maximization model. In each period, adults decide how much of their income to consume and how much to save based on their current wealth, family size, interest rates, and expectations about future childbearing, mortality conditions, and earnings. We make no allowance for intergenerational transfers, that is, parents make no bequests to their children and adult children provide no support to their parents. (Lee *et al.* (forthcoming) analyze the impact of transfers in steady-state models.)

Our integration of demographic factors into the life-cycle saving model is a straightforward extension of earlier work. Each couple calculates the present value of future lifetime earnings, including the earnings of co-resident children. The present value of expected lifetime household consumption is constrained to equal this amount. Couples distribute household consumption over time so as to maximize their lifetime utility. Given the lifetime utility function employed, household consumption per equivalent adult consumer rises at a rate equal to $(r - \rho)(1/\gamma)$, where r is the real rate of interest, ρ is the rate of subjective time preference, and $(1/\gamma)$ is the intertemporal elasticity of substitution. In our simulations, we take ρ to be 0. For $(1/\gamma)$ we use an estimate of 0.6 for Taiwan by Ogaki, Ostry, and Reinhart (1996). We assume that the weight of children in consumption calculations by their parents rises with the children's age, and averages 0.5. Additional elements of the simulation model are described in the appendix to Lee, Mason, and Miller (forthcoming).

For life-cycle planning, it is anticipated future values of the demographic and economic variables that matter. We assume that couples correctly anticipate their fertility and the survival of all family members. These expectations take the form of proportions or probabilities, but we assume that all the uncertainty around these average rates is absorbed by institutions, whose exact nature we do not consider. We would like to experiment with the assumption that couples base their planning on current period life tables rather than foreknowledge of future life tables, but have not yet done this.

Earnings in each year are determined by changes in the general wage level, the productivity growth rate, and a fixed cross-sectional age-earnings profile. The profile is equal to the average shape over the years 1976 to 1990 in Taiwan calculated from the Family Income and Expenditure Survey. The level of this profile shifts according to the assumed rate of productivity growth. We depart here from the standard implementation of the life-cycle model, which has assumed that the longitudinal earnings profile

Table 6.2. *Equilibrium Demographic Variables Related to Saving*

Variable	Pre-transition	Post-transition	Ratio
Population growth rate	1.1%	0.0%	—
Life expectancy at birth	28.3	78.8	2.8
Retirement years/working years	0.078	0.361	4.6
Total fertility rate	6.0	2.0	0.3
Average number of children	3.1	2.0	0.6
Pop (0–19)/Pop	49%	26%	0.5
Pop (50+)/Pop (20+)	21%	50%	2.4
Wealth/income	1.6	5.4	3.4
Saving/income	4.0%	8.3%	2.1

has a fixed shape. We believe our specification to be preferable on both theoretical and empirical grounds as discussed in Lee, Mason, and Miller (1999).

For the interest rate and productivity growth rate, we do not assume perfect foresight. We instead make the ad hoc assumption that people base their expectations on the average experience of the past four years. Then, rather than assuming this rate to continue for the rest of their lives, they expect the rate to tend exponentially toward a long-run target rate, which is their long-run future expectation. These we have taken in our baseline simulation to be $r = 0.03$, and productivity growth $= 0.015$. Our thought is that long-term interest rates will converge to international levels as global capital markets are increasingly integrated and that productivity growth will depend only on technological advance at a rate similar to those experienced in mature economies once the economy reaches equilibrium.

The simulation results presented below are disequilibria outcomes that occur over the demographic transition. But the starting and ending points are equilibrium outcomes that are of interest in their own right. The sharp difference between demographics in a pre-transition and a post-transition population and the consequences for saving and wealth, are summarized in Table 6.2. The expected number of years lived at old ages is substantially greater in a post-transition population, the average number of children reared is smaller, and the percentage of the population concentrated at older ages is greater. Each of these demographic factors pushes the demand for wealth higher and, in concert, dramatically so. The equilibrium wealth/income ratio is higher by 3.4 times at the end of the transition as compared with the beginning. The equilibrium saving rate doubles.[6]

The impact of the demographic transition on equilibrium output is shown in Figure 6.5 for a closed economy and Figure 6.6 for a small open economy. There are no international capital flows in a closed economy and the capital stock is equal to the wealth held by residents. Output per worker and capital per worker are in equilibrium at the intersection of two curves: the production function that determines

---

[6] The rate of technological progress is 0.015 and both pre- and post-transitions satisfy the equilibrium condition that $K/Y = s/(\lambda + n)$.

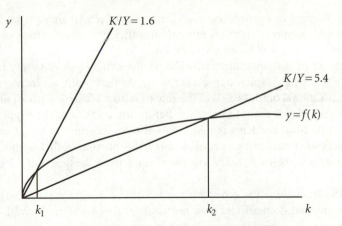

Figure 6.5. *Closed Economy Equilibria*

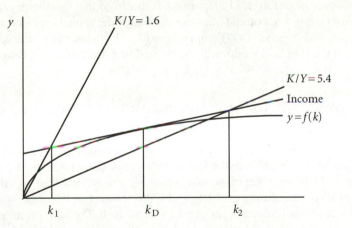

Figure 6.6. *Open Economy Equilibria*

the relationship between output per worker and capital per worker and the supply of capital (i.e. the demand for wealth by households) which in equilibrium is represented by a ray with slope of Y/K. Employing the results reported in Table 6.2, the equilibrium supply of capital increases in the post-transition economy. The slope of the equilibrium supply curve changes from 1/1.6 in the pre-transition economy to 1/5.4 in the post-transition economy.

Equilibrium output per worker increases over the demographic transition, as shown. Of course, with technological innovation output and income per worker will grow at the rate of technological innovation.

In a small open economy, the capital stock is determined by international conditions, namely the worldwide rate of return to capital. If the domestic supply of capital is insufficient, rates of return in the domestic economy exceed those available externally. Foreign investment increases until rates of return are equalized. Similarly, if the domestic supply of wealth is more than sufficient, rates of return are depressed and domestic wealth will be invested abroad.

The impact of demographic transition on the small open economy is shown in Figure 6.6. Domestic capital per worker is k_D. At that point, an increase in capital produces additional output equal to the rate of return available abroad, that is, $f'(k)$ is equal to the global rate of interest, r. Before the transition, the supply of capital $(K/Y = 1.6)$ from residents is well below the equilibrium level and capital flows in from abroad. Total output is equal to $y(k_D)$. A portion of that output accrues to foreign investors, $r(k_D - k_1)$. The income of residents is the height of the income line at k_1.

After the transition, the economy has become a capital exporter. The amount of capital invested domestically does not change. Any additional wealth is invested abroad at rate r. National income, output plus net returns on foreign investment, is the height of the income line at k_2, determined by the intersection of the income line and the supply of wealth, K/Y. Figure 6.6 is drawn so that the country in question moves from being a net capital importer to being a net capital exporter in line with Williamson and Higgins (1997) empirical work. This need not be the case, but an increase in the supply of wealth will clearly lead to a decrease in net dependence on foreign capital.

DYNAMIC SIMULATION RESULTS: 'TAIWAN' CASE

Figures 6.7 and 6.8 chart the trend in saving and wealth from 1900 to 2050 for the baseline simulation and several alternatives. In the baseline scenario growth in output per worker varies in a highly stylized representation of Taiwan. The pre-transition rate of growth is 1.0 percent. Rapid increase beginning around 1950 leads to a peak rate of growth of 5.5 percent during the 1970s and 1980s. Thereafter, the rate drops gradually eventually reaching 1.5 percent per annum around 2050. The most prominent feature of the baseline simulation is the very substantial swing in saving that begins about 1975. The saving rate increases by almost 15 percentage points, doubling the 1975 rate by the time it peaks. The increase in the baseline is followed by an even greater decline in the saving rate. The large swing in saving is a phenomenon that is missed entirely by steady-state analyses but noted above as a possible outcome of rapid demographic transition. Higgins (1994) also notes the possibility of a swing in saving based on his overlapping generations model. The swing in saving rates is accompanied by a rapid increase in K/Y.

A second important feature of the saving simulation is the dip in saving that occurs in the 1960s and early 1970s. The decline is a consequence of reduced saving and increased consumption by young adults who are anticipating the decline in their childbearing and child-rearing costs.

In the baseline simulation, demography, interest rates, and productivity growth rates are all changing and influencing the outcome. The direct impact of demography is isolated by a simulation which holds the interest rate and productivity growth

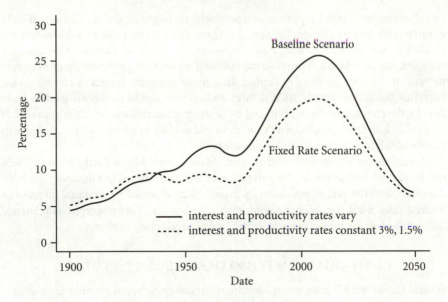

Figure 6.7. *Savings Rate: Taiwan, 1900–2050*

Notes: Scenario 1. Interest rate = productivity rate + 1.5%; productivity rate = 1% (pre-1950), 5.5% (1950–99), 4.5% (2000–9), 3.5% (2010–19), 2.5% (2020–9), 1.5% (2030–).
Scenario 2. Interest rate = 3.0%, productivity rate = 1.5%.

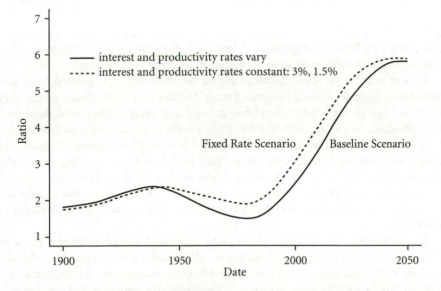

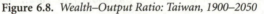

Figure 6.8. *Wealth–Output Ratio: Taiwan, 1900–2050*

Notes: Scenario 1. Interest rate = productivity rate + 1.5%; productivity rate = 1% (pre-1950), 5.5% (1950–99), 4.5% (2000–9), 3.5% (2010–19), 2.5% (2020–9), 1.5% (2030–).
Scenario 2. Interest rate = 3.0%, productivity rate = 1.5%.

rate constant at 3 and 1.5 percent, respectively, throughout the simulation. If only demographic factors change, the saving rate reaches a lower peak and declines more modestly than in the baseline. Note, however, the artificial nature of assuming a constant rate of interest (return to capital) and a constant productivity growth rate in light of the large increase in capital. In a more complete model of the economy, currently being developed, interest rates and growth would be determined in large part by the changes in capital induced by demographic factors. As K/Y approaches its equilibrium level, productivity growth would decline to a lower long-term growth governed solely by technological innovation.

More detailed results reported in Lee, Mason, and Miller forthcoming, assess the impact of variations in the interest rate and the rate of productivity growth. An increase in the rate of productivity growth accompanied by an equal increase in interest rates leads to a higher saving rate. The impact of demography is relatively independent of the rate of interest or the rate of productivity growth.

COMPARISON WITH OTHER RECENT STUDIES

Several recent studies have examined the relationship between population and saving. Williamson and Higgins (forthcoming) analyze pooled cross-section, time-series aggregate saving data using an overlapping generations model to capture the dynamic aspects of the life-cycle framework also modeled here. Their econometric results are similar to the Lee, Mason, and Miller simulation results (LMM) summarized in the previous section. Williamson and Higgins (WH) find that changes in age structure produce a very large swing in saving that begins somewhat earlier and is somewhat greater in magnitude than found in our simulation results. Kelley and Schmidt (1996) also employ a macro-based approach. They conclude that demographic factors matter, but the size of the effects are more moderate than in the WH estimates.

Deaton and Paxson (1997, 2000) employ a very different, micro-based approach. Relying on Taiwan's annual National Family Income and Expenditure survey they construct age profiles of consumption, income, and saving. They hold these profiles constant, consistent with the life-cycle model *in equilibrium*, and determine how changes in age structure would influence aggregate household saving. In their 1997 analysis, Deaton and Paxson find that demographic change essentially has no impact on saving. Their more recent analysis deals with several technical issues that arise in their earlier work and concludes that demographic change has a modest effect on saving. Results from the more recent analysis are displayed in Figure 6.9.

The Williamson and Higgins (WH) and Deaton and Paxson (DP) results are of particular relevance to the work presented here because both studies provide estimates specific to Taiwan. Indeed, the Deaton and Paxson analysis uses the same data for Taiwan that are used to construct some of the underlying parameters of our dynamic simulation model.

The results of these alternative approaches are compared to each other and to actual trends in saving in Taiwan in Figure 6.9. The Williamson and Higgins estimates track

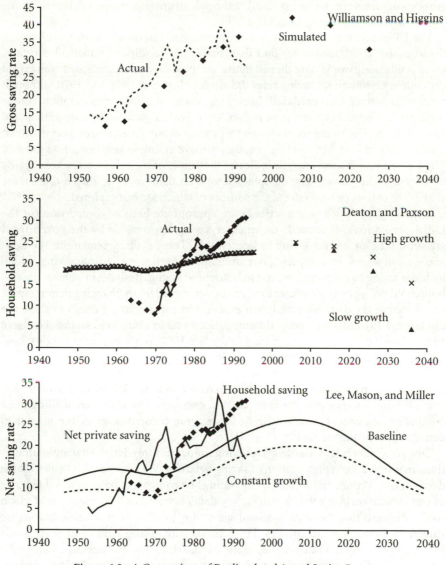

Figure 6.9. *A Comparison of Predicted and Actual Saving Rates*

Source: See text.

the actual gross saving rate quite well and suggest that essentially all of the increase in saving rates in Taiwan are accounted for by changing demographics. There are, of course, short-term fluctuations that are unrelated to longer-term demographic processes. The greatest discrepancy appears to be the downturn in the late 1980s. None of the analyses suggests that demographic factors account for the downturn in gross saving rates (or net saving rates), although all analyses suggest that early in the twenty-first century saving rates will decline.

The DP predictions show a much more attenuated response of saving to changing demographic conditions. They find that, had other conditions remained constant, household saving would have dipped in the late 1960s as a consequence of rising child dependency. Household saving rates did decline between 1964 and 1970, although more substantially than predicted. Beginning in the late 1960s, demographic conditions pushed household saving to higher levels with a peak saving rate anticipated around 2005. The swing from trough to peak is about 7 percentage points, much smaller than in WH, but still large enough to have an important impact on growth. The Deaton and Paxson analysis indicates that most of the rise in household saving in Taiwan is due to non-demographic factors. In their analysis, they ascribe these changes to cohort or time effects, the sources of which are not explored.

It is not clear which saving series is the appropriate basis of comparison for the LMM simulations. It depends on whether saving by firms or by the government are substitutes or not for saving by households. There is disagreement on the issue and we will skirt it by comparing our simulations both to net private saving, which includes saving by corporations, and to household saving. Both net private saving and household saving increased faster than can be accounted for by changing demographic conditions in the dynamic simulation model. Net private saving does not show the dip around 1970 that we find in the simulations and in household saving. The large decline in net private saving beginning in the late 1980s is not mirrored in household saving rates nor in the simulations.

Our results fall quite clearly between the WH and DP findings. Our simulations show a swing in saving rates that is almost twice that of the DP swing between 1970 and 2005, but substantially less than the WH estimates. Obviously, reconciling these competing assessments would help to forge some consensus about the impact of demographic factors on saving.

One possibility is that the life-cycle saving model employed in the dynamic simulations may be a poor representation of saving behavior. We consider this issue in some detail in Lee, Mason, and Miller (forthcoming) by comparing more detailed features of our simulations with the Taiwan survey data also used in the Deaton and Paxson study. We show that the cross-sectional age-saving profiles from our simulations are similar to Taiwan's actual profiles. Households with young heads and older heads have higher saving rates than in our simulations. However, it is unclear whether the differences indicate behavior inconsistent with our simulations or whether it reflects selectivity problems associated with living arrangements and identification of the head in multi-generation households.

A second issue highlighted in several recent studies is the tendency for consumption to track income (Carroll and Summers 1991; Paxson 1996). In the standard life-cycle model, the path of consumption is independent of current income (except in so far as changes in income affect total expected lifetime income). Attanasio considers this issue in his research and shows that demographic factors and uncertainty can also lead to tracking in a life-cycle saving model. We examine this issue with respect to our simulation model and show that our model generates consumption and income trajectories that are very similar to those presented in Deaton and Paxson (1997: 104).

One feature of the Deaton and Paxson analysis may have a particularly important bearing on the difference between their results and ours. Deaton and Paxson (1997) find large cohort effects (later born cohorts have substantially higher saving rates than earlier born cohorts), but they attribute these to non-demographic factors. If we replicate their statistical analysis using our simulated data, we find very similar cohort effects caused by changes in demographic variables, for example, increased life expectancy and lower lifetime childbearing. Our simulated saving rates rise much more rapidly than those in Deaton and Paxson, because of these cohort effects. In Deaton and Paxson (forthcoming) the cohort effects are constrained to zero. (They include time effects.) Again this has the effect of excluding from consideration the impact of trends in life expectancy and lifetime childbearing on saving. A more complete accounting might well lead to the conclusion that demographic factors played a more important role in the rise in Taiwan's saving rates.

It is interesting to note that the three studies share a similar view about the likely impact of demographic changes in the future. Our simulations assume that life expectancy and fertility will change little in the future; hence, changes in population age structure are primarily driving the future decline in saving rates. Given that the DP analysis captures these same changes in age structure, the similarity in the forecasts is reassuring. Caution about these forecasts should be exercised, however. There is a great deal of uncertainty about whether or not life expectancy will stabilize. Alternative simulations which we do not present show that a continued rise in life expectancy at a plausible rate could offset the impact of age structure and lead to rising rather than declining saving rates.

RAPID OR SLOW TRANSITION: DOES IT MATTER?

In this section we examine how saving and wealth dynamics are influenced by the features of the demographic transition. In all of the simulations presented below, we vary only the demographics (fertility and mortality) in ways that will be described. The rate of growth of output per worker is held constant at 1.5 percent per annum and the interest rate at 3.0 percent per annum. The earnings profile and other model parameters are based on Taiwan as detailed above. The purpose then is to ask how saving and wealth dynamics would have varied had Taiwan been subject to a demographic transition that was different than the one actually experienced.

First, we look at the speed of the transition by repeating simulations for Taiwan. The fast transition simulation assumes that the transition to a high life expectancy and low fertility required only 65 years to complete (1900–65) rather than 130 years to complete. Mortality and fertility rates decline twice as fast. The delay between the onset of mortality decline and fertility decline is reduced by half. The slow transition simulation assumes that the 260 years were required to complete the shift to high life expectancy and low fertility; mortality and fertility rates take twice as long to achieve any given level.

The saving and wealth simulations are presented in Figures 6.10 and 6.11 The more rapid the transition, the greater the peak in the saving rate. This is not surprising because in a rapid transition, the equilibrium wealth–income ratio must be reached over a shorter period of time. Higher rates of saving are required to accomplish that task. Because our alternative transitions all begin at the same date, the faster

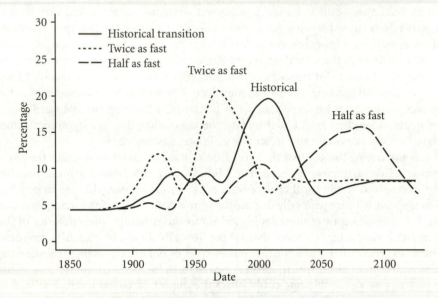

Figure 6.10. *Savings Rate: Taiwan, 1850–2125*

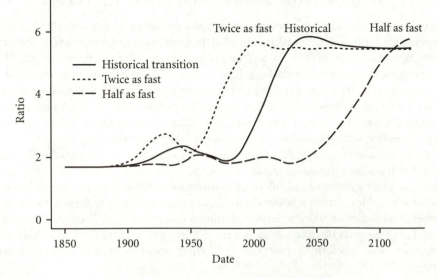

Figure 6.11. *Wealth/Output: Taiwan, 1850–2125*

transitions also complete the transition in an earlier year. If we date any transition by its mid point, the fast transition is centered on 1932, the historical transition on 1965, and the slow transition on 2030. By these rough calculations, the fast transition occurs about 30 years earlier than the historical transition; the slow transition about 65 years later than the historical transition. The peaks in the saving rates are separated by similar lengths of time as are the paths of the wealth/income profiles. The patterns for the historical and fast transition saving rates are quite similar. More rapid changes in fertility and mortality influence household behavior, but age structure is greatly affected by the past and relatively unresponsive to the changes in vital rates that distinguish the historical and rapid transition cases. A slow transition produced a swing in saving rates with a smaller amplitude but one that is longer lasting.

The wealth–income ratios reflect the saving rate trends. The wealth–income ratio increases as rapidly in the historical projection as in the fast projection. This suggests that a more rapid transition in Taiwan would have caused incomes to begin increasing at an earlier date but the rate of growth would not have been any more rapid. On the other hand, the wealth–income ratio rises more slowly, as would income, given the slower demographic transition.

A few East Asian countries have had demographic transitions with a duration as short or shorter than Taiwan's, but the great majority of countries have had slower transitions. Fertility decline has been particularly rapid in East Asia. In one recent empirical assessment, Feeney and Mason (forthcoming) conclude that the transition from high to replacement fertility is taking twice as long among Latin American countries as has been true of Taiwan or several other East Asian countries. Demographic transitions in the industrialized countries have also been very different. They began much earlier, but mortality conditions improved much more slowly, fertility rates dropped much more gradually, population growth rates did not reach such high levels, and age structures changed less radically.

We look first at the implications of a Western-style demographic transition using demographic data from the United States and France. To maintain our focus on demographic transition, the US demographics are purged of the post-World War II baby boom by assuming that fertility remained at replacement level after 1937. In the United States and France, for example, life expectancy at birth was around 50 at the beginning of the twentieth century, almost twice the Taiwan level. The gap remained wide until after 1950 but Taiwan has converged rapidly during the last four decades. Fertility declined in the United States and France throughout the nineteenth century, reaching replacement even before fertility decline began in Taiwan. French fertility was much lower than US fertility throughout the nineteenth and the first half of the twentieth century. Population growth rates were quite low in France throughout the last two centuries. In the United States, population growth rates were close to 3 percent per annum in 1800 and dropped steadily falling below 1 percent around the 1920s. In contrast Taiwan's era of rapid population growth began about that same time.

The impact on saving and wealth of these very different demographic histories are shown in Figures 6.12 and 6.13. Note that the US simulation does not include the effects of the baby boom so as to maintain our focus on demographic transition. For

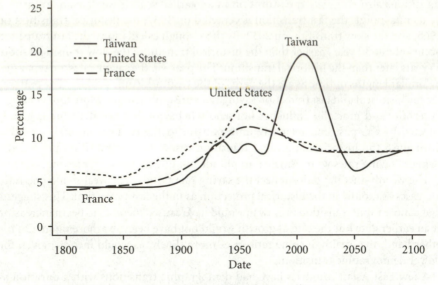

Figure 6.12. *Savings Rate: Taiwan, United States, and France, 1800–2100*

Note: Interest rate = 3.0%, productivity rate = 1.5%.

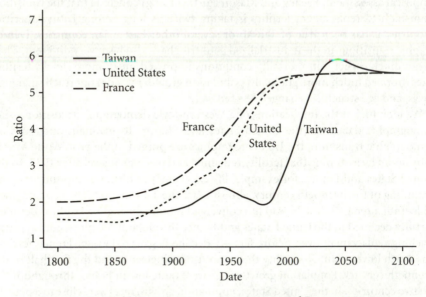

Figure 6.13. *Wealth Output: Taiwan, United States, and France, 1800–2100*

Note: Interest rate = 3.0%, productivity rate = 1.5%.

the purposes of this comparison we have assumed that the total fertility rate remained at replacement level after 1937.

Simulated saving rates increase gradually in France starting around 1800 and in the United States from 1850 to peak in around 1950 in both countries. French

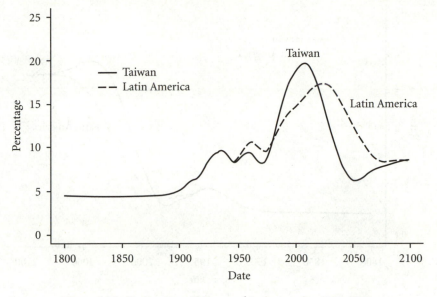

Figure 6.14. *Savings Rate: Taiwan and Latin America, 1800–2100*

Note: Interest rate = 3.0%, productivity rate = 1.5%.

demographics produce a swing in the saving rate from 1900 to the peak of about 5 percentage points. The saving rate reaches only 12 percent of income. The US saving rate peak is 14 percent of income, 6 percentage points greater than the level in 1900. In contrast, Taiwan's demographics produce a peak saving rate of almost 20 percent of income and the swing between 1960 and 2000 is about 12 percentage points.

The French and US wealth–income ratios have moved in parallel fashion with the French ratio higher than the US ratio. The ratios began to increase much earlier and grew more slowly than in Taiwan. Thus, one would expect economic growth that began earlier, was slower, but more sustained given the US-type transition.

The final comparison we make is with the 'Latin American' scenario (Figures 6.14 and 6.15). Fertility decline begins in about the same year as in the Taiwan scenario; however the transition to replacement fertility takes twice as long in the Latin American scenario, 60 instead of 30 years.

The results are very much in accord with the simulations presented earlier. A large swing in saving is produced in either a rapid or a more moderate fertility transition, but the peak saving rate is lower and occurs later when fertility declines at a slower pace. A higher rate of saving is sustained over a longer period. The ratio of wealth to output rises much faster in the Taiwan scenario and the rate of economic growth would be correspondingly more rapid. The Latin American transition eventually produces the same wealth–output ratio as in Taiwan and output per worker and income per capita will be the same, but Taiwan reaches a high income level several decades earlier.

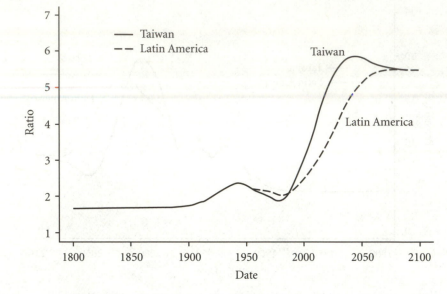

Figure 6.15. *Wealth/Output: Taiwan and Latin America, 1800–2100*

Note: Interest rate = 3.0%, productivity rate = 1.5%.

CONCLUSIONS

The chapter examines how changes in demographic variables that occur over the demographic transition affect saving and wealth, and consequently standards of living. The analysis supports the following conclusions.

First, the demand for material wealth relative to income, if met through savings rather than transfers, is much higher given a modern demographic regime rather than a traditional one. The change reflects the impact of lower rates of childbearing and longer life expectancy on household saving behavior and the influences of population age structure on aggregate wealth and saving. Given widely accepted views about the importance of capital accumulation to development, an increase in the demand for wealth is accompanied by an increase in output per worker or per capita income.

Secondly, the transition to a wealthy society is not a smooth one. Particularly in countries experiencing rapid demographic transitions, saving rates reach historically high levels for a period of several decades. This leads to a correspondingly rapid increase in capital and income. Countries proceeding through their demographic transitions more slowly experience a more moderate swing in saving and rates of economic growth. Demographic transitions as slow paced as those experienced in the West also produce swings in saving and growth but ones that are much more modest than in a country like Taiwan.

The simulations that lead to these conclusions do not, by themselves, prove anything. We have not offered any formal empirical analysis. Rather, we have drawn out the implications of a particular behavioral model or set of assumptions. By doing so, we produce quite dramatic results that have not been appreciated by those whose empirical work is based on the life-cycle saving model. The simulations also establish the possibility that life-cycle saving motives, interacting with the demographic transition, may account for a substantial portion of the rise of East Asian savings rates to unprecedentedly high levels.

Questions remain about the validity of the life-cycle model. In recent work, described briefly here, we have explored in more detail whether important empirical features of saving in Taiwan are consistent with our model. Our model produces cross-sectional profiles that are similar to those found in Taiwan. Moreover, cohort-specific trends produced by our model are also similar to those found in Taiwan. There are, however, ambiguities in the data that leave important issues unresolved.

A particularly important issue not adequately addressed to this point is the change in support systems. The shift from a traditional family system in which family transfers are used to solve life-cycle problems to a system of self-reliance has important implications for the impact of demographic factors on saving. In some countries the shift has been rapid and encouraged by government policy. In Singapore and Malaysia, for example, the creation of funded public pension programs essentially mandates that material wealth rather than transfer wealth be accumulated to deal with the life-cycle needs of an ageing society. Recent social security reform in Chile has similar effects. The United States and many European and Latin American countries, however, have implemented pay-as-you-go programs that mandate the accumulation of transfer wealth rather than material wealth. This issue is important to policy but also to improving empirical analysis of the impact of demographic change.

Earlier in this chapter, we noted the multiplicity of saving motives and acknowledged that people may accumulate wealth in order to leave bequests to their children or to protect themselves from uncertainty or for other reasons. But in this chapter we have only explored how aggregate saving rates change when all saving is motivated by life-cycle purposes. We have experimented with non-standard models that contain elements of life-cycle saving, but which build on simpler 'rule of thumb' specifications, modified by demographic factors. One such model, we have examined, assumes that households save a fixed proportion of income throughout their lives until 'retirement', with the amount set to provide a retirement income equal to 70 percent of their average income in the preceding five years. In this set-up, the presence of children has no effect on saving behavior (contrary to reality), but there is still a substantial effect of the demographic transition on saving rates and wealth due to longer life and the changing age distribution of household heads. There is obviously room for a good deal more work exploring the implications of demographic change when saving is governed by other motives. But any realistic model must conform to an important empirical reality, that wealth rises with age. So long as that is the case, changes in age structure accompanying the demographic transition will lead to a greater demand for wealth.

Reaching a consensus about the impact of demographic factors on saving requires consistency with empirical analyses such as those by Deaton and Paxson and

Williamson and Higgins. The simulation analysis presented here may contribute to that effort by demonstrating that the relationship between aggregate saving and demographic variables, fertility, mortality, or population growth, is quite complex. Age-structure variables have been used most successfully in empirical studies of saving. However, the impact of age structure on saving depends on the underlying age profile of saving, which itself is influenced by life expectancy and childbearing. Reconciling micro and macro empirical analyses with each other and with our results will be possible only when they incorporate these effects.

Finally, the research reported here, like Tobin's (1967) earlier work, demonstrates the importance of moving beyond the simple neoclassical growth model that treats the saving rate as an exogenously determined variable. The assumption of a constant saving rate in the Solow growth model is without theoretical foundation. Once the connections between demographic variables and saving rates are acknowledged, the simple relationship between per capita income and population growth implied by the Solow model no longer holds. If our model accurately characterizes that relationship, then population growth has a greater impact on standards of living than implied by the standard neoclassical model. However, if life-cycle problems were resolved entirely or primarily through transfer systems, then population growth would have a more modest effect. This point also bears on empirical studies of economic growth that often treat saving rates as exogenous variables, thereby providing a biased assessment of the impact of population on economic growth.

References

Attanasio, Orazio P., James Banks, Costas Meghir, and Guglielmo Weber. 1997. 'Humps and Bumps in Lifetime Consumption'. Unpublished paper of University College London, Institute for Fiscal Studies and NBER.

Carroll, Christopher D., and Lawrence H. Summers. 1991. 'Consumption Growth Parallels Income Growth: Some New Evidence'. In B. Douglas Bernheim and John B. Shoven, eds., *National Saving and Economic Performance, A National Bureau of Economic Research Report*. Chicago: The University of Chicago Press, 305–43.

Coale, Ansley J., and Edgar Hoover. 1958. *Population Growth and Economic Development in Low-Income Countries: A Case Study of India*. Princeton: Princeton University Press.

Deaton, Angus, and Christina Paxson. 1997. 'The Effects of Economic and Population Growth on National Saving and Inequality'. *Demography* 34 (1), 97–114.

—— —— 2000. 'Growth, Demographic Structure, and National Saving in Taiwan'. In C.Y. Cyrus Chu and Ronald Lee, eds., *Population and Economic Change in East Asia*, a supplement to *Population and Development Review*. 26, 141–73.

Feeney, Griffith, and Andrew Mason. Forthcoming. 'Population in East Asia'. In Andrew Mason, ed., *Population Change and Economic Development in East Asia: Challenges Met, Opportunities Seized*. Palo Alto, Calif.: Stanford University Press.

Fisher, Irving. 1930. *The Theory of Interest as Determined by Impatience to Spend Income and Opportunity to Invest it*. New York: The Macmillan Company.

Harberger, Arnold C. 1998. 'A Vision of the Growth Process'. *American Economic Review.* 88 (1) (Mar.), 1–32.

Higgins, Matthew D. 1994. 'The Demographic Determinants of Savings, Investment and International Capital Flows'. Ph.D. dissertation, Harvard University.

Hurd, Michael D. 1997. 'The Economics of Individual Aging'. In Mark R. Rosenzweig and Oded Stark, eds., *Handbook of Population and Family Economics*, vol. 1B. Amsterdam: Elsevier, 892–966.

Kelley, Allen C., and R. M. Schmidt. 1996. 'Saving, Dependency and Development'. *Journal of Population Economics.* 9 (4), 365–86.

Kim, Jong-Il, and Lawrence J. Lau. 1994. 'The Sources of Economic Growth of the East Asian Newly Industrialized Countries'. *Journal of the Japanese and International Economies.* 8: 235–71.

—— —— 1995. 'The Role of Human Capital in Economic Growth of the East Asian Newly Industrialized Countries'. *Asia-Pacific Economic Review.* 1: 3–22.

Lee, Ronald D. 1993. 'Modeling and forecasting the Time Series of US Fertility'. *International Journal of Forecasting.* 9: 187–202.

—— and Lawrence R. Carter. 1992. 'Modeling and Forecasting U.S. Mortality'. *Journal of the American Statistical Association.* 87: 659–71.

—— Andrew Mason, and Timothy Miller. 1999. 'Rejoinder', Andrew Mason, Thomas Merrick, and R. Paul Shaw, eds., *Population Economics, Demographic Transition, and Development: Research and Policy Implications*, WBI Working papers. Washington: World Bank Institute, 134–9.

—— —— —— 2000. 'Life Cycle Saving and the Demographic Transition: The Case of Taiwan'. In C. Y. Cyrus Chu and Ronald Lee, eds., *Population and Economic Change in East Asia*, a supplement to *Population and Development Review.* 26, 194–219.

—— —— —— Forthcoming. 'Saving, Wealth, and the Demographic Transition in East Asia'. In Andrew Mason, ed., *Population Change and Economic Development in East Asia: Challenges Met, Opportunities Seized.* Palo Alto, Calif.: Stanford University Press.

Mason, Andrew. 1987. 'National Saving Rates and Population Growth: A New Model and New Evidence'. In D. Gale Johnson and Ronald D. Lee, eds., *Population Growth and Economic Development: Issues and Evidence.* Madison: University of Wisconsin Press, 523–60.

Modigliani, Franco, and Albert Ando. 1957. 'Test of the Life Cycle Hypothesis of Saving'. *Bulletin of the Oxford University Institute of Statistics.* 19 (May), 99–124.

—— and Richard Brumberg. 1954. 'Utility Analysis and the Consumption Function: An Interpretation of Cross-Section Data'. In K. Kurihara, ed., *Post-Keynesian Economics.* Princeton: Princeton University Press.

Ogaki, Masao, Jonathan Ostry, and Carmen Reinhart. 1996. 'Saving Behavior in Low- and Middle-Income Developing Countries: A Comparison'. *International Monetary Fund Staff Papers.* 43 (1) (Mar.).

Ogawa, Naohiro, and Robert D. Retherford. 1993. 'Care of the Elderly in Japan: Changing Norms and Expectations'. *Journal of Marriage and the Family.* 55 (3) (Aug.), 585–97.

Paxson, Christina. 1996. 'Saving and Growth: Evidence from Micro Data'. *European Economic Review.* 40: 255–88.

ROC (Republic of China) CEPD (Council for Economic Planning and Development). 1997. *Taiwan Statistical Data Book, 1997.* Taipei.

Solow, Robert M. 1956. 'A Contribution to the Theory of Economic Growth'. *Quarterly Journal of Economics.* 70 (1), 65–94.

Tobin, James. 1967. 'Life Cycle Saving and Balanced Economic Growth'. in William Fellner, ed., *Ten Economic Studies in the Tradition of Irving Fisher.* New York: Wiley Press, 231–56.

Weinstein, W., T. H. Sun, M. C. Chang, and R. Freedman. 1994. 'Co-Residence and Other Ties Linking Couples and their Parents'. In Arland Thornton and Hui-Li Sheng Lin, eds., *Social Change and the Family in Taiwan.* Chicago: The University of Chicago Press.

Williamson, Jeffrey, and Matthew Higgins Forthcoming. 'The Accumulation and Demography Connection in East Asia'. In Andrew Mason, ed., *Population Change and Economic Development in East Asia: Challenges Met, Opportunities Seized.* Palo Alto, Calif: Stanford University Press.

World Bank. 1993. *The East Asian Miracle: Economic Growth and Public Policy.* New York: Oxford. University Press.

—— 1999. World Development Indicators. CD-ROM. Washington.

Young, Alwyn. 1992. 'A Tale of Two Cities: Factor Accumulation and Technical Change in Hong Kong and Singapore'. In *NBER Macroeconomics Annual 1992.* Cambridge, Mass.: MIT Press, 13–56.

7

Cumulative Causality, Economic Growth, and the Demographic Transition

DAVID BLOOM AND DAVID CANNING

1. INTRODUCTION

In recent years, studies of economic growth have underemphasized the impact of population issues. Giving demographic variables a prominent place in a framework that treats economic and social development as a complex system considerably strengthens our understanding of economic growth.

There is now strong evidence that demographic change has a major impact on the course of economic growth. Rising life expectancy tends to increase savings and education rates, boosting investment in physical and human capital. However, the mortality decline is not spread evenly across the population. Initially, it is concentrated among infants and young children, creating a 'baby boom'. Subsequently, fertility rates fall through increased use of contraception, creating a large cohort of young people that steadily works its way through the age distribution.

When this cohort enters the labor force, it produces a period of 40 to 50 years in which there is a relatively high ratio of workers to dependents, thus creating a potential boost to income per capita. Eventually, this effect disappears as the cohort ages, but it can have a notable significance while it lasts. In 1965–90, for instance, the working-age population of East Asia grew nearly ten times faster than the dependent population, a substantial factor in creating the East Asian 'miracle'.

The equally strong evidence that fertility and mortality rates follow income levels, however, must also be considered. In other words, causality runs in both directions, from the economy to demography and from demography to the economy. The interaction is a dynamic process, with each side affecting the other.

History relates that the relationship between demography and economic growth is not necessarily constant over time. For example, the negative association between income levels and fertility has become stronger between 1870 and 1988. This suggests that developments in contraceptive technology do not lower fertility directly, but allow women to achieve lower fertility more easily, as incomes rise and desired fertility falls.

Equally, the effect of economic growth on mortality rates seems to have weakened. Mortality rates still fall with income, but they have also fallen throughout the world regardless of income. It has been argued that recent falls in mortality are due mainly to health-care technology, with economic growth a somewhat less important factor.

The authors are grateful for the financial support provided by the Economics Advisory Service of the World Health Organization.

The Malthusian model saw population pressure as having an essentially dampening effect on economic growth. However, changes in health technology and contraception have made it easier for population change to have a positive exogenous effect on economic growth, noticeable during the baby-boom cohort's working lives when the ratio of workers to total population is high. Once growth is under way, an endogenous multiplier effect may develop, with positive feedback between economic growth and demographic change. This can allow substantial gains to be achieved in a short period of time, with an economy switching rapidly from an undeveloped to a developed state.

Historically, the demographic transition in Europe took about 200 years. Steady improvements in health were matched by slowly rising living standards and falling fertility. The same process in East Asia spans around 50 years from the end of World War II to the present time. The economic-'miracle' East Asia can only be understood when viewed in association with its rapid fertility decline. These two processes went hand in hand.

Conversely, there is the possibility of being held down by a poverty trap, in which high mortality rates and high fertility keep incomes persistently low. Sub-Saharan Africa has recorded impressive increases in life expectancy over the last 50 years, though from a very low base, and it still lags developing countries in other regions. While life expectancy has improved, fertility remains high, and incomes stagnate. As long as income levels and female education remain so low in Africa it is hard to see fertility falling; the problem is high desired fertility not lack of contraception. The high fertility on the other hand creates a very high youth dependency rate, giving low levels of workers per capita, low savings rates, and low school enrollment rates.

Our view is that economic growth is a system with many different entry points. Technological advance, demographic change, or capital accumulation can all give economic growth an important initial impetus. Western Europe, for instance, provides an example where income growth triggered a demographic transition. In East Asia, however, it seems that advances in public health may have triggered a demographic shift that, in turn, generated the dramatic economic growth of the latter half of the twentieth century.

Section 2 begins with an overview of the traditional role demography has played in studies of economic growth. In Section 3, we lay out and explore the 'new demography' that suggests that demographic variables may be much more important than traditionally has been found. Section 4 discusses the size, speed, and causes of the demographic transition in developing countries. In Section 5, we examine the feedback between demographic change and economic development, and the issues of cumulative causality and poverty traps. In Section 6, we discuss the policy implications of our analysis.

2. THE ROLE OF POPULATION IN ECONOMIC GROWTH

Approaches to understanding economic growth have varied widely, dating back at least as far as Adam Smith. For many years population pressure was seen as a key, if not *the* key, force determining income levels. Thomas Malthus (1798) conjectured that population growth, if unchecked, would be geometric, due to our inability to limit the number of our offspring. In a world with fixed resources for growing food, and slow (arithmetic) technical progress, food production would quickly be swamped by population pressure. The available diet would then fall below the subsistence level, until population growth was halted by a high death rate.

This model implies that income growth cannot be sustained. While technological advances, or the discovery of new resources, will increase income per capita temporarily, this will trigger rapid population growth, forcing income levels back down to subsistence levels. This bleak outlook led economics to be labeled 'the dismal science'.

For many years, this view seems to have been a reasonably good description of how the world actually worked. The introduction of high-yielding technologies in agriculture, such as irrigation in China, and the potato in Ireland, accompanied vast increases in population, with little or no increase in living standards. Up until 1700 income gaps between countries were fairly small, and even by 1820 the 'advanced' European countries enjoyed real income levels only about double those found in Africa, Asia, and Latin America (Maddison 1995).

The phenomenal sustained economic growth of many countries over the last three centuries cannot be explained in the Malthusian model. We now live in a world where growth in living standards is so commonplace as to be the norm. In the industrialized countries, population pressure is not seen as a barrier to growth; indeed the opposite is true, the threat is seen as the problem of a low birth rate and too few workers relative to the number of retirees.

If the Malthusian trap is not operating at present in developed countries, the situation is less clear in the developing world, where some argue that increases in population density will depress income per capita in the long run. In addition, population pressure and economic growth may lead to the depletion of natural resources, creating environmental pressures that act to increase poverty. This 'population pessimist' school of thought continues to uphold the Malthusian premise that population increases reduce economic well-being (see e.g. Coale and Hoover 1958; Ehrlich 1968).

An alternative view is that a higher level of population actually increases income per capita. The pressure of increasing population may inspire the invention or adoption of more efficient technologies (see Boserup 1981; Simon 1981). Increasing returns to scale, and increases in the stock of scientific knowledge with an increasing number of geniuses, who are assumed to be a constant proportion of the population, are two other mechanisms through which increases in the size of the population may have a beneficial effect on incomes (see Kuznets 1967 and Simon 1981).

A middle ground, which has come to be known as 'population neutralism', asserts that population growth rates do not matter. This theory arises from the neoclassical growth model (Solow 1957), which attempts to explain the historically unprecedented economic growth seen since the Industrial Revolution. The key assumptions in the simple Solow model are that population behavior is determined outside the model and that all factors of production are reproducible. It follows that technological progress and savings can raise income levels in the long run, since any increase in income generated has no feedback into population growth. The absence of a fixed factor means that the level of population has no effect—countries with higher populations simply need to accumulate more capital.

The Solow model shifts the focus away from the size of the population and concentrates instead on the rate at which the population is growing. Population growth *does* depress income levels, as existing capital is shared among a greater number of workers. However this effect is only temporary. As the population stabilizes, capital adjusts to the new population level.

These effects have been examined empirically in dozens of studies over the past half century (see e.g. Coale 1986; Bloom and Freeman 1986; Kelley 1988; and Kelley 1995). Some of these studies focus simply on cross-country and time-series correlations between population growth and economic growth. Others use multiple regression analysis to estimate the correlation between these variables, holding constant the effect of other factors that might influence economic growth. Although the empirical specifications vary quite widely, most of the studies done over the past 15 years report a similar finding: population growth has a small but statistically insignificant effect on the rate of economic growth.

This empirical result has had a considerable influence on policy-makers in developing countries and on the international development community. It has also helped steer the modern literature on economic development away from serious consideration of demographic factors as a major factor in economic growth. We believe that it is now time to challenge population neutralism and to create a more carefully nuanced theory. This theory relies on moving beyond the growth of the population as a whole and placing an increased emphasis on the age structure of the population.

3. THE NEW DEMOGRAPHY AND ECONOMIC GROWTH

The importance of the age structure of a population can be seen in various ways. Perhaps the simplest is to consider separately the effects of fertility and mortality on economic growth, and then to compare these with the effect of population growth as a whole. The population growth rate is, of course, equal to the crude birth rate minus the crude death rate, plus net immigration. In what follows we ignore the effect of international migration; while migration is important in a number of countries, for most countries it is not a significant factor.

Bloom and Freeman (1988), Barlow (1994), Brander and Dowrick (1994), and Kelly and Schmidt (1995) find that while the overall population growth rate has little effect, the birth rate and death rate entered separately into growth regressions do have effects on economic growth. Countries with low death rates and low birth rates tend to do well in terms of economic growth, while those with high death rates and high birth rates do badly. However, both types of countries could have similar population growth, so emphasizing this as a factor could mask important changes. It is also quite possible that population growth arising from increases in the birth rate may have a quite different effect on the economy than that arising from decreases in the death rate.

Theorists tend to treat birth and death rates symmetrically when they are thinking about population pressure. In practice, most focus on reductions in fertility as the way to decrease population growth, with few arguing that the answer is to raise the death rate. However, during the Irish famine of 1845–50, economists did advise against famine relief on Malthusian grounds.[1] They argued that famine relief would simply prolong the agony, as deaths were needed in order to allow survivors' incomes to rise to subsistence levels. Even in the Solow model, a high death rate has the same beneficial influence on income as a low fertility rate.

There is some evidence to support the view that high death rates lead to an income boost. Herlihy (1997) and Hirshleifer (1987) argue that the plague of 1348–50 in Europe reduced the population by over 25 percent, but caused a spurt in living standards due to an increase of resources, particularly land, in per capita terms. However, it should be equally obvious that this view does not hold true in current circumstances. There are few people arguing that the AIDS crisis now facing many developing countries will lead to a rise in living standards (Bloom and Mahal 1997).

The basis of Malthusian pessimism has proved weak on two grounds. We have the emergence of low birth rates and also exponential (rather than arithmetic) growth in productivity through technical progress. The fundamental structure of production has changed: technological progress has led to an emphasis on industry and services, and lowered the importance of agriculture. Traditionally, it is in agriculture that the problem of fixed resources looms largest, though even here the 'Green Revolution' led to substantial improvements in productivity, while biotechnology promises much for the future. In the 1970s there was a great deal of worry about fixed natural resources of raw materials at the global level, though this problem now seems less urgent. The main argument that the Malthusian story is still appropriate today comes in the form of concerns about irreversible damage to the environment, through global warming and depletion of the rain forest.

The importance of age structure can be seen still more clearly when the different impact of the birth of a baby and the survival of a 30-year-old worker are considered. Each adds one to population, but will have very different economic effects. We explore three mechanisms: (1) a labor-market effect; (2) an effect on savings and capital accumulation; (3) an effect on educational enrollment and human capital.

The labor-market effect looks at how populations with different age structure have more or less people available to work. Clearly, having a greater number of workers in the prime working-age group relative to dependents (the young and the old) raises inputs into production per capita, and so raises income per capita. A reduction in

---

[1] Jonathon Swift (1729) satirized these views a century before the Irish famine in his 'Modest Proposal for Preventing the Children of Poor People in Ireland, from being a Burden on their Parents or Country, and for Making them Beneficial to the Publick'. Swift proposed that infants should be eaten at the age of 1, relieving population pressures, increasing the ratio of working-age people, and providing a valuable resource for the population.

the number of young or old should lead to a proportional improvement in income per capita. An increase in the numbers of workers, meanwhile, is likely to dilute the amount of capital available per worker and lead to less than proportional gains, at least in the short term.

Exploring this area empirically presents some difficulties. Births, of course, increase the number of youth dependents (for a period at least) and it is possible to measure whether these depress income per capita. The effects of death rates, however, are more difficult to ascertain. Is the person dying young, of working age, or elderly? A more direct way of looking at labor-market effects has been by adopted by Sheehey (1996), Bloom and Williamson (1997), Williamson (1997), Bloom and Williamson (1998), Bloom, Canning, and Malaney (1999), and Kelley and Schmidt (1995, 1999). This uses the dependency ratio directly, rather than birth and death rates separately. It then compares the effect of the growth rate of working-age population against that of the total population. From this approach, significant age-structure effects on economic growth have been demonstrated.

It is important to realize that these changes cannot simply be explained by the 'accounting effect', whereby economic growth results purely from the growth in the number of workers. If income per worker were steady there would be a one-for-one effect of increasing workers per capita. Bloom and Williamson (1998) find a much larger effect on growth over a 25-year period from reductions in the dependency ratio than suggested by the accounting effect, while Bloom, Canning, and Malaney (1999) show this effect persists even if we exclude the reverse causality from economic growth to the age structure.

The accounting effect seems to be joined by a strong behavioral element, though the mechanisms by which this is achieved are unclear. One possibility is that reduction in dependency ratios may free home-carers to enter the formal labor market. As people shift from unpaid work in the home, to paid work in the formal labor market, measured income will rise. Note, however, that this is more of a measurement issue than a substantive increase in welfare.

Changes in the age structure of the population may also reflect changes in the ages at which people are dying, which in turn is an indicator of their health. By including age-structure effects, therefore, we are also including a proxy for the overall health of workers. Strauss and Thomas (1998) have shown that healthier workers are more productive, so, as death rates fall, not only do we have more workers, we also have more productive workers.

The savings and capital accumulation effect is the second mechanism through which age structure has an impact on economic growth. The East Asian example is instructive, with its exceptionally high rates of physical and human capital accumulation seen as a major factor behind its economic success (see Krugman 1994; Young 1994, 1995). If this is so, the question remains as to why East Asian savings and education rates were so much higher than in other developing countries. In fact, while savings rates in East Asia were remarkably high, education levels in Latin America are comparable with those in East Asia, while Sub-Saharan Africa has made substantial progress in education, despite its low income level.

First, it is important to remember that higher savings do not necessarily translate into higher local investment. With completely open international capital markets, only worldwide demographic factors should have an impact on worldwide investment, with investment always flowing to where it can find highest returns. Markets are far from perfect, however, and there is strong evidence that national savings and national investment are roughly equal.

Given that savings facilitate local investment, the life-cycle hypothesis argues that age will have an impact on saving rates. This assertion is modestly backed by data from household surveys (see Paxson 1996 and Deaton and Paxson 1997), which shows peak savings rates among people of around 45 years of age. There is also a dip in savings rates for people in their early thirties, which may be due to the consumption needs of people with young families, as suggested by Coale and Hoover (1958).

However, even very old people save a significant proportion of their income. This contradicts the simple life-cycle model, in which people save when young, and consume their savings when old. The old may be saving to leave bequests to their children, or because the age of their death is uncertain and they are protecting themselves against using all their savings before they die. The variations in savings rates by age are therefore not large, and by themselves cannot account for large swings in saving rates. Deaton and Paxson (1998) find that if the amount people save at a specific age is assumed to remain constant, then changes in the age structure can account for only a small proportion of Taiwan's very large rise in the savings rate over the last 30 years.

The relationship between age structure and aggregate savings is quite interesting (see Leff 1969; Mason 1981, 1987; Webb and Zia 1990; Kelley and Schmidt 1996; Higgins and Williamson 1997; and Higgins 1998). This takes into account changes in the distribution of income between generations, as well as shifts in the population's age structure. Higher income for age groups that have higher savings rates will increase aggregate savings, for example. In this way, researchers can show significant age-structure effects, particularly when they take account of expected economic growth, which tends to raise the lifetime expected income of the young relative to the older generation. While these age-structure effects on aggregate savings agree with our intuition from the life-cycle model of savings, in practice results from cross-country savings studies are fragile and should be treated with caution.

In recent work, Mason (1998) has proposed a different demographic mechanism for explaining the increase in savings rates in East Asia—a very rapid increase in life expectancy. If the retirement age is constant, this creates a greater need for retirement income and may lead to higher savings rates at all ages for those in work. A simulation model of this effect for the Taiwanese economy, calibrated using plausible parameter values, explains most of the rapid increase in observed saving. Importantly, this is a temporary effect, which will only last for one generation. The sudden increase in life expectancy makes the young save at high rates, while there are no old to spend their savings. In the future, aggregate savings return to equilibrium, as the young save and (according to this model) the old spend their savings. Aggregate savings in East Asia are therefore likely to become much more like those seen in Western Europe and North America today.

One caveat to this approach is that it assumes that the retirement age is fixed. A reasonable argument could be made that higher life expectancy should lead people to work longer, postponing retirement. If this happens, there is no need for savings rates for workers to rise. However, empirically, there is a tendency for life expectancy to rise over time, while average retirement ages tend to fall. It seems unlikely, therefore, that demand for higher retirement savings is being met by a longer working life. In addition, Kalemli-Ozcan, Ryder, and Weil (1998) show that, in theory, the optimal response to longer life expectancy, particularly when it is rising from low levels, may be to retire earlier. They argue that when life expectancy is low, death rates are high, and it is optimal not to plan for a retirement one has a small chance of reaching. People in low life-expectancy countries may simply work indefinitely and not take retirement. As life expectancy rises, however, the prospect of reaching old age becomes more likely and planning for retirement at a future, and perhaps fixed, date becomes sensible.

The story that savings rates are mainly driven by life expectancy, and the need for retirement income, is plausible, and is likely to be an important part of the wider picture. It needs to be tested against alternative explanations, however. For example, reductions in fertility and increased labor mobility may increase savings rates, as people are unable to rely on their family to supply old-age security. Non-demographic explanations may be important, too. For instance, the development of financial markets and regulations aimed at protecting depositors may be needed in order to encourage people to save. Further study is clearly needed to understand how important the role of age structure is on investment and to identify different mechanisms more precisely.

Finally we turn to the third possible mechanism: the effect of demographic changes on education. A high youth dependency ratio may reduce parents' ability to finance educational investments. There is some microeconomic evidence showing a negative effect of family size on school enrollment rates and educational attainment (see Knodel *et al.* 1990; Rosenzweig 1990, Knodel and Wongsith 1991; and Hanushek 1992). Cheng and Nwachukwu (1997), meanwhile, attempt to find a causal link from education to fertility in Taiwan, but instead find evidence that the causality runs the other way, from fertility to education rates. However, the evidence is not universally all in favor of this hypothesis (Kelley 1996) and, despite its plausibility, it should be treated as a conjecture rather than an established fact.

Longer life expectancy may also affect rates of return to education, a possibility examined by Meltzer (1995) and Kalemli-Ozcan, Ryder, and Weil (1998). The value of education depends on future earnings gains: gains which can only be realized if a person lives long enough. Psacharopoulos (1994) finds that estimated rates of return to education are broadly similar across countries. However, these estimates are calculated under the assumption that people are infinitely long lived (see Mincer 1974). Kalemli-Ozcan, Ryder, and Weil (1998) have shown that having a finite life time, with uncertain time of death, can have a significant impact on the rate of return to education. Meltzer (1995) calibrates a model, using empirical age-specific mortality profiles to estimate the effect of mortality on the rate of return, and argues that enrollment rates are quite sensitive to the rate of return. Behrman, Duryea, and Székely (1999) find that life expectancy is a robust predictor of school enrollment rates in a cross-country study. While it is clear that mortality rates will affect the rate of return to education, the magnitude of this effect on school enrollment rates needs further study.

Taken together, these three mechanisms suggest that reductions in the death rate, particularly the death rate of adults, have a significant positive effect on economic growth. Reductions can increase the labor force per capita, generate higher levels of savings for retirement, and increase the returns to education. Eventually, a low death rate leads to a higher proportion of old-age dependents, but this need not be a drain on income per capita if old people live off their accumulated capital; even less so if they continue to save. In fact the presence of an old generation living off their capital increases the wages of young workers, whose productivity rises due to the high level of capital intensity. Of course, this rosy picture may be reversed in a pay-as-you-go pension system where the old live off transfer payments from the young and they do represent a burden on those working (see Bloom and Williamson 1997).

On the other hand, high rates of population growth due to high fertility, or low infant mortality, may depress the growth of income per capita, increasing the number of people to be fed, clothed, and housed, in the short run at least, while adding little to the productive capabilities of the economy. In an agricultural setting children can work from a young age and may represent a net income gain for parents (Caldwell 1982). This may help explain the high rate of desired fertility in Africa. However, in more urban settings children usually represent a net cost to their parents.

While the new demography focuses on age structure, there have also been developments on the older question on the effect of population density and resource constraints, versus economies of scale. Most studies find little effect of population density on long-run economic growth; the success of countries with low-population density such as the United States and Australia is matched by successes in some high-density countries, such as Japan, and particularly Singapore and Hong Kong.

While population density does not seem very significant averaged over all countries, Gallup and Sachs (1999) and Bloom and Sachs (1998) find that high population density does seem to promote economic growth in coastal regions, while it seems to impede growth in inland areas. Coastal regions (those near the sea or navigable rivers) have greater access to trade routes and can relieve resource constraints quite cheaply by exchange with other countries. They then exploit the scale economies that come from specialization, without the impediment of local resource constraints. For example, Singapore is so densely populated that it needs to import not only food but also fresh water, but this has not seemed to impose any real resource constraint on its growth.

This result can be compared to what we know about the income advantages enjoyed in cities relative to rural areas. Cities essentially enjoy the benefits of specialization while acquiring raw materials through trade. Since trade is cheaper by sea or river, large cities tend to be located on coasts or rivers, or near raw materials with high transport costs. Countries seem able to benefit from the same advantages, when their location is favorable and they are open to trade.

While coastal countries may find high population density beneficial, inland areas may face the Malthusian problem. They may find trade more costly and have greater reliance on local resources. This may limit their ability to enjoy economies of scale and specialization, both through their lack of access to markets and through the limits the local resource constraints impose on population levels. Globally, too, the situation may be more Malthusian. Whether such local congestion effects in isolated economies, and global pressure on natural resources and raw materials through higher population, will weaken economic growth are still open questions.

Interestingly, there is evidence that an abundance of resources can actually impede growth. When natural resources, other than land, are studied, there is evidence that countries with greater natural resource abundance per capita do worse in terms of economic growth (Sachs and Warner 1995). While greater natural resources abundance clearly raises *potential* wealth, in practice it may reduce average income by generating rent-seeking activities, activities that may benefit the individual but add nothing to total output. People may attempt to benefit from the royalties on the natural resource, rather than undertake productive employment; more time is devoted to fighting over the division of the pie than to creating the pie. Natural resource abundance may also lead to high exports of raw materials, promoting exchange rate overvaluation, thereby reducing competitiveness in the labor-intensive manufacturing sectors which often lead the process of economic growth.

4. THE SIZE AND SPEED OF THE DEMOGRAPHIC TRANSITION

The size of the impact of demographic change on income depends on two factors. First, the total impact is likely to be larger, the larger the demographic changes that occur. Secondly, the impact will be greater, the greater the degree of sensitivity of economic outcomes to demographic change. The claim that demographic factors exert a large influence on economic performance requires both these factors to be present.

There *has* been enormous change in the demographic structure throughout the world over the last 50 years. Figure 7.1 shows life expectancy in Africa, Latin America, South-Central Asia, and East Asia between 1950 and 1995. Life expectancy has increased rapidly in all regions, though this process has happened particularly fast in East Asia and Latin America. Life expectancy has also risen substantially in Africa, though from a much lower base.

Figure 7.2 shows total fertility rates in the same regions over the same period. Fertility rates have come down most sharply in East Asia and Latin America, with evidence of the start of a decline in South-Central Asia. However, fertility rates remain high in Africa.

The consequences of these changes on the age distribution are shown in Figure 7.3, where we plot the ratio of working age (15–64) to dependent population (both young, 0–14, and old, 65 and over) over the period. In developing countries dependents are primarily the young, with a significant number of old people only now starting to

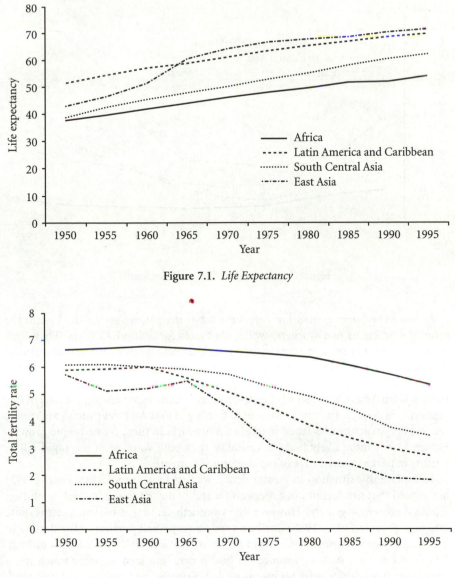

Figure 7.1. *Life Expectancy*

Figure 7.2. *Total Fertility Rate*

appear in East Asia. It can be seen that increases in life expectancy, which come mainly from reductions in child and infant mortality, tend initially to increase the dependency ratio. The population as a whole is increasing, but the number of young people is increasing more rapidly. However, if fertility rates fall, the number of the young being born eventually declines, creating a 'baby-boom' generation, where the population contains a cohort of exceptionally large size.

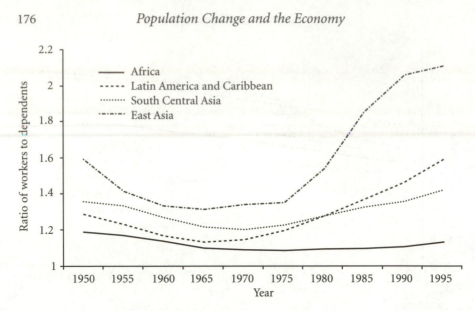

Figure 7.3. *Ratio of Workers to Dependents*

As this baby-boom generation enters the labor market, we see an increase in the ratio of workers to non-workers, which continues for around 45 years. They then leave the labor market and enter retirement. This demographic pattern lies behind the enormous growth in the ratio of workers to dependents in East Asia, from around 1.3 in 1965 to about 2.1 by 1995. No other region has seen anything comparable, though Latin America and South-Central Asia are clearly experiencing the start of this process. It is possible that the reduction in fertility in East Asia was purely exogenous, causing age-structure and labor-market effects which, in turn, created rapid growth. However, it is more likely that the causality runs both ways, with the rapid fall in fertility in part a consequence of rapid economic growth.[2]

To explore this situation in greater detail, we first look at mortality. Fogel (1993) has argued that the declines in European mortality during the industrial revolution followed economic growth. However, the twentieth century experience seems quite different. Preston (1975, 1980) attributes only a very small portion of the decline in death rates observed around the world between 1930 and 1970 to economic growth. Exogenous factors, such as advances in health care, are seen as being much more important. This debate is by no means settled. Pritchett and Summers (1996) work with data from 1960 for developing countries and find a significant effect on infant mortality from both income and education. They argue that this is a causal relationship, though they find overall life expectancy seems to evolve exogenously. Wang and Jamison (1997), meanwhile, find an independent effect for female education levels, in

---

[2] Fertility and mortality are more likely to be linked to the level of income than the growth rate. However, over the 30-year time period we consider, differences in growth rates between countries lead to large differences in income levels.

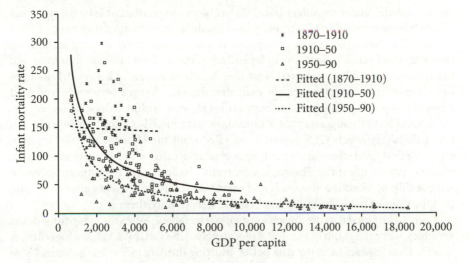

Figure 7.4. *Infant Mortality Rate by GDP per capita*

addition to the overall impact of education and income. They emphasize the changing nature of the relationship between the factors affecting infant mortality over time. More work is clearly needed, in particular to understand the direction of causation within the system.

Our own analysis uses data spanning the period 1870–1988 for a cross-section of countries. The data on real GDP levels are from Maddison (1995) while the data on population, vital statistics, and age structure are from Mitchell (1992, 1993, 1995). A problem with looking at crude death rates is that it is difficult to disentangle the effects of falling mortality rate at each age from the effects of a changing population age structure. While it would be possible to overcome this problem by using age-specific death rates, these data are generally unavailable. However, data are available for infant mortality rates (up to age 1). Figure 7.4 plots infant mortality rates against GDP per capita for the three time periods, again pooling data from each period. During the period 1870–1910, infant mortality rates are high and decline only slightly with rising incomes. Between 1911 and 1950, there is a sharp steepening of the relationship as infant mortality rates fall in high income countries. After 1950, infant mortality rates appear to be low for all countries, with dependence on income level for the lower income countries. These results again point to the importance of improvements in public health, of the kind that initially had an impact on richer countries but have eventually became widespread.

Our statistical analysis follows the model of Jamison *et al.* (1996) and Jamison, Bos, and Vu (1997), in that we try to establish how the relationship between income and mortality changes over time. Our analysis, however, is carried out with data spanning a much longer time frame. One important factor in interpreting Figure 7.4 is that the number of countries in the data set increases over time, so when looking at differences between time periods there may be variation induced by changing the set of countries under consideration. This problem can be overcome by using a fixed effects framework to allow for country-specific differences in mortality rates.

Table .7.1 shows the results of regression analysis using log infant mortality as the dependent variable, with the independent variables being decade dummies and log income per capita interacted with the decade dummies. This model assumes the relationship is constant within each decade, but changes between decades; it amounts to pooling observations from different years within a decade. Testing the three specifications suggests that a random effects model is most appropriate (an F test decisively rejects OLS against fixed effects but the Hausman test of random effects against fixed effects gives a chi-square value of 0.76 (with 5 degrees of freedom, which is not significant)). The regression results indicate that a significant negative relationship between income levels and infant mortality only occurs after 1900, and that the slope of the relationship has become steeper since then.

It should be noted that the regression analysis in Table 7.1 uses the logarithms of the variables, while the graph in Figure 7.4 plots levels of the variables. While a logarithmic specification appears to fit the data better, plotting the data in levels emphasizes how big the absolute differences are in infant mortality between developed and developing countries. The relationship between income and infant mortality shown in Figure 7.4 appears to flatten out in the period 1950–88, while the regression results in Table 7.1 indicate an increasing sensitivity of infant mortality to income over time. This means that while infant mortality rates are getting closer in levels (and are approaching zero in richer countries), the ratio of infant mortality rates in poor countries to that in rich countries is increasing.

The most important point about Figure 7.4 and Table 7.1 is the decline in infant mortality rates over time, apparently independent of the effect of rising incomes. The results suggest that infant mortality in poor countries is now 10 to 30 times lower than in countries at comparable levels of income in 1870. This points toward both an exogenous shift, and an endogenous component in the determination of mortality rates. One story that might fit the data is the discovery of new techniques that are applied first in developed countries and then diffuse slowly to developing countries.

There appears to be an upward movement of the intercept over time in the infant mortality regressions in Table 7.1, which may give the misleading impression that infant mortality is increasing in very poor countries. However, what is really happening is that the relationship is becoming steeper over the actual range of incomes we observe. It is easy to show that the results imply rising infant mortality over time only in countries with annual incomes of less than 1 cent per year (in 1985 dollars at purchasing power parity). It follows that even in very poor countries (which are well above this threshold) there has been a tendency for infant mortality rates to fall over time.

If we wish to compare the magnitudes of the income effect with the exogenous change taking place over time, we can calculate the change in income that would have been required to generate a reduction in infant mortality of the same magnitude as the exogenous shift in the relationship in infant mortality between 1870 and 1980. Using the relationship between income and infant mortality in 1980, we can calculate that the downward shift in the curve between 1870 and 1980 has had roughly the

Table 7.1. *Results of Infant Mortality Regressions (Dependent Variable: log of infant mortality per 1,000 births)*

Independent variables	Ordinary least squares	Fixed effects	Random effects
D(1870)	4.46	3.48	3.71
	(1.52)	(0.900)	(1.17)
D(1880)	3.56	3.35	3.51
	(1.08)	(0.700)	(0.932)
D(1890)	4.21	3.71	3.90
	(1.17)	(0.723)	(0.857)
D(1900)	4.61	3.11	3.40
	(1.26)	(0.796)	(0.875)
D(1910)	6.49	3.85	4.20
	(1.44)	(0.878)	(0.886)
D(1920)	6.13	3.63	4.05
	(0.712)	(1.49)	(0.690)
D(1930)	6.34	3.79	4.21
	(0.467)	(1.13)	(0.524)
D(1940)	7.39	4.42	4.85
	(0.599)	(1.17)	(0.533)
D(1950)	6.36	4.40	4.76
	(0.741)	(0.845)	(0.433)
D(1960)	6.66	4.72	5.13
	(0.696)	(0.764)	(0.459)
D(1970)	7.19	4.69	5.15
	(0.731)	(0.832)	(0.495)
D(1980)	8.96	5.55	6.07
	(0.824)	(0.918)	(0.541)
D(1870) $\times$ ln y	-0.2655	-0.1030	-0.1368
	(0.198)	(0.120)	(0.155)
D(1880) $\times$ ln y	-0.1399	-0.0767	-0.1011
	(0.137)	(0.091)	(0.121)
D(1890) $\times$ ln y	-0.2359	-0.1379	-0.1650
	(0.147)	(0.093)	(0.110)
D(1900) $\times$ ln y	-0.2813	-0.0630	-0.1026
	(0.158)	(0.101)	(0.112)
D(1910) $\times$ ln y	-0.5298	-0.1802	-0.2262
	(0.176)	(0.108)	(0.111)
D(1920) $\times$ ln y	-0.5044	-0.1750	-0.2286
	(0.087)	(0.183)	(0.086)
D(1930) $\times$ ln y	-0.5486	-0.2244	-0.2769
	(0.057)	(0.136)	(0.065)
D(1940) $\times$ ln y	-0.6910	-0.3200	-0.3739
	(0.073)	(0.140)	(0.066)
D(1950) $\times$ ln y	-0.5926	-0.3515	-0.3958
	(0.089)	(0.099)	(0.053)

Table 7.1. *(Continued)*

Independent variables	Ordinary least squares	Fixed effects	Random effects
D(1960) × ln y	−0.6579	−0.4258	−0.4754
	(0.080)	(0.087)	(0.054)
D(1970) × ln y	−0.7329	−0.4471	−0.4998
	(0.080)	(0.091)	(0.056)
D(1980) × ln y	−0.9517	−0.5736	−0.6312
	(0.088)	(0.097)	(0.060)
Constant	2.62		2.64
	(0.120)		(0.068)
R-squared	0.81	0.95	0.94
Number of observations	621		
Number of countries	39		

Note: The variable 'y' represents income per capita and standard errors are reported in parentheses below coefficient estimates.

same effect as that of increasing income by a factor of 50. This is just about the limit of the range of income levels we see today between the richest countries in the world (United States, Sweden, and Switzerland) and the poorest (Mozambique and Chad).

Turning to births, there has been debate on the relative importance of family planning programs versus economic development in determining fertility. Gertler and Molyneaux (1994), Schultz (1994), and Pritchett (1994) show that desired fertility, as determined by economic forces, such as the education levels and wage rates of women, play a significant role in a fixed effects framework, while family planning activity seems less important. If these results are correct, fertility decline may be an endogenous factor, following economic growth rather than causing it: although as we have shown, it still has the potential to play its part in an important multiplier effect.

Figure 7.5 shows the relationship between fertility rates (births per 1,000 women aged 15–45) and GDP per capita in the three time periods. While income levels seem to have little effect on fertility in the nineteenth century, there is a strong negative relationship between fertility and income after 1910. However, the lack of a clear relationship in the data before 1910 may well be because the range of incomes across countries in this time period was fairly small. Table 7.2 shows regression results using log fertility rates as the dependent variable. Due to a smaller data set, the explanatory variables in this regression are dummy variables for 20-year periods, and these dummies interacted with log income per capita. Again, statistical analysis finds random effects to be the preferred model (we can once again decisively reject OLS against fixed effects, but a Hausman test of random effects against fixed effects gives a chi-square value of 0.95 (with three degrees of freedom), which is not significant). Fertility appears not to have had a significant relationship with income before 1890, but there is a significant negative association thereafter. While there appear to be movements in the intercept, these do not follow a regular pattern. Surprisingly, there

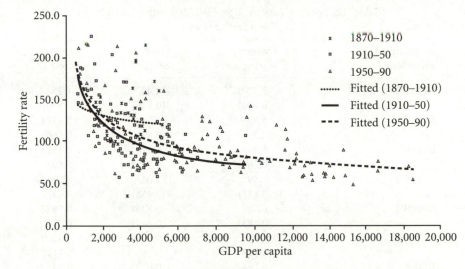

Figure 7.5. *Fertility Rate by GDP per capita*

does not seem to be any clear evidence of technological progress in birth control having an exogenous impact on fertility rates. There is no downward trend in the relationship over time; in particular the introduction of significant new birth control methods in the 1970s and 1980s are not reflected in reductions in the fertility level.

These suggestive results should be qualified in two important ways. A more comprehensive study would require the inclusion of further explanatory variables such as education levels, particularly for females, and the availability of contraception. The regressions are mainly intended to demonstrate the existence of feedback from income levels to fertility and mortality: they are not intended to imply that we believe that only income matters in determining fertility. In addition, it would be desirable to find an instrument for income levels, in order to ensure the robustness of the results to the presence of reverse causation. Bloom, Canning, and Malaney (1999) adopt an instrument variables approach to do this, using only data from after World War II, but find similar results to those presented here.

Bearing these caveats in mind, these empirical results suggest that the relationship between fertility, mortality, and income levels has changed over the last 130 years. A possible cause for these changes has been technological developments in both health care and contraceptive methods. Such changes will tend to reduce mortality and allow actual fertility to more closely approximate desired fertility. Such technological effects are not likely to impact on all countries equally. Rich countries may be alone in being able to afford the improvements offered by health technology, while desired fertility may vary across countries. It follows that technological advances can change the slope, as well as the intercept, of our relationships.

It would be a simpler story if demographic change was exogenous, and had an economic impact; or if economic development were exogenous, and determined

Table 7.2. *Results of Fertility Regression (Dependent Variable:*
Log Total Fertility Rate)

Independent variables	Ordinary least squares	Fixed effects	Random effects
D(1870)	3.52	−1.44	−1.55
	(0.705)	(0.726)	(0.890)
D(1890)	5.86	0.5688	0.4394
	(0.505)	(0.685)	(0.766)
D(1910)	6.98	0.3241	0.2513
	(0.361)	(0.505)	(0.495)
D(1930)	7.89	1.06	0.9949
	(0.437)	(0.458)	(0.437)
D(1950)	6.58	−0.8284	−0.7988
	(0.483)	(0.444)	(0.394)
D(1970)	7.41	0	0.3209
	(0.398)	0	(0.311)
D(1870) × ln y	0.1945	−0.0773	−0.0452
	(0.088)	(0.081)	(0.106)
D(1890) × ln y	−0.1315	−0.3561	−0.3219
	(0.066)	(0.085)	(0.091)
D(1910) × ln y	−0.2808	−0.3336	−0.3072
	(0.046)	(0.075)	(0.062)
D(1930) × ln y	−0.4098	−0.4424	−0.4177
	(0.542)	(0.068)	(0.054)
D(1950) × ln y	−0.2315	−0.1950	−0.1824
	(0.056)	(0.063)	(0.049)
D(1970) × ln y	−0.3352	−0.3015	−0.2865
	(0.043)	(0.0606)	(0.048)
Constant			6.88
			(0.471)
R-squared	0.53	0.82	0.79
Number of observations	245		
Number of countries	33		

Note: The variable 'y' represents income per capita and standard errors are reported in parentheses below coefficient estimates.

demographic change. But the truth appears to be that each affects the other. The relationship between economic development and the demographic transition can only be understood as a process in which causality runs in both directions.

5. MODELS OF THE DEMOGRAPHIC TRANSITION AND ECONOMIC DEVELOPMENT

The richest countries of the world have around 50 times the income per capita of the poorest, in purchasing power parity terms. Even ignoring the very poorest countries, for example, Chad and Mozambique, whose problems have been compounded by civil war, rich countries have about 20 times the income levels of the poorer developing countries. A central question is why such a large gap exists. Two types of answer are possible. One argues that countries are fundamentally different and these differences account for their different economic performance. For example, Gallup and Sachs (1999) emphasize the role of geography in economic growth. The second argues that countries are really quite similar, but that economic development involves positive feedback: countries that do well tend to get further gains, creating wide gaps in outcomes across countries, from very small differences in initial conditions.

The neoclassical Solow model assumes diminishing returns to capital, and so predicts relatively small differences in income levels for countries with different savings rates. Rich countries may have higher levels of capital per worker, but diminishing returns imply that this has only a small impact on income levels. It is difficult for the model to generate the vast differences in real income levels we observe across the world.

Endogenous growth theory is a response to this problem. If the elasticity of output with respect to capital is one, so that a 1 percent increase in capital stock leads to a 1 percent increase in output, capital accumulation becomes a very powerful force in the growth process. With no diminishing returns to capital, economies need not slow down as they get richer and growth can continue indefinitely. Klenow and Rodriguez-Clare (1997) and Prescott (1998) argue that, based on microeconomic evidence exploring the returns on physical capital and education, the elasticity of output with respect to aggregate capital is estimated as 0.5. If this is true, endogenous growth theory lacks an explanation of the wide differences in income levels across countries.

An alternative approach to explaining the wide income differences is to argue that there may be cumulative causality between income growth, mortality decline, and declines in fertility. To understand this process we require a model in which demographic factors can affect economic growth, and income levels can have an impact on demographic variables. In many ways this is a return to the basic approach used by Malthus, who had a theory of production and technological progress, and a theory of fertility and mortality. It is the interaction of these mechanisms that makes the Malthusian model so rich.

Modern models go beyond Malthus by describing how fertility can fall as well as rise with income. Barro and Becker (1989), for instance, argue that, as wages increase, time has a rising opportunity cost. Child-rearing is time-intensive and they are therefore able to introduce the negative effects of income on fertility into a standard neoclassical growth model. This model then generates multiple equilibria, with country income able to settle at a higher or a lower level. Becker, Murphy, and Tamura (1990) argue that, as income growth depresses fertility, there is more human capital per child. If the returns from education are great enough, this in turn leads to further gains in income. This model has a poverty trap at low income levels, where there are large numbers of children, a lack of education, and a relatively low value for time. However, escape from this trap may lead to a phase of endogenous growth, based on ever-increasing levels of income and education.

What is needed is an exogenous stimulus to start this exogenous process, and reductions in mortality offer one such mechanism. Ehrlich and Lui (1991) argue that lower child mortality may lead to lower fertility (if the number of surviving children families desire is constant). In their model, this leads in turn to higher levels of education per surviving child, since education is no longer 'wasted' on children who die before entering the labor market, which can set off a virtuous spiral of rising income and education. In practice, a decline in infant mortality is likely to lead to an increase in the youth dependency ratio in the short run, until fertility behavior adjusts. However, in the longer run, the reduction in fertility may be more than one for one, since the decline in infant mortality also reduces the uncertainty about the number of surviving children, allowing even greater resources per child to be made available for education.

Quah (1997) supports the idea of a development trap, with growth only occurring after a critical level of income. He shows that there are two distinct groups of countries, the poor and the rich, with very few countries in the middle income range. Many ideas have been put forward as to why these two groups, and the multiple equilibria they imply, should exist (see Azariadis 1996). Most depend on the notion that endogenous growth is possible but it is difficult to get started on such a path at low income levels. For example, the multiple equilibria in models presented by Becker, Murphy, and Tamura (1990) and Ehrlich and Lui (1991) arise from an interaction between fertility and education in models where there are no decreasing returns from education. The endogenous growth phase essentially relies on increasing returns. Strulik (1997), meanwhile, also produces multiple equilibria in a model with endogenous population growth and learning-by-doing, essentially using learning-by-doing to produce dynamic increasing returns to scale, once growth is under way.

We argue that demography plays an important part in understanding the process of economic growth. However, the interaction between demography and economic growth must be approached within a system framework, in which each variable affects the others. To an extent this is a trivial observation: there is little dispute that these forces do interact. At a deeper level however, the system approach changes the way we must view causality within the system, but only if the links between variables are sufficiently strong.

Figure 7.6 sets out a schematic diagram that shows our view. We believe that demography influences output directly, through its effects on labor supply, and indirectly, through its effect on capital accumulation. On the other hand, income levels and the capital stock have effects on fertility and mortality. The links at the bottom of the graph, showing the effects of capital accumulation on income and the effects of income on further capital accumulation through savings, are the links that have been most extensively examined by economists.

The schematic could be extended to include other forces. For example, political scientists might see the political process as both a cause and a consequence of economic development and add a box labeled 'politics', with arrows connecting it to all the other variables. However, for the moment, we have taken politics and other

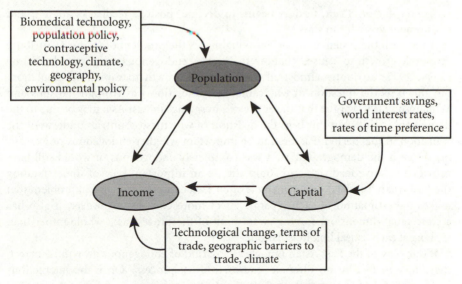

Figure 7.6. *Demography and Growth*

factors as exogenous to the system and focused on the interaction between capital accumulation, economic growth, and demographic change.

The system approach throws new light on the wide dispersion in income levels that lies at the center of the growth debate. Any changes to the exogenous factors in the model will have repercussions for all the endogenous variables. For example, a family planning program may slow down the rate of population growth. This will have an impact on income per capita directly, through its effects on the dependency ratio and the labor force. The ratio of working age to non-working age populations will rise in the short run, while, in the longer run, the lower population may lead to a higher capital–labor ratio. It will also have an indirect impact on income through capital accumulation, perhaps increasing investment in education per child, since there are fewer children. Of course, family planning in the form of contraception distribution programs may itself be endogenous and related to income and education levels. After all, contraception is most demanded where the demand for children is waning; and this occurs at higher levels of income education and development.

In order to elaborate the simple models set out here, it will be necessary to decompose population growth into birth rates and death rates. As incomes rise, both death rates and birth rates tend to decline. However, there may be a threshold effect whereby as mortality falls, a reasonably high income level is required before fertility is affected. There is also evidence that in the initial stages of a demographic transition, rising incomes actually increase fertility, while also reducing child mortality. Taken together, these effects create a take-off problem, deepening the low-level poverty trap. As in Nelson (1956) and Leibenstein (1978), escape from this Malthusian world may only be possible if income levels are pushed slightly above subsistence levels due to some exogenous factor. Then, fertility begins to decline, positive feedbacks are felt, and endogenous growth can start.

A focus on the system approach also highlights the problem of trying to attribute economic growth to 'causes' that are themselves endogenous. For example, Young (1994, 1995) attributes almost all of East Asia's growth to capital accumulation, but this begs the question of why capital accumulation was so high. Higgins and Williamson (1997) argue that the entire rise in savings in East Asia may be due to the demographic shift, but this begs the question of why these countries underwent the transition in this period. Factors can be important whether endogenous or exogenous. Even if the demographic shift was completely endogenous, it would still have provided positive feedback and could still be an important part of understanding the East Asian 'miracle'. Endogeneity is often seen as a purely technical problem that makes the estimation of each separate effect more complex. However, it also has a conceptual dimension, forcing us to think of the process as a whole rather than looking at each causal link in isolation.

If our view of the East Asian miracle as a period of endogenous growth is correct, there may in fact be no ultimate 'causes', only a 'process'. Once the interactions in Figure 7.6 become very strong, the final outcome in terms of the endogenous variables may not depend on the exogenous variables in a unique way. We may need to understand growth as a process of cumulative causation rather than a mapping from causes to effects.

The model also serves to highlight a possible difference between the recent economic success of East Asia and the original Industrial Revolution in the United Kingdom. It may be that the relatively slow population growth rate in the United Kingdom during the industrial revolution was essentially due to a slow, but steady, increase in income levels over a period of 200 years, as suggested by Crafts (1998). However, improvements in medical technology, our understanding of public health, and advances in contraceptive technology, may mean that, in the twentieth and twenty-first centuries, the feedback from income level to demography is much stronger. The transition from a low income economy to a high income economy could now involve a jump between steady states, a jump that may only take one generation.

6. POLICY IMPLICATIONS

There are three distinct areas in which the models for the 'new demographics', which emphasize age-structure effects rather than total population, have potential policy applications.

The first is rooted in the realization that demographic changes only have a *potential* economic impact. The benefits of the 'demographic dividend' require that desired changes in labor supply, savings, and educational attainment actually come about in practice. Any adverse effect of population pressure can be mitigated through the smooth functioning of markets and the price mechanism. Appropriate economic policies are therefore essential.

The baby-boom generation will certainly increase the size of the workforce, but this will only provide higher output if these people find productive work. If the labor market fails to absorb the large cohort, then the potential gains will probably be wasted. Equally, increases in life expectancy will lead people to save more, but only if they have sufficient trust in a well-regulated and efficient financial sector. These savings must then be invested in a way that benefits the economy. Again, demand for education is likely to increase, as people demand schooling for their children and consider returning to education themselves. But this demand may require public intervention, particularly at the primary- and secondary-school level since poor families lack the funds to finance educational investments, and have difficulty borrowing.

In Table 7.3 we report fairly standard growth regressions, explaining growth in per capita income over the period 1965 to 1990 for a cross-section of countries, including demographic factors. Definitions and summary statistics for the variables we use in our cross-country regressions, and a list of countries in the dataset are given in Tables 7.5, 7.6, and 7.7. Initial demographic factors, measured at the beginning of the period, are taken to be exogenous. However, all population growth rates measured over the period are assumed to be endogenous. We instrument these in the regression with log of the fertility rate and the youth dependency rate in 1965 and the lagged growth rates (i.e. between 1960 and 1965) of working age and total population. Since demographic change is instrumented with variables measured before the period of growth begins, we can argue that these instruments are immune from reverse causality. There are several problems with treating 'prior' variables as exogenous. The first is that economic growth rates may be correlated over time so that countries with high growth rates in the period 1965 to 1990 also had high growth rates over the period 1960 to 1965. If this is the case, even if causality runs entirely from economic growth to demography, our instruments will have a spurious correlation with growth in the period we are trying to explain. However, in practice there is very little persistence in economic growth rates over time and essentially zero correlation between current growth rates and lagged growth rates (see Easterly *et al.* 1993). The second problem is that, if economic growth is expected, it can have an effect on fertility behavior and demographic change even before it occurs, so that the arrow of causality may run backwards in time. While we cannot rule this effect out, it seems unlikely that, in practice, uncertain predictions of future rates of economic growth have a large effect on current decisions. If we accept these arguments, our instruments control for reverse causality and give estimates of the effect of population growth on economic growth.

We find that total population growth entered on its own does not have a statistically significant effect of economic growth. However, adding the growth of working-age population, and the total population growth rate, gives a significant improvement in the fit. The effects of working-age growth and total population growth appear to be equal and opposite; it seems to be the differential growth rate that matters. This is reported in column three of Table 7.1. In this specification, we also find that growth is higher, the higher the initial ratio of workers per capita. This implies that the steady-state level of income per capita is higher if the ratio of workers per capita is higher.

Table 7.3. *Basic Specification for Growth, 1965–1990*

	Regression 1.1 (2SLS)	Regression 1.2 (2SLS)	Regression 1.3 (2SLS)
Constant	−0.407	9.777	9.608
	(−0.07)	(2.08)	(2.15)
Log of initial GDP per capita	−2.114	−1.896	−1.913
	(−5.45)	(−5.74)	(−6.18)
Log of ratio of population aged	−8.639	4.655	6.117
15 to 64 to total population	(−1.72)	(0.82)	(2.26)
Percentage of land area	−0.614	−0.850	−0.862
in the geographical tropics	(−1.30)	(−2.28)	(−2.39)
Log of average years	0.532	0.204	0.202
of secondary schooling	(1.84)	(0.75)	(0.76)
Openness indicator	1.635	1.332	1.332
	(3.67)	(3.71)	(3.77)
Index of institutional quality	0.268	0.144	0.145
	(2.84)	(1.86)	(1.91)
Log of life expectancy	2.946	1.870	2.065
	(1.43)	(1.19)	(1.75)
Growth rate of total	−1.000	−3.008	
population*	(−1.44)	(−4.38)	
Growth rate of population		2.826	
aged 15 to 64*		(3.90)	
Difference between growth rate of			2.928
population aged 15 to 64			(4.62)
and total population*			
R-squared	0.57	0.72	0.73
Number of observations	80	80	80
F-Statistic	11.5	20.2	24.5

Notes: *The growth rate of total population, the growth rate of population aged 15 to 64, and the difference between the two were instrumented using the 1965 infant mortality rate, the log of the 1965 fertility rate, the 1965 youth dependency ratio, average growth of total population from 1960 to 1965, and average growth rate of population aged 15 to 64 from 1960 to 1965.
**All results were using heteroskedastic-consistent t-ratios.
2SLS = two-stage least squares.

When we include demographic factors in growth regressions, as in column three of Table 7.3, the education variable (log of average years of secondary schooling) tends to become statistically insignificant. We interpret this not as meaning that education does not matter, rather education may be being driven by the demographic factors (life expectancy and school enrollment are highly correlated), so that demographic change is working partly through its effect on enrollment rates. If demographic change explains school enrollment, education levels do not have an independent explanatory role in regression analysis. Of course, it could be that the real problem is that our education data are very poor, measuring quantity rather than quality (see Behrman and Birdsall 1983), or that the relationship between education and growth is more complex (Birdsall and Londono 1997).

Table 7.4 reports growth regressions in which we include policy variables both on their own and interacted with the differential growth rate of working age and overall

Table 7.4. *Policy Interaction Specification for Growth, 1965–1990*

	Regression 2.1 (2SLS)	Regression 2.2 (2SLS)	Regression 2.3 (2SLS)	Regression 2.4 (2SLS)	Regression 2.5 (2SLS)
Constant	6.084	8.173	6.043	4.782	2.806
	(1.35)	(1.70)	(1.37)	(1.16)	(0.55)
Log of initial GDP	−1.799	−1.929	−1.792	−1.710	−1.272
per capita	(−6.04)	(−6.36)	(−5.62)	(−5.49)	(−2.30)
Log of ratio of population	5.030	5.295	5.048	4.971	4.952
aged 15 to 64 to total	(1.88)	(1.87)	(1.87)	(1.94)	(1.80)
population					
Percentage of land area in	−1.058	−0.956	−1.059	−1.058	−1.001
the geographical tropics	(−3.27)	(−2.82)	(−3.28)	(−3.27)	(−3.06)
Log of average years	0.284	0.281	0.282	0.235	0.279
of secondary schooling	(1.12)	(1.10)	(1.11)	(0.90)	(1.10)
Openness indicator	0.443	1.188	0.415	3.835	1.335
	(0.93)	(3.24)	(0.70)	(1.34)	(3.81)
Index of institutional	0.106	0.052	0.111	0.156	0.909
quality	(1.28)	(0.56)	(1.22)	(1.69)	(1.74)
Log of life expectancy	2.666	2.432	2.663	2.791	2.485
	(2.37)	(1.95)	(2.35)	(2.61)	(2.13)
Difference between growth	1.449	−0.013	1.621	1.467	−0.730
of population aged 15 to 64	(1.48)	(−0.01)	(0.80)	(1.69)	(−0.46)
and total population*					
Log of initial income times				−0.414	
openness				(−1.14)	
Difference times openness	2.849		2.977	2.346	
	(2.61)		(1.66)	(2.35)	
Log of initial income times					−0.110
institutional quality					(−1.67)
Difference times		0.465	−0.038		0.541
institutional quality		(1.90)	(−0.10)		(2.81)
R-squared	0.74	0.74	0.74	0.75	0.74
Number of observations	80	80	80	80	80
F-statistic	22.3	22.1	19.7	20.5	20.1

Notes: *The difference between the growth rate of population aged 15 to 64 and the growth rate of total population was instrumented using the 1965 infant mortality rate, the log of the 1965 fertility rate, the 1965 youth dependency ratio, average growth of total population from 1960 to 1965, and average growth rate of population aged 15 to 64 from 1960 to 1965.
2SLS = two-stage least squares.

Table 7.5. *Descriptive Statistics*

All countries	Mean	Standard deviation	Minimum	Maximum	Number of observation
GROWTH	1.79	1.84	−2.24	7.41	80
YO	7.59	0.89	5.92	9.32	80
LWA	−0.60	0.10	−0.76	−0.39	80
TROPICAR	0.57	0.47	0.00	1.00	80
LSYR	−0.71	1.16	0.00	4.48	80
OPEN	0.38	0.43	0.00	1.00	80
INST80	5.79	2.22	2.27	9.98	80
LLIFE	4.01	0.22	3.51	4.31	80
GDIF	0.22	0.34	−0.36	1.24	80
GPOP	2.06	0.99	0.21	4.13	80
GPOW	2.28	1.01	0.25	4.25	80

Table 7.6. *Definitions and Sources*

Growth: Average growth rate of GDP per capita 1965–90.
  Source: Penn World Tables 5.6

Y_o: Log GDP per capita 1965 (purchasing power parity) in 1985 dollars.
  Source: Penn World Tables 5.6.

Tropical: Proportion of land area in the geographic tropics.
  Source: Gallup, Sachs, and Mellinger (1998).

LSYR: Log of average years of secondary schooling in the working age
  population. Source: Barro and Lee (1994).

OPEN: Percentage of years country is open between 1965 and 1990.
  Source: Sachs and Warner (1995).

INST 80: Index of the quality of government institutions in 1980.
  Source: Knack and Keefer (1995).

LLIFE: Log Life expectancy in 1965. Source: World Bank, World Tables.

GPOP: Average growth rate of total population, 1965–90.
  Source: World Bank, World Tables.

GWA: Average growth rate of working age population, 1965–90.
  Source: World Bank, World Tables.

LWA: Log of ratio of working age to total population.

GDIF: GWA–GPOP.

population. We use institutional quality and openness to trade as policy variables, though ideally we would like to have included separate indicators for the efficiency of the labor market, the financial market, and the educational system. Even using our simple proxies, however, we see that good policy (as expressed by high quality institutions and openness to trade) leads to higher growth, and the impact of demographic change is greater when institutions are better. It is, of course, always important to get policies right, but it may be more so when the baby boom is occurring.

Table 7.7. *Countries used in Cross-Country Regressions*

Algeria	Kenya
Argentina	Korea, Rep.
Australia	Madagascar
Austria	Malawi
Bangladesh	Malaysia
Belgium	Mali
Bolivia	*Mexico*
Brazil	Morocco
Burkina Faso	Mozambique
Cameroon	Netherlands
Canada	New Zealand
Chile	*Nicaragua*
Colombia	Nigeria
Congo, Rep.	Norway
Costa Rica	Pakistan
Côte d'Ivoire	Papua New Guinea
Denmark	*Paraguay*
Dominican Republic	*Peru*
Ecuador	Philippines
Egypt, Arab Rep.	Portugal
El Salvador	Senegal
Finland	Sierra Leone
France	Singapore
Gabon	South Africa
Gambia	Spain
Ghana	Sri Lanka
Greece	Sweden
Guatemala	Switzerland
Guinea	Syrian Arab Republic
Guinea-Bissau	Thailand
Honduras	Togo
Hong Kong	*Trinidad and Tobago*
India	Tunisia
Indonesia	Turkey
Ireland	Uganda
Israel	United Kingdom
Italy	*Uruguay*
Jamaica	*Venezuela*
Japan	Zambia
Jordan	Zimbabwe

One caveat to these results is that it is difficult to estimate the interaction of demographic change with multiple policies. In columns one and two of Table 7.4, when we interact with openness of the economy and institutions separately, we find significant effects. However, when we interact with both policies at the same time, in column three, neither is significant. While the 'demographic dividend' is greater when good policies are in place, cross-country data are not rich enough to tell us which policies are most important. Note, however, that when we add interactions between policies and initial income level we get some evidence that policies matter more in poor countries, but the interaction between policies and demographic change remains significant.

The interaction effects we estimate are not only statistically significant, they are large in magnitude. In countries with the worst policies (zero openness and institutions), we find no significant effect of changes in the age structure. In countries with the best policies, we find very large effects. For example, the interaction between demographic change and policies translates into a 2 percentage-point gap between economic growth in East Asia relative to Latin America over the period due to the faster demographic transition, and better economic policies in East Asia. This is a substantial part of the observed growth differential of just over 5 percentage points a year.

In many cases, when we add the interaction effects between policy and demography, the coefficients on the original level terms representing policy and demography become statistically insignificant, and often change sign. This does not mean we have no demographic or policy effects. For example, the effect of an increase in the rate of demographic change (measured as the differential growth of the working age to total population) is the coefficient on the demography variable *plus* the coefficient on the interaction term times the level of the relevant policy variable. In general this will be positive even if the coefficient on the level term is zero. In fact, the 'average' effect of demographic change, that is, the effect in a country with 'average' levels of the policy variables, is exactly what is calculated in Table 7.3 when we do not allow policy interactions. In countries with the very worst policies (giving policy values of zero on our measures), we do not find any effect of demography in our specifications, but this should not be especially surprising.

The second implication of the new demographics is for health policy. Better health and increased life expectancy clearly have a direct impact on human welfare. However, if life expectancy promotes economic growth, public health measures may have an indirect impact on welfare by encouraging economic growth. Our results in Tables 7.3 and 7.4 find life expectancy to have a significant impact on economic growth. This is one of the most robust results in the growth literature. While there is a problem that life expectancy may merely be acting as a proxy for the overall level of human development, it may be that health policy should be given a greater priority; it may have a double dividend, increasing welfare directly and also promoting long-run economic growth. It is obvious that the AIDS epidemic represents an enormous human tragedy for the people of Sub-Saharan Africa, as does the recent decline in life expectancy for the population of Russia. The economic bad news, however, may only be beginning to be felt.

Finally, our results have important implications for population policy, by which is usually meant family planning through the control of fertility. One view is that there is a trade-off between the number of children and economic growth, with fewer children leading to greater growth. However, we do not wish to imply that people would be better off with fewer children, as it is essential not to confuse economic growth with human welfare.

One issue is how (and whether) policy-makers should calculate a trade-off between potential children and the well-being of those already born. We can side-step this difficult philosophical question if we follow Barro and Becker (1989) and assume that parents are altruistic toward their children. Parents already calculate a trade-off between having more children and having fewer, but providing them with a higher standard of living and education. If they have knowledge of, and access to, family planning, the number of children born will reflect this trade-off. It is therefore unclear what more policy-makers can do. This leads to the view that the correct aim for family-planning policy is to inform parents of the trade-offs involved and to provide methods of making actual fertility match desired fertility. Reducing births below the desired level might increase income growth, but would reduce welfare.

The argument for going further is based on situations where there are externalities to the number of children born. For example, if an extra child in one family reduced the welfare of children in another, perhaps through pressure on scarce public resources, it is possible to make both families better off if birth numbers are restricted. In this situation, each family is in a situation known as the prisoners' dilemma, first formulated by mathematician Albert W. Tucker in the 1950s (see Axelrod 1984). The dilemma is that each family is best off if the other does not have a child and worst off if the other family has a child and they do not. Between these two poles, they are slightly worse off if both have children and slightly better off if neither do. However, the situation is different when examined globally, with all families better off overall if the number of children is limited. The latter is a cooperative strategy and it may be possible for policy-makers to influence more families to choose it for the mutual good.

Macroeconomic analysis is not well placed to decide whether externalities exist or whether benefits of fewer children accrue only to families making that decision. Detailed microeconomic studies at the family level are needed to find the private trade-off between child quantity and quality, and to compare that to the macroeconomic effects. Only if there is a clear social, rather than private, trade-off can we justify societal intervention to influence the fertility decisions taken by individuals.

7. CONCLUSION

Why are income levels so different across the world? Why do the differences show no sign of narrowing?

These are fundamental questions. Endogenous growth models in economics have tended to answer them by arguing from the existence of very high returns to capital, and a process of cumulative causation, whereby countries that invest more (in physical capital, human capital, and research and development) grow much faster than others.

There is another possibility, however. The interaction of economic growth with population dynamics can create a poverty trap. There may be two clubs, one with low income and high population growth rates, the other with high income and low population growth rates. Transition between these clubs may be rare, but when it occurs it may happen very fast, due to the positive feedbacks between growth and demographic change, and be seen as a growth 'miracle'.

This model depends on the interactions between income levels, demographic changes, and capital accumulation being sufficiently strong. Evidence is emerging that these linkages may be fairly strong, but a great deal more empirical research is required. In addition, the overall behavior of the system can only be understood as a whole. This requires an integration of demographic studies of the effect of income and education levels on fertility and mortality, with economic studies of the effect of demographic variables on capital intensity, labor force participation rates, savings rates, and school enrollment rates.

References

Axelrod, A. 1984. *The Evolution of Cooperation.* New York: Basic Books.

Azariadis, C. 1996. 'The Economics of Development Traps'. *Journal of Economics Growth.* 1: 449–85.

Barlow, R. 1994. 'Population Growth and Economic Growth: Some More Correlations'. *Population and Development Review.* 20: 153–65.

Barro, R. J., and G. S. Becker. 1989. 'Fertility Choice in a Model of Economic Growth'. *Econometrica.* 57: 481–501.

—— and J. W. Lee. 1994. 'Sources of Economic Growth'. *Carnegie–Ruchester Conference Series on Public Policy.* 40: 1–46.

Becker, G. S., K. M. Murphy, and R. Tamura. 1990. 'Human Capital Fertility and Economic Growth'. *Journal of Political Economy.* 98: S2–S37.

Behrman, J. R., and N. Birdsall. 1983. 'The Quality of Schooling—Quantity Alone is Misleading'. *American Economic Review.* 73: 928–46.

—— S. Duryea, and M. Székely. 1999. 'Human Capital in Latin America at the End of the 20th Century'. Mimeo, University of Pennsylvania.

Birdsall, N. and J. L. Londono. 1997. 'Asset Inequality Matters: An Assessment of the World Bank's Approach to Inequality Reduction'. *American Economic Review.* 87: 32–7.

Bloom, D. E., D. Canning, and P. N. Malaney. 1999. 'Demographic Change and Economic Growth in Asia'. *CID Working Paper No. 15.*

—— and R. B. Freeman. 1986. 'The Effects of Rapid Population Growth on Labor Supply and Employment in Developing Countries'. *Population and Development Review.* 12: 381–414.

—— —— 1988. 'Economic Development and the Timing of Economic Growth'. *Journal of Policy Modeling.* 10: 57–81.

—— and A. Mahal. 1997. 'AIDS, Flu, and the Black Death: Impacts on Economic Growth and Well-Being'. In D. Bloom and P. Godwin, eds., *The Economics of HIV and AIDS: The Case of South and South East Asia.* United Nations Development Programme, Oxford University Press, 22–52.

—— and J. Sachs. 1998. 'Geography, Demography, and Economic Growth in Africa'. *Brookings Papers on Economic Activity.* 2: 207–73.

—— and J. G. Williamson. 1997. 'Demographic Change and Human Resource Development'. In *Emerging Asia: Changes and Challenges.* Asian Development Bank, 141–97.

—— —— 1998. 'Demographic Transitions and Economic Miracles in Emerging Asia'. *World Bank Economic Review.* 12 (3): 419–55.

Boserup, E. 1981. *Population and Technological Change: A Study of Long-Term Trends*. Chicago: Chicago University Press.

Brander, J. A., and S. Dowrick. 1994. 'The Role of Fertility and Population in Economic Growth: Empirical Results from Aggregate Cross National Data'. *Journal of Population Economics*. 7: 1–25.

Caldwell, J. C. 1982. *Theory of Fertility Decline*. London: Academic Press.

Cheng, B. S., and S. L. S. Nwachukwu. 1997, 'The Effects of Education on Fertility in Taiwan: A Time Series Analysis'. *Economics Letters*. 56: 95–9.

Coale, A. J. 1986. 'Population Trends and Economic Development'. In J. Menken, ed., *World Population and U.S. Policy: The Choices Ahead*. New York: Norton.

—— and E. Hoover. 1958. *Population Growth and Economic Development in Low-Income Countries*. Princeton: Princeton University Press.

Crafts, N. 1988. 'Forging Ahead and Falling Behind: The Relative Decline of the First Industrial Nation'. *Journal of Economic Perspectives*. 12: 193–210.

Deaton, A. S., and C. H. Paxson. 1997. 'The Effects of Economic and Population Growth on National Savings and Inequality'. *Demography*. 34: 91–114.

—— —— 1998. 'Growth, Demographic Structure, and National Savings in Taiwan'. Mimeo, Princeton University.

Easterly, W., M. Kremer, L. Pritchett, and L. H. Summers. 1993. 'Good Policy or Good Luck—Country Growth-Performance and Temporary Shocks'. *Journal of Monetary Economics*. 32: 459–83.

Ehrlich, I. and F. T. Lui 1991. 'Intergenerational Trade, Longevity, and Economic Growth'. *Journal of Political Economy*. 99: 1029–59.

Ehrlich, P. 1968. *The Population Bomb*. New York: Ballentine.

Fogel, R. W. 1993. 'Economic Growth, Population Theory, and Physiology: The Bearing of Long Term Processes on the Making of Economic Policy'. Nobel Lecture, The Nobel Foundation.

Gallup, J. L., and J. Sachs. 1999. 'Geography and Economic Development'. *CID Working Paper No. 1*.

Gertler, P. J., and J. W. Molyneaux. 1994. 'How Economic Development and Family Planning Programs Combined to Reduce Indonesian Fertility'. *Demography*. 31: 33–63.

Hanushek, E. A. 1992. 'The Trade-Off between Child Quantity and Quality'. *Journal of Political Economy*. 100: 84–117.

Herlihy, D. 1997. *The Black Death and the Transformation of the West*. Cambridge, Mass.: Harvard University Press.

Higgins, M. 1998. 'The Demographic Determinants of Savings, Investment and International Capital Flows'. *International Economic Review*. Forthcoming.

—— and J. G. Williamson. 1997 'Age Structure Dynamics in Asia and Dependence of Foreign Capital'. *Population and Development Review*. 23: 261–93.

Hirshleifer, Jack. 1987. *Economic Behavior in Adversity*. Chicago: University of Chicago Press.

Jamison, D. T., E. Bos and M. T. Vi. 1997. 'Poverty and Mortality among the Elderly: Measurement and Performance in 33 Countries'. *Tropical Medicine and International Health*. 2.

—— J. Wang, K. Hill, and J.-L. Londono. 1996. 'Income, Mortality and Fertility in Latin America: Country-Level Performance, 1960–1990'. *Revista de Analisis Economico*. 11: 219–61.

Kalemli-Ozcan, S., H. E. Ryder, and D. N. Weil 1998. 'Mortality Decline, Human Capital Investment and Economic Growth'. *Working Paper No. 98-18*. Department of Economics, Brown University.

Kelley, A. C. 1988. 'Economic Consequences of Population Change in the Third World'. *Journal of Economic Literature*. 27: 1685–728.

—— 1995. 'Revisionism Revisited: An Essay on the Population Perspective'. Forthcoming in R. Ohlsson, ed., *Population, Development and Welfare Symposium in Economics*. Berlin: Springer-Verlag.

—— 1996. 'The Consequences of Rapid Population Growth on Human Resource Development: The Case of Education'. In A. Dennis, A. Kelley, A. C. Mason, and K. Oppenheim, eds., *The Impact of Population and Growth on Well-Being in Developing Countries*. Population Economics Series. New York: Springer, 67–137.

—— and R. M. Schmidt 1995. 'Aggregate Population and Economic Growth Correlations: The Role of the Components of Demographic Change'. *Demography*. 32: 543–55.

—— —— 1996. 'Savings, Dependency and Development'. *Journal of Population Economics*. 9: 365–86.

Klenow, P. J., and A. Rodriguez-Clare. 1997. 'The Neoclassical Revival in Growth Economics: Has it Gone Too Far?' Mimeo, Graduate School of Business, University of Chicago.

Knodel, J., N. Havanon, and W. Sittitrai. 1990. 'Family Size and the Education of Children in the Context of Rapid Fertility Decline'. *Population and Development Review*. 16: 31–56.

—— and M. Wongsith. 1991. 'Family Size and Children's Education in Thailand: Evidence from a National Sample'. *Demography*. 28: 119–31.

Krugman, P. 1994. 'The Myth of Asia's Miracle'. *Foreign Affairs*. 73: 62–78.

Kuznets, S. 1967. 'Population and Economic Growth'. *Proceedings of the American Philosophical Society*. 111: 170–93.

Leff, R. D. 1969, 'Dependency Rates and Savings Rates'. *American Economic Review*. 59: 886–96.

Leibenstein, H. 1978. *General X Efficiency Theory and Economic Development*. New York: Oxford University Press.

Maddison, A. 1995. *Monitoring the World Economy, 1820–1992*. Paris: Organisation for Economic Co-operation.

Malthus, T. R. 1798. *An Essay on the Principle of Population*. London: W. Pickering, 1986.

Mason A. 1981. 'An Extension of the Life-Cycle model and its Application to Population Growth and Aggregate Saving'. *East-West Institute Working Paper*. No. 4. Honolulu.

—— 1987. 'National Saving Rates and Population Growth: A New Model and New Evidence'. In D. G. Johnson and R. Lee, eds., *Population Growth and Economic Development: Issues and Evidence*. Madison: University of Wisconsin Press.

Meltzer, D. 1995. 'Mortality Decline, the Demographic Transition, and Economic Growth'. Mimeo, Brigham and Women's Hospital and NBER.

Mincer, J. 1974. *Schooling, Experience and Earnings*. New York: NBER.

Mitchell, B. R. 1992. *International Historical Statistics: Europe, 1750–1988*. New York: Stockton Press.

—— 1993. *International Historical Statistics: The Americas, 1750–1988*. New York: Stockton Press.

—— 1995. *International Historical Statistics: Africa, Asia and Oceania, 1750–1988*. New York: Stockton Press.

Nelson, R. R. 1956. 'A Theory of the Low-Level Equilibrium Trap in Underdeveloped Economies'. *American Economic Review*. 46: 894–908.

Paxson, C. H. 1996. 'Savings and Growth: Evidence from Micro Data'. *European Economic Review.* 40: 255–88.

Prescott, E. C. 1998. 'Needed: A Theory of Total Factor Productivity'. *International Economic Review.* 39: 525–51.

Preston, S. 1975. 'The Changing Relation between Mortality and the Level of Economic Development'. *Population Studies.* 29: 231–48.

—— 1980. 'Mortality Declines in Less Developed Countries'. In R. Easterlin, ed., *Population and Economic Change in Developing Countries.* Chicago: University of Chicago Press.

Pritchett, L. H. 1994. 'Desired Fertility and the Impact of Population Policies'. *Population and Development Review.* 20: 1–55.

—— and L. H. Summers 1996. 'Wealthier is Healthier'. *Journal of Human Resources.* 31: 841–68.

Psacharopoulos, G. 1994. 'Returns to Investment in Education: A Global Update'. *World Development.* 22: 1325–43.

Quah, D. T. 1997. 'Empirics for Growth and Distribution: Stratification, Polarization, and Convergence Clubs'. *Journal of Economic Growth.* 2: 27–59.

Rosenzweig, M. R. 1990. 'Population Growth and Human Capital Investments: Theory and Evidence'. *Journal of Political Economy.* 98: S38–S70.

Rostow, W. W. 1960. *The Stages of Economic Growth: A Non-Communist Manifesto.* Cambridge: Cambridge University Press.

Sachs, J., and A. Warner. 1995. 'Economic Reform and the Process of Global Integration'. *Brookings Papers on Economic Activity.* 1: 1–118.

Schultz, T. P. 1994. 'Human Capital, Family Planning, and their Effects on Population Growth'. *American Economic Review, Papers and Proceedings.* 84: 255–60.

Sheehey, E. J. 1996. 'The Growing Gap between Rich and Poor Countries: A Proposed Explanation'. *World Development.* 24: 1379–84.

Simon, Julian. 1981. *The Ultimate Resource.* Princeton: Princeton University Press.

Strauss, J., and D. Thomas. 1998. 'Health, Nutritional and Economic Development'. *Journal of Economic Literature.* Forthcoming.

Strulik, H. 1997. 'Learning-by-doing, Population Pressure, and the Theory of Demographic Transition'. *Journal of Population Economics.* 10: 285–98.

Summers, R., and A. Heston. 1991. 'The Penn World Table (Mark5): An Expanded Set of International Comparisons, 1950–1988'. *Quarterly Journal of Economics.* 106: 327–68.

Swift, J. 1729. *A Modest Proposal for Preventing the Children of Poor People in Ireland, from being a Burden on their Parents or Country, and for Making them Beneficial to the Publick.* Dublin: S. Harding.

Wang, J., and D. T. Jamison. 1997. 'Education and Income as Determinants and Fertility: Regional and Temporal Variation in Effects'. Mimeo, World Bank.

Webb, S., and H. Zia. 1990. 'Lower Birth Rates = Higher Savings in LDCs'. *Finance and Development.* 27: 12–14.

Williamson, J. 1997. 'Growth, Distribution and Demography: Some Lessons from History'. *NBER Working Paper.* No. 6244. Cambridge: National Bureau of Economic Research.

Young, A. 1994. 'Lessons from the East Asian NIC's: A Contrarian View'. *European Economic Review.* 38: 964–73.

—— 1995. 'The Tyranny of Numbers: Confronting the Statistical Realities of the East Asian Growth Experience'. *Quarterly Journal of Economics.* 110: 641–80.

PART III

FERTILITY, POVERTY, AND THE FAMILY

In this part we explore the effects of demographic change on poverty, looking at the relationship between demographic change and poverty both at the macro or economy-wide level and at the household level.

Thomas Merrick starts things off with a review of a substantial literature on the effect of high fertility on household poverty. Merrick begins by noting the virtually universal finding that large families and low incomes are highly correlated, at whatever level of aggregation. The question is about causality: does high fertility itself drive families into poverty? On the one hand, poor families may have high fertility because it makes sense for them. Parents may be hoping children will work and add to family income, or provide old-age security, or they may simply be trading off a large family against other forms of consumption. On the other hand, there is another possibility: that poor parents have many children even when it is not in their own long-term interest—among reasons studied because women, who absorb most of the costs of children in some settings, have limited control over the decision to become pregnant.

Eastwood and Lipton address the question of whether high fertility worsens poverty by looking at the relationship between declines in fertility and declines in poverty across some 45 countries. Their estimates suggest that declines in fertility reduce absolute levels of poverty by increasing overall economic growth (accounting for about one-half of the increase) and by changing the distribution of consumption in favor of the lowest income groups (accounting for the other half). Why would high fertility affect the distribution of consumption? The authors note the possible Malthusian connection: past high fertility affects the current supply of workers (and may increase relatively the supply of unskilled workers if past high fertility was concentrated among the poor)—which in turn may reduce employment possibilities and wage levels for the poor. In addition, a family's own fertility (and mortality) may affect its own chances of being poor or not—for example by reducing a mother's labor-force participation or simply by raising the overall consumption needs of the family. Eastwood and Lipton also show that the poorer the country and the higher its initial poverty level, the greater the effect of reducing fertility on subsequent poverty levels.

Hausmann and Székely explore the same set of links—affecting fertility, education, and labor-force participation—among family decisions, at the micro level. Using household-level data from Latin America, they show how these decisions (be they explicit family decisions or not) are deeply interrelated. A change in the economic environment that affects any one of these decisions can reverberate through the household and across generations to affect the others, in turn affecting poverty at the family level and in the aggregate. For example, an increase in the demand for unskilled labor (say because trade liberalization opens up new markets for rural agriculture), by pulling women into the formal labor force, can set off a cascade of other family decisions about the number and schooling of children. Those decisions in turn will affect the economic well-being of the parents and their children. They demonstrate how in Latin America the mutually reinforcing feedbacks among these three sets of factors are working—illustrating at the micro level the way the macro feedbacks suggested by Bloom and Canning operate.

Paes de Barros and his colleagues then show how the combination of those family decisions has reduced poverty in Brazil from what it would otherwise be. Using a decades-long series of cross-section household surveys they show how poverty has declined in part as a function of declines in the number of children per household and resulting increases in the number of working adults per household and in income per adult. They estimate that the poverty level of the cohort born in 1970 is 25 percent instead of the 37 percent it would have been had it experienced the fertility rate of the cohort born in 1900—an effect equivalent to a 0.7 percent increase in per capita GDP.

8

Population and Poverty in Households:
A Review of Reviews

THOMAS MERRICK

1. INTRODUCTION

This chapter provides a reading of evidence about linkages between household demo-graphics and well-being as reported in a series of review articles, including background papers by Lipton (1983) for the World Bank's 1984 *World Development Report* on population and by King (1987) for the National Research Council's (1986) report on population and development, articles in the *Handbook of Development Economics* (1988–95), contributions produced either for or as a follow-up to the 1994 International Conference on Population and Development (ICPD), and a selection of other items. After gleaning some of the main findings in these reviews, the chapter will conclude with a reflection on the implications of those findings for what govern-ments might do to more effectively link population policies and programs to poverty reduction. This was one of the principal recommendations of the ICPD Program of Action.

The topic holds interest because one of the rationales for public-sector interventions in population is to reduce poverty. This parallels macro-level discussion of rationales for such intervention based on externalities and market failures. These occur when, for a variety of reasons, the costs of reproductive behaviors by individuals and house-holds are not fully borne by them. One puzzle that needs to be addressed in discussing these linkages at the individual/household level is how reproductive behaviors that people perceive to be beneficial to themselves could also be leading them into poverty or making it more difficult for them to escape it.

As Birdsall (1994) notes,

high fertility in poor families does not reflect irrational decisions on the part of poor par-ents, even though it reduces family resources per capita in the short run. On the contrary, it can reflect reasonable decisions on their part—to ensure greater future family income once children start working, or to ensure their own security in old age via support from their children. . . . It may also reflect parent's decisions to enjoy children rather than other forms of consumption.

In either case, individual children may get less health and education, an intergenera-tional externality through which parents pass some of the costs of their high fertility along to their children and, in cases where there is a gender bias to this process, more of those costs fall on daughters.

While most studies of household-level linkages between population and economic variables have focused on determinants of behaviors affecting demographic and reproductive health outcomes, there is also a literature on how household demographics affect well-being and poverty status. The association between high fertility and low income at the country level is paralleled by a similar association between larger household size and poverty, whether measured by consumption or income per person.[1]

There is little debate about whether poverty and household size are correlated. As Lipton noted in 1983, 'almost every study, at whatever level of disaggregation, for either a particular group or for a total population, shows the incidence of poverty and mean household size increasing together'. The problem then, and now, is whether it is possible to demonstrate a direct causal relationship between poverty and large families or to establish the direction of causality. Many of the correlates of high fertility (illiteracy, poor health) are also associated with poverty. Recognition of the multiple paths through which the population-poverty nexus could be working opens the discussion in many possible directions. To focus, it is helpful to frame the discussion both in terms of which 'poverty' and 'population' variables are on the table.

Most discussions of population and poverty go beyond consumption and income to bring in other correlates of poverty, including illiteracy and poor health, as well as lack of physical (land, housing) and human-capital (education) assets. Similarly, the 'population' variables in such discussions go beyond household size and/or high fertility to examine other aspects of household composition (number/ages/sex of adults and children in the household, timing and spacing of births, and so on). Earlier studies have focused on one or more of these linkages, and many have noted the problems of disentangling relationships where the variables in question may be interacting with each other or are being jointly affected by other variables inside and outside the household. More recent studies have delved more deeply into intra-household dynamics, recognizing that some members, particularly women and girls, may be more adversely affected than their husbands and brothers.

2. REVIEWS FROM THE 1980s

Lipton (1983) provides a comprehensive review of work on linkages between household-level demographics and poverty in more and less developed countries, including those that examined such linkages at earlier stages of the more developed countries. The review documents the consistently negative correlation between expenditure per person and household size and makes a number of recommendations

---

[1] There has also been much discussion of household-poverty measurement issues, including weighting of household members by age and sex to account for differences in consumption needs. See Lipton (1983) and Lipton and Ravallion (1995).

about the design of population and anti-poverty policies and programs that remain valid today. A basic message is that policies should take account of the differential effects of interventions on households of different sizes. Governments can improve their anti-poverty policies by looking for ways to help or induce large families with high child–adult ratios 'to alter the nature or timing of their non-demographic behavior (mainly job search and choice, asset size and structure, consumption patterns and intra-household distribution) in ways that reduce the risk of and from poverty, and especially, ultra-poverty'.

Governments may also seek to change attitudes, incentives, laws, technologies (including contraceptive technology), or delivery systems in the hope of causing potentially poor households to change size, structure, or associated demographic parameters in ways that help to reduce the risk of poverty. Lipton's focus on risk factors affecting the outcomes of the household anticipates a number of later studies that focus on specific contextual factors which affect the chances that 'rational decisions' by poor households will lead to the improvements in well-being that they expected to result from such decisions.

King's (1987) review of studies on the effects of population on household welfare reports findings on linkages between family size, birth order, and spacing of children on three clusters of welfare variables: investments in children as measured by their education, health, and nutrition, the health of the mother, and families' consumption and production decisions. These are that:

- Children in large families perform less well in school and less well in intelligence tests than children from small families. When economic class is controlled for, the correlation is approximately halved, but remains significantly negative.
- Children in large families tend to have poorer health and lower survival probabilities; infants born less than 24 months after a sibling are less likely to survive than those born after longer intervals.
- Large family size also appears to inhibit physical development, possibly through lower quality maternity care and poorer nutrition.
- Linkages between family size and measures of parental welfare are less clear and vary over the life cycle; effects on the mother's allocation of time between child-rearing, market work, and leisure depend on the compatibility of market work opportunities with child care. High parity increases the exposure of mothers to the risk of maternal death over the reproductive life cycle, and there is some evidence regarding 'maternal depletion' associated with high parity (a finding challenged by more recent research).

King cautions against causal interpretations based on the negative association between family size and children's physical health and/or intellectual performance reported in many studies because family size and child quality are simultaneously determined choices. In her view, the question to answer is 'whether, for families who do not possess much in the way of land or other productive assets, the addition of extra children exacerbates or alleviates poverty'. And while the studies she reviewed show that siblings and parents suffer from a large family size, particularly in poorer settings where the distribution of food resources favors males over females and adults over children, many of these adverse consequences turned out to be temporary, with surviving children growing up to be net contributors to the family's resources.

Rosenzweig (1990) reviews earlier efforts to untangle the simultaneity of household-level decisions on fertility and investments in children and reports findings from three country studies based on quasi-natural experiments in micro data for households with twins to identify the effects of couple's inability to control fertility on their allocation of resources to children. His analysis of evidence from three countries (India, Indonesia, and Malaysia) confirms that contraceptive control was not perfect and that the inability to control fertility lowers human-capital investments in children. He notes that the range of estimates, from 8 to 34 percent due to an exogenously induced extra child, is due both to differences in methodology across the studies and to cross-country differences in contraceptive efficiency, costs, or preferences. He cautions against policy to increase public funding for contraception without further information on the interaction between these household-level decision processes, market structures, and government behavior.

The discussion of micro-level linkages between population and economics in Birdsall's (1988) review for the *Handbook of Economic Development* focuses mostly on determinants of fertility, but addresses the effects of fertility decisions on societal and family welfare as a dimension of the interdependence of household decisions about childbearing, consumption and production, their responsiveness to signals coming from the larger system, and the possibility of market failures in this process. Institutional factors as well as government policies (lack of property rights and/or policy-induced market distortions that discourage labor-using technology) can contribute to a divergence between marginal private and social benefits by sending signals that undermine or distort decisions that poor households perceive to be in their best interest and may lead to a loss rather than a gain in welfare. She suggests that it would be useful to consider whether societal-level variables, including rapid population growth itself, contribute to institutional failures to adapt to the resultant pressures of larger numbers or to policies such as technology restrictions that limit the capacity of poor households to adapt to change.

This point is also addressed in Kelley's (1988) review of the economic consequences of population, which examines evidence about the macro-level effects of population and notes that one of the main effects of population growth has been to reveal the consequences of bad policies sooner and more dramatically. Among the policies mentioned are those that encourage production patterns at variance with comparative advantage and under-utilize abundant supply. Examples are taxes on farm outputs, international trade policies that encourage capital-intensive industries, and subsidies that favor urban over rural dwellers. Such policies can increase the costs and reduce the benefits of growth in labor supply at the macro level and undermine strategies of households who expect that additional children will improve rather than worsen their welfare.

More recently, Kelley (1996) reviewed evidence on linkages between family size and educational outcomes at both the macro and micro levels. A cross-national analysis of 30 countries showed no direct impact of demography (population growth, age structure) on the share of GDP devoted to education and led him to conclude that the impact of population on attainment is likely to operate mainly through the efficiency of resource allocations within the education sector. He notes Schultz's earlier (1987) finding that while enrollment rates were not affected by the size of school-age cohorts, expenditures per pupil are negatively related to that variable. In their work on Asian countries, Tan and Mingat also found that allocations within the sector (for example, between primary and other levels of education) were a more important determinant of educational attainment than the age-structure impact on overall expenditures, and that outcomes varied considerably by country. These findings raise the further question as to whether the distribution of benefits among richer and poorer families within countries was affected by rich–poor differences in family demographic characteristics.

Kelley also reviewed findings on the impact of the number of children per household on the level and distribution of education within households from 36 studies using household-level data from developing countries. He reports that the overall impact of family size on school enrollments and years attained is mixed, though a small negative impact is the most representative result in the studies in which effects are statistically significant. As already noted, the jointness issue leads to biased estimates, and studies that attempt to account for jointness find that the impact of demographic factors is much reduced. Two further observations are that the impact of family size appears to be greatest in comparing relatively large with relatively small families, and that the negative impact appears to be least in countries that are relatively poor and/or at early stages of their demographic transitions. Kelley's findings reinforce the need for caution in interpreting both cross-national and household-level data showing negative correlations between population and educational investments. At the same time, they suggest the need to look more closely at differential experiences of richer and poorer households as societies pass through their demographic transitions.

3. ADVANCES DURING THE 1990s

More recent work has expanded in a number of directions from earlier approaches: looking more closely at factors outside the household that influence allocations within the household; exploring the implications of non-traditional definitions of households and recognizing that household members may not all share the same needs, goals, and power to make decisions; and focusing on gender dimensions of these considerations, particularly as they affect the life chances of the next generation during the critical formative years of childhood and adolescence.

Dasgupta's (1995) review of population and economics emphasizes the need to look beyond the household as a collective decision-making unit and recognize the social mechanisms in which a 'myriad of individual household decisions can lead to outcomes that are a collective failure'. These include:

- differences across cultures about what constitutes a household and how it functions;
- cultural and institutional factors that lead to differing interests among household members and unequal capacity to participate in household decisions, particularly for women;
- differing and often rapidly changing economic and natural-resource bases on which household consumption and production depend.

He contrasts the unitary view of household decision-making that is constrained by income, prices, and quality/quantity trade-offs with the reality in many low-income settings of gender imbalances in the capacity to decide whom and when to marry, who in the household gets access to health care and education, when and what kind of contraception to use, and the power to negotiate safe sex when the risk of sexually transmitted diseases and HIV/AIDS infection is high.

Another aspect of variation in household composition relates to the roles/ responsibilities assumed or not assumed by men and women in child-rearing. Hobcraft (1997) examines the difficulties that women face in balancing child-rearing roles with those of provider under a range of household structural conditions: for example contrasting situations where the male acts as parent and provider, where the male is absent but provides support, and where the woman alone has to provide support as well as care for children. The paper presents a revealing illustrative allocation of time and income for two- and one-parent family models under different assumptions about the amount of support provided by the partners. While he examines these differences from the perspective of female empowerment and its impact on child well-being, Hobcraft's findings add to our understanding of the linkages between gender inequities in society and household well-being. There are negative consequences for children from partnership breakdown and extra-partnership childbearing as well as added benefits for girls in more gender-equitable contexts.

The broader approach to household decision processes has been undertaken by investigators working in more developed country settings. For example, Behrman and colleagues (1995) expand on earlier studies of how parents allocate resources (particularly education) among children by looking at whether parents favor boys over girls, first-borns over younger sibs, and so on. While they find less gender bias than is common in such settings as South Asia, their work demonstrates that even in rich countries outcomes are influenced by institutional forces. In settings (or groups) with low intergenerational mobility, a child's economic destiny is largely determined by the family into which the child is born. This and a series of related issues highlight the importance of the larger economic and social context in analyzing the effects of intra-family allocations on intergenerational economic mobility.

Behrman (1996) also explores possible flaws in households' capacity to adjust their intergenerational allocations during times of rapid societal change. As countries move through the transition from high to low fertility, they experience changes in the age structure at both the societal and household levels, moving from high child dependency through periods of rapid growth in the young adult and mature adult populations and eventually to rising old age dependency. Much of the recent discussion of macro-level economic/demographic linkages is focused on the temporary windows of opportunity for the accumulation of physical and human capital afforded by these age shifts. There are parallels at the household level. Those groups in society that are at the leading edges of such change, and can take advantage of them by educating their children and finding good jobs, will benefit in terms of income and asset accumulation.

The poor, who are typically the last group in society to experience fertility decline, may miss out on such opportunities. They may find themselves relatively worse off at the end of the transition, particularly if they miss the signals that large families may no longer be as beneficial to them as in the past. Lipton (1995) refers to this as a

cycle of poverty, not in the usual connotation (to blame victims and absolve the rich and the State), but because inequality and inadequate, or inappropriate, state action creates harsh circumstances in which poor, undernourished and undereducated parents cannot avoid 'rational choices' to produce many children like themselves. (Emphasis in original)

Attention to contextual factors has also been emphasized in recent work on links between population and education. Jejeebhoy's (1996) review of links between education, women's autonomy, and reproductive outcomes documents the expected strong association between levels of educational attainment and such population variables as desire for small families and use of contraception. At the same time, she notes that the strength of the effects depends on the autonomy that women have in making reproductive decisions, which varies substantially in different cultural contexts. In settings characterized by a high degree of gender stratification, effective decision-making comes only with relatively high levels of education, if at all. In more egalitarian settings, even modestly educated women are likely to participate in important family decisions, whether they be economic (working outside the home, spending money) or non-economic (child care, sexual abstinence, fertility regulation).

Lloyd's (1994) paper on investing in the next generation reviews more recent evidence on the relationship between large family size and investment in children, with strong emphasis on the point that effects are context specific and not gender neutral. The studies cited in her review suggest that the level of development, the level of social expenditures by the state, the culture of the family, and the phase of the demographic transition are critical determinants of the relationship between fertility and the level of child investment.

1. Some level of development appears to be required before family size has an impact on child investment; in environments without schools and health clinics, parents have few ways to impact materially on their children's health or schooling, whether their resources are spread among few or many. Similarly, at a given level of development, the greater the extent to which child services are subsidized by the state, the less important parental resource constraints are for child investments.
2. Cultural and institutional factors affect the process in a variety of ways. While mothers may be more child-oriented in their expenditures than fathers, their

capacity to act on this will depend on their access to resources and their autonomy in using household resources. In cultures where responsibilities for child support extends beyond children's own parents to grandparents, aunts and uncles, and others, the number of siblings may be a less important determinant. Where child fostering is common, the impact of additional children is spread across a wider kin network.

3. The phase of the demographic transition also conditions these effects. The linkage between child mortality and fertility has long been recognized, including the possibility of excess fertility as a result of the expectation that more children would die than actually did when infant mortality was declining. As parents gain confidence that both they and their children will survive long enough to reap the returns on investments in child quality, investments in children may rise.

In settings where older siblings share child-care responsibilities, girls are more likely than boys to carry such responsibility, and are more likely to drop out of school for this reason. Gender bias can be more direct in societies where education of girls is valued less by parents (and teachers) than for boys, or where conditions in schools (lack of privacy in bathrooms or lack of personal security, for example) are an obstacle for girls, particularly as they approach early adolescence. More recent work by Mensch and Lloyd (1998) examines gender differences in the schooling experiences of adolescents in Kenya with a view to illuminating some of the factors that may present obstacles for girls. They found that girls did less well in school than boys, in part because of negative attitudes and discriminatory practices in school and also because while attendance at school increases their risk of early sexual activity, little guidance and information is provided to help them deal with this risk.

Unwanted pregnancy can undermine investments in schooling by disrupting parents' plans for investing in children already born. Gage (1995) reminds us that it is also one of the main reasons why girls drop out of school. Montgomery and Lloyd (1997) examined the effects of departures from family-size goals in four countries and found evidence suggesting that unwanted and excess births reduced educational attainment in two countries (the Dominican Republic and the Philippines) but found no such effect in two others (Kenya and Egypt). Both contextual and family-level factors are suggested as explanations of this. They argue that the positive benefits of reductions in unwanted fertility are more likely to show up in countries in later stages of the transition to lower fertility (total fertility rates (TFR) were around 4 in the Dominican Republic and the Philippines). In Kenya (where the TFR was above 5), the capacity of families to spread the costs of unanticipated childbearing among relatives may explain why the effect is not observed there.

This last point is buttressed in further analyses by Mensch, Bruce, and Green (1998), who reviewed findings from a range of studies and data sources on the experiences of adolescent girls in the developing world. They report that the driving forces behind early marriage and childbearing are girl's social and economic disadvantages. Their movements outside the household are restricted in many settings, and their domestic duties are meant to prepare them for a lifelong role as wife and mother. This affects their social contacts and chances for education at a time when boys are being encouraged to develop some degree of autonomy and independence from the family. In many settings, particularly Sub-Saharan Africa and South Asia, girls' school enrollment declines steeply during adolescence because of rising school fees, distance to be traveled, parents' fears about safety and their daughters' reputation, and the expectation that the benefits of education will accrue to the family into which the girl marries rather than their own.

In Latin America, where gender differentials in school enrollment have not been as great as in Africa and South Asia, Hausmann and Székely's (1998) analysis of household-level data for 14 countries seeks to determine whether household demographics contribute to an intergenerational transmission of inequity and, if so, how it happens. Their data show that parent's education is a key determinant of the number and educational attainment of children, and that the extent to which this contributes to inequality among households depends largely on factors outside the household, labor markets, and the returns to education of women, which vary by country. Again, context matters.

4. POLICY AND PROGRAM IMPLICATIONS

While demographers continue to find negative correlations between household size and structure, high fertility, unwanted fertility, and a range of measures of house-hold well-being and/or poverty status, it remains difficult to draw strong conclusions. Exceptions to generally accepted empirical relationships almost inevitably turn up. Economists remind us that (1) causal relationships are difficult to identify because fertility and related household-level resource allocation decisions are jointly deter-mined and (2) households are not acting irrationally in trading what they perceive to be the short-term costs of high fertility for the longer-term contributions that those children will make to household income, old-age security, and the other benefits that children bring.

Recent studies broadened the scope of inquiry into the links between household demographics and welfare, with particular focus on factors affecting gender relations in society and within the households. They reveal an interplay of forces that are far more complex than the links between family size and welfare outcomes and point to a number of reasons why parental expectations about the benefits and costs of rearing another child may not be realized or could lead to a reduction in their and their children's well-being rather than improve it. Some of the reasons that this might happen are that:

- Public policies may distort markets, particularly for low-income labor, and lead poor households to expect higher returns from their children's labor than is actually possible.
- Market conditions on which decisions are based (e.g. the value of the labor of an extra child) may be changing rapidly as a result of changing demographics (rapid changes in age composition associated with fertility decline at the societal level) and economic conditions (new technologies, globalization).

- Because they are usually at the trailing rather than leading edge of the economic, demographic, and institutional change processes affecting outcomes of household decisions, the poor are more likely to be losers (and the rich to be winners) in the longer run.
- The poor have less access to information or fewer of the physical and human capital assets needed to take advantage of the windows of opportunity afforded by such changes.
- In certain cultural and institutional environments, women and children may be in less powerful bargaining positions than men and boys in the resource allocation process and will thus bear a disproportionate share of the costs of high fertility.

The effort to understand linkages between population dynamics and poverty at the household level is motivated by the desire to identify policy and program directions that will help the poor adapt more effectively to change and/or cope more effectively with the risks associated with rapid change, or to ensure that when they make household reproductive decisions that they perceive to be in their best interest, those decisions do not in fact reduce their welfare.

To be effective, interventions need to address specific needs such as the reduction in unwanted fertility and keeping girls in school as well as to combine services with support for income and employment for women. An example of the latter is the micro-enterprise programs such as BRAC in Bangladesh. As noted in the review by Khandker and Khalily (1996), BRAC's social development programs build on a basic core of micro-credit with interventions in health care, basic education, legal services, and skill development for its members, most of whom are women. The way in which the programs are designed and implemented may enhance the synergistic effects by seeking to ensure that women have control over money, that their information networks are broadened through contacts that reach beyond the traditional boundaries for poor women in Bangladesh, and by reinforcing positive human development practices and values in regular meetings of members.

In Africa, social action programs and social funds have proved themselves to be valuable means of support for multi-sectoral initiatives to reduce poverty and contribute to positive reproductive health and population outcomes (Marc *et al.* 1995). Targeted on the poor rather than specific sectoral inputs, they have mobilized community support and funding for family planning and reproductive health services as well as credit and job creation for rural women. Malawi's social action program has had direct effects on population and reproductive health outcomes through health and family planning services as well as indirect effects through gender-focused initiatives in education, credit, and employment schemes.

These synergies do not just happen. Achieving multi-sectoral effects that empower poor households requires special institutional capacity over and above that required to deliver services. Even when sectoral ministries do relatively well in designing and delivering the services for which they are responsible, they often miss opportunities to address multi-sectoral opportunities. Experience has shown that attempts to run such initiatives from within sectoral ministries usually fail because other sectors do not have a sense of ownership or because the implementing sectoral ministry does not really grasp what kind of multi-sectoral outreach is needed to achieve these effects. Some countries have attempted to address multi-sectoral dimensions of population policy through national population councils or similar intra-governmental units, but there are few success stories. A recent Population Council/Overseas Development Council (1997) seminar concluded that the population community needed to reach out and involve new individual and institutional talent if the multi-sectoral dimensions of population are to be effectively addressed.

Because governments and international organizations organize themselves along sectoral lines, they find it difficult to reach effectively across sectoral boundaries. Foundations and non-governmental organizations are potentially better equipped to help both governments and aid donors do better in this arena. As 'Cairo-plus-five' events unfold, it would be useful to focus the effort to build and strengthen the partnerships being called upon to implement the Cairo Program of Action on this important aspect of that agenda.

References

Ahlburg, D. A. 1994. 'Population growth and poverty'. In Cassen *et al.* 1994.

—— A. C. Kelley, and K. O. Mason, eds. 1996. *The Impact Population Growth on Well-Being in Developing Countries*. Berlin: Springer-Verlag.

Anand, S., and J. Morduch 1996. 'Population and Poverty'. In IUSSP. 1995.

Behrman, J. 1996. 'Demographic Change, Poverty, and Income Distribution'. *Occasional Papers Series No. 4*. Washington: Overseas Development Council.

—— and T. N. Srinivasan, eds. 1995. *Handbook of Development Economics: volume 3*. Amsterdam: Elsevier.

—— R. Pollack, and P. Taubman. 1995. *From Parent to Child: Intrahousehold Allocations and Intergenerational Relations in the United States*. Chicago: University of Chicago Press.

Birdsall, N. 1988. 'Economic Approaches to Population Growth'. In Chenery and Srinivasan 1988.

—— 1994. 'Government, Population and Poverty; A Win-Win Tale'. in Cassen *et al.* 1994.

Cassen, R. and contributors. 1994. *Population and Development: Old Debates, New Conclusions*. New Brunswick and Oxford: Transaction Publishers.

—— with Bates, L. 1994. *Population Policy: A New Consensus*. Washington: Overseas Development Council.

Chenery, H., and T. N. Srinivasan, eds. 1988. *Handbook of Development Economics: volume 1*. Rotterdam: North-Holland.

Dasgupta, P. 1992. 'Population, Resources and Poverty'. *Ambio*, 21: 95–101.

—— 1995. 'The Population Problem: Theory and Evidence'. *Journal of Economic Literature*. xxxiii: 1879–902.

Gage, Anastasia. 1995. 'The Social Implications of Adolescent Fertility'. In IUSSP 1995.

Hausmann, R., and M. Székely. 1998. 'Inequality and the Family in Latin America'. Office of the Chief Economist, Inter-American Development Bank.

Hobcraft, J. 1997. 'The Consequences of Female Empowerment for Child Well-Being'. In Seminar on Female Empowerment and Demographic Porcesses: Moving beyond Cairo. Lund, Sweden: Lund University and International Union for the Scientific Study of Population.

International Union for the Scientific Study of Population (IUSSP). 1995. *Demography and Poverty*. Florence: IUSSP.

Jejeebhoy, S. J. 1996. 'Women's Education, Autonomy and Reproductive Behavior: Assessing what we have Learned'. Honolulu: East–West Center Program on Population.

Johnson, D. G., and R. D. Lee. 1987. *Population Growth and Economic Development: Issues and Evidence*. Madison: University of Wisconsin.

Kelley, A. C. 1988. 'Economic Consequences of Population Change'. *Journal of Economic Literature*. xxvi: 1685–728.

—— 1996. 'The Consequences of Rapid Population Growth on Human Resource Development: The Case of Education'. In Ahlburg *et al*. 1996.

Khandker, S., and B. Khalily. 1996. 'The Bangladesh Rural Advancement Committee's Credit Programs: Performance and Sustainability'. *World Bank Discussion Papers No. 324*. Washington: The World Bank.

King, E. M. 1987. 'The Effect of Family Size on Family Welfare: What do we Know?' In Johnson and Lee 1987.

Lipton, M. 1983. 'Demography and Poverty'. *World Bank Staff Working Papers No. 623*. Washington: The World Bank.

—— 1995. 'Population and Poverty: How do they Interact?' In IUSSP 1995.

—— and M. Ravallion. 1995. 'Poverty and Policy'. In Behrman and Srinivasan 1995.

Lloyd, C. B. 1994. 'Investing in the Next Generation: The Implications of High Fertility at the level of the Family'. In Cassen *et al*. 1994.

Marc, A., Carol Graham, Mark Shakter, and Mary Schmidt. 1995. 'Social Action Programs and Social Funds: A Review of Design and Implementation in Sub-Saharan Africa'. World Bank Discussion Paper No. 274.

Mensch, B. S., and C. B. Lloyd. 1998. 'Gender Differences in the Schooling Experiences of Kenyan Adolescents'. *Studies in Family Planning*. 29: 167–184.

—— J. Bruce, and M. E. Greene. 1998. *The Uncharted Passage: Girls' Adolescence in the Developing World*. New York: The Population Council.

Montgomery, M. R., and C. B. Lloyd. 1997. 'Excess Fertility, Unintended Births and Children's Schooling'. In *Policy Research Division Working Paper No. 100*. New York: The Population Council.

National Research Council. 1986. *Population Growth and Economic Development: Policy Questions*. Washington: National Academy Press.

The Population Council and the Overseas Development Council. 1997. 'What can be Done to Foster Multi-sectoral Population Policies?' New York and Washington: The Population Council and Overseas Development Council.

Rosenzweig, M. R. 1990. 'Population Growth and Human Capital Investments: Theory and Evidence'. *Journal of Political Economy*. 98: S38–S71.

Schultz, T. P. 1987. 'School Expenditures and Enrollments, 1960–1980: The Effects of Income, Prices, and Population Growth', in Johnson and Lee 1987.

Tan, J.-P., and A. Mingat. 1992. *Education in Asia: A Comparative Study of Cost and Financing*. Washington: The World Bank.

9

Demographic Transition and Poverty: Effects via Economic Growth, Distribution, and Conversion

ROBERT EASTWOOD AND MICHAEL LIPTON

1. THE HEART OF THE MATTER

Demographic transition affects poverty in several ways. The literature concentrates on one aspect of the transition—population size, as it is increased by population growth and as it increases population density—and on one effect of this, on poverty[1] via economic growth. The effect of the size aspect of transition on poverty is probably important and usually negative—but it is controversial, because contingent on socio-economic circumstances and scarcities in ways that render it variable in space, and not very robust over time. More robust and important may be another aspect of the transition—changing age-structure—as the main driving force behind two other effects on poverty: via the distribution of consumption and income (CI), and via the efficiency with which the poor and near-poor convert CI into well-being.

Growth effects of demographic transition, especially of changing fertility, on poverty, should be explored with both micro- and macro-level evidence. But the effect of high fertility on poverty via income distribution should be explored mainly at *macro* level; the main transmission mechanism—postulated by Malthus—is through macro markets for labour and food. (When unskilled labourers' mean fertility is high, a labouring family cannot, just by its own prudential restraint, safeguard itself against dear food and cheap work.) Conversion effects are best explored mainly at micro level.

The modern demographic transition is manifested as sharp falls in child mortality and, significantly later, in fertility. These falls (1) first sharply raise, then lower, the rate of population growth—the population-*size* aspect; and (2) first substantially

---

[1] While this does not prove causality, hundreds of empirical studies confirm that in today's developing countries larger households have higher poverty incidence (Krishnaji 1984; Lloyd 1994; Lipton 1983*a*, 1994: 12–13). For example, in urban Colombia in the 1970s, in the poorest decile of households, 78% contained 8 or more persons, as against only 12% for all households (Birdsall 1979). Recent evidence suggests that there are no large regional exceptions, as was sometimes claimed for West Africa, for example; the household surveys in Ghana, the Ivory Coast (Glewwe 1990; Kakwani 1993: 53–4) and Mauritania (Coulombe and Mackay 1994: 48), show a strong positive link of household size to poverty *incidence*. Probably all, or almost all, the 41 developing countries with reliable household surveys show this relationship in both urban and rural areas. Poverty *intensity* also often increases with household size (e.g. Bauer and Mason 1993: 34).

raise, then gradually but substantially lower, the ratio of children to adults—the age-structure aspect. These two aspects of the transition might each affect poverty in three ways: by altering the rate of growth of consumption or income (CI) per person, the growth effect; by altering distribution of CI, the distribution effect; or by altering the well-being or capabilities of the poor at a given CI, the conversion effect.[2]

Recent controversy has concerned the growth effect on poverty from changing population size, especially via the rate at which fertility falls after an initial decline in mortality. While most evidence is that faster fertility-induced rises in population size worsen poverty by slowing CI growth—so that speeding up the fertility transition helps the poor by retarding population size—this may not be very robust.[3] The distribution effect and conversion effect of demographic transition on poverty are at least as harmful to poverty reduction in early transition, and as helpful as fertility declines later, as the growth effect; and the poverty impact of the three effects via age structure is at least as harmful in early transition (and as helpful when the trends reverse later) as via population size.

New data (Eastwood and Lipton 1999; hereafter EL) show that the distribution effect, on a nation's poverty incidence, of higher fertility is harmful, and about as large as the growth effect. Other evidence (Bloom and Williamson 1997) shows that changing age structure largely mediates the effect of demographic transition on international variations in economic growth; these explain 35–50 percent of variance in rates of poverty reduction (Ravallion and Chen 1996; Lipton 1998*b*).

The evidence on the conversion effect is less rigorously comparable, but the number of careful household-based analyses is impressive. Poorer couples—acting rationally—start families earlier, have more and closer-spaced children, and over-compensate for the high child mortality caused by poverty (and worsened by these harsh decisions) with even higher fertility and population increase, relative to richer couples. Almost certainly, high fertility reduces conversion efficiency for the poor and near-poor, that is, sib crowding effects outweigh economies of scale in consumption for them.

Table 9.1 guesses at the relative size and robustness of possible paths from high fertility to slower progress against poverty, and from fertility slow-down to faster progress. In interpreting it one should recall Malthus's recognition (1824)—based on census results, especially for Norway and Switzerland, showing that low death rates induced lower birth rates—that, as poor people raised their target for minimum adequate subsistence, they would substitute quality for quantity in children (much as in Becker and Lewis 1973). However, the poor enjoy falling child deaths and rising prospects for female education and modern employment—the main determinants of fertility reduction (Easterlin and Crimmins 1985)—later than the rich in the same country, and thus (Daly 1985) rationally delay their fertility transitions; so poverty reductions from those transitions are also lagged.

---

[2] Definitions of poverty, transition, etc., and evidence, are left until later.

[3] The key macro evidence from cross-national data (Kelley and Schmidt 1994), and confirmatory micro evidence (from India: Evenson 1993), is discussed below, but remains contingent.

Table 9.1. *Tentative Hypotheses: From Population to Poverty*

Effects of population change as manifested in:	Effects on the poor via changes in:		
	Economic growth	CI distribution	Conversion efficiency
Early transition: fast population growth			
Fertility	−−, nr	−−, r	−−, nr?
Age structure	−−−, r	−, r?	−, nr?
Late transition: much slowed growth population			
Fertility	++, nr	++, r	++, nr?
Age structure	+++, r	−/+, nr?	+, r?

Notes: '+' means 'favourable to the poor or to poverty reduction', '−' means 'unfavourable'. The more signs, the more effect. 'r' and 'nr' mean robust, or not, to economic conditions.

2. DEFINITIONS AND APPROACH

Let us initially define 'poor persons' both narrowly and meanly, as 'persons in households where consumption, per equivalent adult (EA), is below a level—the poverty line—expected to be just sufficient to provide adequate food-energy'.[4] The extent of consumption *poverty* in any community can then be measured as 'incidence', that is, the proportion of persons who are poor; as 'intensity', that is, incidence *times* the proportion of poverty-line consumption by which the average poor person falls short of that line; or as 'severity', that is, intensity adjusted to give more weight to more extreme poverty.[5]

Population change, in a given area, is here divided into changes in size and in structure, especially age structure. A particular common sequence of changes in size and age structure of a population of a given area—changes first consequent on, and later also causing, falling child mortality followed by falling fertility—comprises the '*demographic transition*'. Other changes in population structure can also affect poverty and inequality, but are not seen as part of the demographic transition. This is because at national level such structural population change is either small and gradual (e.g. change in gender structure, except during wars), or—as with the rural–urban structure of population[6]—more contingent, less 'biological', than age structure in its interaction with changes in population size.

[4] See Lipton and Ravallion (1995) for fuller discussion and references.
[5] See Lipton and Ravallion (1995) for fuller discussion and references.
[6] Falling rural shares in population normally bring falling mortality, faster-falling fertility, and hence slower population growth. But exceptions such as Pakistan show that this sequence is not pre-ordained. In the initial stages it depends on gender-selective migration of young persons from a big rural sector to a small urban sector, which becomes highly 'unbalanced' between genders in the child-producing age groups. As this imbalance falls, townward migration continues to retard population growth only to the extent that such migration reduces fertility incentives, i.e. to the extent that health care, educational chances, and above all gender equality are significantly more in urban than in rural areas.

Demographic transition can affect trends in any measure of poverty in three ways.

- It can alter the *growth* rate of CI per EA. Growth is the product of (1) extra output per unit of investment in—that is, the total marginal product of—physical and human capital and (2) the proportion of output that is saved (domestically, or by attracting net foreign savings to finance an import surplus). So we can separate the demographics → growth → poverty sequence into effects via (1) the efficiency of extra capital, human or physical, generated by savings and (2) the savings rate.

- Demographic transition can also alter *inequality* as it affects poverty: via income distribution between poor and non-poor (especially near-poor), and also (if intensity or severity is the poverty measure) between just-poor, poorer, and very poor.[7] Poverty is not directly affected by 'any old' inequality, for example, by the gap between the top 1 percent and the next-richest 9 percent.[8] Section 3, using EL, shows that the demographics → inequality → poverty sequence can operate in two ways, here termed the dependency effect and the acquisition effect.

- Thirdly, and almost ignored in the literature, each 'dose' of demographic change may have a once-for-all effect on current consumption poverty by altering the consumption–income ratio of the poor and near-poor.

So the effects of demographic transition on poverty are complex partly because 'poverty', 'transition', and 'effects' each have several connotations:

1. Poverty is measured by (*a*) incidence, (*b*) intensity, or (*c*) severity.[9]
2. Each of the three measures in a country can be affected by either of two demographic transition aspects: changing (*a*) population size or (*b*) age structure. (They are linked, but the links shift: age-specific fertility and mortality vary over space and time).
3. Each of the two demographic transition aspects can influence each of the three poverty measures via five effects: by changing: *Economic growth*, as the transition alters (*a*) savings rates or (*b*) the total derivative of output to physical and/or human capital; *low-end inequality*, as the transition alters, differently for the poor (or near-poor) and the non-poor, (*c*) dependency ratios, or (*d*) incentives per

---

[7] If many of the non-poor are near-poor, this hugely increases the impact of regressive redistribution (if it pushes many such people even very slightly below the poverty line) on poverty incidence, though the effect on intensity and severity may be tiny. Because incidence is a bad (though popular) measure of poverty, its use leads to counter-intuitive inferences about the effects on poverty incidence of redistribution (whether or not due to demographic change). Redistributing consumption from the very poor to those just below the poverty line, i.e. regressively among the poor, will push some of the just-poor above the line and thus reduce poverty *incidence*. Redistributing income from the just-poor to the rich does not increase poverty incidence, 'only' intensity and severity.

[8] It does, however, have a disproportionately large effect on the Gini coefficient. It may well be the main mechanism at work in those few cases where a Kuznets curve has been verified (Lecaillon *et al.* 1983). This underlines the need *not* to use Gini, Theil, etc. coefficients to measure inequality when we consider it as a cause, effect, or correlate of poverty. (It may be that top-end inequality affects poverty *indirectly*—e.g. if such inequality arises from concentration of market power to buy unskilled labour and/or to sell items consumed by the poor.)

[9] This assumes we measure absolute poverty at one poverty line. Matters become even more involved with different (absolute) poverty lines, or relative or subjective measures.

worker to acquire income; or (*e*) the part of poor people's incomes that they consume, as the transition alters low end consumption income ratios.

So there are at least 3 × 2 × 5, or 60, paths from demographic transition to poverty. Not one is clearly unimportant!

Two more bricks must be put in place. *Differential demographic transition* means, among other things, that the poor usually experience declining mortality and subsequently falling fertility later, and with a longer lag between them, than the non-poor (see above). *Mutual causation* means that rapid population growth—with its usual accompaniments of early first births, large families, high child–adult ratios and near spacing of siblings—may be not only a cause of poverty through the above mechanisms, but also a consequence of poverty—probably due largely to constraints on, and rational behavior by, the poor.

In this example, faster demographic transition is assumed to reduce poverty levels, and this reduction is assumed to accelerate transition. In fact, either part of the mutual causation might work the opposite way. More people could bring economies of scale of various sorts, for example, making it pay in some African economies to put in transport links that led to farm intensification; if this path is genuine, rapid demographic transition would slow down progress along it, toward faster growth and hence poverty reduction. Similarly, if faster population growth permits 'infection effects' and economies of scale in research (Simon 1986), this process too would be slowed down by faster demographic transition. It is also possible to envisage circumstances where poverty reduction leads to faster, rather than slower, population growth; this was Malthus's initial position, though one he drastically modified in his later work.

Partha Dasgupta (2000) has argued persuasively that—especially if we add the interaction of environmental change—it is not feasible to sort out the mutual demographic-economic chains (from or to population, via growth and distribution, to or from poverty) by normal economic empirics. We seem to be reduced either to exchanging examples and anecdotes, or to econometrics inevitably dependent—because of degrees-of-freedom problems, if nothing else—on selecting some variables (and some functional forms) and omitting others. Also time series for poverty are scarce, and usually on a time scale shorter than that of demographic change (for which normally only decennial census data are available—household surveys being usually one-off).

The rest of this chapter is structured as follows. Section 3, the bulk of the chapter, condenses the results of EL (1999), indicating large negative growth and distribution effects—of similar size—of high fertility on poverty. Section 4 argues that the 'conversion effect' of high fertility on poor and near-poor people's capacity to turn a *given* CI into capabilities and well-being is also negative and large. Section 5 suggests that the distribution and conversion effects of fertility on poverty are likely to be more robust and universal than the growth effect. Section 6 shows how these interactions between fertility and poverty are strengthened in the context of various 'virtuous circles' that have begun to emerge as centre-pieces of the new development economics—which can itself be strengthened by becoming less of a demography-free zone. Section 7 glances—very superficially—at possible implications for development policy, optimal population, and the welfare economics of inheritance.

3. GROWTH AND DISTRIBUTION EFFECTS OF FERTILITY CHANGE ON POVERTY

3.1. *Main Results Summarized—and the Intellectual Context*

EL, using cross-national regressions for 45 developing and transitional economies, show that fertility (crude birth rate net of infant deaths) increases absolute poverty (defined with respect to a 1985 dollar-a-day private consumption standard) both by retarding economic growth and by skewing distribution against the poor. The average country in 1980 had poverty incidence of 18.9 percent; had it reduced its fertility by 5 per 1,000 throughout the 1980s (as did many Asian countries), this figure would have been reduced to 12.6 percent. The growth and distribution effects are roughly equally responsible for this reduction. This analysis neglects effects on conversion efficiency of CI into well-being among poor and near-poor people; such effects almost certainly increase these people's gains from fertility reduction, as do 'virtuous circle' effects discussed in Section 6 below.

What is the context of these results? Malthus's mature work, based on new Census evidence, reversed his earlier view that 'schemes of improvement'[10]—by increasing the CI of the poor—would necessarily induce higher fertility. However, he maintained his view that higher fertility would raise the supply of unskilled labour and the demand for food, pushing real wage rates down, and thus increasing poverty through *distribution effects*, on which his analysis[11] clearly centers. He questioned the capacity of liberalization to reduce poverty (absent reduced family-size norms among the poor), not to increase economic growth. Yet, oddly, Malthus's approach is explored in modern economics mainly in the debate between neo-Godwinians such as Julian Simon (1986) and others about the *growth effect* of fertility; the key papers are Kelley and Schmidt (hereafter KS) (1994, 1995).[12]

---

[10] Including not only the redistributive proposals of Godwin and Condorcet, but also the trade liberalization proposed by Adam Smith (see Lipton 1990 for further discussion and references).

[11] As opposed to caricatures of it; and minus his assumptions about contraception, and his unfortunate heuristic device of contrasting geometric population growth against (allegedly) arithmetic growth in food output. Malthus's changing responses to evidence, especially his 1824 summing-up, are much closer to modern economic demography than is his 'undergraduate essay' of 1798. See Lipton (1990).

[12] References are to KS (1994) unless otherwise stated. KS (1995) should be consulted on choice of lags and on isolation of birth-rate and death-rate effects. In a paper perhaps written before these results, and certainly before those of Datt and Ravallion (1996) or Lipton (1998a) on the effects of growth on poverty, Ahlburg (1996: 218) emphasizes that there is 'little direct evidence' on Malthus's argument that high fertility worsens *poverty*; his literature review concludes that a negative impact 'is reasonably clear [but its importance] is unclear'. Time-series analysis for 13 Indian States from 1959/60 to 1970/71 concluded that a 10% rise in rural population raised the incidence of rural poverty by about one-tenth of a percentage point; thus the impact, while significant at the 5% level and causally structured, was not large, though in some States a larger impact (up to 1 percentage point) was found (ibid. 242; van der Walle 1985). Van der Walle conjectures that this is due to adverse shifts in rural income distribution because of higher unemployment.

On the former, KS analyze cross-sections[13] of both developing and developed countries for the 1960s, the 1970s, and the 1980s, showing that high birth rates reduce current growth of real GDP per person, but accelerate it after 10 to 15 years, as the extra new-borns grow up and become workers and net savers. In each decade the net effect of higher birth rates on growth was negative, but so was that of higher death rates. Both effects usually appear substantial, significant, robust, and causally structured; but they have opposite implications for the relationship between population growth and the rate of growth of GDP per person, so that stability in this relationship is not to be expected, and is not found.[14] The link from fertility to growth, like almost all the KS results, is stronger for developing countries. Their results imply that the fertility fall actually achieved in the 1980s by the median developing country raised the growth rate of GDP per capita by about 1.4 percentage points.[15] EL strengthen the inference that higher fertility damages growth, since—unlike KS—their more recent and improved data show no offset from higher lagged fertility (or from lower death rates). To estimate poverty effects through the growth channel, EL combine these results with estimates of the impact of growth on poverty. They thus estimate the size of damage from higher fertility,[16] via slower economic growth and lower mean GDP (or private consumption), to poverty.

EL further show that higher fertility also increases poverty through the distribution channel, as Malthus believed. The effect is of similar size to that through the growth channel, and comprises (1) the acquisition effect of higher fertility, in reducing the relative ability or willingness of poorer households to acquire a given level of total

Evenson (1993; see fn. 41 below) confirms the distributional effect with data for Indian Districts (but shows that it works largely through real wage rates), as do the results of this chapter globally. Squire (1993) found no significant cross-national linkage between population growth and changes in poverty incidence, but could not fully explore causal structure or omitted-variables problems, partly for lack of time-series data.

[13] Time-series data are preferable. But poverty time series in developing countries are few, and except in India too close together and for too short periods to test the impact of long-run demographic change. Hence KS and EL use cross-section data.

[14] KS find an indeterminate relationship for the 1960s and 1970s and a negative relationship in the 1980s, for two reasons. First, international variation in the death rate has become much smaller since 1980, so that the (still large) variation in the birth rate has become a relatively more important component of differences in the rate of population growth Secondly, the effect of fertility differences on economic growth became stronger in the 1980s: much higher real long-term interest rates, and debt-related and other finance constraints since 1980 make it likelier that growth has been finance-constrained in developing countries, increasing the importance of (1) the life-cycle savings effect, on growth, of high birth rates, (2) immediate negative effects of birth rates relative to long-term positive effects.

[15] Computed using the equation from KS reported as eqn 2 below. Other relevant evidence: (1) Bloom and Williamson (1997) show that late demographic transition accounts for about half of East Asia's 'excess growth' of real GDP per person in 1970–90 (actual growth was 5.5% per year, 3.5 percentage points above their figure for the long-run sustainable rate of 2% per year). After 1970 past high fertility and falling child mortality, plus fertility decline, raised the working and saving proportions of East Asian populations— a demographic 'gift' to economic growth. In this apparently robust model, the age-structure aspect of transition, not the size aspect, is what drives 'excess' economic growth. (2) Robinson and Srinivasan (1997: 1186–7) note that since 1988 'more recent work . . . has found a small negative relationship' between population growth, especially as influenced by birth rates, and economic growth.

[16] We use 'fertility' henceforth to refer to birth rates, often 'net' of infant deaths, and sometimes lagged or adjusted, as indicated by the context.

household consumption (e.g. via regressive effects of extra child costs and falls in the real wage) and (2) the dependency effect of higher fertility, in diluting given household consumption more in poorer households, because their higher overall fertility raises their dependency burden proportionately more than for other households.

3.2. *Data and Methods*[17]

Data Choices On *poverty*,[18] there are three issues. EL's *choice of concept* is 'narrow' absolute private consumption poverty, PCP. A person suffers PCP if and only if she falls below a fixed level of private consumption—the poverty line—in the country and year of survey. Consumption indicates command over resources more reliably and stably than income. It would be desirable to include free or subsidized consumption of state-provided, collective, or non-price-excludable public goods, but this is seldom available from surveys, and raises valuation problems; hence per-person 'paid-for' (private) consumption[19] is used. EL's choice of poverty line is the widely available, though arbitrary, 'POV30': a level of private consumption that, if exchanged into dollars at rates adjusted for purchasing-power parity, could command $30 per person per month (in 1985 prices) of the bundle of goods and services consumed in 1985 by an average citizen of 'Earthia'.[20] For adding up poverty below the line, EL use incidence and intensity (incidence times proportion by which the average poor person's consumption falls below the line).

EL also need to measure *real resource flows* per person—to isolate the effect of fertility on distribution, and to act as dependent variable in analyzing the effect of fertility on growth. EL report equations using two such indicators: mean real GDP, because its growth is a policy target, and indicates a nation's resource flow; and AVCON, because its variance does significantly better than variance of real per capita GDP in explaining international differences in poverty.[21]

The right measures and lags for *fertility* depend on the effects hypothesized on poverty, whether via growth or distribution. Possible indicators are: crude birth rate;

---

[17] For full discussion, see EL.

[18] A cross-section of the most recent available nation-wide household survey data—all post-1980 and in all but five cases post-1987—is used for both poverty and AVCON. The data were kindly made available to EL by Ravallion and Chen, who have screened them for reliability and nation-wide coverage (1996). Data are for 59 countries, 46 developing and 13 transitional.

[19] In surveys used by EL, consumption includes peasant household enterprises' self-consumed product (mostly staple crops), usually at retail value. Consumption per equivalent adult is preferable, but raises measurement problems (Deaton and Muellbauer 1980), is often unobtainable, and where obtainable seldom ranks large groups differently from consumption per person.

[20] Comparisons among countries of real average consumption (AVCON), real average GDP, and poverty lines are made using purchasing-power parities from the latest (5.6) version of the Penn World Tables.

[21] EL use AVCON, alongside fertility indicators, to predict national poverty levels through the distribution channel. However, KS (and EL where they analyze the poverty effect of fertility through the growth channel) also use fertility indicators to predict not AVCON but mean real GDP, and there they also estimate the elasticity of AVCON with respect to mean real GDP.

net birth rate, that is, crude birth rate net of infant deaths; dependency ratio; and total fertility rate. The net birth rate represents durable additions better, especially since many infant deaths (in developing countries often 10–20% of all births) occur in the first few weeks of life. The net birth rate is used in KS's analysis of the fertility-to-growth link, and in EL's analysis of the growth channel.[22]

Data Types   Why did EL decide to test fertility-to-poverty links with macro data? Probably only household surveys—often, only panels—can provide data to estimate individual decisions underlying changes in fertility, and also in many socioeconomic variables, such as labour supply, that affect poverty (Schultz 1981). However, a data set on PCP at an internationally comparable norm has recently become available; it is for countries. Even if we can get household-level poverty data, comparable data for fertility are hard to come by; vital events are infrequent, even in quite large sub-samples. Official fertility data from large samples, such as India's Sample Registration Survey, are never made available at household level and seldom even at reasonably disaggregated levels such as an Indian District (typically 2–5 million people). But all this merely says that it is easier to look for a lost key where there is a street-light–little use if it is elsewhere. There is a more positive reason for using macro data: that the main posited links between fertility and poverty operate only at national level, or via large interacting markets. The Malthus hypothesis—that population growth increases poverty by depressing real wage rates, bidding up market labour supply and food demand—cannot be tested by using micro data that reveal only the impact of population characteristics on each household's labour supply, food demand, and poverty. Further, internal migration weakens effects at subnational level, even in large geographical units; for instance, if an Indian State has higher fertility than its neighbors and this threatens higher poverty, one would expect migration to other States, diffusing the effect. Only cross-national analysis can capture such effects in macro markets.

EL use *cross-section data* because on time series on poverty are inadequate. Ravallion and Chen (1996) find pairs of observations on national poverty for 42 developing and transitional economies, but most of the pairs are separated by five years or fewer; only very few countries have reliable estimates of demographic change over such short periods.[23] Until more long-term poverty (or more short-term demographic) data sets are available, international comparative work on the links between poverty and demography must rely on cross-section data.

Econometric Issues—Causality   In assessing whether there is reciprocal causation between the birth rate and poverty incidence, a problem arises: for the vast majority

---

[22] In modeling the distribution channel we tried a range of fertility indicators, and two other demographic indicators (net death rate, namely, crude death rate less infant deaths, and population growth rate. Again net birth rate does best in a statistical sense, for reasons discussed in Sect. 3.3).

[23] The only widespread empirical base for fertility data is decennial censuses. Except in a few cases such as India's Sample Registration Surveys, annual data are inevitably arbitrary interpolations, giving no genuine information about fertility changes over short periods.

of developing countries, reliable nation-wide PCP estimates are few and recent. Thus we cannot, for example, test whether lagged values of the birth rate add anything to an explanation of poverty in terms of its own history (Granger causality). Just using lagged demographic variables in the poverty equations does not eliminate the problem: an association between poverty and the lagged birth rate might be attributed to reverse causation via (1) dependence of poverty on its own history, (2) dependence of the birth rate on its own history, and (3) contemporaneous dependence of the birth rate on poverty. So we run poverty regressions with *both* the current and the lagged birth rates as regressors. If causation ran mainly from poverty to the birth rate, poverty should be more strongly associated with the current birth rate than with the lagged birth rate. When, conversely, we find that the association with the lagged birth rate is much stronger, we infer that the dominant causal process is from the birth rate to poverty.

The problem of joint causation has been used as a basis for criticizing the use of aggregate relationships in studying links between economic and demographic variables (Schultz 1981). For example, faster economic growth may help to explain lower fertility in a statistical sense, but it is reasonable to attribute this to joint causation, in the absence of any apparent causal process running from growth to fertility. The aggregate relationship is accordingly uninformative, as well as being of little use to a policy-maker wanting to know which growth-promoting policies are also fertility-reducing and which are not. However, plausible causal processes from lagged demography to poverty are identifiable.

Econometric Issues—Structure and Robustness EL's approach to the functional relationship between 'poverty' and the independent variables (average GDP or consumption, and demographic indicators) was pragmatic. They experimented with several forms (linear, double log, with and without interaction terms) and were guided by results of statistical tests of functional form and normality of residuals.[24] Except as indicated, all reported equations passed both tests at the 5 percent significance level.

To test the robustness of results EL tried regional dummies, and other potential determinants of poverty ('social variables').[25] Regional dummies were sometimes significant when entered individually, but in the interests of robustness we required them to retain significance when other regional dummies were also included.[26] The

---

[24] Ramsey's RESET test of functional form and Bera and Jarque's test for normality as described in Pesaran and Pesaran (1991). Using the normality test as a criterion, rather than merely as an indicator of whether significance tests are to be relied upon, may perhaps be justified by reference to the Central Limit Theorem.

[25] It has become standard procedure (Levine and Renelt 1992; KS 1994: 40–1; Clarke 1995) to test equations predicting economic growth by seeing what happens to the statistical significance of the explanators (and to the size of their effect) when the standard 'Barro variables' are added to the right-hand side. Since we aim to predict national poverty incidence rather than growth, our 'social variables' are somewhat different from the Barro variables.

[26] EL examined their regressions for outliers. One country (Guinea-Bissau) emerged, and somewhat harmed the results for poverty intensity, but not for incidence. This is because the survey was in a year of near-total harvest failure, with dollar poverty far higher than in any other of the 59 countries reported.

'social variables' comprised two indicators of health provision, two of education provision, and the Gini coefficient of operated land inequality.[27] The aim was both to assess their significance, jointly and severally, and to observe the effects of their inclusion on the size and significance of the demographic effects.

Econometric Issues: Significance Tests and Heteroskedasticity   Both poverty and growth equations contain interaction terms; for example, poverty is measured as a function of net birth rate, surveyed consumption per person, and the product of the two. Thus testing for the significance of a given explanatory variable requires a Wald test of the null hypothesis that both the level and the interaction term can be eliminated. EL therefore place most weight on the Wald statistics in such cases, paying little attention to the t-statistics on the 'level' terms.

EL found heteroskedasticity only in the equations for intensity of poverty ('poverty gap index'). Here, significance tests are based on White-corrected estimated standard errors.[28]

3.3. *New Results: Distribution Channel from Fertility to Poverty*

EL's preferred equation for the impact on the percentage incidence of PCP below $30 per month in standardized 1985 purchasing power (PWT 5.6)[29] is eqn 1 in Table 9.2. This gives incidence as a linear function of the natural logarithm of real consumption expenditure per head (LAVCON), the ten-year lagged net birth rate (NBR10), an interaction term (the product of the first two regressors) and a dummy for Latin American countries. The Wald tests (for LAVCON and NRB10) and the t-test for the Latin American dummy show that all variables are highly significant. Before discussing the effects identified in this equation, EL review its credibility, using the other equations in Table 9.2.

Equation 2 confronts the issue of causality by introducing the current net birth rate (NBR) as well as NBR10. The Wald tests give p-values of 0.592 and 0.101 respectively. For NBR10 to be almost significant at the 10 percent level when contending with NBR—despite a 0.968 correlation coefficient between NBR and NBR10—strongly suggests that the principal causal process runs from lagged births to poverty.[30]

---

[27] The Ginis of operated land (derived from FAO agricultural censuses, fairly reliable at national level, and a reasonable proxy for owned land distribution), cleaned and standardized across countries, were kindly supplied to us by Klaus Deininger of the World Bank.

[28] We looked for heteroskedasticity by regressing squared residuals both on squared fitted values of the dependent variable and, separately, on population. An inverse relation between error variance and population is to be expected if large countries are, in effect, agglomerations of independent regions (Blanchet 1988). We found no evidence of this in our data.

[29] Results for the impact on poverty intensity, and on incidence below $21 per month, are given in Appendix A4.

[30] In view of the high correlation between NBR and NBR10, replacing NBR10 with NBR in eqn 1 produces a very similar result: our only statistical basis for choosing the specification with NBR10 is that provided by eqn 2.

Table 9.2. *POV$30 Set of Regressions*

Independent variables	Regressions						
	1	2	3	4	5	6	7
1. LAVCON	−8.13 (−0.93)	−9.82 (−1.09)	−21.94 (−3.54)	−2.78 (−0.28)	−0.68 (−0.07)	6.27 (0.36)	6.42 (−0.75)
2. NBR		1.87 (0.57)					
3. NBR10	3.41 (3.23)*	1.59 (0.48)		3.29 (2.99)*	3.47 (2.86)*	5.41 (2.44)**	0.45 (3.35)*
4. NDR					−17.44 (−2.23)**		
5. NDR10				2.67 (1.09)	18.73 (2.43)**		
6. POPG10			24.85 (2.39)*				
7. LAVCON*NBR		−0.52 (−0.69)					
8. LAVCON*NBR10	−0.64 (−2.67)*	−0.14 (−0.19)		−0.62 (−2.47)**	−0.67 (−2.26)**	−1.1 (−2.26)**	0.65 (−2.74)*
9. LAVCON*NDR					3.71 (1.96)		
10. LAVCON*NDR10				−0.67 (−1.17)	−4.13 (−2.18)**		
11. LAVCON*POPG10			−4.37 (−1.84)				
12. DUMLATAM	9.97 (3.78)*	10.19 (3.8)*	8.69 (3.13)*	8.92 (2.83)*	7.11 (2.31)**	6.83 (1.62)	9.86 (3.82)*
13. DUMGB						−0.18E-3 (−0.41)	16.62 (1.83)
14. PHYSIC						0.17E-3 (0.28)	
15. NURSE						0.12 (1.64)	
16. PRIMENR						−0.13 (−1.14)	
17. SECENR						−0.41 (−0.03)	
18. LANDGINI							
Adj. R²	0.854	0.851	0.843	0.852	0.866	0.814	0.860
Wald tests	LAVCON 197.99 (0)* NBR10 31.57 (0)*	LAVCON 190.42 (0)* NBR 1.05 (.592) NBR10 4.58 (0.101)	LAVCON 234.9 (0)* POPG10 25.76 (0)*	LAVCON 157.04 (0)* NBR10 27.77 (0)* NDR10 1.43 (0.489)	LAVCON 179.07 (0)* NBR10 26.34 (0)* NDR 7.41 (0.025)** NDR10 7.81 (0.020)**	LAVCON 71.35 (0)* NBR10 7.42 (0.024)** social variables 7.54 (0.183)	LAVCON 162.81 (0)* NBR10 34.86 (0)*

Notes: (a) Sample size = 59, except for regression 6 where s = 38; (b) values in parentheses next to the coefficients are t-ratios; they are p-values for the Wald statistics; (c) all regressions are free from statistical problems (tests outlined in fn. 25); (d) Wald tests: in each case a joint test is performed of the null hypothesis that the coefficient on that term, and those on all interaction terms including it, are zero. Thus, if POV$30 = $\alpha 1 + \alpha 2$*LAVCON + $\alpha 3$*NBR10 + $\alpha 4$*(LAVCON*NBR10), then the Wald test of the significance of NBR10 uses the null: $\alpha 3 = 0$ and $\alpha 4 = 0$; (e) variable definitions in the Appendix.

Equation 3 shows that lagged population growth can replace lagged net births quite successfully.[31] EL therefore consider whether the international differences in poverty are being driven, not by NBR, but by net death rate (NDR) (with which NBR is highly correlated across countries), in eqns 4 to 5, which may be compared to eqns 1 to 2. NDR10 is insignificant in eqn 4, yet when both NDR and NDR10 are included (in eqn 5), both appear significant. EL conclude that the problem of causation makes eqn 5 uninterpretable; not only are there are plainly good reasons to expect two-way causation between net deaths and poverty,[32] but the Wald test statistics, unlike those for eqn 2, give no grounds for asserting that causation runs principally in one direction.

Equation 6 introduces the set of social variables to eqn 1. They achieve significance neither individually nor collectively (but see the discussion of the Latin American dummy below). Equation 7 introduces a dummy variable for Guinea-Bissau. This dummy fails to achieve significance at the 5 percent level, yet the very large estimated excess poverty incidence is worth noting (and becomes significant for measures of poverty intensity, and incidence at $21).

The effects are summarized in Tables 9.3 and 9.4. Because of the interaction between NBR10 and LAVCON, the parameter estimates in eqn 1 are not directly interpretable as marginal effects: for example, the marginal effect of a change in NBR10 on POV$30 depends on the level of LAVCON. The negative sign on the interaction term implies, reasonably, that the poorer the country, the more POV$30 is raised by extra net births. Table 9.3 reports the marginal effects of NBR10 on POV$30 at the 25th, 50th, and 75th percentile values of LAVCON: the effect at the median of LAVCON is of the order of 0.6 (corresponding to an elasticity of about 1.1). This may be put in context: the semi-interquartile range of NBR10 is about 7 births per 1,000 and the median of NBR is about 4 per 1,000 below the median of NBR10. So, for example, it is predicted that a hypothetical country at the medians of NBR10, NBR, and LAVCON would attain, by virtue of the fall of 4 per 1,000 in the net birth rate in the pre-survey decade, a fall of some 2.4 percent in POV$30 in the next decade via the distribution channel alone. For a country at the 25th percentile of the LAVCON distribution, the predicted fall would be about 3.4 percent. The (diagnostic) eqn 2 apart, Table 9.3 also shows that the estimated effects of changes in NBR10 on POV$30 via distribution are fairly stable to specification changes.

Table 9.4 reports the response of POV$30 to changes in LAVCON. Quite apart from changes in NBR10, the functional form of our equation implies that the *elasticity* of

---

[31] Experimentation with the total fertility rate (TFR) and the dependency ratio (DR) produced poor results. In the case of TFR the explanation probably lies in the long and diffuse lag between this variable and CBR. For DR, as explained in Section 3.4, it is high variability of this variable across households—rather than its average value—which would be expected to be associated with high poverty at constant AVCON.

[32] The poor have higher death rates, both because they have a higher proportion of persons in the 'death-prone' age group 0 to 5 (because they marry younger and have higher family-size norms) and because their nutrition and sanitation increase age-specific mortality: thus poverty causes net deaths. Poor households also feature higher death rates among workers, making a causal link from lagged net deaths to poverty probable also.

Table 9.3. *POV$30 Set of Regressions: Effect on the Level of POV$30 (in percent) of a Unit Change in the Demographic Variables*

LAVCON	Regression number						
	1	2	3	4	5	6	7
At 25th percentile	NBR10: 0.85	NBR: −0.21 NBR10: 1.03	POPG10: 7.37	NBR10: 0.81 NBR10: −0.01	NBR10: 0.79 NDR: −2.6 NDR10: 2.21	NBR10: 1.01	NBR10: 0.85
At 50th percentile	NBR10: 0.61	NBR: −0.41 NBR10: 0.98	POPG10: 5.71	NBR10: 0.57 NDR10: −0.26	NBR10: 0.54 NDR: −1.19 NDR10: 0.64	NBR10: 0.59	NBR10: 0.60
At 75th percentile	NBR10: 0.33	NBR: −0.63 NBR10: 0.92	POPG10: 3.83	NBR10: 0.31 NDR10: −0.55	NBR10: 0.25 NDR: 0.41 NDR10: −1.14	NBR10: 0.12	NBR10: 0.32

Note: These level effects are partial derivatives computed at the 25th, 50th, and 75th percentile value of LAVCON, e.g.: $\delta POV\$30/\delta NBR10 = 3.41 + (-0.64*4.38)$ for regression 1 row 2. Table 9.2, col. 1 and Appendix A1.

Table 9.4. *POV$30 Set of Regressions: Effect of Changes in* LAVCON

	Regression number						
	1	2	3	4	5	6	7
Level effect at median	−28.89	−29.15	−32.47	−28.53	−30.47	−29.40	−27.18
Elasticity at median	−1.53	−1.55	−1.72	−1.51	−1.62	−1.56	−1.44

Notes: (*a*) Level effects are partial derivatives computed at the median value of the demographic variable, e.g.: δPOV$30/$\delta$LAVCON $= -8.13 + (-0.64{*}32.43)$ for regression 1; (*b*) elasticities in row 2 are calculated with median values of POV$30 ($= 18.86\%$).

POV$30 with respect to AVCON rises in absolute value as POV$30 falls. Put another way, a 10 percent rise in AVCON has the same absolute effect on poverty incidence whether it occurs in a rich country with low POV$30 or in a poor country with high POV$30. This is intuitive; the experiment entails a greater *absolute* rise in AVCON in the richer country.[33] In Table 9.4, we give both the estimated effect on POV$30 of a 1 percent change in AVCON and the elasticity calculated at the median of POV$30.[34]

Note the strong effect of the Latin American dummy At face value, POV$30 is 10 percentage points higher than would be expected from LAVCON and fertility alone. Land inequality is high in this region. In eqn 6, inclusion of the land Gini and other social variables halves the coefficient of the regional dummy, and renders it insignificant.[35] However, since the social variables are also insignificant in eqn 6, it is not clear what should be inferred. It is disappointing not to have been able to eliminate the regional dummy from the equation by identifying what 'true' causal processes it is obscuring, but exclusion of the dummy has almost no effect on the size or significance of the link from NBR10 to POV$30, so that for this link—our main concern—the problem is of limited importance.

3.4. *Explaining the Distribution Channel: Dependency and Acquisition Effects*

The dependency effect means that higher national fertility may worsen the distribution of consumption if the extra births are concentrated in the poorer households, raising dependency ratios among the poor disproportionately. Mean household

[33] There is a special problem when POV$30 becomes negligible, because successive small identical proportionate rises in AVCON would eventually bring POV$30 incidence below zero; this is one reason why the double-log form is often used (Chen *et al.* 1993; Ravallion and Chen 1996), but its diagnostics are unsatisfactory for our data set.

[34] Our reasonably stable estimate of about −1.5 for the elasticity is close to (but slightly above) that of Ravallion and Chen (1996) in a model without demographic variables.

[35] Further investigation revealed that that there was little to choose in statistical terms between the Gini index of land inequality and the Latin American dummy: each was significant when included without the other (and without the other social variables) and both were insignificant, the Gini rather more so, when included together.

consumption is equal to consumption per non-dependent[36] divided by the dilution ratio: the ratio of household members to non-dependents (one plus the dependency ratio). A rise in fertility raises the dilution ratio in both poor and non-poor households, but we speak of a positive dependency effect only if the ratio is raised proportionately more in poor than in non-poor households. In other words, a positive dependency effect will raise poverty even if the distribution of consumption per non-dependent and national mean consumption do not change. If there is no dependency effect, then higher fertility can worsen the distribution of consumption only by worsening the distribution of consumption per non-dependent—by differential effects on the ability or willingness of non-dependents to acquire income or via differential savings effects. If such worsening does occur, we refer to a positive acquisition effect of the rise in fertility. If both the dependency and acquisition effects are zero then the distribution effect (the effect of higher national fertility on poverty at constant AVCON) is necessarily also zero.[37]

To gather evidence on the dependency effect, EL searched 56 World Bank Poverty Assessments, and in 18 they could identify separate dependency ratios for 'poor' and 'non-poor'. This data set gave only a slight indication that the dependency effect was responsible for the distribution-channel linkage between higher fertility and greater poverty: as the dilution ratio for the poor rises, the proportionate rise in the dilution ratio for the non-poor is only slightly smaller (the estimated elasticity is 0.94, insignificantly different from +1). Although this is weak evidence, probably a strong effect in respect of just young dependents is present, but obscured by the fact that our data do not separate young and old dependents for the poor (or non-poor). In worse-off developing countries (with higher dependency ratios among poor and non-poor alike), a smaller proportion of dependents is over 65, and most of these old dependents are in non-poor households (Lipton 1983*a*, 1988). This suggests that, if our data had separated young and old dependents, the estimated elasticity for the young-end dilution ratio alone would have been below 0.94. Since over-65s make a greater economic contribution to the household than under-15s,[38] a 'young-end' dependency effect may be an important part of the distribution channel from high fertility to poverty.

As regards the acquisition effect, there seem to be four principal ways in which high fertility might worsen the distribution of consumption per non-dependant: through (1) child costs, (2) labour supply, (3) savings, or (4) factor rewards.

1. Marginal child costs consist of the costs associated with the presence of an extra child in the household and those associated with infant mortality. Each may skew consumption against poorer households. One cost of the presence of an extra child is the direct or opportunity cost of child care. Suppose that this cost is fixed independently

---

[36] Meaning 'total household consumption averaged across non-dependents'.

[37] For example, consumption per non-dependent may have risen uniformly by, say, 10% while a rise in fertility has led to dilution ratios also rising uniformly by 10%: the distribution of mean consumption at the household level has not changed. Our analysis neglects possible intra-household effects, as do the poverty measures with which we are working.

[38] Bloom and Williamson (1997) find that extra persons under 15 reduce growth of GDP per head, while extra over-65s slightly but significantly enhance it.

of household characteristics. If household income and savings are unaffected by the extra birth, then mean household consumption is lowered proportionately more in poorer households, resulting in a positive acquisition effect.[39] But how do marginal child-care costs depend on household affluence? Marginal child care may be provided by the diversion of household labour resources from production, by 'buying-in', or in extended families, by a non-working relative such as a grandparent. Households able to utilize the last of these options will have lower marginal costs than do others. Extended families are much less common among low-income households (Lipton 1983*a*). Thus marginal child-care costs may be lower in richer households, strengthening the acquisition effect. The relevance of infant mortality is that, since it is higher in poorer households, they require more births to generate a net addition to the family: therefore the costs associated with 'wasted' pregnancies are higher in poorer households, further strengthening the acquisition effect.

2. The previous paragraph assumed household income constant. But there is evidence dating back to district-level data from Russia in the 1880s (Chayanov 1924) that the pressure of extra dependents in a household induces greater labour supply from non-dependents (see also Hunt 1978). This effect is poverty-dependent: household studies show that age- and gender-specific participation rates tend to increase with falls in consumption per person, eventually reaching an upper limit (Lipton 1983*b*). Therefore higher fertility squeezes mean household consumption more in poorer households, leading to a positive acquisition effect.

3. Fertility may also cut household accumulation. A simple analysis suggests that households able to reduce saving in response to extra children will tend to do so, initially skewing the distribution of consumption against asset-poor households. But there will be offsetting effects over time because of effects on wealth accumulation. At any given horizon, therefore, the sign of the impact of fertility, via savings, on the distribution of consumption is indeterminate.

4. The immediate effect of higher fertility on labour supply is indeterminate, since the child-care and Chayanov effects work against one another. However, over time the child-care effect declines and the extra children begin to enter the labour force, so that labour supply rises. This will tend to depress real wages and earnings, especially among low-income rural groups, who are heavily concentrated in unskilled agricultural labour.[40] Higher-income groups earn a larger share of labour income via (*a*) skilled and/or non-farm activity, which is less affected by the Malthusian effect, and (*b*) land management and overview, where earnings per person-hour may be positively affected when extra births raise the demand for land and the supply of labour. Finally, better-off groups earn larger proportions of income from land or

---

[39] Household size also affects this calculation, but not if we consider (as we should) an experiment which raises *dilution* equiproportionally in all households so as to abstract from the dependency effect. If M is the original value of mean household consumption and K the cost of caring for an extra child, then $\triangle M/M$ can be shown to be proportional to $-(1 + K/M)$ for a fixed dilution of the household (i.e. the addition of a number of children proportional to household size). $\triangle M/M$ falls in absolute value as M rises.

[40] Evenson (1993) has demonstrated that Indian Districts with faster growth of labour supply (given other relevant variables) have slower growth of unskilled real wage rates.

assets, where the rates of reward are raised, relative to labour, by Malthusian effects. Other things equal, these factor reward changes imply a positive acquisition effect.

3.5. *Updating KS's 'Growth Channel' from Fertility to Poverty*

EL have shown that poverty is higher in countries with (i) higher birth rates lagged ten years given AVCON—the 'distribution channel'; or (ii) lower AVCON given the lagged birth rate. EL now estimate the growth channel, that is, (iii) the impact that demographic variables would have no poverty via the growth rate of (mean GDP and thus) AVCON, even if distribution were unchanged. This involves estimating impacts of (1) fertility and population growth on growth of GDP per person, that is, updating KS;[41] (2) growth of GDP per person on growth of AVCON; (3) growth of AVCON on level of AVCON, and hence on poverty at a given horizon.

For (1), EL use similar methods to KS, but with updated data, and a perhaps more appropriate sample. EL further reduce ambiguity about the direction of causation—from high current fertility to slower growth of GDP per person—and confirm a large and significant effect, not, contrary to KS, offset by faster growth of GDP per person resulting from other aspects of population increase (namely, lower death rates, or delayed effects of earlier high birth rates on growth, perhaps via extra labor input or savings). So the net negative impact of population increase on growth of GDP per person is more clear-cut than in the KS estimates.

For (2), EL estimate the relationship between growth of GDP and growth of AVCON. For (3)—using the fact that (1) and (2) give the path from differences in the birth rate to differences in growth of AVCON over the next ten years—EL calculate the effect, on the level of AVCON after ten years, of this slower growth rate, and hence the effect of a sustained shift in a country's net birth rate on poverty via the growth channel alone, ten years later.

From Fertility to GDP   Following KS, we estimated trend growth of real GDP per head, 1980–90, as a linear function of (i) its initial (1980) level and the square and cube of that level; (ii) mean net birth rate and net death rate in the period 1980–90, PNBR and PNDR; (iii) net birth rate 15 years previously, that is, in 1965–75, PNBR15;[42] (iv) interaction effects between GDP per head and the demographic

---

[41] The 1980s are used (1) because census demographic data are more reliable than interpolations, (2) for comparability with the KS results. In predicting AVCON growth from GDP growth we must use the years of nation-wide household surveys from which AVCON growth can be calculated (Ravallion and Chen 1996).

[42] (1) These PNBRs and PNDRs differ somewhat from the NBRs and NDRs in Sect. 3.3. The poverty equations of Sect. 3.3 sought to explain international differences in *levels* of poverty given AVCON, in a particular survey year. Hence the levels of NBR and NDR, in that year or ten years earlier, were used as explanators. But the growth equations of Sect. 3.5 seek to explain differences in the *growth* of GDP per person, and hence of AVCON and thus poverty, over the period 1980–90. Hence net birth rates over the period (e.g. PNBR), over the 1980s or over the decade 15 years prior, are used as explanators. (Of course PNBR and PNBR15 are not very different from, respectively, NBR in 1985 and NBR in 1970).

(2) The choice of lag length is somewhat arbitrary. We chose a ten-year lag for our poverty equations on the grounds that a longer lag would obscure the dependency effect (many poor people become workers

variables. As before, these interaction effects—vital to avoid imposing assumptions of independence and thus biasing the estimates—mean that the impact of the coefficients cannot be directly, that is, independently, interpreted from their size, nor their significance from their t-statistics. Accordingly we present the equation, predicting GDP growth from GDP level and the demographic variables, and then—allowing for interactions—the Wald statistics (indicating significance level of the explanators), and elasticities of growth to the explanators at the median net birth rate of the 1980s.[43] We present only the equation, from our data, that most closely follows the original KS work for developing countries; we have tried other formulations without improving on this.[44] Next, we compare results from KS. We then discuss the results.[45]

Equation 1: EL's Growth Equation for the 1980s

$$GDPGR = c - 6.75(GDP)[-1.59] + 10.58(GDP^2)[1.19]$$

$$- 8.13(GDP^3)[-1.12] - 4.5(PNBR)[-2.17]^{**}$$

$$+ 0.95(GDP^*PNBR)[0.93] + 0.91(PNBR15)[0.44]$$

$$- 0.15(GDP^*PNBR15)[-0.18] - 0.03(PNDR)[-0.01]$$

$$+ 0.60(GDP^*PNDR)[0.59] \tag{1}$$

Adj. R^2 = 0.418; standard error = 1.96; 46 observations. Wald (PNBR) = 10.65 (0.005)*; Wald (PNBR15) = 0.38 (0.827); Wald (PNDR) = 0.63 (0.731); Wald (GDP) = 8.21(0.223).

Equation 2: KS's Growth Equation for the 1980s[45]

$$GDPGR = c + 2.94(GDP)[1.46] + 1.97(GDP^2)[0.73] - 1.6(GDP^3)[0.83]$$

$$- 4.67(PNBR)[4.48]^* + 0.68(GDP^*PNBR)[1.28]$$

$$+ 4.24(PNBR15)[3.5]^* - 1.3(GDP^*PNBR15)[2.44]^{**}$$

$$+ 2.78(PNDR)[1.31] - 3.25(GDP^*PNDR)[2.74]^* \tag{2}$$

Adj. R^2 = 0.370; 66 observations. Wald (PNBR) = (0.000)*; Wald (PNBR15) = (0.002)*; Wald (PNDR) = (0.005)*; Wald (GDP) = (0.000)*

around age 10); we try (and, as it happens, reject) a 15-year lag in the growth equation to provide results directly comparable to those of KS, recognizing that their choice of lag length was reasonable given their main posited mechanism by which lagged birth rates might (positively) affect growth, namely, life-cycle savings.

[43] Chosen because this is the only significant explanatory variable; see below.

[44] Our sample (46 here) is smaller than that used by KS (66). There are 41 developing and 5 transitional countries in our sample; these comprise all those in the 59-country sample, used in Sect. 3.3, with reliable PWT 5.6 and demographic data for the 1980s. Our sample thus includes all feasible countries where we can later align the findings with reliable household-survey data on poverty. KS omit countries that are 'historically planned', highly resource- or remittance-dependent, or with incomplete or grossly problematic data (KS 1994: 86, 92). Also we use PWT 5.6 data for growth of GDP per person, which improve upon the PWT 5.5 data available to KS.

[45] Reproduced from column 9 of Kelley and Schmidt (1994, table C4: 102).

Notes: (*a*) values in square brackets are t-statistics and those in parentheses are p-values; * means significant at 1%, ** at 5%. Equation 1 passed standard tests for heteroskedasticity, normality and functional form. (*b*) Wald statistics, except for Wald (GDP), refer to tests of the null that all terms including the named variable can be omitted (e.g. PNBR and GDP*PNBR in the case of PNBR). In the case of Wald(GDP) the null excludes only GDP, GDP^2, and GDP^3, in accordance with KS. For eqn (1) we also tested the hypothesis that all six terms including GDP could be excluded; this Wald statistic was calculated to be 8.21 [0.221]. If KS had reported a test entailing the exclusion of all terms including GDP, the data would have rejected this even more strongly. KS report only p-values, not the Wald statistics themselves.

(*A*) We confirm KS's estimate of a large and significant negative impact of current PNBR on growth of mean GDP in the 1980s. A fall of 5 in 1,000 in the net birth rate in 1980, maintained throughout the 1980s, would have raised trend annual growth of GDP per head in the 1980s by 1.36 percentage points in a country at the median of GDP per capita. KS's equation implies a somewhat larger estimate of 1.70 percentage points. The coefficients on the level and interaction terms in eqns 1 and 2 are similar for PNBR, implying a similar estimated dependence of the growth effect on initial GDP per capita in the two cases. (*B*) Unlike KS, we find no evidence that this negative effect of higher population growth on growth of GDP per person in the 1980s, through higher current birth rates, is offset by positive effects through falling death rates or higher pre-1980 birth rates (compare the Wald p-values in eqns 1 and 2 for PNDR and PNBR15).

Finding (*A*) implies that the gain to growth of GDP per person in developing countries in a period, from a lower PNBR in that period, is somewhat less than in KS, but still large. Finding (*B*) implies that slower population growth does *more* for economic growth than KS suggest because (i) there are no losses to economic growth from a lower PNBR in previous periods, raising the long-run net gain to growth from reducing the birth rate; (ii) there is no growth impact of NDR.[46]

From Growth of GDP to Growth of AVCON   EL used the Ravallion and Chen (1996) data set for AVCON growth between successive household surveys in 42 developing and transitional countries. These data, in 1985 standardized purchasing power using PWT 5.6, were matched with similar data for GDP per head, but the latter were not available for 13 transitional economies, which had to be excluded. We were thus left with 80 observations on 29 countries.[47] This was modeled using a fixed-effects specification, with the results indicated in eqn 3.

---

[46] (*a*) Both KS and EL results depend on the rejection of reverse causation. EL used the Hausman–Wu test (Berndt 1991: 379–80), instrumenting PNBR with PNBR15, and found no evidence of endogeneity of PNBR in eqn 1. (*b*) The differences between EL and KS results cannot be attributed to the fact that EL's sample, unlike KS's (1994: 87), includes transitional economies: inserting an intercept dummy for these economies has no effect on EL's conclusions. (Only five transitional economies have data for both fertility and poverty, so there are too few degrees of freedom to insert a slope dummy.)

[47] We omit one of the four observations on Poland (1989–93) which appears to be a transcription error. We average the two somewhat different AVCON values available in 1990 for China. Post-1992 PWT 5.6 data

Equation 3: Double-log Regression of AVCON *on GDP per head (OLS/IV)*

(a) OLS :   LAVCON $= 0.890(\text{LGDP})[6.45]^*$ adjR$^2 = 0.454$

(b) IV :   LAVCON $= 0.854(\text{LGDP})[6.40]^*$ adjR$^2 = 0.453$

Notes: (*a*) These equations are reported in 'deviation from means' form, i.e. data are centered round country mean values to eliminate the country fixed effects. (*b*) In the IV regression, one-year lagged values of the logarithm of GDP per head were used as instruments. (*c*) Both regressions passed standard specification tests. (*d*) t-statistics in square brackets, * = significant at 1%.

The IV regression allows for interdependence between the AVCON error and GDP per head. While the OLS and IV estimates of the elasticity are fairly close, the fact that the OLS estimate is larger hints at simultaneity bias, and we use the IV estimate in what follows. Hence our estimate that a sustained fall of 5 per 1,000 in the birth rate at median GDP per head produces a fall of 1.36 percent in the annual trend growth rate of mean GDP (p. 232) implies an estimated fall of some 1.16 in the annual percentage trend rate of growth of AVCON.

From Growth of AVCON *to Poverty—The Growth Channel*   The growth equation implies that a once-for-all, but sustained, fall in fertility has an effect on the level of AVCON that increases through time. Therefore, from the poverty equation, the effect on poverty via the level of AVCON also increases through time. Moreover, the growth effect on poverty at a given horizon is the product of two components, each of which depends on country characteristics as a result of the interaction terms in the equations. The effect of fertility on the growth rate of GDP per head depends on the initial level of GDP per head, having the biggest impact in the poorest countries; the effect of a level change in AVCON on poverty depends on initial fertility, the effect being biggest in high fertility countries. In sum, the growth effect on poverty is biggest in high-fertility, low-income countries. These points are illustrated in Table 9.5, which shows the estimated growth effect, on $30 poverty incidence at the end of a decade, of a once-for-all decline of 5 per 1,000 in the initial net birth rate, sustained throughout the decade. This effect is shown for the 25th, 50th, and 75th percentiles of the fertility and GDP per head distributions. The estimated effect is almost 5 percentage points in the high-fertility low-income case.[48]

on GDP are not yet available; in the few cases where AVCON was surveyed later than 1992, we estimate PWT 5.6 GDP in the survey year by multiplying national-accounts GDP by the 1992 ratio of PWT 5.6 GDP to national-accounts GDP. Where a survey year was given as, for instance, 1986–87, the mean of GDP per person for 1986 and 1987 from PWT 5.6 was matched with the given value of AVCON.

[48] This is the product of dPOV30/dLAVCON at the 75th percentile of NBR10 (equals −32.15 from Table 9.2, eqn 1 and the percentile values of NBR10 given Appendix A) and dLAVCON/dLGDP $*$ dLGDP/dPNBR$*$dPNBR, where LGDP denotes the natural logarithm of GDP per capita at a ten-year horizon. dLAVCON/dLGDP is estimated as 0.854 from eqn 3; dLGDP/dPNBR is calculated as 0.1 $*$ dGDPGR/dPNBR, this derivative being obtained from the growth equation as −3.55 = −4.50 + 0.95 $*$ 1.0, the very last number (1.0) being the 25th percentile value of the index of GDP/capita. dPNBR = −0.5.

Table 9.5. *Growth Effect on POV$30 of a 5 per 1,000 Fall in Net Birth Rate: 10-Year Horizon*

Percentage points	25th percentile of GDP per capita	Median of GDP per capita	75th percentile of GDP per capita
25th percentile of fertility	−3.44	−2.76	−1.61
Median fertility	−4.03	−3.23	−1.88
75th percentile of fertility	−4.82	−3.86	−2.25

Note: Equivalent tables referring to POV$21 and POVGAP30 are available from the authors on request. The results are similar: the estimates equivalent to those in the central cells of Tables 9.5 and 9.6 are 2.30 and 4.45 for POV$21 and 1.25 and 3.07 for POVGAP30.

3.6. *Combined Results: Impact of National Fertility on Poverty at a Ten-Year Horizon*

The distribution effect is itself higher at lower levels of AVCON, as a result of the negative coefficient on the interaction term in the poverty equation: the estimated effect on $30 poverty incidence at the 25th, 50th, and 75th percentiles of AVCON of a fall in the net birth rate of 5 per 1,000 can be calculated from Table 9.3 as 4.25, 3.05, and 1.32 percentage points respectively. Adding these numbers to those in Table 9.5 gives estimates of the total effect shown in Table 9.6. It is large. The absolute effect on P$30 incidence is highest for poor countries with high fertility.[49] Tables 9.5 and 9.6 show that the growth and distribution channels from fertility to poverty are of similar size. EL use a fall of 5 per 1,000 in the net birth rate to generate these numbers because this is similar both to the average fall achieved by the countries in the sample in the ten years preceding the survey, and to the semi-interquartile range. So it is not absurd to imagine that a change of this order might be achievable over 10 to 15 years in countries still experiencing high fertility.

The estimates depend on numbers derived from the poverty and growth equations and on the estimated elasticity of AVCON to GDP per head—all subject to error. But alternative specifications of the growth and poverty equations generate similar coefficients to those that underlie Table 9.6, and computations of the array of total effects based on such alternatives produce broadly similar numbers.

The element in which EL have least confidence is the level/growth distinction that characterizes the distribution and growth effects. As far as the poverty equation is concerned, insufficiency of time-series data on poverty forced us into a 'levels' specification. This excuse is not available for the growth equation, but there a comparison of EL's results with those of KS reveals some doubt about whether per capita GDP growth should be thought of as depending on the level or the change in fertility.[50] The latter specification is equivalent to a 'levels' model with a time trend and country

---

[49] So, of course, is their initial poverty incidence, in the last table, the 9.07% fall in absolute incidence in the bottom-left corner is likely to represent a smaller proportion of those in '$30 poverty' than does the 2.93% figure in the top-right corner.

[50] The role of PNBR15 in KS implies that the fastest growing countries are those where fertility has fallen.

Table 9.6. *Total Effect on the POV$30 of a 5 per 1,000 Fall in Net Birth Rate: 10-Year Horizon*

Percentage points	25th percentile of GDP per capita	Median of GDP per capita	75th percentile of GDP per capita
25th percentile of fertility	7.69	5.81	2.93
Median fertility	8.28	6.28	3.20
75th percentile of fertility	9.07	6.91	3.57

fixed effects.[51] While more extensive time-series data on poverty would be useful, it would be unduly optimistic to expect even good data to discriminate finely between alternative dynamic specifications of the link from fertility either to GDP per capita or to (conditional) poverty.[52]

4. THE ISSUE OF CONVERSION EFFICIENCY

Does high fertility affect household conversion efficiency—that is, capacity to transform a given CI, per equivalent adult (EA), into welfare or capabilities (e.g. health, schooling) per EA? Because poor families rationally choose more offspring[53] (Sect. 4.1), this boils down to another issue. Are 'economies of scale in consumption' more, or less, important than 'sib crowding' in their effects on poor households' conversion efficiency (Sect. 4.2)? There is a clear, large net negative effect in education (Sect. 4.3) and health and nutrition (Sect. 4.4). The evidence on transient and chronic poverty illuminates this debate (Sect. 4.5). Finally, declining state activity may interact with high fertility in reducing the conversion efficiency of the poor (Sect. 4.6).

These demographic effects on CI damage mainly women and children. The differential effect on women—together with the fact that the 'double day' and educational disadvantage locks female, more than male, poor into chronic poverty and non-empowerment—may justify the general perception that women are poorer in the developing world, even though most careful surveys find little difference in PCP between men and women, or male-headed and female-headed households. Children's concentration in large, poor households—30 to 35 percent of persons are below a national poverty line in recent Indian NSS data, but 40 to 45 percent of children—also

---

[51] i.e. $dy/dt = a + b\,dx/dt$ integrates to $y = \text{constant} + at + bx$.

[52] This does not imply that better time-series data on poverty would not be useful; in particular, such data allows country fixed effects to be removed by differencing (as in Ravallion and Chen 1996).

[53] Above, we argued that cross-national data showed that the causal chain from high fertility to poverty was statistically much more important than the reverse causation, when the process was mediated via low and maldistributed CI. Here, we argue that individual households in food poverty are likely rationally to prefer higher fertility than are the better-off, so that reverse causation is important when the fertility-to-poverty process is mediated via low conversion efficiency of CI into welfare and capabilities. There is no inconsistency. However, since the former process works substantially via income distribution through food and labour macro markets, it has to be investigated largely with macro data, and this is feasible if reverse causation is less important; whereas the latter process involves two-way causation at household level and appears to require mainly micro analysis, preferably with panel data.

interacts with their greater vulnerability to the effects of poverty-induced undernutrition: once again, the effects of high fertility on measures of CI poverty are amplified by the effects in reducing conversion efficiency.

4.1. Poor Couples' Many-Offspring Strategy is Rational,[54] but Tactics Harm Conversion

The poor rationally attach high value to the benefits from many children, low value to the costs, and small probability to satisfactory alternatives. Benefits tend to be high from many children, as the food-poor need them to ensure the 'durable consumer good' of dynastic survival; food poverty interacts with unhealthy water, bad sanitation, and shortage of affordable health care (especially competent midwifery) to raise child mortality. Also, the food-poor rationally attach high value—even survival value—to 'investment income' from many children as sources of child labor, and later from adult offspring's remittances. As for costs, the food-poor face fairly low costs of child-rearing—especially opportunity costs of women's time.[55] The alternative of fewer children, better-educated, and thus with better prospects to earn (Becker and Lewis 1973), seems remote to the food-poor, requiring unaffordable savings, delayed (and heavily discounted) and risky returns, and having high current opportunity cost (forgone child labor income). Nor are pensions, or social charity, a safe alternative in old age to support from at least one child; the often desperate situation of old and childless widows in India and Bangladesh (Drèze 1990) suggests, to couples that anticipate food poverty, that they should have many children.

Yet the specific tactics of poorer couples in their rational pursuit of this option, while child mortality and education prospects are so bad—damage conversion efficiency. Poorer couples start the family earlier; and first births substantially raise the risks to mother and child only if they follow early (i.e. adolescent) pregnancies. Poorer couples have more closely spaced children, and this too interacts with low CI to produce low conversion efficiency; in Mali in 1987, the extra risk of malnutrition associated with birth intervals below two years was significant only in the group of households with 'little property' (Lalou and Mbacké 1993: 216).[56] Poorer couples feature high hoarding and replacement fertility; and for high-order births the risks of death, ill-health, and bad school performance rise sharply. For instance, in Pakistan, 'eliminating all births after the fifth would reduce maternal mortality by half' (Allison *et al.* 1989: 36).

---

[54] See note 1 for evidence on the dramatic results (of this and reverse causal sequences). In Pakistan's 1984–85 household survey, the poorest quintile of households by income-per-person averaged 4.3 children, and the least poor 1.5 (Allison *et al.* 1989: 41; Visaria and others reported in Lipton 1983a).

[55] In Pakistan, until children are 15, the saving out of their earnings is much too little to offset the reduction of parental savings to pay for children's consumption (Allison *et al.* 1989: 47).

[56] Lloyd (1994) shows that some of the 'misery' consequences of poverty (linked to large household size) appear only as state services are provided—i.e. more in middle-income than in low-income countries. If there are hardly any health or education services, then poverty—whether or not associated with household size—cannot much affect access to them.

4.2. *Economies of Scale in Consumption*

These exist for the enlarging household (e.g. Lazear and Michael 1980; Lanjouw and Ravallion 1995). They have two sources. There are household-level public goods, such as a common door or vehicle, or a household well for drinking water. There are also external economies, such as reach-me-down clothes for younger siblings. This suggests that high fertility may increase conversion efficiency, and later demographic transition may harm it.

Yet strong evidence (see below), and some reasoning, points in the opposite direction. Very large families create rising marginal congestion costs, rapidly reducing net marginal returns from once-public goods and rendering them rivalrous; external economies are offset by diseconomies from infection; and both sequences are likeliest in poor households. Sib crowding is likelier to do harm in their small, crowded dwellings; and, since over 70 percent of CI near the poverty line is food consumption, there is less room for economies of scale (for discussion see also King 1987: 389). In a study in rural and urban Philippines and Thailand, assumptions about scale economies, and methods of calculating equivalence scales, do not alter the finding of 'very substantial impact of family size on poverty'[57] (Bauer and Mason 1993: 24, 30).

The issue of scale economies in consumption is usually discussed too aggregatively. They are clearly much more important for a family owning substantial shared durable consumer goods than for one that spends 70 percent or more of income on food; for a family that adds 'persistent' members with learning effects, than for one that must offset frequent fixed costs from child deaths, pregnancies, and births; and for a household enlarging from two to three, four or five, than for one enlarging from to six to eight or ten. Yet these very large households, where congestion and infection effects of enlargement are almost certain to outweigh public-goods and external-economy effects, are common among the poorest households, for which durable consumer-type public goods are least significant. In urban Colombia in the 1970s, in the poorest decile of households, 78 percent contained eight or more persons, as against only 4.8 percent for the other 90 percent (i.e. 12% for all households) (Birdsall 1979).

4.3. *High Fertility and Education-Based Loss of Conversion Efficiency*

Even given real income per person, children in larger households enjoy worse educational prospects; evidence of the causal sequence from high fertility to worse and less education appears for numerous countries in King (1987), for Thailand in Knodel (1993), and for the Philippines in DeGraff *et al.* (1993).[58] The work on twins in rural India by Rosenzweig and Wolpin (1980) shows that unplanned, and therefore non-endogenous, increases in fertility cause reductions in the older siblings' access to

---

[57] Consumption per child falls by a somewhat smaller multiple of consumption per adult in the rural Philippines.

[58] The latter study is unusual in showing the worst effects on older male siblings.

education. Such relationships, apply much more strongly to households in the poverty zone than to wealthy households. In most studies, high fertility and large households especially damage the educational prospects of girls (Lloyd and Gage-Brandon 1993, for Ghana; Shreeniwas 1993, for Malaysia; implicitly, Greenhalgh 1985 for Taiwan; see also Lloyd 1994).[59]

4.4. *Health, Nutrition, and the Impact of High Fertility on Conversion Efficiency*

Large households tend to be less healthy and worse nourished, and to discriminate more among members. Larger households provide less care per child, less access to health care, and more gender discrimination in food distribution (King 1987; Desai 1993: 179; Mahmud and McIntosh 1980; Lloyd 1994). Much greater risk of undernutrition appears in larger households, for example, in the Philippines, Bangladesh, and Mali (King 1987). 'In 12 of 16 countries the addition of a sibling under age 5 has a significant negative impact on children's height-for-age standardized scores' (Desai 1993: 165). In one suggestive study, larger household size (and associated greater poverty risk) brings more damage to nutrition[60] in villages where average consumption is relatively low (Mahmud and McIntosh 1980). As for health, 'competition between children [and] exhaustion of the mother' are quantified 'explanatory factors[61] for the same reality: poverty' in Mali. Lloyd (1994) shows that the links are subtle—not just via female exhaustion and sib crowding, but because larger household size induces authoritarian, less equal, less altruistic households, more hierarchical by age and gender.

4.5. *Relevance of Transient and Chronic Poverty*

The mechanics of high fertility, as a reducer of conversion efficiency among low-income households, is illuminated by growing evidence from household panels about the extent, nature, and life-cycle victims of transient poverty. Typically, 25 to 40 percent of persons in PCP (private consumption poverty) in the year before a survey are not normally in PCP (Ryan and Walker 1990). The transient poor are much likelier to be ultra-poor than the chronic poor (Gaiha and Kazmi 1987). 'Churning' down from near-poverty towards ultra-poverty is likeliest when a household contains several under-fives and one worker; and in economic adjustment a household's risk of being thus 'churned down' is greatly increased by an extra birth, which also

---

[59] The educational harm from high fertility, especially for girls, is usually more in towns, because there is less to damage. In general, where few people, especially few girls, are educated, the effect of sib numbers on their prospects is smaller, as in Pakistan (Lloyd 1994; Allison *et al.* 1989: 38–9).

[60] The study is in Bangladesh, where (as in North India and Pakistan) there is evidence of gender discrimination against little girls in food provision or health care. In such circumstances the nutritional damage, associated with larger and poorer families, appears to fall especially on these girls.

[61] Lloyd (1994) has a more nuanced, socially contextualized account of how large families induce child deprivation.

cuts its prospects of joining the (many) poor households who *escape* poverty during adjustment (Grootaert 1996; Grootaert *et al.* 1997; Glewwe and Hall 1998).

In short, the evidence from panel data about transient poverty seems to be that time distributions of a given (integral of household lifetime) poverty over household life cycles concentrate it when members are pregnant or lactating women, or under-fives, and thus most exposed to irreversible consequences. For those with large or rising child numbers, declines in near-poverty CI are thus converted into larger proportionate declines in welfare or capability. So fertility reduction, apart from effects on PCP, reduces damage from given levels of poverty. If families with low PCP are helped to control fertility,[62] their children benefit even if overall PCP indicators do not improve. In Thailand, children's education improved with falling household size, with 'household wealth level' (not an ideal indicator of poverty) constant (Knodel 1993: 289).

4.6. *State Retreat may Catalyse the Damage of High Fertility to Conversion Efficiency*

Ruttan (1993) points out a 'time warp': the fiscal crises, and the disillusionment with the state, of the early 1980s have impaired public-sector activities such as agricultural research, perhaps for a shortish period, but with long-term results. A similar time warp may have harmed children in big, poor households. Such children are especially dependent on public provision to correct their parents' below-average ability to provide them with these semi-public goods. This has been shown for primary education in Ghana (Lloyd and Gage-Brandon 1993) and preventive health care (Desai 1993: 178) in many countries. Where adjustment causes governments to withdraw from providing child-related services, transient poverty 'is likely to increase the vulnerability of children in large families' (ibid. 178–9).[63]

The delayed-action effect of undiscriminating anti-statism, therefore, homes in on big, and often therefore poor, families seeking to maintain or upgrade their children's human capital. That makes it less likely that couples can, or will, escape poverty by choosing smaller families with better prospects of survival, health, or education.

5. FERTILITY → POVERTY: CONVERSION AND DISTRIBUTION EFFECTS VERSUS GROWTH EFFECTS

The economics that the most intelligent *literary* figures come to take for granted suggests that the effect of fertility on poverty via distribution and conversion efficiency is deeply intuitive. The distribution effect is based on price theory (in labor and staples markets) so old, elementary, and apparently non-controversial that it was famously

---

[62] Such help will usually take the form of changing incentives to favor high family size norms (e.g. via better access to education for poor girls), and may sometimes also involve lowering the costs of contraception.

[63] A commentator (Andrea Cornia) suggests that in Eastern Europe and the former Soviet Union the rapid reduction of state provision may have reduced fertility and 'linked' poverty to smaller family size.

declared by Coleridge to provide scant grounds for Malthus's repute. The conversion effect—being based on sib crowding, and on the constraints that children, however much desired, place on poorer parents' progress—also has literary testimony to its self-evidence (e.g. in the tragic suicide note of the children in *Jude the Obscure*: 'because we was too many').

The growth channel depends on two links. The link from growth to reduced poverty incidence and intensity is clear (though there are big differences among the few available national-level time-series elasticities—the African numbers are generally about half those in Asia). More contingent, even controversial, is the link from high fertility to slow growth. This link is clearly context-dependent.

Over time, Simon and Gobin (1980) found no cross-national link between population growth and economic growth prior to the mid-1970s, and KS—who disaggregate population growth into fertility and mortality components—also find a clear net effect only after about 1975 (see above, fn. 14). There are good reasons why the age-structure aspect of such a linkage (Bloom and Williamson 1997) should have emerged after the mid-1970s, alongside tightening finance constraints and the consequently greater importance of domestic life-cycle savings. Also, standard diminishing-returns models—even with technical progress—suggest that congestion effects of increasing workforces on growth of output per head would, over time, begin to dominate scale economies (in production).

The universality over space of the fertility-to-poverty link, at any given period, is also questionable. Holden and Binswanger (1998) have argued that in several African countries low population density (even if there is not a lot of land in efficiency units per person) makes it uneconomic to install the infrastructure for agro-rural development, so that population and workforce increase are required to make faster growth of GDP per person feasible. This has to be true in some cases, though the non-significance of the African regional dummy in Section 3.3 above suggests it is not true overall. Simon (1986) has modeled plausible sequences in which, in some cases, economies of scale in invention and in the diffusion of research could lead to positive growth responses to higher fertility. Finally, the gloomy population literature of the 1930s and 1940s recalls the possibility that—though normally the high child–worker ratios (associated with high-fertility regimes) might harm growth by cutting the savings rate—such cuts could be a blessing in places or times of depressed aggregate demand and spare productive capacity.

During the past 20 to 25 years, there is strong evidence for the growth effect, both at micro and at macro level. Probably, this means that the effect is coming to be felt in most parts of the developing world. But it is more dependent on place and time than the distribution and conversion effects, which have a firmer theoretical basis.

6. WHAT IF THE RESULTS ARE TRUE? VIRTUOUS CIRCLES AND SEQUENCES

Section 3 advises caution about taking too literally the size (or timing) of the effects on poverty attributed to fertility in the equations. There is another reason why assaults on high fertility—measured as in the above regressions—are not a cheap or easy 'magic pill' against poverty. The main measure is NBR, defined as CBR net of infant deaths. In the demographic transition, CBR falls along with, and partly because of, the fall in the infant mortality rate, IMR. Policy initiatives involving female education and employment or access to family planning, for instance, may well reduce infant deaths, thus producing modest falls in NBR even if CBR is lowered substantially. But this argument—that even if the poverty impact of significant NBR declines is large, such declines are likely to be small because of 'drag' from falling IMR—cannot be pushed very far. The fall of 5 per 1,000 in NBR used in EL's tables is not much above the median fall in the sample.

Further, Tables 9.5 and 9.6 may *under*state the effects of fertility decline on poverty reduction, because they do not allow for a cumulative impact of such effects due to recent findings about interactions among five variables: growth, reduction of inequality, poverty reduction, greater economic openness, and provision of basic social services. These interactions are mainly positive (sometimes cumulatively, with reciprocal causation), sometimes neutral, and seldom negative. So the impression is 'positive feedback' among the five variables. But the tests, on which this impression is based, do not include demographic variables. Positive sequences from fertility reduction to growth or poverty reduction, and even more to both, mean that adding fertility reduction to the above five variables could strengthen positive feedback—including the longer-run impact of fertility reduction on poverty reduction.[64]

The recent conclusions on 'positive feedback', with which a link from fertility to poverty may require to be 'interacted', include the following propositions:[65]

1. Contrary to earlier findings, there is no 'Kuznets curve' (Anand and Kanbur 1993). A country's level (or growth rate) of real GDP per head, or real AVCON, appears *as such* to have no influence on the resulting level (or rate of change) of that country's distributional indicators, or its ranking in an international ordering of such indicators (Hongyi *et al.* 1995; Bruno *et al.* 1996; Ravallion and Chen 1996).[66]

2. However, as illustrated for Asia by De Haan and Lipton (2000), the elasticity of poverty indicators to growth shows considerable variation across regions, countries,

---

[64] Positive sequences from fertility reduction to poverty reduction also suggest that models of growth—whether endogenous or conditionally convergent—need to include interactions with fertility. So, even more, do attempts to model the impact of growth, overall or in respect of its sectoral or regional composition, on inequality or poverty.

[65] The conclusions arise from time-series and cross-section work, intra- and international, micro and macro, and draw on big recent data improvements—both new and carefully screened household surveys, and improved national-accounts sources such as PWT. The above conclusions are more firmly rooted than the brilliant conjectures, inevitably drawing on a far weaker data base, that they replace (the Kuznets curve, the need for inequality so that rich people's savings might finance growth, etc.).

[66] This result follows through whatever index of inequality is used (Gini, Theil, share of richest 20%, ratio of the latter to share of poorest 20%, etc.), and appears to be true whether consumption or income, or per-person or per-household, measures are used. Deininger and Squire (1996) present a standardized database of inequality indicators from a carefully screened set of nation-wide household surveys of acceptable quality.

growth sectors, and policies. For example, cross-State and time-series analysis for India in 1958–91 shows that agricultural growth substantially reduced poverty, but industrial growth did not (Datt and Ravallion 1996).[67]

3. If policy-makers choose an 'unequalizing' growth path, they do not accelerate subsequent economic growth. Contrary to earlier views, countries with initially more unequal income or consumption probably experience slower subsequent growth.[68] There is wider consensus that very unequal access to education (Birdsall *et al.* 1995) or operated farmland (Deininger, personal communication, 1997) retards subsequent growth.

4. Most evidence suggests that two sets of policies can be identified as growth-promoting: 'openness', that is, policies that reduce market distortions and other barriers, especially against international trade and investment; and creation of infra-structures, both human (mass health and education) and physical, for economic development.[69] Such policies may not perform well in particular cases due to civil violence, institutional failure, obstructed foreign markets, or remote or difficult terrain. However, across large cross-sections of countries and in the long run, both 'openness' and 'infrastructure' (or human capital) seem important in explaining growth, whether technical progress is interpreted endogenously to it (Romer 1986) or exogenously as in conditional convergence models (Barro 1991; Radelet *et al.* 1997).

5. The above points are parts of the new consensus, to be 'interacted' with the fertility–growth–poverty nexus. To them has to be added another point, which is at once controversial and puzzling: it is not clear that adjustment policies, notably increased 'openness', are poverty-reducing. In low-income economies with high labor–capital ratios, such policies should, through the Heckscher–Ohlin mechanism, redistribute income toward the plentiful factor, labor, and thereby improve low-end income distribution. Yet, even for countries with the highest labor–capital ratios, the controversy is about whether adjustment policies damage the poor (by worsening inequality more, and more surely, than they accelerate growth) (Cornia *et al.* 1987) or are neutral toward poverty and thus, in the long run, helpful to the poor as growth picks up (see point 3 above) (Sahn *et al.* 1996). Almost nobody argues that adjustment and liberalization, because they reduce low-end inequality, help the poor even if they do not promote growth. Yet Heckscher–Ohlin implies just that.[70]

[67] That may be due to the greater labour intensity of agriculture, to labour-intensive agricultural progress (the spread of irrigation followed by the 'Green Revolution'), or to protectionist and other policies rendering industry capital-intensive.

[68] Alesina and Rodrik (1994); Persson and Tabellini (1994); Clarke (1995); Bruno *et al.* (1996); but cf. Hongyi *et al.* (1995).

[69] Government size, perhaps because 'good' for educational and communications infrastructure but 'bad' for price neutrality and openness, is not robustly associated with good—or bad—subsequent economic performance (Levine and Renelt 1992).

[70] One explanation of this puzzle is that 'openness' does not reduce low-end inequality because it attracts private foreign investment which brings globally generated, labor-saving technology. Another is that the poorest countries lack the spread of education required for trade-expanding labor-intensive to openness (Wood 1994).

Probably the most serious deficiency in these 'big new ideas' of development economics is their empirical base in studies that, except for Bloom and Williamson (1997), exclude demographics. The fertility transition is a central feature of development, and is interwoven with growth, distribution, and induced technical progress. Incorporating changes in human fertility, as causes and as effects of economic change, into the above 'stylized facts' therefore seems likely to be central to the research agenda of development economics. This task cannot even be commenced here. But how might the 'new consensus' be affected, if indeed poverty reduction in developing countries now depends importantly on reduced fertility?

1. Table 9.6 calculates the effects of fertility change upon poor people by adding its effects in changing (i) distribution between poor and non-poor of a given level of real resource flows per head, (ii) the latter's rate of growth. This ignores any possible direct feedback from growth to distribution. If, as used to be believed, there was a Kuznets curve, then a low-income country that achieved faster growth would tend to worsen its income distribution. So a cut in fertility would lead to faster growth, but this would carry a distributional penalty, so the poverty effects in Table 9.6 would be overestimates. If proposition 1 above is correct, this possibility can be put aside. If anything, feedbacks excluded from the model in Section 3 above are likely—over a longer time horizon—to enhance the poverty effects. Though EL's and KS's tests identified fertility change as cause, much more than effect, of short-run or concurrent economic change, economic growth and income equalization are normally associated with events that reduce fertility in the long run: most growth paths are associated with a rising opportunity cost of women's time, and with better prospects and incentives for couples to produce fewer children; more equal income distribution also appears to be associated, in the long term, with lower subsequent fertility (Lam 1997; Repetto 1979). The elements of a virtuous circle are therefore present, an initial fall in fertility leading via faster growth and more equal distribution to further fertility declines later on. This may be dubbed the 'fertility amplifier'.

2. The findings reported in the previous paragraph, together with Section 3 above, suggest that governments that choose policies leading to equalizing growth will find longer-term benefits from the fertility amplifier. Equalizing growth will, *ceteris paribus*, reduce fertility. This will lead to improvements in both growth and distribution.

3. This would lose much of its force if the policy choice were between faster growth and more equality. Then, the fertility effect of choosing more equality would be ambiguous. Conversely, our findings interact positively with evidence that inequality retards growth of AVCON and mean GDP, the implication being that a country may become locked into a cycle of high inequality, high fertility, and slow growth.[71]

4 and 5. Theory indicates 'two-way' gains to the poor—via faster growth, and via more equal distribution of given resource levels—from appropriate policy (openness, physical and human infrastructure-building) in developing countries. Evidence

---

[71] Note that our results imply a statistical association between faster growth and more equality, to the extent that both follow a fall in fertility.

supports theory, except that increased openness has apparently not made distribution more equal in low-income countries; gains from specialization and trade do not appear to have raised the share of the poor via Heckscher–Ohlin redistribution toward unskilled workers. Could demographics be part of the explanation?

Even processes of growth 'led' by increased openness and mass education appear to leave behind groups of hard-core, uneducated poor, unable to leave ill-favored jobs or regions. Such groups enjoy little, if any, of either the growth impact or the distributive impact on poverty. They therefore lack the incentives to lower fertility that might set up the 'second round' of poverty reduction via the growth and distribution channels. This does not mean that specialization, growth, and Heckscher–Ohlin redistribution—especially with the above 'fertility amplifier'—are not better for the poor than stagnation and forced import substitution would have been. Yet, in much of East Asia (China, Thailand, probably Malaysia), inequality grew in the middle and late 1980s to such an extent that poverty reduction stalled, despite quite rapid growth and increasing economic openness (Lipton and de Haan 1997). When the poor in 'lead' regions and jobs have been pulled out of poverty, the less growth-responsive poor are left. These may well lack incentives and institutions permitting them to 'substitute quality for quantity' by having fewer, but healthier and more educated, children. Laggards, especially in remote regions, may be left out of the 'virtuous circles' and their amplification via fertility reduction. The 'new consensus' is not the whole story of requirements for poverty reduction.

7. TWO (EVEN MORE) TENTATIVE AND IMPERTINENT THOUGHTS ON POLICY AND THEORY

The first thought necessarily repeats the obvious. This chapter, KS, and EL are *not* 'Son of Enke—more about the astronomical returns to family planning'. Despite Bangladesh, the key task is to reduce the poor's family size norms. These (though jointly real-wage-depressing) are rational for most individual poor couples. To make lower norms rational is costly (it means providing clean water, sanitation, schooling) and difficult (because of interactions with female empowerment).

The second thought—taking off from Birdsall *et al.* (1995) and Lipton (1998*a*)—is really a plea for certain sorts of research. How should we follow up the findings about virtuous circles between distribution and growth—findings that may be hugely strengthened by inserting the demographic component, as this chapter tries to do? It is really somewhat tiresome to debate whether inequality in general is good or bad for growth in general. Clearly, some sorts of inequality reward hard work; other sorts reward special skills and other market-place contributions; others again reward activities that society condemns, such as successful production and sale of heroin and cigarettes.

But a huge component of measured inequality, in almost all societies, is due to inheritance. This is also the main cause of land inequality, especially in countries of Latin America, where inherited land inequality is plainly a major constraint on farm productivity and rural growth, as well as on poverty reduction and (if this chapter is correct) on fertility reduction too. In Brazil, it is in the north-east that the gaps between the rich and the poor in fertility—as well as in land access—are the greatest (Daly 1985). The virtuous circles, described above, seem to await unlocking.

Yet almost every society has inheritance rights. On one view, these are basic property rights, respecting the animal wish to benefit one's offspring, and the human skill to construct and earn tangible property. Yet the degree to which such rights are taxed varies hugely among societies. And, in another view, inheritance rights are rights, on grounds of parentage, to tax the incomes of others. They encourage savings from the bequest motive; but they discourage savings by rich children who feel they can depend on, or borrow against, unearned inheritances. These are plainly a tax on incentives; a Friedmanite could with perfect consistency advocate 100 percent death duties, and might command wider respect if he or she did.

The research issue is that inheritance rights and demographic sequences, such as those discussed in this chapter, interact fairly fundamentally. For example, some societies encourage or compel primogeniture, others the division of estates, and some (in Africa) ultimogeniture. What are the income-distributional and demographic effects of the options? How should governmental treatment of inheritance, and of gifts *inter vivos*, be affected by the virtuous circles connecting fertility reduction, growth, and some forms of equality—together with the near-certainty that other forms of inequality, those that reward inventiveness and risk-taking, are needed for growth?

A final impertinent thought concerns optimal population, and, linked to this, Parfit's 'repugnant conclusion'. If higher fertility worsens income distribution, its effect on poverty is greater than if the effects on growth—the only relevant ones quantified previously—were the whole story. The cumulative causation examined in Section 6 makes the effects greater still. This means two things. If one is ready to be pushed toward the repugnant conclusion, then the optimal level of fertility is reduced. And, at any given level of fertility, the size of the population sustainable if the repugnant conclusion is accepted becomes smaller, because the associated unrestrained fertility increases inequality and thus poverty, reducing population through higher child mortality.

Appendix A1. List of Variables

Poverty equation: Section 3.3 (full sample of 59 countries, except for 'social variables'—38 countries)

Variable	Description	Source	Mean value	Standard deviation	25th percentile	Median	75th percentile
POV$30	Incidence of poverty under a poverty line of $30 PPP 1985 (PWT 5.6) per capita per month	Ravallion latest data set (1996), pers. comm.	25.25	22.27	5.95	18.86	43.79
POV$21	Incidence of poverty under a poverty line of $21 PPP 1985 (PWT 5.6) per capita per month	Ravallion latest data set (1996), pers. comm.	16.48	18.52	1.33	10.1	24.37
POVGAP	Poverty gap index under a poverty line of $30 PPP 1985 (PWT 5.6) per capita per month	Ravallion latest data set (1996), pers. comm.	9.91	12.06	1.1	5.0	14.7
AVCON	Mean expenditure ($/capita/month) in 1985 PPP $ (PWT 5.6), from household surveys	Ravallion latest data set (1996), pers. comm.	89.44	44.95	54.71	80.1	122.93
LAVCON	Natural log of mean expenditure ($/capita/month) in 1985 PPP $ (PWT 5.6), from household surveys	Computed from Ravallion latest data set (1996), pers. comm.	4.35	0.58	4.0	4.38	4.81
POPG10	Population growth rate, lagged 10 years from the year of survey	World Bank (1995), *World Development Indicators 1995*, Washington, CD Rom	2.27	0.99	1.73	2.41	2.88
NBR	Net birth rate per 1,000 population on the year of survey (= crude birth rate minus infant mortality rate)	World Bank (1995), *World Development Indicators 1995*, Washington, CD Rom	28.89	10.28	21.55	28.44	37.18
NBR10	Net birth rate lagged 10 years from the year of survey (= crude birth rate lagged 10 years minus infant mortality rate lagged 10 years)	World Bank (1995), *World Development Indicators 1995*, Washington, CD Rom	32.34	9.90	26.32	32.43	40.67
NDR	Net death rate per 1,000 population on the year of survey (= crude death rate minus infant mortality rate)	World Bank (1995), *World Development Indicators 1995*, Washington, CD Rom	8.23	3.43	5.38	7.2	11.19
NDR10	Net death rate lagged 10 years from the year of survey (= crude death rate lagged 10 years minus infant mortality rate lagged 10 years)	World Bank (1995), *World Development Indicators 1995*, Washington, CD Rom	9.09	3.29	6.32	8.42	11.43

'Social variables' used in poverty equation

Variable	Description	Source					
LANDGINI	Gini coefficient of land ownership inequality at the year of survey	Deininger and Minton (1997), pers. comm.	0.65	0.17			
NURSE	Population per nurse at the year of survey	World Bank (1997), *World Development Indicators 1997*, Washington, CD Rom	3,207.8	2,989.0			
PHYSIC	Population per physician at the year of survey	World Bank (1997), *World Development Indicators 1997*, Washington, CD Rom	10,107.1	17,019.6			
PRIMENR	Primary school enrollment rate (% gross), lagged 10 years from the year of survey	World Bank (1997), *World Development Indicators 1997*, Washington, CD Rom	86.66	30.44			
SECENR	Secondary school enrollment rate (% gross), lagged 10 years from the year of survey	World Bank (1997), *World Development Indicators 1997*, Washington, CD Rom	3.50	21.68			

Growth equation: Section 3.5 (sample of 46 countries)

Variable	Description	Source					
GDP	GDP per capita level in 1980 (average of the 1979, 1980, and 1981 values)	Penn World Tables Mark 5.6, Internet	2.25	1.52	1.0	1.88	2.93
GDPGR	GDP per capita growth over 1980–90 in % (instantaneous growth rate)	Computed from Penn World Tables Mark 5.6, Internet	0.06	2.57	−1.68	0.12	−.47
PERNBR	Net birth rate per 100 population, average over 1980–90 (= crude birth rate minus infant mortality rate)	United Nations (1987, 1993), *Demographic Yearbook 1986 and 1992*, New York	3.29	0.93	2.79	3.27	4.12
PERNBR15	Net birth rate per 100 population, average over 1965–75 (= crude birth rate minus infant mortality rate)	United Nations (1975), *Demographic Yearbook 1974*, New York	3.56	0.78	3.21	3.63	4.03
PERNDR	Net death rate per 100 population, average over 1980–90 (= crude death rate minus infant mortality rate)	United Nations (1987, 1993), *Demographic Yearbook 1986 and 1992*, New York	0.82	0.35	0.55	0.73	−.03

Note: PERNBR, PERNBR15, and PERNDR are expressed per 100 people (and not per 1,000 people as usual); this is to match Kelley and Schmidt's usage so that the regressions coefficients are directly comparable.

Appendix A2. Lists of Samples

(a) *Poverty equation (59 countries, subsample used for regressions with 'social variables' in italics)*

Algeria (1988), *Bolivia (1990–91)*, *Botswana (1985–86)*, *Brazil (1989)*, Bulgaria (1992), Chile (1992), China (1993), *Colombia (1991)*, *Costa Rica (1989)*, *Côte d'Ivoire (1988)*, Czech Republic (1993), *Dominican Republic (1989)*, *Ecuador (1994)*, *Egypt (1990–91)*, Estonia (1993), *Ethiopia (1981–82)*, *Guatemala (1989)*, *Guinea (1991)*, Guinea-Bissau (1991), *Honduras (1992)*, *Hungary (1993)*, *India (1992)*, *Indonesia (1993)*, *Jamaica (1993)*, *Jordan (1992)*, *Kenya (1992)*, Kyrgyz Republic (1993), *Lesotho (1986–87)*, Lithuania (1993), *Madagascar (1993)*, *Malaysia (1989)*, *Mauritania (1988)*, Mexico (1992), Moldova (1992), Morocco (1990–91), *Nepal (1984–85)*, *Nicaragua (1993)*, *Niger (1992)*, Nigeria (1992–93), *Pakistan (1991)*, *Panama (1989)*, Peru (1994), *Philippines (1988)*, *Poland (1993)*, Romania (1992), Russia (1993), Rwanda (1984–85), *Senegal (1991–92)*, Slovakia (1992), South Africa (1993), *Sri Lanka (1990)*, *Tanzania (1993)*, *Thailand (1992)*, *Tunisia (1990)*, Turkmenistan (1993), *Uganda (1989–90)*, *Venezuela (1991)*, Zambia (1993), Zimbabwe (1990–91).

(b) *Growth equation (46 countries)*

Algeria, Bolivia, Botswana, Bulgaria, Brazil, Chile, China, Colombia, Costa Rica, Côte d'Ivoire, Dominican Republic, Ecuador, Egypt, Guatemala, Guinea, Guinea-Bissau, Honduras, Hungary, India, Indonesia, Jamaica, Kenya, Lesotho, Madagascar, Malaysia, Mauritania, Mexico, Morocco, Nicaragua, Niger, Nigeria, Pakistan, Panama, Peru, Philippines, Poland, Romania, Rwanda, Senegal, Sri Lanka, Thailand, Tunisia, Uganda, Venezuela, Zambia, Zimbabwe.

(c) *LAVCON/LGDP equation (29 countries)*

China (1985, 1990, 1992), Indonesia (1984, 1987, 1990, 1993), Malaysia (1984, 1989), Philippines (1985, 1988), Bulgaria (1988, 1992), Hungary (1989, 1993), Romania (1989, 1992), Yugoslavia (1985, 1989), Brazil (1985, 1989), Chile (1990, 1992), Colombia (1988, 1991), Costa Rica (1981, 1989), Guatemala (1986–87, 1989), Mexico (1984, 1992), Peru (1985–86, 1994), Jordan (1986–87, 1992), Morocco (1984, 1990), Tunisia (1985, 1990), Sri Lanka (1985, 1990), Nigeria (1985–86, 1992–93), Zambia (1991, 1993), Thailand (1981, 1988, 1992), Ghana (1987, 1988, 1991), Poland (1985, 1987, 1989, 1992), Venezuela (1981, 1987, 1989, 1991), Bangladesh (1983–84, 1985–86, 1988–89, 1991–92), Côte d'Ivoire (1985, 1986, 1987, 1988), Jamaica (1988, 1989, 1990, 1991, 1992, 1993), India (1983, 1986–87, 1987–88, 1988–89, 1989–90, 1990–91, 1992).

Appendix A3. World Bank Poverty Assessments

Used for investigation of dependency ratios; * indicates that poverty-specific dependency ratios were found, and used in the regression reported in Section 3.4.

*13318-AR	*Argentina.* Argentina's Poor: A Profile (27.06.95)
7946-BD	*Bangladesh.* Poverty and Public Expenditures: An Evaluation of the Impact of Selected Government Programs (16.01.90)

15380-BY	*Belarus.* An Assessment of Poverty and Prospects for Improved Living Standards (28.06.96)
12706-BEN	*Benin.* Towards a Poverty Alleviation Strategy (05.08.1994)
8643-BO	*Bolivia.* Poverty Report (03.10.90)
14323-BR	*Brazil.* A Poverty Assessment (2 vols.) (27.06.1995)
*13167-CM	*Cameroon.* Diversity, Growth, and Poverty Reduction (04.04.95)
13126-CV	*Cape Verde.* Poverty in Cape Verde: A Summary Assessment and a Strategy for its Alleviation (30.06.94)
10409-CHA	*China.* Strategies for Reducing Poverty in the 1990s (29.06.1992)
*12673-CO	*Colombia.* Poverty Assessment Report (2 vols.) (08.08.1994)
13401-COM	*Comoros.* Poverty and Growth in a Traditional Small Island Economy (29.09.94)
8519-CR	*Costa Rica.* Public Sector Social Spending (23.10.1990)
13619-DO	*Dominican Republic.* Growth with Equity: An Agenda for Reform (15.05.1995)
9838-EGT	*Egypt.* Alleviating Poverty During Structural Adjustment
*12315-ES	*El Salvador.* The Challenge of Poverty Alleviation (09.06.1994)
11306-ET	*Ethiopia.* Towards Poverty Alleviation and Social Action Program (28.06.93)
11486-GH	*Ghana.* 2000 and Beyond: Setting the Stage for Accelerated Growth and Poverty Reduction (06.11.92)
14504-GH	*Ghana.* Poverty Past, Present and Future (29.06.95)
12313-GU	*Guatemala.* An Assessment of Poverty (17.04.1995)
13317-HO	*Honduras.* Country Economic Memorandum/Poverty Assessment (17.11.1994)
ISN 157101	*Hungary.* Poverty and Social Transfers (14.03.1996)
8034-IND	*Indonesia.* Poverty Assessment and Strategy Report (11.05.1990)
12702-JM	*Jamaica.* A Strategy for Growth and Poverty Reduction: Country Economic Memorandum (12.04.94)
12675-JO	*Jordan.* Poverty Assessment (28.10.94)
13152-KE	*Kenya.* Poverty Assessment (15.03.95)
*13171-LSO	*Lesotho.* Poverty Assessment (18.08.1995)
*14044-MAG	*Madagascar.* Poverty Assessment (2 vols.) (28.06.96)
*15437-MAI	*Malawi.* Human Resources and Poverty: Profiles and Priorities for Action (19.03.96)
8667-MA	*Malaysia.* Growth, Poverty Alleviation and Improved Income Distribution in Malaysia: Changing focus of Government Policy Intervention (01.91)
*11842-MLI	*Mali.* Assessment of Living Conditions (30.06.1993)
12182-MAU	*Mauritania.* Poverty Assessment (06.04.94)
13215-MAS	*Mauritius.* CEM: Sharpening the Competitive Edge (12.04.95)
*8770-ME	*Mexico.* Mexico in Transition: Towards a New Role for the Public Sector (22.05.91)
*15723-MOG	*Mongolia.* Poverty Assessment in a Transition Economy (27.06.1996)
11918-MOR	*Morocco.* Poverty, Adjustment and Growth (2 vols), (01.1994)
9510-NAM	*Namibia.* Poverty Alleviation with Sustainable Growth (29.10.91)
*8635-NEP	*Nepal.* Relieving Poverty in a Resource-Scarce Economy (15.08.90)
*14038-NI	*Nicaragua.* Poverty Assessment (2 vols.) (01.06.95)
15344-NIR	*Niger.* Poverty Assessment: A Resilient People in a Harsh Environment (28.06.96)

*14733-UNI	*Nigeria.* Poverty in the Midst of Plenty: The Challenge of Growth with Inclusion: A World Bank Poverty Assessment (31.05.1996)
14397-PAK	*Pakistan.* Poverty Assessment (25.09.95)
12293-PA	*Paraguay.* Poverty and the Social Sectors in Paraguay: A Poverty Assessment (29.06.94)
10193-PA	*Paraguay.* Public Expenditure Review—The Social Sectors (16.06.92)
11191-PE	*Peru.* Poverty Assessment and Social Policies and Programs for the Poor (05.05.1993)
7144-PH	The *Philippines.* The Challenge of Poverty (17.10.88)
13051-PO	*Poland.* Understanding Poverty in Poland (14.09.94)
12465-RW	*Rwanda.* Poverty Reduction and Sustainable Growth (1994)
13431-CE	*Sri Lanka.* Poverty assessment (1995)
15526-TO	*Togo.* Overcoming the Crisis, Overcoming Poverty: A World Bank Poverty Assessment (25.06.1996)
11380-UG	*Uganda.* Growing out of Poverty (31.05.1993)
*14313-UG	*Uganda.* The Challenge of Growth and Poverty Reduction (30.06.95)
*9663-UR	*Uruguay.* Poverty Assessment: Public Social Expenditures and their Impact on the Income Distribution (04.05.93)
*9114-VE	*Venezuela.* Poverty Study: From Generalized Subsidies to Targeted Programs (05.06.1991)
*13442-VN	*Vietnam.* Poverty Assessment and Strategy (23.01.1995)
*12985-ZA	*Zambia.* Poverty Assessment (2 vols.) (10.11.1994)
13540-ZIM	*Zimbabwe.* Achieving Shared Growth: Country Economic Memorandum (2 vols.) (21.04.1995)

Appendix A4. Equations for POV$21 (incidence relative to a $21 poverty line) and POVGAP (intensity relative to a $30 poverty line)

Table A.9.1. *POV$21 Set of Regressions*

Independent variables	Regressions					
	1	2	3	4	5	6
1. LAVCON	5.77 (0.71)	7.1 (0.84)	−2.64 (−0.45)	1.42 (0.15)	8.45 (0.80)	20.07 (1.25)
2. NBR		−2.95 (−0.84)				
3. NBR10	3.89 (4.0)*	6.78 (1.9)		4.44 (4.2)*	5.05 (4.13)*	5.93 (2.89)*
4. NDR					−2.65 (−0.32)	
5. NDR10				−4.18 (−1.15)	−0.86 (−0.09)	
6. POPG10			39.79 (4.15)*			
7. LAVCON* NBR		0.57 (0.70)				
8. LAVCON* NBR10	−0.79 (−3.54)*	−1.34 (−1.64)		−0.90 (−3.78)*	−1.09 (−3.69)*	−1.23 (−2.74)**
9. LAVCON* NDR					0.16 (0.08)	
10. LAVCON* NDR10				0.88 (1.05)	0.54 (0.23)	

Table A.9.1. (Continued)

Independent variables	Regressions					
	1	2	3	4	5	6
11. LAVCON* POPG10			−8.01 (−3.69)*			6.07 (1.562)
12. DUMLATAM	8.66 (3.55)*	8.35 (3.38)*	7.54 (3.10)*	7.62 (2.62)**	7.13 (2.40)**	
13. DUMGB	31.66 (3.7)*	36.76 (3.61)*	42.29 (4.78)*	44.89 (3.21)*	39.19 (2.52)**	
14. PHYSIC						−0.19E-3 (−1.60)
15. NURSE						0.32E-3 (0.58)
16. PRIMENR						0.11 (1.62)
17. SECENR						−0.07 (−0.70)
18. LANDGINI						−1.94 (−0.17)
Adj. R²	0.820	0.819	0.826	0.819	0.821	0.730
Wald tests	LAVCON	LAVCON	LAVCON	LAVCON	LAVCON	LAVCON
	110.89 (0)*	112.52 (0)*	144.15 (0)*	99.87 (0)*	99.71 (0)*	46.71 (0)*
	NBR10	NBR	POPG10	NBR10,	NBR10	NBR10
	29.2 (0)*	1.93 (0.380)*	32.21 (0)*	29.03 (0)*	25.82 (0)*	9.34 (0.009)*
		NBR10		NDR10	NDR	social variables
		7.76 (0.021)**		1.81 (0.405)	2.59 (0.275)	8.34 (0.139)
					NDR10	
					1.21 (0.546)	

Notes: (a) Sample size = 59, except for regression 6 where s = = 38; (b) As Guinea-Bissau is not contained in sample 38, there is no DUMGB in regression 6; (c) values in brackets next to the coefficients are t-ratios; they are p-values for Wald tests (see notes to Table 9.2); (d) * means significant at 1%; and ** at 5%; (e) all regressions are free from statistical problems, apart from regressions 4 and 5 which suffer from a problem of incorrect functional form (the test used in Ramsey's RESET test, 5% significance level); (f) variable definitions in the Appendix.

Table A.9.2. *POV$21 Set of Regressions: Effect on the Level of POV$30 (in percent) of a Unit Change in the Demographic Variables*

LAVCON	Regression number					
	1	2	3	4	5	6
At 25th percentile	NBR10: 0.73	NBR: −0.67 NBR10: 1.42	POPG10: 7.75	NBR10: 0.84 NDR10: −0.66	NBR10: 0.69 NDR: −2.01 NDR10: 1.3	NBR10: 1.01
At 50th percentile	NBR10: 0.43	NBR: −0.45 NBR10: 0.91	POPG10: 4.71	NBR10: 0.50 NDR10: −0.33	NBR10: 0.28 NDR: −1.95 NDR10: 1.51	NBR10: 0.54
At 75th percentile	NBR10: 0.09	NBR: −0.21 NBR10: 0.33	POPG10: 1.26	NBR10: 0.11 NDR10: 0.05	NBR10: −0.19 NDR: −1.88 NDR10: 1.74	NBR10: 0.01

Table A.9.3. *POV$21 Set of Regressions: Effect of Changes in lavcon*

	Regression number					
	1	2	3	4	5	6
Level effect at median	−19.85	−20.15	−21.94	−20.36	−21.20	−19.82
Elasticity at median	−1.97	−2.0	−2.17	−2.02	−2.10	−1.96

Note: Elasticities in row 2 are calculated with median values of POV$21 (= 10.1%).

Table A.9.4. POVGAP *Set of Regressions*

Independent variables	Regressions					
	1	2	3	4	5	6
1. LAVCON	6.68 (1.15)	5.60 (1.03)	9.31 (1.55)	7.56 (1.33)	13.59 (1.33)	12.41 (1.21)
2. NBR			−4.80 (−1.94)	−3.71 (−1.58)		
3. NBR10	2.63 (2.97)*	2.62 (3.08)*	7.32 (2.91)*	6.25 (2.62)**	3.63 (2.77)*	3.53 (2.69)**
4. NDR						
5. NDR10						
6. POPG10						
7. LAVCON*NBR			1.0 (1.76)	0.75 (1.39)		
8. LAVCON*NBR10	−0.54 (−2.70)*	−0.54 (−2.81)*	−1.52 (−2.63)**	−1.27 (−2.33)**	−0.75 (−2.60)**	−0.73 (−2.55)**
9. LAVCON*NDR						
10. LAVCON*NDR10						
11. LAVCON*POPG10						
12. DUMLATAM		5.13 (3.88)*		4.73 (2.87)*		2.58 (1.04)*
13. DUMGB	28.32 (8.14)*	27.90 (8.40)*	36.17 (5.02)*	34.12 (5.02)*		
14. PHYSIC					−0.18E-3 (−2.32)**	−0.17E-3 (−2.26)**
15. NURSE					0.26E-3 (0.73)	0.25E-3 (0.68)
16. PRIMENR					0.06 (1.40)	0.06 (1.31)
17. SECENR					−0.06 (−0.84)	0.05 (−0.81)
18. LANDGINI					4.67 (0.79)	0.40 (0.06)
Adj. R²	0.770	0.801	0.784	0.810	0.682	0.682
Wald tests	LAVCON 71.15 (0)* NBR10 22.87 (0)*	LAVCON 90.99 (0)* NBR10 24.37 (0)*	LAVCON 81.35 (0)* NBR 5.55 (0.062) NBR10 13.02 (0.001)*	LAVCON 100.14 (0)* NBR 4.64 (0.098) NDR10 11.8 (0.003)*	LAVCON 36.94 (0)* NBR10 8.92 (0.012)** social variables 16.62 (0.005)*	LAVCON 38.03 (0)* NBR10 8.15 (0.017)** social variables 11.0 (0.051)

Notes: (*a*) Sample size = 59, except for regressions 5 and 6 where s = 38. As Guinea-Bissau is not contained in the sample 38, there is no DUMGB in regressions 5 and 6; (*b*) values in parentheses next to the coefficients are t-ratios; they are p-values for the Wald tests (see notes to Table 9.2); (*c*) * means significant at 1% and ** at 5%; (*d*) all regressions are free from statistical problems, apart from regressions 2 and 4 which suffer from a problem of incorrect functional form (the test used in Ramsey's RESET test, 5% significant level), and regressions 1 and 2 which suffer from heteroskedasticity of residuals (Harvey test, 5% significance level). White's heteroskedasticity-consistent t-ratios are given in brackets for these two regressions, instead of the usual t-ratios.

Table A.9.5. POVGAP *Set of Regressions: Effect on the Level of POVGAP (in percent) of a Unit Change in the Demographic Variables*

LAVCON	Regression number					
	1	2	3	4	5	6
At 25th percentile	NBR10: 0.47	NBR10: 0.46	NBR: −0.8 NBR10: 1.24	NBR: −0.71 NDR10: 1.17	NBR10: 0.63	NBR10: 0.61
At 50th percentile	NBR10: 0.26	NBR10: 0.25	NBR: −0.42 NBR10: 0.66	NBR: −0.43 NDR10: 0.69	NBR10: 0.35	NBR10: 0.33
At 75th	NBR10: 0.03	NBR10: 0.02	NBR: 0.01 NBR10: 0.01	NBR: −0.10 NBR10: 0.14	NBR10: 0.02	NBR10: 0.02

Table A.9.6. POVGAP *Set of Regressions: Effect of Changes in* LAVCON

	Regression number					
	1	2	3	4	5	6
Level effect at median	−10.83	−11.91	−11.54	−12.30	−10.73	−11.26
Elasticity at median	−2.17	−2.38	−2.31	−2.46	−2.15	−2.25

Note: Elasticities in row 2 are calculated with median values of povgap (= 5%).

References

Ahlburg, D. 1996, 'Population Growth and Poverty'. In D. Ahlburg, A. Kelley, and K. Mason, eds., *The Impact of Population Growth on Well-being in Developing Countries*. Berlin: Springer.

Alesina, A., and D. Rodrik. 1994. 'Distributive Politics and Economic Growth'. *Quarterly Journal of Economics*. 109: 465–90.

Allison, C., K. C. Cheong, and L. Yap. 1989. *Rapid Population Growth in Pakistan: Causes and Consequences*. Report No. 7522-PAK (EMENA). Washington: World Bank.

Anand, S., and R. Kanbur. 1993. 'The Kuznets Process and the Inequality-Development Relationship'. *Journal of Development Economics*. 40: 25–52.

Barro, R. 1991. 'Economic Growth in a Cross-Section of Countries'. *Quarterly Journal of Economics*. 106 (2), 407–43.

Bauer, J., and A. Mason. 1993. 'Equivalence Scales, Costs of Children and Poverty in the Philippines and Thailand'. In Lloyd 1993.

Becker, G., and H. Lewis. 1973. 'On the Interaction between the Quantity and Quality of Children'. *Journal of Political Economy*. 81 (2), pt. 2.

Berndt, E. 1991. *The Practice of Econometrics: Classic and Contemporary*. Addison-Wesley.

Birdsall, N. 1979. 'Siblings and Schooling in Urban Colombia'. New Haven: Yale University, Ph.D. Unpub.

—— D. Ross, and R. Sabot. 1995. 'Inequality and Growth Reconsidered: Lessons from East Asia'. *World Bank Economic Review*. 9 (3), 477–508.

Blanchet, D. 1988. 'Estimating the Relationship between Population Growth and Aggregate Economic Growth in LDCs: Methodological Problems'. In *Consequences of Rapid Population Growth in Developing Countries*. New York: Taylor and Francis.

Bloom, D., and J. Williamson. 1997. 'Demographic Transitions, Human Resource Development, and Economic Miracles in Emerging Asia'. Background paper for Asian Development Bank Emerging Asia Study. HIID Working Paper. Cambridge, Mass.: Harvard Institute for International Development.

Bruno, M., L. Squire, and M. Ravallion. 1996. 'Equity and Growth in Developing Countries: Old and New Perspectives on the Policy Issues'. Working Paper No. 1563, Poverty Analysis and Policy Division. Washington: World Bank.

Chayanov, A. 1924. *Theory of Peasant Economy*, ed. D. Thorner, tr. B. Kerblay. Homewood, Ill.: Irwin, 1966.

Chen, S., G. Datt, and M. Ravallion. 1993. 'Is Poverty Increasing or Decreasing in the Developing World?' Working Paper No. 1146, Poverty Analysis and Policy Division. Washington: World Bank.

Clarke, G. 1995. 'More Evidence on Income Distribution and Growth'. *Journal of Development Economics*. 47 (2), 403–27.

Cornia, G., R. Jolly, and F. Stewart. 1987. *Adjustment with a Human Face, Vol. I: Protecting the Vulnerable and Promoting Growth*. Oxford: Clarendon Press, for UNICEF.

Coulombe, H., and A. McKay. 1994. 'The Causes of Poverty: A Study based on the Mauritania Living Standards Survey 1989–90'. In T. Lloyd and O. Morrissey, eds., *Poverty, Inequality and Rural Development*. Basingstoke: Macmillan.

Daly, H. 1985. 'Marx and Malthus in North-East Brazil: A Note on the World's Largest Class Difference in Fertility and its Recent Trends'. *Population Studies*. 39 (2).

Dasgupta, P. 2000. 'Population and Resources: An Exploration of Reproductive and Environmental Externalities', *Population and Development Review*, 26 (Dec.).

Datt, G., and M. Ravallion. 1996. 'Why have some Indian States done Better than Others at Reducing Rural Poverty?' Working Paper No. 1594, Poverty Analysis and Policy Division. Washington: World Bank.

Deaton, A., and J. Muellbauer. 1980. *Economics and Consumer Behaviour*. Cambridge: Cambridge University Press.

DeGraaff, D., R. Bilsborrow, and A. Herrin. 1993. 'The Implications of High Fertility for Children's Time Use in the Philippines'. In Lloyd 1993.

De Haan, A., and M. Lipton. 2000 'Poverty in Emerging Asia: Progress, Poverty and Log-jams' *Asian Development Review*. 16 (2), 135–76.

Deininger, K., and L. Squire. 1996. 'Measuring Income Inequality: A New Data Base.' Policy Research Department. Washington: World Bank.

Desai, S. 1993. 'The Impact of Family Size on Children's Nutritional Status: Insights from a Comparative Perspective'. In Lloyd 1993.

Drèze, J. 1990. 'Widows in Rural India'. DEP No. 26. London: London School of Economics, Development Economics Research Programme.

Easterlin, R., and E. Crimmins. 1985. *The Fertility Revolution: A Supply-Demand Analysis*. Chicago: University of Chicago.

Eastwood, R., and M. Lipton. 1999 'The Impact of changes in Human Fertility on Poverty'. *Journal of Development Studies*, 36 (1), 1–30.

Evenson, R. 1993. 'India: Population Pressure, Technology, Infrastructure, Capital Formation, and Rural Incomes'. In Jolly and Torrey 1993.

Gaiha, R., and N. Kazmi. 1987. 'Aspects of Poverty in Rural India'. Mimeo. Delhi: University of Delhi, Faculty of Management Studies.

Glewwe, P. 1990. 'Investigating the Determinants of Household Welfare in Côte d'Ivoire'. Working Paper No. 71. Washington: World Bank, Living Standards Measurement Study.

—— and J. Hall. 1998. 'Are some groups more vulnerable to Macroeconomic Shocks than Others: Hypothesis Tests on Panel Data from Peru'. *Journal of Development Economics*, 56.

Greenhalgh, S. 1985. 'Sexual Stratification: The Other Side of 'Growth with Equity' in East Asia'. *Population and Development Review.* 11 (2).

Grootaert, C., with contributions by L. Demery and R. Kanbur 1996. *Analysing Poverty and Policy Reform: The Experience of Côte d'Ivoire.* Aldershot: Avebury.

—— R. Kanbur, and G.-T. Oh. 1997. 'The Dynamics of Welfare Gains and Losses: An African Case-Study'. *Journal of Development Studies.* 33 (5), 635–57.

Holden, S. and H. Binswanger, 1998.'Small-Farmer Decisionmaking, Market Imperfections, and Natural Resource Management in Developing Countries'. In E. Lutz, P. Hazell, and A. McCalla eds., *Agriculture and the Environment: Perspectives on sustainable Rural Development.* World Bank, Nov.

Hongyi, L., L. Squire, and H. Zou. 1995. 'Explaining International and Intertemporal Income Inequality'. Working Paper, Policy Research Department. Washington: World Bank.

Hunt, D. 1978. 'Chayanov's Model of Peasant Household Resource Allocation and its Relevance to Mbere District, Kenya'. *Journal of Development Studies.* 15 (1), 59–86.

Jolly, C., and B. Torrey, eds. 1993. *Population and Land Use in Developing Countries.* Washington: National Academy for National Research Council.

Kakwani, N. 1993. 'Measuring Poverty: Definitions and Significance Tests with Application to Côtre d'Ivoire'. In M. Lipton and J. Van der Gaag, eds., *Including the Poor.* Washington: World Bank.

Kelley, A., and Schmidt. 1994. 'Population and Income Change: Recent Evidence'. Discussion Paper No. 249. Washington: World Bank.

—— —— 1995. 'Aggregate Population and Economic Growth Correlations: The Role of the Components of Demographic Change'. *Demography.* 32 (4), 543–55.

King, E. 1987. 'The Effect of Family Size on Family Welfare: What do we Know?' In D. Gale Johnson and R. D. Lee, eds., *Population Growth and Economic Development: Issues and Evidence.* Madison: University of Wisconsin Press.

Knodel, J. 1993. 'Fertility Decline and Children's Education in Thailand: Some Macro and Micro Effects'. In Lloyd 1993.

Krishnaji, N. 1984. 'Family Size, Levels of Living and Differential Mortality in Rural India: Some Paradoxes'. *Economic and Political Weekly.* 9 (6).

Lalou, R., and C. Mbacké. 1993. 'The Micro-consequences of High Fertility on Child Malnutrition in Mali'. In Lloyd 1993.

Lam, D. 1997. 'Demographic Variables and Income Inequality'. In Rosenzweig and Stark 1997.

Lanjouw, P., and M. Ravallion. 1995. 'Are Larger Households really Poorer?' *Economic Journal,* 105.

Lazear, E., and R. Michael. 1980. 'Family Size and the Distribution of Per Capita Income'. *American Economic Review.* 70 (1).

Lecaillon, A., F. Paukert, C. Morrison, and D. Germidis. 1983. *Income Distribution and Economic Development.* Geneva: International Labour Office.

Levine, R., and D. Renelt. 1992. 'A Sensitivity Analysis of Cross-Country Growth Regressions'. *American Economic Review.* 75.

Lipton, M. 1983*a*. *Demography and Poverty.* Staff Working Paper No. 623. Washington: World Bank.

—— 1983*b*. *Labor and Poverty.* Staff Working Paper No. 616. Washington: World Bank.

—— 1988. The 'Poor and the Poorest'. Discussion Paper No. 25. Washington World Bank.

Lipton, M. 1994. 'Growing Points in Poverty Research: Labour Issues'. Discussion Paper No. 66. Geneva: International Institute of Labour Studies.

—— 1990. 'Responses to Rural Population Growth: Malthus and the Moderns'. In Geoffrey McNicoll and Mead. Cains, eds., Rural Development and Population: Institutions, Issues and Policy. New York: Oxford University Press.

—— 1998a. 'Interactions between Population and Poverty'. In M. Livi-Bacci and G. de Santis, eds., *Population, Distribution and Development*. Oxford: Oxford University Press.

—— 1998b. *Successes in Anti-poverty*. Geneva: International Labour Office.

—— and M. Ravallion. 1995. 'Poverty and Policy'. In S. Behrman and T. N. Srinivasan, eds., *Handbook of Development Economics: Vol. 3B*. Amsterdam: North-Holland.

Lloyd, C. B, ed. 1993. *Fertility, Family Size, and Structure*. New York: Population Council.

—— 1994. 'Investing in the Next Generation: The Implications of High Fertility at the Level of the Family'. New York: Population Council, Working Paper No. 63.

—— and A. Gage-Brandon. 1993. 'Does Sibsize Matter? The implications of Family Size for Children's Education in Ghana'. In Lloyd 1993.

Mahmud, S., and J. McIntosh. 1980. 'Returns to Scale from Family Size—Who Gains from High Fertility?' *Population Studies*. 34 (3).

Malthus, T. R. 1798. *An Essay on the Principle of Population*. In T. R. Malthus, *On Population*, ed. G. Himmelfarb. New York: Modern Library, 1803.

—— 1824. 'Population'. London: Encyclopaedia Britannica, 1830. In F. Osborn, ed. *Three Essays on Population*, 1960.

Persson, T., and G. Tabellini. 1994. 'Is Inequality Harmful for Growth?' *American Economic Review*. 84: 600–21.

Pesaran, M., and B. Pesaran. 1991. *Microfit 3.0*. Oxford: Oxford University Press.

Radelet, S., J. Sachs, and J.-W. Lee. 1997. 'Economic Growth in Asia'. Harvard Institute for International Development, Development Discussion Paper 609.

Ravallion, M., and S. Chen. 1996. 'What can New Survey Data Tell us about Recent Changes in Living Standards in Developing and Transitional Economies?' Working Paper, Poverty and Human Resources Division. Washington: World Bank.

Repetto, R. 1979. *Economic Equity and Fertility in Developing Countries*. Baltimore: Johns Hopkins.

Robinson, J., and T. N. Srinivasan. 1997. 'Long-Term Consequences of Population Growth'. In Rosenzweig and Stark 1997.

Romer, P. 1986. 'Increasing Returns and Long-Run Growth'. *Journal of Political Economy*. 94: 1002–37.

Rosenzweig, M., and O. Stark, eds. 1997. *Handbook of Population and Family Economics: Vol, 1B*. Amsterdam: North-Holland.

—— and K. Wolpin. 1980. 'Testing the Quantity-Quality Fertility Model: The Use of Twins as a Natural Experiment'. *Econometrica*. 48: 227–40.

Ruttan, V. 1993. 'Population Growth, Environmental Change, and Innovation: Implications for Sustainable Growth in Agriculture'. In Jolly and Torrey 1993.

Ryan, J., and R. Walker. 1990. *Village and Household Economies in India's Semi-arid Tropics*. Baltimore: Johns Hopkins.

Shreeniwas, S. 1993. 'Family Size, Structure, and Children's Education: Ethnic Differentials Over Time in Peninsular Malaysia.' In Lloyd 1993.

Sahn, D., P. Dorosh, and S. Younger. 1996. 'Exchange-Rate, Fiscal and Agricultural Policies in Africa: Does Adjustment Hurt the Poor?', *World Development*. 24 (4), 719–47.

Schultz, T. P. 1981. *Economics of Population*. Reading, Mass.: Addison-Wesley.

Simon, J. 1986. *Theory of Population and Economic Growth.* Oxford: Blackwell.

—— and R. Gobin. 1980. 'The Relationship between Population and Economic Growth in LDCs'. *Research in Population Economics.* 215–35.

Squire, L. 1993. 'Fighting Poverty'. *American Economic review.* 83 (2), 377–82.

van der Walle, D. 1985. 'Population Growth and Poverty: A New Look at the Indian Time-Series Data'. *Journal of Development Studies.* 21 (3), 429–39.

Wood, A. 1994. *North–South Trade, Employment and Inequality: Changing Fortunes in a Skill-Driven World.* Oxford: Clarendon Press. IDS Development Studies Series.

10

Inequality and the Family in Latin America

RICARDO HAUSMANN AND MIGUEL SZÉKELY

INTRODUCTION

Latin America is the region with the greatest income inequality in the world. It is the region where the richest 5 percent of the population concentrate the highest proportion of resources (more than 26% of total income on average), and where the poorest 30 percent receive the lowest proportion (less than 8% on average).[1] Within the region there are some differences. For instance, while the Gini coefficient in Uruguay is 0.44, in Brazil, Ecuador, and Paraguay it reaches almost 0.60, but still, all the countries for which recent reliable data is available register inequality indexes above the world average of 0.41.

Why is inequality in Latin America so high? The structure of the economy, geography, culture, ethnicity, and many other general and social factors are important explanations,[2] but when one looks at the personal characteristics of the rich and poor, there are three key variables that make the difference: fertility, female participation, and education.[3] With regards to fertility, household survey data from 16 countries in the region around 1995 reveal that the average family in the top 10 percent of the distribution in the region has 1.4 children, while the typical family from the poorest 30 percent has 3.3.[4] So, as is well known, the poor not only get lower incomes than the rich, but they share this income among more individuals, resulting in greater

---

[1] See Inter-American Development Bank (IDB) (1998).

[2] IDB (1998). See also Gavin and Hausmann (1998).

[3] It could be argued that the reason why these characteristics are more important is because of the definition used to separate the rich from the poor. Specifically, since they are ordering households according to household per capita income, they should observe (almost by definition) large differences in participation and number of children because income per capita is already a product of participation and household size. To verify how sensitive the conclusions are to the ordering according to per capita income, we used household survey data to order households by the income of the head of household (the results are presented in Table A.10.1). The interesting result is that in some cases the differences in these three variables are somewhat smaller than those in IDB (1998), but even so, the use of this new ordering still yields very large differences in the number of children (the 30% poorest still has around 1.2 children more than the richest 10% in all 16 countries for which data is available), and female participation is still significantly higher among the rich in 11 out of the 16 cases. Differences in schooling are magnified by this ordering. So, it cannot be said that these characteristics appear to be important just because of the way in which the population is being ordered.

[4] This will be documented in more detail later in the text.

income per capita inequalities.[5] What makes this fact more interesting is that total fertility rates in Latin America have declined dramatically from 6 percent in 1960, to 2.9 percent by 1995,[6] but clearly, the reductions in fertility have not reached all sectors of the population and have not reached all countries in the same way.

The second characteristic that makes the households in the top 10 percent of the distribution different from the poorest 30 percent, is labor market participation.[7] Male participation varies little across countries and along the income distribution, but surprisingly, the difference comes from the fact that female participation is much lower among poor women than among those in households in the top decile.[8]

The third characteristic is education. The average Latin American adult in the richest 10 percent of the distribution has seven more years of education than the adult in the poorest 30 percent but more importantly, the education that these adults are able to provide for their children is also very different. As shown by Duryea and Székely (2000), the difference in education attainment among 21 year olds in the richest and three poorest deciles, is almost six years. It has been estimated that if there were no education inequality, 30 to 40 percent of the total observed inequality would be eliminated.[9]

One interesting aspect about fertility, labor market participation, and education attainment, is that these are strongly interrelated decisions made within the family (and not only at the individual level). For instance, given the traditional role that women play in the household in Latin America, the decision for females of whether or not to participate in the labor market is strongly dependent on the number of children in the household. Similarly, the amount of education invested in each child is a function of the number of children that the household has to educate. To close the circle, the number of children that a couple decides to have is strongly related to the education level that their own parents were able to provide them with. One complication is that the causality between these three variables is obviously very difficult to disentangle.

The purpose of this chapter is to shed some light on the causes behind the large differences in fertility between countries; and between poor and rich households within the same country. The central argument we develop is that the critical factor is not just the education of the parents (and specifically of the mother), but the potential returns to female education in the labor market. Fertility differences within and between countries are not solely affected by family characteristics. There are underlying conditions in the Latin American economies that are greater than the families themselves and their characteristics that affect fertility differences within

---

[5] On average, the Gini coefficient for total household income of the 16 countries for which household surveys are available to us, is around 13 percent smaller than the Gini for household per capita income.

[6] According to UN population statistics (UN 1997).

[7] We show detailed evidence on this in Section 2 of this chapter.

[8] As will be stressed later, this does not imply that poor women work less than the rich (in fact it is perfectly compatible with the idea that the poor actually spend more hours working than the rich). It only means that the activities performed by the rich have a higher probability of being remunerated in the labor market.

[9] Several works point in this direction. See for instance, Psacharopoulos *et al.* (1993) and IDB (1998).

and between countries. Some of them come from the functioning of labor markets, technological progress, factor endowments, and other factors at the country level. For instance, when the returns to education in the labor market are less differentiated, so that the income gap between uneducated and educated workers is smaller, the differences in fertility between poor and rich are smaller. Therefore, what matters the most for fertility are the returns to unskilled labor. This has strong implications for income inequality.

Since fertility cannot be understood properly without looking also at participation decisions and the education of the current and future generations, we look at the three issues together. As in the case of fertility, the other two family choices are also strongly influenced by the opportunities that women face for using their human capital in the labor market. These opportunities are shaped by the economic context and trigger a set of family decisions that vary widely within and between countries. The most important relative price is the earning capacity of a woman in the job market relative to the value that the family attaches to her housework. This relative price changes very significantly across countries and implies that two similar persons would experience radically different inequality and would be enticed to make very different choices about how many children to have and how much to educate them, depending on the particular country in which they live. The different relative prices will cause families to evolve along very different paths over the generations.

In the rest of this work we rely heavily on household survey data for 15 Latin American countries to develop our argument.[10] In Section 1, we begin by looking at fertility and try to identify what drives the difference in the number of children between poor and rich households. We argue that the opportunity cost of work for the market versus work in the house changes very drastically along the income distribution, explaining the different choices made by these households. Section 2 focuses on labor force participation and its relation to fertility. Section 3 focuses on the connection between fertility, participation, and the education attainment of the new generations. Section 4 brings our story together by estimating a simultaneous equations model that includes the fertility, participation, and education decisions that households make. Section 5 concludes by arguing that personal characteristics do not exclusively determine the fundamental choices that people make. The characteristics interact with the surrounding conditions to generate choices. Specifically, the relative prices with which each economy confronts the individual and his or her family are key determinants of fertility decisions, female participation, and investment in human capital.

1. FERTILITY, FAMILIES, AND INEQUALITY

As mentioned in the introduction, household survey data confirms the well-known fact that family size changes quite dramatically along the income distribution. The rich live in much smaller families. Table 10.1 shows the percentage of people in the

---

[10] See Duryea and Székely (2000) for details on the data.

Table 10.1. *Share of Population by Household Size and Income*

Country	Top 10% of the distribution				Bottom 30% of the distribution			
	1	2–3	4–6	7 or more	1	2–3	4–6	7 or more
Argentina	14.26	46.81	36.68	2.25	0.36	17.82	49.46	32.37
Bolivia	4.13	26.08	59.75	10.03	0.68	7.92	52.39	39.01
Brazil	5.53	40.91	51.05	2.52	0.49	12.73	52.76	34.01
Chile	4.63	35.30	55.87	4.2	0.77	14.19	62.64	22.40
Colombia	3.91	31.08	50.60	14.42	0.42	11.43	56.78	31.37
Costa Rica	4.63	36.41	53.57	5.39	1.56	12.4	54.24	31.80
Ecuador	4.84	27.15	57.18	10.83	0.79	8.52	45.9	44.79
El Salvador	3.35	31.23	56.48	8.93	0.79	9.11	41.65	48.45
Honduras	3.12	23.84	55.98	17.07	1.17	7.79	37.86	53.19
Mexico	4.63	30.82	58.60	5.95	0.68	6.95	42.64	49.73
Panama	7.19	40.10	48.54	4.17	1.56	11.66	47.86	38.93
Paraguay	5.62	28.46	53.12	12.8	0.38	8.09	36.63	54.90
Peru	5.08	25.66	56.49	12.75	0.42	5	43.67	50.91
Uruguay	11.41	49.21	38.22	1.15	1.3	19.93	56.04	22.73
Venezuela	3.53	31.22	52.52	12.72	0.48	6.85	43.02	49.65
Average	5.72	33.62	52.31	8.35	0.79	10.69	48.24	40.28
United States	27.87	59.75	12.37	0	6.47	32.14	48.08	13.31

Source: Authors' calculations.

top decile and the bottom three deciles that live in single-person households. It shows that the top decile is very significantly overrepresented in single-person households, especially in Argentina and Uruguay where over 10 percent of the top decile live alone. However, it is interesting to note that these numbers are dwarfed by the US experience, where almost 28 percent of the top decile live by themselves. The poor, on the other hand, very rarely live on their own in Latin America although this is not the case in the United States. A similar pattern is apparent for three-person households, in which, throughout the region, between a fifth and a quarter of the rich live but barely one-tenth of the poor do so. By contrast, in the United States all segments of the income distribution have a similar probability to live in three-person households. The situation is dramatically reversed for households with seven or more members. Here we observe that barely one-tenth of the top decile live in such large families, while a striking 40 percent of the poor do so.

Theories about the economics of family formation have two potential explanations for the relationship between family size and income. The first is related to the effects of income and the second is related to fertility. The income effects are seen as the consequence of two opposing forces. First, it is argued that there are economies of scale in consumption, so that two persons living together can share the same appliances and physical space and thus gain more benefits out of their resources. However, as more people share space there ensues some loss of freedom for each

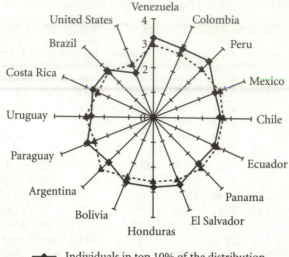

— Individuals in top 10% of the distribution
--▲-- Individuals in bottom 30% of the distribution

Figure 10.1. *Adults per Household (Individuals 18 Years Old and over)*

Notes: Data are for 1995 except for Argentina, Honduras, and Peru (1996) and Chile and Mexico (1994).

one. Hence, one would expect the rich to use their resources to 'buy freedom' by living in smaller households while the poor cannot afford to bestow the economies of scale in consumption provided by larger households. The alternative story relates to demography. As fertility declines, there are simply fewer children in each home so the average size of households is smaller and the proportion of older people in the population increases. Thus, in Argentina, Uruguay, and the United States, the over-65 population is much larger and is significantly overrepresented in single-person households because they are at a later phase of the demographic transition.

Separating the number of adults and children in a home can disentangle the income and demographic stories. If what's important is economies of scale in consumption, then more adults will live together as we go down the income distribution ladder. If the effect were generated by fertility, then the story would be reflected in the number of children. Figure 10.1 shows that there is no consistent pattern in the way the number of adults changes along the income distribution. While in the United States and Argentina there is a weak relationship between income and the number of adults, in most other countries the number of adults is smaller in both rich and poor households compared to the average of the population. While the number of adults does not exhibit a strongly consistent pattern, the number of children shows very stark contrasts (Fig. 10.2).[11] Here the differences are quite large and consistent throughout

---

[11] Household survey data only seldom provides direct information on fertility. We have used the number of children in the household as a proxy variable for the fertility of the parents.

Figure 10.2. *Children per Household (Individuals 17 Years Old and Younger)*

Notes: Data are for 1995 except for Argentina, Honduras, and Peru (1996) and Chile and Mexico (1994).

the region. Even in countries that have low fertility rates such as the United States, Argentina, and Uruguay there is a difference of about two children between the top decile and the bottom 30 percent of the population. In higher fertility countries such as Central America, the Andean Region, and Paraguay, the rich have between 1.5 and two children while the poor have between three and four children.

Many hypotheses about poverty have centered on the issue of family and family values. It has often been argued that in the United States, poverty is strongly associated with single-parent households, while the non-poor live in nuclear or traditional families. While this is very much a US story, the data suggest that it is not primarily a Latin American one. Family structures change surprisingly little along the income distribution. True, the rich are disproportionately represented among those living alone. It is also true that they are overrepresented among those living as couples without children. But the traditional family remains the dominant form in Latin America. As shown in Table 10.2 most Latin American children live in (pure or extended) nuclear families, that is, in families with a parent, a spouse, and children (pure), which may also include other relatives (extended),[12] while the proportions are lower in the United States.

In the typical model, raising children is a costly activity in terms both of the resources spent on each child, and of the income that family members (typically the

---

[12] Note that we cannot determine if the spouse is the parent of all children present.

Fertility, Poverty, and the Family

Table 10.2. *Share of Children Living in Nuclear and Single Parent Households by Country and Income Level*

Country	Top10%	Bottom 30%	Top 10%	Bottom 30%
Argentina[1]	80.84	82.61	7.29	13.11
Bolivia	86.19	74.16	12.57	15.37
Brazil	79.01	74.85	9.80	16.89
Chile[2]	62.54	67.35	9.07	18.01
Colombia	83.08	67.35	12.78	19.31
Costa Rica	82.63	80.47	10.94	20.93
Ecuador	85.83	79.96	11.72	15.13
El Salvador	90.37	49.53	13.71	28.89
Honduras	70.92	81.28	13.69	26.90
Mexico[2]	91.87	72.78	10.89	10.50
Panama	76.28	85.73	9.91	25.97
Paraguay	87.55	85.57	14.72	11.75
Peru[1]	85.1	75.57	13.50	9.90
Uruguay	79.56	63.93	8.62	18.99
United States	75.36	65.92	6.82	41.12
Venezuela	87.26	74.5	15.28	27.26

Notes: Data are for 1995 except for [1]1996 data [2]1994 data.

Source: Calculations from household survey data.

mother) have to forgo to take care of them.[13] If a higher market wage is available for women, the cost of raising children is also larger and this induces lower fertility. On the contrary, the lower the relative market value of women's labor, the lower the cost of raising children.[14] This leads to a trade-off between the quality and the quantity of children.

There is a widely observed negative relationship between parents' schooling and fertility, which is not surprising, since education is one of the main determinants of earnings.[15] Figure 10.3 shows the average relationship between number of children

---

[13] There are several theories in the extensive literature on this issue, all of which suggest that the fact that the poor decide to have more children reflects the outcome of a cost-benefit rational analysis. Galor and Weill (1996), for instance, argue that through the process of development, women's wages increase and this raises the cost of raising children more than it adds resources to the household. Therefore, development induces lower fertility. From this perspective, the poor have more children because of the lower relative market value of the labor they can offer in the market. Another channel that has been suggested by Becker *et al.* (1990) is that poor families have higher fertility rates because the rate of return on education is lower than the return on children (the quality vs. quantity hypothesis). In the same line, Neher (1971) argues that poor people may choose to have more children as a result of old-age security. Thus, children are viewed as an investment. The process of economic development (and urbanization) opens opportunities for children from rural or poor families to enjoy higher lifetime income outside the parent's unit. Thus, it erodes the importance of that motive.

[14] See e.g. Galor and Weil (1996).

[15] Lam and Duryea (1999) is a recent example of the analysis of these relations in a Latin American country.

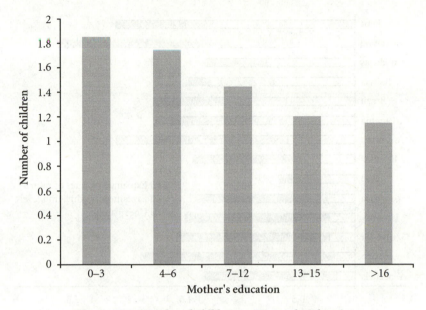

Figure 10.3. *Number of Children per Woman by Education*

and education level for 15 Latin American countries. There is a very consistent pattern: women with six years of schooling or less have 0.7 more children than those with more than 13 years of schooling. The economic explanation is that income has two opposing effects on fertility. First, if children are 'normal' goods, there should be a positive relationship between fertility and parent's education and income. However, child-rearing requires resources which have an opportunity cost related to the value of a woman's work in the market. The higher the education level the more income a woman forgoes by retiring from work in order to take care of her children. If a woman's potential income in the market is low, then staying at home is relatively cheap, and once at home, taking care of one more child is not that costly. The higher this opportunity cost, the fewer the number of children. Hence, a recurrent feature we find in Latin America, and one that is consistent with this theory and with the vast empirical evidence, is that while the education and income of the father increases the number of children, that of the mother reduces it.[16]

The number of children may vary across countries for potentially many reasons. Tastes might be different. But one alternative explanation is that relative prices for women's human capital are systematically different across countries. To check this hypothesis we ran regressions of the number of children on the opportunity cost

[16] We obtained the statistical relationship between the number of children in the household and the education of the parents by controlling for geographic area, age of the household head, and the presence of adults in the household. As would be expected, we confirmed that in all of the 15 Latin American countries for which the estimation is performed, the mother's education has a strong negative effect over the number of children in the household, while the education and income of the father has a positive (weaker) effect.

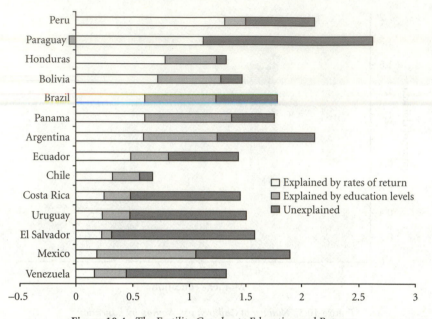

Figure 10.4. *The Fertility Gap due to Education and Returns*

Notes: The fertility gap is calculated as the difference in the number of children per household in the top decile and the bottom three deciles.

of a woman's income-generating capacity, as it emerges from earnings equations. The model used for the estimation is presented in the Appendix, and the basic idea is that the demand for children depends on the market value of the educational endowments of the parents.[17] This allows us to simulate the following experiments. How much of the difference in the number of children in poor and rich households is due to differences in the opportunity cost that rich and poor women face? Would the number of children change if the household faced other relative prices?

Figure 10.4 summarizes the results from these experiments. The figure shows that if all households had the same education, a low proportion of the differences in El Salvador, Uruguay, Mexico, and Venezuela would be eliminated. However, in Honduras, Peru, Bolivia, Chile, and Paraguay they would reduce the difference in the number of children by around one-half.

The second experiment consists of measuring the impact of having different education levels, but additionally, we allow the prices to vary across countries. Figure 10.4

[17] The simulations that follow use econometric estimates performed in two stages. First, an earnings regression that uses education, experience, and the geographic location of the household is estimated separately for working-age men and women. The coefficients are used to predict the income that each individual would earn, given his or her labor market experience, education, and location. In other words, this is an estimate of the income-generating capacity. The predicted incomes are used in a second stage regression where the dependent variable is the number of children in the household, and the independent variables are the estimated income-earnings potential. See the Appendix for a discussion of the methodology.

shows that when we allow the opportunity cost of participating in the labor market faced by rich and poor parents to vary, we account for 60 percent of the differential in the number of children that they have. However, in Honduras, Bolivia, Chile, Panama, Peru, and Brazil, the explanatory power of prices and quantities of education is much higher and reaches around 80 percent of the differences between rich and poor.

The difference between the results of the first and second experiments suggests that in most countries, quantities are important, but that the differences in relative prices faced by rich and poor parents—and which are shaped by the economic environment—play a key role in the decision of how many children to have. In countries like Honduras, Bolivia, and Chile, these relative prices account for most of the differences between rich and poor households. So, the mother's education is not the only critical factor. The potential returns to her education in the labor market—which are determined by the economic context—are as important. Fertility differences across the income distribution and between countries are therefore due to factors greater than the personal characteristics of individuals. If the returns to education in the labor market were less differentiated, the differences in fertility between poor and rich would also be smaller.

2. LABOR FORCE PARTICIPATION

Section 1 argued that the opportunities faced by a woman in the labor market are strong determinants of fertility decisions. Women that receive a low relative remuneration for the human capital they own tend to have more children. However, fertility in itself has an effect on the participation of adults in the labor force. In this section we explore this link.

Table 10.3 documents the fact that labor force participation rates change quite systematically along the income distribution. Household survey data reveals that the poor participate systematically less than the rich in all countries. The difference in participation is overwhelmingly explained by female participation, which remains substantially below male rates throughout the region. The gap between the genders in this respect is substantially higher than in the industrial countries. This difference is particularly large in the Central American countries, Mexico, Panama, Venezuela, and Chile.

While male participation is relatively constant and high along the income distribution, female participation varies strongly with income in all countries except Paraguay and Peru (Table 10.3). While on average only 34 percent of women in the top decile are out of the labor force, among the poorest three deciles, over 55 percent are not working.[18]

---

[18] Household surveys ask individuals directly about their time use. The low participation rates among females presented in Table 10.3 reflect the fact that when women are asked about their activities, a larger proportion of females in poor households declare that they use their time in activities other than performing a job in the labor market. Therefore, not participating does not imply that a woman doesn't work and the differences between poor and rich do not mean that poor women work fewer hours than the rich. They only reveal that a higher proportion of the rich receive a remuneration in the labor market for the time

Table 10.3. *Labor Force Participation Rates by Income Decile (Ages 18 to 65)*

Country	Total							Informal					
	Total			Top 10%		Bottom 30%		Total		Top 10%		Bottom 30%	
	All	Males	Females	Males	Females	Males	Females	Males	Females	Males	Females	Males	Females
Argentina[1]	65.5	83.2	48.8	88.5	68.1	80.9	39.6	35.1	22.2	18.0	12.8	48.2	27.6
Bolivia	63.4	76.2	51.5	80.2	57.6	72.8	44.6	38.0	36.6	21.0	20.7	45.0	38.5
Brazil	69.2	86.8	52.5	85.8	61.7	85.9	44.8	48.2	20.0	32.6	17.8	56.8	18.4
Chile[2]	58.1	80.0	37.5	78.5	55.7	78.3	21.3	33.1	14.3	17.4	13.5	37.2	12.9
Colombia	62.3	84.5	42.1	87.2	52.2	82.8	27.2						
Costa Rica	62.0	86.0	38.0	86.0	57.0	82.0	25.0	42.0	17.6	21.2	10.9	52.8	17.0
Ecuador	72.3	89.1	55.8	90.2	69.6	87.7	50.4	54.7	44.4	29.7	27.9	68.5	52.0
El Salvador	61.4	82.4	43.4	84.2	62.4	78.3	23.1	46.3	30.2	24.4	23.4	60.6	23.9
Honduras[1]	63.1	88.4	39.7	86.6	61.7	86.5	24.1	55.9	30.2	34.4	21.8	72.3	31.5
Mexico[2]	N.A.	84.2	37.9	82.4	52.3	85.1	29.9	58.2	28.8	30.7	19.5	67.7	33.2
Panama	60.2	80.4	40.0	83.5	63.8	79.6	24.3	39.2	15.2	11.7	6.6	63.8	19.6
Paraguay	60.1	90.8	72.8	84.9	60.2	83.0	89.0	64.8	52.8	36.1	34.9	88.1	65.1
Peru[1]	78.7	84.1	59.8	90.8	72.8	93.6	64.7	49.6	44.3	28.8	29.5	53.7	46.7
Uruguay	71.7	85.3	57.0	88.7	67.2	83.6	48.3	27.5	22.7	16.6	12.9	35.3	28.1
Venezuela	70.3	82.3	39.6	86.6	59.3	76.5	24.7	41.1	18.5	29.4	13.9	43.7	19.3
Industrial Countries	61.2	94.0	73.0										

Notes: Data are for 1995 except for [1] 1996 data [2] 1994 data.

Source: Calculations from household survey data.

When poor women participate, they do so mainly in the informal sector. This is clear from Table 10.3 where the share of informal employment among women of working age is shown. It is clear that the proportions change dramatically along the income distribution. For example, while poor women in Paraguay, Peru, and Ecuador have high participation rates, they are conspicuously absent from the formal sector. By contrast, women in the top decile that participate twice as much as poor women, on average, have a much smaller presence in the informal sector and an overwhelming presence in the formal sector.

Why do the poor participate less than the rich do? There is a very large literature that tries to understand what drives the kinds of results described above.[19] Economic theory explains them by arguing that female participation involves a choice between work at home and work for the market. As with all economic choices, these reflect relative returns. A woman's work will be more valued at home, the lower the productivity of housework and the higher the demand or need for it. Hence, things like access to running water and electricity, which permit the use of appliances for washing, cooking, and cleaning free time that can be offered in the market in exchange for a monetary income. By the same token, the larger the number of children that need taking care of, the less time will be left for market work. Alternatively, the higher the returns to market work, the more women will consider freeing up time to be offered in that attractive market, and maybe arrange for somebody else to do some of the house chores. She might even consider having fewer children (as discussed in Section 1). But if the husband is already making a good living, then it might make sense to stay at home and improve the supply of those home-made goods and services that cannot be bought in the market.

Hence, a woman's participation in the labor market should depend positively on some measure of her earning capacity, such as education, and negatively on the husband's earning capacity and the number of children. These relationships are very strongly borne out by the available evidence. Figure 10.5 shows the rate of female participation by education level. There is a strong and clear pattern between educational attainment and participation. In fact the differences are quite sharp. While only some 40 percent of women with four years or less of schooling participate in the labor market, over 78 percent of those with higher education do. The contrast is much sharper with respect to female participation in the formal sector where the differences in participation are even larger. These differences are also apparent when comparing men and women as a whole (Fig. 10.6).

We also observe a similar pattern between participation and the number of children (Fig. 10.7). The number of children has a negative effect on participation and the

---

they spend working. In fact, poor women tend to spend more time working in household tasks, which are not remunerated and therefore do not count as participation. It should be borne in mind that the participation rates will be underestimated when female respondents understate their work activities, and that some types of activities such as working informally in family businesses, which are more common among the poor, are more prone to this problem.

[19] See e.g. Psacharopoulos and Tzannatos (1992) for an analysis of Latin American countries, and the volume by Birdsall and Sabot (1991).

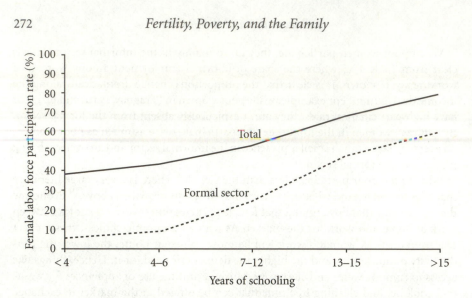

Figure 10.5. *Female Labor Force Participation Rate by Education in Latin America*

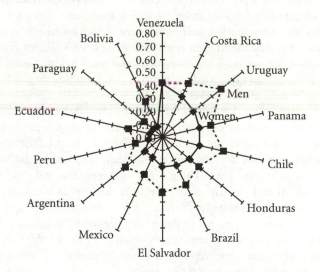

Figure 10.6. *Share of Formal Sector Participation for Men and Women with Four to Six Years of Schooling*

Notes: Data are for 1995 except for Argentina, Honduras, and Peru (1996) and Chile and Mexico (1994).

impact is sharper in the formal sector. On average, women with five or more children participate almost 10 percent less than do women with less than two children.

It is reasonable to assume that women have more difficulty entering the formal sector because formal employment requires a commitment to work a certain number of hours a day, on fixed schedules, and with severe limitations on absenteeism. Any of

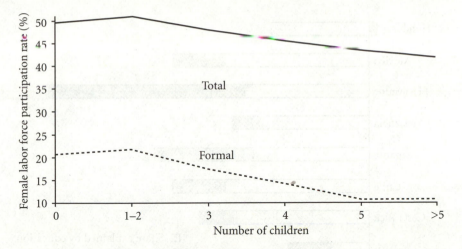

Figure 10.7. *Female Labor Force Participation Rate by Number of Children in Latin America*

the many problems that can arise at home may make a potentially reliable worker into an unreliable one. Women who do work in the formal sector must rely on a network of support that can help deal with unpredictable events at home. This support may involve relatives or domestic servants and may be costly. Hence, only women who can have access to this network will find it efficient to work in the formal sector. Given the traditional role of women in Latin America, this restriction applies to women but much less to men, and is one reason why men have less difficulty in joining the formal sector.

So, there is a clear relationship between education, the number of children (our proxy for fertility), and the decision of women to participate in the labor market. Other factors such as the relative age of the children, the earning potential of the household head, the presence of other adults and that of retired persons (over 65) may also affect these choices by making housework more demanding or by providing additional resources with which to accomplish those tasks. Our estimates (not presented here) show, however, that they are not as important as education and the number of children.

To find our way in terms of the relative relevance and importance of these factors we estimated a participation model that allows women to make three decisions: stay at home, work in the informal sector, or work in the formal sector. The model is presented in the Appendix. We use the model here to simulate some experiments that point to the relative importance of each factor.[20] First, in eight out of the 14

[20] The simulations that follow use econometric estimates performed in two stages, similar to those in Section 1. First, an earnings regression that uses education, experience, and the geographic location of the household is estimated separately for men and women. The coefficients are used to predict the income that each individual would earn, given his or her labor market experience, education, and location. In other words, this is an estimate of the income-generating capacity. The second stage consists of estimating

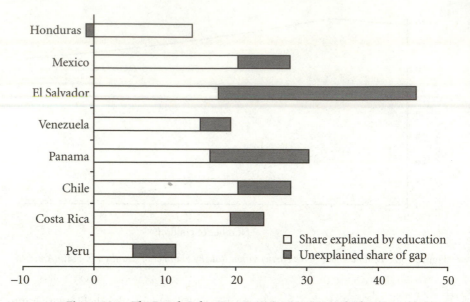

Figure 10.8. *The Female Labor Force Participation Gap and Education*

Notes: The gap is calculated as the difference between female labor force participation rates in the top 10% and the bottom 30% of the income distribution. Only countries with a gap of 10% or more are included. Data are for 1995 except for Honduras and Peru (1996) and Chile and Mexico (1994).

countries in the estimation, the gap in labor force participation between high and low income women exceeded 10 percent. Of these eight countries, the difference in educational levels of high income and low income women explained around 40 percent (see Fig. 10.8). The only exception is Honduras, where education levels explain the whole gap.

By contrast, the number of children under 6 years of age is statistically significant but has a smaller impact on the participation gap between rich and poor. After taking education and other factors into consideration, the number of children explains around 2 percent of the labor force participation gap. In fact, the association between participation and the number of children is due mainly to the association of both variables with the education of the woman. Controlling for education, the number of children loses some of its effect on the decision. On average, each additional child under 6 reduces the participation rate by 4.1 percentage points. By contrast, each additional year of schooling increases participation by 2.1 percent. Hence, while the

a multinomial logit regression to predict the probability that each person has for not participating in the labor market, participating in the informal sector, or participating in the formal sector. This regression uses the number of children in the household and the estimated income-generating capacity of the individual in question as independent variables. The simulations consist of using the coefficients from the regressions to evaluate the probabilities by using different mean values of each variable, depending on the experiment in question. The Appendix shows the coefficients of the multinomial regression and provides a more detailed discussion.

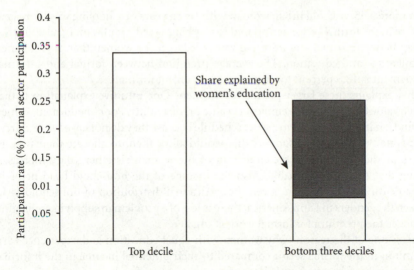

Figure 10.9. *Women's Formal Sector Participation due to Education*

difference in years of schooling between the rich and the poor typically exceeds six years, the difference in the number of children under 6 is around one. Therefore, education dominates over the number of children in explaining participation along the income distribution, but as we will see later, the number of children also has an effect on education. So, part of the effect of education on participation is related to fertility indirectly.

While education has a large effect on participation, it has an even larger impact on work in the formal sector. Using our model we simulated the effect of giving women in the lower 30 percent the same education as those in the top 10 percent and measured the effect on participation. The results are quite dramatic, with most of the gap in formal employment being eliminated in most countries (Fig. 10.9). The probability of working in the informal sector declines by an average of 6 percentage points when we simulate giving poor women the same education as the rich.

The earning potential of the household head also has an impact on participation, although smaller. If we were to give the poorer 30 percent of women the same income of the male household head as that of the rich, their participation would increase by an average of 5 percentage points. Alternatively, giving the household heads where poor women live the same education as that of the household heads of the rich would reduce informal employment by an average of 5 percentage points.

Now, other things being equal, it is generally the case that the formal sector pays women more than the informal sector. How much is this premium worth? To find out we estimated another set of earnings equations[21] and used them to estimate how

[21] These simulations are similar to the previous ones. We first estimate earnings regressions, and use the coefficients to predict each person's income based on their personal characteristics. Secondly, we use the coefficients to evaluate the function at other mean levels, and recompute the predicted income.

much more a 35-year-old urban woman with seven years of schooling would make if she were in the formal sector as opposed to working as self-employed. In all countries the gap between formal and informal wages is larger for women than it is for men of similar age and education. The average premium between formal and informal employment is 18.5 percent for women and 7 percent for men.

What explains these larger premia for women? One intuitive explanation is that women value flexibility while employers value predictability. Poor uneducated women may find it harder to commit to a strict schedule because they do not have the resources to generate the network of support that would allow them to allocate their time in a more predictable way. As the education of the woman rises her salary increases, making that network affordable. Also the income of the household head helps in this same direction. For men, given the traditional distribution of household tasks between the genders in Latin America, there is less of a problem in supplying reliability and hence the premium for formal work is smaller.

This is one of the reasons why women with equal education and experience earn a premium in the formal sector compared to their potential income in the informal sector and why this premium is larger for women than for men of otherwise equal characteristics.

In sum, a woman's earning capacity and the number of children in the household are key determinants of where she will end up working: at home, in the informal sector, or in the formal sector. As opposed to men, there is a very strong relationship between female participation and income and this effect is even stronger when we consider participation in the formal sector.

3. CHILDREN'S EDUCATIONAL ATTAINMENT

As with the link between fertility and participation, there is a circular relation between fertility and educational attainment of the new generations. As seen in Section 2, the economic opportunities that a woman faces and therefore, the fertility decisions, depend on her human capital and the returns to education. However, the possibility of acquiring human capital within the family for the new generations, in turn, depends on the number of children that the household has to support. This section looks into this issue.

The educational attainment of children also changes systematically along the income distribution. Education gaps (measured as the difference between the number of years of education a child is expected to have given his or her age, and the actual number of years attained) are not very evident at age 12, where in many countries the differences in attainment along the income distribution are less than half a year (see Fig. 10.10 and Duryea and Székely 2000). However, in some countries the education gaps are much larger such as Brazil, El Salvador, and Paraguay. In these countries, there is already an important gap in attainment between rich and poor, but enroll-ment rates at this age remain relatively high in most of the region, with an attendance rate of almost 90 percent for the bottom 30 percent of the income distribution.

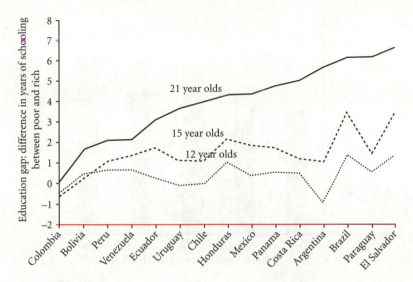

Figure 10.10. *Difference in Education Gap by Age between Children in Poor and Rich Households*

Notes: Data are for 1995 except for Argentina, Honduras, and Peru (1996) and Chile and Mexico (1994).

The picture changes quite dramatically by age 15, a time at which most children are expected to be in high school. At this early age, the differences in attainment and enrollment start to be quite sharp. At this age, children are expected to have between eight and nine years of schooling, which most of the children in the top decile tend to get. While in many countries the gap in attainment between rich and poor is about a year, in El Salvador, Honduras, and Brazil the gap is almost four years, while it is around two years in Mexico, Panama, and Paraguay. However, by this time many of the poorer children have already left school and will not be acquiring more schooling. Enrollment among the 15 year olds of the poorest 30 percent of the population is barely 32 percent in Honduras, 42 percent in Paraguay, and 50 percent in El Salvador and Ecuador. Interestingly, in spite of the fact that in Brazil this group of children have attained barely 3.5 years of schooling, 68 percent are still enrolled.[22]

By age 21 we observe an accumulated education gap as shown in Figure 10.10. In countries like Peru and Venezuela the differences are only about two years. By contrast, the gap exceeds six years in Brazil, Paraguay, and El Salvador and averages about four to five years in Mexico, Panama, Chile, and Costa Rica. Also, by age 21 less than 20 percent of the bottom three deciles are enrolled in school in all countries except Peru, Chile, and Venezuela. By contrast the top 10 percent present enrollment rates in excess of 50 percent in Uruguay, Costa Rica, Argentina, El Salvador, Panama, and Chile.[23]

---

[22] See Duryea and Székely (2000) for more details.   [23] Ibid.

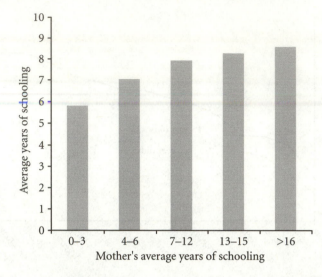

Figure 10.11. *Children's Education by Mother's Education (15 Year Olds)*

Educational attainment of the children has an even tighter relationship with the education of the parents.[24] This is patently clear in Figure 10.11 where we present the educational attainment of 15 year olds by the education of the mother.[25] In fact, the education of the parents is better at predicting the attainment of the children than is income. One interpretation is that the parents' schooling plays a pedagogical and exemplary role for their children. An alternative hypothesis is that attainment depends not on the income of the period in which the survey was conducted, but instead on the income over the years in which the schooling was accumulated. From this point of view, a person's education may be a better predictor of lifetime earnings than the income in any given month. Moreover, a mother's education may be more closely related to schooling not because of any distinct pedagogical function played by mothers, but instead because a mother's labor force participation is strongly related to her education. Hence, the higher the education of the mother, the more likely it is that the household has two incomes. We tested this idea by asking whether the educational attainment of children was positively or negatively associated with whether the mother was in or out of the labor force. If the story is a pedagogical one, we would expect that mothers that do not participate in the labor market have more time to improve their children's schooling. Nevertheless, what we found was that children of mothers that participate had higher educational attainment than those of mothers out of the labor force. Table A.10.3 in the Appendix shows that even after controlling for the effect

[24] This strong association is well documented in the vast literature on the subject. The most comprehensive surveys can be found in Behrman (1997) and Behrman and Knowles (1997).

[25] A similar picture emerges if one considers instead the education of the father, as there is a very high correlation between the two. Econometrically, there is a tighter link between mother's education and school attainment of the children, which will be explained below.

of the number of children in the household, gender, parent's education, household income, urban–rural location, age of the child, and the presence of elderly members in the household, participation in the labor market by a child's mother increases the probability of attending school. In 13 out of the 15 Latin American countries for which we have information, the positive effect of mother's participation on her child's attainment is positive and statistically significant (the only exceptions are Argentina and Peru). On average, if the mother participates in the labor market, the probability that her child remains in school increases by around 5 percent.

An additional element that is strongly related to attainment is the number of children in the household. More children implies that it will be harder to finance the education of each one. This idea is strongly borne out by the data (Fig. 10.12, and Table A.10.3 in the Appendix). Twenty-one year-old children in households with six children or more have on average two years less of education than children in households with one or even three children. This reflects the trade-off between quantity and quality of children. The higher the demand for quantity, the harder it will be to have them achieve more schooling. Hence, quantity makes quality more expensive. But as we saw in the previous section on fertility, the higher the potential income of the mother in the market, the lower the demand for quantity. It is just one more logical step to note that if the parents opt for fewer children because of the mother's career opportunities, then they will have all the more resources to invest in the education of the children they do have. Hence, the relationship between education of the mother, number of children, and attainment.

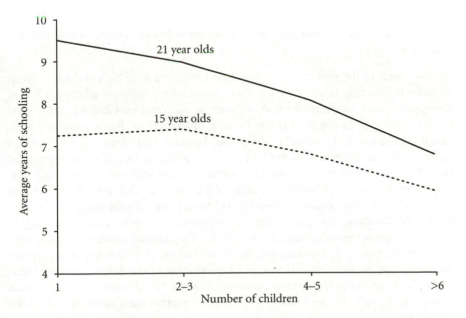

Figure 10.12. *Child's Education by Number of Children of the Mother and Age*

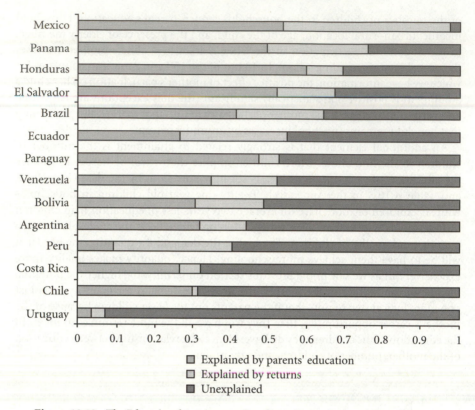

Figure 10.13. *The Educational Attainment Gap due to Parents' Education and Returns*

How much of the difference in educational attainment of high and low income children is due only to the fact that their parents have different education levels? Using our model, we estimated that, on average, the variations in the parents' level of education explain about 30 percent of the differences in their children's educational attainment. In El Salvador, Honduras, Panama, and Mexico, the proportion of the difference explained reaches 50 percent (see Fig. 10.13). After accounting for the differences attributed to parental education, economy-wide factors also contribute to the gap in children's educational attainment. One important factor is how much the labor market values an additional year of schooling, that is, the return to education. Unequal returns to education between primary and higher education across countries indeed account for a significant amount of the educational attainment gap. On average, the combination of disparities in returns to education and parental education explain 55 percent of the difference in the educational attainment of high and low income children. However, in Mexico, Panama, Honduras, El Salvador, and Brazil, these factors explain close to 80 percent of the difference.

3.1. *The Intergenerational Transmission of Inequality*

Since education and other endowments of the parents have such a strong relationship to their children's school attainment, it is important to ask if such links condemn us to reproduce, generation after generation, the same inequality. This question can be formally studied by estimating the intergenerational transmission of schooling.

The principle of the calculation is the following. We know that the education of the children depends to a large extent on that of the parents. When today's children become parents, their children's education will also depend on theirs, and so on. One question that can be asked is whether this process converges toward equilibrium or is explosive, and whether different segments of society are moving toward the same education or toward different levels of education in the long run.

We present the essential intuition in graphic form in Figure 10.14. On the horizontal axis we have the education of today's parents. On the vertical axis we have that of today's children. A 45° line is drawn. Points on this line indicate that parents and children have the same education. Another line is drawn, which cuts the 45° line from above. That is the line that relates the attainment of today's children to their parents' education. Notice that if this line were constant across the generations, society would eventually converge to an education level equal for all at point E. If a family starts at point A, with very little education, then the next generation would get to point B, and the following to point C. By contrast, if a family starts with a lot of education, such as point X, then the next generation would move to point Y, and so on. Point E is the only single equilibrium for the educational long run. However, a different picture

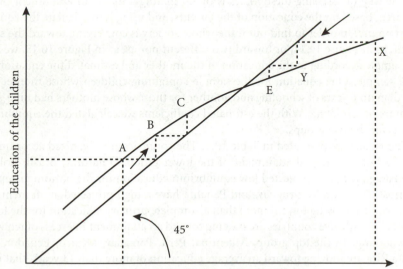

Figure 10.14.

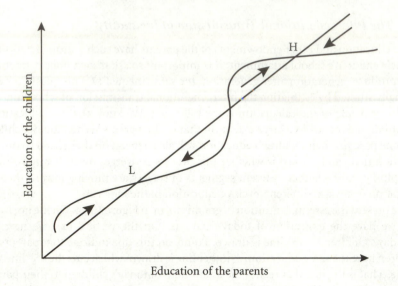

Education of the children

Education of the parents

Figure 10.15.

would emerge if the curve had cut the 45° line from below. Then society would be pulled to the extremes with some people having more education in every generation while others would have less. A final possibility is that shown in Figure 10.15 where the educational attainment line crosses the 45° line at two points, one low, L, and one high, H.

One way of assessing these forces is by estimating a model of attainment of the children, based on the education of the parents, and using it to calculate the equilibrium points. In order to find out if the whole society is converging toward the same point, as in Figure 10.14, or toward two different points, as in Figure 10.15, we split the sample according to the education of the mother and estimated the equation for each sample. One equation for the sample containing children whose mother had less than nine years of schooling and another for those whose mothers had nine years or more of schooling. With the estimated coefficients we calculated the equilibrium points for the two groups.

The results are presented in Table 10.4. The countries are organized according to the level of educational attainment of the lower group. Honduras, Brazil, Bolivia, and Paraguay have a projected low equilibrium education for the bottom group. By contrast, Peru, Chile, Uruguay, and Panama have a high projected attainment. All countries are moving toward more than a complete primary education for the lower group, but only five countries are moving toward an attainment in excess of ten years of schooling. In the top group, Argentina, Peru, Paraguay, Mexico, Ecuador, and Costa Rica are moving toward an average education of more than 13 years, that is, at least two years of higher education. In general, there is an association between the level of education of the bottom group and the gap between the two groups. Looking at the relationship between these two variables we can see that there is a strong negative

Table 10.4. *Estimated Education Equilibrium for the Two Education Groups*

	More educated	Less educated
Argentina[1]	14.29	9.63
Bolivia	12.19	8.07
Brazil	11.10	7.62
Chile[2]	12.95	11.41
Colombia	12.73	9.76
Costa Rica	13.35	9.83
Ecuador	13.35	9.83
El Salvador	12.76	8.93
Honduras[1]	10.77	6.58
Mexico[2]	13.65	9.98
Panama	13.28	10.38
Paraguay	13.81	8.64
Peru[1]	14.13	11.84
Uruguay	12.38	10.81
Venezuela	11.77	9.51

Notes: Data are for 1995 except for [1] 1996 data [2] 1994 data.

Source: Estimations based on regression results.

association. Countries with low attainment at the bottom will tend also to have high education inequality.

4. PUTTING THE STORIES TOGETHER

We have shown that fertility, participation in the labor market, and educational attainment of the children vary strongly along the income distribution and that the earning potential of women, as measured by their own educational attainment, plays a central role in all of these decisions. However, this earning potential depends not only on the educational attainment itself but also on the returns to that attainment generated by the economy as a whole. Moreover, choices about fertility, labor market participation, and attainment also include other elements, such as those that affect the productivity of household work (e.g. availability of water, electricity, and urban transport), the availability and total cost of child care, and the quality of education. These elements vary across countries and across localities of the same country and are hard to measure directly. However, they come into the explanation of why some countries are more unequal than others, and why some have more fertility than others.

To put all these stories together, we estimated a recursive model of earnings, participation, number of children, and attainment of those children and estimated it for 14 Latin American countries. The technical presentation of the model is presented in

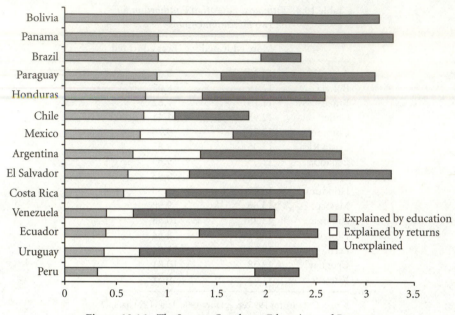

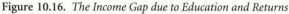

Figure 10.16. *The Income Gap due to Education and Returns*

the Appendix.[26] Here we will play with some simulations of the model to illustrate the mechanisms of inequality across the region.

To provide a clearer picture of the dynamics of the model, in Figure 10.16 we show the proportion of the differences in per capita income between rich and poor families that can be accounted for simply by the lower education level of poor parents, and by the fact that the returns to a year of low education are much lower than the return to a year of higher schooling. On average, we find that if the only difference between the poor and the rich were the quantities of education of the parents (in this case the return of each year is equal across countries and education levels), we would explain 26 percent of the per capita income differences. However, the prices paid for different types of education are not the same, and when we account for this, we are able to explain around 60 percent of the differences between rich and poor. In the case of

---

[26] The method for the simulations is similar to the one we already employed to estimate participation and the number of children in the household. The difference is that in this case, we have three kinds of decisions (rather than one), that are taken simultaneously. The simulation method is as follows: at a first stage, earnings equations are estimated based on experience, education, and geographic location. The coefficients from the regressions are used to predict each person's income-earnings potential, based on personal characteristics. The estimated income feeds into three simultaneous equations that determine the number of children per household, the probability of participating formally and informally in the labor market, and children's education attainment. By using the coefficients from the regressions and evaluating each equation at certain mean values, the estimated per capita income of the members of the household can be obtained. See the Appendix for more details.

Brazil, Peru, Mexico, and Bolivia, the differences in relative prices and quantities of education for parents actually explain more than 60 percent of the disparities in per capita income between the rich and the poor. The lesson we derive from this is that personal differences between one person and another matter, but that the magnitude of the difference is determined by the economic environment where they live.

4.1. *Two Couples on a Trip across Latin America*

Imagine two couples who always decide to live in urban areas. The Altamira couple (Family A) is composed of two 35-year-old people each with 12.1 years of schooling (the average in the top 10% for the 14 countries in our sample). The Bajares couple (Family B) is also 35 years of age but each has only 5.04 years of schooling. We will use these two fictional families to ask the following questions. How unequal would they be if they lived in different countries of the region? How many children would they decide to have? How different would their choices about labor market participation be? And how much education would their children get?

Notice that in this experiment we are keeping the people constant and are only changing the environment in which they are making their decisions. If there are large differences in the choices they make and in the inequality they experience, we cannot blame it on their education differences *per se*, which are the same, by design. Hence, the inequality must be coming somehow from the environment.

Table 10.5 shows the results from the estimation. Fertility decisions vary quite markedly. Almost everywhere, Family B would have more children. Fertility would be highest in El Salvador, Mexico, and Venezuela and lowest in Brazil and Peru. The differences exceed one child for Argentina, Bolivia, Brazil and Honduras. They are lowest in Uruguay, Chile, and Ecuador.

The table also shows the estimated probability that Mrs Altamira and Mrs Bajares will be in the labor market. Participation would be lowest in Brazil followed by Peru, Mexico, Bolivia, and Argentina and highest in Uruguay, Honduras, El Salvador, and Panama. Mrs Altamira would have a 90 percent probability of working in Uruguay's formal sector, but would only have a 35 percent chance of doing so in Brazil. In Brazil, she would have a 34 percent probability of being in the informal sector and an 11 percent probability of being in the formal sector.

Mrs Altamira's maximum chance of being out of the labor force is in Paraguay, with 22 percent probability. Mrs Bajares's maximum chance of being in the formal sector is in Bolivia and Peru with 30 percent. By contrast, Mrs Altamira's maximum chance of being in the formal sector is in Uruguay with 91 percent, while Mrs Bajares's maximum chance of being in the informal sector is in Uruguay with 90 percent, followed by Panama (77%) and Honduras (75%).

The expected wage they would receive in the formal and informal sectors would also vary quite dramatically across the region.

The estimated schooling attainment of the children in each country is also shown in the table. On average, the children of the Altamira family will get 9.8 years of schooling while those of the Bajares family will get only 9. Family A would achieve its

Table 10.5. *The Altamiras and Bajares: Women's Formal Labor Force Participation Rate, Number of Children, and Children's Educational Attainment by Country and Income Level*

	Labor force participation rate		Number of children		Children's educational attainment	
	Top 10%	Bottom 30%	Top 10%	Bottom 30%	Top 10%	Bottom 30%
Argentina[1]	49.67	20.19	1.10	2.69	10.68	9.42
Bolivia	49.78	30.05	1.19	2.18	10.45	10.07
Brazil	34.49	11.10	0.83	1.81	9.14	6.96
Chile[2]	54.90	10.36	2.27	2.04	10.07	10.03
Costa Rica	57.38	8.78	1.84	2.11	8.65	8.40
Ecuador	5.36	25.68	2.09	2.44	9.09	8.90
El Salvador	72.91	14.59	3.27	3.32	8.58	8.03
Honduras[1]	75.42	10.45	1.03	2.23	8.36	7.58
Mexico[2]	41.70	16.18	2.96	3.57	10.54	9.17
Panama	79.75	5.70	1.44	2.44	10.20	8.88
Paraguay	46.94	28.14	1.43	2.49	8.88	8.51
Peru[1]	45.71	29.68	1.37	2.00	10.40	9.97
Uruguay	90.82	5.11	2.42	2.14	9.34	9.30
Venezuela	62.96	10.52	3.29	3.59	8.37	8.05

Notes: Data are for 1995 except for [1]1996 data [2]1994 data.

Source: Calculations from household survey data.

highest attainment in Argentina and its lowest in Venezuela. Family B would achieve its highest attainment in urban Bolivia followed by Peru and its lowest attainment in Brazil, which is the country that would exhibit the largest gap in education between the two families.

The choices for the number of children and the educational attainment exhibit some elements of the quantity versus quality trade-off in these simulations. However, Brazil generates an unusually large gap due to low achievement in the Bajares family, while Argentina also shows a large gap caused by high achievement of the Altamiras family.

To show whether the distribution of schooling or the returns to education are driving these results, we performed an experiment with the equations we used for explaining participation and fertility decisions. In this case, we asked what would be the differences in attainment between rich and poor children in each country if all families faced the same relative prices across countries and across the income distribution. This is equivalent to asking how much of the differences in attainment of rich and poor children are only due to the fact that their parents have different educational levels. We estimate that, on average, the differences in the parents' level of education explain around 30 percent of the differences in children's attainment. In El Salvador, Honduras, Panama, and Mexico, the proportion of the difference explained reaches 50 percent.

Allowing the returns to education to vary is equivalent to asking how much of the difference in attainment is due to the differences in prices and quantities of the parent's education. We estimate that on average, these prices and quantities explain 55 percent of the difference between poor and rich children's attainment. However, in Mexico, Panama, Honduras, El Salvador, and Brazil, the explanatory power is close to 80 percent.

5. CONCLUSIONS

We have seen in this chapter the interrelated nature of critical choices that vary systematically along the income distribution: participation, fertility, and educational attainment. We identified the critical role played by the opportunity cost for women to enter the labor market. A high return to female market work generates high participation, a lower demand for children, and higher attainment by those children. That is the virtuous circle. However, we found that this process depends not only on the educational attainment of the mother; but also on the potential returns to her education in the labor market, which vary quite dramatically across the region. We found these variations by simulating a model in which we left constant the educational differences between two hypothetical families. Different countries generated very different levels in the inequality these families would experience. Hence, their specific education *per se* cannot explain the large and changing level of inequality they would experience across the different countries of Latin America. Something else in the structure of the economy is making fertility differentials large in some countries and small in others. Something is making wage gaps vary, and making the same type of women stay at home in some countries, work by themselves in the informal sector in others, or have relatively easy access to the formal sector. Choices of attainment also change drastically.

What could explain these differences? Part of the answer is in the returns to schooling, which reflect the structure of demand and supply of education by the rest of the economy. Hence, high returns reflect in part low educational attainment by the population as a whole. However, low attainment must itself be explained by elements that in the past have affected the choices of fertility and attainment of the previous generations. The same elements that came into determining the steady-state equilibrium gaps we estimated previously affect the rewards that different people receive for the same education in different countries. Part of the answer lies in the difference in the earnings equations which reflect to a large extent the demand for labor and skills in the economy. Part of the answer also has to do with the relative sensitivities to those relative prices when making participation, fertility, or attainment decisions.

Hence, by travelling this microeconomic road we have hit upon the macroeconomic boundary. It is things larger than the characteristics of the families that are driving the returns to education and the economic opportunities available for women; things that make similar people choose differently in different countries. If something generates very unequal earnings, then these will feed back into very different choices of fertility, and also on participation and attainment so that over time households will also be more unequal in their family characteristics.

What are these things? A full answer is not available, but IDB (1998) has argued that the *stage of development* of each country—including the demographic transition, urbanization, the development of labor markets, and the accumulation of physical and human capital, *factor endowments* (including the abundance of natural resources), and *geographic characteristics* are some of the key determinants of the relative prices that households face. Although it could be argued that some of the above elements are difficult (or even impossible) to change, it is important to identify them. Identifying them is a necessary condition for designing policies that guarantee that the standard of living of the Altamira and Bajares families will start to converge, rather than following two diverging paths over future generations.

Appendix

Fertility Decisions

One limitation of household survey data is that it does not always contain information about all the children that a woman has had. Typically we are able to count the number of children living in a household and we are able to identify their mother, but we do not know if the woman has other children living elsewhere. Therefore, rather than strictly looking at fertility, we can only focus on the number of children in the household, and try to determine if this number is significantly correlated with other variables.

To perform the simulations on fertility discussed in the main text, we conduct an exercise in two stages. In the first stage, we estimate wage regressions of the following form:

$$\ln(y_i) = c + \beta_1 e_i + \beta_2 exp_i + \beta_3 (exp_i)2 + \beta_4 urb_i + u_i$$

where the dependent variable is the logarithm of the income of each earner, *e* represents the number of years of education of person 'i', *exp* denotes experience (measured as the age minus six, minus the years of education),[27] exp^2 is its squared value, and *urb* is a dummy variable for urban areas. The regression is performed separately for men and women, correcting for sample selection bias.[28]

We use the estimated coefficients (corrected for sample selection bias) to predict the income (denoted y^*) that each person would obtain if he or she participated in the labor market by using their education, experience, and location. These predicted incomes are denoted y_m^* and y_f^* (for males and females, respectively) and then used in a regression where the dependent variable is the number of children in the household, and the independent variables are y_m^* and y_f^* and the urban–rural location dummy.[29] With these two equations we can simulate the number of children that a prototype person would have, and we can test for the sensibility of that result to the education of the mother, to the education and income of the male spouse or male household head, and so on, by multiplying the regression coefficients by the mean values of the variables in question.

[27] To measure experience we take into consideration the number of children each woman has. The assumption is that a woman loses one year of labor market experience per child.

[28] In the case of Argentina, Bolivia, and Uruguay, we only have urban data, so the dummy variable is not included.

[29] This second-stage regression was only estimated for the sample of 35–40-year-old females.

Female Labor Market Participation Decisions

Female participation decisions have been studied extensively in the literature. One of the problems of econometric estimations is data availability and specifically, that it is difficult to obtain a good measure of the opportunity cost that a woman faces when deciding whether to participate actively in the labor market or not. One way of tackling the issue is to produce a variable that gives some idea about the income that a person would obtain in the labor market if he or she were to participate, and then use this to see if the decision to participate is statistically associated with this measure. This is the approach followed here.

The exercise requires a two-stage process. The first stage is identical to the wage regression in the fertility equation previously discussed. Then we use y^* as an independent variable in a multinomial logit equation of the following form:

$$\ln(p_i) = c + \gamma_1 nkids_i + \gamma_2 y_f^* + \gamma_3 y_m^* + \gamma_4 urb_i + \gamma_5 age_i$$

where *nkids* is the number of children each female has, y_f^* is the predicted income of the female in question, y_m^* is the predicted income of the male spouse or male household head, and *age* is a dummy variable for age p_i is a variable that takes the value of 0 if woman 'i' is not participating in the labor market, 1 if she participates in the informal sector, and 2 if she participates in the formal sector of the economy.

The coefficients from the multinomial logit estimation are presented in Table A.10.2.

With these two equations we performed several simulations. For example, given the coefficients and the mean value of the wage regression one can estimate the income of a prototype person by simply multiplying the coefficients by the assumed education, experience, and location. With this information we predict y_m^* and y_f^* respectively, and if we had the number of children that each woman has, her age, and her rural–urban location, we could multiply them by the coefficients of the multinomial logit regression to obtain the predicted probabilities of being types 0, 1, or 2.[30] With this method, one can vary the education of the woman, the education or income of the male head or male spouse, the number of children, and the age to assess the impact on the probabilities of participating in the labor market.

Obviously, this kind of exercise is subject to econometric problems such as endogeneity. This is the case especially with variables such as the number of children in the household. Unfortunately it is difficult to get around this problem with the information from household surveys because it is almost impossible to construct good instrumental variables. Several robustness tests were performed on the estimates presented in Table A2 to check whether the conclusions changed when attempting to substitute the variable *nkids* with constructed instruments. The conclusions we derive from the results did not vary significantly in any of these estimations.

Putting the Stories Together

To put the decision-making process of the family together, regarding participation, fertility, and children's education, we estimated a recursive model of earnings, participation, number of children, and attainment of those children and estimated it for 14 Latin American countries. Since all these are interrelated decisions, we estimate a simultaneous equation system following

---

[30] To assess the probabilities we obviously make the corresponding transformations to the coefficients so that they yield the predicted probabilities.

these steps:

1. First, we run earnings regression of the following form

$$\ln(y_i) = c + \beta_1 e_i + \beta_2 exp_i + \beta_3 (exp_i)2 + \beta_4 urb_i + u_i$$

with which we predict y_m^* and y_f^* (corrected for sample selection bias) as in the exercises previously described.

2. The predicted variables y_m^* and y_f^*, which represent the income-generating potential of a person with certain education, experience, and location, feed into the following regression:

$$nkids = c + \alpha_1 y_m^* + \alpha_2 y_f^* + \alpha_3 urb_i + u_i$$

where the idea is that the coefficients of this regression can be used to predict the variable *nkids* for each household, based only on the opportunity cost (proxied by the earnings potential variables) and location. We denote *nkids** the number of children in each household predicted by y_m^* and y_f^* and *urb*. From this perspective, the only reason why two couples in the urban sector would choose to have a different number of children is because they have different education levels, and because the returns to their education (the opportunity cost) differs.

3. Thirdly, we re-estimate the multinomial logit described previously in this Appendix, by running the following regression

$$\ln(p_i) = c + \gamma_1 nkids_i^* + \gamma_2 y_f^* + \gamma_3 y_m + \gamma_4 urb_i + \gamma_5 age_i$$

where *nkids* has been substituted by *nkids**. With the coefficients from this regression and the average values for y_m^*, y_f^*, *nkids**, *urb*, and the age of each female, we can predict the probability of being out of the labor force, participating in the formal sector, or in the informal sector, which we label p_i^*.

4. Fourthly, we estimate earnings equations of the same form as in the first stage regression above, but we run them separately for men and for women in the formal and informal sectors, respectively. The coefficients allow us to predict the following income-earnings potentials:

$y_{m,f}^* =$ income of males in the formal sector

$y_{m,i}^* =$ income of males in the informal sector

$y_{f,f}^* =$ income of females in the formal sector

$y_{f,i}^* =$ income of females in the informal sector

5. Fifthly, we estimate the income per capita of each family through the following formula:

$$ypc_i^* = \{y_m^* + [p_i^*(1)]y_{f,i}^* + [p_i^*(2)]y_{f,f}^*\}/(nkids^* + 2)$$

The formula says that the estimated income per capita (ypc^*) of family 'i' is calculated by adding up the predicted income of a male with certain education, experience, and geographic location, and the income of the female computed as the estimated probability of being in the informal sector times the informal sector predicted income (the income is also predicted based on education, experience, and rural–urban location), plus the estimated probability of being in the formal sector times the formal sector predicted income. All this is divided by the number of children we would expect a couple with certain education, experience, and rural–urban location to have.

6. Finally, we estimated the education attainment of each family through the following regression:

$$educh_i^* = c + y_m^* + [p_i^*(1)]y_{f,i}^* + [p_i^*(2)]y_{f,f}^* + nkids^* + sex + u_i$$

where $educch_i^*$ represents the predicted attainment of the child, and sex is a dummy variable for the gender of the child.

Therefore, the system of equations uses the number of years of education, experience, and geographic location as exogenous variables, and with this information it predicts the income-earning potential in the formal and informal sectors, the probability of females being out of the labor force, or in the formal or informal or informal sectors, the number of children that a couple with the above characteristics would have, and their attainment. The main advantage is that, as explained in the text, the methodology allows us to simulate several scenarios by making an explicit distinction between the effects of the number of years of schooling (the quantity effect), and the returns to education (the price effect).

Table A.10.1. *Number of Children, Female Participation, and Education of the Adults Living in the Household, by Socioeconomic Level*

Country	Number of children per household[1]			Female labor force participation			Education of adults in the household		
	Richest 10%	Poorest 30%	Total	Richest 10%	Poorest 30%	Total	Richest 10%	Poorest 30%	Total
Argentina	1.75	2.46	2.04	48.66	37.94	40.78	14.34	7.13	9.40
Bolivia	2.52	2.92	2.91	57.88	57.95	56.56	13.71	7.09	9.28
Brazil	1.77	2.69	2.23	55.05	47.74	50.36	11.40	2.10	5.06
Chile	2.05	2.18	2.11	50.85	31.82	36.06	13.83	5.74	8.64
Colombia	1.77	2.78	2.32	56.49	38.43	43.94	12.76	3.56	6.65
Costa Rica	2.34	2.91	2.57	43.23	33.06	37.54	12.35	4.27	6.99
Ecuador	2.42	3.27	2.90	62.41	61.28	59.20	12.15	4.25	7.11
El Salvador	2.57	3.33	2.92	55.56	39.25	46.43	10.82	1.97	5.01
Honduras*	3.08	3.80	3.50	52.62	43.34	44.32	9.81	2.31	4.80
Mexico	2.27	3.34	2.82	40.11	46.92	41.51	14.05	3.67	7.18
Nicaragua*	1.93	2.69	2.29	52.51	37.66	44.18	9.57	2.22	4.90
Panama	3.06	4.19	3.64	58.58	31.45	40.75	14.47	5.32	8.59
Paraguay	2.57	3.63	3.15	67.11	69.01	66.95	11.69	3.64	6.11
Peru*	2.61	3.67	3.09	45.08	80.08	63.20	12.25	5.82	8.41
Uruguay	2.22	2.95	2.82	58.04	47.49	52.78	12.88	5.17	7.79
Venezuela	1.95	2.09	1.99	44.74	38.66	40.80	11.43	4.63	6.95

Notes: Data are for 1995 except for Argentina, Honduras, Mexico (1996); Chile (1994); Colombia, Peru (1997); and Nicaragua (1993). [1]Calculated only for households where the head is between 30 and 45 years of age.

Table A.10.2. Coefficients from Multinomial Logit Regression

Independent variable	Argentina 96	Bolivia 95	Brazil 95	Chile 94	Costa Rica 95	Ecuador 95	El Salvador 95	Honduras 96	Mexico 94	Panama	Paraguay	Peru 96	Uruguay 95	Venezuela 95
Dependent variable, female labor market participation (Baseline, p = 0)														
p = 1														
nkids	-0.11	-0.00	-0.03	-0.14	-0.05	-0.06	-0.04	-0.06	-0.01	-0.04	0.01	-0.09	-0.06	-0.07
y_f	-1.28	-2.23	-0.10	-0.61	0.19	-0.75	-0.39	0.12	-0.11	-0.44	-0.37	-2.46	-0.72	-0.59
y_m	-0.45	-0.24	-0.19	-0.14	-0.19	-0.13	-0.21	-0.34	-0.36	-0.39	-0.01	-0.21	-0.06	-0.14
urb		0.57	0.57	1.07	0.16	0.28	0.97	0.46	0.10	0.27	-0.74	0.04		0.57
age2	0.19	0.63	0.17	0.25	0.15	0.28	0.38	0.47	0.52	0.30	0.22	0.19	0.18	0.29
age3	0.53	0.74	0.24	0.49	0.05	0.27	0.75	0.45	0.43	0.77	0.55	0.29	0.30	0.52
age4	0.47	0.92	0.19	0.62	0.24	0.33	0.43	0.46	0.26	0.61	0.46	0.41	0.38	0.42
age5	0.25	0.78	0.14	0.36	-0.13	0.28	0.37	0.16	0.26	0.43	0.41	-0.02	0.22	0.13
age6	0.00	0.38	-0.01	0.11	-0.52	-0.34	0.08	-0.03	-0.05	0.31	0.32	-0.24	-0.04	-0.39
age7	-0.64	-0.39	-0.37	-0.35	-0.99	-0.43	-0.28	-0.07	-0.38	-0.47	0.21	-0.58	-0.78	-0.66
cons	3.49	5.69	-1.65	2.94	-1.39	7.34	0.38	-0.24	0.09	-0.38	3.60	5.92	7.68	2.91
p = 2														
nkids	-0.19	0.02	-0.17	-0.17	-0.11	-0.03	-0.05	-0.06	-0.18	-0.11	-0.03	0.05	-0.17	-0.04
y_f	2.37	3.07	1.05	2.07	2.04	1.94	2.21	2.54	1.92	2.54	1.97	2.76	1.59	2.11
y_m	-0.45	-0.23	-0.26	-0.13	-0.24	-0.12	-0.27	-0.43	-0.38	-0.33	-0.07	-0.20	-0.06	-0.15
urb			1.27	0.19	0.28	-1.33	0.32	0.38	-0.29	0.21	-0.68	-2.23		-0.05
age2	-0.12	0.08	-0.13	-0.13	-0.28	0.05	0.13	-0.25	0.20	0.09	-0.28	-0.12	-0.01	0.22
age3	-0.11	-0.17	-0.27	-0.23	-0.34	0.18	0.29	-0.09	-0.09	0.53	-0.26	-0.22	0.00	0.42
age4	-0.26	-0.41	-0.51	-0.37	-0.61	0.10	-0.60	-0.76	-0.40	0.00	-0.18	-0.26	-0.12	0.24
age5	-0.79	-0.87	-0.98	-0.95	-0.84	-0.65	-0.80	-0.67	-0.84	-0.22	-1.07	-0.49	-0.64	0.05
age6	-0.91	-1.62	-1.47	-1.21	-1.66	-0.51	-1.31	-1.41	-0.99	-1.05	-0.90	-1.07	-0.99	-0.58
age7	-1.72	-2.36	-1.98	-1.89	-2.71	-1.18	-2.23	-1.60	-2.33	-2.95	-0.58	-1.74	-1.92	-1.52
cons	-5.36	-8.89	-3.84	-15.03	-13.20	-16.21	-7.26	-7.51	-5.31	-4.96	-18.02	-4.75	-16.56	-13.80

Note: * Age groups start at 20 years of age. Age2 represents 25–30 years of age. The rest are successive five-year groups.

Table A.10.3. *Dependent Variable: Probability of being Enrolled in School*

Independent variable	Argentina	Bolivia	Brazil	Chile	Colombia	Costa Rica	Ecuador	El Salvador	Honduras	Mexico	Panama	Paraguay	Peru	Uruguay	Venezuela
Kid's Age	−0.0891**	−0.0292**	−0.0811**	−0.0382**	−0.0785**	−0.0911**	−0.0643**	−0.0963**	−0.1466**	−0.1446**	−0.0571**	−0.1070**	−0.0691**	−0.0518**	−0.0937**
Gender	−0.0186	−0.0026	−0.0329**	−0.0224**	−0.0737**	−0.0693**	−0.0110	−0.0024	−0.1104**	−0.0705**	−0.0350**	0.0463*	0.0087	−0.0612**	−0.0955**
Father's educ	0.0131**	0.0071**	0.0119**	0.0043**	0.0223**	0.0174**	0.0225**	0.0126**	0.0217**	0.0201**	0.0052**	0.0171**	0.0102**	0.0144**	0.0086**
Mother's educ.	0.0242**	0.0051**	0.0210**	0.0177**	0.0412**	0.0326**	0.0335**	0.0271**	0.0287**	0.0303**	0.0140**	0.0269**	0.0071**	0.0114**	0.0253**
Log of household pc income	0.0841**	−0.0056	0.0299**	0.0092*	−0.0021	−0.0033	0.0013	0.0118	0.0277**	−0.0036	0.0314**	0.0119	−0.0166**	0.0538**	−0.0213**
urban–rural	−0.0482**	−0.0050**	−0.0079**	−0.0209**	−0.0197**	−0.0347**	−0.0279**	−0.0045	−0.0096	−0.0363**	−0.0187**	−0.0173**	−0.0185**	−0.0279**	−0.0146**
# other kids in hh			0.0970**	0.0730**	0.0623**	0.1618**	0.1943**	0.2472**	0.1881**	0.1263**	0.1394**	0.2141**	0.1438**		0.1196**
Mother participates	−0.0579	0.0258**	0.0432**	0.0050	0.0765**	0.0561**	0.0416**	0.0593**	0.0605**	0.0442**	0.0208	0.1302**	−0.0105	0.0534**	0.0054
# elderly members of hh	−0.0481	0.0478**	0.0259**	0.0437**	0.0437**	0.0740**	0.1074**	0.0593**	0.0546**	0.0643**	−0.0218	0.0779**	−0.0019	0.0518**	0.0782**

Notes: **Statistically significant at the 99% level. *Statistically significant at the 95% level.

References

Becker, G. 1991. '*The Economics of the Family*' Boston: 2nd edn. Harvard University Press.

—— M. Murphy, and R. Tamura. 1990. 'Human Capital, Fertility and Economic Growth'. *Journal of Political Economy*. 98 (5).

Behrman, J. R. 1988. 'Intrahousehold Allocation of Nutrients in Rural India: Are Boys Favored? Do Parents Exhibit Inequality Aversion?' *Oxford Economic Papers*. 40.

—— 1997. 'Women's Schooling and Child Education: A Survey'. Philadelphia, University of Pennsylvania. Mimeo.

—— and J. Knowles. 1997. 'How Strong is Child Schooling Associated with Household Income?' Philadelphia, University of Pennsylvania. Mimeo.

Birdsall, N., and R. Sabot, eds. 1991. 'Unfair Advantage: Labor Market Discrimination in Developing Countries'. The World Bank.

Bourguignon, F., and P. Chiappori. 1992. 'Collective Models of Household Behavior'. *European Economic Review*. 36. North-Holland.

Cigno, Alessandro. 1991. *Economics of the Family*. Oxford: Clarendon Press.

Connelly, A. *et al.* 1996. 'Women's Employment and Child Care in Brazil'. *Economic Development and Cultural Change*. 619–56

Dahan, M., and M. Tsiddon. 1998. 'Demographic Transition, Income Distribution and Economic Growth'. *Journal of Economic Growth*. Mar.

Deutsch, R. 1998. 'Does Child Care Pay?: Labor Force Participation and Earnings Effects of Access to Child Care in the Favelas of Rio de Janeiro'. Poverty and Inequality Advisory Unit. Washington: Inter-American Development Bank. Mimeo.

Duryea, S., and M. Székely. 2000. 'Labor Markets in Latin America: A Look at the Supply-Side'. *Emerging Markets Review*.

Engle, Patrice L. 1991. 'Maternal Work and Child Care Strategies in Peri-Urban Guatemala: Nutritional Effects'. *Child Development*. 62: 954–65.

Galor, O., and S. Weil. 1996. 'The Gender Gap, Fertility and Growth'. *American Economic Review*. 86.

Gavin and Hausmann, 1988. 'Nature, Development, and Distribution in Latin America: Evidence on the Role of Geography, Climate and Natural Resources'. Working Paper 378. Office of the Chief Economist, Inter-American Development Bank.

Gonzales de la Rocha, M. 1994. *The Resources of Poverty*. Oxford: Blackwell Publishers.

Haddad, Lawrence, and Kanbur Ravi. 1992. 'Intrahousehold Inequality and the Theory of Targeting'. *European Economic Review*. 36. North-Holland.

Kapteyn, Arie, and Kooreman Peter. 1992. 'Household Labor Supply: What Kind of Data can Tell us How Many Decision Makers There Are?' *European Economic Review*. 36. North-Holland.

Katz, Elizabeth. 1997. 'The Intra-Household Economics of Voice and Exit: Evaluating the Feminist-Institutional Content of Family Resource Allocation Models'. Columbia University. Mimeo.

Lam, D., and S. Duryea. 1999. 'Effects of Schooling on Fertility, Labor Supply, and Investments in Children, with Evidence from Brazil'. *Journal of Human Resources*, Winter.

Londoño, J. L., and M. Székely. 2000. 'Persistent Poverty and Excess Inequality: Latin America 1970–1995'. *Journal of Applied Economics*. 3(1) (May), 93–134.

Pitt, Mark, and Mark R. Rosenzweig. 1986. 'Agricultural Prices, Food Consumption, and the Health and Productivity of Indonesian Farmers'. In Singh *et al.* 1986.

Psacharopoulos, G., and Z. Tzannatos. 1992. *Women's Employment and Pay in Latin America.* Washington: The World Bank.

—— S. Morley, A. Fiszbein, H. Lee, and B. Wood. 1993. 'Poverty and Income Distribution in Latin America: The story of the 1980s'. Latin America and the Caribbean Technical Department Regional Studies Program. Report No. 27.

Sen, A. 1984. 'Economics and the Family'. chapter 6 in *Resources, Values and Development.* Cambridge: Cambridge University Press.

Singh, I., L. Squire, and M. Strauss. 1986. 'The Basic Model: Theory, Empirical Results and Policy Conclusions'. *Agricultural Household Models.* Cambridge: Cambridge University Press.

Sorrentino, C. 1990. 'The Changing Family in an International Perspective'. *Monthly Labor Review.* 41–58.

Székely, M. 1998. *The Economics of Poverty, Inequality and Wealth Accumulation in Mexico.* London: Macmillan.

United Nations. 1997. *Population Statistics.* New York.

Wong, R., and R. Levine. 1992. 'The Effect of Household Structure on Women's Economic Activity and Fertility: Evidence from Recent Mothers in Urban Mexico'. *Economic Development and Cultural Change.* 41 (1), 89–102.

11

Demographic Changes and Poverty in Brazil

RICARDO PAES DE BARROS, SERGIO FIRPO,
ROBERTA GUEDES BARRETO, AND PHILLIPPE GEORGE PEREIRA LEITE

1. INTRODUCTION

Poverty is a consequence of economic and demographic conditions. The degree of poverty a society might experience depends on the volume and distribution of resources and on the size and distribution of the population among households. These two basic determinants of poverty, however, are not independently determined. On the one hand, the size and age structure of a population are consequences of fertility decisions taken over past decades which were influenced by the prevailing economic conditions. On the other hand, the volume of resources available today is influenced by the size and age composition of the labor force.

In this study we present evidence of the impact of demographic factors on the level of poverty based on the Brazilian experience. Two demographic factors are investigated: (1) the size and (2) the age composition of the population. The goal is to estimate the impact of changes in these two factors on the distribution of income and consequently on the level of poverty.

Demographic factors have a direct and an indirect impact on the distribution of income. As the size and age composition of the population change, the relative size of the labor force and the number of dependents also change, modifying the dependency ratio of families, and therefore their level of poverty. This is the direct effect of demographic changes. It captures the effect that demographic changes have on quantities: number of children, size of the labor force, and the number of elderly persons.

These changes in quantities, however, will in general influence prices in the economy. In particular, changes in the rate of growth of the population and in the age structure may have important impacts on labor supply and on savings. As a consequence, demographic changes may have considerable impact on the level of wages and on interest rates. Since these prices are important determinants of family income, they are bound to have a profound influence on the level of poverty. These are the indirect impacts of demographic changes on poverty, since they occur through the indirect effects of demographic changes on the level of labor supply, savings, wages, and interest rates.[1]

---

[1] Examples of empirical and theoretical studies of these indirect effects can be found in the works of R. Willis, 'Life Cycles, Institutions, and Population Growth: A Theory of the Equilibrium Rate of Interest in an Overlapping Generations Model'; A. Cigno, 'Some Macroeconomic Consequences of the "New

There are essentially three approaches to investigating the impact of demographic changes on poverty. The first approach is based on macro regressions relating poverty to its determinants. In general, these regressions are estimated using cross-national panel data.[2] This approach has the advantage of offering estimates of the overall impact of demographic changes including all direct and indirect effects. The approach, however, faces two difficulties. First, it has either to assume that the demographic changes were exogenous or to base the inference on debatable choices of instrumental variables. Secondly, since this approach cannot separate direct from indirect effects of demographic changes on poverty, it can only provide estimates for the overall effect.

A second approach is to use micro simulations based on household surveys to estimate the direct effect of demographic changes on poverty. This is the approach used in this study. It consists essentially of three steps. First, one must select alternative scenarios for the size and age composition of the population. Secondly, one must express the per-capita family income as a function of the size and age structure of the family and of the average income of members by age group. Thirdly, one can simulate the direct impact of demographic changes, computing new values for the per-capita income that would be observed if average income by age were the same but the demographic composition followed the alternative scenarios selected in the first step. Given the new per-capita income for every family, the level of poverty can then be immediately recomputed. The major limitation to this approach is the fact that it cannot be used to estimate the indirect effect of demographic changes on poverty. Nevertheless, it provides an almost ideal procedure to estimate its direct effect.

A third approach that could be used to obtain separate estimates of the direct and indirect effects of demographic changes on poverty would be to use a computable general equilibrium (CGE) model. In this case, conditional on the correctness of the specification and parameters of the model, it is possible to obtain separate estimates for the direct and indirect effects of demographic changes on poverty. The main difficulty with this approach is precisely how to find a convincing procedure to specify and obtain estimates of the parameters of the model. Since the final estimates of the impact of demographic changes can be quite sensitive to the model specification and the choice of parameter values, the uncertainty behind these choices may become a serious limitation of the procedure.

Throughout this study we make use of a simple but useful expression, which connects family per-capita income to the average income of family members by age and the family age structure. To obtain this expression we first have to divide the age spectrum into *m* non-overlapping age groups. Then we can write the family per-capita

Home Economics".' In Arthur Lee and Rodgers, eds., *Economics of Changing Age Distributions in Developed Countries.* Oxford: Oxford University Press, 1995; R. Lee, 'Population Dynamics: Equilibrium, Disequilibrium, and Consequences of Fluctuations'. *Handbook of Population and Family Economics.* Amsterdam, North-Holland, 1997.

[2] See Ch. 9, for an example of this procedure.

income, y^f, as

$$y^f = \frac{\sum_{i=1}^{m} n_i^f y_i^f}{\sum_{i=1}^{m} n_i^f}$$

where n_i^f denotes the number of members of family f in the age group i and y_i^f the average income of family members in this age group.[3] According to this specification, the vector $(n_1^f, \ldots, n_m^f)$ captures the demographic factors (i.e., the size and age composition of the population), while the vector $(y_1^f, \ldots, y_m^f)$ captures market prices and assets held by the family.

In this study we pursue the impact on poverty of a series of alternative demographic scenarios. In Section 2, we investigate what poverty would look like today if demographic conditions were equal to those prevailing in previous decades. In other words, we investigate the impact of temporal changes in the size and age composition of the population on the level of poverty. In Section 3, we turn to investigate the impact of regional differences in demographic conditions on poverty. In Section 4, we then investigate to what extent poverty can be explained by demographic differences, both between and within income classes, with particular emphasis given to the demographic differences between rich and poor families. Finally, Section 5 presents a summary of the main findings of the study and its main conclusions.

2. LONG-TERM DEMOGRAPHIC CHANGES

In this section we present estimates of the direct effect of long-term demographic changes in Brazil on its level of poverty. Estimates are presented both for the country as a whole, as well as separately for the main regions of the country. The regional analysis is important since, due to very different levels of economic development, the regions began their demographic transition at very different points in time and proceeded through the transition at different speeds.

To estimate the direct effect of long-term demographic changes on the level of poverty, we estimated what poverty today would be in Brazil if the size and age structure of the population were equal to that observed decades ago. In performing this counter-factual simulation we kept constant the average income of each age group in every family. For this reason the estimated impact captures only the direct effect of the demographic changes.

This section is organized in three subsections. In the first, we present in detail the methodology being used. The second describes the demographic changes that have occurred in Brazil over the past 50 years. Finally, in the third subsection we present the results of the counter-factual simulation, aiming to estimate the impact of these secular demographic changes on poverty.

---

[3] If there is nobody in the family in a given age group we let $y_i^f = 0$.

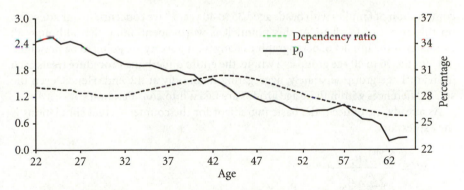

Figure 11.1. *Dependency Ratio and P_0 by Age of Household Head*

Note: Dependency ratio is: number of persons under 22 and above 64 divided by number of persons between 22 and 64 years.

Source: Based on *Pesquisa Nacional por Amostra e Domicilios* (PNAD), 1996.

2.1. *Methodology*

Since over the life cycle of families[4] the level of poverty varies as the dependency ratio varies, as can be seen in Figure 11.1, the overall level of poverty is influenced by the distribution of families according to their positions in the life cycle.[5] Hence, demographic changes have a direct effect on poverty through two channels: (1) first, by modifying the demographic composition of families over their life cycle—*the internal effect*; (2) secondly, by modifying the distribution of families according to their positions in their life cycle—*the composition effect*.

In studying the direct impact of demographic changes on poverty, it is of fundamental importance to sort out these two effects, since the internal effect is of much greater substantive importance than the composition effect. Although the composition effect does influence the overall level of poverty at a given point in time, it has no effect on the evolution of the poverty level of a cohort of families over their life cycle. Hence, it has no effect on the lifetime level of welfare of families.

To concentrate attention on the internal effect, one must either standardize the distribution of families according to their positions in the life cycles or focus only on families at a given point in the life cycle. For the sake of simplicity we opt for the second alternative. In other words, to isolate the internal effect, we limit our investigation only to families with heads in a narrow age group. Since the demographic changes occurring in Brazil over this century had their stronger effects on the demographic

---

[4] A common procedure for determining the location of a family in its life cycle is the age of the head. That is the procedure being used in this study.

[5] David Lam has a similar study, in which he is concerned, however, with how income inequality is influenced by the distribution of families according to their positions in the life cycle David Lam, 'Demographic Variables and Income Inequality'. *Handbook of Population and Family Economics*. Amsterdam: North-Holland, 1997.

composition of families with heads aged 36 to 40 years,[6] we concentrate our attention on this group of families. At this point, it is worth mentioning that although all estimates of the impact of demographic changes on poverty are going to be presented only for the 36 to 40 age group as a whole, the entire underlying procedure treats each individual age group separately, aggregating them only at the end. Hence, even the small differences within these age groups are taken into consideration.

As already introduced, the basic ingredient for the counter-factual simulations is the expression

$$y^f = \frac{\sum_{i=1}^m n_i^f y_i^f}{\sum_{i=1}^m n_i^f};$$

for per-capita family income. In order to fully specify this expression it is necessary to choose a partition for the age spectrum. Our choice was to divide the age spectrum into four groups: (1) 0 to 14, (2) 15 to 21, (3) 22 to 64, and (4) 65 and more.

The goal of the counter-factual simulation is to compare the level of poverty based on y^f (the original poverty level), with the level of poverty that would prevail if per-capita family income were given by

$$y_t^f = \frac{\sum_{i=1}^4 n_{it}^f y_i^f}{\sum_{i=1}^4 n_{it}^f};$$

where n_{it}^f is chosen in order to ensure that the aggregated size and age composition of members of family f match that of the cohort born t years ago. More specifically, we made

$$n_{it}^f = \frac{n_i^f N_{it}}{N_i},$$

where N_i is the number of members in age group i per family today. Note that N_i is simply the average value of n_i^f. N_{it} is the corresponding average t years ago. As a consequence, one has by construction that the average of n_{it}^f equals to N_{it}, indicating that after the transformation from n_i^f to n_{it}^fs the aggregated family size and age composition match that observed t years ago. This transformation is conducted separately for families at each point in the life cycle.

This transformation captures the overall change in family size and age composition. A similar procedure can be used to isolate the change at each age group and its specific impact on poverty. To isolate the effect of changes in age group j we constructed the following counter-factual family per-capita income

$$y_{jt}^f = \frac{\sum_{i \neq j, i=1}^4 n_i^f y_i^f + n_{jt}^f y_j}{\sum_{i \neq j, i=1}^4 n_i^f + n_{jt}^f}.$$

[6] See e.g. Ricardo P. Barros *et al.*, *Family Structure and Behavior over the Life Cycle in Brazil* (in progress).

Note that in this expression only one of the n_{it} has been changed, allowing the effect on poverty of the changes in this specific age group to be evaluated.

These expressions revealed that to implement the counter-factual simulations it is necessary to count with estimates for N_{it} for as many points in time as one wished to simulate. We opted for going back 50 years in time. In other words, we investigated the impact on poverty of the demographic changes that took place over the last 50 years. We estimated not just the situation 50 years ago but also how it has evolved over the past five decades. As a result, we ended up with estimates of the entire evolution over these decades of the impact that demographic changes had on poverty. Based on this information, it is possible, for instance, to identify when the impact of demographic changes on poverty was particularly important.

To measure poverty we used three poverty measures: (1) the headcount ratio, P_0, (2) the average income gap, P_1, and (3) the average squared income gap, P_2. These measures are the first three members of the Foster, Greer, and Thorbecke[7] family. They are defined via

$$P_\alpha = \frac{1}{n} \sum_{i=1}^{q} \left(\frac{Z - Y_i}{Z}\right)^\alpha;$$

where $\alpha = 0$, 1, or 2, Z is the poverty line, q is the number of persons living in families below the poverty line (the poor), and n the size of the overall population. For the poverty line we use R\$60 per person per month. Since the exchange rate was close to 1.00 R\$/US\$ in 1996, this poverty line is close to US\$2 per day per person.

Next, we discussed how estimates for N_i were obtained covering the past 50 years. From a current household survey it is possible to obtain estimates for n_i^f for the family f. The average value of n_i^f is then an estimate of N_i. In principal, estimates for N_{it} can be obtained applying the same procedure to a corresponding household survey collected t years ago. Since the Brazilian Annual Household Survey (PNAD) has been collected on a regular basis only over the past 20 years, this procedure could only provide a partial answer. Some kind of extrapolation became necessary.

To describe the procedure used to extrapolate, we change our notation, momentarily letting N_{ist} denote the average number of members in age group i in families with heads aged s at time t. Based on the 18 available household surveys covering the period 1976–96 we obtained estimates of N_{ist} for all age groups ($i = 1, \ldots, 4$), for families with heads aged 20 to 80 years old, and for all years between 1976 and 1996. Based on this information we estimated the following regression:

$$\ln(N_{ist}) = a_i + b_i{}^*s + c_i{}^*h + d_i{}^*s^2 + e_i{}^*sh + f_i{}^*h^2 + u_{ist};$$

where $h = t - s$ is the year of the birth of the head. Since all coefficients are allowed to vary by age group, we actually estimate a separate regression for each age group. Table 11.1 shows the coefficients for these regressions. Based on these regressions we

---

[7] J. Foster, E. Greer, and E. Thorbecke, 'A Class of Decomposable Poverty Measures'. In: *Econometrics*, 52, 1984.

Fertility, Poverty, and the Family

Table 11.1. *Regressions Coefficients—Brazil (Dependent Variable: Log of the Average Number of People in Each Age Range)*

Regressors	Dependent variables							
	0 to 14 years		15 to 21 years		22 to 64 years		65+ years	
	Coefficient	P-value	Coefficient	P-value	Coefficient	P-value	Coefficient	P-value
Intercept	−442.52	0.78	3225.92	0.48	592.21	0.76	−4915.18	0.18
Age	47.98	0.55	−126.09	0.59	−11.29	0.91	196.62	0.29
Birth date	451.49	0.78	−3248.11	0.48	−602.27	0.75	4973.32	0.17
Age[2]	−3.90	0.00	−0.85	0.78	−3.75	0.00	1.08	0.65
Birth date[1]	−115.50	0.77	817.07	0.48	152.41	0.75	−1258.98	0.17
Age * birth date	−21.85	0.59	65.31	0.57	9.57	0.84	−100.58	0.28
Number of observations	1008		1008		1008		1008	
R squared	0.84		0.14		0.71		0.89	

Notes: [1] The variable 'birth date' is the calendar year divided by 1,000. [2] The variable 'age' is the age of head divided by 50.

Source: Based on *Pesquisa Nacional por Amostra e Domicílios* (PNAD) of 1996.

were able to obtain estimates for the evolution of N_{ist} over the past 50 years via

$$N_{ist} = \exp(a_i + b_i{}^*s + c_i{}^*h + d_i{}^*s^2 + e_i{}^*sh + f_i{}^*h^2 + \bar{u}_{ist});$$

where $\bar{u}_{ist}$ is the average of the regression residuals across all birth cohorts with available information relative to a given age group, i, and family position in the life cycle, s. This average error term was included in the estimates for N_{ist} to reduce the difference between these estimates and the values actually observed.

To obtain regional estimates, N_{istr}, we enlarged the regression model as follows:

$$\ln(N_{istr}) = a_{ir} + b_{ir}^*s + c_{ir}^*h + d_i{}^*s^2 + e_i{}^*sh + f_i{}^*h^2 + u_{istr};$$

where, as above, $h = t - s$ is the year of birth of the head. Table 11.2 shows the coefficients for each age group regression. Based on this regression we obtain estimates for N_{istr} for any point in time via

$$N_{istr} = \exp(a_{ir} + b_{ir}^*s + c_{ir}^*h + d_i{}^*s^2 + e_i{}^*sh + f_i{}^*h^2 + \bar{u}_{istr});$$

where $\bar{u}_{istr}$ is the average of the regression residual across all birth cohorts with available information for a given age group, i, family position in the life cycle, s, and region r.

This specification imposes that the parameters of the quadratic terms are common to all regions. Only the intercept and the parameters of the linear terms are allowed to vary across regions. This parsimonious assumption was imposed in order to improve the ability of the model to provide reliable estimates outside the sample range. When we relaxed this assumption, in many cases non-plausible estimates were obtained for N_{istr}.

Table 11.2. *Regression coefficients—Region (Dependent Variable: Log of the Average Number of People in Each Age Range)*

Regressors	Explicative variables							
	0 to 14 years		15 to 21 years		22 to 64 years		65 + years	
	Coefficient	P-value	Coefficient	P-value	Coefficient	P-value	Coefficient	P-value
Intercept	−109.68	0.91	2693.61	0.20	509.87	0.58	−3349.82	0.09
Age	31.91	0.50	−90.44	0.39	−9.75	0.84	122.28	0.23
Birth date	118.93	0.90	−2715.47	0.19	−517.12	0.58	3396.93	0.09
Age^2	−3.90	0.00	−1.52	0.26	−3.77	0.00	2.57	0.05
Birth date[1]	−32.55	0.89	683.77	0.19	130.40	0.58	−861.95	0.09
Age * Birth rate	−13.62	0.57	47.56	0.37	8.79	0.71	−63.80	0.21
Regions								
North	0.67	0.00	0.50	0.00	0.05	0.00	0.00	0.90
Northeast	0.57	0.00	0.34	0.00	−0.03	0.07	0.03	0.36
South	0.00	0.79	−0.03	0.38	−0.06	0.00	0.03	0.39
West Central	0.26	0.00	0.22	0.00	−0.03	0.01	−0.27	0.00
Number of observations	5039		5034		5039		4865	
R squared	0.80		0.21		0.68		0.84	

Notes: [1]The variable 'birth date' is the calendar year divided by 1,000. [2]The variable 'age' is the age of head divided by 50.

Source: Based on *Pesquisa Nacional por Amostra e Domicílios* (PNAD) of 1996.

2.1.1. *Data Sources*

The data were obtained from *Pesquisa Nacional por Amostra de Domicílios*—PNAD (The Brazilian Annual National Household Survey) for the years 1976 to 1996, which are available for the public in magnetic files. This is an annual national household survey performed in the third quarter that interviews 100,000 households every year. It is conducted by IBGE, the Brazilian Census bureau. It began at national level in 1971 and underwent a major revision between 1990 and 1992. This revision makes it difficult to have compatibility between PNAD concepts before and after 1992.

This survey contains extensive information on personal characteristics, including information on all sources of income, labor force participation, and educational attainment and attendance. Being a household survey it also contains detailed information on family structure. The large number of PNAD surveys and their large sample sizes make them, like the demographic censuses, very useful for isolating life-cycle variations from time trends.

In addition to a basic questionnaire, which is repeated every year, most PNADs have a supplement considering a special topic. Many of these supplements have a considerable amount of retrospective information on fertility, marriage, and educational outcomes among others that can be particularly useful in describing the life cycle of the family structure and the demographic change in Brazil.

2.2. *Demographic Changes*

Estimates, based on the methodology previously exposed, for the evolution of N_{ist} over the past 50 years for families with heads aged 36 to 40 years are presented in Figures 11.2 to 11.5.[8] These estimates are the base of the counter-factual simulations investigated in this section. Hence, before discussing the results of these simulations, we first present a short description of the basic patterns of the demographic changes over the past decades.

All these figures consider only the case of families with heads aged 36 years old. The patterns for families with heads of other ages than those in the bracket 36 to 40 are not presented here, since they are almost identical to those for families with heads in the chosen age group. It is worth mentioning that, except for this subsection, throughout the study all results are for age groups in the bracket 36 to 40.

These figures reveal a clear decline in the number of persons per family in all age groups, except for the oldest (65 and more). Figure 11.2 reveals that families with heads born near the beginning of the century (1910) had, on average, 3.5 members under 15, while those with heads born around 1960 had just two members under 15 years of age.

Figure 11.3 reveals a similar pattern for the number of teenagers per family. In fact, households whose heads were born near the beginning of the century (1910) had on average 2.5 members aged 15 to 21, while those with heads born around 1960 had just 0.5 members in this age group. These two figures taken together indicate a sharp decline in the number of persons under 22 per family, with the number of persons per family in this age group going from 6.0 to 2.5 over a period of five decades.

The same decline in size is also observed for the working-age group—persons aged 22 to 64 years old. As Figure 11.4 reveals, the decline for this age group was much less intense, with the number of persons per family in this age group declining from 2.5, for families headed by persons born at the beginning of the century (1910), to 1.9, for those whose heads were born in 1960.

The results for the oldest group presented in Figure 11.5 indicate a reverse trend, with the number of elderly persons per family increasing over time. The relative importance of this group is, however, still extremely limited, with the average number of persons in this age group being smaller than 0.1 per family.

As a result of these temporal patterns, the size of families and the dependency ratio declined considerably over this five decades. Looking at Figures 11.2 to 11.5 as a whole, one can see that the family size declined from 8.5 to 4.5, while the dependency ratio (defined as the ratio between the number of family members younger than 22 or older than 64 and the working-age family members) also declined considerably from 2.10 to 1.20. In sum, over these five decades both the family size and the dependency ratio declined considerably, reaching at the end of the period values close to one-half of its initial value. The impact of these trends on poverty is bound to be

---

[8] Although we calculated estimates for the evolution of N_{istr}, they are not shown here, for editorial reasons. The mimeo version of this chapter contains them and it can be obtained directly from the authors.

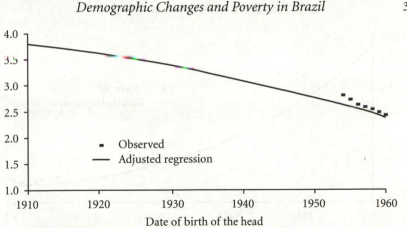

Figure 11.2. *Average Number of People 0 to 14 Years of Age in Families whose Head is between 36 and 40 Years Old—Brazil*

Source: Based on *Pesquisa Nacional Por Amostra e Domicilios* (PNAD), 1976–96.

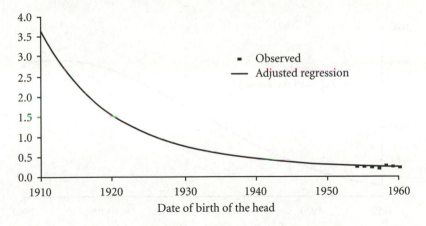

Figure 11.3. *Average Number of People 15 to 21 Years of Age in Families whose Head is between 36 and 40 Years Old—Brazil*

Source: Based on *Pesquisa Nacional Por Amostra e Domicilios* (PNAD), 1976–96.

significant. An assessment of this impact is precisely the objective of the following subsection.

The regional patterns are very similar to the overall pattern for Brazil, showing no great differences between Brazilian regions apart from the family-size reduction movement. These patterns are summarized in Table 11.3. This table shows that the greatest changes occurred in the Northeast and West Central regions, where the dependency ratio fell by about 50 percent in half a century.

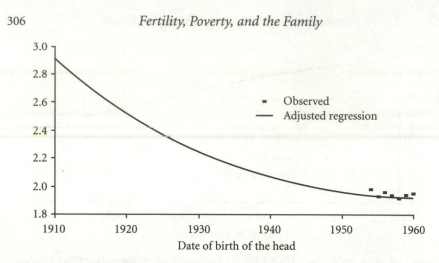

Figure 11.4. *Average Number of People 22 to 64 Years of Age in Families whose Head is between 36 and 40 Years Old—Brazil*

Source: Based on *Pesquisa Nacional Por Amostra e Domicilios* (PNAD), 1976–96.

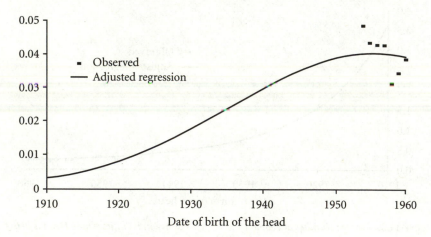

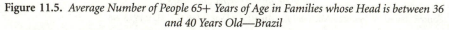

Figure 11.5. *Average Number of People 65+ Years of Age in Families whose Head is between 36 and 40 Years Old—Brazil*

Source: Based on *Pesquisa Nacional Por Amostra e Domicilios* (PNAD), 1976–96.

2.3. *Demographic Changes and Poverty*

We discuss first the results for the country as a whole, followed by the specific regional results.

2.3.1. *Brazil*

Figure 11.6 presents how poverty would be today among families with heads aged 36 to 40 years old if the number and age composition of the family members were the

Table 11.3. *Average Number of People by Age Group in Families whose Head is between 36 and 40 Years Old*

	Brazil	South	Southeast	North	Northeast	West central
Heads born in 1910						
0–14	3.64	4.41	4.22	5.45	5.91	4.67
15–21	1.54	1.06	1.14	1.90	1.50	1.37
22–64	2.49	2.56	2.55	2.54	2.52	2.50
65+	0.01	0.02	0.02	0.02	0.02	0.01
Dependency ratio	2.08	2.15	2.11	2.90	2.95	2.42
Heads born in 1960						
0–14	2.08	1.90	1.82	2.35	2.55	2.01
15–21	0.24	0.20	0.21	0.35	0.28	0.26
22–64	1.95	1.93	1.93	1.92	1.90	1.89
65+	0.03	0.03	0.03	0.04	0.03	0.02
Dependency ratio	1.20	1.10	1.07	1.43	1.50	1.21
Absolute variation						
0–14	−1.56	−2.51	−2.40	−3.10	−3.36	−2.66
15–21	−1.31	−0.87	−0.93	−1.54	−1.22	−1.12
22–64	−0.55	−0.63	−0.63	−0.62	−0.62	−0.61
65+	0.02	0.01	0.01	0.01	0.01	0.01
Dependency ratio	−0.88	−1.04	−1.04	−1.47	−1.44	−1.21

Source: PNAD (1976–96).

same as *t* years ago. This figure reveals that the headcount ratio (average income gap) would be 7 (5) percentage points higher today if the number and age composition of family members were that prevailing 50 years ago.

In the same figure we also presented by how much the income of all family members would have to be reduced annually in order to simulate the effects of maintaining the demographic structure on poverty of *t* years ago. Since the time evolution of poverty in this case would be very similar to that resulting from the demographic change, we concluded that the effect of the demographic change on poverty over the past 50 years was equivalent to an additional 21 percent growth in per-capita income. In fact, if there had been no demographic changes over the past 50 years, but an additional growth in per-capita income of 0.4 percent per year, then the evolution of poverty would have remained almost the same.

The results just presented are estimates of the impact on poverty of all changes in the size and age composition of families. Next, we present estimates of the impact on poverty of changes in the size of each age group. Estimates of these partial effects are presented in Figures 11.7 to 11.10. These figures present how poverty would be today among families with heads aged 36 to 40 years old if the number of family members in age group *i* were the same as *t* years ago. From these figures it is possible to identify which demographic group is responsible for the greatest impact on poverty.

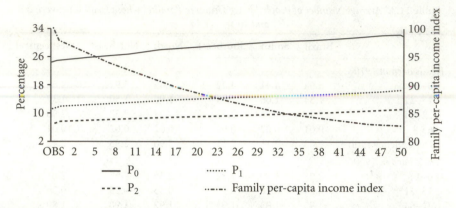

Figure 11.6. *Counter-factual Poverty Measures: Effects on Poverty of the Maintenance of the Age Structure of t Years Ago—Brazil*

Note: Poverty line: R$60.00, 1996.

Source: Based on *Pesquisa Nacional por Amostra e Domicilios* (PNAD), 1976–96.

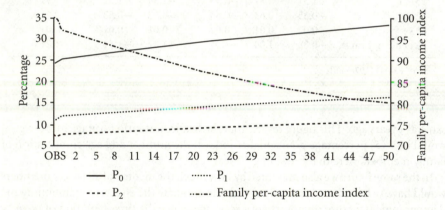

Figure 11.7. *Counter-factual Poverty Measures: Effects on Poverty of the Maintenance of the Average Number of People between 0 and 14 Years Old per Family of t Years Ago—Brazil*

Note: Poverty line: R$60.00, 1996.

Source: Based on *Pesquisa Nacional por Amostra e Domicilios* (PNAD), 1976–96.

These figures reveal that the greatest impact on poverty comes from the reduction in the number of younger (0–14) family numbers. This change alone is responsible for a decline in the headcount of 6 percentage points. Despite this fact, Figure 11.8 reveals that the decline in the number of family members aged 15 to 21 years old has also been responsible for a significant (4 percentage points) reduction in poverty, although smaller than the impact of the reduction in the number of younger family members.

On the other hand, the reduction in the number of family members aged 22 to 64 has led to an increase in the headcount of 3 percentage points, as Figure 11.9 shows.

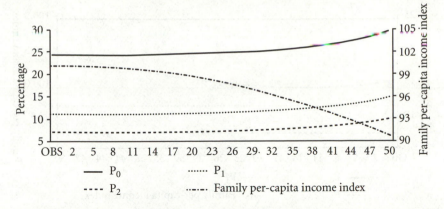

Figure 11.8. *Counter-factual Poverty Measures: Effects on Poverty of the Maintenance of the Average Number of People between 15 and 21 Years Old per Family of t Years Ago—Brazil*

Note: Poverty line: R$60.00, 1996.

Source: Based on *Pesquisa Nacional por Amostra e Domicilios* (PNAD), 1976–96.

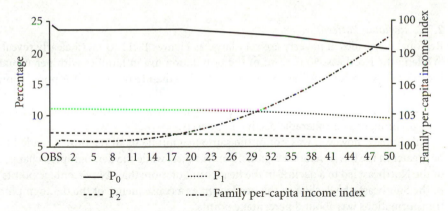

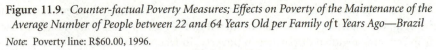

Figure 11.9. *Counter-factual Poverty Measures; Effects on Poverty of the Maintenance of the Average Number of People between 22 and 64 Years Old per Family of t Years Ago—Brazil*

Note: Poverty line: R$60.00, 1996.

Source: Based on *Pesquisa Nacional por Amostra e Domicilios* (PNAD), 1976–96.

Finally, it is worthy noticing that for the group whose members were aged, 65 or more, the demographic changes were too small to have any significant impact on poverty.

In sum, the demographic changes over the past 50 years led to a decline in the headcount ratio of 7 percentage points. This change, however, is the result of two opposing forces. On the one hand, the decline in the number of young dependents (persons younger than 22) brought a decline of 10 percentage points in the headcount. On the other hand, the decline in the number of working-age members (22–64) led to an increase in the headcount of 3 percentage points.

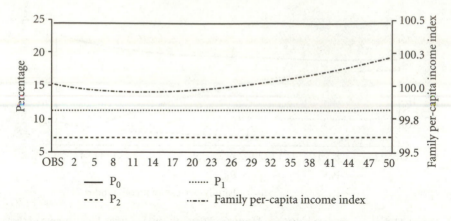

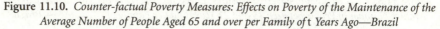

Figure 11.10. *Counter-factual Poverty Measures: Effects on Poverty of the Maintenance of the Average Number of People Aged 65 and over per Family of t Years Ago—Brazil*

Note: Poverty line: R$60.00, 1996.

Source: Based on *Pesquisa Nacional por Amostra e Domicilios* (PNAD), 1976–96.

2.3.2. Regional Patterns

Regional disparities in poverty are very large as Figures 11.11 to 11.15 clearly reveal. While in the Northeast 50 percent of the population live in families with per-capita income below the poverty line, in the Southeast, less than 15 percent of the population is below the poverty line.[9] These figures reveal that the demographic changes that occurred over the past 50 years benefitted all regions. In all of them, the demographic changes brought a considerable decline in poverty.

This impact, however, was not of the same magnitude in all regions. It tended to be greater in the less developed regions. For instance, while the demographic changes in the Northeast led to a decline in the headcount of more than 14 percentage points, in the Southeast, the decline in the headcount as a consequence of the demographic transformations was about 8 percentage points.

As a consequence of this differential impact favoring the less developed regions, the demographic transformations that occurred in the past 50 years were a relevant factor in reducing regional disparities in poverty. In fact, over this period demographic transformations have been working in the direction of eliminating regional disparities in poverty.

3. CONTEMPORANEOUS REGIONAL DISPARITIES

As mentioned in the previous section, regional disparities in Brazil are large. While in the Northeast 50 percent of the population are poor, in the South only 15 percent are

---

[9] Estimates of the impact on poverty of changes in the size of each age group for each region were calculated. Once more the interested reader can find them in the mimeo version of this chapter.

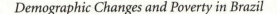

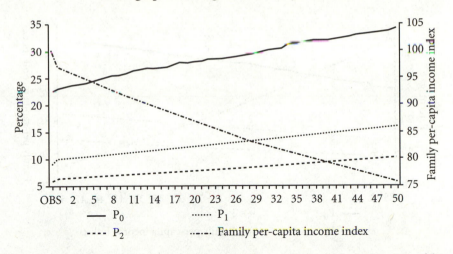

Figure 11.11. *Counter-factual Poverty Measures: Effects on Poverty of the Maintenance of the Age Structure of t Years Ago—West Central*

Note: Poverty line: R$60.00, 1996.

Source: Based on *Pesquisa Nacional por Amostra e Domicilios* (PNAD), 1976–96.

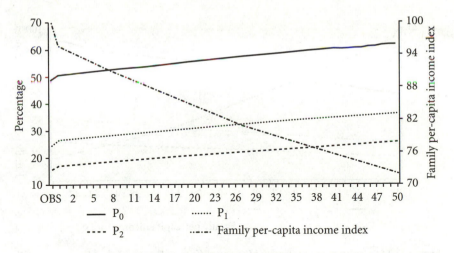

Figure 11.12. *Counter-factual Poverty Measures: Effects on Poverty of the Maintenance of the Age Structure of t Years Ago—Northeast*

Note: Poverty line: R$60.00, 1996.

Source: Based on *Pesquisa Nacional por Amostra e Domicilios* (PNAD), 1976–96.

below the poverty line. The objective of this section is to investigate to which extent these sharp differences are caused by concomitant demographic differences.

Figure 11.16 presents some evidence on the size and age composition of families in Brazil for each age group. This figure reveals important regional demographic

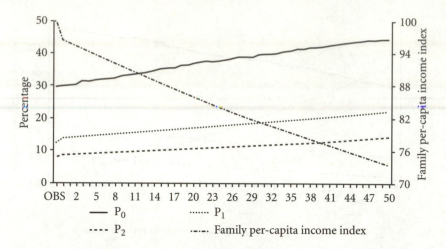

Figure 11.13. *Counter-factual Poverty Measures: Effects on Poverty of the Maintenance of the Age Structure of t Years Ago—North*

Note: Poverty line: R$60.00, 1996.

Source: Based on *Pesquisa Nacional por Amostra e Domicilios* (PNAD), 1976–96.

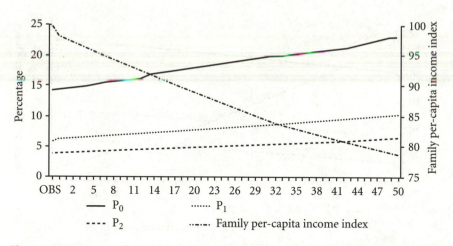

Figure 11.14. *Counter-factual Poverty Measures: Effects on Poverty of the Maintenance of the Age Structure of t Years Ago—Southeast*

Note: Poverty line: R$60.00, 1996.

Source: Based on *Pesquisa Nacional por Amostra e Domicilios* (PNAD), 1976–96.

disparities, which are clearly related to the level of economic development. In the more developed regions (South and Southeast) the average number of young dependents per family (persons under 22 years of age) is well below the average for the less developed regions (North and Northeast). There are also regional differences in the

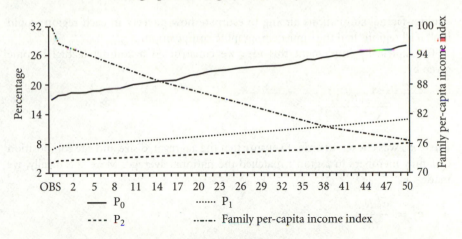

Figure 11.15. *Counter-factual Poverty Measures: Effects on Poverty of the Maintenance of the Age Structure of* t *Years Ago—South*

Note: Poverty line: R$60.00, 1996.

Source: Based on *Pesquisa Nacional por Amostra e Domicilios* (PNAD), 1976–96.

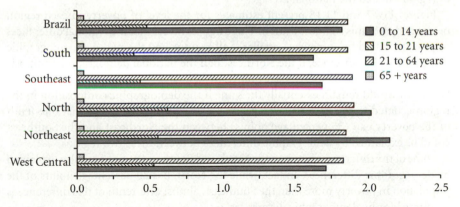

Figure 11.16. *Average Number of Members of Each Age Group per Family*

Source: Based on *Pesquisa Nacional por Amostra e Domicilios* (PNAD), 1996.

number of persons per family in the working-age group favoring the more developed regions. These differences, however, are relatively smaller.

As a consequence of these demographic differences, the dependency ratio is considerably greater in the less developed regions than in the more developed ones. Next we investigate to what extent these sharp regional differences in demographic composition are the main cause of the concomitant large regional differences in poverty.

In order to estimate the impact of regional differences in the size and age distribution of the population on the concomitant differences in poverty, we perform counter-factual simulations aiming to estimate how poverty in each region would look if all regions had the same demographic composition.

To empirically implement this idea we constructed a counter-factual income given by

$$y_r^f = \frac{\sum_{i=1}^4 n_{ir}^f y_i^f}{\sum_{i=1}^4 n_{ir}^f};$$

where n_{ir}^f was chosen in order to ensure that the aggregated size and age composition of family members in region r matched the national average. More specifically, we made

$$n_{ir}^f = \frac{n_i^f N_i}{N_{ir}};$$

where N_i is the average number of members in age group i per family for the country as a whole and N_{ir} is the corresponding average for region r. As a consequence, one has by construction that the average of n_{ir}^f in region r equals to N_i, indicating that, after the transformation, the aggregated size and age composition of family members in region r match the national average.

Figures 11.17 and 11.18 present estimates for the level of poverty in each region before and after this standardization. These figures reveal that the regional differences in poverty would be somewhat smaller if all regions had the national demographic composition. For instance, if the Northeast had the national demographic composition, poverty would be 3 percentage points smaller, whereas the level of poverty in the Southeast would remain essentially the same if the demographic composition in the region equated to the national average. As a consequence, we found that one-tenth of the poverty gap (35 percentage points) between the Northeast and the Southeast could be explained by demographic differences between these two regions.

Some of the differences between the North and Southeast regions are also explained by demographic differences. In fact, while the North has 20 percentage points of the population in poverty more than the Southeast, almost one-tenth of this difference is accounted for by demographic differences.

Demographic differences also explain some of the differences in poverty between the Southeast and the Center-West and between the Southeast and the South. In this case, however, the original disparities are smaller, as is the contribution of demography in explaining these differences.

Finally, Figures 11.19 and 11.20 present how the elimination of regional differences in demographic structure would affect the overall level of poverty in the country, that is, what the level of poverty in Brazil would be if all regions had an identical demographic composition. These figures reveal that the elimination of regional differences in demographic composition would have a very small effect on the overall level of poverty. More specifically the elimination of these disparities would reduce the headcount ratio just from 24 percent to 23 percent.

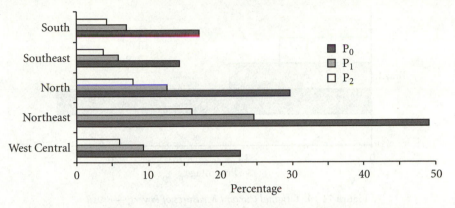

Figure 11.17. *Original Regional Poverty Measures*

Note: Poverty line: R$60.00, 1996.

Source: Based on *Pesquisa Nacional por Amostra e Domicilios* (PNAD), 1996.

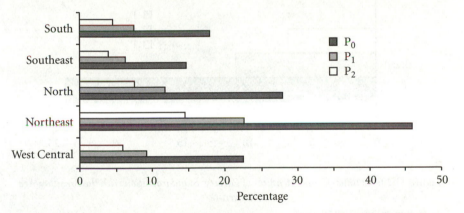

Figure 11.18. *Counter-factual Regional Measures of Poverty: Standardization with the Brazilian Age Structure*

Note: Poverty line: R$60.00, 1996.

Source: Based on *Pesquisa Nacional por Amostra e Domicilios* (PNAD) 1976–96.

4. DEMOGRAPHIC DIVERSITY AND POVERTY

In the previous section we illustrated the relationship between regional differences in demographic structure and regional differences in poverty. Regional differences, however, are just one example of demographic diversity. In this section we further explore this connection between demographic diversity and poverty.

Two aspects of the demographic diversity are investigated. First, we investigate to what extent poverty would be reduced if all income groups had on average the same demographic composition. In other words, we investigate the impact of eliminating

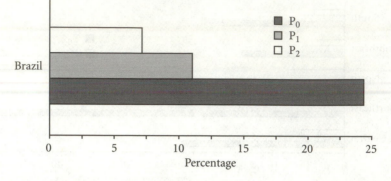

Figure 11.19. *Original Current Measures of Poverty—Brazil*

Note: Poverty line: R$60.00, 1996.

Source: Based on *Pesquisa Nacional por Amostra e Domicilios* (PNAD), 1976–96.

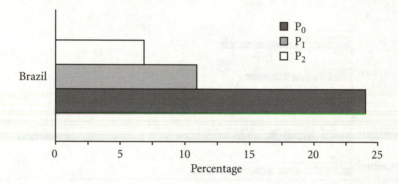

Figure 11.20. *Counter-factual Measures of Poverty: Standardization with the Brazilian Age Structure*

Note: Poverty line: R$60.00, 1996.

Source: Based on *Pesquisa Nacional por Amostra e Domicilios* (PNAD), 1976–96.

all demographic differences between income groups on the level of poverty. Secondly, we investigate to what extent poverty would be reduced if all families had exactly the same demographic composition, that is, we investigate the effect on poverty of eliminating all demographic diversity.

4.1. *Eliminating Demographic Differences between Income Groups*

In this section we examine the effect on poverty of eliminating demographic differences between rich and poor families. To implement this objective we have to divide families into income groups. To construct these income groups we have to choose a notion of income to construct a partition of the income spectrum.

The natural choice for income may seem to be the family per-capita income. Nevertheless, this income is itself heavily influenced by demographic aspects. It derives from the fact that the family per-capita income incorporates the earnings of child labor. In its turn, child labor tends to occur more frequently in families with a large number of children, which is one of the demographic indicators used.

In order to avoid this problem, we decided to construct income groups based on the average income of adults (people aged 22 to 64) in the family. This decision also has a normative justification. We are interested in classifying families as rich or otherwise taking into consideration only the income of people of working age, since children's earnings, although increasing the family income, must reflect a family welfare loss. We also decided to split the income spectrum into 100 non-overlapping groups using the percentiles of the distribution as boundaries.

We equated the average demographic composition of all income groups to the overall average and recomputed the level of poverty to assess the impact of differences in demographic composition between income groups on poverty. In order to implement this objective we constructed the following counter-factual income:

$$y_d^f = \frac{\sum_{i=1}^4 n_{id}^f y_i^f}{\sum_{i=1}^4 n_{id}^f};$$

where n_{id}^f was chosen in order to ensure that the aggregated size and age composition of family members of income group d match that prevailing in the overall population. To ensure that this property holds, we make

$$n_{id}^f = \frac{n_i^f N_i}{N_{id}};$$

where N_i is the average number of members in age group i per family in the population and N_{id} is the corresponding average for families in the income group d. As a consequence, by construction, the average of n_{id}^f among families in the income group d equals N_i indicating that the transformation from n_i^f to n_{id}^f ensures that the aggregated size and age composition of family members in income group d match that observed in the overall population.

Estimates of N_{id} are presented in Figure 11.21. This figure reveals that the number of children (persons younger than 14 years old) and the number of teenagers (persons aged 15 to 21 years old) are decreasing functions of income, that is, the richer the family the smaller the number of young dependents in the family. More specifically, this figure reveals that the number of young dependents per family is close to 3.0 among very poor families and close to 1.7 among very rich families. At the same time, the number of persons of working age per family tends to increase with the income level, going from 1.7 among the very poor to more than 2.0 among the very rich.

Figures 11.22 to 11.24 present estimates of poverty before and after we eliminated the demographic differences between income groups. These figures reveal that, similar to the regional analysis, differences between income groups have little effect on

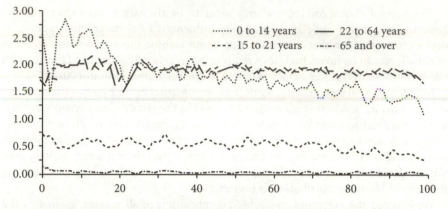

Figure 11.21. *Average Number of Family Members per Income Centile*
Source: Based on *Pesquisa Nacional por Amostra e Domicilios* (PNAD), 1996.

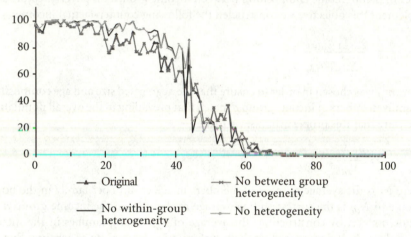

Figure 11.22. P_0 *by Family Per-Capita Income of Adults Distribution*
Source: Based on *Pesquisa Nacional por Amostra e Domicilios* (PNAD), 1996.

poverty. More specifically one can see that, for almost all income groups as well as for all groups taken together, the impact on poverty of eliminating demographic differences between income groups is almost insignificant. This result is rather important. It says that poverty is not, by any significant amount, a consequence of differences in demographic structure between poor and rich families.

4.2. *Eliminating All Demographic Differences*

In the previous section we obtained the rather unexpected result that differences in demographic structure between rich and poor families were not important in explaining poverty. In this section we pursue further the connection between demographic

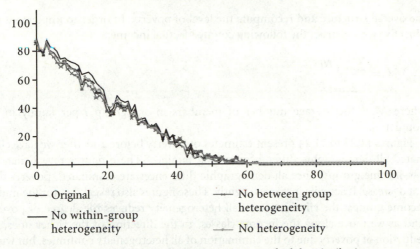

Figure 11.23. *P₁ by Family Per-Capita Income of Adults Distribution*

Source: Based on *Pesquisa Nacional por Amostra e Domicilios* (PNAD), 1996.

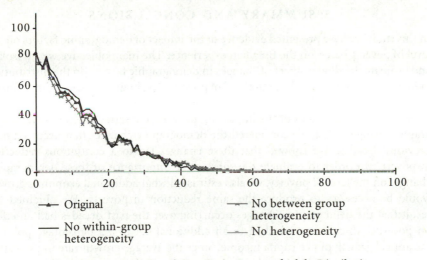

Figure 11.24. *P₂ by Family Per-Capita Income of Adults Distribution*

Source: Based on *Pesquisa Nacional por Amostra e Domicilios* (PNAD), 1996.

diversity and poverty. More specifically, in this section we investigate the effect on poverty of eliminating all differences among families, in size and age composition.

Since overall disparities can always be decomposed between groups and within groups, we can also contrast the results of this section with those obtained in the previous section, to obtain measures of the impact of demographic disparities within income groups.

To assess the impact on poverty of eliminating all differences in demographic composition among families we equate the demographic structure of all families to the overall structure and recompute the level of poverty. In order to implement this objective we construct the following counter-factual income:

$$\bar{y}^f = \frac{\sum_{i=1}^{4} N_i y_i^f}{\sum_{i=1}^{4} N_i};$$

where N_i is the average number of members in age group i per family in the population.

Figures 11.22 to 11.24 present estimates of poverty before and after we have elim-inated all demographic differences among families. These figures reveal that, for low-income groups, once all demographic differences are eliminated, poverty does not decrease. It actually increases slightly. These figures also reveal that for the middle income groups, the elimination of all heterogeneity reduces the degree of poverty. And as we move along the income classes, in the direction of the richer ones, the reduction of poverty due to the elimination of all heterogeneity continues, but with a lower impact.

5. SUMMARY AND CONCLUSIONS

In this study we have presented evidence of the impact of demographic factors on the level of poverty based on the Brazilian experience. The main objective was to isolate and estimate the *direct* impact of changes in demographic factors on the distribution of income and consequently on the level of poverty. To obtain estimates of this impact we rely on micro simulations based on a series of household surveys.

We presented estimates of the impact on poverty of a series of alternative demo-graphic changes. First, we considered the demographic changes that occurred over previous decades. We showed that these changes led to a continuous reduction in poverty. In order to evaluate the substantive importance of these demographic changes on the level of poverty, we also estimated what additional economic growth would be necessary to produce the same reduction in poverty. We obtained the result that the demographic changes occurring over the past decades had an effect on poverty, which was equivalent to an additional 0.4 to 0.5 percentage point in the annual growth of per-capita income. Since the average growth rate in per-capita income in Brazil over this period was close to 3.0 percent per year, the demographic change in the period had an important *direct* impact on reducing poverty. In sum, the estimated direct impact of the demographic transition had an impact on poverty which was close to 15 percent of the corresponding impact of economic growth.

We also investigated the importance of regional differences in demographic con-ditions for explaining concomitant differences in poverty. We showed that despite some important regional differences in the timing and in the speed of the demo-graphic transition, current demographic regional differences explained only a very small fraction of the sizeable regional differences in poverty.

Finally we investigated to what extent poverty can be explained by demographic differences between poor and rich families. We found that when families are ranked by their average income per adult, the demographic differences between poor and rich families are very small. As a consequence, these demographic differences proved unimportant in explaining the level of poverty.

In sum, accordingly to our estimates, overall secular demographic changes tend to have much greater impact on poverty than differences in the time and the speed of the demographic transition across regions and between poor and rich families.

PART IV

POPULATION, AGRICULTURE, AND NATURAL RESOURCES

The impacts of population growth on natural resource use and on the environment are exceptionally complex. John Pender's chapter in this part illustrates that complexity in one domain: the impact of population change on the productivity of agriculture. The central lesson applies to other natural resource and environmental issues. It is that population change is seldom the principal cause of problems and seldom if ever the focal point for a solution. Rather, population 'amplifies' or 'exacerbates' the costs of institutional and market failures that plague use of natural resources—and are an unfortunate but defining feature of developing countries.

Pender provides an exhaustive list of the potential responses—positive and negative—of agricultural production and systems to population pressures. He then illustrates with the study in Honduras the mechanisms and the tools needed to unbundle their effects. On the one hand, the potential negative effect of population growth has been and can be mediated by policy and practices, including collective action. On the other hand, as Pender puts, it, *without* collective action, population density can make things worse. Collective action includes the capacity of societies to develop the necessary policies, for example protection of property rights and appropriate pricing of water, and the necessary institutions, including rules for sustainable use of common property resources.

Though theory and the concepts are clear, a simple and general conclusion about the effect of population on natural resource use and sustainability remains elusive. This is unfortunate. Estimates of the costs of environmental damage in developing countries often reach several percentage points of GDP, thus qualifying the record of economic growth in developing countries. To the extent that population does play a role in environmental damage, it represents a further externality far from individual couples' calculus (implicit or explicit) affecting their fertility behavior. Thus, reducing the rate of population growth may well produce another kind of demographic bonus.

Meanwhile, the one point that is clear is the following: the effects of markets and institutions—sometimes good, sometimes bad—can easily swamp the effect of population change on resource use, degradation, and depletion. The implications for policy thus go far beyond the traditional 'population' arena.

12

Rural Population Growth, Agricultural Change, and Natural Resource Management in Developing Countries: A Review of Hypotheses and some Evidence from Honduras

JOHN PENDER

1. INTRODUCTION

The impacts of population growth on agriculture and natural resource management have been debated at least since the time of Malthus. Although the dismal predictions of Malthus regarding the inability of agricultural production to keep pace with population growth have not come to pass in the industrialized nations, agricultural production per capita has fallen and poverty has increased in many developing countries in recent decades (especially in Africa). In addition, there are serious and growing concerns about the impacts of rapid population growth on natural resources, including forests, land, water, biodiversity, and other resources (World Commission on Environment and Development 1987; Ehrlich and Ehrlich 1990).

In contrast to the dire predictions of the neo-Malthusian perspective, a more optimistic perspective has arisen in recent decades as well, following from the work of Ester Boserup and others. Boserup (1965, 1981), Ruthenberg (1980), and others have emphasized the responses of households, communities, and societies to pressures induced by population growth, including reduction in fallow periods, intensified use of labor and capital per unit of land, development and adoption of labor-intensive technologies, and institutional changes (such as development of more specific and individual property rights and development of markets). It is generally accepted that such responses, to the extent that they occur, should increase agricultural production per unit of land, though their impacts on labor productivity, output per capita, and

The author gratefully acknowledges the financial support of the Swiss Development Cooperation and the Inter-American Development Bank for this research, and institutional support from the International Food Policy Research Institute and the Inter-American Institute for Cooperation in Agriculture. I am grateful to my colleague, Sara Scherr and to the Honduras study team—Guadalupe Durón, Fernando Mendoza, Carlos Duarte, Juan Manuel Medina, Oscar Neidecker-Gonzales, and Roduel Rodriguez—for their valuable contributions to this study. I am especially grateful to the many farmers and others in Honduras who generously agreed to respond to our many questions.

poverty have been debated (e.g. Robinson and Schutjer 1984; Salehi-Isfahani 1988; Krautkraemer 1994). The impacts on natural resources are also debated (Blaikie and Brookfield 1987; Lele and Stone 1989; Panayotou 1994).

The evidence on these issues is mixed. For example, an often cited study of the Machakos district in Kenya found that between the 1930s and the 1990s, per capita income had increased, erosion was much better controlled, and trees were more prevalent in the landscape, despite a fivefold increase in population (Tiffen *et al.* 1994), supporting the Boserup perspective. Numerous other studies have also found positive associations between population growth, agricultural intensification, and investments in land improvement and resource conservation (see Templeton and Scherr 1999, and the references cited therein). However, many studies have also found population growth to be associated with various aspects of resource degradation, including deforestation, overgrazing, soil erosion, soil nutrient depletion, and other problems (see studies cited by Templeton and Scherr 1999; Panayotou 1994; Kates and Haarmann 1992).

Part of the difficulty in reaching definitive conclusions about the relationship between population growth and natural resource conditions is due to the fact that there are many complex and interdependent ways in which population growth may affect agricultural and natural resource-management decisions by households, communities, and societies. Population growth may affect natural resource management by affecting household decisions about land use, labor or capital intensity, product choice, technology adoption, off-farm employment, migration, or fertility (Bilsborrow and Carr 1998; Panayotou 1994; Boserup 1965). It may affect natural resource management by affecting community and societal decisions relating to collective management of common property resources (Baland and Platteau 1996); development or adaptation of technology (Boserup 1965; Hayami and Ruttan 1985); investments in infrastructure (ibid.); development of property rights, land tenure relations, markets or other institutions (ibid.; North 1990; Scherr and Hazell 1994); or development of organizations (Pender and Scherr 1999).

By affecting poverty, distribution of wealth, or other outcomes, population growth may also cause changes in resource management through feedback effects from these outcomes. For example, poverty may increase resource degradation by causing people to have a short time horizon in their decisions (Pender 1996; Holden *et al.* 1998), or may promote labor-intensive investments in resource conservation by farmers who have few alternative investment opportunities or low opportunity cost of family labor (Pender and Kerr 1998).

Adding to the complexity of the issue is the fact that the impacts of population growth likely depend on many site-specific conditioning factors, such as agricultural potential, fragility of the resource base, market integration, initial population density, local human and social capital endowments, and other factors (Pender, Place, and Ehui 1999; Pender, Scherr, and Durón 1999; Lopez 1998; Tiffen *et al.* 1994; Panayotou 1994). Moreover, resource degradation or improvement is a multi-dimensional and site-specific concept; improvements in one type of resource or in resources in one location may be associated with degradation of other resources or resources in another location. For example, intensification of crop production may reduce pressure on forests but increase problems of soil erosion and nutrient depletion; enclosures of common grazing areas may lead to regeneration in enclosed areas but more rapid degradation of other grazing areas.

The purpose of this chapter is to sort through these complexities by reviewing key hypotheses about the impacts of rural population growth on agriculture, natural resource management, and related impacts on poverty in developing countries. I will consider factors conditioning the hypotheses, different aspects of resource management, and some of the evidence available with respect to these hypotheses. The emphasis of this chapter is on the impacts of rural population growth. I do not consider in detail the broader set of linkages resulting from urban population growth, industrial development, and the feedback effects on the agricultural and rural sectors, since I assume these issues will be adequately addressed by other chapters in this volume. I have not conducted an exhaustive literature review of the evidence, but rely on some of the excellent literature reviews that have recently been completed (e.g. Templeton and Scherr 1999; Panayotou 1994). I then present results of recent field research conducted by the International Food Policy Research Institute (IFPRI) on some of these issues in Honduras.

2. HOUSEHOLD RESPONSES TO RURAL POPULATION GROWTH

I will proceed by considering possible responses to rural population growth, beginning with those that involve the least departure from the ways of doing things in the past (e.g. extensification of agriculture using the same methods), and considering later those that involve more investment, collective action, and/or reorganization of social relations (e.g. changes in institutions such as property rights). A general hypothesis consistent with the evolutionary perspective of Boserup is that the responses requiring greater investment and accommodation are likely to come later, though this may not always hold if the pressures for change are very rapid or sudden, or if certain favorable factors exist (e.g. the opening up of a road may create a sudden increase in demand for private land titles, and this may be fulfilled if a land titling program happens to be already in place).

I consider responses mainly at the household and local community level. This is not to assert that responses occur only at these levels. Responses of course occur at the individual level, and household production decisions may not be adequately reflected by a unitary household model (Udry 1996). Important responses are also made above the community level; for example, by policy-makers. I abstract from those complications to keep the task manageable, though this is not to argue that these other levels are unimportant.

For each type of response, I propose hypotheses about the factors favoring or inhibiting it, and the expected impacts of the response on indicators of agricultural productivity (including land productivity and labor productivity), human welfare (income and welfare per capita and distribution of welfare), and natural resource conditions (including impacts on forests, soil erosion, soil fertility, water availability and quality). Many other indicators of natural resource conditions (such as biodiversity) or human welfare (such as per capita food consumption) could also be suggested; I do not consider them for reasons of space and the possibility that the impacts on these may be largely reflected in the indicators mentioned. For example, the qualitative direction of impacts on biodiversity may be very similar to the impacts on forests.

The general types of household-level responses to rural population growth include extensification of agricultural production using traditional methods, intensification of labor per unit of land using traditional methods (i.e. shortening fallow cycles), adoption of more labor-intensive methods of production (e.g. hand hoeing and weeding, mulching, composting), labor-intensive investments in land (e.g. soil and water conservation structures), adoption of capital-intensive methods (e.g. use of draft animals, equipment, purchased agricultural inputs), knowledge-intensive responses (e.g. development or adaptation of new techniques, such as biological conservation measures, integrated pest management, or integrated soil nutrient management), changes in product mix (e.g. adoption of more labor-intensive crops, integration of crops with livestock products, adoption of higher value products), changes in occupation (e.g. development of off-farm income), migration, and reduction in fertility. The hypotheses about these responses are summarized in Table 12.1.

2.1. *Extensification*

Extensification of agricultural production using traditional methods of shifting cultivation is the first response one would expect to population growth in situations of low population density with large amounts of open access land available, of relatively good quality for agricultural production, and relatively accessible (Boserup 1965; Binswanger and McIntire 1987). All of the conditioning factors are important. There are many situations (most common in Latin America) of low population density where agricultural expansion by smallholders is not possible because most suitable and accessible land is owned and protected by large farmers or ranchers. There are also many places where open access land exists, but agricultural expansion is limited because they are not well suited to agriculture (e.g. much of the humid tropics of Africa, where problems of pests and disease inhibit agricultural expansion) and/or remote (e.g. much of the Amazon region). In most areas of high population density, little open access land usually remains. An exception is where state or community ownership of land prevails but is not well enforced, leading to a situation of *de facto* open access. This situation is common in many state forests in developing countries (Otsuka 1998). Not surprisingly, such forests are rapidly disappearing.

Where extensification is possible and the available land is relatively suitable for agricultural production, extensification is expected to have little impact on agricultural productivity per unit of land used or per unit of labor. In this situation, there will also be little impact on income per capita (including the value of subsistence production)

Table 12.1. *Hypotheses about Household Responses to Rural Population Growth*

Response	Conditioning factors	Productivity		Human welfare			Natural resource conditions			
		Land	Labor	Income per capita	Welfare per capita	Distribution of welfare	Forest	Soil erosion	Soil fertility	Water
Extensification	Low population density Open access land available and accessible Land relatively homogeneous in quality	0	0	0	0	0	−	−	0/−	−
Shorter fallow	Rising population density Open access land becoming unavailable Emphasis first on better quality land Alternative opportunities for labor limited	−	−	0/−	−	0/−	−	−	−	−
Labor intensive practices	Rising population density Open access land becoming unavailable Emphasis first on better quality land Alternative opportunities for labor limited	+	−	0/−	−	0/−	+	+	0/+	+/−
Labor-intensive land investments—near term	High population density Land tenure security Agroecological suitability Commercialization (+/−) Off-farm opportunities (+/−) Land market development Access to credit Poverty	0/−	−	0/−	−	+/−	+	0/+	0/+	+/−

Table 12.1. (*Continued*)

Response	Conditioning factors	Productivity		Human welfare			Natural resource conditions			
		Land	Labor	Income per capita	Welfare per capita	Distribution of welfare	Forest	Soil erosion	Soil fertility	Water
Labor-intensive land investments—long term	(same)	+	+	+	+	+/-	+	+	+	+/-
Capital intensification—draft animals/plow	Medium population density Elimination of woody fallows, increased demand for bottomland with heavy soils Climate and disease (humid tropics limit adoption) Longer growing season or irrigation Market access Access to credit	0/+	+	+	+	0/-	-	-	+/0	-
Capital intensification—purchased inputs	Complementarity to labor Climate risks, irrigation Access to roads, markets Commercialization, production of high value crops Access to credit Government trade, exchange rate, marketing policies (+/-)	0/+	0/+	+	+	0/-	+/-	+/-	+/-	-
Knowledge intensification	Changing factor scarcities (induced innovation hypothesis) Growing population (reduces per capita costs of innovation)	0/+	0/+	+	+	0/-	+/-	+	+	0/+

	+/-	+/-
	+/-	+/-
	+/-	+/-
	0/+	+/-
	0/-	

Determinant / factor					
Change in product mix—adoption of labor intensive products	+	—	0/-		+/-
Mechanisms to share costs of innovation or reward innovators for external benefits					
Similar to factors affecting labor intensification					
Change in product mix—increased specialization	+	0/+	+		+/-
Higher population density					
Development of infrastructure and markets					
Education and training	—	+	0/+		+/-
Changes in occupation/migration			0/+		0/+
Opportunities for labor in other occupations					
Infrastructure development					
Labor mobility					
Land tenure security					
Land and housing market development					
Availability of social services in urban areas					
Reduction in fertility—effects on age structure	+	0/+	+/-		0/+
Costs and availability of education, food, health care	—		+/-		
Expected wage levels					
Availability of open access resources					
Property rights/land tenure arrangements					
Means to assure security in old age					
Education and status of women; family planning					

or the distribution of income, since land of suitable quality is available to all. The main impacts of this response will be on resource conditions, and these will mainly be negative. Forest resources will be depleted as agriculture expands. In hilly terrain, this will likely lead to increased soil erosion as land cover is reduced through slash and burn. The reduction in forest cover and increase in soil erosion can lead to reduced availability of water in the local ecosystem by increasing run-off, and reducing the capacity of the ecosystem to store and recycle water through uptake by plants and evapotranspiration. Erosion and run-off can reduce the quality of water downstream and cause increased problems of flooding and sedimentation of rivers and reservoirs. Soil fertility will decline as a result of erosion, leaching, and crop production without full recycling of the nutrients. However, fertility can again recover provided that the cropping cycle is short enough and the fallow cycle long enough to allow woody fallow to return (Vasey 1979).

Once extensification has proceeded to where the land available is less suitable for agricultural production, further extensification may be slowed and farmers may have an incentive to intensify production on the better quality lands instead. To the extent that extensification continues to be pursued, it is likely where it is a lower cost option to intensification, though production costs will probably be higher than where land is of better quality. This is because farmers may have to work harder to clear the land, clear more land to achieve the same production, or plant crops for a shorter period due to more rapidly declining fertility. Production per unit of land cropped is likely to fall (especially in the second case), as is production per unit of labor (in all cases). Although productivity is likely to fall, production per capita may not, since farmers may work harder to maintain subsistence consumption. As long as this response is possible and continues, there will be little impact on income per capita or its distribution, although household welfare will decline as a result of lower labor productivity and increased labor input. The qualitative effects on resources will be similar to the effects discussed above for the case of uniform land quality, except that the magnitude of effects is likely to become greater as extensification proceeds into lands that are more susceptible to degradation, such as steeply sloping lands, or lands where soil fertility is low or apt to decline rapidly.

In summary, extensification likely represents the least cost response to population pressure from the farmers' perspective, where open access land of suitable quality is available and accessible. The costs in terms of depletion of unpriced resources may be very large, however. These costs, as well as the costs to the farmer, are expected to rise as such land begins to be used up, and lower quality or more remote land must be used. As population continues to increase, the costs of continuing expansion eventually become greater than the costs of more intensive production on better quality or more accessible land, and intensification eventually begins to occur. Of course, there may still be land available for extensification (though at higher cost), and as intensification proceeds and as the costs of this strategy rise, some extensification may continue to occur. Thus, intensification and extensification may occur simultaneously for some time, as long as some open access land is still available.

2.2. *Shortening the Fallow Cycle*

When intensification first begins, farmers are likely to simply shorten the fallow cycle on better quality (or less remote) lands, returning to them sooner rather than expanding to lower quality lands (Boserup 1965). As fallow periods shorten, forest fallow is eventually replaced by bush and then grass fallow, since the forest is not given time to regenerate.[1] Soil fertility is given less chance to recover, and the length of the cropping period must also be reduced.

The factors favoring this change are mainly the rising population density and declining availability of good quality land where extensification can occur. Insecurity of future access to better quality lands may accelerate the process, since land left fallow may be claimed by other users (Otsuka 1998). A factor that may inhibit this change (or any of the other aspects of labor intensification discussed below) is the availability of more remunerative opportunities for labor elsewhere. If there are opportunities to migrate to take advantage of available land elsewhere (extensification) or off-farm employment opportunities (locally or through migration), the process of intensification may proceed slowly or be halted by the flow of labor out of agriculture. We have examined the implications of the extensification strategy above, and will consider the off-farm employment and migration strategies later.

This strategy will lead to declining land productivity, due to declining soil fertility. There may be offsetting impacts on labor productivity, since declining productivity due to declining soil fertility may be offset to some extent by the reduced labor requirement to clear fallow fields, which will have less vegetation to clear (Vasey 1979). However, one would expect farmers to have voluntarily reduced fallow periods earlier, if doing so increased labor productivity (since labor is likely the constraining factor in an extensive fallow system). Thus, our expectation is that if population pressure forces farmers to reduce fallow periods, the declining productivity effect outweighs the labor-saving effect, and labor productivity will begin to decline. As long as there is still sufficient land available, however, production per capita can still be maintained if each farmer cultivates more land, and thus there may not be distributional effects on production and income per capita. Since cultivating more land with lower labor productivity requires more effort, farmer welfare decreases however.

Many of the expected impacts of shorter fallow cycles on resource conditions are similar to the impacts of extensification. To the extent that forest fallow existed prior to shortening the fallow cycle, this shortening will lead to less forest fallow land, which is likely to have similar impacts to a reduction in primary forest. Forest fallow can serve many of the same environmental functions as primary forests, including preventing soil erosion, recycling water and nutrients, and preserving biodiversity. The expansion of crop land relative to fallow of any kind increases the rate of soil nutrient depletion and possibly of soil erosion, since most types of fallow likely provide better vegetative

---

[1] This of course applies only to areas where the original climax vegetation is forest. Where the original vegetation is bush or grassland, declining fallow periods would still be expected to alter the original vegetative composition and to lead to declining soil fertility.

cover of the soil than most crops (possibly excluding some perennial crops) during periods of erosive rainfall.

2.3. *Adoption of More Labor-Intensive Methods*

At higher levels of population density, and low levels of wages and off-farm opportunities, adoption of more labor-intensive methods of agricultural production begin to become economical. Use of hoeing and hand weeding can replace burning to clear crop fields, both because vegetation is reduced by declining fallow periods, and because the amount of labor available per unit of land is rising. Planting density may increase, as may the care given to planted crops through various labor-intensive methods to improve soil fertility, such as application of compost or mulch.

Greater labor intensity likely increases productivity per unit of land, but reduces labor productivity as a result of diminishing returns to labor (unless complemented by increased capital intensity or technical change, as discussed below). As with shortening fallow periods, farmers may compensate for reduced labor productivity by working harder, so that production and income per capita do not decline. Again, however, welfare does decline as a result of declining labor productivity. As land becomes increasingly scarce, the distributional impacts of access to better quality land increase, with greater welfare achieved by occupants of the better quality land, as predicted by the Ricardian theory of rent.

The impacts of increased labor intensity on resource conditions may be mixed, though generally positive. More intensive practices and reduced use of burning will reduce the rate of deforestation and the problems associated with it. These also may result in greater vegetative cover being kept on the land (relative to the impacts of burning), reducing problems of erosion. Adoption of labor-intensive soil fertility management practices may improve soil fertility, though these may be insufficient to offset the increased outflow of soil nutrients resulting from increased amounts harvested per unit of land (Smaling 1998; Buresh *et al.* 1997).

2.4. *Labor-Intensive Investment in Land*

Rising population density and declining value of labor relative to land also may lead to labor-intensive investments in land improvement, such as construction of terraces, bunds, check dams, live barriers, or other structures to conserve soil and water. Land tenure security is likely a critical conditioning factor for such investments. Without secure tenure, farmers risk losing the benefits of such investments and thus may not make them even if the potential benefits are high (Feder *et al.* 1988). The impact of tenure insecurity may be reversed, however, if the act of making such investments actually increases tenure security (Otsuka 1998; Besley 1995).

Other factors conditioning such an investment response include agroecological conditions, the extent of commercialization, the extent of off-farm opportunities, the nature of local factor markets (especially for land, labor and credit), and poverty.

Agroecological conditions may have more effect on the types of investments that become economical than on whether land improvements eventually occur as population pressure increases. For example, in drier environments, live barriers may have difficulties in becoming established or may compete with crops for water, whereas physical structures such as stone or soil bunds may yield high benefits (Herweg 1993). In more humid environments, by contrast, such physical structures may be less effective than biological approaches.

Commercialization may have mixed effects on land improvements. On the one hand, it increases the value of land, but on the other it may also increase the value of labor. The net effect on the relative value of land to labor will determine whether commercialization promotes or inhibits labor-intensive land improvements. Similarly, commodity prices have ambiguous effects on land improvements and land degradation (LaFrance 1992; Pagiola 1996).

Off-farm opportunities likely increase the value of labor and thus tend to inhibit labor-intensive investments (Pender and Kerr 1998; Clay *et al.* 1998). On the other hand, off-farm income tends to increase farmers' liquidity and reduce their discount rates thus tending to promote investments, particularly where there is a functioning labor market (ibid.).

The existence of a land market may promote land improvements by reducing the irreversibility associated with such investments (since farmers would have the option to recoup some or all of the value of their investment by selling or leasing the land) (Pender and Kerr 1999). A land market and the ability to mortgage land may also promote investment by increasing farmers' access to credit (Feder *et al.* 1988; Pender and Kerr 1999). Credit constraints may cause farmers to have high discount rates, thus reducing incentives to invest in land improvements with high initial costs and limited near term benefit (Pender 1996; Holden *et al.* 1998).

Poverty may have the same effect of shortening farmers' time horizons (ibid.). On the other hand, poorer farmers may be more likely to invest in labor-intensive land improvement because the opportunity cost of their time is lower (Pender and Kerr 1998) or because they have fewer profitable alternative investment alternatives.

Such land improvements can be expected to eventually increase land and labor productivity (or they would not be voluntarily adopted by farmers). However, they may reduce production in the near term by displacing land that otherwise would have been used in production. Thus they may lead to reduced production per capita in the near term but higher production per capita in the longer term. They may also reduce farmers' ability to take advantage of off-farm employment opportunities, because of the labor required to construct and maintain them, thus reducing off-farm income. The distributional impacts of such investments depend mainly on who is able to benefit from them, as determined by the conditioning factors noted above. If poverty and credit constraints are major factors inhibiting such investment, then the distribution of income and wealth may become more unequal as a result of differences in investment between rich and poor. On the other hand, distribution may become more equal if poorer people are more able to make such investments because of the lower opportunity costs of their time.

The impacts of labor-intensive land improvements on resource conditions are likely positive in general, though this may not always be the case. Such investments can help to reduce erosion, reclaim degraded land, and reduce pressure on more marginal lands. By helping to reduce erosion, they may reduce the outflow of soil nutrients and give farmers greater incentive to use fertilizers, manure, or other means of improving soil fertility (to the extent that such investments and soil fertility measures are complementary). By helping to control run-off and conserve soil moisture, they can help to recharge groundwater aquifers, contribute to regeneration of vegetation, and reduce problems of flooding downstream. However, such investments can also contribute to problems such as accelerated run-off and downstream erosion if not properly planned or maintained. For example, investments in drainage from one farmer's fields may channel run-off into a neighbor's fields or accelerate the rate of flow downstream. Poorly constructed or maintained bunds or other barriers may concentrate water flows and lead to gully formation. Conversely, water-harvesting structures may increase the availability of water to farmers who have constructed them at the expense of downstream water users. Thus, achieving positive net social (as opposed to private) benefits of such investments may require collective action at the village level or higher, to assure that such externalities are taken into account.

2.5. *Adoption of Capital-Intensive Methods*

Population growth may stimulate adoption of capital-intensive methods of production as well, particularly those that are complementary to labor (i.e. their productivity is greater when combined with more labor input). This may include use of draft animals and farm equipment, and some types of purchased inputs. The factors conditioning these and their impacts may be different, so I consider them separately.

The use of draft animals and plows is likely after population density has reached a high enough level that forest or bush fallow are no longer practiced (Pingali *et al.* 1987). In these systems, the costs of removing tree stumps and maintenance of animals is high, relative to the costs of using fire and hand implements to prepare fields. Once the transition to grass fallow has occurred, the costs of using animals and plows are substantially reduced. At the same time, the value of manure as a source of soil fertility rises as fallow periods become shorter, and the availability of grass as a fodder source increases, so that the benefits of using animals rises. Another factor promoting increased use of animal power and plowing is increased use of bottomlands with heavy soils as a result of population pressure.

Other factors that condition the transition to animal draft power include climate and disease constraints, soil conditions, market access and the extent of commercialization, and the availability of credit. In humid tropical climates, adoption of draft animals is often prevented by tropical diseases, such as trypanosomiasis in humid Sub-Saharan Africa (McIntire *et al.* 1992). Adoption likely occurs earlier where the growing season is longer or irrigation is possible, allowing for greater capacity utilization of draft animals and equipment (Pingali *et al.* 1987). Adoption also likely occurs earlier where soils are heavier, as noted above. Where market access is good and prices of meat are attractive, the returns to raising animals for meat as well as draft power may promote earlier adoption (ibid.). Access to credit to finance animal purchases may also promote earlier adoption of draft animals and plows, where other factors assure that their use is profitable.

Adoption of draft animals and plowing does not necessarily increase land productivity, but it increases labor productivity by reducing labor requirements per unit of land (ibid.). If additional land is available or land can be used more intensively (e.g. through irrigation and multiple cropping), the increase in labor productivity can lead to an increase in agricultural output per capita. Agricultural output per capita may also rise if labor is able to migrate out of agriculture as a result of the labor savings. Even without an increase in production per capita of a given crop, the value of output per capita may rise if the labor savings enable farmers to shift into higher value crops which may require more labor and plowing. Per capita incomes may increase even without an increase in the value of per capita production, since labor saved may be employed in off-farm activities. Farmers' welfare may thus increase because of greater value of production, off-farm income, leisure, or a combination of the three. The distribution of welfare benefits may be quite unequal, however, depending upon differences in farmers' abilities to finance acquisition and maintenance of animals and implements, and in the amount of land they operate, which will determine the extent of capacity utilization.

After the initial benefits of adoption of draft animals and plows are realized, further intensification of their use resulting from further population growth is likely to eventually face diminishing returns (holding technology constant). Thus income and welfare per capita are not likely to continue to rise as population continues to grow, unless this induces technological or other changes as discussed below.

The impacts of adoption of draft animals and plowing on resource conditions are complex and mixed. Animal manure can contribute to soil fertility, though this may be merely recycling nutrients, if the animals are fed only crop residues and grass from farmers' own fields. To the extent that animals graze or are fed materials from outside the farm and their manure is kept on the farm, this represents a net addition to the fertility of the soil on the farm, though this may be at the expense of soil fertility on common grazing lands. As livestock populations grow, overuse of such common grazing lands may occur, particularly if their use is not adequately regulated, leading to declining productivity of the commons. Overgrazing can also cause serious problems of soil compaction and erosion. Plowing also can cause serious erosion problems, especially on sloping lands, if adequate measures are not used to prevent it. The demand for fodder for growing livestock herds may induce further deforestation to clear land for grazing. Increasing animal numbers also increases demands on available water supplies and can cause water pollution problems resulting from animal wastes. At the same time, the labor saving provided by use of draft animals can enable farmers to invest more effort in soil and water conservation measures; while the animals may contribute labor to such efforts as well.

Adoption of purchased inputs, such as chemical fertilizer, improved seeds, and pesticides may be influenced in complex ways by population growth. To the extent that such inputs are complementary to labor, one would expect population growth to promote their adoption. This may be the case with chemical fertilizer and improved seeds, though the evidence is not clear on these. Herbicides are more likely to be substitutes for labor, so one would not expect population growth to promote their use, unless population growth induces a change in farming system that favors their use. For example, the transition from forest to grass fallows and sedentary farming may favor adoption of herbicides, since they may be more cost effective than burning to control weeds in the latter types of situations. In addition, problems of weeds and pests may increase as agricultural intensification proceeds, as a result of declining soil fertility and diminished habitat for the natural predators of pests. Thus, even for inputs that are not complementary to labor, there may be an increase in demand for their use as population grows.

Farmers' incentive and ability to use purchased inputs in response to population growth are largely conditioned by the returns to and risks of such inputs (determined by agroclimatic factors, crop choice, and management practices) and the costs, accessibility, and ability to purchase these inputs (determined by market access, extent of commercialization, development of the input market, government policies, access to credit and/or off-farm income, and poverty). In drought-prone areas, use of chemical fertilizers can be very risky, unless adequate soil moisture can be assured through irrigation, water conservation, or other methods. Returns to use of such inputs will generally be higher with higher value or higher yielding crops. In addition, many such crops may be more susceptible to damage by insects or weeds than more traditional varieties, thus generating greater demand for pesticides. Commercial production of cash crops also facilitates access to the income needed to purchase such inputs. This is of course dependent upon access to markets, which also increases the availability and reduces the costs of inputs. Development of a competitive input market also facilitates use of inputs. Government policies, particularly those relating to foreign trade, exchange rates, input subsidies and distribution, and regulation of importers, wholesalers, and retailers of agricultural inputs, can have a large impact on the development of the input market and the availability and cost of such inputs. Farmers' access to credit and/or off-farm income may determine whether and how much they are able to purchase of inputs. Without sufficient access to credit (and even with it), poverty may prevent farmers from taking advantage of profitable opportunities to use inputs, due to financial constraints as well as extreme risk aversion.

The expected impact of such inputs, where adopted, is to increase land and/or labor productivity. To the extent that both are increased (e.g. by improved seeds and fertilizer), agricultural production per capita is likely to increase. Labor-saving inputs such as herbicides may not increase land productivity directly, though the labor saved may be used to increase land productivity by more intensive labor use in other crop activities. Use of purchased inputs may also enable production of higher value crops, thus increasing the value of output per capita. These effects will lead to increased average welfare per capita among farmers, compared to what would occur without adoption of such inputs. The distribution of the benefits may be very unequal, however, depending upon differential access to suitable land, markets, credit, and/or sufficient income to finance such purchases.

It should be emphasized that the increase in per capita income resulting from such capital intensification flows from the increase in capital used per farmer, and not from population growth itself. Improved access to markets and commercialization can induce adoption of such practices without rural population growth, and population growth reduces the amount of capital used per worker if production exhibits diminishing returns to scale (Pender 1998). Even in the case of constant returns to scale, a faster population growth leads to less steady-state capital intensity per worker than a slower growth rate (ibid.; Solow 1956). Thus population growth beyond the point which induces adoption of new capital-intensive technology is not expected to lead to welfare benefits (unless the technology exhibits increasing returns to scale), even though the adoption of such technology may yield welfare benefits.

The expected impacts of purchased inputs on natural resources are mixed. Increased use of chemical fertilizers can improve soil fertility, especially if used in conjunction with measures to preserve or restore soil organic matter (Sanchez *et al.* 1997). The use of such valuable inputs can also increase farmers' incentive to control soil erosion, lest such valuable inputs be washed away. The additional crop residue and other biomass made available through improved soil conditions (as well as improved seeds) may reduce the pressure on grazing lands and forests, by providing alternative sources of fodder and fuel. Additional fodder availability may in turn allow greater use of animals, which may further improve soil fertility through manure availability. Thus, such purchased inputs may help to catalyze a virtuous cycle of soil improvement and productivity enhancement. On the other hand, if farmers use purchased inputs as a substitute for efforts to improve soil conditions more generally, their use may only mask the effects of land degradation. In this case, the vicious cycle of land degradation, declining productivity, and poverty may continue unabated. In addition, increased use of agricultural chemicals (especially pesticides) without proper training and precautions can contribute to problems of water contamination, human health problems, species extinction, and other environmental problems.

2.6. *Knowledge Intensification*

Increasing the 'knowledge intensity' of agriculture, by invention of new production technologies or adaptation of existing techniques to new conditions, is another possible response to population pressure or other pressures. The induced technical innovation hypothesis (Hayami and Ruttan 1985) posits that technical innovation taking advantage of relatively abundant factors will be induced by changes in relative factor endowments. In much of the literature on induced technical innovation, innovation is seen as being supplied primarily by agricultural research organizations. However, farmers themselves may also be important sources of technical innovation (Boserup 1965, 1981; Richards 1985). For example, population growth may induce farmers to invent or adapt labor- (and knowledge-) intensive methods, such as new indigenous soil and water conservation measures, new organic soil fertility management practice, or integrated pest management approaches. It is difficult to draw a clear distinction between knowledge intensification and simple changes in factor intensity, since many changes in labor or capital intensity involve a strong element of adaptation and learning by doing. Similarly, changes in product choice or occupation (discussed below) also involve learning and adaptation, and thus some degree of knowledge intensification.

Although the distinction between induced technical change and simple changes in factor proportions is difficult to draw in many practical situations, the conceptual distinction is important. In the absence of some learning or invention, constant or diminishing returns to scale in agriculture will imply that labor and capital intensification will be insufficient to improve human welfare as population grows (Pender 1998). However, the non-rival nature of new knowledge, and positive externalities associated with investments in human capital and learning by doing, can cause increasing returns to scale, providing the basis for sustainable long-term growth in incomes and welfare per capita (Romer 1990; Lucas 1988; Arrow 1962). If there are increasing returns to scale, population growth may contribute to more rapid technical change and welfare improvement if it enables economies of scale and specialization to be realized.[2] For example, the per capita costs of inventing a new method of production will decline with population growth, since the total costs of such invention are likely unaffected by population growth. If mechanisms are in place (or are induced to develop) to share such costs or internalize the external benefits among a growing population, technical innovation is likely to occur simply because the per capita costs are declining.

Whether population growth does in fact lead to technical innovation thus depends critically upon whether institutional or organizational mechanisms exist to allow such economies of scale and positive externalities to be realized. One way to do this is by taxing people to pay for the costs of agricultural research or experimentation. This is of course an important response at the national or state level, but is likely limited at the local level. Sharing costs and risks of innovation at the local level may occur through local farmer organizations, such as community mutual support groups or savings and credit groups that serve to pool risks. Another approach is to compensate farmer innovators for some or all of the external benefits that arise from innovations. For many kinds of innovation in developed countries, this is done by assigning intellectual property rights (e.g. parents and copyrights). However, such formal mechanisms likely are of limited applicability to most of the subtle and often site-specific innovations that farmers in developing countries generate, and the transaction costs of such formal approaches are likely prohibitive. But less formal mechanisms to reward innovators may be quite important, such as providing them greater status in the community, prizes through local production contests, and so on. Many factors affect the prospects for such institutional or organizational development. These factors are considered below in the discussion of collective responses.

[2] Recall Adam Smith's famous dictum: 'The division of labor is limited by the extent of the market'.

The impacts of knowledge intensification in agriculture for agricultural productivity and human welfare are expected to be positive. Total factor productivity is expected to increase, so that the average productivity of labor, land, and capital may all increase. This can increase income per capita directly as well as by promoting greater investment in land and/or capital (since returns to investment will increase). The distribution of benefits will depend upon how (and how much) innovators are compensated, how widely knowledge of the innovation spreads, and how applicable the innovation is to different farmers' circumstances. Where innovators are compensated more through status or other non-economic mechanisms, where information is widely available, and where the innovation is applicable to a wide range of circumstances, the economic benefits of innovation will be more widely distributed.

The impacts of innovation on resource conditions will depend of course on the nature of the innovation as well as other factors, and may be mixed. For example, development of a new technology that increases the profitability of farming may reduce pressure on forests if the technology is more suited to labor-intensive production than to extensive production, if the elasticity of demand for food is low and the technology increases food production, or if labor supply is relatively inelastic (Angelsen and Kaimowitz 1998). Conversely, if the technology reduces the cost of clearing forests or if factor supplies and output demand are elastic, the increased profitability of farming may lead to increased deforestation. To the extent that innovations are induced by factor scarcity, one would expect population growth to result in labor-using, land-saving innovations, which should promote land improvement. Soil fertility should therefore tend to be enchanced and soil erosion reduced by population-induced innovation. However, as mentioned earlier, such land improvements will depend critically upon the security of land tenure, and on other factors such as local agroecological conditions and the extent of commercialization. Since scarcity of other resources such as water also increases with population growth, induced innovation is likely to emphasize conservation or improvement of water supplies as well.

2.7. *Changes in Product Mix*

Population growth may also induce changes in the mix of products produced by farmers. Increases in labor to land ratios make adoption of products requiring greater labor intensity and producing higher returns per unit of land likely. At lower levels of population density, population growth may induce a change from extensive livestock or cereal production to integrated crop-livestock systems that use labor more intensively and take advantage of complementarities between crop and livestock production (McIntire *et al.* 1992). At higher levels of population density, further population growth may induce a return to specialization as a result of increasing competition between crops and livestock for land and water, and development of infrastructure and markets making specialization more profitable (ibid.). Adoption of highly labor-intensive crops, such as rice or vegetables under irrigated conditions, may enable much fuller utilization of available land but leave less land or labor available for the maintenance of livestock (except perhaps draft animals). On the other hand, intensive livestock operations, such as commercial dairy or poultry operations, may develop in areas close to urban markets as population density rises to high levels.

Many of the factors conditioning the transition from specialized extensive crop or livestock production to integrated crop-livestock systems were discussed above, in discussing adoption of draft animals. Topography, soils, climate conditions, and the extent of infrastructure and market development condition the comparative advantage of specialized crop or livestock production relative to integrated systems. Where topographic and/or soil conditions are not well suited to plowing (e.g. on steep slopes), adoption of draft animals may be limited. Good access to roads and urban markets, or significant local variations in comparative advantage, will favor continued specialization and trade as population grows, particularly at higher population densities where problems of competition between crops and livestock become more severe. The transition to intensive irrigated crops of course depends upon the potential for irrigation as well as the availability of inputs such as fertilizer, seeds and pesticides, access to credit, and access to markets (particularly for perishable crops such as vegetables). Development of commercial dairy or poultry production depends upon the availability of low-cost feed, as well as close proximity to markets. Particularly with perishable products such as milk or vegetables, development of organizations (such as cooperatives) or institutional mechanisms (such as contract farming) to ensure access to inputs and credit, an assured market for sellers, and quality control for buyers, may be very important.

As with adoption of more labor-intensive methods of production, adoption of more labor-intensive products can be expected to increase the value of output per unit of land, but may be associated with reduced value per unit of labor input, unless some element of learning or technological change is associated with the change in product mix. Where shifts in product mix are brought about by new opportunities, such as new technology, development of infrastructure, or expansion of markets for high-value products, increases in the value of labor as well as land are likely. Only in such cases can one expect the shift in product mix to improve incomes per capita and welfare, and population growth will be responsible for the improvement only to the extent that it led to the expansion of such opportunities.

The impacts of changes in product mix on resources can be complex. The adoption of more labor-intensive products can be expected to reduce pressure on forests or other marginal lands, as long as the supply of labor is not perfectly elastic. Adoption of such products may involve better management of land in some respects. For example, investments in soil and water-conservation structures may be promoted by adoption of irrigated crops (Pender and Kerr 1998). On the other hand, continuous multiple cropping of such crops may create problems for soil fertility and structure, while frequent plowing may cause problems of severe soil erosion. Problems of soil fertility and structure may be aggravated as integrated crop-livestock systems are replaced by specialized crop production at high population density, since reduced availability of manure may reduce soil organic matter and nutrients. Farmers may compensate for reduced manure by using chemical fertilizers, but this may not address the problems associated with low soil organic matter. Increased use of fertilizers and pesticides in such intensive crop systems also may cause water quality and health problems, as mentioned previously.

2.8. *Changes in Occupation and Migration*

Declining land availability and labor productivity resulting from population growth may induce people to seek alternative sources of income. At the same time, development of infrastructure and markets, and the process of agricultural intensification itself may create new opportunities for non-farm employment. For example, adoption of plows or other implements will generate demand for tool makers. Opportunities for specialization and trade will increase as the size of the potential market grows, as originally argued by Adam Smith. While many opportunities may develop within rural communities, a large share of the new opportunities will likely occur in developing urban centers, facilitating rural to urban migration.

Key factors influencing this response include education and training opportunities, labor mobility, land tenure security, land and housing markets, the development of infrastructure, the pace of investment and growth in the industrial sector of the economy, the presence of social services in the urban sector, and poverty. Education and training are obviously important for more skilled occupations. Labor mobility is of course necessary for rural people to take advantage of non-farm employment opportunities in urban areas. Such mobility may be inhibited by explicit policies to restrict migration (e.g. requirements of residence permits), but may also be retarded by the absence of housing in urban areas, land tenure insecurity that may arise by leaving the rural area, limited ability to sell or lease out farmland, poor living conditions and social services in urban areas, or the risks associated with migration, which may be very high for very poor people. Many of these factors may cut the other way, however. Displaced people from rural areas may find it easier to establish squatters' rights in urban shanty towns than in less anonymous rural communities. Poverty and desperation may drive people to such areas, despite the risks. Urban-biased policies, better social services, and/or higher wages in urban areas may attract migrants to urban areas, even if unemployment is greater there (Lipton 1977; Harris and Todaro 1970).

Movement of labor out of agriculture and into other occupations can have positive impacts on productivity in agriculture. By reducing the stock of labor in agriculture, average productivity of the labor (but not of land) remaining in agriculture should increase, unless surplus labor exists in the agriculture sector (Lewis 1954). To the extent that labor shifts into other occupations with productive linkages to agriculture (such as supplying tools or production inputs), this can also contribute to productivity improvement. By increasing off-farm demand for food and other agricultural products, migration out of agriculture can stimulate market development and increase relative prices of agricultural products, promoting investment in farm improvement. Off-farm employment by rural residents or by family members in urban areas can provide a source of income and savings to finance purchase of inputs or investments in agriculture (Reardon *et al.* 1994). These effects are expected to contribute to increased per capita incomes and generally increased welfare in rural areas. Distributional impacts will favor those with less or no land, since wages will tend to rise relative to land rents as a result of employment of labor outside agriculture.

There can also be negative impacts on agriculture and resource management as well. As off-farm opportunities and rural wages increase, labor-intensive investments in land management and improvement become less attractive, and even existing investments may be less well maintained.[3] As a result, existing systems of production may become unsustainable, and a process of agricultural dis-intensification may occur (Goldman 1995). The qualitative impacts of this on natural resource conditions may be the opposite of the impacts of agricultural intensification (both positive and negative). For example, labor-intensive methods of soil fertility management (such as composting or mulching) may be abandoned and soil and water conservation structures may not be maintained, contributing to reduced soil fertility and increased erosion in the near term. However, if dis-intensification leads to a return to longer-term fallows, it may result in regeneration of soil fertility and woody vegetation in the longer term. The point, well articulated by Goldman (ibid.), is that changes in population density may change what constitutes sustainable agricultural practices. Once agricultural systems and practices adjust to the new circumstances, the system may again become sustainable, although substantial resource degradation may occur during the transition from one system to another.

2.9. *Changes in household fertility decisions*

The final household-level response to population growth that I consider is change in household fertility decisions.[4] According to the modern economic theory of fertility decisions, fertility is determined by the interaction of demand and supply factors. Households' demand for children is influenced by the costs of raising, caring for, and educating children; the economic benefits that they may provide for the household over their lifetime (including their contribution to household income and providing old-age security for parents); and of course the non-economic benefits or costs that people associate with children (Becker and Lewis 1973; Schultz 1981). The supply of children is influenced by biological factors that may be influenced by the nutrition and health of women (Easterlin 1980).

Population growth may have effects on both demand and supply factors, many of which suggest that population growth should induce declining fertility. If population

[3] The effect of increased wages on land investment may be offset by the liquidity-enhancing effect of off-farm income, which may enable farmers with off-farm income to hire workers to make investments (Pender and Kerr 1998; Clay *et al.* 1998).

[4] I do not consider mortality rates to be a choice variable for households, but rather something they try to minimize. Thus mortality rates may respond to population growth, as originally argued by Malthus, but are not properly considered a household behavioral response.

growth results in lower wages and less available open-access resources that can be readily exploited, the benefits of having many children may tend to decrease. As resource
and food supplies become scarce, the costs of raising children are also increased. If
population growth is a result of declining child mortality, parents will find that they
need to have fewer children to ensure that some will survive, be productive, and contribute to their old-age security, and may decide to substitute 'quality' for 'quantity'
(Becker and Lewis 1973). To the extent that population growth increases poverty and
reduces the nutrition and health of women, this may also induce declining fertility for
biological reasons (Easterlin 1980). Furthermore, if children are seen as an investment
with near-term costs and long-term benefits, population-induced poverty may reduce
fertility by increasing the discount rate and shortening households' time horizon.

However, there are many factors that may cause fertility rates not to decline as a
response to population growth. Continuing poverty may cause parents to continue
to desire a large number of children to ensure their old-age security, even if child
mortality rates fall. Children may be seen as more productive assets in farming than in
other occupations; thus the demand for children may remain high as long as farming
is the dominant activity of households. Agricultural intensification and technical
change may increase the productive benefit of having children and thus slow the
decline in fertility (Vosti *et al.* 1994). Low education levels and status of women may
continue to foster early marriage and childbearing. Lack of information or access
to family-planning options may limit the ability of households to convert a decline
in demand for children to a decline in fertility. Religious and cultural norms about
family size, land inheritance rules, and other sociocultural factors may also inhibit a
fertility response (ibid.).

To the extent that a decline in fertility occurs as a result of population growth, this
will tend to mitigate any of the impacts of increased population size discussed above.
An additional effect is to change the age distribution of the population.[5] In the near
term, a decline in fertility will reduce the dependency ratio, leading to increased production and welfare per capita. This will increase households' ability to save and invest,
which also contributes to growth in income and welfare per capita. This increase in
income and savings per capita will help to ensure the old-age security of parents, and
will be needed since they will have fewer children in the working population as a result
of declining fertility. To the extent that parents invest in greater quality of education
and health care of their children as a result of substituting 'quality for quantity', there
may be an intergenerational transfer of wealth from parents to children.

The impacts of the changing age structure following a decline in fertility on
resources are likely to be generally positive, though there may be negative impacts as
well. By enabling greater investment, this will encourage investment (per capita) in
improved natural resources as well as other forms of capital, particularly if different
forms of capital are complementary (Pender 1998). Increased wealth per capita may

---

[5] The impact on age structure of an acceleration in population growth caused by a decline in mortality
at the beginning of a demographic transition is just the reverse of the impact of a decline in fertility. The
impacts of such a change in age structure will thus be the opposite of those considered here.

reduce households' discount rates and increase their access to credit, and thus also promote investment in resources (Pender 1996). Increased investment in children's education may lead to a greater awareness of resource and environmental problems. On the other hand, increased wealth and education may cause people to have higher opportunity costs of labor and better alternative investment opportunities than to invest in land or other resource improvement. The positive effects of the changing age structure and dependency ratio on investment in resource improvement may be offset by increasing wages, which will reduce incentives to make labor-intensive investments. Thus, as with most other responses, the predicted impacts of fertility decline on resource conditions are mixed.

3. COLLECTIVE RESPONSES TO RURAL POPULATION GROWTH

The responses to population growth that may occur at a community or higher level include investments in infrastructure, changes in collective action to manage resources (e.g. management of common property resources), changes in institutions (e.g. property rights and land tenure arrangements, development of markets), and changes in organization and social roles (e.g. establishment of organizations to protect common resources or achieve economies of scale in marketing). Our hypotheses about these responses are summarized in Table 12.2.

3.1. *Investments in Infrastructure*

Investments in rural infrastructure may be promoted by population growth. The costs of infrastructure such as roads, irrigation systems, and electricity networks are largely fixed costs, so that the costs per capita decline as population grows (Boserup 1965). As with technical innovation (discussed previously), the ability to take advantage of such economies of scale will depend critically upon the development of institutions and organizations. Thus, the development of cost-sharing mechanisms, such as a tax system or collective investment in infrastructure development, is needed. The potential for local collective action to achieve these scale economies is of course much greater for investments that do not require much technical input or sophisticated capital (e.g. construction of rural feeder roads or hand-dug wells). A functioning system of public finance will be necessary to finance more technological and/or capital-intensive projects such as large dams and electricity networks. The factors determining such institutional and organizational development (discussed below) are thus critical.

Infrastructure development (particularly roads and irrigation) can have large positive impacts on agricultural productivity and rural incomes by increasing access to and reducing costs of inputs, increasing farm-level prices of outputs, providing access to irrigation water, enabling production of higher value perishable products, improving access to technical assistance and education, increasing specialization and trade, and increasing off-farm employment opportunities. Thus, rural welfare will tend to increase in general, though there may be adverse distributional impacts. Households with land displaced by road or irrigation projects may not be adequately compensated. Construction of irrigation projects may increase access to water for upstream users at the expense of downstream users. Differential access to roads or irrigation may increase the inequality of income, and promote acquisition of land or other resources by advantaged farmers at the expense of poorer ones. The extent to which such negative impacts arise and are compensated depends upon the nature of the process used to decide on, plan, and implement them. The more the process includes potentially affected people, the more likely that negative distributional impacts can be avoided. There may be a trade-off, however, between avoiding negative distributional impacts and achieving aggregate social gains, since transaction costs, imperfect information, and incentive problems may limit the ability to identify and adequately compensate losers.

The impacts of infrastructure development on resource conditions may be very mixed. Where roads or other infrastructure are established near forest areas, they may promote deforestation if open-access land exists, farmers are acting as profit maximizers, immigration is relatively easy, and the elasticity of demand for the agricultural products from these areas is high (Angelsen 1999). On the other hand, if farmers are subsistence oriented, labor is locally constrained, or the elasticity of demand for agricultural production is low, increased production made possible by increased access to roads or irrigation may cause farmers to intensify production on a smaller area of land, thus reducing pressure on forests or marginal lands (ibid.). The increased value of land caused by infrastructure development will tend to promote labor-intensive investment in land conservation and improvement if land values rise more than wages. It will also tend to promote greater capital intensity, unless improved market access increases people's investment opportunities elsewhere to a greater extent than locally. Knowledge intensity in agriculture is also likely to increase as a result of improved access to markets, information, technical assistance, and education. Increases in labor, capital and knowledge intensity and shifts in product mix and occupations brought about by infrastructural development can have both positive and negative impacts on resources and the environment, as discussed earlier.

3.2. *Changes in Collective Action*

Population growth may cause changes in collective action related to natural resources at the community or other levels. At very low levels of population density, the relative abundance of land and other resources may require little action (whether collective or private) to manage resources. As population grows, increasing scarcity increases the potential rents that can be achieved by protecting and intensively managing land and other resources. At the same time, the costs of organizing may fall as population density grows from low levels, as people begin to live closer together (Templeton and Scherr 1997).[6] Economies of scale in protecting resources at a collective rather than

---

[6] If wages fall as a result of declining labor productivity resulting from population growth, this will also tend to reduce the costs of organizing.

Table 12.2. *Hypotheses about Collective Responses to Rural Population Growth*

Response	Conditioning factors	Productivity		Human welfare			Natural resource conditions			
		Land	Labor	Income per capita	Welfare per capita	Distribution of welfare	Forest	Soil erosion	Soil fertility	Water
Investments in infrastructure	Growing population (reduced per capita costs)	+	+	+	+	+/−	+/−	+/−	+/−	+/−
	Mechanisms to share costs (collective action, institutional and/or organizational development)									
Collective action to manage resources	Moderate population density (economies of scale in protection, diseconomies in collective management)	+/−	+/−	+	+	+/−	+/−	+/−	+/−	+/−
	Moderate population growth (stability of resource users group)									
	Extent of externalities									
	Transaction costs of private bargaining									
	Number and heterogeneity of resource users									
	Geographic and social proximity of users									
	Time horizons of users									
	Risks and risk aversion									
	Norms of cooperation or equity									
	Presence of organizations									

Institutional change	Changes in factor scarcity (induced institutional innovation)	+/−	+/−	+/−	+/−	+/−	+/−	+
	Changes in technology /opportunities							
	Private costs and benefits of political entrepeneurs, powerful groups							
	Collective action and organizational change							
	Cultural factors (e.g. norms of equity, cooperation, religion, ideology)							
	Education							
Organizational change	Similar to factors affecting collective action and institutional change	+/−	+/−	+/−	+/−	+/−	+/−	+

private level may outweigh incentive problems associated with collective (relative to private) management at low to moderate levels of population density, particularly since management and investment requirements may be fairly limited when intensity of resource use is still relatively low. Thus establishment of common property resources with collective protection and management may become the optimal strategy for managing scarce resources as population density grows to moderate levels.

As population density grows to high levels, the benefits and costs of collective action relative to private action may begin to change. The beneficial effect of increasing population density in reducing organizational costs will decline in importance where people already live in close proximity. At the same time, the need to organize larger numbers of people and the increasing scarcity of resources will make attaining collective action more difficult, since the costs of monitoring and enforcement and the benefits of violating collective restrictions on resource use will be rising. As resource management and investment requirements become greater with increasing use intensity, the incentive problems associated with collective (relative to private) management will increase. Eventually, the net benefits of private management will exceed the benefits of collective management as population grows, promoting a shift in management systems. This shift may occur without a shift to private property—economies of scale in resource protection may favor keeping resources under communal ownership, even though they may be privately managed.

As management decisions become increasingly private in nature, externalities caused by private management decisions of households (e.g. impacts of irrigation or drainage investments by upstream farmers on downstream farmers) may still require some form of collective action, unless transactions costs are sufficiently low that bargaining between rights holders to resolve the externalities is feasible (Coase 1960). The transactions costs of such an approach may be prohibitive for externalities that affect large numbers of people, and such externalities may proliferate as population density and intensive land management increases. Thus, collective action may evolve from collective protection and management of resources toward regulating or taxing specific types of negative externalities or promoting specific community-level investments that generate positive externalities (e.g. community watershed management investments).

The ability to attain collective action in managing resources may depend upon many factors, including the nature of the resource, the nature of the uses of the resource, the nature of the users of the resource, and the existing institutional and organizational strucure within the community (Ostrom 1990; Rasmussen and Meinzen-Dick 1995). Collective resource management is more likely to arise and be effective where costs of exclusion are lower but economies of scale in exclusion exist (thus inhibiting privatization); where the benefits of cooperation relative to non-cooperation are greater; where there are fewer users; where the interests of users are more homogeneous,[7] where membership in the users group is less open and more stable; where users are

---

[7] Note that homogeneity of wealth does not necessarily imply homogeneity of interests, and wealth heterogeneity may favor collective action (Olson 1965; Baland and Platteau 1996).

closer to one another physically and socially; where users have longer time horizons; where risks and risk aversion increase the benefits of pooling risks; where norms of cooperation and/or equity exist among users; or where there already exist cooperative organizations upon which efforts to attain collective action can build (ibid.; Baland and Platteau 1996).

Population growth may promote collective action through its effects on many of these factors. It may reduce the per capita costs of protection of the resource, if there are economies of scale in this. It tends to increase the benefits of cooperation, since it increases the scarcity rents achievable by good management. It may increase the geographic and social proximity of resource users by increasing population density.

On the other hand, population growth also may detract from collective action for many reasons. Since it increases resource rents, it also increases the benefits to be gained by cheating on collective agreements. It increases the number of resource users and perhaps their diversity of interests. It reduces the stability of membership of the users group, particularly if population growth is rapid and/or there is significant immigration or emigration from the community. Related to this, population growth may also undermine group stability and incentives to cooperate to the extent that it promotes infrastructure and market development. To the extent that population growth increases poverty, it may cause people to have higher discount rates and shorter time horizons. Increasing scarcity and rapid population change may erode norms of cooperation and equity, particularly where migration and commercialization are substantial.

As I have argued above, the balance of these factors is expected to weigh in favor of collective action at moderate levels of population density and growth. However, at very high levels of population density or growth, the factors tending to undermine collective action appear likely to dominate. Thus, we may observe an inverted U-shaped relationship between population density or population growth and collective action for resource management.

To the extent that collective action for natural resource management follows from increased demands generated by population growth, it will tend to promote greater welfare and improved resource conditions for the members of the collective, although this may involve some near-term sacrifice on the part of individuals for the sake of greater collective gains. However, there may be adverse distributional impacts on weaker members of the collective groups, or on outsiders. For example, collective grazing restrictions may be established that allow farmers to cut and carry fodder grasses to feed draft animals, but limit access of goats and sheep to grazing areas. Such restrictions may benefit the wealthier members of the community at the expense of poorer ones, who may own fewer draft animals and may be more dependent upon small ruminants for their livelihoods. There can also be adverse impacts on resources outside of those collectively managed. For example, establishment of a protected grazing area as mentioned above may increase grazing pressure on unprotected areas. Thus collective action may displace rather than solve resource management and poverty problems, unless the action is sufficiently encompassing of affected groups and resources.

3.3. *Institutional Change*

Closely related to the development of collective action is the prospect of institutional change, particularly regarding changes in property rights and land tenure relations. As population pressure and intensity of land use increase, the demand for more secure rights to specific pieces of land or other resources will increase (Boserup 1965; Demsetz 1967; Ault and Rutman 1979; Binswanger and McIntire 1987; Platteau 1996). This demand may be accommodated within customary land tenure systems by allowing households long-term use and inheritance rights to specific resources. As relative factor scarcities change, the demand for land and other factor transactions may increase. Land leasing and sharecropping may arise, allowing more efficient use of available factors of production, which may differ across households. Where capital intensification is occurring, increased demand for credit will increase the demand to be able to mortgage land. Customary rights to mortgage or even sell land may evolve (Platteau 1996). In short, customary land rights may evolve from communal to more private forms. This evolution may proceed without external intervention, although it is often assumed that formal land-titling arrangements are necessary for this process to occur (ibid.).

The demand for other forms of institutional innovation is likely to increase as population grows as well. In addition to land markets, other markets are also likely to arise. Markets for labor are likely to develop as increasing land scarcity causes land-poor households to seek employment elsewhere, whether on other farms or in off-farm activities (particularly where land quantity or quality are unevenly distributed). Markets for capital inputs, such as draft animals, farm equipment, and purchased inputs, are also likely to develop as the demand for such inputs develops. The demand for credit services will also increase as the use of capital inputs increases. As labor moves out of agriculture and into other activities, increased trade in food and other agricultural products will be needed, promoting development of product markets. To the extent that population growth promotes investment in transportation infrastructure, this will also help to promote commercialization and market development.

The demand for non-market institutions may also rise as population grows (Hayami and Ruttan 1985). For example, the demand for regulation of the use of resources is likely to increase as population pressure increases externality costs. The demand for institutions to share the costs of infrastructure investment, which will be declining on a per capita basis as population grows, will also increase. Similarly, the demand for institutions to share the costs of agricultural innovation or internalize some of the positive externalities resulting from innovation will also be growing as population grows.

Many factors condition whether the supply of institutional innovation is consistent with the changing demand (ibid.). Where political entrepreneurship is needed to bring about institutional change, the factors influencing the private costs, benefits, and risks faced by such entrepreneurs are likely to be critical. The relative power of particular interest groups may prevent institutional changes from occurring, even if their potential net social benefits may be very high. For example, a shift from communal to private property rights may be prevented by a village chief, whose power and status would be reduced by losing the ability to allocate land rights. Conversely, 'rent-seeking' forms of institutional innovation may occur where these serve the interests of powerful groups, despite the fact that they may not promote greater welfare in general. It has been argued that land-titling efforts are sometimes of this nature, providing an opportunity for well-connected elites to claim land used by weaker or less well-informed households (Platteau 1996).

Cultural factors may also have a strong impact on the supply of institutional innovation (Hayami and Ruttan 1985). For example, cultures which foster strong norms of cooperation and reciprocity are likely to find it easier than other cultures to develop institutions to share the costs of infrastructural development or innovation. On the other hand, strong egalitarian norms may cause animosity toward complete privatization of property rights, particularly the elimination of common lands available to the poorest people, or the alienation of an individual's right to land through sale or foreclosure on a mortgage (Platteau 1996). Education may also have a strong influence on the receptivity of people to institutional innovation, and on the likelihood that the innovations that come about are efficiency improving (Hayami and Ruttan 1985).

Clearly there is much more to institutional change than a simple response to changes in net social benefits. Much of the challenge in understanding modern economic history is in understanding why institutional innovations that promote greater efficiency and economic development are adopted in some circumstances while seemingly inefficient institutions persist over very long periods in others (North 1990). The role of differential power relations, cultural factors, education, and other location-specific conditioning factors may explain a large fraction of the variance in outcomes. But North also pointed to the nature of the process of institutional innovation itself as a source of divergence. Institutions condition the nature of expectations and the range of permissible activities, and those expectations and activities may reinforce the strength of the institutions. Thus institutional change may be a self-reinforcing process characterized by multiple equilibrium outcomes and path dependency (ibid.). Even small differences in initial conditions between different societies may lead to large and persistent differences in their pathways of institutional change. Thus, for example, the pressure of population growth may lead to a smooth transition from common property to private property in some circumstances, while in others the pressure may cause a breakdown in the common property system leading toward unregulated open access. Differences in people's initial expectations about the path that development may take and their assurance that others will respect property rights may account for the differential outcomes. The differences in impacts on natural resource conditions and human welfare between these different scenarios may be very extreme.

In general, the impacts of institutional change for welfare and resource conditions will occur via its impacts on the conditioning factors affecting all of the previous responses considered. Thus, for example, development of more private and secure property rights will inhibit extensification, favor investments in land improvements, promote use of inputs (to the extent that private land rights promote access to credit), and perhaps facilitate migration and changes in occupations. The expected impacts of all of these changes on human welfare and resource conditions are, as we have seen, diverse. In general, however, to the extent that institutional innovation is responding to changes in net social (as opposed to private) benefits, it will lead to increases in general welfare, although there may be adverse distributional consequences.

3.4. *Organizational Change*

Also closely related to collective action and institutional change is organizational change, which may also be stimulated by population growth. Following Uphoff (1986), I distinguish organizations, defined as 'structures of recognized and accepted roles' from institutions, defined as 'complexes of norms and behaviors that persist over time'. One may see the roles established in organizations as largely determined by the nature of institutions and technology, since these will tend to define the set of possible roles that may be served by organizational structures and the costs and returns of alternative structures. However, technological and institutional change may also be affected by organizational change. For example, establishment of farmers' cooperatives may reduce the costs or increase the benefits of extending new technologies and thus promote greater technical innovation. The presence of cooperatives may also facilitate institutional innovation; for example, they may facilitate collective action needed to establish effective regulation of externalities caused by private farming practices.

Population growth is expected to affect organizational development for most of the same reasons that it may affect collective action and institutional development. Since organizational development requires collective action, the factors affecting collective action are also relevant for organizational development. Factors favoring collective action, such as the homogeneity of interests of the members, the stability of the group, proximity of the members, the ability to exclude outsiders, and so on, will also tend to favor organizational development by reducing the costs of such development. The demand for new types of organizations serving different functions will also tend to increase as population grows and new economic roles are required. For example, increased use of capital inputs in agriculture may promote not only new institutions such as mortgageable land and markets for such inputs, but it also requires new organizations such as rural banks and input wholesalers and traders.

As with institutional development, organizational development may be affected by power relations, cultural and other factors, and may be subject to path dependency as well. Also, organizational development may not be socially beneficial even where it benefits the members, since organizations may arise to serve rent-seeking motives rather than efficiency enhancement (Olson 1982). Thus the impacts of organizational development on welfare and natural resources may be quite diverse. Organizations such as water- or pasture-users groups may improve the management of common property resources for the benefit of all. On the other hand, such groups may be dominated by powerful elites who use the organization as a way of capturing rents for themselves at the expense of other members or those who may be excluded from the group. As with institutional development, organizational development will improve social welfare to the extent that it responds to efficiency motives, although there may be adverse distributional implications.

3.5. *Summary*

To summarize the hypotheses, I have argued that population growth may stimulate a wide variety of responses at the household and collective level. Many of these responses are strongly conditioned by the nature of technology, infrastructure, institutions, and organizations. In the absence of development of these factors, population growth is likely to lead to declining labor productivity and human welfare, as a result of diminishing returns. The expected impacts on resource conditions are more mixed and dependent upon the conditioning factors, with population growth inducing agricultural extensification and deforestation in low population density settings with open access land available, but promoting labor-intensive investments in land improvement at higher population densities where land tenure is secure.

The larger impacts of population growth in the long term may be via its impacts on development of technology, infrastructure, institutions, and organizations. As emphasized in the literature on induced innovation, population growth may reduce the per capita costs and increase the benefits of innovations in these different areas, leading to welfare and resource-improving changes. However, the supply of such innovations and their impacts may be very dependent upon the distribution of wealth and power, cultural factors, education, and other context-specific conditions, and these developments may be subject to a substantial degree of path dependency. Thus, very large differences in the impacts of population growth for agricultural productivity, human welfare, and natural resource conditions may occur in communities and households embarked upon different pathways of development. Much of the challenge of empirical policy research on these issues is to identify the factors that lead to different pathways of institutional and technological change, and policy interventions that may help more productive, welfare-enhancing and resource-improving pathways to evolve.

Given the importance of so many complex and site-specific conditioning factors and the possibility of path dependence in responses, the impacts of rural population pressure may be very different in different contexts. I now consider evidence of such impacts in the context of the hillsides of central Honduras.

4. EVIDENCE FROM CENTRAL HONDURAS

Recent research conducted by IFPRI in hillside communities of central Honduras provides evidence on some of the hypotheses discussed above.[8]

---

[8] This section is based on Pender, Scherr, and Durón (1999) and Pender and Scherr (1999).

4.1. *Methods*

The evidence is based on a survey of 48 villages in the central region of Honduras, selected through a random sample stratified by population density and distance to the dominant market in the region (Tegucigalpa). The survey collected information about changes in agriculture and natural resource management between 1975 and 1996, and about the causes and effects of those changes. The survey included a group questionnaire and participatory mapping of community boundaries and resources, augmented by analysis of available aerial photographs, maps, and village-level data from the 1974 and 1988 population censuses.

Econometric analysis was used to identify the factors influencing changes in agriculture and natural resource management, and the impacts of those factors on indicators of changes in outcomes, including agricultural productivity, poverty, and natural resource conditions. The response variables analyzed included (among others) indicators of agricultural extensification (change in forest area between 1975 and 1996), change in fallow use, labor intensification (change in use of burning, use of various soil fertility management practices in 1996), labor-intensive land investments since 1975 (terraces, live barriers, stone walls, tree planting), capital intensification (change in use of oxen, plows, and purchased inputs), change in product mix or occupation (classification of communities by 'development pathway', based on information on occupation and product mix),[9] collective action (whether or not the community had invested collectively in improving common lands or controlling run-off), and local organizational development (number of local organizations). The outcome variables analyzed included indicators of land and labor productivity (levels and changes in maize yields and wages), poverty (levels and changes in percentage of households with a dirt floor and percentage of households whose last child had died), and natural resource conditions (land use on steep lands and perceived changes in crop-land quality, forest quality, water availability, and water quality).

The econometric model used was determined by the nature of the dependent variable. In most cases, the dependent variables were measured as ordinal variables, either representing a change between 1975 and 1996 (e.g. whether use of a particular practice had increased, stayed the same, or declined; whether the condition of a particular type of resource had improved, stayed the same, or degraded) or the condition of the variable in 1996 (e.g. an ordinal index representing the extent of adoption of particular conservation measures, ranging from 0 (no one uses) to 6 (everyone uses)). Ordered probit analysis was used to analyze the factors affecting such dependent variables. In some cases (e.g. changes in wages and indicators of poverty), the dependent variables

---

[9] Six development pathways were identified based on information on change in occupation and product choice, including (1) expansion of basic grains production, (2) stagnation of basic grains production, (3) adoption and expansion of horticultural production, (4) expansion of coffee production, (5) specialization in forestry, and (6) high and increasing importance of non-farm employment. Basic grains production was important in all of the surveyed communities; communities were distinguished more by the other occupations/product choices. See Pender, Scherr, and Durón (1999) for more details on the classification of communities by development pathway.

were measured as continuous variables, and least squares estimation was used. In one case (collective action) the dependent variable was measured as a binary discrete choice; binary probit analysis was used in this case. In one other case (pathway of development), the dependent variable is a choice among several discrete outcomes, and multinomial logit analysis was used.

The variables used to explain determinants of development pathways included factors affecting agricultural potential (altitude and number of rainfall days), population density, access to markets (distance to the urban market and to the nearest road), and access to technology (presence of a technical assistance program since 1975). The variables used to explain changes in household agricultural practices and changes in outcomes included the development pathways, change in population density, whether road access had improved or stayed the same since 1975, change in the adult literacy rate between 1974 and 1988, and the presence of various types of agricultural programs (technical assistance, credit, agrarian reform, or land titling) since 1975. The specification was similar for the cross-sectional analysis of conservation measures and levels of outcomes, except that population density and literacy rate were included as explanatory variables instead of changes in these, and distance to the nearest road and to the urban market were used instead of indicators of change in road access. The determinants of organizational development and collective action were similar, but also included total village population (as a factor affecting demand for collective action), the population growth rate and growth rate squared (to investigate the hypothesis of an inverted U-shaped relationship between population growth and collective action), and the percentage of the village that had been born in the same municipality (to investigate whether stability of village population affects collective action).[10]

Possible endogeneity of some explanatory variables—particularly population growth, the development pathways, and government programs—could lead to biased estimates. In all regressions including these explanatory variables, we ran the regressions twice, using predicted and actual values of these variables, to investigate the robustness of the results.[11] We report which results are significant and robust below. In all regressions, the standard errors were corrected for sample weights, stratification, and finite population, and are robust to heteroskedasticity.

---

[10] See Pender, Scherr, and Durón (1999) and Pender and Scherr (1999) for more details on the econometric specifications.

[11] The pathway variables are predicted using the multinomial regression described previously. Population growth and the presence of government programs were predicted using 1974 population density, indicators of agricultural potential (altitude and average number of rainfall days), distance of the village from Tegucigalpa, and indicators of wealth and access to various services in 1974 (proportion of households with a dirt floor, access to potable water, sanitation, electricity, radio, or a sewing machine in 1974; adult literacy rate in 1974). Standard errors were not corrected for the use of predicted values of explanatory variables in these regressions because of the difficulty of deriving an analytical formula for the covariance matrix for such complex models (e.g. multinomial logit, probit, and least squares used in the first stage regressions, ordered probit in the second stage). Bootstrapping was also judged not to be appropriate because of the small number of observations per stratum (12). Thus, Pender, Scherr, and Durón (1999) did not report the results of the multistage regressions, but only used them to check the robustness of the findings.

4.2. *Results*

Impacts on Responses   The empirical results concerning the impacts of population pressure on household and collective responses in central Honduras are summarized in Table 12.3. As hypothesized, we find that population growth is significantly and robustly associated with agricultural extensification, as measured by the likelihood of decline in forest area. Population growth is also associated with collective action and organizational development, and the relationship has the hypothesized inverted-U shape. A higher population level is also associated with collective action and organizational development (though the result is robust only for organizational development), consistent with the hypothesis that higher population implies higher demand for such collective responses. As expected, higher population density is associated with some labor-intensive practices and land investments, including use of cattle manure and investments in live barriers and trees. Lower initial population density was positively associated with expansion of basic grains (maize, beans, and sorghum) production and expansion of horticultural production (although the result was robust only for horticultural expansion). Higher population density is associated with less likelihood of collective action to improve common lands and control run-off, consistent with the expectation that resource scarcity may undermine collective action.

None of the statistically significant results is inconsistent with our expectations, as noted above. However, the lack of a significant impact of population pressure on many responses is also notable, particularly with regard to changes in the fallow system and adoption of several labor-intensive practices and land investments. Reductions in use of fallow and adoption of labor-intensive measures were much more strongly influenced by access to technical assistance and other government programs, and the development pathway being pursued. In general, technical assistance programs promoted more labor-intensive practices, especially conservation practices. Other programs had mixed effects on such practices. Adoption of labor-intensive measures varied greatly across development pathways, with different measures apparently suited to different pathways.

Capital intensity was also not significantly affected by population pressure, and much more affected by road access and the development pathways. Road access favored all kinds of capital intensification. Adoption of purchased inputs was more common in more commercialized pathways, while use of oxen and plowing was less common in the more peri-urban non-farm employment and horticultural pathways.

Although population pressure did not have a statistically significant direct effect on many aspects of intensification in the econometric analysis, this does not prove that population pressure had no impact on these aspects. Given the relatively small number of observations, the statistical power to discern such effects was relatively low, especially for responses that did not vary greatly within the sample (such as qualitative changes in use of particular practices, which were generally in the same direction, or adoption of conservation measures, which was generally low).

Table 12.3. *Evidence of Responses to Population Pressure in Central Honduras*

Response	Indicator	Effect of	Effect
Extensification	Change in forest area (1975–96)	Change in population density (1974–88)	−®
Shorten fallow cycle	Change in use of fallow	Change in population density	0
Labor intensification	Change in use of burning	Change in population density	0
	Use of contour planting (in 1996)	1988 population density	0
	Use of mulching		0
	Use of incorporation of crop residues		0
	Use of cattle manure		+®
Labor-intensive land investments	Constructed terraces (since 1975)	1974 population density	0
	Planting live barriers		+®
	Constructing stone walls		0
	Planting trees		+®
Capital intensification	Change in oxen use	Change in population density	0
	Change in use of plow		0
	Change in use of insecticides		0
Change in product mix/occupation (development pathway)	Basic grains expansion	1974 population density	−
	Horticultural expansion		−®
	Coffee expansion		0
	Forestry expansion		0
	Non-farm employment expansion		0
Collective action	Collective investment to control run-off/improve common lands	1974 population	+
		1974 population density	−®
		Population growth rate (1974–88)	+®
		Population growth rate squared	−®
Organizational development	Number of local organizations	1974 population	+®
		1974 population density	0
		Population growth rate (1974–88)	+®
		Population growth rate squared	−®

Notes: + means a positive and statistically significant effect at the 5% level.
− means a negative and statistically significant effect at the 5% level.
0 means effect is not statistically significant at the 5% level.
® means the effect is also statistically significant at the 10% level if population growth (where applicable), government programs, and development pathways are replaced by their predicted values in the regression.

Source: Pender, Scherr, and Durón (1999); Pender and Scherr (1998).

Furthermore, population pressure may have indirect effects on intensification via its effects on other factors, such as the development pathways, government programs, or infrastructure development. For example, since lower initial population density appears to have favored horticultural expansion, and horticultural expansion is associated with adoption of purchased inputs, population pressure may indirectly reduce use of purchased inputs by undermining horticultural expansion. Lower initial population density is also associated with the presence of technical assistance programs and road development, perhaps because people are wealthier and more politically connected in less densely populated areas.[12] Paradoxically, lower population density communities may thus have been encouraged to adopt more labor-intensive methods by technical assistance programs than in higher population density communities where such programs were less present. Lower population density also appears to have favored adoption of capital-intensive methods, to the extent that this contributed to road development. These indirect effects do not support the hypothesis of population-induced intensification of labor or capital.

Impacts on Outcomes   The impacts of population pressure on outcomes in central Honduras are summarized in Table 12.4. Population density is found to have a negative association with maize yield and with the presence of forest on steep land (having slope greater than 30%), and a positive association with cultivation on steep lands. The negative association of population density and maize yield is not consistent with our expectations of the effects of population-induced labor intensification, and suggests that population pressure is associated with land degradation. This is consistent with the estimated impact of population growth on changes in maize yields and perceived cropland quality, although these impacts were not statistically significant at the 5 percent level. The associations of population density with forest and cultivated area on steep lands are consistent with the hypothesis of population-induced expansion onto marginal lands, and also with the results on forest area discussed earlier. Generally, the evidence suggests that population pressure is causing land degradation in central Honduras.

We do not find evidence of a significant and robust impact of population density or population growth on indicators of labor productivity or poverty. Surprisingly, population growth is positively associated with wage growth, but this effect is not robust when predicted population growth is used in the regression. This suggests that the positive association is due to the endogeneity of population growth, and that population growth responds positively to rising wages (via migration), rather than the other way around.

As discussed above, the insignificant impacts of population pressure in these regressions do not prove that it has no effect. The statistical power of the regressions is low,

---

[12] This result is from the regressions used to predict the presence of government programs. Population density did not have a significant effect on the presence of other government programs. These regression results are available upon request.

Table 12.4. *Evidence of Outcomes of Population Pressure in Central Honduras*

Outcome	Indicator	Effect of	Effect
Productivity	Maize yield, 1996	Population density, 1988	− [®]
	Ln(high male wage), 1996		0
Change in productivity	Change in maize yield, 1975–96	Change in population density, 1974–88	0
	Change in ln(male wage)		+
Resource conditions	Forest on steep land, late 1970s	Population density, 1974	−[®]
	Cultivation on steep land, late 1970s		+[®]
Change in resource conditions	Perceived change in cropland quality, 1975–96	Change in population density	0
	Perceived change in forest quality		0
	Perceived change in water availability		+
	Perceived change in water quality		+
Poverty	Proportion of houses with a dirt floor, 1988	Population density, 1988	0
	Proportion of households where last child died		0
Change in poverty	Change in proportion of houses with a dirt floor, 1974–88	Change in population density, 1974–88	0
	Change in proportion of households where last child died		0

Notes: +means a positive and statistically significant effect at the 5% level.
− means a negative and statistically significant effect at the 5% level.
0 means effect is not statistically significant at the 5% level.
[®] means the effect is also statistically significant at the 10% level if population growth (where applicable), government programs, and development pathways are replaced by their predicted values in the regression.

Source: Pender, Scherr, and Durón (1999).

as noted above. Furthermore, the impacts of population growth may be dispersed by migration. For example, changes in wages and poverty may be similar across communities as a result of migration, even though population growth may be having a generalized impact on wages and poverty in the central region of Honduras as a whole. It is difficult to identify such effects in a study conducted in a single, relatively integrated labor market.

Table 12.5. *Predicted Effects of Population Pressure and Market Access on Outcomes*

| Factor | Effect | Productivity, 1996 | | Resource conditions, late 1970s | | | Poverty, 1988 | |
		Maize yield (kg/ha)	ln (male wage) (Lps/day)	Percentage of steep land in forest	Percentage of steep land de-vegetated	Percentage of steep land cultivated	Percentage of houses with dirt floors	Percentage of households where last child died
Higher population density (by 1 person/km^2)	Direct	−31.3	0.0037	−0.55	0.32	0.25	−0.22	0.02
	Indirect	6.6	0.0028	−0.37	0.29	0.03	−0.09	0.00
	Total	−24.7	0.0065	−0.92	0.61	0.28	−0.31	0.02
Further from road (by 1 km)	Direct	−119.4	−0.0615	−0.91	2.64	−1.17	−0.51	0.24
	Indirect	−366.2	−0.0930	2.52	−4.14	1.22	1.01	0.35
	Total	−485.6	−0.1545	1.61	−1.50	0.05	0.50	0.59

Source: Pender, Scherr, and Durón (1999).

To the extent that population pressure affected the development pathways (and other factors), it may have had indirect effects on outcomes. Table 12.5 presents the results of simulations of the direct and indirect effects of changing population density and road access on various outcomes, assuming the indirect effects are due to the effects on development pathways.[13]

The indirect impacts of population pressure are smaller in magnitude than the direct effects in all cases, and in the same direction as the direct effects in all but one case (effect on maize yield). The predicted overall effects of population pressure are unfavorable for land productivity and pressure on steep lands, favorable for wages and housing quality, and negligible for child mortality. In general the predicted impacts are relatively small, particularly in comparison to the impacts of road access. If improvements in road access were undermined by population pressure (recall the negative association between initial population density and road construction noted above), population pressure may have had additional indirect impacts which would have helped to reduce deforestation on steep land but also reduced productivity and increased poverty.

5. CONCLUSIONS

There are many possible household and collective responses to rural population pressure. These responses are affected by many site-specific factors, may interact in complex ways, and may be subject to path dependency. It is therefore difficult to predict what impacts rural population pressure will have on agriculture and natural resource management, agricultural productivity, poverty, or natural resource conditions. I have considered a large number of plausible hypotheses about these impacts, arguing that the impacts of population growth are more likely negative when there is no collective response than when population growth induces infrastructure development, collective action, institutional or organizational development. Beyond this general proposition, the impacts of population pressure, particularly on natural resource conditions, may be very different in different contexts. Thus careful empirical work is required in different contexts before general conclusions can be drawn.

Despite the large volume of literature and debate concerning the relationship between population pressure and resource conditions in developing countries, there is still a paucity of empirical evidence from which to draw general conclusions. Much of the evidence that is cited is based on case studies that, though useful, may not be generalizable. In this chapter, I have reported results from two recent studies of these issues in central Honduras, based on a survey conducted in a representative sample of villages. Conducting similar studies in different agroecological and socioeconomic environments would help to overcome the present gap in empirical knowledge about

---

[13] I do not estimate the indirect effects of population pressure on outcomes via its impact on the presence of government programs, because of the insignificance (and sometimes implausible signs) of the coefficients of government programs in the outcome regressions. I do not estimate the predicted effects of population growth on measures of changes in outcomes because most of these measures are ordinal variables (except changes in poverty measures), making the interpretation of predicted values problematic.

the impacts of rural population growth on natural resource management and their implications.

The results from Honduras support the concern that population pressure leads to land degradation in a situation of relatively low population density and available land, by encouraging expansion of agricultural production onto marginal steep lands and causing lower land productivity. We also found that population pressure promoted adoption of some labor-intensive soil fertility management practices and land improvements, although the adoption of such practices remained low and was largely determined by the presence of technical assistance programs. Moderate population growth was found to promote collective action to manage common resources and organizational development, consistent with the induced innovation hypothesis. Despite these impacts, we found that population pressure had a statistically insignificant impact on wages and poverty, and that the magnitude of the estimated impacts were relatively small. Even when indirect impacts of population pressure on occupational and product choice were considered, the impacts remained relatively small.

The results from central Honduras suggest that other factors besides population pressure have been more important in determining agricultural change, resource management practices, wages, and poverty. Notable among these are road development and technical assistance programs. Although induced innovation theory suggests that both of these types of interventions would be more likely in more densely populated settings, we found just the opposite—that is, these interventions were more likely in less densely populated communities. This may have been an anomalous result of the particular political setting of Honduras. Nevertheless, it emphasizes the point that such 'induced' policy responses are by no means automatic, nor necessarily in the direction one might expect. It also suggests that policies may not have been efficient; for example, by promoting labor-intensive practices through technical assistance programs focused in less densely populated areas.

The evidence from central Honduras suggests the importance of considering the complex array of conditioning factors that influence the responses of communities and households to population growth or other pressures. Particularly important among these are the factors leading to differences in changing comparative advantage, as summarized by the pathways of development. Within particular development pathways, the processes of induced technological, institutional, and organizational development may proceed differently, with different long-term implications for resource management and human welfare. Further research is needed to explore these issues in different agroecological and socioeconomic contexts.

References

Angelsen, A. 1999. 'Agricultural Expansion and Deforestation: Modelling the Impact of Population, Market Forces and Property Rights'. *Journal of Development Economics*. 58: 185–218.

—— and D. Kaimowitz. 1998. 'When does Technological Change in Agriculture Promote Deforestation?' Paper presented at the AAEA International Conference on Agricultural Intensification, Economic Development, and the Environment, Salt Lake City, 31 July–1 Aug. 1998.

Arrow, K. J. 1962. 'The Economic Implications of Learning by Doing'. *Review of Economic Studies.* 29 (June), 155–73.

Ault, D. E., and G. L. Rutman. 1979. 'The Development of Individual Rights to Property in Tribal Africa' *Journal of Law and Economics.* 22 (1), 163–82.

Baland, J.-M., and J.-P. Platteau. 1996. *Halting Degradation of Natural Resources: Is there a Role for Rural Communities.* Oxford: Clarendon Press.

Becker, G., and H. Lewis. 1973. 'On the Interaction between the Quantity and Quality of Children'. *Journal of Political Economy,* 81 (2), pt. 2.

Besley, T. 1995. 'Property Rights and Investment Incentives: Theory and Evidence from Ghana'. *Journal of Political Economy.* 103 (5), 903–37.

Bilsborrow, R. E., and D. L. Carr. 1998. 'Population, Agricultural Land Use and the Environment in Developing Countries'. Paper presented at the AAEA International Conference on Agricultural Intensification, Economic Development, and the Environment, Salt Lake City, 31 July–1 Aug. 1998.

Binswanger, H. P., and J. McIntire. 1987. 'Behavior and Material Determinants of Production Relations in Land Abundant Tropical Agriculture'. *Economic Development and Cultural Change.* 36 (1), 73–99.

Blaikie, P., and H. Brookfield, eds. 1987. *Land Degradation and Society.* London and New York: Methuen.

Boserup, E. 1965. *The Conditions of Agricultural Growth.* New York: Aldine Publishing Co.

—— 1981. *Population and Technological Change: A Study of Long-Term Change.* Chicago: University of Chicago Press.

Buresh, R., P. A. Sanchez, and F. Calhoun, eds. 1997. *Replenishing Soil Fertility in Africa.* SSSA Special Publication No. 51. Madison: Soil Science Society of America.

Clay, D., T. Reardon, and J. Kangasniemi. 1998. 'Sustainable Intensification in the Highland Tropics: Rwandan Farmers Investments in Land Conservation and Soil Fertility'. *Economic Development and Cultural Change.* 46: 351–77.

Coase, R. 1960. 'The Problem of Social Cost'. *Journal of Law and Economics.* 3 (Oct.), 1–44.

Demsetz, H. 1967. 'Towards a Theory of Property Rights'. *American Economic Review, Papers and Proceedings.* 57 (2), 347–59.

Easterlin, R. A., ed. 1980. *Population and Economic Change in Developing Countries.* National Bureau of Economic Research. Chicago: University of Chicago Press.

Ehrlich, P. R., and A. H. Ehrlich. 1990. *The Population Explosion.* New York: Simon and Schuster.

Feder, G., T. Onchan, Y. Chalamwong, and C. Hongladaron. 1988. *Land Policies and Farm Productivity in Thailand.* Baltimore. Johns Hopkins University Press.

Goldman, A. 1995. 'Threats to Sutainability in African Agriculture: Searching for Appropriate Paradigms'. *Human Ecology.* 23 (3), 291–334.

Harris, J. R., and M. P. Todaro. 1970. 'Migration, Unemployment and Development: A Two-Sector Analysis'. *American Economic Review.* 60 (Mar.), 126–42.

Hayami, Y, and V. W. Ruttan. 1985. *Agricultural Development: An International Perspective,* 2nd edn. Baltimore: Johns Hopkins University Press.

Herweg, K. 1993. 'Problems of Acceptance and Adoption of Soil Conservation in Ethiopia'. *Topics in Applied Resource Management.* 3: 391–411.

Holden, S., B. Shiferaw, and M. Wik. 1998. 'Poverty, Credit Constraints, and Time Preferences: Of Relevance for Environment Policy?' *Environment and Development Economics*. 3: 105–30.

Kates, R., and V. Haarmann. 1992. 'Where the Poor Live: Are the Assumptions Correct?' *Environment*. 34 (May), 4–28.

Krautkraemer, J. A. 1994. 'Population Growth, Soil Fertility, and Agricultural Intensification'. *Journal of Development Economics*. 44: 403–28.

LaFrance, J. T. 1992. 'Do Increased Commodity Prices lead to More or Less Soil Degradation?' *Australian Journal of Agricultural Economics*. 36 (1), 57–82.

Lele, U., and S. W. Stone. 1989. 'Population Pressure, the Environment and Agricultural Intensification in Sub-Saharan Africa: Variations on the Boserup Hypothesis'. MADIA Discussion Paper No. 4. Washington: World Bank.

Lewis, W. A. 1954. 'Economic Development with Unlimited Supplies of Labor'. *The Manchester School*. 22 (May), 139–91.

Lipton, M. 1977. *Why Poor People Stay Poor: Urban Bias in World Development*. Cambridge, Mass.: Harvard University Press.

Lopez, R. 1998. 'Where Development Can or Cannot Go: The Role of Poverty-Environment Linkages'. *Annual World Bank Conference on Development Economics 1997*. Washington: World Bank.

Lucas, R. E. 1988. 'On the Mechanics of Economic Development'. *Journal of Monetary Economics*. 22: 3–42.

McIntire, J., D. Bourzat, and P. Pingali. 1992. 'Crop-Livestock Interactions in Sub-Saharan Africa'. Washington: World Bank.

North, D. C. 1990. *Institutions, Institutional Change and Economic Performance*. Cambridge: Cambridge University Press.

Olson, M. 1965. *The Logic of Collective Action: Public Goods and the Theory of Groups*. Cambridge, Mass.: Harvard University Press.

—— 1982. *The Rise and Decline of Nations*. New Haven: Yale University Press.

Ostrom, E. 1990. *Governing the Commons: The Evolution of Institutions for Collective Action*. Cambridge: Cambridge University Press.

Otsuka, K. 1998. 'Land Tenure and the Management of Land and Trees in Asia and Africa'. Paper presented at an International Food Policy Research Institute Policy Seminar, 3 Sept. 1998, Washington.

Pagiola, S. 1996. 'Price Policy and Returns to Soil Conservation in Semi-arid Kenya'. *Environmental and Resource Economics*. 8: 251–71.

Panayotou, T. 1994. 'Population, Environment, and Development Nexus'. In R. Cassen, ed., *Population and Development: Old Debates, New Conclusions*. Washington: Overseas Development Council.

Pender, J. 1996. 'Discount Rates and Credit Markets: Theory and Evidence from Rural India'. *Journal of Development Economics*. 50(2), 257–96.

—— 1998. 'Population Growth, Agricultural Intensification, Induced Innovation and Natural Resource Sustainability: An Application of Neoclassical Growth Theory'. *Agricultural Economics*. 19: 99–112.

—— and J. Kerr. 1998. 'Determinants of Farmers' indigenous Soil and Water Conservation Investments in India's semi-arid tropics'. *Agricultural Economics*. 19: 113–25.

—— —— 1999. 'The Effects of Land Sales Restrictions: Evidence from South India'. *Agricultural Economics*. 21: 279–94.

—— F. Place, and S. Ehui. 1999. 'Strategies for Sustainable Agricultural Development in the East African Highlands'. Environment and Production Technology Division Discussion Paper 41. Washington: International Food Policy Research Institute.

—— and S. J. Scherr. 1999. 'Organizational Development and Natural Resource Management: Evidence from Central Honduras'. Environment and Production Technology Division Discussion Paper 49. Washington: International Food Policy Research Institute.

—— —— and G. Durón. 1999. 'Pathways of Development in the Hillsides of Honduras: Causes and Implications for Agricultural Production, Poverty, and Sustainable Resource Use'. Environment and Production Technology Division Discussion Paper 45. Washington: International Food Policy Research Institute.

Pingali, P., Y. Bigot, and H. P. Binswanger. 1987. 'Agricultural Mechanization and the Evolution of Farming Systems in Sub-Saharan Africa'. Baltimore: Johns Hopkins University Press.

Platteau, J. P. 1996. 'The Evolutionary Theory of Land Rights as Applied to Sub-Saharan Africa: A Critical Assessment'. *Development and Change*. 27: 29–86.

Rasmussen, L. N., and R. Meinzen-Dick. 1995. 'Local Organizations for Natural Resource Management: Lessons from Theoretical and Empirical Literature'. Environment and Production Technology Division Discussion Paper 11. Washington: International Food Policy Research Institute.

Reardon, T., E. Crawford, and V. Kelly. 1994. 'Links between Nonfarm Income and Farm Investment in African Households: Adding the Capital Market Perspective'. *American Journal of Agricultural Economics*. 76: 1172–76.

Richards, P. 1985. *Indigenous Agricultural Revolution: Ecology and Food Production in West Africa*. Boulder, Colo.: Westview Press.

Robinson, W. C., and W. Schutjer. 1984. 'Agricultural Development and Demographic Change: A generalization of the Boserup Model'. *Economic Development and Cultural Change*. 32 (2), 355–66.

Romer, P. M. 1990. 'Endogenous Technological Change'. *Journal of Political Economy* 98, S71–S102.

Ruthenberg, H. 1980. *Farming Systems in the Tropics*, 3rd edn. Oxford: Clarendon Press.

Salehi-Isfahani, D. 1988. 'Technology and References in the Boserup Model of Agricultural Growth'. *Journal of Developmental Economics*. 28 (2), 175–91.

Sanchez, P. A., K. D. Shepherd, M. J. Soule, F. M. Place, R. J. Buresh, A.-M. Izac, A. U. Mokwunye, F. R. Kwesiga, C. G. Ndiritu, and P. L. Woomer. 1997. 'Solid Fertility Replenishment in Africa: An Investment in Natural Resource Capital'. In Buresh *et al.* 1997.

Scherr, S. J., and P. Hazell. 1994. 'Sustainable Agricultural Development Strategies in Fragile Lands'. EPTD Discussion Paper No. 1. Washington: International Food Policy Research Institute.

Schultz, T. P. 1981. *Economics of Population*. Reading. Mass: Addison-Wesley Publishing Co.

Smaling, E. M. A., ed. 1998. 'Nutrient Balances as Indicators of Productivity and Sustainability in Sub-Saharan African Agriculture'. *Agricultural Ecosystems* & *Environment*, Special Issue, 71 (1, 2, 3).

Solow, R. M. 1956. 'A Contribution to the Theory of Economic Growth'. *Quarterly Journal of Economics*. 70: 65–94.

Templeton, S., and S. J. Scherr. 1999. 'Effects of Demographic and Related Microeconomic Changes on Land Quality in Hills and Mountains of Developing Countries'. *World Development*. 27(6), 903–18.

Tiffen, M., M. Mortimore, and F. Gichuki. 1994. *More People, Less Erosion: Environmental Recovery in Kenya*. Chichester: John Wiley and Sons.

Udry, C. 1996. 'Gender, Agricultural Productivity and the Theory of the Household'. *Journal of Political Economy*. 104 (5), 1010–46.

Uphoff, N. 1986. *Local Institutional Development: An Analytical Sourcebook with Cases*. West Hartford: Kumarian Press.

Vasey D. E. 1979. 'Population and Agricultural Intensity in the Humid Tropics'. *Human Ecology*. 7 (3), 269–81.

Vosti, S. A., J. Witcover, and M. Lipton. 1994. 'The Impact of Technical Change in Agriculture on Human Fertility: District-Level Evidence from India'. Environment and Production Technology Division Discussion Paper 5. Washington: International Food Policy Research Institute.

World Commission on Environment and Development. 1987. *Our Common Future*. Oxford: Oxford University Press.

PART V

SOME ECONOMICS
OF POPULATION POLICY

The preceding four parts of this book focus on the consequences of demographic change for economic growth, for poverty reduction, and for use of natural resources. This part addresses the following question: do those consequences—which we have shown to be negative in certain circumstances—warrant public policy intervention to change the behavior of individuals? And if so, what kinds of interventions under what circumstances?

Economists have been cautious over the last several decades about exaggerating in any way the negative consequences of rapid population growth, for fear that policy-makers would use those results to intervene in family decisions in ways that would be misguided, and would end up reducing overall well-being rather than increasing it.

In his chapter Behrman emphasizes that evidence at the macro level about the consequences of population growth is not useful for making policy unless it is based on micro-foundations. The evidence at the macro level needs to reflect some underlying understanding of the decisions of individuals in response to the incentives, the 'prices' the social and economic and other constraints they face. Only with that understanding is it possible to imagine developing a policy or program that would alter those incentives, prices, or environment in a way that leads individuals to alter their behavior in their own interests.

In the concluding chapter, Birdsall links that conclusion to the earlier chapters in the volume. Those chapters indicate that in developing countries there have been and are costs of high fertility and accompanying high population growth (as well as of high mortality, which of course, all other things the same, reduces the rate of population growth). Those costs are borne by parents, especially the poor, and by society as a whole, in the form of lower economic growth than there could have been at least during some transition period (the period of the demographic bonus), and in terms of reduced success in eliminating poverty. So lower aggregate fertility, as long as it reflects individual decisions that are fully informed and freely taken, has and is likely for some time to improve the lot of the poor in most developing countries. She then sets out five types of interventions that join the macroeconomic analysis of economic consequences with the microeconomic emphasis on maximizing the well-being of individuals and families. All are likely to be effective in some measure, since all assist the poor directly by allowing them to reduce their own unwanted fertility, and indirectly by reducing the societal burden—in developing countries where fertility is still high—of that high fertility.

13

Why Micro Matters

JERE R. BEHRMAN

INTRODUCTION

Why are we interested in population change and economic development? One major reason is simply to understand better what broad trends in population and economic development have been occurring and are likely to occur in the future, conditional on other future changes. A second major reason, and one that primarily motivates most of those present at the conference for which this chapter was written, is to help formulate better policies related to population change and economic development.

The basic proposition of this chapter is that:

For both good conditional predictions and good policy formation regarding most dimensions of population change and economic development, a perspective firmly grounded in understanding the micro determinants—at the level of individuals, households, farms, firms, and public sector providers of goods and services—of population changes and of the interactions between population and development is essential.

Only considering aggregate patterns in variables related to population and economic development is *not* likely to be sufficient for a wide range of questions related to population change and economic development. In particular, only considering aggregate patterns is *not* likely to provide a sufficient basis for good conditional predictions nor for good policy formation and analysis. That is the case because critical behavioral decisions regarding population and development are made at the micro level—by households, by individuals, and by other entities—given the resources under the control of the decision-makers and the market and policy environments in which these decisions are made. The resource, price, and other constraints under which these decisions are made are likely to change in the development process, and thereby induce changes in micro behaviors including those related to population. Important aspects of policies, moreover, are likely to be determined by aspects of local micro, or perhaps mezo, conditions. Important policy concerns, further, go beyond concerns about averages of aggregates such as per capita income to the distribution of outcomes among members of society, perhaps further identified by demographic characteristics, such as gender or ethnic group, or economic status, such as being below a poverty line. What determines whether many people are poor, for example, reflects their micro behaviors under constraints that may be severe but that may change with the process of development (e.g. Birdsall 1994). For all of these reasons, I claim, not only does a micro perspective matter, but for many—probably most—questions regarding population change and economic development, it is essential.

In this chapter I sketch out the basis for this proposition and give some illustrations related to studies of aspects of population and development and some specific related policies. Section 1 presents some fundamentals for thinking about population change and development at the micro level and for empirically assessing aspects of population change and development. Section 2 presents some fundamentals for thinking about policies. Section 2.1 considers the efficiency/productivity rationale for policy interventions, Section 2.2 considers the distribution rationale, and Section 2.3 considers choices among policy alternatives. Section 3 then presents some illustrations of these fundamentals for thinking about the specific implications of policies for population change and economic development and summarizes selected empirical micro studies that build on such frameworks to illuminate what we know about critical aspects of population change and economic development and policies. In Section 3.1 I review some empirical estimates on selected topics related to micro aspects of population change and economic development to illustrate what we do and, equally important, do not know from systematic empirical approaches and how being systematic in such approaches in the sense of grounding the analysis firmly in the conceptual frameworks of Sections 1 and 2 may make a substantial difference in our understanding of these topics. Because of the difficulties in obtaining good empirical estimates, however, often policies have to be formulated considerably on the basis of a priori frameworks. In Section 3.2 I review a priori considerations, grounded in the frameworks of Sections 1 and 2, for selected policy issues related to population change and economic development.

1. FUNDAMENTALS OF MICRO BEHAVIORS CHANGE RELATED TO POPULATION AND ECONOMIC DEVELOPMENT

The assumption from which I start is that at the micro level decision-makers are currently making the decisions that they perceive maximize their welfare over time discounted to the present, given the resources over which they have control, the prices that they currently face and expect to face in the future, the policies that they currently face and expect to face in the future, the informal networks they have and expect to have in the future, and their knowledge of markets, social norms, production processes, and other relevant matters. With no apologies, this basically is the standard assumption made by economists. Some are uncomfortable with such an assumption because they perceive that people are not always making calculations so as to maximize their welfare. But, as I discuss in some respects below, these objections generally can be accommodated. If they can be accommodated, there still is the objection that such an assumption should not be characterized as an interesting theory because it is not clear how to falsify it. Given the lack of direct observations on welfare levels, almost any behavior can be interpreted as reflecting some aspects of unobserved preferences. This objection has some merit. But there is nevertheless a strong case for such an approach if parsimonious models can lead to a range of testable predictions. Moreover the alternative maintained assumption is that people who think that they have choices between A and B with A increasing their welfare more than B, consciously chose B, which does not seem very plausible.

It is useful to elaborate somewhat on what is being assumed here with regard to what is being maximized, on what are the constraints that limit such maximization, and on what are some of the implications for micro behavioral relations related to population change and economic development.

Consideration of Some Critiques of this Approach   Some elaboration of some of the assumptions is useful because it illustrates that what some people consider to be strong criticisms of such an approach are based on factors that in fact can and often are accommodated within its framework without changing its essence. I consider several examples of such critiques.

1. 'People simply do not make rational cost-benefit calculations of every decision that they make.' Making decisions in itself has costs, including time costs and costs due to balancing off alternatives. For such reasons of course people do not continuously make cost-benefit calculations. Such costs may imply, in fact, that most people most of the time will follow certain behavioral patterns out of habit because it simply is not worth the cost of reviewing constantly such decisions. But if there are large changes in the constraints that people face, it may be worth evaluating possible changes in behaviors. Such a perspective that most people do not make continuous cost-benefit decisions for most behaviors can be accommodated within this framework by recognizing the costs of such decisions.

2. 'Many people do not know what is best for them so they could not possibly behave as posited.' The assumption that I make is not that people do what is best for them in the judgment of others, including 'international experts', but that they do what yields the greatest welfare for themselves in their own perceptions, given what they perceive to be the options and constraints. There are some people, including infants and children and some adults with certain types of mental limitations, nevertheless, that other members of their own societies might agree do not know what is best for themselves so institutions, including importantly families, exist to provide care and guidance for them. There are difficult questions about how to consider the welfare of such individuals that I do not try to address here because considering them would divert from the basic thrust of the chapter.

3. 'This is an individualistic approach that ignores that people care about other people.' A special case of this approach is individualistic. But that is a special case. There is nothing in the way that this approach is stated above that precludes people being altruistic or concerned about what other people think (i.e. norms). If an altruistic decision-maker's welfare depends on the consumption or the welfare of other people, then whatever improves the consumption or welfare of those people also improves the welfare of this decision-maker—which easily fits into this framework.

4. 'Some people do not have any choices.' Some people have very limited choices. Hopefully the process of development will increase their choices. But most people, even very poor people, do have choices and do make decisions that affect their behaviors. An example is provided by the calorie consumption response of poor people who experience small income increases. Because most poor people in the developing world are thought to be malnourished, it might seem—and many have argued that it is the case—that if their income is increased a little the extra income would go exclusively or primarily to consuming more calories. Some have suggested that such poor people 'would have no choice' but to increase their calorie consumption by about 10 percent, for example, if their income increases by 10 percent. But careful studies over the past decade or so find that such people, if their income increases by 10 percent, do *not* choose to increase their calorie consumption by 10 percent, or even 8 or 6 percent. Instead they choose to increase their calorie consumption by 1 to 3 percent by choosing to consume more expensive calories in foods that offer greater variety, greater convenience, more status, better taste, and/or more micro nutrients (e.g. Bouis and Haddad 1992).

Constraints on Such Maximization   Individual decision-makers cannot maximize their welfare without limit. They face constraints on their actions, perhaps in many cases severe constraints. The resources that they have at a point in time limit substantially their choices. These resources include physical (e.g. land, livestock), financial (e.g. savings accounts, pension plans), and human resources (e.g. genetic endowments, time, health, education, work experience, number of children, social networks). These resources in important part reflect past investment decisions. At the center of the process of successful economic development is an increase in such resources.

What the resources yield (or are expected to yield) in terms of increased options for the individuals who control them depends importantly on what are current and expected future prices broadly defined. 'Prices' include all of the monetary, time, and other costs of purchases and the returns to ownership of resources (e.g. wages for labor time with particular skill levels, the rental value of land or of other production inputs). Because prices so defined include non-monetary costs, primarily time costs, resources to which individuals have access through subsidized (including 'free') public provision and through networks also have non-zero prices. All of these prices might be expected to change with the process of development. And expected prices are important for the investment decisions associated with both economic development and population change. If, for example, with the process of development, the rates of return on education are expected to increase and if children are viewed in part as expected providers of old-age support or if parents have interest in the welfare of their children for altruistic or sociobiological reasons, price incentives effectively are expected to shift toward inducing having fewer but better educated children. If, for another example, with the process of development there are expected to be better options for investing financial resources because of capital market developments and development of pension and social security systems and children are likely to be less reliable sources of old-age support because of increased mobility for children and weakening of social norms for children fulfilling parental support roles; to the extent that children are desired for old-age support purposes, price incentives have changed toward having fewer children and perhaps greater financial investments. Thus, with the process of development, aggregate resources and options are likely to increase at least for most individuals. At the same time the composition of resources is likely to change because of changes in relative prices and some resources are likely to decline (e.g. the dependence on low-skilled children for parental old-age support).

The knowledge of decision-makers definitely constrains choices for increasing their welfare. This knowledge includes knowledge of production processes (whether for the production of crops, of children, or of health), knowledge of market options, knowledge of options through using public services, and knowledge of future developments. Increases in knowledge of any type increases the range of choices available and is generally thought to be an important part of the development process. Knowledge thus can be viewed similarly to other resources from the point of view of individual decision-makers in that the stock of knowledge of an individual can be increased through investments in knowledge, but such investments have costs such as not using for other purposes the time or other resources involved in knowledge acquisition.

Implied Micro Behavioral Relations Related to Population Change and Economic Development If individual decision-makers do behave as if they are maximizing their welfare given their resources broadly defined and the constraints that they face, they will make investments at the level at which the additional (marginal) present discounted value of the *private* benefit of the investment equals its additional (marginal) present discounted value of the *private* cost.[1] Investments include any use of current resources with expectations of increasing future welfare. Examples of such investments include population changes such as having children or migrating as well as human resource, physical, and financial asset accumulation. Figure 13.1 provides an illustration for one type of investment for one individual. The marginal private benefit curve depends on the expected private gains from an investment as perceived by an individual investor. These reflect expected welfare gains from various dimensions of the returns from the investments, which often reflect in part expected prices related to returns from the investment but also include direct welfare effects such as parents liking to have children *per se*. The marginal private benefit curve is downward-sloping because of diminishing returns to such investments (e.g. benefits do not increase

---

[1] Discounting reflects the fact that a benefit received now is worth more than an equal benefit received in the future if it can be invested to obtain a return over time. For example, if benefits are measured in pesos, prices do not change, and the interest rate is 10% per year, the present discounted value of a benefit that is received in one year is 90.48 pesos because if 90.48 pesos are invested at 10% they yield 100 pesos in one year. (More generally, the present discounted value of a benefit of 100 pesos received in t years with an interest rate r is $100/e^{rt}$.) Similar considerations relate to costs. The use of expected values abstracts from uncertainty regarding future outcomes. Considerations of the impact of uncertainty may modify and complicate some of the analysis, though the basic thrust of it will remain the same. For simplicity, however, I refer to marginal benefits and marginal costs hereafter without qualifications about expected presented discounted values of future marginal benefits and costs (or their related marginal welfare effects).

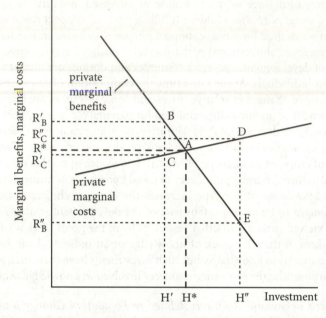

Figure 13.1. *Private Marginal Benefits and Private Marginal Costs of Investment for an Individual*

proportionately with additional investments due, for example, to fixed genetic endowments). The marginal private cost curve will be increasing if, for example, there are increasing opportunity costs to devoting additional time to such investments as in the case of education or if there are increasing marginal costs of obtaining financial resources for such investments.

Private returns net of costs are maximized at level H*, where private marginal benefits are equal to private marginal costs. This can be seen by considering first a level of investment H' to the left of H*, at which investment level the marginal benefit R'_B exceeds the marginal cost R'_C; therefore welfare gains can be made by increasing the investment to H*. The net gain for a small increase in investment from H' to H* is equal to the total additional benefit minus the total additional cost, which is the triangle ABC in the figure. Consider next a level of investment H'' to the right of H*, at which investment level the marginal benefit R''_B is less than the marginal cost R''_C; therefore welfare gains can be made by decreasing the investment to H* with the net gain for a small decrease in investment from H'' to H* equal to the triangle ADE in the figure.

This framework implies that private decision-makers will tend to change their investments in response to changes in the private marginal benefits or the private marginal costs. Figure 13.2 illustrates the impact of an increase in private marginal benefits from the solid to the dashed line to that the optimal investment increases from

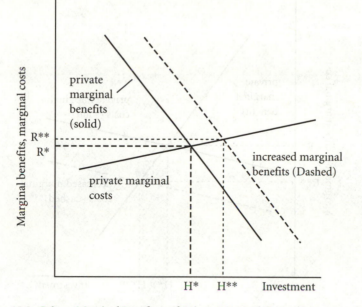

Figure 13.2. *Private Marginal Benefits and Private Marginal Costs of Investment for an Individual with Increased Marginal Benefits (Dashed Line)*

H* to H**. Figure 13.3 illustrates the impact of a decrease in private marginal benefits from the solid to the dashed line so that the optimal investment increases from H* to H***. Importantly among the elements underlying both the marginal benefits and marginal costs are prices and expected prices. Analyses that ignore prices, as in many aggregate characterizations of population and development, may be misleading in their interpretations of causal effects (an example is given in the second paragraph below).

The process of economic development is likely to change the marginal benefits and marginal costs for micro investments related to population change as well as other micro investments such as in human, physical, and financial resources. The marginal benefits curve for having children from the perspective of potential parents, for example, is likely to shift downward if there are reduced expected rates of returns (wages, productivities) for unskilled labor and increased alternatives to children for parental old-age support due to improved capital markets and increased formal pension systems. But the marginal benefits curve is likely to shift upwards if, as part of the development process, the life expectancy for children increases or if parents want to use their increased income in part to obtain more 'child services'. The marginal cost curve for having children from the perspective of parents is likely to shift upwards due to increased time costs of raising children due to higher wages, but there may be tendencies in the other direction because, for instance, of lower financing costs due to improved capital markets and to lower private schooling and health-care costs due to

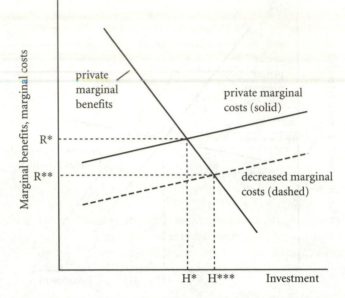

Figure 13.3. *Private Marginal Benefits and Private Marginal Costs of Investment for an Individual with Decreased Marginal Costs (Dashed Line)*

expansion of social services related to education, health, and nutrition. Whether the tendencies for increasing or decreasing the number of children dominate with economic development within any particular market, policy, and institutional context is an empirical question. Widespread experience suggests, however, that the factors inducing parents to choose fewer children predominate, while at the same time investments in the human resources of children (and of adults) and in physical and financial assets tend to increase. Note that if fertility is endogenous as much micro literature suggests, analysis that assumes that fertility is exogenous (or that related demographic phenomena that are heavily dependent on fertility rates such as the age structure of population are exogenous—see Ch. 3, this vol.) is difficult to interpret.

In such a context it also may be difficult to identify what are the causal effects except conditional on an explicit model of behavior. For example, suppose that there are basic changes—such as a shift in political power toward a group with stronger interests in economic growth or the institution of new policies that increase prospects for income growth—that improve the functioning of capital and labor markets and increase expectations of economic growth. From the point of view of potential parents, the improved capital and labor markets and expectations of increased economic growth may lead to increased investments in fiscal and physical capital and reduced investments in number of children because the former have become better options than the latter and the latter have become more expensive. If the increased growth expectations are realized, the result is a negative correlation between fertility and economic growth. But it would be wrong from such a correlation to infer that reduced fertility and population growth caused the increased economic growth.

Individual versus Collective Decision-Making   To this point I have referred to individual decision-makers. But individuals are joined together into collectives such as families and households. And members of such collectives, while generally sharing many interests, also may have important divergences of interests. For example, a number of observers claim that mothers on average care more about human resource investments in children than do fathers (e.g. Thomas 1990). Other observers suggest that women may have a greater interest in limiting fertility than do men. If there are divergences of interests, then both social norms and relative bargaining power may be important. If relative bargaining power depends on control over resources, then when the above framework is applied to collectives such as couples, families, or households, it may be important to identify who controls each resource.

2. FRAMEWORK FOR EVALUATING POLICIES RELATED TO POPULATION CHANGE AND ECONOMIC DEVELOPMENT

Often analyses of policies related to population change and economic development are undertaken without consideration of the general rationale for policies. It is just presumed that policies that say, increase family planning or education or savings or improve health and nutrition must be good. But such analyses are of little help in convincing skeptics that scarce resources should be allocated for these purposes, given the many competing alternative uses. Moreover they may not provide much in the way of guidelines for choosing among policy alternatives. Therefore it is useful to begin by asking why policy interventions related to population change and economic development (and in other areas) might be desirable. For most economists the two possible justifications for governmental policy interventions in these and other areas are: (1) to increase efficiency/productivity and (2) to redistribute resources. As I discuss below in Section 3.2, these two justifications include some other common concerns about policies, such as questions of access and quality of services and sustainability of overall economic development and of particular programs.

The policy justifications based on efficiency and on distribution are both firmly rooted in micro dimensions of behaviors as outlined in Section 1 and thus are intimately tied in to 'why micro matters'—the focus of this chapter. That is the case because *both of these standard economic motivations for policy are concerned ultimately with the welfare of individuals as judged by those individuals*. I emphasize this last statement by placing it in italics because economic efficiency is viewed by some as a concern about allocation of things and technical and financial concerns, but *not* a concern about people. But this reflects a fundamental misunderstanding. To the contrary, economic efficiency ultimately is a concern with the welfare of people as judged not by policy-makers or international experts, but by the individual decision-makers involved. In addition there is a separate important concern about the distribution of decision-making powers. But it is important to recognize that the efficiency motive for policy, far from being purely a mechanical or technical concern of 'dismal scientists' devoid of concerns about people, is based fundamentally on people's perceptions of their own welfare.

2.1. *Efficiency/Productivity*

Resources are used efficiently in the economic sense of the term if they are used to obtain the most product possible given the quantities of the resources and the available production technologies at a point of time and over time and if the composition of that product increases the welfare of members of society as much as is possible given the resource and technological constraints and the distribution of resource ownership. It is important to note that efficiency is not just a concern about the static use of resources at a point in time, but also is a concern about the use of resources over time and thus productivity and productivity growth over time. An investment (or expenditure) related to population change or economic growth is efficient if the marginal *social* benefit of the last unit of that investment just equals its marginal *social* cost.[2] If the marginal social benefit of a particular investment is greater (less) than the marginal social cost, society is not investing enough (is investing too much) and would benefit from increasing (decreasing) the level of investment until the marginal social benefits and costs are equalized.

Although applying the above rule maximizes social gains, private maximizing behavior leads to investments related to population change and economic development at the level at which the marginal *private* benefit of the investment equals its marginal *private* cost under the assumption that, given the information available to them and the constraints that they face, individuals act in what they perceive to be their best interests, as is discussed in Section 1. Figure 13.1 provides an illustration for investments related to one individual decision-maker.

Now consider what happens if the private incentives for investments related to population change and economic development differ from the social incentives for such investments, first with respect to the marginal benefits and then with respect to the marginal costs.

Let the dashed line in Figure 13.2 now represent the marginal *social* benefits for investments related to population change and economic development that are drawn to be greater than the marginal *private* benefits (rather than the changed

---

[2] Three points should be noted. First, economic efficiency is not the same as engineering efficiency because of the incorporation of marginal benefits and marginal costs rather than focusing exclusively on technological efficiency. Secondly, these marginal conditions for efficiency may not hold if there are, for example, large discontinuities in production processes. In such cases choices may have to be made among a number of different alternatives, using an explicit welfare function to compare the alternatives. Thirdly, the considerations noted above in Section 1 about expected present discounted values and about uncertainty hold for this discussion as well.

marginal private benefits as in the discussion in Section 1).[3] In this case the private incentives are to invest at level H*, which is less than the socially optimal (efficient) level of investment at level H**. Therefore there is an efficiency argument for policies to induce or to require private investments at level H** instead of level H*.

Why might marginal social benefits exceed marginal private benefits for investments related to population change and economic development? Among the most frequent answers to this question are:

1. Investments in education are thought to have not only private benefits to the person being educated through increasing his or her productivity in various activities, but, by adding to society's stock of knowledge, social benefits beyond the private benefits that include enhanced possibilities for desired population change and economic development.[4]

2. An investment in fertility control is thought to have not only private benefits in enabling individuals (couples) to attain better their desired levels of fertility with their desired spacing among births, but also social benefits if it reduces their number of children because of social costs of having children that are not reflected in market prices (and thus the private incentives for having children), such as some aspects of congestion, of environmental degradation, and of demands for subsidized social sector services.

3. Some health and nutrition interventions, in addition to their direct impact on the individual's own productivity and welfare, may reduce susceptibility to contagious diseases that, if contracted, may spread to others. This is a particularly relevant consideration in the case of investments in the prevention and treatment of infectious diseases.

4. Information on which private investment decisions are made may misrepresent the private rates of return to these investments because it is incomplete or incorrect. This is an important consideration in the case of investments related to population change and economic development because actual and potential consumers are often not well informed about many of the private benefits and costs, and thus may underinvest in comparison with what they would do with better information. [5]

---

[3] The marginal social benefits also could be lower than the marginal private benefits so that the marginal social benefits curve is below the marginal private benefits curve, and policies to attain efficiency would have to reduce the private incentives to the social levels.

[4] When investments in one individual's education affect the productivity and welfare of others other than in ways that are reflected in market prices, this investment is said to generate 'externalities'—i.e. effects that are external to what is transmitted through markets. If at least some individuals do not fully consider the external effects of their own decisions on the welfare of others, a purely private market solution leads to underinvestment from society's standpoint in activities that generate positive externalities (e.g. knowledge, immunizations) and an overinvestment in the case of negative externalities (e.g. use of antibiotics). Such 'externalities' are one case of a broader category of 'market failures' (other examples are discussed below).

[5] The 'public good' nature of information (i.e. that the marginal cost of providing information to another consumer is virtually zero) leads to underproduction of information from a social point of view by private markets because private providers cannot cover their costs if they price information at the social marginal cost as required for efficiency.

5. There may be social gains beyond the private gains to investments related to population change and economic development if such changes are viewed by society as inherently valuable in themselves (e.g. to facilitate catching up with other rapidly growing economies) in addition to their effects on individual economic productivity, consumption, and welfare.

6. The combination of uncertainty, risk aversion, and imperfect insurance markets may result in private incentives to underinvest in human, financial, and physical assets that enhance economic development from a social point of view because from a social point of view the risks are pooled.[6]

Now let the dashed line in Figure 13.3 represent the marginal social costs for investments related to population change and economic development (rather than alternative marginal private costs, as in Section 1) that are drawn to be less than the marginal private costs.[7] In this case the private incentives are to invest at level H*, which is less than the socially optimal (efficient) level of investment at level H***. Therefore there is an efficiency argument to consider the possibility for policies to induce or to require private investments at level H*** instead of at level H*.

Why might marginal social costs be less than marginal private costs for investments related to population change and economic development? Among the most frequent answers to this question are:

1. There may be capital market imperfections for investments—particularly for investments in human resources (in part because human capital is not recognized as collateral) such that the marginal private costs for such investments exceed their true marginal social costs, probably more so for individuals from poorer families who cannot relatively easily self-finance such investments. This may be a problem, for example, for risky investments in such areas as some types of education or in safe motherhood (e.g. emergency obstetric services) that involve substantial outlays with some of the benefits reaped only with considerable delays under conditions in which capital and insurance markets do not function well or are non-existent.

2. The sectors that provide population and human resource services may produce inefficiently because institutional arrangements do not induce efficient production of an efficient basket of commodities. This may be mainly a problem where services are provided directly by governments that operate under incentive schemes that do not encourage efficiency; but it can also be an outcome of monopoly pricing, particularly in isolated communities.

3. The sectors that provide population and human resource services may produce inefficiently because regulations preclude efficient production of an efficient basket of

---

[6] These are major reasons for a divergence to arise between private and social marginal benefits for investments related to population change and economic development, though there may be other factors as well (e.g. the social discount rate may be lower than the private discount rate, wage and price rigidities may preclude wages and prices from reflecting social marginal benefits and costs, income taxes may cause private marginal returns to human capital investments to be lower than social marginal returns).

[7] The marginal social costs also could be higher than the marginal private costs, in which case the marginal social cost curve would be above the marginal private cost curve, and policies to attain efficiency would have to reduce the private incentives to the social levels.

commodities. For example, regulations that limit contraceptive choices or abortion or that impose quality standards based on different conditions in other economies (e.g. standards established by the United States Food and Drug Administration may not be appropriate for other economies) or that limit provision of services to public providers all may result in much greater costs of attaining specific outcomes related to population and development than would be possible with lessened regulations (see also Chomitz and Birdsall 1991). This is not to say that all regulations are bad. In some contexts regulations may be the most efficient means of attaining a goal, particularly if there are certain types of information problems (e.g. those related to the quality of goods and services that cannot easily be discerned by consumers). But often regulations, no matter how good might be their intent, are not very effective policy tools (see Sect. 2.3 for further consideration of policy choices).

2.2. *Distribution*

Distribution is a major policy motive distinct from efficiency. Distributional concerns, at least officially, often focus on the command over resources of the poorer members of society. Society might well want to assure, for example, that everyone has basic social services even at some cost in reduced efficiency. Sometimes family planning, education, health, and nutrition services are viewed as 'merit goods' that are socially desirable in themselves.

Though distributional concerns often are characterized by focus on the distribution of income or other resources *among* households, there also may be important distributional considerations *within* households. Household decision-makers are not likely to consider equally the preferences of all household members in allocating household resources. For example, if women have preferences for fewer or more widely spaced children, safer childbirth, or using more resources to invest in children than do their husbands, these preferences may not be weighed equally as those of their husbands in decisions made by their husbands. Moreover, even if some households as aggregates have sufficient resources to cover what society considers to be basic needs, certain types of individuals in households may not be allocated what society considers to be sufficient resources for their individual satisfaction of basic needs. For example, there are many suggestions that women (and even more so widows), infants and children (particularly females and high birth orders), and the elderly may have relatively limited resources allocated to them by household decision-makers.

2.3. *Policy Choices to Increase Efficiency and to Improve Distribution*

Consider first efficiency. If all other markets in the economy are operating efficiently and there are differences between marginal private and social incentives in markets related to population change and economic development so that private incentives are to invest at level H* instead of at level H** in Figure 13.2 or level H*** in Figure 13.3, policies that increase the investment to the socially efficient levels increase efficiency.

If all other markets in the economy are *not* operating efficiently, then policies that narrow the differences between private and social incentives in markets related to population change and economic development do *not* necessarily increase efficiency and productivity. It is conceivable that the distortion between private and social incentives in the particular market that results in the discrepancy between the private and the social optimal investments in Figures 13.2 or 13.3 is just offsetting some distortion elsewhere, so that the economy will become less efficient and less productive if this distortion by itself is lessened.[8] Because there always are distortions between private and social incentives elsewhere in the economy, this may seem to be bad news for establishing an efficiency/productivity basis for policy. But, in the absence of specific information to the contrary, such as the existence of two counterbalancing distortions, a reasonable operating presumption is that lessening any one distortion between social and private incentives is likely to increase efficiency and productivity. With perfect information, one could know for sure and only make policy changes that in fact improve efficiency. In the real world in which policy-makers (and everyone else) have very imperfect information, probabilistic statements must instead be made about policy changes that are likely to improve efficiency.

That still does not indicate what policies would be best to induce investments related to population change and economic development at level H** in Figure 13.2 or level H*** in Figure 13.3. There is a large set of possibilities, including governmental fiats, governmental provision of social services such as schools and health clinics at heavily subsidized prices, price incentives in the markets for population and human resource-related services, price incentives in other markets, and changing institutional arrangements in various markets. To choose among alternatives, there are two important considerations.

First, it is necessary to realize that policies have costs. These costs include the direct costs of implementing and monitoring policies and the distortionary costs introduced by policies that may encourage socially inefficient behavior (including rent-seeking[9] by both public and private entities).[10] Often policy-makers focus only on the direct costs and ignore the distortionary costs that may be much greater because only the direct costs have obvious and visible direct ramifications for governmental budgets. In fact the costs may be sufficiently high that it is not desirable to try to offset some market

---

[8] These considerations are part of the 'theory of the second best'. For example, eliminating monopoly pricing that restricts output in an industry that is a heavy polluter might not improve efficiency because output might expand and therefore pollution might expand enough to more than offset the efficiency gains due to increased market pressures on pricing of the product of the industry.

[9] Economic 'rents' are returns to fixed supplies. Because the supplies are fixed, the rents gained by the owners of them do not affect the quantities supplied. If supplies are fixed, for example, by regulations, rents are created by the supply restrictions, so there are incentives for various private and public entities to try to obtain these rents ('rent-seeking'). Rent-seeking uses resources and transfers income among various groups, but does not add to production.

[10] Behrman and Knowles (1998a, sect. 3.2) provide an example of distortionary costs arising in connection with the provision of emergency obstetric care insurance in Indonesia.

failures by policies.[11] But, if it is desirable to do so, there is a case generally for making policy changes that are directed as specifically as possible to the distortion of concern because that tends to lessen the distortion costs. A *policy hierarchy* can be defined in which alternative policies to attain the same improvement in efficiency in a particular market are ranked according to their social marginal costs, including direct and distortion costs. A policy is higher in the policy hierarchy if it has lower social marginal costs for the same direct effect. This hierarchy indicates the preferential ordering of policies to deal with particular divergences between private and social incentives. For example, it sometimes is argued that female schooling should be subsidized because more-schooled women have fewer children which relieves budgetary pressures on subsidized schooling and health services. But it is not clear that increasing female schooling through such subsidies is high in the policy hierarchy. It would seem, for instance, that higher in the policy hierarchy might be the elimination of any public subsidies that are not warranted by the marginal social benefits exceeding the marginal private benefits as would seem to be the case in many societies for the production of a number of goods and services (e.g. public transportation, curative health, tertiary schooling, fuel, fertilizer).

Secondly, there are tremendous information problems regarding exactly what effects policies have, particularly in a rapidly changing world. This is an argument in favor of policies that are as transparent as possible, which generally means those higher in the policy hierarchy with regard at least to distortion costs because more direct policies are likely to be more transparent.[12] Information problems also provide an argument for price policies (taxes or subsidies) because if there are shifts in the underlying demand and supply relations they are likely to be more visible in a more timely fashion to policy-makers if they have an impact on the governmental budget than if they only change the distortions faced by private entities as tends to happen with quantitative policies such as quotas and restrictions on production or use.[13] Finally information problems in the presence of heterogeneities across communities point to the possible desirability of decentralization and empowerment of users of social services in order to increase the efficacy of the provision of those services, though such considerations must be balanced against possible economies of scale, higher quality

[11] If the policies involve public expenditures as do most policies, it is important to consider the cost of raising the necessary tax revenue to finance the policy. In the United States, for example, it has been estimated that the distortionary cost (often called the 'deadweight loss') of raising a dollar of tax revenue ranges from $0.17 to $1.00, depending on the type of tax used (e.g. Feldstein 1995).

[12] This also is an argument for considering an experimental approach to evaluating policy alternatives when possibly—e.g. rather than introducing a reform country-wide, introduce variants of reforms for health clinics, schools, and other social services in randomly selected sites with careful monitoring of the results for both the experimental groups and the control groups.

[13] Nevertheless there are likely to be some cases, such as providing information regarding the quality of goods and services associated with investments related to population change and economic development, for which quantitative regulations may be higher in the policy hierarchy than price policies because of the nature of the information requirements. For example, the problems in consumers being able to discern the quality of certain foods and medicine may mean that regulations requiring the provision of certain information and monitoring to assure quality control may be high in the policy hierarchy.

of staff, and possibly lower levels of corruption at more centralized levels, as well as inter-community distributional concerns.

Thus, for efficiency/productivity reasons, particularly given that in the real world information is imperfect and changes are frequent, there is an argument generally for choosing policies as high as possible in the policy hierarchy defined by the extent of marginal direct and distortionary costs—and thereby using interventions that are as focused directly on the problem as possible.[14] Note in particular that this means that if there is a good efficiency reason for public support for investments related to population change and economic development, that does *not* mean that the best way to provide that support is through governmental provision of the relevant services. Higher in the policy hierarchy than direct governmental provision of such services, for example, may be subsidies or taxes that create incentives for the efficient provision of these services, whether the actual providers are public, private, or some mixture. On the other hand, policies that discriminate against one type of provider—for example, by making the availability of such subsidies dependent on whether the provider is public—are generally likely to be lower in the policy hierarchy than policies that do not have such conditions.

Now consider distribution. Generally speaking, the subsidization of specific goods and services (and even less, the direct provision by governments of goods and services at subsidized prices) is *not* a very efficient way of lessening distributional problems. Because subsidies are designed to lower prices to consumers, they induce inefficient consumption behavior (i.e. consumption at a point to the right of point H* in Fig. 13.1). Instead, it generally is more efficient (and thus less costly in terms of alternative resource uses) to redistribute income to consumers, allowing them to allocate the income in ways that lead to efficient patterns of consumption.[15] Nevertheless, there are some cases in which subsidization of selected goods and services may be defensible to attain distributional objectives. For example, in cases where it is difficult (and therefore costly) to target the poor, subsidizing certain goods and services that are mainly consumed by the poor may be the most efficient policy alternative. A second example is if policy-makers believe that there is a serious problem of intra-household distribution (e.g. women and children are disadvantaged relative to adult males). In such circumstances, subsidies directed to goods and services consumed mainly by those who are viewed as disadvantaged within households may serve to improve their welfare more than cash payments directed to the household.[16]

Rather than being concerned with the general command over resources of its poorer members, as noted above, society may deem it desirable that everyone enjoy

---

[14] In Section 3, I discuss an example of a fertility control policy that is not well focused (i.e. charging fees for obstetric delivery care only for third and subsequent births) and that has negative distributional and health effects.

[15] However, even redistributing income may lead to inefficiency because it can affect the work effort of those on both the tax-paying and tax-receiving sides.

[16] However, household decision-makers may reallocate resources so that the intended beneficiaries of such policies receive much smaller benefits than intended (e.g. children receiving subsidized food at school may be fed less at home).

basic population and human resource-related (and other) services.[17] That is, society may decide to behave paternalistically by designing policies to assure consumption of certain goods and services even if their consumption results in less welfare for the private decision-makers affected than would consumption of other goods and services requiring the same aggregate resources—perhaps because of concern about intra-household distribution.[18] Or, as noted in Section 2.1, society as a collective might gain welfare if every member of the society has certain minimal human resources beyond those that individual members of society would choose were they only concerned with their own private welfare gains from their own human resources. Such objectives might be obtained through many means. But presumably it is desirable to assure that everyone has these basic options or minimal human resource levels at as little cost in terms of productivity (and therefore economic development) as possible. Therefore, rather than ignoring efficiency considerations, it is desirable to choose policies as high as possible in the policy hierarchy and still assure that the basic service objectives are met. Efficiency goals thus play an important role in interaction with the pursuit of distributional goals, not as independent considerations.

3. SOME ILLUSTRATIONS CONCERNING MICRO ASPECTS OF POPULATION CHANGE AND DEVELOPMENT AND RELATED POLICY CONCERNS

For either prediction or for examining policies it would be desirable to have good micro estimates of critical relations pertaining to population change and development. It would be desirable because, as noted in Section 1, a priori there may be many effects and some of these effects may be working in the opposite direction from others. Crude descriptions of average associations in aggregate data between indicators of population change and economic development give some idea of the magnitude of the net associations, but they are not likely to be very informative about the underlying causal effects nor be very good guides for policy choices.

But good empirical estimates of the underlying micro relations are also very difficult to obtain. One basic problem is that behavioral data, rather than experimental data, generally must be used. Therefore unobservable variables that affect behaviors—such as innate abilities, genetic health endowments, and expected prices—must be controlled to obtain estimates of causal effects. If they are not controlled, the estimated effects are likely to be contaminated (biased) by including effects of unobserved variables in addition to the effects of the variables of interest. Moreover, at times the questions of interest are what is the effect of one behavioral choice variable on another—for example, what is the effect of nutrient consumption on health. In

[17] In the context of such an objective it is important for governments to decide whether success is to be measured in outcomes (i.e. health status), utilization (health clinic use), or access (ability to consume a package of basic services at all income levels).

[18] For example, society might decide that more resources should go to children and less to adult goods such as jewelry and alcohol than the parents would choose.

such cases the estimation procedure must control for what determines the former behavioral variable; if there is not control for what determines it, its estimated effect will again be contaminated by including not only the true effect but also the effects of its determinants. Yet another problem is that for the efficiency motive for policy, what is of interest are divergences between private and social optimal behaviors, but identifying those divergences in many cases is very difficult. For this combination of reasons, the most informative empirical research is conditional on an explicit model of the underlying behaviors—which in turn can be viewed as a special case of the general model sketched out in Section 1—with the empirical estimates tied tightly to that model and the interpretations of those estimates conditional on that model.

In Section 3.1 I review some empirical estimates on selected topics related to micro aspects of population change and economic development to illustrate what we do and, equally important, do not know from systematic empirical approaches and how being systematic in such approaches in the sense of grounding the analysis firmly in the conceptual frameworks of Sections 1 and 2 may make a substantial difference in our understanding of these topics. Because of the difficulties in obtaining good empirical estimates, however, often policies have to be formulated to a considerable extent on the basis of a priori frameworks. In Section 3.2 I review a priori considerations, grounded in the frameworks of Sections 1 and 2, for selected policy issues related to population change and economic development.

3.1. *Review of Empirical Estimates on Selected Topics Related to Micro Aspects of Population Change and Economic Development*

In this section I provide selected illustrations of some of the difficulties in making empirical inferences about micro relations relating to population change and development and related policies. The explicit examples that I consider are (1) the impact of schooling on population change and on productivities, (2) targeting policies toward particular demographic groups and collective versus unitary household decisions, (3) the role of expectations regarding future developments within dynamic optimizing models of micro behavior on population change and economic development, and (4) distributional analysis of policies.

Impact of Schooling on Population Change and on Productivities   I start with schooling because it is widely perceived that schooling is tied in intimately with a number of important aspects of population change and development and that schooling is susceptible to a range of policy influences. More schooling and better schooling is associated with what many people consider to be 'good' outcomes—higher productivities in a wide range of activities, fewer children, better health and nutrition, and lower mortality rates. For many of these outcomes female schooling has been emphasized as being particularly important.

There are literally hundreds of micro studies that purport to investigate the impact of schooling on economic (e.g. wages, agricultural productivity) productivity and non-market productivity in developing countries (see the surveys in Behrman 1990*a*, 1990*b*, 1997; King and Hill 1993; Psacharopoulos 1994; Schultz 1988; Strauss and Thomas 1995). An effective way to summarize many of the studies on wages has been through the calculation of the real rates of return to the costs incurred in schooling which permits comparisons among a wide range of investments, both within the schooling sector and elsewhere in the economy. Typically these rates of return have been calculated by comparing the direct economic outcomes for individuals with different amounts or types of schooling and calculating the rate of return to the private costs (primarily the time costs but perhaps also tuition, books and materials, and other private costs) and to the social costs (the private costs plus public subsidies) to obtain, respectively, the so-called 'private' and 'social' rates of return to schooling. These estimates are widely interpreted to imply that in developing countries:

(1) the rates of return to schooling are high,[19]
(2) they do not decline very rapidly with the level of development,
(3) the impact of schooling, particularly for females, on non-market outcomes is considerable and generally greater than that of males,
(4) the social rates of return decline with schooling levels (though the private rates of return do not necessarily do so because of relatively high per student subsidies to higher schooling levels), are higher for general as opposed to technical vocational schooling, and are at least as high on average for female as for male schooling,
(5) variability in schooling is associated with the variability in income distribution and more schooling is associated with less probability of being below the poverty line,[20] and

---

[19] Such estimates imply, in fact, that investment in schooling is such a high return investment that they are not completely credible on these grounds alone. Investments with a real annual rate of return of 16–24% (the social rate of return to primary school in the four developing regions given in Psacharopoulos 1994) given reinvestment of the proceeds of such investment imply that society can double the real invested assets in 2.9 to 4.3 years, and the social real rate of 11–18% on secondary schooling implies the possibility of doubling real assets in 3.8 to 6.3 years. These estimates, moreover, understate the true social rates of return and overstate the true time that social assets could be doubled by marginal schooling investments if there are positive externalities to schooling as often is claimed. If developing countries have available such investment opportunities on a fairly broad scale (i.e. in most of its children), furthermore, it would seem that much higher economic growth would be observed than ever has been experienced for any sustained period of time.

[20] Psacharopoulos *et al.* (1992), for example, examine the relation between schooling and income inequality and poverty in the Latin American and Caribbean region. A decomposition of the inequality in the distribution of workers' income (including only individuals over 15 years of age in the labor force with positive income) indicates that variations in schooling attainment are associated with about a quarter of the income inequality. Also low schooling attainment is the characteristic observed in the data that is most associated with being in the bottom 20% of the distribution of workers' income; on average those with no schooling have a 56% probability of being in the bottom 20% of the workers' income distribution, while those with primary schooling have 27% probability, those with secondary schooling 9% probability, and those with university schooling 4% probability. These results are characterized by Psacharopoulos *et al.* (1992: 40, 48) to indicate 'the overwhelming preeminence of education' and that 'clearly ... education is the variable with the strongest impact on income inequality'.

(6) there is not likely to be an equity-productivity trade-off in expanding schooling in the most productive way because the returns are highest for basic (primary, then secondary) schooling for which further expansion is likely primarily to enroll more children from very poor families and the total returns are higher for females than for males.

Under the assumption that wages are strongly associated with productivities, these conclusions generally are interpreted to carry over to the impact on productivity.[21] Conclusions of this sort are used to guide policy recommendations by many, including the World Bank (1991), for increasing policy support for schooling, particularly for basic (primary and lower secondary) schooling and particularly for females.

But the systematic empirical basis for these policy recommendations is weak in a number of respects. First of all, there are a number of well-known possible problems with the methodology sketched out above for estimating the impact of schooling. Most of the existing studies of the impact of schooling do not control well for the behavioral decisions that determine who goes to what type of school for how long with what degree of success. Simple analytical frameworks for school investments as in Becker's (1967) Woytinsky Lecture, as well as casual observations, suggest that individuals with higher investments in schooling are likely to be individuals with more ability and more motivation who come from family and community backgrounds that provide more reinforcement for such investments and who have lower marginal private costs for such investments and lower discount rates for the returns from those investments and who are likely to have access to higher quality schools. That effectively means that, in Figures 13.2 and 13.3, the private marginal benefit curves are likely to be higher for individuals who are from 'better' family backgrounds (i.e. because they have more inherited abilities, greater motivations for material rewards, better family connections) and the private marginal private costs are likely to be lower for such individuals (i.e. investments in their schooling is likely to be less constrained by capital/insurance market imperfections). Therefore most studies that (usually implicitly) assume that schooling is distributed randomly among sample members probably suffer from omitted variable biases that cause substantial upward biases in the estimated impact of schooling. The association of schooling with outcomes such as wage rates, agricultural productivity, fertility, and child health does not necessarily represent causality because in most estimates years of schooling is representing not only time in school, but also factors that are correlated with years of school such as abilities, discount rates, family backgrounds, and schooling qualities. To obtain insight into the impact of years of school on such outcomes, one needs to control for these other factors, as do to a certain extent some—but not many—of the existing studies.

Some 'revisionist' studies for developing countries, parallel to a similar literature for developed economies, have explored the impact of some of these estimation

---

[21] The third conclusion and a small subset of the studies underlying the other conclusions use direct measures of productivity, not wages, as the dependent variables.

problems on estimated schooling returns with data or specification modifications of the standard earnings function framework by controlling for: school quality (Behrman and Birdsall 1983), unobserved shared family background of adult siblings and of members of the same household (Behrman and Wolfe 1984; Behrman and Deolalikar 1993), usually unobserved abilities through new tests (Boissiere *et al.* 1985; Knight and Sabot 1990; Glewwe 1996), selectivity (Schultz 1988), dropout and repetition rates (Behrman and Deolalikar 1991),[22] measurement error, school quality, and behavioral choices regarding school attendance (Alderman *et al.* 1996). Likewise a smaller number of studies control for various characteristics such as women's childhood family background or the nature of the extended household environment or access to information which reduces substantially the estimated impact of women's schooling on outcomes such as health and nutrition and fertility (e.g. Barrera 1990; Behrman and Wolfe 1987, 1989; Strauss 1990; Thomas *et al.* 1991; Wolfe and Behrman 1987). Those studies that incorporate such controls for developing countries tend to find that the 'standard estimates' (i.e. those without such controls) may overstate the impact of schooling attainment by as much as 40 to 100 percent, probably more so for primary schooling, and underestimate the relative importance of school quality improvements (Behrman 1990*a*, 1990*b*).[23,24] At this point I perceive that the 'standard' estimates for developing countries probably overstate the true schooling returns substantially but that there remain some open questions about this literature to which further studies of developing economies are likely to continue to contribute. But because of such estimation problems, there may be substantial misunderstanding among policy-makers of what are the true returns to schooling as opposed to associations with schooling.

For such reasons policy-makers and other observers may overstate, perhaps substantially, the impact of schooling on population change and development as related to the second major policy motive discussed in Sect. 2, distribution. But perhaps more important, such studies and parallel studies using aggregate data—even if there are no estimation problems—have nothing to say about the efficiency motive for

---

[22] Grade repetition is substantial in many developing countries (e.g. Latin America and the Caribbean have a first grade repetition rate of 42%, and an overall primary school repetition rate of 29% according to recent estimates based on a special UNESCO/OREALC survey) so the failure to control for grade repetition and school dropouts in standard estimates may be quite important.

[23] Such factors are controlled generally by linking data used for the standard estimates with other information about characteristics such as school quality, family background, and ability or by using special data on adult siblings or family or community members to control for common unobserved characteristics (e.g. the estimate of the difference in wage rates regressed on the difference in schooling for adult siblings controls for the additive effect of common family and community background shared by the siblings).

[24] The recent ferment in studies of such questions for the United States (see Card 1999 for a survey) has re-emphasized the point that random measurement error and other estimation problems may mean that some of these studies may not overestimate schooling attainment effects as much as I suggest. Recent studies for the United States and Australia that use adult identical twins to control perfectly for genetic endowments at the time of conception and for all common family background and use reports by others to control for random measurement errors, however, still indicate that standard estimates overstate the schooling impact by from 12% to 100% due to the failure to control for 'ability' genetic endowments and correlated aspects of family background (Behrman and Rosenzweig 1999).

policies to support schooling. Why? Because such studies have nothing to say about the possibility that the solid and dashed lines in Figures 13.2 and 13.3 differ (with the dashed lines representing marginal social benefits and costs, respectively, as is discussed in Sect. 2.1). The impact of schooling on some outcome may be large, but with little or no divergence between optimal private and optimal social schooling and therefore little or no reason for policy interventions justified on efficiency grounds. Or, the opposite may be the case: the impact of schooling on some outcome may be small, but with a large divergence between optimal private and optimal social schooling and therefore considerable reason for policy interventions justified on efficiency grounds.

There are a few exceptions in the empirical literature that do find some evidence of differentials between private and social returns to schooling. For example, a few recent studies (e.g. Besley and Case 1994; Foster and Rosenzweig 1995, 1996; Munshi 1997; Rosenzweig 1995, 1997), based on data from the 'Green Revolution' adoption of new agricultural seeds, analyze the causal effect of schooling on the adoption of new technologies, with incorporation of estimates of learning through observing neighbors as well as learning from one's own experiences (with the former resulting in the social returns exceeding the private returns). Learning about appropriate allocations of inputs was a challenge to farmers formerly engaged in traditional practices. The continual introduction of new seeds permanently raised the returns from skills in information decoding. The new technologies were more complex than previous technologies because the new seeds were considerably more sensitive to appropriate use of fertilizer and water than were traditional varieties. So the margin for error was greater. The empirical estimates from these studies indicate that the costs of delays in adoption while learning about complex new technologies may be considerable. Over the first five years, the average loss due to slow adoption and misuse of the new technologies in comparison with their subsequent experienced use averaged 3.7 times the pre-Green Revolution annual income. These studies also indicate that farmers learned over time about the micro characteristics of the new technologies from their own experiences and from the experiences of neighboring farmers. Farmers with primary schooling had a very small initial advantage over farmers with no schooling that translated into about 5 percent greater profits in the first year. But farmers with primary school had more rapidly increasing profits with experience than did those with no schooling—an 18 percent greater effect on profits in the second year per acre-year of prior experience. Moreover there are spillover effects of schooling, with an unschooled farmer reaching full specialization in the new technologies in four years rather than five if he had schooled rather than unschooled neighbors.

Assessing the relevance and extent of such 'social' learning is critical for understanding policy implications for subsidizing schooling based on the efficiency motive for policy. That such studies find support for such externalities, however, in itself does not address the question of which policies are high in the policy hierarchy discussed in Section 2.3. They provide no insight at all, for example, into the answer to the sometimes contentious question of whether direct subsidies to public schools or direct subsidies to students and their families is higher in the policy hierarchy, though a priori reasoning based on the welfare considerations in Section 2 suggests that the latter may be more effective in creating desirable incentives for the right types of schooling.

Targeting Policies towards Particular Demographic Groups and Collective versus Unitary Household Decisions   Because many of the critical decisions regarding population change and economic development occur at a micro level, understanding how relevant micro units function is important for both conditional predictions and for policy analysis related to efficiency as well as to distribution. The critical unit in many cases is the household or the family. Some studies find that if women have greater household income shares, children have better education, health, and nutrition.

Thomas (1990), for example, explores whether there are different effects of men's and women's unearned income on child survival rates, anthropometric measures, and nutrient intakes for children using 1974–75 Brazilian data for over 25,000 urban households. Unearned income (not wages) is used and parents' education is controlled in order to focus on the income effects alone, without the price effects that wages would entail. The estimates indicate a much larger effect on child survival and child anthropometric measures of women's unearned income than of men's, with some further gender differentiation in that mothers' unearned income has greater impact on daughters than on sons, while fathers' unearned income has greater impact on sons.[25] He also reports that the estimated effects of both women's and men's unearned income are positive, but decline as income increases. But the estimated impact of women's unearned income is about seven times that of men's, for both calories and proteins. Thomas concludes that these results reject the consensus preference model of households often used for economic analysis,[26] and suggest that mothers' income is much more important in shaping children than is fathers' income.

Schultz (1990) explores whether there are different effects of men's and women's unearned income on female labor supply and recent fertility using over 8,000 households with adults between 25 and 54 in age from the 1980–81 Thai Socioeconomic Survey. He finds that women's non-earned income has significantly different effects (i.e. reducing more) than men's non-earned income on women's labor supply, but not for men's labor supply. He also finds that women's non-earned income has a significant positive effect on the number of co-resident children under 5 years of age (a proxy for recent fertility) but men's unearned income does not. However he notes

[25] There are some anomalies, such as the indication that unearned income of non-parents has much greater impact on anthropometric measures for boys than either mothers' or fathers' unearned income. Also in the household demand relation for calories, other unearned income has a possibly puzzling *negative* estimated impact, declining with income. Nancy Birdsall has suggested that the puzzle may be due to reverse causality—i.e. that those who are most at nutritional risk are more likely to receive transfers from other households. This is an interesting possibility. But it is not clear that such transfers would be counted in these data as unearned income of other household members rather than of the mothers and/or of the fathers as would seem to be needed for this to be the explanation.

[26] Though he also notes that ratios of income effects are not significantly different from each other, which is consistent with the common preference model if income is measured with error, as well as consistent with differential intra-household preferences that are homogenous in the relative preference weights that mothers and fathers have for the child health outcomes.

that his relation may reflect reverse causality if women with more children are likely to receive more transfers from their families and other sources. Schultz concludes that this paper 'has rejected one of the restrictions implied by the neoclassical model of family demand behavior, that for female labor supply' (and, with more qualifications, perhaps that for fertility).

What do these and similar studies mean with regard to the nature of household decision-making? McElroy (1992: 12) interprets these and related studies to be part of the 'strong results favoring bargaining models'. Alderman *et al.* (1995) suggest that such results imply that it is 'time to shift the burden of proof' to those who favor the consensus assumption. One important implication is that, if women have preferences that favor socially desirable goals (the usual examples include more investments in children and less fertility) more than do men, then policies that shift resources to women will be more effective in attaining those goals.[27] If those goals are based on efficiency considerations, then there is an efficiency reason in addition to any distributional reasons, for targeting women with policies. In some countries policies have been designed to direct resources to women based explicitly on this literature (e.g. the PROGRESA program for improving education, health, and nutrition in rural Mexico).

But there are problems with the interpretation that these results reject the pooling assumption of the consensus preference model. To test that assumption what one would like to do would be to conduct an experiment in which extra income were distributed randomly to males and females and then to observe whether the marginal propensities to use such income differed depending upon who is the recipient. However neither Schultz or Thomas (nor, to my knowledge, anyone else) uses such data for these tests of micro income pooling. Instead they use individual 'unearned' income. They explicitly use unearned income rather than earned income or total income in order to abstract from price (i.e. opportunity cost of time) or preference effects that wages would represent. But is there any reason to think that unearned income is orthogonal to wages and unobserved productivity and preferences? The answer depends in part on what are the sources of unearned income. In the data for both studies the sources are largely pensions and social security, both of which are related to past wages and productivity. Even earnings from assets may reflect past wages and productivity if such assets were acquired out of past labor earnings. Therefore unearned income may in part represent preferences regarding time use and productivity in labor market activities associated with household activities pertaining to

---

[27] There is an interesting question regarding why women might have preferences that favor human resource investments in children relative to men. An explanation based in sociobiology might be that women are more limited in the number of biological children that they can have than are men so they have greater incentives than do men to invest more in the quality of their children—and the gene pool therefore has relatively more representatives of women with preferences that favor higher quality children and of men with preferences that favor more children because these are the strategies (differentially by gender) for gene perpetuation that have proved effective. Given that the genes of children are inherited from both parents, this would require an interaction between the child's gender and her or his genes that determine her or his innate preferences.

health, nutrition, fertility, and time allocations. If so, these results do not necessarily mean that shifting income to women would have more positive effects on, say, child health than shifting equal income to men, but simply may reflect that more productive women or women with different preferences have more positive effects on their children's health. These results, in fact, are consistent with the true effects involving income pooling, but unearned income coefficient estimates being biased differentially by proxying for unobserved productivity and preference endowments given gender specialization in household tasks.

More recent empirical research suggests, however, that what really may be relevant may be what determines each individual's options if the collective dissolves (i.e. what determines each marriage partner's options outside marriage if the marriage fails) as would be expected from formal models of bargaining within households (e.g. McElroy 1990). For example, empirical estimates for the United States suggest that all resources are pooled within households at least in states with common property laws for divorce settlements, but that nevertheless the parental family resources on which a marriage partner can rely should a divorce occur affect the use of the couple's resources within the marriage (Behrman and Rosenzweig 1998). Likewise analysis of the change in child benefit laws in the United Kingdom from payments to household heads to payments to mothers finds impacts on intra-household allocations (Lundberg *et al.* 1997). Though I am unaware of similar studies for developing countries, these results reinforce the point of the collective model that who receives resources (or who potentially would receive resources if the marriage were to dissolve) in the household affects significantly how those resources are used.

Role of Expectations regarding Future Developments within Dynamic Optimizing Models of Micro Behavior on Population Change and Economic Development The discussions of micro decisions regarding population change and economic development in Section 1 note that such decisions depend not only on present prices, policies, and other determinants, but also on expectations regarding future developments. Incorporation of such expectations within the framework of such models may change relevant empirical estimates in important ways and thereby our understanding of significant phenomena related to population change and economic development. But considerations of expected future developments usually are not incorporated into analyses, in major part because it is often hard to know how to incorporate such expectations into the analysis.

One recent exception is the study by Eckstein, Mira, and Wolpin (1998) on fertility dynamics in Sweden over two and a half centuries. They note that many have argued that a reduction in infant and child mortality is a necessary precondition for fertility decline in the demographic transition theory, but that a recent extensive survey of the relevant literature in Cohen and Montgomery (1998) concludes that 'a mountain of evidence refutes such a simple description of "real-world events". Eckstein, Mira, and Wolpin note that simple correlations between fertility and infant and child mortality over two and a half centuries in Sweden are also not strong—there is a strong positive upward secular trend over the entire period in survival rates but basically constant fertility rates at a level that implies more than four children for birth cohorts born before 1856 and at a level that implies about two children for birth cohorts born after 1901, but with a sharp fall between these two birth cohorts. But they suggest that such a correlation, like the available empirical studies, may not be very informative on this topic because neither such a correlation nor previous studies are well based in a dynamic model of optimal life-cycle fertility decisions that incorporates, *inter alia*, forward-looking behaviors within a dynamic optimizing model of fertility behavior. They fit such a model to fertility decisions in Sweden for 43 five-year birth cohorts between 1736 and 1946 and use the model to decompose the determinants of the fertility decline that commenced in the last half of the nineteenth century (e.g. with declines of 0.77 in completed fertility between the 1871 and 1886 birth cohorts and of 0.97 between the 1886 and 1901 birth cohorts after a long period with completed fertility more or less stable above 4, with that for the 1856 birth cohort only 0.04 less than that for the 1751 birth cohort). Their results suggest that both wage increases and reductions in infant and child mortality contributed to the fertility decline, with the former accounting for less than a fifth of the decline and the latter being much more important. They also test whether a model estimated only with data on birth cohorts up to 1856 would predict well the subsequent fertility transition despite the fairly stable high fertility rates for over a century (and probably much longer) before then. They find that the model estimated with these data indeed predicts a substantial fertility decline—in fact somewhat overpredicts the actual decline. Thus simple associations in the data and empirical studies that did not incorporate dynamic forward-looking behavior both miss what in a dynamic optimizing fertility model with incorporation of forward-looking behavior is a substantial impact of reduced infant and child mortality on completed fertility.

Distributional Analysis of Policies   Much of the literature on population change and economic development has placed considerable emphasis on distribution as an important motive for policies. This literature, of course, means that analysis of policy impact cannot be just aggregate, but must take into account the distribution of the policy effects among micro units, such as among households. There are also many empirical studies that attempt to characterize the relations between policies associated with human resources as well as other outcomes and distribution. But, perhaps surprisingly, such characterizations are relatively rare for policies related directly to population change.

For this reason I summarize here a characterization of the distributional dimensions of family planning in Vietnam based on Behrman and Knowles (1998*b*). Vietnam has had a strong anti-natalist population policy since 1963, but only since 1993 has the government made substantial investments in family planning. The program recently has made available more contraceptive methods, has implemented a large information and education component, and has developed an administrative structure with paid staff down to the commune level and with thousands of volunteers at the village level. The total fertility rate has fallen from about 6.4 in 1960–64 to about 3.3 in 1989–93. Current demographic objectives include limiting couples to one or two children, achieving replacement level fertility by the year 2015, and achieving a stable population by the year 2050. The government regards the family planning program as one of its most important development programs.

Vietnam has an extensive, but poorly funded, governmental health system. A limited number of relatively well-funded central government hospitals operated by the Ministry of Health, almost all of which are located in urban areas, are at the top of the system. These facilities are generally acknowledged to provide the best quality health care. Although their inpatient services are in principle available to the entire population, their extensive outpatient services are practically accessible only to urban and suburban populations, and because of the relatively high fees they charge, are mainly used by upper-income groups and senior governmental officials. Provinces operate a system of provincial and district hospitals, with the former being considerably larger and providing a broader range of higher quality services than the latter. Provinces also operate polyclinics (health centers staffed by several doctors) in a few areas with poor access to district hospitals. The lowest level of the governmental health system (and in fact not formally a part of it) consists of commune health centers operated and financed almost entirely by communes. They are typically staffed by either one doctor or assistant doctor and one or two nurses and/or midwives. The government's family planning program provides services through the existing health infrastructure, and unlike most other health services (including prenatal care, obstetric delivery care, abortions, and menstrual regulations) there is usually no charge for either family planning services or contraceptives.

Estimates of the utilization of family planning services by per capita income quintile[28] indicate that current contraceptive use is 66 percent among the poorest women, 75 to 78 percent among women in the next three quintiles, and 70 percent among women in the richest quintile. Perhaps surprisingly, there is no systematic variation observed between quintiles in rates of modern contraceptive use, which is 57 percent among the poor and 55 percent among the rich. There is also relatively little variation in the method mix between women in different per capita consumption quintiles, although poorer women tend to rely more on the IUD and less on traditional methods. There is, however, substantial variation observed in the source of contraceptives. More than half of the poorest women (54 percent) obtained their contraceptives from commune health centers, compared to only 21 percent of women in the richest quintile. In contrast, almost one-quarter (24 percent) of the rich obtained contraceptives from hospitals, compared to only 11 percent of poor women. Since the unit costs of family planning services (which are equal to unit subsidies in this case) are much higher in hospitals, these data suggest that the rich may be capturing proportionately more family planning program subsidies than the poor.

Because one of the reasons most often given for subsidizing these services is to help the poor, an important question to ask is what share of the total subsidy is reaching its

---

[28] Consumption expenditures are used to represent income in this study and in much of the literature because they better represent longer-run income constraints than does measured annual income if there are large transitory income fluctuations and if households can smooth consumption somewhat over time.

target. The poorest per capita income quintile receives 15 percent of the total governmental family planning benefits (i.e. public subsidies). Although this is less than their
share of the population (20%, by definition of a quintile), it is substantially more than
their share of total private consumption (9%).[29] The poorest two quintiles receive
36 percent of the total benefits, almost as much as their share of the population (40%)
and substantially more than their share of total private consumption (22%). The main
source of inequality in the distribution of family planning benefits received stems from
the greater use of more heavily subsidized governmental providers (i.e. hospitals) by
the higher income quintiles. For example, 26 percent of contraceptive users in the
richest quintile obtain their contraceptives from governmental hospitals, compared to
only 11 percent of those in the poorest quintile. In contrast only 21 percent of contraceptive users in the richest quintile obtain their services at a commune health center
(the least expensive source), compared to 54 percent of those in the poorest quintile.
In addition to differences in the source mix, differences in contraceptive prevalence
(relatively small in Vietnam) and in the proportion of married women of reproductive
age in the population (18 percent of the richest quintile, compared to 14 percent of
the poorest quintile) also contribute to the inequality in the distribution of benefits.
Partly offsetting these factors is the fact that 29 percent of those in the richest quintile
obtain their services from the relatively lightly subsidized private sector (i.e. private
sector subsidies are limited to the government's social marketing program).

A policy of charging fees for the relatively high-cost family planning services provided by hospitals would be likely to improve the distribution of family planning
benefits in Vietnam.[30] At present, the government provides much higher subsidies
(in absolute terms) to family planning services obtained from hospitals than it provides for services obtained from commune health centers, polyclinics, and family
planning centers. Since the relatively well-off urban population lives relatively close
to hospitals, they are in a better position to (and do in fact) capture the bulk of
these relatively generous subsidies. If instead the subsidy per acceptor at hospitals
were reduced to the same level as that received by acceptors at commune health centers and family planning centers, the share of subsidies received by the poorest two
quintiles would increase from 36 to 41 percent (i.e. more than their share of the
population), while the share received by the richest quintile would decrease from
29 to 21 percent (i.e. program benefits would be distributed almost proportionately
across quintiles). In addition, such a policy change would be likely to shift some rich
acceptors away from more expensive sources of family planning services (since they

[29] It is also about the same share as the poorest quartiles of the population were estimated to receive
in two other studies of family planning program benefit incidence in Cebu, Philippines, and Indonesia
(Committee on Population 1995).

[30] However, in making such a policy change, it is important to introduce fees that recover most, if not
all, of program costs. Otherwise, the effect of introducing fees may further limit access of the poor to the
most heavily subsidized services (in absolute terms), so that an even higher share of program subsidies
accrues to the rich. Such an adverse consequence of user fees actually occurs in the case of safe motherhood
services in Vietnam (Behrman and Knowles 1998a).

would be receiving more appropriate price signals), simultaneously improving overall program efficiency.

3.2. *A priori Considerations for Selected Policy Issues Related to Population Change and Economic Development*

As Section 3.1 illustrates, good empirical information about micro aspects of development are difficult to obtain. Therefore conditional predictions and policy analysis must be made under considerable uncertainty—for which reason a priori models (whether so called or not) must provide guidance. Therefore I discuss briefly in this section the relations between selected issues that are prominent in policy discussions relating to population change and economic development and the frameworks of Sections 1 and 2—namely, (1) the role of regulatory policies, (2) pricing and cost recovery in programs related to population change and human resource development, (3) access to programs and quality of programs related to population change and human resource development, and (4) overall and program sustainability.[31]

Role of Regulatory Policies   Many people and organizations who are interested in improvements in human resource and population programs advocate increased regulations to obtain the goals that they deem desirable. They apparently perceive that regulations are the most direct, and therefore the most effective, means of obtaining desired goals. If, for example, better schools and better health programs are desired, then they should be mandated—and educational and health services should be provided by the public sector so that it can be assured that the mandates are followed. But the implication of the discussion in Sections 1 and 2 is that in most cases regulations are likely to be relatively low in the policy hierarchy. In most cases they are likely to increase inefficiencies and reduce welfare and often impact negatively particularly on poorer members of the society who can with least ease get around the regulations. They also are likely to establish privileged positions for certain suppliers of goods and services that lessen the pressures for efficient provision of these goods and services through the competition of actual or potential new providers of these goods and services. It is true, as noted above, that there may be some important exceptions in which regulation is high in the policy priority, such as providing information about the quality of foods and drugs and other items, the quality of which is not easily discernible by consumers. But an important implication of the framework presented above is that generally regulations are not high in the policy hierarchy. This is the case because they tend to lessen private options for improving efficiency and improving welfare, have increased distortionary effects with other changes in the economy with little feedback

---

[31] This discussion builds in part on discussions about family planning and reproductive health policies in Behrman and Knowles (1998a), where, in addition, there are discussions of some other policy issues related to family planning and reproductive health (e.g. targets, incentives, and unmet needs and the role of the private sector).

that causes appropriate adjustments, and create vested interests in maintaining and increasing the regulations. Therefore the working presumption should be that regulations are generally not high in the policy hierarchy and not the policy tools of choice unless there are particular reasons in the particular context being considered to presume that they are.

Pricing and Cost Recovery in Programs Related to Population Change and Human Resource Development   Many human resource and family planning programs provide services free of charge or with substantial subsidies to the entire population. Financing these programs has become burdensome in many developing countries. One response has been to consider charging fees for these services. Although charging fees has the potential to recover a significant share of costs, concern is often expressed that it will reduce use levels and impose a burden on the poor. Other issues relate to how high fees should be (i.e. what percentage of costs should be recovered) and how fees should be set for different services (e.g. for different health services or different contraceptive methods).

The policy framework presented in Section 2 suggests that from an efficiency perspective all human resource-related services (including family planning services), whether produced by the government or by the private sector, should be priced so that the marginal social benefit of the last unit consumed is equal to its marginal social cost. Unless a situation such as that depicted in Figures 13.2 or 13.3 exists, the normal operation of competitive markets should ensure that this occurs. If not, methods such as those illustrated in Behrman and Knowles (1998a: sect. 3.1) should be used to find an appropriate level of subsidy (or tax). If a case can be made for subsidizing governmental services on efficiency grounds, the same subsidy should be provided to private providers. Failure to extend the same subsidies to the private sector as the public sector receives puts the private sector at a competitive disadvantage and risks losing the potential gains in efficiency that may be obtained by strengthening competition between public and private sector producers.

The same guidelines should be used to determine subsidies, if any, from an efficiency perspective for different services and goods, such as individual contraceptive methods or different pharmaceuticals or different types of schooling. In general, these guidelines imply that prices (and subsidies) for different options should be roughly proportional to their marginal cost, so, for example, the fee charged for a sterilization or implant should in most cases be significantly higher than that for an IUD insertion. For a given option, the same absolute subsidy should be given to each provider (including private providers). Actual pricing policy often departs from these principles, however, as the Vietnam example above illustrates; more expensive options and services typically receive higher subsidies to make them affordable. In many programs, all services regardless of cost are provided free. Varying the subsidies from one option or source to another, other than as dictated by applying the principles presented in the policy framework of Section 2, creates the wrong incentives for consumers and encourages inefficient choices.[32,33] It can also exacerbate distributional inequities, as the example above illustrates and is illustrated by the large subsidies per student in many societies for upper levels of education that are attained primarily by students from middle and upper-income families.

It is certainly true that pricing human resource and population-related services according to efficiency guidelines may hurt the poor in comparison with free provision (just as competitive pricing of food, housing, and clothing may hurt the poor in comparison with free provision). They will be hurt whether they reduce their consumption of the service or not. At times it is suggested that they will be hurt more if they reduce their use of such services a lot due to price increases (e.g. Gertler *et al.* 1987). But in fact the implication of the framework in Section 1 is that they will be hurt more by increased prices due to 'cost recovery' applied to services that induce no or little reduction in utilization following the price increase (i.e. demand is inelastic) than they are by price increases that result in large reductions of quantities demanded (i.e. for which there are close substitutes so demand is elastic). If the poor can readily substitute other goods and services (e.g. additional food purchases) for human resource services or family planning if the price of the latter increases, this may be of concern to the public health specialist and the family planning worker. But it may be of less concern to the poor themselves because they are able to substitute consumption of other goods and services with little loss of welfare.

That the poor may reduce their use of human resource and family planning services because of price increases as part of cost recovery efforts, however, does not imply that continuing to subsidize all such services necessarily helps the poor. If certain services have a high income elasticity of demand, for example, most of the subsidy will be captured by upper-income groups, as for hospital-based subsidies in the example for Vietnam discussed above. In such cases, the poor would be better off if the funds were used to subsidize the goods and services of which they consume proportionately more or if the subsidies can be targeted better so that indeed the poor are the primary beneficiaries (though such targeting, if successful, may reduce political support for the subsidies).

Access to Programs and Quality of Programs Related to Population Change and Human Resource Development The human resource and family planning

---

[32] In some cases there may be a strong rationale in terms of the framework in Section 2 for subsidizing certain options more heavily. The condom, for example, provides protection against STDs and AIDS. Its use generates significant externalities to other consumers in the form of reduced risk of contracting these illnesses.

[33] Even if paternalistic policy-makers decide that the basic policy objective should not be increasing welfare of the populace but some goal such as reducing population growth, and long-term contraceptive methods are perceived to be more cost-effective in reducing fertility, the underlying private household behaviors that are discussed in Section 1.1 and the behaviors of suppliers need to be taken into account in devising the structure of subsidies. A subsidy will be ineffective if demand for or supply of the method is highly inelastic (i.e. a price reduction does not encourage much additional demand or much additional supply—Hammer and Berman 1995).

communities frequently identify 'access' and 'quality' as program objectives in addition to efficiency, distribution (or equity), and 'sustainability' (discussed below). 'Access' is usually defined as the absence of economic and physical barriers that keep a prospective client away from a service delivery point; 'quality' is usually defined as the factors that determine whether the care is effective and acceptable to the client once she or he walks through the door. Optimal levels of access and quality are defined in this literature to be those that maximize utilization and impact. Thus, for example, medical services and contraceptives are delivered free of charge to a client's doorstep (taking access to the limits), and governmental human resource and family planning programs are criticized for their poor quality if they do not provide a full range of options or highly trained staff, citing studies that utilization increases with quality defined by such indicators.

I do not see, however, that these concepts add to the perspective of the framework in Section 2. 'Access' and 'quality' considerations are already included in the concept of efficiency. The framework presented in Section 2 is consistent with improved access (e.g. bringing services closer to clients) up to the point where the marginal social benefits of doing so are equal to the marginal social cost. Goods and services of varying qualities are effectively distinct goods and services, and the normal functioning of competitive-like markets (assuming consumers are well informed) provides an optimal mix of goods and services of different qualities (i.e. that mix that responds to consumer demand). Unless a situation such as that depicted in Figures 13.2 or 13.3 is present, the normal operation of competitive markets should result in optimal 'access' and 'quality'. If this is not the case, the optimal levels of subsidies (or taxes) should then be applied to all producers, public and private. If consumers cannot be relied upon to make 'good' quality choices in markets for human resource and family planning services because they do not have as much information as is warranted by the same efficiency guidelines (i.e. to the point at which the marginal social benefit equals the marginal social cost of information), subsidization of more information is likely to be higher in the policy hierarchy than emphasis on access and quality *per se.*

If governments have an effective monopoly in the provision of certain services, which can easily occur if they are financed mainly out of governmental budgets, problems of poor access and quality often arise. Decisions about the location of governmental human resources and other facilities, for example, are often made on the basis of political considerations, rather than on the basis of efficiency and distribution. Governmental providers have little incentive to provide good quality services; and they tend to provide a more limited range of service quality than do private providers. The poor quality of governmental services often is a consequence of a lack of competition from private providers. Policies that subsidize governmental providers, and not private providers, are the source of the problem. Providing subsidies, if any are warranted on efficiency or distributional grounds, equally to all providers is the solution. Special quality improvement programs directed to governmental providers are not nearly as high in the policy hierarchy as solutions to problems of poor-quality governmental services.

Sustainability 'Sustainability' seems to have two different meanings in the population change and economic development literatures.

The first meaning of sustainability concerns the overall process of development and whether it is sustainable in the sense that it is supported by the evolving resource base of an economy. This might be referred to as overall sustainability of the development process to distinguish it from the second meaning discussed below. There is concern, for example, that the development process in some contexts cannot be continued in the long run because of environmental degradation in many forms ranging from water pollution to solid-waste disposal to soil run-offs. Many seem to think that this concept of sustainability adds another basic policy motivation beyond efficiency and equity.

But, again, I do understand why. All of the concerns that I understand are covered by this meaning of sustainability are already incorporated in the concept of efficiency, including efficiency over time (or dynamic efficiency). If an economy is efficient but the rate of development is not maintainable I do not see what insights the concept of overall sustainability has to offer. Any changes suggested by this concept would, by definition, only make people worse off by reducing welfare. If an economy is not efficient, then—whether or not the rate of development is maintainable (sustainable)—welfare improvements can be made (at least in the probabilistic sense discussed above) by making it more efficient, by bringing marginal private incentives more into alignment with marginal socially desirable incentives. If there is a divergence between the private and the social marginal benefits or costs, for example, because there is pollution or resource degradation that is not incorporated into private calculus at the margin, the implication of the efficiency motive for policy is that there would be gains from changing the private behavior (perhaps by changing prices through taxes and subsidies) so that the optimal private decision (e.g. H* in Figs. 13.2 and 13.3) coincides with the optimal social decision (e.g. H** or H*** in these figs.). What does the concern with overall sustainability have to add beyond that?

The second meaning of sustainability that is encountered frequently in the human resource and population and some other development communities is much narrower. It concerns the capacity of a donor-funded project to continue producing the benefits it is expected to provide (e.g. those that were projected in the project's cost-benefit analysis) beyond the period for which financing and other inputs are provided by a donor. This might be characterized as project sustainability to distinguish it from the overall sustainability discussed above. For example, if the project provides funds for a capital investment, will the beneficiary agency (e.g. usually a government or non-governmental organization (NGO)) be able to mobilize the recurrent expenditure to operate the capital investment when project support terminates? Although the primary focus of this meaning of sustainability is financial, the concept has been broadened to consider the beneficiary's institutional and managerial capacity to continue generating projected benefits of an investment beyond the life of an externally funded project period. It is widely accepted that projects that provide support for recurrent expenditures are more difficult to sustain than those that provide support only for capital investments.

Sustainability is a major problem for many development projects and programs, including those directly related to human resources and population. One reason for such concerns is that donor projects in these areas often provide support to recurrent expenditure in the form of donated pharmaceuticals, contraceptives, and other supplies. Some projects also supplement staff salaries and administrative costs, particularly in the case of projects involving NGOs. A desire to get services out to clients as quickly and reliably as possible is often the basis for funding a broader range of inputs. It is also true that in the early stages of governmental programs support is often relatively weak, and there is no presumption that the necessary recurrent expenditure would be forthcoming in the absence of donor funding.

Given ongoing concerns for the sustainability of such programs, some donors have funded entire projects designed to promote sustainability. The problem is perceived to be particularly acute in the case of NGOs, which tend to receive a very high share of their recurrent budgets from donor funding and have only limited opportunities available for obtaining alternative sources of funding. Cost recovery is often advocated or strengthened as one way to replace donor funding. One problem is that as fees rise, the characteristics of the clients served tend to change, with the result that a smaller share of the remaining subsidies reaches the poor (as is illustrated in benefit incidence studies, such as that summarized above on family planning in Vietnam). 'Cross-subsidization' is another common sustainability strategy frequently supported by sustainability projects. An example is for an NGO to establish a clinic or a school in a relatively high-income location and to charge fees there that more than cover its costs, using the surplus to support its operations in low-income areas. Cross-subsidization activities, although they are sometimes generously funded by donors, rarely succeed (Janowitz and Gould 1993).[34]

In the context of the policy framework presented in Section 2, however, project or program sustainability poses less serious problems. To begin with, governments should not in most cases necessarily provide population change and economic development-related services directly.[35] Even from a distributional perspective, the policy options that have heavily subsidized governmental providers servicing the poor while a self-sufficient private sector services the rich and middle-income groups are not likely to be high in the policy hierarchy. If governmental financing is justified on either efficiency or distribution grounds, the preference should be for demand-side subsidies (e.g. vouchers) provided directly to target groups of consumers (e.g. the poor). In addition to fostering competition and therefore efficiency, the use of targeted demand-side subsidies also helps to resolve the problem of

---

[34] There is little reason to expect they would succeed because in competitive (and even monopolistically competitive) markets there is no reason to expect producers to enjoy long-run profits. If activities in high-income markets are profitable (i.e. generate revenue above actual costs), other investors are attracted into the market and the increased supply drives prices down to the point where price is equal to average cost (i.e. zero profit). This has in fact been the experience of many donor-funded cross-subsidizing ventures.

[35] If governments do provide these services directly (and most do), they should be made to compete with the private sector on an equal basis, i.e. the private sector should receive the same level of subsidies received by governmental providers.

sustainability. In the case of NGOs, for example, those that are able to control their costs and compete effectively for consumers' business (including the business of those consumers who are equipped with vouchers) will survive; the rest will fail. Governmental programs probably should disappear if they show themselves less able to compete with commercial and NGO providers on a level playing field.

4. CONCLUSIONS AND SUMMARY

The basic proposition of this chapter that was presented in the introduction and that I repeat again here is that:

> *For both good conditional predictions and good policy formation regarding most dimensions of population change and economic development, a perspective firmly grounded in understanding the micro determinants—at the level of individuals, families, and other such micro entities—of population changes and of the interactions between population and development is* essential.

I maintain that only considering aggregate patterns in variables related to population and economic development is *not* likely to be sufficient for a wide range of questions related to population change in economic development. In particular, only considering aggregate patterns is *not* likely to provide a sufficient basis for good conditional predictions nor for good policy formation and analysis. I claim that is the case because critical behavioral decisions regarding population and development are made at the micro level—by households, by individuals, and perhaps by other entities—given the resources under the control of the decision-makers and the market and policy environments in which these decisions are made. Important aspects of policies, moreover, are likely to be determined by aspects of local micro, or perhaps mezo, conditions. Important policy concerns, further, go beyond concerns about averages of aggregates such as per capita income to the distribution of outcomes among members of society, perhaps further identified by demographic characteristics, such as gender or ethnic group, or economic status, such as being below a poverty line. I claim that for such reasons not only does a micro perspective matter, but for many—probably most questions regarding population change and economic development—it is essential.

I sketch out the basis for this proposition and give some illustrations related to studies of aspects of population and development and some specific related policies. I begin with the presentation of some simple fundamentals for thinking about population change and development at the micro level and for empirically assessing aspects of population change and development. These fundamentals are based on the proposition that individual decision-makers make decisions as if they are maximizing their own welfare subject to what they perceive are their own best interests. I discuss some aspects of this approach, including that it does not mean that people are continuously consciously making cost-benefit calculations and that it does not mean that people are not altruistic.

I then turn to considering some fundamentals for thinking about policies. I first consider the efficiency/productivity rationale for policy interventions. Two important points from this discussion are that (1) efficiency is based on individual decision-maker welfare maximization, not some abstract or technical notion of resource allocation rules and (2) central to the case for policy changes on efficiency grounds is the existence of discrepancies between privately and socially optimal behaviors at the margin. I then consider the distribution rationale, and emphasize that distribution is a fundamental justification for considering policy interventions, just as is efficiency, and that distribution relates to distribution among individuals in a society, not just among households. I next consider choices among policy alternatives. I note that different policy options that might attain the same direct objective may have widely varying costs, that the relevant costs include not only the direct budgetary costs but also importantly the distortion costs, that there is a policy hierarchy in terms of increasing marginal costs, that policies with less costs tend to be more focused on the problem that is being addressed and use price (tax, subsidy) means rather than fiats or regulations, that governmental provision of services need not be and often is not high in the policy hierarchy, and that policies to address distributional issues may have efficiency costs but the policy hierarchy still is relevant because it is desirable to attain a given distributional goal at as little efficiency/productivity cost as possible.

I then present some illustrations of these fundamentals for thinking about the specific implications of policies for population change and economic development and for evaluating selected empirical micro studies that build on such frameworks to illuminate what we know about critical aspects of population change and economic development and policies. I first review some empirical estimates on selected topics related to micro aspects of population change and economic development to illustrate what we do and, equally important, do not know from systematic empirical approaches and how being systematic in such approaches in the sense of grounding the analysis firmly in the conceptual frameworks earlier presented may make a substantial difference in our understanding of these topics. The explicit examples that I consider are (1) the impact of schooling on population change and on productivities, (2) targeting policies toward particular demographic groups and collective versus unitary household decisions, (3) the role of expectations regarding future developments within dynamic optimizing models of micro behavior on population change and economic development, and (4) distributional analysis of policies. These examples illustrate how inferences drawn without a systematic guiding framework may be hard to interpret and substantially misleading, that good systematic empirical studies are difficult to undertake, that most empirical studies even if they are not plagued by biases do not provide insight into the efficiency justification for policies because they do not illuminate the extent of discrepancies between privately and socially optimal behaviors at the margin, and that in some areas of concern, including policy evaluations related directly to population change, there has been very little systematic concern with the distribution justification for policies.

Because of the difficulties in obtaining good empirical estimates, however, I note that often policies have to be formulated considerably on the basis of a priori frameworks. I therefore then review a priori considerations, grounded in the frameworks summarized before for individual behavior and for policy analysis, for selected policy issues related to population change and economic development—namely, (1) the use of regulations related to population change and development, (2) pricing and cost recovery in programs related to population change and human resource development, (3) access to programs and quality of programs related to population change and human resource development, and (4) overall and program sustainability. I note that from the perspective of the previously presented policy framework there seems to be a lot of confusion in discussions of these topics. Many regulatory and pricing and cost recovery programs, for example, seem oblivious of efficiency guidelines for pricing, distort incentives by limiting any subsidies (even if warranted on efficiency grounds) to certain types of providers (e.g. only governmental suppliers), create vested interests in their perpetuation, and are rationalized on the grounds that they redistribute more resources to the poor but in fact benefit primarily middle and upper income classes. The concerns about program access, program quality, and overall sustainability, moreover, are best considered not as policy justifications separate from efficiency and distribution, but basically are aspects of efficiency—but if they are used as guidelines for policy formation without recognizing their implications for efficiency, the result is likely to be higher costs than recognized in terms of other societal objectives.

References

Alderman, Harold, Jere R. Behrman, David Ross, and Richard Sabot. 1996. 'The Returns to Endogenous Human Capital in Pakistan's Rural Wage Labor Market'. *Oxford Bulletin of Economics and Statistics*. 58 (1) (Feb.), 29–55.

——Pierre-Andre Chiappori, Lawrence Haddad, John Hoddinott, and Ravi Kanbur. 1995. 'Urinary versus Collective Models of the Household: Time to Shift the Burden of Proof?' *World Bank Research Observer*. 10: 1–19.

Barrera, Albino. 1990. 'The Role of Maternal Schooling and Its Interaction with Public Health Programs in Child Health Production'. *Journal of Development Economics*. 32 (1) 69–92.

Becker, Gary S. 1967. 'Human Capital and the Personal Distribution of Income: An Analytical Approach'. Ann Arbor: University of Michigan, Woytinsky Lecture, republished in Gary S. Becker, *Human Capital*. New York: NBER, 2nd edn 1975, 94–117.

Behrman, Jere R. 1990a. *Human Resource Led Development?* New Delhi, India: Asian Regional Training and Employment Programme/International Labour Organization.

——1990b. *The Action of Human Resources and Poverty on One Another: What We Have Yet to Learn*. Washington: Population and Human Resources Department, World Bank.

——1997. 'Women's Schooling and Child Education: A Survey'. Philadelphia: University of Pennsylvania. Mimeo.

——and Nancy Birdsall. 1983. 'The Quality of Schooling: Quantity Alone is Misleading'. *American Economic Review*. 73: 928–46.

——and Anil B. Deolalikar. 1991. 'School Repetition, Dropouts and the Returns to Schooling: The Case of Indonesia'. *Oxford Bulletin of Economics and Statistics*. 53 (4) (Nov.), 467–80.

Behrman, Jere R., and Anil B. Deolalikar. 1993. 'Unobserved Household and Community Heterogeneity and the Labor Market Impact of Schooling: A Case Study for Indonesia'. *Economic Development and Cultural Change.* 41 (3) (Apr.), 461–88.

—— and James C. Knowles. 1998a. 'Population and Reproductive Health: An Economic Framework for Policy Evaluation'. *Population and Development Review.* 24 (4) (Dec.), 697–738.

—— —— 1998b. 'The Distributional Implications of Government Family Planning and Reproductive Health Services in Vietnam'. Prepared for the Rockefeller Foundation. Philadelphia: University of Pennsylvania. Mimeo.

—— and Mark R. Rosenzweig. 1998. 'In-Law Resources, Parental Resources and Distribution Within Marriage'. Philadelphia: University of Pennsylvania. Mimeo.

—— —— 1999. ' "Ability" Biases in Schooling Returns and Twins: A Test and New Estimates'. *Economics of Education Review.* 18: 159–67.

—— and Barbara L. Wolfe. 1984. 'The Socioeconomic Impact of Schooling in a Developing Country'. *Review of Economics and Statistics.* 66 (2) (May), 296–303.

—— —— 1987. 'How Does Mother's Schooling Affect the Family's Health, Nutrition, Medical Care Usage, and Household Sanitation?' *Journal of Econometrics.* 36: 185–204.

—— —— 1989. 'Does More Schooling Make Women Better Nourished and Healthier? Adult Sibling Random and Fixed Effects Estimates for Nicaragua'. *Journal of Human Resources.* 24 (4) (Fall), 644–63.

Besley, Timothy, and Anne Case. 1994. 'Diffusion as a Learning Process: Evidence from HYV Cotton'. Princeton: Princeton University. Mimeo.

Birdsall, Nancy. 1994. 'Government, Population and Poverty: A Win-Win Tale'. In Robert Cassen, ed., *Population and Development: Old Debates, New Conclusions.* Washington: Overseas Development Council, 253–74.

—— and Kenneth M. Chomitz. 1993. 'Population Growth, Externalities, and Poverty'. Washington: World Bank, Population, Health and Nutrition Policy Research Paper 1158.

Boissiere, Maurice, John B. Knight, and Richard H. Sabot. 1985. 'Earnings, Schooling, Ability and Cognitive Skills'. *American Economic Review.* 75: 1016–30.

Bouis, Howarth E., and Lawrence J. Haddad. 1992. 'Are Estimates of Calorie-Income Elasticities Too High? A Recalibration of the Plausible Range'. *Journal of Development Economics.* 39 (2) (Oct.), 333–64.

Card, David E. 1999. 'New Developments in the Economics of Schooling', in Orley Ashenfelter and David Card, eds., *Handbook of Labor Economics,* iv. Amsterdam: North-Holland.

Chomitz, Kenneth M., and Nancy Birdsall. 1991. 'Incentives for Small Families: Concepts and Issues'. *Proceedings of the World Bank Annual Conference on Development Economics 1990.* 309–39.

Cohen, Bernard, and Mark Montgomery. 1998. *From Birth to Death: Mortality Decline and Reproductive Change.* Washington: National Academy Press.

Committee on Population. 1995. 'Resource Allocation for Family Planning in Developing Countries'. Report of a Meeting. Washington: National Research Council.

Eckstein, Zvi, Pedro Mira, and Kenneth I. Wolpin. 1998. 'A Quantitative Analysis of Swedish Fertility Dynamics: 1751–1990'. Tel Aviv: Tel Aviv University. Mimeo.

Feldstein, Martin. 1995. 'Tax Avoidance and the Deadweight Loss of the Income Tax'. Cambridge, Mass.: National Bureau of Economic Research Working Paper No. 5055.

Foster, Andrew, and Mark R. Rosenzweig. 1995. 'Learning by Doing and Learning from Others: Human Capital and Technical Change in Agriculture'. *Journal of Political Economy.* 103 (6) (Dec.), 1176–209.

Foster, Andrew, and Mark R. Rosenzweig. 1996. 'Technical Change and Human-Capital Returns and Investments: Evidence from the Green Revolution'. *American Economic Review.* 86 (4) (Sept.), 931–53.

Gertler, Paul, Luis Locay, and Warren Sanderson. 1987. 'Are User Fees Regressive? The Welfare Implications of Health Care Financing Proposals in Peru'. *Journal of Econometrics.* 36: 67–88.

Glewwe, Paul. 1996. 'The Relevance of Standard Estimates of Rates of Return to Schooling for Education Policy: A Critical Assessment'. *Journal of Development Economics.* 51 (2) (Dec.), 267–90.

Hammer, Jeffrey S., and Peter Berman. 1995. 'Ends and Means in Public Health Policy in Developing Countries'. In Peter Berman, ed., *Health Sector Reform in Developing Countries.* Cambridge, Mass.: Harvard University Press.

Janowitz, Barbara, and Brian J. Gould. 1993. 'Options for Financing Family Planning'. Draft report for UN Fund for Population Activities. Family Health International, Research Triangle Park, NC.

King, Elizabeth M. and A. Anne Hill, eds. 1993. *Women's Education in Developing Countries: Barriers, Benefits, and Policies.* Baltimore and London: Johns Hopkins University Press for the World Bank.

Knight, John B., and Richard H. Sabot. 1990. *Educational Productivity and Inequality: The East African Natural Experiment.* New York: Oxford University Press.

Lundberg, Shelly J., Robert A. Pollak, and Terence J. Wales. 1997. 'Do Husbands and Wives Pool Their Resources? Evidence from the United Kingdom Child Benefit'. *Journal of Human Resources.* 32 (3) (summer), 463–80.

McElroy, Marjorie B. 1990. 'The Empirical Content of Nash-Bargained Household Behavior'. *Journal of Human Resources.* 25 (4), 559-83.

—— 1992. 'The Policy Implications of Family Bargaining and Marriage Markets'. Durham, NC: Duke University. Mimeo.

Munshi, Kaivan. 1997. 'Farmers as Econometricians: Social Learning and Technology Diffusion in the Indian Green Revolution'. Boston: Boston University. Mimeo.

Psacharopoulos, George. 1994. 'Returns to Investment in Education: A Global Update'. *World Development.* 22 (9) (Sept.), 1325–44.

—— Samuel Morley, Ariel Fiszbein, Haeduck Lee, and Bill Wood. 1992. *Poverty and Income Distribution in Latin America: The Story of the 1980s.* Washington: World Bank.

Rosenzweig, Mark R. 1995. 'Why Are There Returns in Schooling?' *American Economic Review.* 85 (2) (May), 153–8.

—— 1997. 'Social Learning and Economic Growth: Empirical Evidence'. Philadelphia: University of Pennsylvania. Mimeo. Background paper for *World Development Report 1998.*

Schultz, T. Paul. 1988. 'Education Investments and Returns'. In Hollis Chenery and T. N. Srinivasan, eds., *Handbook of Development Economics,* Amsterdam: North-Holland, 543–630.

—— 1990. 'Testing the Neoclassical Model of Family Labor Supply and Fertility'. *Journal of Human Resources.* 25 (4) (Fall), 599–634.

Strauss, John. 1990. 'Households, Communities and Preschool Children's Nutrition Outcomes: Evidence From Rural Cote d'Ivoire'. *Economic Development and Cultural Change.* 38 (2), 231–62.

—— and Duncan Thomas. 1995. 'Human Resources: Empirical Modeling of Household and Family Decisions'. In Jere R. Behrman and T. N. Srinivasan, eds., *Handbook of Development Economics,* vol. 3A. Amsterdam: North-Holland, 1883–2024.

Thomas, Duncan. 1990. 'Intrahousehold Resource Allocation: An Inferential Approach'. *Journal of Human Resources*. 25 (4) (Fall), 635–64.

—— John Strauss, and Maria Helena Henriques. 1991. 'How Does Mother's Education Affect Child Height?' *Journal of Human Resources*. 26 (2) (spring), 183–211.

Wolfe, Barbara L., and Jere R. Behrman. 1987. 'Women's Schooling and Children's Health: Are the Effects Robust with Adult Sibling Control for the Women's Childhood Background?' *Journal of Health Economics*. 6 (3), 239–54.

World Bank. 1991. *World Development Report: The Challenge of Development*. Oxford: Oxford University Press for the World Bank.

14

New Findings in Economics and Demography: Implications for Policies to Reduce Poverty

NANCY BIRDSALL

There have now been more than four decades of debate about the consequences of rapid population growth for economic growth in poor countries. In his review of that debate (Ch. 2), Allen Kelley notes that on the whole the role of economists has been to advocate moderation. For one thing, even if rapid population growth has negative overall consequences, economists have viewed those consequences as small and generally short-lived as societies develop compensating technology and institutions. This emphasis on compensating and offsetting factors, and thus on moderation, comes naturally to economists whose models at the macro level build in general equilibrium effects in large markets, so that a perturbation in one part of any system is likely to generate a compensating response elsewhere.[1]

The chapters in this volume, while they stand firmly in that careful tradition, nonetheless highlight new and surprisingly stronger conclusions about the negative effects of rapid population growth—or more precisely, about the potential positive effect of reductions in the rate of population growth. On the basis of those conclusions, should economists today then express stronger or clearer views about the potential role of governments in encouraging lower fertility? The answer is yes—again, however, with moderation.

In the Introduction to this volume, we pointed out that new and more convincing evidence that high fertility constrains economic growth does not *in itself* provide a rationale for public interventions to reduce fertility; indeed economic growth is not an end in itself but a means to the larger objective of improved well-being.[2] A coercive policy to change behavior is only the most extreme example of an approach that makes no sense, since it compromises the current well-being and rights of individuals for a benefit to society as a whole that is both uncertain and comes in a future that should in any event be discounted. The only real justification for any intervention to change behavior is the existence of a difference between the private and social costs

---

[1] Similarly, economic theory at the micro level emphasizes that human behavior responds to incentives and constraints such that an increase in the cost of children (e.g. if land becomes more scarce) will naturally induce couples to have fewer of them.

[2] Economists participating in the Bellagio Symposium emphasized this point. See also the opening paragraphs of Chapter 8, referring to Birdsall (1994), and the concluding observations of Chapter 7.

and benefits of such behavior. That difference is usually the result of some market failure—the classic case is pollution, where the polluter does not fully absorb the costs of pollution but passes those costs to others. In the case of fertility, if parents absorb fully the costs of their children, the reduction in their per capita income (and in aggregate per capita income) does not in itself justify a public intervention.

But if parents either cannot or will not absorb fully[3] the cost of their children, or where they are bearing children in excess of their desired fertility goals, there may be a justification for non-coercive policies that encourage—or make it easier for parents to attain the goal of—smaller families. One example where parents may not bear the full costs of their children is in the use of natural resources. For given levels of consumption, more people put more stress on natural resources, including both sources (forests, water) and sinks (the air which receives pollution). In the absence of prices that reflect the true scarcity value of these sources and sinks, there is likely to be excessive consumption of these 'goods' from society's point of view. Excessive consumption is multiplied the more people there are.

The chapters in this volume do not directly address the question of whether parents absorb the full costs of children. They do suggest that there are costs—to the parents and/or society as a whole, in terms of lower economic growth and in many countries of the Third World, in terms of reduced success in eliminating poverty. In their entirety they put together a newly compelling set of arguments and evidence indicating that high fertility at the economy-wide level exacerbates poverty or, said another way, that high fertility makes poverty reduction more difficult and less likely. This suggests that in fact lower aggregate fertility, as long as it reflects individual decisions that are fully informed and freely taken, does not in itself pose any trade-off between the current individual welfare and future common welfare of the poor in most of the Third World.[4] On the contrary lower aggregate fertility has and is likely for some period to improve the lot of the poor. Thus concern about population growth and change in the Third World can be directly linked to concern about the welfare of parents, children, and families.

The arguments and associated evidence for this point can be divided, crudely, into three categories.

First, constant high fertility at the country level prevents the one-time but signal shift in age structure now documented as contributing to economic growth in some parts of the developing world. This matters for poverty reduction because economic growth is a critical ingredient for poverty reduction at the country level.[5] So high

---

[3] i.e. the complete marginal cost.

[4] Here I refer to the situation in most countries of the Third World, where fertility rates are not close to replacement level. The situation in a few countries, especially China, is different. In China, the benefits of reduced youth dependency are fast being overtaken by the costs of rising old-age dependency, as the cohorts born in the period of emphasis on the one-child system enter working age and are relatively small.

[5] This point is virtually uncontested in the development literature; see e.g. World Bank (1990). That literature, linking growth to poverty reduction, has not incorporated the effect of demographic change on growth and thus on poverty reduction, nor the effect of growth on poverty reduction through growth's effect on demographic change (in the two-way causation assessed by Bloom and Canning in Ch. 7).

fertility exacerbates poverty by slowing economic growth. (This is also of course true for high mortality, which also prevents the change in age structure that contributes to growth.[6]) The effect is indirect but substantial—in Eastwood and Lipton's analysis accounting for one-half the 'damage' (to use those authors' words) that high fertility implies for increased poverty.

Secondly, high fertility reduces the chances for the poor to escape poverty and may also reduce their *relative* welfare. At the country level, higher levels of fertility in the past are associated with a higher incidence and intensity of poverty, presumably because, as Malthus suggested, higher past fertility increases the availability and reduces the wages of workers and, all other things the same, raises the demand for and the price of such 'wage goods' as food.[7] It may also be, as Eastwood and Lipton note, that higher fertility at the country level reflects *differentially* higher fertility among poor households, and that the resulting high dependency ratio in households at or below the poverty line increases the incidence and severity of poverty measured at the country level. Higher fertility in poor households may also reduce non-child consumption, given child costs, if it reduces the working hours of adults.

Finally, there is the growing evidence both that the high fertility of poor families may not be optimal for family welfare even when it is apparently consciously chosen, and that some fertility among the poor is unwanted or unintended. The irony is that circumstances that may make high fertility among the poor bad for family welfare may often occur at times when economic and social gains are spreading. In a rapidly changing environment, with new opportunities to accumulate human capital and other assets, the poor may end up worse off with more children because they are unaware of or unable to respond to changed signals about the costs and benefits of children to them, and of siblings to their children.[8] These circumstances almost always reflect one or another market failure that disproportionately harms the poor.

Economists conclude that unwanted fertility and market failures together justify some policies and interventions, as long as they can be shown to improve the situation of poor families. Which policies and interventions are appropriate depends on a hierarchy in which no particular policy or program should be dominated by more effective or efficient means to accomplish the same end.[9] In their microanalysis, economists (including Behrman in Ch. 13) put particular emphasis on the relative costs and benefits of alternative programs for achieving a particular goal, and thus on

[6] The chapters in this volume document this point. Moreover, reductions in mortality, despite the initial effect of increasing youth dependency, appear to be necessary if not sufficient to bring reductions in fertility, at least in the modern postwar world.

[7] In small completely open economies changes in fertility would not necessarily affect the price of a traded good such as food.

[8] Behrman (1996) discusses the difficulties households face in adjusting allocation of resources between parents and children when economic and social circumstances are changing rapidly. Birdsall (1994) notes that poor parents may have access to less information about, for example, increasing returns to family investments in children's education.

[9] This broad but critical statement summarizes a central conclusion of the participants in the Bellagio Symposium.

the ideal of a hierarchy of interventions. Birdsall (1994) in addition, places particular emphasis on the logic of policies and programs that reduce fertility *because* they create new options and opportunities, especially for the poor. (These programs and policies of course include many that are not targeted directly to changing fertility behavior.)

The problem, of course, is the extraordinary difficulty, even given the specific objective of reducing fertility, of adequately assessing the costs and benefits of alternative approaches (the hierarchy referred to above) to changing the environment of the poor (and the non-poor) in a manner that improves their well-being and as a result reduces their fertility. The difficulty is compounded by the obvious fact that many programs that meet this criterion serve other objectives—indeed their primary objective may be to improve access to education or to deepen credit markets. Even with their effects on fertility a by-product, they may be more cost-effective than programs targeted specifically at fertility reduction, or even if not cost-effective in reducing fertility they may have higher ratios of benefits to costs given their multiple benefits.

Still, even in the absence of analysis of the costs and benefits of different interventions that would generate the ideal hierarchy, there is an important set of policies and programs implied in the analyses of economists—a set that joins the macroeconomic analysis of economic consequences of aggregate demographic change with the microeconomic emphasis on maximizing the well-being of individuals and families. That set includes the following.[10]

1. The highest priority should go to *undoing* any existing policy-induced distortions, such as those that actively limit access to education (including education of girls) or access to information or services about health and family planning (such as government restrictions on private provision) or that actively discriminate against women. These reduce welfare independent of their effect on fertility; they probably also help maintain high fertility and high mortality.

2. Second is a range of economic policies that strengthen land, labor, and financial markets and encourage broad-based income growth. These are likely to reduce fertility (and mortality) not only indirectly because they are associated with faster income growth, but directly by for example undoing the constraint that families face where they cannot accumulate financial savings because capital markets are poor, and thus turn to children as a form of old-age security, or the constraint that poor owners of land face where property rights are not legally protected so that they turn to sons to physically defend their land rights.[11] In addition, deeper and better functioning markets and institutions bring the offsetting and moderating forces that are central to minimizing any negative effects of high fertility and rapid population growth (e.g. in the case of agriculture, as illustrated in Ch. 12, this volume). Properly functioning markets should also help guarantee (consistent with the evidence of Kelley and Schmidt 1995) that the change in age composition associated with mortality

---

[10] This discussion builds on Birdsall (1994), while reflecting the spirit if not the details of the discussion at the Bellagio Symposium.

[11] Cain (1978) makes this point for widows in Bangladesh.

and fertility decline ends up making a substantial contribution to economic growth because it interacts positively with sound economic policies—as apparently happened in East Asia.[12]

3. Third is a range of social programs, including education and health programs. The evidence is that more education and better health lead to lower fertility. In any event, some public financing of these, particularly if targeted at the poor, can probably be justified in most settings, independently of any demographic impact, on the grounds that they help close the gap between private and social costs and benefits of family spending on child education and health. Here the question of the optimal hierarchy of programs is most difficult—what combination of resource-taking health, education, and other services should command public financing? Given the multiple benefits of these programs, convincing analysis is unlikely, and in most societies decisions about allocations to these programs are therefore usually made through a political process, and are best made through a reasonably democratic and decentralized process.[13]

4. There is in addition the range of policies and programs that improve the status of women, including for example special access for women to micro credit. The evidence is that in some settings women are not full partners in childbearing decisions. To the extent that they bear more of the costs and receive fewer of the benefits of childbearing, it may be that their greater participation in the decision would ultimately reduce fertility. There is a logic of policies and programs that strengthen their ability and willingness to participate actively in those decisions anyway; the possibility that the result would be lower fertility suggests an additional benefit given the evidence in this volume that lower fertility can bring faster economic growth and more poverty reduction.

5. Finally there is the specific issue of family planning information and services. For decades the justification for family planning programs as a means to reduce fertility has been contentious. Unlike the case of health, where it is straightforward to assume that virtually all families want lower mortality, in the case of fertility it is presumptuous at best and dangerous at worst to make assumptions about private fertility choices. To the extent that family planning has health benefits (via better spacing of children for example) it can be included in the statement above. More fundamentally, to the extent that there are social benefits of lower fertility, both for growth and for poverty reduction, and given the considerable evidence of unwanted fertility and market

---

[12] The effect of the policy environment in influencing the linkage between population dynamics and economic performance has not, however, emerged in many other econometric analyses. See Bloom and Williamson (1998). The region with the most marked reduction in dependency, East Asia, has also had the best economic performance and, until the financial crisis of 1997–98, was widely viewed as having an excellent policy environment (World Bank 1993). Behrman *et al.* (1999) explicitly considered how relations between age structures and outcomes associated with economic growth differ depending on policy regimes.

[13] For given resources, analysis of cost-effectiveness of alternative inputs to a given goal is of course possible and useful. Analysis of the relative costs and benefits of alternative inputs, where the range of benefits and the weight one would put on each in a social welfare analysis is itself not agreed, is immensely more difficult.

failures that limit private access to family planning,[14] an economic case can be made for non-coercive programs of reproductive health and family planning.

More generally, given the difficulty of constructing a hierarchy of policy interventions, the practical reality is that a range of policies and programs are likely to make sense—because they have other social and economic benefits while also reducing fertility and mortality, and because they introduce no trade-off in terms of improving individual well-being. Many of these policies and programs are relatively low in cost (or even costless in the case of good economic policies and the elimination of distortions that constrain individual choices) and have multiple social benefits that probably exceed private benefits. This is most obviously true of basic education, especially for girls, and of primary health care.

*   *   *

The chapters in this volume focus primarily on the consequences of demographic change without much direct allusion to policy implications. However, combined with some simple welfare economics and a bit of common sense about the goals of development, they strengthen the argument for public support of policies and programs that improve the environment in which the poor too often make constrained decisions about childbearing. Most broad development policies, from deepening of financial markets and rationalization of labor market regimes to expansion of girls' education and of reproductive health and family planning services, meet this test. The most difficult issue is less whether they make sense at all and more their costs and benefits relative to each other. All are likely to be effective in some measure, since all assist the poor directly by allowing them among other things to reduce their own unwanted fertility, and indirectly by reducing the societal burden of high fertility. Moreover, to this justification for policy based on the congruence of efficiency gains along with gains in well-being, we can add the additional justification that policies to improve the environment in which the poor make fertility choices are likely also to move societies closer to the 'right' distribution of well-being.[15]

References

Behrman, Jere R. 1996. *Demographic Changes, Poverty and Income Distribution*. Washington: Overseas Development Council.

[14] For evidence of unwanted fertility, see Bongaarts (1990). For a discussion of market failures that limit private access to family planning, see Chomitz and Birdsall (1990) who cite failures in the market for information, and in credit and insurance markets, and the externality associated with the high costs of early adoption of contraception and of new contraceptives faced by early adopters. See also Birdsall and Griffin (1993), who note that there may be redistributive social programs (such as family planning) that would improve overall welfare, including of the rich, through their effect on the fertility of the poor.

[15] The 'right' distribution depends ultimately on the appropriate social welfare function. See Sen (1999).

—— Suzanne Duryea, and Miguel Székely. 1999. 'Aging and Economic Opportunities: Major World Regions at the Turn of Century'. OCE Working Paper Series No 105, Research Department, Inter-American Development Bank, Oct.

Birdsall, Nancy. 1994. 'Government, Population and Poverty: A Win-Win Tale'. In Robert Cassen, ed., *Population and Development: Old Debates, New Conclusions.* Washington, Overseas Development Council. 253–274. Also published in Kerstin Lindahl-Kiessling and Hans Landberg, eds., 1994. *Population, Economic Development, and the Environment.* New York and Oxford: Oxford University Press, 1994: 173–98.

—— and Kenneth Chomitz. 1990. 'Incentives for Small Family Size: Issues and Options'. Proceedings of the World Bank Conference on Development Economics, Supplement to the *World Bank Economic Review* and the *World Bank Research Observer.*

—— and Charles Griffin. 1993. 'Population Growth, Externalities and Poverty'. In Michal Lipton and Jacques van der Gaag, eds. *Including the Poor.* New York: Oxford University Press for the World Bank.

Bloom, David, and Jeffrey Williamson. 1993. 'Demographic Transition and Economic Miracles in Emerging Asia'. *World Bank Economic Review.* 12 (3) (Sept.), 419–55.

Bongaarts, John. 1990. 'The Measurement of Unwanted Fertility. *Population and Development Review.* 16 (3) (Sept.), 487–506.

Cain, Mead. 1978. 'Household Lifecycle and Economic Mobility in Rural Bangladesh'. *Population and Development Review.* 4 (3) (Sept.). 421–38.

Chomitz, Kenneth, and Nancy Birdsall. 1990. 'Incentives for Small Family Size: Issues and Options'. Proceedings of the World Bank Conference on Development Economics, Supplement to the *World Bank Economic Review* and the *World Bank Research Observer.*

Sen, Amartya. 1999. 'The Possibility of Social Choice'. *American Economic Review.* 89 (3) (June), 349–78.

World Bank. 1993. *The East Asia Miracle: Economic Growth and Public Policy.* Washington: World Bank.

Index